T*ravellers*
S*urvival*
K*it*

India

Travellers **S**urvival **K**it

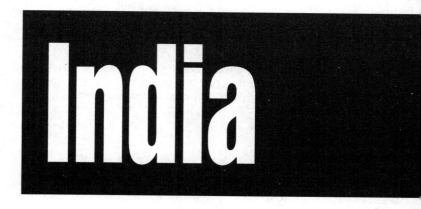

India

JOHN & COLETTE LEAK

Published by
VACATION WORK, 9 PARK END STREET, OXFORD

TRAVELLERS SURVIVAL KIT: INDIA

by John and Colette Leak

Copyright © Vacation Work 1997

ISBN 1 85458 174 0

Cover Design:
Miller Craig & Cocking Design Partnership

Maps by Andrea Pullen

Chapter headings by Nigel Casseldine

Other drawings by Alison Musker

The publisher acknowledges that the plans on pages 88, 89, 139 and 331 are based
on plans that originally appeared in *A Handbook to India, Pakistan, Burma and
Ceylon*, published by John Murray.

Printed by Unwin Brothers Ltd, Old Woking, Surrey, England

Contents

THE NORTHERN PLAINS

CENTRAL INDIA

WESTERN INDIA

SOUTH-WESTERN INDIA

SOUTH-EASTERN INDIA

NORTH-EASTERN INDIA

MAPS

Abbreviations

The following abbreviations are used in the listings sections that appear throughout this book:

SR	Single room	Exp	Expensive
DR	Double room	Rest	Restaurant
SWB	Single with bathroom	Ind	Indian
DWB	Double with bathroom	Chi	Chinese
A/C	Air-conditioned	Cont	'Continental'/ Western
SC	Service charge	Veg	Vegetarian
Mod	Moderate		

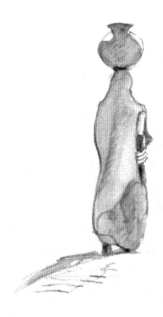

Acknowledgements

We would like to thank all those people and organisations who have helped during the research for this book. We would also like to thank Simon Calder and Dr Dandapani and colleagues at SD Enterprises for their helpful comments on the manuscript.

While every effort has been made to ensure that the information contained in this book is as up-to-date as possible, some details are bound to change within the lifetime of this edition, and readers are strongly advised to check facts and credentials themselves.

The *Travellers Survival Kit: India* will be revised regularly. We are keen to hear comments, criticisms and suggestions from both natives and travellers. Please write to the author at Vacation Work, 9 Park End St, Oxford OX1 1HJ. Those whose contributions are used will be sent a complimentary copy of the next edition.

Preface

We are often asked why we like India or why we went there in the first place nearly 20 years ago. The simple answer is that we don't know, we simply wanted to go. We still like it so we keep going. When pressed we might joke about having spent a previous incarnation there, or point out that India has everything: fabulous beaches, rain forests, sandy deserts, the highest mountains in the world, stunning monuments and, last but not least, friendly and generous people. Actually, the more we think about it the more we wonder why anyone would want to go anywhere else.

A lot has changed in India in the last decade and a half. Two prime ministers have been assassinated. Guerilla wars have broken out in Punjab and Kashmir. More and more revelations of corruption are made. Natural disasters have struck. The population has grown by another 200 million to something over 900 million. And yet India carries on; ramshackle maybe, but boasting a true democracy, improving standards of living and life expectancy, and better prospects for everybody. And, above all, it is a very safe country to travel in, which is more than you can say of some Western countries these days.

The change most visible to the traveller is a social one. The newly emerged middle class is not afraid of conspicuous consumption as in the past, and this shows up in better shops and a huge amount of house building. More important perhaps, you see a lot more smiling faces in India these days, and this is one of the main signs of a new national self-confidence. Another is the way that Indians now enter into serious conversation with foreign visitors. Not so many years ago they would make a statement conditioned by their social standing or, more likely, what they thought you wanted to hear, and leave it at that. Now you can really learn something about India and its people the best way, by talking to them.

Some things change, others seem never to. Away from the towns and cities, India goes its quiet, timeless and peaceful way. India in all its many aspects is truly the most interesting and rewarding country in the world for the traveller.

John and Colette Leak
Cumbria, May 1997

INDIA AND ITS PEOPLE

India is a large country of nearly 3.3 million square miles, smaller only than Russia, Canada, China, the USA, Brazil and Australia. The population at the 1991 census was 844 million, second only to China and rapidly catching up.

THE LAND

The extremes of India are roughly 3200km/2000 miles north to south and 3000km/ 1875 miles east to west. Cape Comorin (Kanniyakumari) is 8° north of the equator and the northernmost part of Kashmir 38°N, the latitude for instance of Athens, the toe of Italy and San Francisco. This span matches that from Cape York to Wilsons Promontory in Australia, from Gibraltar to Archangel in northern Russia, and from the 49th parallel down to Mexico City. Part of Gujarat is further west than Kabul in Afghanistan, and Assam is further east than Rangoon and part of Sumatra.

India encompasses huge variations of landscape and climate. Rain forest, sandy desert, lush farmland, beautiful beaches and the highest mountains in the world; India has them all.

For convenience this book divides India into seven areas; in the geographical sense there are four.

The Himalayas

Forming the northern border of the sub-continent are the Himalayas, a formidable barrier readily passable only in the north-west. At one end the hills and jungles of Assam and Burma consolidate this natural barrier, and at the other end is the Thar Desert. The great rivers of northern India — the Ganges, Yamuna, Indus and Brahmaputra — rise here and provide a water supply safe from the vagaries of the monsoon. The mountains also prevent the icy air of Tibet and Siberia spilling over onto the plains.

The northern plain

The northern plain stretches almost from the Khyber Pass on the border between Afghanistan and Pakistan right across India and into Bangladesh. The fertile alluvial soil supports nearly two-thirds of India's population and produces most of the country's cereals and pulses.

The Deccan

The southern border of this plain is formed by the Vindhya Mountains, and south of these is the Deccan, an upland savannah that occupies most of peninsular India. Divided from the coastal areas by the hills of the Eastern and Western Ghats rainfall is low, and this is the area (with Rajasthan and Saurashtra) that really suffers when

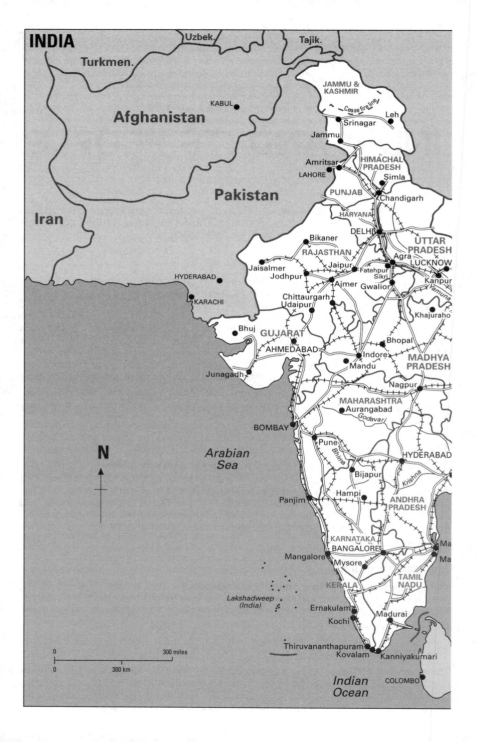

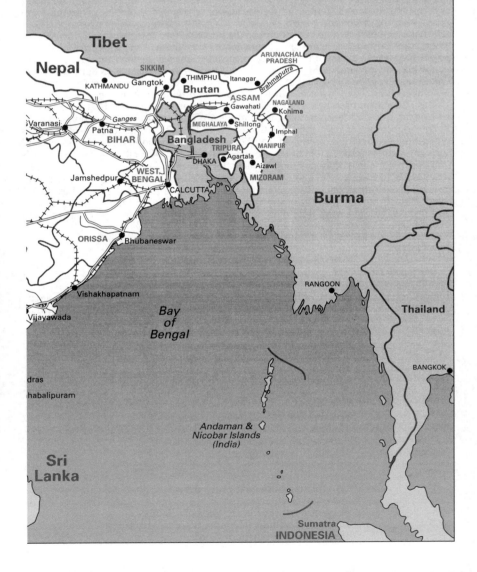

The international boundary on this map does not claim to be correct and is not recognised to be authentic by the Survey of India

the monsoon fails. Much of India's wealth, in the form of gold, silver and diamonds, came from this area and it is still the source of many valuable minerals.

The coastal plains

Below the Ghats are the southern coastal plains. Very fertile, they have adequate rainfall and support the highest population density in India.

CLIMATE

The weather in all of India (except for the Himalayas) follows three seasons: cool, hot and wet. In the north, temperatures are extreme; Agra, for instance, varying from little over zero at night in winter to nearly 50°C/122°F before the monsoon breaks in late June. The best time to visit is during the cool weather from November to March, when the days are clear and sunny and the nights crisp. April is hotter, 30–35°C/86–95°F in daytime and still pleasantly cool at night. May and June are fiendishly hot, day and night, with very low humidity. Temperatures in September and October are similar to April, but humidity is high. In the south there is less variation in temperature — it is warmer in winter and slightly less hot in summer.

The Himalayan area has a more conventional four seasons. The best time to visit is from May to October, though the foothills are affected by the monsoon.

The monsoons are a controlling factor in Indian life. A good monsoon means prosperity and a national sense of well-being; a failed monsoon means bankrupt and starving farmers, electricity shortages and depression in the cities. Most of India is influenced by the south-west monsoon, which breaks in Kerala around 1 June, reaches Delhi towards the end of June, and lasts until the end of August. The north-east monsoon affects mainly just Tamil Nadu in November and December. Quite apart from frequent heavy rain showers, the constant high humidity is unpleasant, and insects, absent in the hot weather, abound. Travel (both land and air) is often disrupted.

HISTORY

A brief chronology

2000BC	Indus valley civilisation (Dravidian). Highly developed society in towns of Mohenjo Daro and Harappa (Pakistan) and Lothal (Gujarat).
1500	Aryan invasions. Indus valley towns destroyed (–900BC).
518	Indus valley and Punjab annexed to Persia by Darius I (–486BC).
326	Invasion by Alexander the Great of Greece.
321	Maurayan empire founded by Chandragupta.
273	Accession of Ashoka. Maurayan empire extended to Afghanistan and all but southernmost India. Buddhism adopted as state religion.
184	Collapse of Maurayan empire. Successive invasions by Greeks and central Asian Scythians and Kushans.
AD225	End of Kushan empire.
319	Gupta dynasty founded by Chandragupta II at Patna, and extended by later rulers. India's 'Golden Age' of literature and art. Indian mathematicians devise decimal system, introduce zero, and evaluate π.
450	Start of new wave of invasions by Huns.
c600	Revival of Hinduism under various dynasties: Chalukya and Rashtrakuta in northern Deccan, and Pallava to the south.

711	First Muslim invasion. Muhammed ben Kasim in Sind (now Pakistan).
725	Muslims occupy Gujarat.
907	Chola empire based on Thanjavur in south (–1310).
1000	Raids by Mahmud of Ghazni from Afghanistan (–1026).
1190	Hoysalas establish kingdom in Halebid –1326).
1193	Delhi captured by Muslims under Qutb-ud-Din Aibak. Delhi sultanate established (–1526).
1336	Foundation of Hoysala kingdom at Vijayanagar (Hampi) symbolises Hindu resistance in Deccan (–1564).
1398	Tamerlane (Timur) sacks Delhi.
1498	Vasco da Gama (Portuguese) lands at Calicut.
1510	Albuquerque (Portuguese) captures Goa.
1526	Babur, a Mongol descended from Genghis Khan and Tamerlane, takes Delhi and starts Mughal (same word as 'Mongol') dynasty (–1530).
1530	Humayun succeeds Babur. Exiled from Delhi for many years by Sher Shah (–1556).
1556	Akbar, the Great Moghul. Ruled successfully by acknowledging pluralism, married a Rajput princess, and abolished discriminatory taxes on Hindus. Empire enlarged and enhanced by conquest and treaty. Hindus employed in many responsible positions. Highest standard of living ever in India for both courtiers and peasants (–1605).
1600	Founding of (English) East India Company.
1605	Jehangir, great patron of the arts and drunkard. Mughal empire at the height of its power (–1627).
1612	English trading post at Surat in Gujarat.
1627	Shahjahan. Extravagant builder of Taj Mahal and Delhi, but poor administrator (–1665).
1640	English occupy Madras.
1646	Shivaji leads Mahrattas against Muslims (–1680).
1658	Aurangzeb deposes Shahjahan. Subjection of Deccan and capture of Golconda deplete finances, and religious intolerance destroys previous goodwill (–1707).
1668	English establishment at Bombay.
1672	French in Pondicherry.
1707	Death of Aurangzeb. Mughal empire in rapid decline. Constant warfare with Mahrattas who, by 1719, control Mughal emperor.
1739	Nadir Shah, a Persian adventurer, sacks Delhi. General state of anarchy.
1746	Hostilities between British and French. Various campaigns leave Britain dominant foreign power. Clive's action in Bengal after 'Black Hole of Calcutta' establishes British political influence (–1761).
1767	Wars between Britain and Mysore culminating in taking of Seringapatam (–1799).
1803	British take Delhi from Mahrattas and eventually destroy Mahratta power (–1806).
1849	Punjab occupied after Sikh wars.
1857	Great Mutiny of the Bengal Army (the East India Company ruled India through the three Presidencies of Bengal, Madras and Bombay). Rebellion finally put down in the following year with help of Sikhs and Gurkhas.

1858	British Crown assumes government of India from East India Company with later a Viceroy to represent the sovereign.
1885	Formation of Indian National Congress, and tentative beginning of freedom movement.
1906	Muslim League formed to protect interests of Muslim minority in the event of elected government. Seeds of partition sown.
1914–18	First World War. India supports Britain with men and money in anticipation of reforms after war.
1920	Mahatma Gandhi in forefront of independence struggle. New policy of non-cooperation and passive resistance. Limited concessions by British (–1945).
1939–45	Second World War. Indians again support British, fighting Japanese (who had no plans to invade the major part of India), and in North Africa and Italy.
1945	Election of Labour government in Britain. India to be granted independence subject to orderly transfer of power.
1946–47	Serious communal fighting in Punjab and Sind forces British to speed up hand-over. Appointment of Mountbatten as Viceroy. Decision to partition country to produce separate Muslim state of Pakistan in two parts, East and West.
1947	Independence (as a dominion) on 15th August. Jawaharlal Nehru, long a Congress leader, first Prime Minister. War with Pakistan over Kashmir.
1948	Gandhi assassinated by Hindu militant.
1950	India becomes a republic within the Commonwealth. Beginning of industrialisation programmes, and planned development along socialist lines.
1961	Taking of Goa, Daman and Diu from Portuguese. Final end of colonialism.
1962	War with China over disputed territory in Ladakh and Arunachal Pradesh.
1964	Death of Nehru. Succeeded by Lal Bahadur Shastri.
1965	War with Pakistan over Kashmir.
1966	Death of Shastri at Tashkent after negotiating peace with Pakistan. Indira Gandhi (daughter of Nehru, and not related to the Mahatma) takes over as Prime Minister.
1971	India aids secession of East Pakistan and formation of Bangladesh. Further hostilities with Pakistan.
1975	Faced with increasing civil disorder, Mrs Gandhi declares Emergency and assumes near-dictatorial powers. 160,000 political opponents imprisoned.
1977	General election. Congress party defeated, for first time since Independence, by coalition Janata (People's) Party led by Morarji Desai.
1979	Defections and personal ambitions cause collapse of Janata, followed by landslide victory for Mrs Gandhi in new poll.
1980	Mrs Gandhi's son and chosen successor, Sanjay, killed in air crash.
1981	Rajiv, Mrs Gandhi's other son, elected as MP for Amethi (UP). Isolated incidents of terrorism in Punjab.
1982	Communal violence between Sikhs and Hindus in Amritsar and elsewhere.
1983	Violence during state assembly elections in Kashmir. Rapidly escalating violence leads to imposition of President's rule in

1984	**(June)**	Punjab. Army storms Golden Temple with heavy casualties on both sides.
		Collapse of Kashmir state government, sporadic violence, and Sunni-Shia rioting.
	(Oct)	Assassination of Mrs Gandhi by her Sikh bodyguards and accession of Rajiv as Prime Minister. 3000 (mostly Sikhs) killed in rioting following Mrs Gandhi's death, 2400 in Delhi. Police supine, and Cong (I) involved. Rajiv acts decisively to end trouble and broadcasts 'secularism is the bedrock of our nationhood'.
	(Dec)	General election except in Punjab and Assam. Cong (I) win 403 of 513 constituencies contested. Before Mrs Gandhi's assassination its defeat seemed inevitable. Opposition unable to agree strategy and hence annihilated. VP Singh finance minister.
1985	**(May)**	Sikh bombing campaign in Delhi, at least 80 killed. FBI discover plot in US to kill Rajiv, due to visit following month.
1986	**(Jan)**	Militant Sikhs take control of Golden Temple and later declare independent state of Khalistan.
	(Apr)	Army and police invade Golden Temple again to evict militants. Little violence then, but wave of killing follows, mainly of innocent Hindus.
		Unrest in Jammu and Kashmir following court decision allowing Hindus to worship in Ayodhya mosque.
1987	**(Apr)**	Conflict between President Zail Singh and Rajiv over corruption in his government. News of Bofors and other corrupt deals breaks. VP Singh resigns as defence minister over investigation launched by him into defence procurement corruption, apparently involving Rajiv or his close aides.
	(July)	Agreement between Rajiv and Sri Lanka to settle Tamil insurgency there. Indian Peace-Keeping Force (3000 men) deployed, compromised by inability to cut off Indian support for Tamil separatists for political reasons. Chaos as different Tamil groups attack one another and provoke action by IPKF against them. Fighting worsens, heavy casualties on all sides. IPKF eventually grows to 70,000 without really getting on top of problem.
	(Sept)	Raids on *Indian Express* newspaper by tax authorities aimed at blocking its Bofors investigations. Further allegations against Rajiv and his confidantes.
1988	**(June)**	VP Singh elected to parliament in by-election on anti-corruption ticket. Sikh bombs in Delhi, more killing of Hindus in Punjab.
	(July)	Auditor-General damns government over Bofors deal. Opposition MPs resign *en masse*.
	(Aug)	National strike to try to force Rajiv's resignation.
		Sri Lankan pressure for withdrawal of IPKF.
		General election announced for November. First violence over Ayodhya mosque, fomented by VHP (Vishwa Hindu Parishad), 100 killed in various parts of Uttar Pradesh. Formation of Janata Dal, opposition coalition excluding BJP and communists. Inflation, not a problem for a long time, a major factor in election.
		Congress win only 193 of 525 seats contested, opposition still fragmented. VP Singh forms National Front government with support from BJP and others.

1990		Kashmir Liberation Front involved in secessionist violence. Army deployed.
	(Mar)	IPKF finally withdrawn from Sri Lanka; violence continues.
	(Sept)	Unrest throughout northern India over VP Singh's plan to implement Mandal Commission's report on government job reservations for disadvantaged communities.
	(Oct)	LK Advani (leader of BJP) falls out with secular-minded VP Singh by provoking further trouble at Ayodhya and is arrested.
	(Nov)	Singh's government collapses. New National Front government under Chandra Shekhar with Cong (I) support. 3560 killed in Punjab during year.
1991	**(Mar)**	NF government falls apart over Cong (I) demands.
	(May)	Rajiv assassinated in Tamil Nadu by Tamil partisans while campaigning for general election. PV Narasimha Rao elected Cong (I) leader.
	(June)	Cong (I) forms minority government (226 seats out of 545) despite severe losses to BJP in Hindi heartland. Financial and foreign exchange crisis. Trouble continues in Punjab, death toll for year 4768.
1992	**(Feb)**	First elections in Punjab for eight years, Cong (I) successful. Maoist guerillas kill 33 upper caste Hindus in Bihar.
	(Mar)	Reforming budget; import duties reduced, $1300 million of state industries to be privatised, industrial controls and curbs on foreign investment relaxed, and principle of self-reliance eroded.
	(Apr)	Strife in Kashmir and Punjab.
	(May)	200 die in Orissa after drinking methyl alcohol.
1993	**(Feb)**	Government breaks up huge BJP rally in Delhi and arrests 75,000 militants. Deregulation and tax cuts in budget, rupee to be convertible. Huge World Bank loan, mainly to look after workers in unviable state industries.
	(Mar)	250 killed, 1200 injured in bomb explosions in Bombay. Traced to criminal gang with alleged help from Pakistan. Liberalisation of licence raj.
	(Jun)	Rao accused of accepting $320,000 election funding from Bombay stockbroker.
	(Nov)	Big BJP losses in state elections.
	(Dec)	Kashmir militants kill 2600, mostly civilians, in year, and lose 1075 to security forces.
1994	**(Feb)**	Further economic liberalisation despite slower than expected economic growth.
	(Jul)	Ban on sex testing of foetuses passed in Lok Sabha.
	(Dec)	Cong (I) suffer major losses in state elections, mainly because of austerity programme. Ministers resign over corruption allegations.
1995	**(Jan)**	Crisis in Cong (I) over Rao's woolly leadership and party's move away from its traditional supporters. World Bank loan to restructure and modernise certain Indian banks, apparently with view to privatisation.
	(Mar)	More Cong (I) losses in state elections. Renewed speculation on party split.
	(Aug)	Chief Minister of Punjab assassinated.
	(Sept)	Yet another cabinet reshuffle. Rama Rao's personal guru said to

have links to gangs accused of Bombay bombings.

(Nov)	Kentucky Fried Chicken forced to close in Bangalore and Delhi as part of BJP campaign against multinationals; reopened following month.
(Dec)	Mosque at Ayodhya destroyed. Around 1200 deaths in ensuing rioting, almost all Muslims. Government arrests 5000 including BJP leaders.
1996 **(Jan)**	Huge corruption scandal involving former ministers of all parties. Three ministers resign and are charged. Advani and prominent members of other parties resign their seats.
(Feb)	Four more ministers resign. Chief Minister of Delhi resigns. Supreme Court forbids Prime Minister to oversee investigations. Telecoms to be privatised.
(Mar)	Altogether 115 politicians and bureaucrats alleged to have taken $18 million in bribes from just one businessman. General election called for April/May.
(Apr)	Three more ministers resign. Governor of Himachal Pradesh resigns over involvement in Delhi housing scandal.
(May)	Cong (I) routed in elections: BJP 194 seats, National Front–Left Front 179, Cong 139. Atal Behari Vajpayee of BJP named Prime Minister, resigns 2 weeks later unable to form a government. HD Deve Gowda Prime Minister of United Front (new name of National Front–Left Front) government with Cong support.
(June)	Government wins confidence vote and promises higher social spending. Finance Minister cuts spending causing tension in coalition. Cabinet reshuffle. Rao charged with corruption.
(July)	Minister resigns from United Front government over corruption charges.
(Sept)	Rao resigns as Cong president.

Two important features of Indian history are not necessarily obvious in a summary like this. Firstly, unlike the histories of smaller unified countries, there has not been a clear progression and development over the centuries. Dynasties have come and gone, and government, society, the arts and so on have evolved in fits and starts. Secondly, and not surprisingly in so large an area, there have always been many different things going on at the same time. Even Ashoka and the Mughals, who came closer to unifying India than anyone else before the British, had to contend with frequent rebellions in the provinces, as often as not by their own subordinates and co-religionists. The British themselves were content to leave many of the princes, both Hindu and Muslim, to run their own states, and directly controlled little over half the country.

GOVERNMENT AND POLITICS

Before independence in 1947 British India — now India, Pakistan, and Bangladesh — consisted of the British-ruled provinces (roughly 60% of the 4.3 million sq km/1.7 million sq mile land area) and 563 princely states in varying degrees of alliance to the British crown. Initially the (British) Indian Independence Act envisaged a unified country with the princes allowed to carry on much as before, or even becoming fully independent. Lord Mountbatten, appointed as Britain's last Viceroy, had to sort out the mechanics of independence in a hurry against a background of indifference in Britain, agitation for a Muslim state, internecine squabbling between Hindu politicians, and religious massacres.

The inevitable concession of partition into two separate states of India and

Pakistan made further division unthinkable, and thus necessitated the accession of the princely states to one country or the other. This process was accomplished as much by Mountbatten's force of character as by any sincere belief the princes may have had in a democratic India. Some of the methods were a little rough and ready, but one has only to consider a Muslim-ruled state with a predominantly Hindu population in the centre of India allying itself to Pakistan to see the justification. The princes' misgivings proved well founded when Mrs Gandhi arbitrarily terminated their pensions and privileges in 1971.

The external boundaries of British India were natural and historic ones, mostly mountain chains. Creating Pakistan meant determining areas with a Muslim majority and drawing a line on the ground, sometimes cutting villages or even fields in two.

India's internal boundaries at the time of independence were the result of warfare and administrative convenience, cutting across more natural demarcations. The present states evolved over a period of years after independence. The old Bombay Presidency, for instance, first absorbed the princely states within its boundaries and then split into Maharashtra and Gujarat. The basis of this division was a linguistic one, between Marathi and Gujarati speakers. Until 1966 Punjab was a much larger state incorporating the present Haryana and much of Himachal Pradesh. Sikh agitation, ostensibly on linguistic grounds, but actually more religious and political, saw the slimming down to an essentially Sikh state.

Central government

Voters directly elect representatives (MPs) to the lower house (Lok Sabha — People's Assembly) of the central government in New Delhi. This assembly of about 550 members can be dissolved by the President and is subject to a general election after five years at most. The upper house (Rajhya Sabha — Assembly of States) consists mainly of representatives elected by members of the state assemblies and also specialists nominated by the President. This is never dissolved, one third of the members retiring every other year. Both houses are accommodated in Sansad Bhavan, the circular parliament building.

The President is chosen by an electoral college consisting of MPs and MLAs (see below) using a form of proportional representation and weighting for the smaller states. The term is five years, and in the past things have been arranged so that the post tends to alternate between a Hindu and a Muslim.

Union territories are (apart from Delhi) politically sensitive areas considered unready for full local self-government. They are presided over by a Lieutenant-Governor and have an assembly with limited powers.

State government

Each state has its own government, the Vidhan Sabha or legislative assembly; some of the larger states also have an upper house (Vidhan Parishad). The members of the assembly are known as MLAs, and the Council of Ministers in a state is headed by the Chief Minister. Central government delegates certain powers, notably police, education, local taxes, and industry to the states and also appoints the Governor to represent the Union President. The power of the Governor to dissolve the local assembly, a power not always exercised with political impartiality, can cause friction when the state government is a different party from the union one.

Politics

Elections in India are by universal suffrage, the qualifying age now being 18, lowered from 21 in 1988. Voting is on the first-past-the-post principle, candidates needing only a simple majority. The elections are essentially fair, though a certain amount of 'booth capturing', where partisan goondas prevent people voting freely, takes place in remote areas. Blatant vote buying is decreasing as voters become more sophisticated. In this context Indian politicians are having to learn that illiterate is not a synonym for stupid. The cultivation of vote-banks, for instance where a politician prevents clearance of a slum in return for the inhabitants' votes, does not encourage good government.

The one constant factor politically has been the Indian National Congress, known simply as Congress. Founded in 1885 to campaign for self-government, it has ruled India for all but four years since 1947. Personal ambitions have caused it, like other parties, to split into factions, the dominant one of the last twenty years being the Cong (I) founded by Indira Gandhi.

Opposition to Congress has always taken the form of an alliance. To an extent this is inevitable as while Congress presents a (more or less) monolithic face across the country opposition in the states often consists of purely local parties. The success of these parties in national elections ensures a fragmented state of the parties in Delhi, and means decisions on which grouping to support. Such decisions are rarely made on political principle, never mind for the greater good of the country.

The first defeat suffered by Congress at a national level was by the Janata (People's) Party in 1977. Despite two different leaders (Morarji Desai and Charan Singh) that alliance fell apart within two years because of internal bickering over power. An identical fate befell the National Front led first by VP Singh and then Chandra Shekhar in 1988–91.

The last few years have seen the rise of the Bharatiya Janata Party (BJP), an overtly Hindu party and, as such, an unwelcome deviation from India's secular principles.

Interestingly, the recent Congress government under PV Narasimha Rao, widely assumed to be a makeweight, has made the greatest efforts to cut through red tape and liberalise the vast latent power of the Indian economy.

THE ECONOMY

India is an agrarian society with 80% of the population living in 600,000 or so villages. Apart from the necessary artisans most of these people work on the land either as peasant farmers or landless labourers. The countryside has undergone a 'green revolution' in the last 20 years and now produces more food grains per capita than ever before despite the small size of the countless farms. A measure of this success is that India can now afford (in a good year) to export food, though local shortages still occur because of distribution problems. Life remains hard for the land-workers, but at least the spectre of starvation has receded.

Despite having only 20% of the population in the cities India is now a major industrial power with vast mineral resources. The unbelievable inefficiency and corruption of state-owned industries and the dead hand of government control over private industry has severely hampered exploitation and development. Bold government reforms in 1991–2, if maintained, augur well for the future, not least because Indians now realise how smaller and less advantaged East Asian nations have left them behind in the prosperity stakes.

State industries and patronage

It always amazes people used to the industriousness and business success of Indians everywhere else in the world that their own country should be in such an economic mess. The main reason for this has been government intervention.

The socialist principles of India's founding fathers saw to it that both central and state governments played a central role in industrial development. Although India always espoused a mixed economy the result was exactly the same as in the former Soviet bloc: protectionism, high prices, limited production, and shoddy goods.

The biggest disincentive was what became known as licence raj (the rule of licences). Say a small businessman wanted to set up a little factory to make ceiling fans. First he needed a licence; this meant bribes because he would be competing with larger companies and possibly state-owned ones that had influence and simply did not want competition. He would be instructed to buy his raw materials from a state-owned firm that delivered only when bribed, and then delivered sub-standard stuff. The licence stated how many fans he could make, so he would have to bribe more officials not to notice higher production.

Because road transport (privately owned) was not allowed to compete with the railways (state-owned) a very restrictive system of licensing was used. Most trucks were limited to a certain area, so at state borders you would see lorries back-to-back as their cargoes were humped from one to the other. The list is endless, and the result inevitable. Exports were minute, and the Indian consumer got a very raw deal.

Politicians like state-owned industries because of the opportunities for patronage. Directors of state-owned firms were more likely to be chosen for their contributions to party funds than their ability. And, of course, they would be looking for ways to claw back those contributions. Yet more bribes, so what the socialist dreamers envisaged as a virtuous and benevolent state became a mendacious and inefficient one. Privatisation and innate Indian entrepreneurship promise big changes.

THE PEOPLE

The ten-yearly census taken in 1991 showed the population of India to be 844 million. This is more than twice as large as in 1947 and largely accounts for the slow improvement in living standards despite India's massive industrialisation programme. Although the birth rate is now showing a small decline population is still increasing because of improved health care.

Population density over the country as a whole is 267 per sq km, roughly half that in Britain. In the major states the density varies from 766 per sq km in West Bengal to 128 per sq km in Rajasthan, though the actual extremes are a staggering 6319 per sq km in urban Delhi down to 10 per sq km in the mountainous Arunachal Pradesh. The overall literacy rate is 52% (males 64%, females 39%), up from 44% in 1981, and only 34% in 1971. The most literate state is Kerala with 91% (they now claim 99%) and the least (excluding the tiny and scattered population of Arunachal) where you would expect in benighted Bihar and traditionalist Rajasthan (both 39%). Female literacy in these two states is less than one third of the male figure. The overall sex ratio is 929 females to 1000 males, a figure that has steadily worsened since the beginning of the century. Two states, Maharashtra and Punjab, have introduced legislation against prenatal sex testing because wholesale abortion of female foetuses threatened to make the position even worse.

Ethnic background

One of the legacies of India's many invasions is the varied ethnic make-up of the population. The aborigines (Adivasis), surviving in small groups in the hills and jungles, are related to the peoples of Sri Lanka, Sumatra, and Australia. The Dravidians, who probably came from western Asia by way of Baluchistan, supplanted this indigenous population in the Deccan and still dominate in the south. The first wave of Aryans colonised the northern plains around 1500BC, and their descendants are still there. Physical differences are noticeable (though often misleading), Dravidians tending to be both shorter and darker than Aryans.

In the Himalayas are people of Chinese and Tibetan origin, and in the tribal areas of the south are groups of Malay-Negro and Malay-Mongolian descent.

The new middle class

For a long time India lacked a substantial urban middle class with surplus spending power. There has always been plenty of wealth in India, but a turbulent history encouraged saving, preferably in the form of gold buried in the back yard. Suddenly people are no longer afraid of conspicuous consumption, and it shows in greatly increased private car traffic, better quality consumer durables in smarter shops, and better amenities of all kinds. The main sign, though, is the mushrooming of housing colonies around all of India's cities.

The young (yes, there are lots of yuppies in India) are no longer content to live in an extended family in the ancestral home. They have relatives in the West, they see Western films, they visit there themselves and see our lifestyle. They want to emulate it, and in the process they are picking up a few of the good things as well as most of the bad ones. This way of life, of course, contrasts sharply with rural poverty. Young Indians argue, reasonably enough, that they work hard and efficiently. Why should they not enjoy the same fruits as their Western counterparts?

Women in India

One might think that in the first large country to have a woman Prime Minister women's rights would have advanced in India, but this is not the case. Mrs Gandhi, as a conservative brahmin, saw little need for social change, whatever she might promise at election time. She, like the female head of every Indian family, had reached the top of the tree, and that was good enough for her and everyone else. And this is the paradox. Matriarchs have great respect and influence both inside and outside the family, yet women as a whole, almost regardless of caste or economic standing, are disadvantaged from cradle to grave.

Girl children are not welcome. They cannot work as hard as boys, and when they marry they need dowries that can leave a poor family in debt for 20 years. When food is scarce they are the first to go short, and female infanticide is still far from unknown.

After marriage a woman goes to live in the extended family of her husband. There she is likely to be treated as little more than a slave to her mother-in-law. Producing boy children and age gradually improve her status, until eventually she becomes the family matriarch. Having been through the mill herself she sees no reason for change, and so the whole miserable cycle continues.

Marriage in India

Despite other changes virtually all marriages in India are still arranged ones. In the villages professional matchmakers do the work for a fee. The participants, especially the brides, have no say in the matter, and a majority of girls is married well before the government's legal minimum age of 18. Things are more liberal for the urban middle class, and it is now common for both sides to be allowed a veto.

Take a look at the Sunday papers during your stay. They carry pages of matrimonial notices where parents advertise for a match for their children. The requirements are incredibly detailed, going into caste and sub-caste, education, employment, and domestic attainments. Two of the best selling points are 'wheatish complexion' (a fair skin counts for a lot) and, best of all, a 'Green Card', which entitles the holder to residence in the USA.

An interesting social change has occurred in these pages. Fifteen years ago perhaps one advertisement out of a whole page would have the phrase 'No bars' implying that a match from a different caste would be considered. Now as many as 20% of the advertisements say this. Another expression, rarely seen before, is 'decent wedding', which means that the bride's parents are expected to provide a respectable show rather than a ridiculously lavish one.

Wedding celebrations still tend to be extravagant and noisy. Certain times of year are considered auspicious, and it can be hard to find refuge from the bright lights and unbelievably loud music.

Given Indian hospitality you are quite likely to be invited in to a wedding by people you have never met before, and this is an opportunity not to be missed.

'Marriage comes first, love comes later', they say in India. Marriage is also for life. Although legal, divorce is extremely rare and a great social disadvantage, especially for the woman. In theory non-Muslim women divorcing are entitled to a share of the family property. Their chances of getting anything, or custody of boy children, are poor. Muslim women are even worse off. The Congress party has always regarded the Muslim community as one of its vote banks and, to keep them sweet, passed what is called Muslim personal law. At variance with the law for everyone else, amongst other things it denies a divorced Muslim woman any rights at all.

Other social changes

It is not only the bourgeoisie that is becoming more assertive. The masses are at last starting to demand the rights the constitution promised them fifty years ago. Pressure groups have had some success in preventing the illegal logging that is so damaging to the environment; they also protect the rights of poor farmers whose land is taken for dam building.

Indian women, never the shrinking violets Western feminists might believe, are becoming more vociferous too. Despite immense pressure from the booze barons they have forced the reintroduction of prohibition in Andhra Pradesh and Haryana (virtually bankrupting the latter state in the process). The practice of 'wife burning', faking a wife's suicide so that the husband can marry again and claim another dowry, is declining as the police are forced to take action against guilty in-laws, something almost unknown ten years ago.

Sex in India

India does not cater for sexual tourism. Prostitution, though illegal, exists in well defined areas of most cities. These include the area around Ajmeri Gate in Old Delhi and Bombay's notorious cages on Falkland Road; neither welcomes foreigners, and the equivalent district in Calcutta is positively dangerous. Better class call-girls sometimes work the international hotels.

The chances of a male visitor having a fling with a respectable Indian girl are zero. Western women will, of course, find no shortage of offers.

Homosexuality in India

One might think from the number of men who stroll around holding hands that homosexuality is rampant in India. It is not, and this is just a sign of companionship in a country where social contact between unmarried people of opposite sexes is still very rare.

Homosexuality does of course exist, but Indian society has no place for unmarried men, and lesbians are in an even worse position. The admission of homosexual sentiments is deeply unacceptable, and affairs are furtive. Contrary to what the government claims AIDS is a serious problem.

Hijras

One of the odder aspects of Indian society you may encounter on a city street, especially in Delhi, is the hijras or eunuchs. Apparently women, they are conspicuous for their gaudy saris and the uproar that usually seems to accompany their progress in public.

The hijras are in an ambivalent position socially, despised but needed. Traditional families believe that their presence at the birth celebrations for a boy will absorb any homosexual tendencies the child may have. The hijra communities, each under a guru, can be extremely prosperous. Rich Indians pay well for their services, and they also have a neat line in blackmail. They pick on men in the street demanding alms, and anyone who refuses is likely to be shamed by some blatant flashing.

Accounts of the operation are pretty horrific, a common technique being for a barber to tighten a cord round the genitalia and then slice the lot off with a razor. It has been estimated that up to 75% of the men undergoing this die as a result.

The best account of the eunuchs in modern society is in William Dalrymple's *City of Djinns*, which is excellent on other aspects of Delhi as well.

MEETING PEOPLE

This book inevitably spends a lot of time describing temples, forts, and so on. An equally rewarding part of travel is the people you meet. Friendships are quickly formed with fellow travellers; more effort has to be put into meeting Indians in a meaningful way. Indians can be defensive with foreign visitors, possibly because of an old inferiority complex regarding all things Western. A few years ago it was no use expecting serious discussion with an Indian you met casually; you got either a simple pat statement of his stance (determined more by caste or financial standing than thought) or nothing at all. He may have thought you were talking rubbish but would not tell you. Now the younger generation at least really listen to your views, advance their own opinions, and defend them.

This seems to be one of the first signs of a new national self-confidence. Other positive changes include a lot more smiling faces, and not only among the newly affluent.

Many young Indians who have grown up abroad are now backpacking around India just like the rest of us. You get a quite different perspective on things by talking to them, especially the girls.

Dodgy characters

You will be approached by many people, both Westerners and Indians, with hard luck stories. Most are conmen and professional beggars. Do not be taken in by impressive-looking credentials, you can get anything printed in India; especially, take no notice of people claiming to collect for charity, memorial funds, or anything similar.

Gurus and godmen

Seeking enlightenment in India may be less fashionable than in the past, but many people do still have high expectations. Caution is called for. The first thing to grasp is that India is a deeply materialistic country. Never mind all that stuff about dharma and karma, there is a strong incentive to rise above the poverty line and better oneself. The self-centredness of Hindu culture can make Indians unselective about how they achieve this. Gurus and cult leaders are not immune to these rather Western motivations.

It is an unfortunate fact that many of the people attracted to Indian spiritual teachers are unhappy and insecure. The culture shock of India invariably heightens these feelings, and the unscrupulous find literal-thinking Westerners easy prey. Make no mistake about it; many so-called gurus are powerful tantric magicians who can exert a strong influence over your mind, and possess you in the old sense of the word.

Here are three ground rules:

1. Have nothing to do with anyone who wants you to change your name or wear funny clothes; this is part of a process of destroying your identity and self-reliance.

2. Avoid anyone whose portraits are plastered all over the ashram or, worse, are worn on necklaces or badges; this reinforces emotional dependency.
3. Finally, pay little or no more than will cover the simple accommodation and food provided; what need has a holy man for a Mercedes, or any other material possessions for that matter?

Two good books on the subject, *In Search of the Master* by Muz Murray and *Hunting the Guru in India* by Anne Marshall, are out of print but may be found in second-hand bookshops. More readily available is *The Shortest Journey* by Philippa Pullar. The title alludes to the search within for self-enlightenment. One can infer that a person who can't make this journey in his or her own culture and persona is unlikely to achieve it in India.

As an aside, the author's spell-checker objected to the word 'godmen', offering 'admen' in its place.

Women travellers

You should have no real trouble travelling on your own in India, but life will be easier if you understand something of the Asian male's outlook.

Asian men in general, including apparently Westernised ones, have little or no concept of platonic friendship. Free association with the opposite sex is extremely rare in their society. In their eyes, acceptance of a solo dinner invitation, let alone a moonlit stroll round the Taj, can be tantamount to an agreement to sleep with them. This does not mean that you have to pass up every invitation, just be cautious. The safest way is to make sure that there are always other women present. It is not common for Indian women to shake hands with men; certainly any physical contact beyond a handshake is asking for trouble.

The situation is not helped by some very odd beliefs about Westerners and their morals, not least the notion that Western women will not need much persuading before they hop into bed. Even today's emancipated young urban Indians never kiss in public; as little as a quick peck on the cheek or holding hands arouses comment and fuels these silly ideas.

Perhaps as a result of this you will have trouble with gropers through most of South Asia. You can console yourself with the thought that Indian women suffer too. That's what the signs about Eve-teasing in the buses refer to. Modest clothing does reduce the problem. Personal experience suggests that this harassment can be just as much of a strain for a male companion. Even if he catches the offender, thumping him will not help matters and could cause serious trouble.

A limited range of contraceptive pills is now available. Tampons and sanitary towels can be found in all but the smallest towns, though given the rather casual approach to sterility and hygiene, it is a good idea to take your own.

The Indian queue

Queuing is part of the way of life in India. It takes ages to get almost anything done, and in the meantime you queue. Some queues are orderly, others like a rugby scrum. Either way you will literally be rubbing shoulders with your fellow queuers. Indians find it odd that Westerners dislike this sort of contact, which they seem not to notice. Not surprising, perhaps, in a country where only the wealthy can afford privacy. Tempers are not improved by constant attempts at queue jumping and clerks shutting up shop just as you get near the front.

There are only two ways round the queue. Wealthy Indians send a servant to do the business, and you can often find an agent or someone at the hotel to do it for you for a consideration. Or... send your girfriend, wife or whoever. Women are usually allowed to go straight to the front of the queue.

RELIGION

Religion and faith play a crucial part in Indian life. Whether the way of life follows religion or the other way round is a matter for conjecture, but all of the country's problems (and its great strengths) are related pretty directly to religious beliefs. Worship, philosophy, and even conflict are highly stylised. Even in the case of Islam there is considerable blurring of divisions; Hindus willingly accept foreign deities and prophets, and Hindu influence is obvious in the art of other religions — and in the way that they tend to develop caste systems of their own.

Pilgrimages are important to all religions in India. Some are detailed in this book, and you should try to make at least one to sample the unique atmosphere.

Hinduism

Hindu is synonymous with Indian, and an understanding of the religion will account for much of what you see and experience in India. Hinduism is not only a religion, it is a social system, a philosophy, a whole way of life. It is much older than all other major religions, having its origin in the Vedism, or nature worship, brought to India by the Aryans in about 1500BC. The verses called Vedas that explain this are still a basis of Hindu belief. Around 1000BC Brahmanism introduced the concept of a universal god or Brahman, and a class of priests, or Brahmins, whose duties are laid down in the Brahmanas. The following thousand years saw the writing of many other holy works including the Upanishads and the great epic poems, the Mahabharata (tenth century BC) and the rather later Ramayana. The former includes the Bhagavad Gita, which is probably the best known of these works. The most influential, however, was the Law Book of Manu (third century BC), which codified the caste system and the rigid social law that still binds much of India.

Caste. There are thousands of sub-castes, but all belong to one or other of the following:

1. *Brahmins*, or priests and pundits.
2. *Kshatriyas*, warriors, landowners and aristocrats. Generally speaking Rajputs belong to this caste.
3. *Vaisyas*, farmers and tradesmen.
4. *Sudras*, labourers and servants.

There is a racial aspect to this division. The first three castes were Aryan, but the Sudras were Dravidian. Outside the caste system altogether were the untouchables, who got all the really unpleasant jobs. Mahatma Gandhi called these people harijans, or children of God; these days their own preferred term is Dalit. The government now calls them scheduled castes and reserves a proportion of official jobs for them, a system that increases friction because there are always thousands of applicants for each post. In a similar position are the scheduled tribes, who are often primitive aborigines following pre-Vedic animist religions.

Concepts. There are three basic concepts in Hindu belief — samsara, karma and dharma — which also apply (more or less) in Buddhism and Jainism. Samsara is belief in the principle of reincarnation. The idea is that as one body dies the soul migrates to a new one. Whether this new body is higher or lower in the social scale (it can be the body of an animal or insect) depends upon karma.

Karma means action or deeds, and here signifies the belief that one's behaviour in this life determines the status of the soul's new body. Karma, in this sense, is how dharma is followed.

Dharma is the law that governs a Hindu's every action. It is basically a matter of caste, the mode of life being determined by the caste into which one is born. The Gita teaches that it is less harmful to follow your own dharma badly than to excel in some other lifestyle. The only way to progress up the social scale is to fulfil your dharma and achieve a good reincarnation. Eventually, with good karma and countless incarnations one can achieve moksha, oneness with god and freedom from the cycle of death and rebirth. This may be interpreted as leading to a certain degree of social inertia.

The practicalities of dharma are far-reaching. For each caste rituals are laid down for washing, the preparation of food, what to wear, and how to avoid every caste Hindu's greatest fear — pollution by someone lower in the system. A brahmin could be polluted by an untouchable venturing within 40m of him. Things are generally less extreme now, and the system is rapidly breaking down in urban areas. You will still, however, see plenty of people who carry their own cups and packed meals rather than risk contact with something handled by a person lower in the order.

The gods. Worship is very much a personal matter, with few organised services and plenty of choice. Despite the apparent profusion of gods Hinduism is, in effect, a monotheism. As already mentioned Brahman is the all-pervading God, the Atman within each soul. The many different gods are just aspects of Brahman, who is symbolised as the **trinity** of Brahma, Shiva and Vishnu. **Brahma**, the creator, is depicted as having four heads (five until Shiva lopped one off), and his wife **Sarasvati** is goddess of music. Apparently the senior member of the trinity, Brahma in fact has a negligible following; of all the places covered in this book only one, Pushkar, has a Brahma temple.

Shiva, the destroyer and reproducer, has a much wider appeal. You will always be able to spot one of his shrines by the symbols: tridents and lingams. The lingam is a stylised phallus representing Shiva's role as reproducer. In front of most Shiva temples you will find the bull Nandi, which is also revered. Shiva's consort **Parvati** is the goddess of beauty, but also has a more sinister aspect as **Kali**, or **Durga**, who carries out most of Shiva's destructive function. **Ganesh**, the elephant-headed god of wisdom and enterprise, is one of their two sons, the other being **Kartikkeya**, the god of war.

Vishnu, the preserver, is notable for his nine visits to Earth. In each case Vishnu has taken an earthly form to help him rescue mankind from great danger. The inspiration for this belief, which had been adopted in its final form by the 11th century AD, comes from a variety of sources, some quite possibly not Indian. Recognising the avatars makes temple visits more interesting:

1. *The Fish* (Matsya) rescued Manu, a figure analogous to both Adam and Noah, from a flood that engulfed the Earth.
2. *The Tortoise* (Kurma). Among the things lost in this flood was the amrit, or nectar of the gods. Vishnu took the form of a giant tortoise to retrieve the amrit from the bottom of the primeval ocean.
3. *The Boar* (Varaha) killed the demon who had thrown the Earth back into the ocean, and raised it up again on his tusks.
4. *The Man-Lion* (Narasimha) killed an otherwise invincible demon.
5. *The Dwarf* (Vamana) dealt with another demon that had taken over the Earth. Granted one wish by the demon, Vamana demanded as much ground as he could cover in three paces. His three steps encompassed not only Earth, but also heaven and the middle air.
6. *Parasurama* (Rama with axe). Vishnu made his first incarnation in human form to avenge a brahmin robbed and later murdered by Kshatriyas. The story goes that he killed 21 generations of male Kshatriyas — not a popular theme as the princes who endowed most temples came from this caste.
7. *Rama*, perhaps based on a real prince of the eighth century BC, is best known as the hero of the epic poem, the *Ramayana*. Helped by Hanuman, the monkey-faced demigod, he rescued his wife Sita from the demon king Lanka. He took this incarnation, however, to rescue the world from the demon

Ravana. Rama is usually depicted with a dark face and carrying a bow and arrow.

8. *Krishna* is the most popular figure in the Indian pantheon. Best known as a lover of the countryside and patron of herdsmen (and especially herds-women), he is also the hero of the *Mahabharata*. In this epic he vanquishes the forces of evil all over the country and delivers the seminal message of Hinduism, the *Bhagavad Gita*. The huge body of Krishna stories is obviously based mainly on the exploits of a number of real Indian folk heroes, but seems also to draw on themes from as far away as the Near East and Greece. It has even been conjectured that the child-god form derives from missionaries' tales of Jesus.

9. *Buddha* is a comparatively late addition to the list. Traditionally Vishnu took this form to save animals from the ritual slaughter associated with Brahmanical worship. The real reason is probably more prosaic: to encourage Buddhists, who could be seen as non-conformist Hindus, to return to the fold.

10. *Kalkin* will be the next avatar. Vishnu will appear on a white horse and bearing a flaming sword to end the present age of evil and to deliver judgement on all men. This apocalyptic vision has Christian and Parsi parallels, but probably owes more to Buddhist and Jain belief in teachers yet to come.

Representations of the first eight avatars are common and will be seen on many temples; the last two are much rarer. In paintings Krishna is most often depicted with a blue face and playing a flute. His consort Radha was a milkmaid. He is sometimes pictured lifting a mountain to shelter peasants from the Vedic rain god Indra. Vishnu's wife is **Lakshmi**, goddess of wealth.

Tradition and dharma still exert tremendous influence despite laws that have banned, for instance, untouchability and dowry. Sati, the practice of a widow immolating herself on her husband's funeral pyre, was supposedly abolished by the British in 1830 but still occurs occasionally. Dowry causes much bloodshed, and not so long ago a wealthy harijan in Madhya Pradesh who had given a temple Rs45,000 for a new idol was not allowed in to worship it! He got off lightly; there are still places where he would have been killed for entering the temple.

In the cities the more obvious manifestations of caste are declining rapidly. In the countryside it is a different matter, despite the enlightened efforts of many groups and individuals.

Although the constitution designates India as a secular state and guarantees freedom of worship, 85% of the people are Hindu and this obviously has a considerable effect.

Buddhism

Siddhartha Gautama, known as Buddha, is a historical figure. He was born at Lumbini (just over the border in Nepal) in 624BC. The son of a king, he renounced his life of ease at the age of 29 and spent six years as a wandering beggar trying different ways of gaining knowledge. He eventually achieved enlightenment at Bodhgaya and began his ministry.

The basic Buddhist belief is in the **Four Noble Truths**: (i) life is suffering, (ii) suffering is caused by desire, (iii) by ending desire man can end his suffering, (iv) there is a way of ending desire.

The **Eight-fold Path** is the way to end desire, and by following this one can ultimately achieve nirvana, or freedom from the cycle of rebirth.

There is no god in Buddhism, and the reverence of Buddha himself is a development of the **Mahayana** sect to provide a more popular appeal. The **Hinayana** Buddhists maintain the original beliefs and forms. Buddhism spread rapidly and, as state religion under Ashoka (second century BC), covered almost all India and reached as far as Afghanistan. By around AD500 Buddhism was already dwindling by the process of re-absorption into the mainstream of Hinduism, and the Muslim invasions completed the job.

About four million people in India are Buddhists. Of this total perhaps 3.5 million are harijan converts, disciples of the late Dr Ambedkar. Many of the remainder, including the 100,000 Tibetan refugees resident in India, are followers of Tantric Buddhism, or Lamaism, the complex form that has developed in Tibet.

Jainism

Despite being almost unknown outside India and having only 2½ million adherents, Jainism is in many ways the most interesting of the home-grown religions. It is contemporary with Buddhism and was founded in the same area as a reaction against Brahmanical Hinduism and its animal sacrifices. The founder, who is known as **Mahavira** (great hero) or **Jina** (victor), was the last of 24 **tirthankas** or prophets. Statues of the tirthankas are very similar to those of Buddha, and can be distinguished from one another by the symbol (horse, bull, etc.) on the pedestal. The plants you see climbing up the legs of some of the standing images symbolise their immovability and permanence.

Starting as an atheistic monastic order Jainism has developed the trappings of a religion to cater for lay members. There are two sects, the **Svetambaras** and the **Digambaras**. The latter until recently took their asceticism to the extreme of wearing no clothes, their name translating literally as 'sky-clad'. All Jains believe in **ahimsa**, total non-violence, and are vegetarian, the stricter ones not even eating root vegetables as that kills the plant. Priests and members of monastic orders wear masks and sweep the ground in front of them to avoid killing even the smallest living organism. A convocation of holy men requires long planning as the participants will only walk to it; vehicles run over or squash insects.

Jainism allows its followers considerable say in their destiny and, through the principles of Right Faith, Right Cognition and Right Conduct, the chance to attain nirvana during life. This can be seen as more positive than Hindu and Buddhist teaching and, probably as a result of this, Jains tend to be successful and dynamic businessmen.

Buddhists, Jains and Sikhs can all be seen as reformed sects of Hinduism, though the Sikhs at least would vigorously dispute this statement. Hindus certainly take this view, admitting them to temples that are closed to Muslims and Christians and probably, for that matter, Dalits as well. The constitution, of course, guarantees entry to all Indian citizens.

Sikhism

Immediately distinguishable by their carefully wound turbans and uncut hair the Sikhs provide the practical skills that keep India moving. Their religion stems from a 16th century attempt by the first guru, Nanak, to establish a bridge between Hinduism and Islam. It differed, however, in admitting neither predestination nor total subjection to God. Nanak preached against the idol worship of the Hindus and the intolerance of the Muslims. Non-belief in caste was fundamental, an ideal not subsequently lived up to.

Initial friendliness gave way to persecution under later Mughal emperors, and it was the sixth guru, Har Gobind (1606–1645), who built the Lohgarh (Steel Fort) in Amritsar and trained a body of soldiers. Oppression worsened, and the killing of Tegh Bahadur (the ninth guru) by Aurangzeb led his successor, Govind Singh, to establish Sikhism largely as it is known now. Irked by the cowardice of Sikhs who should have supported Tegh Bahadur, he laid down the five k's or kakkas that externally distinguish a Sikh. These are uncut hair (kesh), comb in the hair (kanga), bangle (kara), knife or sword (kirpan), and boxer shorts (kachh). Govind Singh refused to name a successor and advised his followers to read the Granth Sahib (holy book) if they needed guidance.

The emergence of the Sikhs as a military elite led through a century of guerilla, and later full-scale, warfare to the setting up of the Sikh state. This was integrated by Maharaja Ranjit Singh with its capital at Lahore. Ranjit Singh established a friendship with the British (which, despite several traumas, long survived) and helped them in the First Afghan War. However, the chaos after his death in 1839 led to a series of wars with the British (1845–1849) and annexation to British India. Undaunted, the Sikhs helped to put down the Mutiny in 1857 and became a privileged and important part of the British Indian Army. Today, although less than 2% of the population, and despite the disillusion caused by the storming of the Golden Temple, they still provide over 10% of the armed forces' manpower (perhaps an even higher percentage of officers).

The Akalis are a sect of orthodox Sikhs who are in the forefront of the struggle for an autonomous Sikh state. You may also come across the Nihangs, an extraordinary group of men armed to the teeth with traditional weapons, who act as gurudwara guards and each year re-enact a famous battle. They wear distinctive yellow and blue clothes and huge turbans.

Although they do not proselytise the Sikhs happily accept converts; there is little formality, one has simply to adopt a Sikh way of life. Indeed it was a tradition in many Hindu Punjabi families to have a younger son brought up as a Sikh. A substantial community of white Sikhs exists in the USA, and you may encounter them in Delhi. The author has seen local Sikhs totally bemused by American women in militaristic uniforms complete with turban and sword!

Before entering a gurudwara both men and women must cover their heads; a sun hat is acceptable. Shoes and socks must be removed, and hands and feet washed. After doing this you may be allowed to put on a brand new pair of socks to wear inside.

A brief account of the recent troubles in Punjab is given in the section on Amritsar.

Islam

About 12% of the population is Muslim. Visitors tend to associate Islam mainly with the Mughals; in fact it is much older-established. In the century following the foundation of the faith in AD622 it spread rapidly to Spain in the west, and India in the east. By the end of the 13th century conquest had carried it over all of India except the very south. As with Christianity many people freely converted to Islam to escape the caste system.

The very word Islam means total submission to God, and Muslim religious practices, though few, are well defined. A devout Muslim will pray five times a day facing Mecca and will try to visit Mecca at least once in his lifetime. Islam is the one religion, apart from Christianity, that requires its adherents actively to propagate its teaching.

Islam is purely monotheistic, with Allah as the one God, and Mohammed his principal prophet. All Muslims, incidentally, regard Jesus as a prophet, and the Ahmadiyya sect (more numerous in Pakistan) gets a lot of flak from more orthodox Muslims for attaching too much importance to him. Read the section on Srinagar for a little more information.

It is often said that Islam is the least influential of India's minority religions. Muslims' original prestige was based on conquest, and this vanished with the takeover by the infidel British. Their position was further weakened by their tendency to side with the British in their struggle against Hindu nationalism. These days considerable ill-feeling is caused by Muslim 'personal law', which gives them legal dispensations not enjoyed by other communities. They can, for instance, have four wives and avoid paying maintenance to ex-wives. The privilege has been defended by the Congress Party over the years to enable them to keep the Muslims as a 'vote bank'. This all plays into the hands of the Hindu nationalists who find it easy to portray the Muslims as a backward and pampered minority.

Christianity

Christianity was established in India long before the European powers arrived on the scene, and it surprises many people to learn that there are more Christians than Sikhs in the country.

Christians in India follow many branches of the faith and for different reasons. The Syrian Orthodox church still has a wide following, as does the Roman Catholic. Although a few high-caste Hindus were converted, the main appeal has always been to harijans and tribals as a way out of the caste system. Unlike most colonial powers the British discouraged missionaries as far as possible, ostensibly to avoid upsetting local feelings, but possibly also because the idea of equality for all men did not fit their book too well.

Apart from Anglo-Indian communities most Christians are concentrated in the south — you will find more details in the introduction to Kerala. Oddly enough, however, Christians form a majority not where you might expect, in Goa or Pondicherry, but in the hill states of Meghalaya, Nagaland and Mizoram.

The Parsees

Parsees are descendents of Zoroastrians driven from Persia in the seventh century by Muslim intolerance. Popularly regarded as fire-worshippers they actually only revere fire as a symbol of purity. Zoroaster (Zarathrustra) was a prophet of the god Ahura-Mazda, and the religion dates from around 1000BC. Parsees believe that their behaviour in life determines their after-life, and this makes them notable (and non-sectarian) philanthropists. Their respect for the environment makes them unwilling to pollute air or earth by cremating or burying their dead; instead they are exposed in Towers of Silence to be devoured by vultures.

The Parsees have always been outward-looking, eschewing Hindu caste and dietary restrictions, and have played a large part in building up Indian industry. Paradoxically, their lack of cant is working against their community. Only the child of a Parsee father can be Parsee, and their numbers, perhaps now down to 60,000, are falling because of mixed marriages. Matters are not helped by the practice, in some families, of marrying only first cousins.

ART AND ARCHITECTURE

The vitality and continuity of Indian art, combined with its extraordinary ability for assimilation, are exceptional in a world context. The earliest objects surviving belong to the Indus valley civilisation, and most were unearthed at Mohenjo Daro and Harappa. There are figures in limestone, clay, and steatite, and also steatite seals bearing images of gods and animals, including many magnificent bulls. There are notable affinities, stylistically and iconographically, with the contemporary civilisation of Mesopotamia, for instance in the bust of a man who is perhaps a priest-king. Certain truly Indian features are already established however. The fluid naturalism of the limestone torso found at Harappa is a good example, and the wide hips, high breasts, elaborate jewellery and hair of the mother goddesses another. Most of the best finds are exhibited in the National Museum, New Delhi.

The Indus valley civilisation died out around 1500BC, and though the following thousand years saw the basic features of Indian culture develop they have left little in the way of art objects. Wood was the predominant building material so no architecture has survived, though Rajgir (in Bihar) had stone walls by 600BC, of which some parts remain.

Ashoka was responsible for the earliest surviving monumental sculptures, one of the finest being the lion capital now in the museum at Sarnath (which also houses some of the best Gupta figures). The lion capital dates from between 242 and 232BC and betrays strong Persian influence. Indeed, all the external influences came from the west, and it must not be forgotten that the last outpost of the Greek empire was at Gandhara in present-day Afghanistan.

The vogue for cave temples began during Ashoka's reign too, but they remained rather basic for the first couple of hundred years or so. They were becoming more sophisticated by the second century AD from which time the Karla caves (near Bombay) date. The plan of the main temple is basilican, also owing its form to influences from the west. The vaulting is in imitation of the wood architecture still current at this time.

Perhaps the finest monument of this era is the great stupa at Sanchi, dating from the first century AD. It is predated by Barhut and can be seen as a development from it in sculptural style. The Barhut railings are in the Calcutta Museum; they are in lower relief and have less complex composition than the reliefs in Sanchi, but are still very beautiful. Sanchi's reliefs are believed to have been made by ivory carvers, which perhaps explains their marvellous intricacy. The Buddha is represented by symbols and does not appear as a figure until the following century.

A 'classical' period for sculpture then arose with two centres. Gandhara with its evident Greek influence, and Mathura (between Delhi and Agra) with a more purely native style. Gandharan images of Greek gods have been found, but the sculpture was mainly Buddhist in both centres. The two styles co-existed for several centuries and, though the differences are obvious, they shared a quality of stillness and meditation.

Though painting is mentioned in the Vedas (before 1000BC) the earliest examples surviving date from AD600. The frescoes at Ajanta are remarkable for their grace and freshness; those at Bagh, slightly older than Ajanta, have deteriorated badly, but excellent copies can be seen in the Archaeological Museum in Gwalior.

The period between the collapse of the Gupta empire and the arrival of the Muslims is generally classified as medieval. It saw a Hindu renaissance of tremendous vitality culminating in the creation of those temples and sculptures one thinks of as quintessentially Indian, for instance those at Khajuraho, Bhubaneswar, and Konarak. These are Indo-Aryan as opposed to Dravidian, and it is in the latter, at Mahabalipuram, that we see the transition from rock-cut to constructed temples. The works at Mahabalipuram were produced by the Pallava dynasty from about AD600 to 750 in what is now Tamil Nadu. The Pallavas were succeeded by the Cholas whose special contribution to Indian art was superb bronzes, many of which can be seen in Madras Museum. The last great monument to the Dravidian style is the eighth century Kailasha Temple at Ellora — architecture or sculpture?

The temples at Khajuraho date between the 10th and 12th centuries AD. Like Konarak they are famed for their erotic sculpture, but there are many other subjects also. However the whole is imbued with warmth, sensuality, and life. In the museum is a remarkable sculpture of Ganesh dancing, the largest as well as one of the finest ever made. This was also a productive era for the Jains, the glorious temples at Dilwara (Mount Abu in Rajasthan) being built at this time.

Much of northern India was by now under Rajput rule. They were great builders of secular as well as religious buildings, and a wealth of architecture survives at such places as Chitor, Mandu, Amber, Jaipur, and Gwalior. Emperor Babur, no indophile, admired Jodhpur fort in particular.

The Muslim invaders destroyed a great deal but also introduced new ideas from the west. Architects, poets, and artists were brought from Constantinople and Persia, and with them came the dome and the arch. They adorned their buildings with calligraphic and abstract decoration in keeping with the injunctions in the Koran against graven images. The history of these turbulent times is embodied in the architectural monuments of Delhi from the Qutb Minar through the Lodi tombs to Humayun's tomb, which anticipates that greatest of Mughal achievements, the Taj Mahal.

The Mughals kept their identity, but their catholic interest in the arts enabled considerable exchange between native and Persian elements, which added new impetus to the continuing vitality of Indian art. Calligraphy was an important art for the Muslims, appreciated and cultivated in the same way as in China.

There were flourishing schools of painting in Jammu, Kangra, and Rajputana before the coming of the Muslims, and the oldest illuminated manuscripts are Jain texts. The Persian style met the native styles at the court of Akbar, blending to become something unique and richly varied. The Pahari paintings (from the foothills of the Himalayas) are delicately naturalistic, those of southern Rajasthan more stylised with bright areas of colour and pattern, but the movements between courts of the most accomplished artists tended to blur these regional differences. Many artists signed their work, though many paintings were the result of co-operation between a number of artists, this practice being common in Muslim workshops. Akbar was a great admirer of Hindu art, and Jehangir, while not a great builder like his father and his son, was also an enthusiastic connoisseur of painting. Contacts with Europe were established, and European art was seen in engraved reproduction. The influences were reciprocal and Rembrandt, amongst others, admired Indian miniatures. Akbar left us Fatehpur Sikri, a whole city almost perfectly preserved. Shahjahan's architecture appears more purely Persian than his grandfather's and is also more lavishly ornamented.

The Hindu kingdoms of the south were also artistic centres, and fine architecture survives at Vijayanagar despite the efforts of Aurangzeb. Even some paintings remain, most unusually, on the ceiling of the main temple. The arrival of Aurangzeb on the artistic scene was disastrous. He not only dismissed the artists from his court (many sought patronage in the small Hindu kingdoms on the fringe of the Mughal empire) but also destroyed books, paintings, and sculptures wherever he went. Muslim art did not survive this holocaust, and later examples of their architecture tend to be degenerate.

Because there are many similar references in this book it might be remarked here that the Muslims had no monopoly on this kind of destructive behaviour. Protestants wreaked precisely the same kind of damage in European cathedrals during the Reformation, and the English Civil War saw the Roundheads shooting the heads off surviving statues and whitewashing murals.

Despite Muslim iconoclasm the Hindu arts flourished, especially in Rajputana, and one of the finest buildings in Jaisalmer, for example, is 19th century.

The British did little for Indian art. They did, however, put up some fine buildings, such as the neo-gothic railway station in Bombay, and introduced new ideas that sometimes had curious results, like the palace in Mysore.

The last movement of real interest was that of the patriotically nostalgic group of artists headed by the Tagore brothers, who produced exquisite watercolours of which excellent collections can be seen in Delhi, Mysore, and Varanasi. The Hindu University of Varanasi has one of the finest collections of paintings from all periods in India.

The modern scene is depressing. Modern artists in India are few enough; they seem in general to have forgotten their origins and for the most part ape Western art inadequately and meaninglessly. The folk arts have more vitality though some, such as brasswork, are becoming degenerate.

LANGUAGE

Background. There are 14 major languages in India, and many hundred minor ones and dialects. The present state boundaries are drawn mainly on linguistic lines though Urdu, predominant in Pakistan, can be encountered wherever there is a large Muslim community. The northern languages, except for a few of Tibeto-Burmese origin, belong to the Indo-Aryan group and, like most European languages, derive from a proto-Sanskrit. The most common of this group is Hindi, which is also the official language of the country. Most of the northern languages are intelligible to the Hindi speaker, but the southern ones of the Dravidian group are completely different. To give an idea of how confused the whole business of race and language is, some philologists believe the Dravidian languages to be related to those European misfits, Finnish, Estonian and Hungarian.

To further complicate matters, all the major languages have a distinctive script, the most common being Devanagri for Hindi and Rajasthani, and the familiar-looking Persian for Urdu and Kashmiri. There was a plan around the time of Independence to adopt the Roman alphabet for all the languages, but this came to nothing. Whatever the language most signs and directions are translated into English or at least transcribed into Roman characters.

People in the south have proved very reluctant to learn Hindi, and English still enjoys the status of a secondary official language, though it was intended to phase it out as early as 1965. Even now, when a central government officer writes a letter to someone in a state that has not adopted Hindi as one of its official languages he has three options. He can write in the language of the recipient; virtually impossible as he has first to find a secretary who speaks the language and then the appropriate typewriter. If he writes in Hindi he must attach an English translation to the letter so, hardly surprisingly, most adopt the third course and simply write in English in the first place. The sudden growth in access to television, however, may break down this prejudice. Tamils still will not learn Hindi in the classroom but they seem not to mind assimilating it by watching the Ramayana in Hindi!

Getting by. In practice you will find that most of the people you need to deal with have at least a smattering of English.

The position today. Most educated people speak very good English, and take more care over the grammar than we tend to. The mixture of up-to-date slang and 1920s and 1930s idiom can be very entertaining.

Going the other way, between two and three thousand Indian words have found their way into the English language over the years, and we use many of them without realising their origin.

Indian textiles had been famous since the days of Marco Polo, and foreign traders soon adapted the local names. Chintz derives from *chhinta*, which means variegated (before the development of printing, designs were painted on the cloth), and *qtun* (cotton) for your *paejama* is one of several Arabic words that found their way into English via India. Calico comes from Calicut in south India, and cashmere is simply Kashmir, the northernmost Indian state known for its fine woollen shawls (Hindustani, *shal*).

When the working day was over the Englishman in India might return to his bungalow (a corruption of *Bengali*, and meaning a house in that style), put his feet up on the verandah (Bengali again), and smoke a cheroot (Tamil) while waiting for his *kari* (curry, also Tamil), which would, of course, be accompanied by *chatni* (chutney). Sport was one of the compensations the British found for the rigours of life in India. Gymkhana translates literally as ball-house (i.e. rackets court) and came in time to signify any place of exercise. Whether use of the Hindi word for a ball (*goli*) is associated with sport is another matter. Catamaran is Tamil (*kattu*, to bind, plus *maram*, tree), and was originally a raft of logs lashed together and used in Madras to bring passengers and goods ashore through the surf. And a *dinghi* was once a rowing boat on the Ganges.

More seriously, the word thug derives from the cult of Thuggee, a religious sect whose members robbed and strangled travellers as part of their devotions to the goddess Kali. The swastika has similarly unpleasant associations in Europe, and visitors to India are often surprised to see it emblazoned on temples and houses. Yet the hooked cross, deriving from the Sanskrit word *svasti* for well-being or luck, was an auspicious symbol to the Hindus for thousands of years before Hitler misappropriated it.

Things are rarely what they seem in India. Are any words more obviously Chinese than coolie or pagoda? Well, *kuli* (perhaps originally Turkish) was the wages a day-labourer would receive, and pagoda is, believe it or not, the Portuguese corruption of a Persian word for an infidel temple (*bat*, idol, plus *kadah*, house). To confuse you still further, char, or *chai* as the Indians usually pronounce it, really is a Chinese word, Mandarin to be precise.

At least there can't be any doubt about mandarin being Chinese. Or can there? When we speak of a senior civil servant as a mandarin the word we are actually using is *mantrin*, Hindustani for a counsellor. A *brahmin* (another term used for high-flyers in the Civil Service) is one of the top caste of priests, and *pandits* are brahmins expert in genealogy. Pandit Jawarharlal Nehru, first leader of independent India and father of Indira Gandhi, belonged to this caste. And while we are on holy matters it would take a guru to explain the difference between dharma and karma. Both words entered English in the happy, hippy sixties and have been cheerfully confused and misused ever since.

Other words, such as bandana and *jangal* for jungle are pretty obvious. Less likely are bangle (*bangri*, a glass bracelet) and shampoo; *champna* means to press or massage, and possibly acquired its present meaning by association with Turkish baths.

By now it will come as no surprise that one word indelibly associated with India is not of Indian origin at all. Caste, which still permeates most of Indian life, comes from the Portuguese *casta*, itself a derivative of the Latin *castus* for chaste or pure.

Find a copy of *Hobson-Jobson* ('A Glossary of Anglo-Indian Colloquial Words and Phrases', updated by Yule and Burnell) if the subject interests you.

READING

It was once said that 'you only see what you already know', so it is a good idea to get anything you can find on the subject of India from your library and local second-hand bookshops before travelling. The more you read the more you will understand and enjoy the country.

Conventional reading lists tend to be predictable and boring, with most of the books written by Westerners. This is fine if you want to make an academic study. As a Westerner travelling in India, however, you want to see the country (and its attitude to foreigners like yourself) through Indian eyes. That means reading books by Indian writers.

Three Indian authors can give you a really valuable insight into the country: Nirad C Chaudhury, Khushwant Singh, and RK Narayan. Chaudhury's most valuable works (for this purpose) are *The Continent of Circe* and *A Passage to England*. The views expressed in the former are often controversial, but the information is invaluable. *A Passage to England* chronicles better than any other book the author has read the peculiar love-hate relationship between the Indians and the British. His *Clive of India* is a biography of the clerk-turned-soldier who founded the British Empire in India despite the indifference of his employers and the British government. Elegantly written it contains much social comment that shows how little India has changed in 225 years.

Khushwant Singh is India's premier journalist. Collections of his pithy and witty editorials and lectures make amusing and informative reading. He is also the author of the definitive history of the Sikhs.

RK Narayan is a novelist whose work centres on the fictitious South Indian town of Malgudi. He captures to perfection the flavour of small town and rural India. *The Guru* is one of the author's personal favourites. Very cheap editions of both Khushwant Singh's and Narayan's books are on sale all over India.

VS Naipaul, an Indian novelist born and brought up in the West Indies, wrote two excellent books around visits to his homeland, *An Area of Darkness* and *India: A Wounded Civilisation*. Given their rather negative view it may be better to read these two after your visit to see how your observations compare with his. His latest work, *India: A Million Mutinies Now*, is mellower without losing any of the acute perception.

Princess by Vijayaraje Scindia and Manohar Malgonkar and *A Princess Remembers* by Gayatri Devi, both the wives of leading maharajas give a fascinating insight into the life of India's princes in the twilight of the British Raj.

Freedom at Midnight by Collins and Lapierre, a popular history of how India achieved independence, has had a long vogue with budget travellers.

The most accessible serious history is Pelican's *A History of India* in two volumes, the first by Romila Thapar and the second by Percival Spear.

India has captivated many British novelists over the years, and it is fun to read Kipling, Forster, Masters, and Scott while you are in the country. Most of their descriptions and observations are still valid. An acute contemporary observer of the Indian scene is Ruth Prawer Jhabvala.

One of the oddest and most appealing books written about India is *Bengal Lancer* by Francis Yeats-Brown. Alternate chapters contrast the gung-ho life of a cavalry officer and his search for enlightenment. Other personal favourites of the author include *An Indian Summer* by James Cameron and *A Soldier Erect* by Brian W Aldiss.

There are excellent bookshops in most larger towns, and even the pavement and station vendors have all the latest foreign paperbacks, often in cheap rip-off editions. Imported books are sold at the rupee equivalent of the cover price. In Delhi, bookshops in the Janpath tourist bazaar and the underground Palika Bazaar sell coffee-table books on Indian subjects far cheaper than in the West. You will find that you need to buy only a couple of books, after that you can swap with other travellers.

FURTHER INFORMATION

The Government of India publishes a yearbook full of up-to-date statistics on the country.

Specialist magazines in both your own country and India can often provide reprints of old articles and may put you in touch with people who have relevant information.

The India Office Library in London has records relating to the British rule of India and all the births, deaths, and marriage registers of that period. They also have a copy of just about every book published on the subject of India. Reading facilities are provided, and the staff are very helpful. Many of their books are available on loan through your local library, which also has access to the vast British Library collection. The local library is in fact the best place to start any hunt for specialist information. Senior librarians are trained in hunting down information and usually enter into such research enthusiastically.

Information on tourist offices appears on page 83.

PRACTICAL INFORMATION

INDEPENDENT TRAVEL

Independent travellers to India fall into two groups: the there and backers, and those for whom India is one stop on a longer journey. The first group, usually pushed for time, invariably fly and just go for the cheapest fare they can find. The rest, the lucky ones, have a (sadly diminishing) range of options.

Flying

Here are a few thoughts on air tickets. 'Bucket shops' (specialist long-haul agents) offer the cheapest fares, but do make sure you understand the restrictions, which can be very tight indeed; typically, you cannot change dates or destination. If you are making a multiple-stop journey consider the advantages of a full-price economy ticket. This gives you far more flexibility than a cut-price ticket as the mileage allowed is rather more than the direct route, and it can be extended by paying a modest supplementary fare. Full-price tickets allow you to visit off-route destinations and change your plans as much as you like. Round-the-world fares seem popular at the moment; again check the restrictions very carefully.

Surplus seats are not limited to economy class. Airlines sometimes offer a free upgrade to business or even first class if economy is overbooked. Ask when you check in. Preference is given to holders of full-price economy tickets, but it is always worth asking. You need to be smartly dressed to stand a chance.

Scheduled flights from Britain. Many airlines fly between London and Delhi or Bombay, a few to Calcutta, Madras and Trivandrum. Except around Christmas time most have surplus seats, which they unload at substantial discounts. High street travel agents sell these tickets, but the best deals are from the bucket shops. British Airways' economy return fare to Delhi is £820, yet you can buy nearly the same comfort and standard of service for around £350 from a bucket shop. Bucket shops advertise in the weekend papers and magazines like *Time Out* and *TNT*; you can also try page 236 on

ITV Teletext. Always make sure before handing over your money that you will be given either the ticket or a receipt bearing an ATOL number. Probably not the very cheapest, but certainly highly reliable is Trailfinders, 46 Earls Court Road, London W8 6FT (Tel 0171-938 3366).

Few airlines offer non-stop flights from Europe to Delhi and Bombay, and the discounts offered rarely match those on flights staging through the Middle East or the former Soviet Union.

The choice of airline is important. Gulf Air and Emirates are safe and offer high standards. Unlike some others, Emirates lets you fly into Delhi and out of Bombay. Dear old Ariana Afghan, if it ever gets itself organised again, is IATA's answer to the hippy buses of yore. Their fares were always the cheapest, and their champagne half the price of anyone else's. Punctuality was not a strong point, but the crews made up for it by being very easy-going. Ever had a party and drunk the bar dry in a DC10? The natural successor is Turkmenistan Airlines (0181-746 3080), which has weekly services from Heathrow and Birmingham via Ashkabad to Delhi.

Avoid obscure airlines like Egyptair that may have very limited representation in India. Aeroflot is less of a risk now that an involuntary stopover in Moscow does not mean incarceration in a ropey hotel.

Charter flights from Britain. The cheapest flights from Britain at present are the charters direct to Goa and Kerala. Except at peak times your local travel agent can sell you a return flight and two weeks basic bed and breakfast for less than the price of just a fare to Delhi or Bombay. The problem is persuading them to let you stay more than two weeks, and spending 12 hours with your knees under your chin. The charter market is likely to develop further as India becomes a more popular tourist destination. Two of the leading operators are Inspirations (01293-822244) and Somak (0181-423 3000), or try Teletext page 224.

Scheduled flights from the USA and Canada. Discounted fares from the east coast to Delhi and Bombay are around $1000 return. Check the weekend papers for sources. It may be possible to save a little money by taking a cheap flight from New York or Toronto to London, and getting a bucket shop ticket there. From the west coast the fares are around $1400 return. As from the east coast it is possible to save a little by going to Hong Kong and getting an onward ticket there.

Scheduled flights from Australia and New Zealand. Flights are very expensive compared with those originating in Europe, not helped by the best time to visit India coinciding with peak fare time. Try Yellow Pages and expect to pay A$1500 or NZ$1900. Most airlines offer good discounts to anyone under 26, through a range of agents — notably STA Travel, which has offices throughout Australasia.

Alternatively you could get the cheapest flight to Singapore, Bali, or Jakarta and take the traditional overland route to Bangkok, from where you can get a cheap flight to Calcutta or Kathmandu (cheaper).

Flights from Nepal. Coming from Nepal you have a choice of arrival airports. The shortest and cheapest flight is to Patna, a horrible place in the middle of nowhere. Better to pay the extra and fly to Varanasi. The same flight continues to Khajuraho, Agra, and Delhi. Also direct flights to Delhi and Bombay.

Onward and return travel. It is always best to go to India with a return or onward ticket; cheap tickets are hard to find there. Those airlines (not all) permitted to sell tickets are supposed to do so at the same price as Air India, and this amount must be paid in foreign currency. The more enterprising travel agents are prepared to split their commission with you and give you back a certain sum in rupees. Since their 'commission' can be over 50%, this is well worthwhile. The author has dealt several times with Brooks Travels near the Government of India Tourist Office in Janpath, New Delhi and found them efficient and honest. They quoted Rs12,140 (around

£240/$400) for Delhi—London with a rebate of Rs6900 (£140/$230), and Rs6186 (£120/$205) for Bangkok with a rebate of Rs3350 (£65/$110), both on Aeroflot. Most agents are reliable, but be cautious. Don't hand over signed traveller's cheques; go with the agent to the bank, which will take your money and give you a receipt. The airline takes the receipt as proof of payment at the official fare and issues the ticket. Then the agent gives you the refund in cash. Obviously you will need to have spare bank receipts to re-convert the rupees unless you want to spend that much before leaving. Don't forget the airport tax of Rs300 (£6/$10) levied as you leave the country.

Sea routes

There are no longer any regular passenger ship links to India, not even the ferries from Sri Lanka or Penang in Malaysia. India is, however, a major trading nation and it follows that cargo ships from all over the world call at her ports. After a long period of decline there is now an increase in the number of freighters carrying passengers. Hugo Verlomme's *Travel by Cargo Ship* (Cadogan Guides) is a useful source of information, and details of scheduled services will be found in the *ABC Shipping Guide* or can be obtained from local agents. You travel more or less as a personal guest of the captain and officers, so do not expect any bargains.

The most frequented sea route is from the Persian Gulf to Karachi or Bombay. Since a lot of Indian and Pakistani workers in the Gulf travel by sea less formal arrangements are possible, probably on a motorised dhow. This is strictly for men only. Make sure that everyone on the dhow understands that the local police know that you are on the boat and that you are expected at your destination. Do not expect an easy time with immigration at the port of arrival. In the same way one can travel between South India (usually Tuticorin) and Sri Lanka, sometimes under sail.

Overland

The modern version of the classic overland 'hippie trail' to India involves working your way through Turkey, Iran and Pakistan, and then entering India at Amritsar. This avoids Afghanistan, which traditionally formed part of the route, but is now out of bounds. Those with US passports will need to find a way through Asia that avoids Iran — for example, by going through the former Soviet Union and China; the Trans-Siberian railway could form the backbone of such a trip.

Travelling towards Europe you'll sometimes find a freak bus in Kathmandu (off Durbar Square) or in Delhi (Tourist Camp) and, barring terminal breakdowns, these are generally preferable to public transport. Because of licensing requirements these buses cannot be trusted to go further than Istanbul or the Greek border, whatever they say or charge for. Best to get off in Istanbul.

The best way of overlanding is with one of the organised tours. The author went to India for the first time on one of Top Deck's double-decked buses and has nothing but praise for that company. Their route takes you through the most interesting and attractive parts of Turkey and down into Syria and Jordan. The precise route will obviously depend on political and military conditions at the time. A Hann Overland bus, for instance, got through Iran and Afghanistan at the height of the Gulf War with no problems at all. But it only takes one warlord or bureaucrat to change his mind and... Contact Top Deck Travel (Tel 0171-370 4555), Encounter Overland (Tel 0171-370 6951) or Exodus (Tel 0181-675 5550).

The other way of overlanding is by train. With breaks only for Lake Van in Turkey (first-class wagons go on the ferry) and the 240km/150 miles between Kerman and Zahedan in Iran, the rails run all the way from Istanbul to India. Whether there is a train is another matter — check Thomas Cook's *Overseas Timetable* for services east of Istanbul.

Pakistan. The only border crossings in use between India and Pakistan are the railway and road from Lahore to Amritsar. The road crossing is for people with their own vehicles, others take the train (3½hrs), which runs direct between the two cities. Official opening times of the road border vary a lot; unofficially it is often open when the authorities say it is not. As a result of the troubles in Punjab, Kashmir and Sind the status of these crossings is volatile. Be prepared for the expense of an air ticket. Checks are often very thorough on this border, and you will be in real trouble if you are caught with the smallest amount of dope.

Nepal. The two border crossings in common use are Sonauli for Pokhara and Raxaul/Birganj for Kathmandu. Take a bus from Pokhara to Sonauli, where you will probably have to stay overnight, then bus or share a jeep to Gorakhpur on the Indian Railways system. This is easier and faster than using the train between Nautanwa (the rail terminus near Sonauli) and Gorakhpur. See the entry for Sonauli (see page 160) for more information.

It is a spectacular all-day bus ride from Kathmandu to Birganj on the border, though you may like to break the journey at Daman from where there is a good if distant vista of the Himalayas and Mount Everest (lodge available). A rickshaw (Rs20; around 40p/65 cents) takes you from the bus-stand in Birganj over the border to the station or a hotel in Raxaul. For details of onward travel see Raxaul (page 161).

Travelling towards Nepal try to arrive in Birganj in the early afternoon; this gives you a better choice of hotels and buses. Book the bus yourself; it's cheaper and you can make sure you get a good seat in a decent bus. Minibuses are more expensive, little faster, and often have barely adequate legroom.

A crossing near Siliguri links Kathmandu and Darjeeling, but involves a gruelling two-day bus ride. Drivers on this run can be difficult as foreigners cause a delay at the border.

Several other crossings have been in use over the years, but at some you would not even find a road, let alone a bus on the Nepalese side. This is likely to change with the construction of a new east-west all-weather highway through the Terai, the Nepal lowlands. These crossings may be a challenge to the hardened traveller, but the Terai is a desperately poor area short of most amenities.

Bangladesh. Few travellers cross this frontier (few go to Bangladesh at all), and those who try tell of all sorts of hassles. Make sure in Calcutta or Dhaka (Dacca) which crossing point, if any, may be used by foreigners and what papers are required. Double check and then keep your fingers crossed.

Burma. Despite the long frontier there is no land crossing between Burma and India or Bangladesh.

PACKAGE TOURS

Dozens of companies arrange package tours to India ranging from the moderately cheap to the very expensive and mostly aimed at the mainstream tourist. A high street travel agent can offer information on these.

More interesting and adventure tours are arranged by smaller, more specialised companies. Many of the better operators belong to the Association of Independent Tour Operators who will provide an index to the tours organised by their members. Contact AITO Ltd, 133a St Margaret's Road, Twickenham TW1 1RG (Tel 0181-744 9280 Fax 0181-744 3187).

Red Tape

PASSPORTS AND VISAS

A full passport is essential; make sure that it is valid well beyond the planned duration of your trip and has enough blank pages for visas and stamps.

Visas. Every visitor to India needs a visa, obtainable from a high commission (in a Commonwealth country), embassy, or consular office. In countries where India has no representation the British embassy or high commission should be able to help. Check the terms of issue in advance. In London, for instance, visas are issued to callers on the day after application, and office hours are short. Postal applications can take two weeks. Prices vary according to your nationality, the type of visa, and its duration. Unless your length of stay is absolutely fixed go for the longest visa available, usually six months; much simpler than renewing the visa in India. Visa renewals, restricted area permits, and visas for other countries (e.g. Nepal) obtained in India each need two or three passport photos. You save time, if not money, by bringing a supply with you.

Major Indian legations:

UK
High Commission of India
India House, Aldwych, London WC2B 4NA
Tel 0171-836 8484 Fax 0171-836 4331

Consulate-General of India
19 Augustus Street,
Birmingham B18 6DS
Tel/Fax 0121-212 2782

Consulate-General of India
Fleming House, 6th Floor, 134 Renfrew Street, Glasgow G3 7ST
Tel 0141-331 0777 Fax 0141-331 0666

USA
Embassy of India
2107 Massachusetts Ave, NW, Washington DC 20008
Tel 202-939-7000
Fax 202-939-7027

Consulate-General of India
3 East 64th Street,
Manhattan NY 10021
Tel 212-939-7000
Fax 212-988-6423

Consulate-General of India
540 Arguello Bvd, San Francisco CA 94118
Tel 415-668-0662
Fax 415-668-2073

Australia
High Commission of India
3–5 Moonah Place,
Yarralumla ACT 2600
Tel 02-6273 3999
Fax 02-6273 3328

Consulate-General of India
153 Walker Street, Sydney NSW 2060
Tel 02-9955 7055
Fax 02-9929 6058

Consulate-General of India
13 Munro Street, Coburg,
Melbourne Vic 3058
Tel 03-9384 0141 Fax 03-9384 1609

Canada
High Commission of India
10 Springfield Road, Ottawa K1M 1C9
Tel 613-744-3751
Fax 613-744-0913

New Zealand
High Commission of India
180 Molesworth Street,
Wellington
Tel 04-473 6390
Fax 04-499 0665

South Africa
High Commission of India
Sanlam Centre, Johannesberg
Tel 011-333 1525
Fax 011-333 0690

Visa extensions. Now that visas are readily granted for six months in the first place extensions have become even harder to get. Major cities have a Foreigners' Regional Registration Office (FRRO) and this is the place to try. Expect considerable expense, some official, some otherwise, lots of form-filling, and even more hanging around.

Other paperwork

Permits. The land border areas of India and the whole of the north-east comprising Assam and the hill states are restricted areas, and special permits are required for travel there. The same applies to the Andaman and Nicobar Islands and Lakshdweep Islands. Rules for Sikkim have been much relaxed recently, and you can obtain a permit at the Indian Embassy in your own country. Applications for permits for restricted areas should be sent to the Ministry for Home Affairs Foreigners' Section, Lok Nayak Bhavan, Khan Market, New Delhi 110 003. Unfortunately processing can be slow. More information is included in the appropriate sections.

Health card. India does not require inoculations or a health card, but neighbouring countries may; check before travelling.

All-India Liquor Permit. This is issued free on request when you get your visa, or at a Government of India tourist office in India. Its sole purpose is to enable you to buy alcoholic drink in dry states. There are only three of these at present, Gujarat, Haryana, and Andhra Pradesh, and visitors tend to spend little time in any of them.

Registration. Anyone staying in India for more than 90 days is supposed to register at a Foreigners' Registration Office, the same place as for visa extensions; there are offices in most large towns. This rule seems mostly to be honoured in the breach.

Income tax clearance. After an unbroken stay of more than 90 days it is necessary to get Income Tax clearance before leaving India. While this involves only proving that you have exchanged enough foreign currency to support yourself, you may consider it easier to visit one of the neighbouring countries for a few days before the deadline. This clearance is easily obtained in Delhi at what is almost certainly the most efficient and friendly government office in all India; the story elsewhere can be very different. For a fee a travel agent may perform this service for you. Note that while the clearance form is often not checked, people have had a lot of trouble trying to leave the country without one.

Airport tax. And you certainly won't get out if you can't pay the airport tax, currently Rs300 (around £6/$10).

CUSTOMS

Even in the Green Channel you are likely to be stopped for a check. Expensive items such as video cameras are likely to be entered on a Tourist Baggage Re-Export (TBRE) form and your passport. You will have trouble getting the items out of the country without the form, and even more trouble getting yourself out if you have lost the goods or had them stolen. Duty-free allowance is the usual litre of spirits and 200 cigarettes.

Export regulations. Any item more than 100 years old requires an export permit. Export of animal and snake skins is forbidden.

WHAT MONEY TO TAKE

Living costs. At the present time a return air ticket from London to Delhi or Bombay costs between £320 and £800 (at Christmas). Once you have landed in India you can budget anything from £25/$40 per week upwards.

How much money you need depends entirely on how you want to travel and live. At the bottom of the scale younger backpackers cover all their expenses, including travel by bus or 2nd class rail, hotels, and food, on £25–30 per week.

Staying and eating in four and five star hotels, flying wherever possible, and making use of chauffeured hire cars for sightseeing runs to around £500–800/$800–1300 per week for two people. Perhaps a better guide is that we cashed a £100 travellers' cheque each week when working on this book. For the two of us that covered rail travel (first class or air-conditioned two-tier), spartan but clean and comfortable hotels, good food, scooter rickshaws and public taxis for sightseeing, and beer whenever we felt like it. It is worth noting that single hotel rooms in all price brackets are hard to find, and that there is often no reduction for single occupancy of a double room. This means that it is substantially cheaper for two people to travel together. In the same way a chauffeured hire car can be little or no more expensive than two first class rail fares over shorter distances.

MONEY IN INDIA

Rupees. The Indian monetary unit is the rupee (abbreviated to Re in the singular and Rs in the plural), which consists of 100 naye paise (np), always referred to simply as paise. Notes (bills) are in denominations of Re1 and Rs2 and Rs5 (also coins) and Rs10, 20, 50, 100 and 500. Most of these come in two different patterns, both legal. Avoid accepting tatty and torn notes. Coins smaller than 25np are rarely seen these days. You will sometimes hear the expressions '4 annas' and '8 annas'; these are a throwback to pre-decimal days and signify 25 paise and 50 paise respectively.

Values are so different in India that you must get into the habit of 'thinking rupees' and not converting prices into your own currency. If you find this difficult just remember that Rs2000 (around £40/$65) is a fairly normal monthly salary and that an agricultural worker may get as little as Rs10 (20p/35 cents) or Rs20 a day. The standard offering to a beggar is 25np (less than 1p or a cent).

Exchanging money. At the time of writing the exchange rate was:

£1	=	Rs50	Re1	=	2p
US$1	=	Rs30	Re1	=	3.3 US cents
Aus$1	=	Rs23	Re1	=	4.3 Aus cents
NZ$1	=	Rs21	Re1	=	4.8 NZ cents

The rupee is fixed against a basket of currencies in which the US dollar predominates. Its value against sterling and other currencies depends on their strength against the dollar. The current exchange rate can be found in a good newspaper or from a bank or Indian tourist office. Rupees are not legally available outside India.

The only way to carry your money is as travellers' cheques. Get them from a well known bank and have them in sterling; they are often easier and quicker to cash.

Before purchasing check carefully with the bank the terms on which they replace lost or stolen cheques.

Banking hours are 10am–2pm Monday to Friday and 10am–noon on Saturday, though you will find local variations. Banks are always closed on the second Saturday of the month, and there are numerous other holidays throughout the year, so try not to run low on cash. Changing money is a slow process.

When you change money always make sure that the bank gives you a receipt and keep it. Bank receipts are needed for Income Tax clearance and to re-convert surplus Indian currency.

The black market. There is no point in carrying a lot of foreign cash because the black market offers at best a 20% premium, which is not worth the risk of being robbed. Anyone who offers you more than this is bound to be a rip-off artist. Furthermore, the banks give a better rate for travellers' cheques than for currency notes.

Transfers. Take all the money you will need with you; getting a transfer to India can be problematic. Even if your bank telexes to an Indian bank, it can take weeks before you get the cash. While you are tearing your hair out and living on banana butties, someone else is earning interest on your money. However Western Union, American Express and Thomas Cook all advertise rapid-transfer services, although you pay a substantial fee for the convenience.

The best method of transfer is to write or cable to your bank asking them to send an International Money Order to where you are staying or to the nearest post office. This will take only as long as registered mail, four or five days to a major city if you're lucky. Tell your bank to advise you where to cash this. The same Indian bank will sell you sterling travellers' cheques.

Caution. You are likely to be approached by people offering plausible schemes for making you a large and quick profit. They are all thieves; the spiel and technique vary, but the result is always the same. You are taken for a mug and you waste a lot of time trying to get your travellers' cheques replaced. A popular scam is to invite you to invest in shipping musical instruments (or anything else) to an importer in your own country, all legal and above board as the business is to be done through a major bank. At the bank the conman takes your travellers' cheques, ostensibly to see the manager, and skips out of the back door.

TIPPING

Tipping, or bakshish, is part of the way of life in India. Whatever your views on the subject you must remember that wages are low, and many people are dependent on tips for their livelihood. The amounts involved are not large, about 5% of the bill in ordinary restaurants, and 10% in the big tourist hotels. Where a service charge is made on your hotel bill tip only the porter who carries your baggage. People who help you by opening buildings or showing you monuments should be given Rs2 to Rs5 (4–10p/7–16 cents). A similar amount is appropriate in Sikh temples where offerings help to provide food and accommodation for anyone who asks. There is no need to give money in other temples where it is probably just a perk for the custodians. Take no notice of Rs10 notes in offerings dishes, they are bait for the gullible.

Taxi and rickshaw drivers are not tipped, and drivers of private hire cars only if they have been especially helpful. Remember that they get commission on anything you buy, sometimes just for introducing you to a shop, and adjust the tip accordingly.

Bakshish, in the sense of bribery, is a rather more vexed subject. Given the helpful attitude of the vast majority of Indian officials towards foreigners it will rarely be necessary, but Rs20 (around 40p/65 cents) to the conductor should get you a berth on a 'full' train, and Rs100 (around £2/$3.35) a seat on a fully-booked plane. Bakshish can also speed up visa renewals, but always proceed with caution.

WHAT TO TAKE

Baggage. What you take and how you take it depends on your style of travel. Doing things the comfortable way India is like any other civilised country, and you can pack accordingly.

Travellers on a tighter budget need to take more with them. Bedding and towels (and often soap) are not provided in the cheapest hotels and bungalows. From December to March a medium weight sleeping bag, preferably fully zipped, will be needed. A sheet sleeping bag long enough to pull up over your head is useful at any time. This can easily be run up in India, and good-quality towels are very cheap.

The social stigma that once attached to the backpack (read *Hippy Dharma* if you see a copy) has more or less evaporated, and this remains the favourite form of baggage. Choose one with detachable side pockets or none at all, the extra width is a real handicap in fighting your way on to crowded buses and trains. The alternatives include a strong canvas or nylon bag with shoulder strap, which has the merit of fitting more easily under a bus seat, and even a suitcase (preferably old and battered). The latter may seem an odd choice, but it is safer from thieving (if only because it will be assumed to belong to an Indian), and in India there is usually someone to carry it for you. The official charge for porters at railway stations is usually shown on a sign. The Rs3–5 (around 6–10p/10–16 cents) covers carrying your baggage between train and rickshaw or taxi stand. Whatever you use you will want a separate shoulder bag for your camera, lunch, this book, and so on.

Most railway stations and a few major bus-stands have left-luggage offices ('cloakrooms'). These are quite safe, but some will refuse baggage that is not locked because of past accusations of theft.

Oddments. An unbreakable water bottle is invaluable. Ear plugs and the eye shades provided by most airlines are a boon for light sleepers; all Westerners are light sleepers in India. A small torch and/or candles are essential.

Dress. For daytime wear lightweight cotton or cotton/polyester clothes are best. Trousers and a conventional shirt with button pockets are preferable to jeans and T-shirts, and more versatile. A pullover or jacket will be needed on cloudy or breezy days from December to February, and is useful at other times, if only in air-conditioned restaurants and hotels. In December and January warm clothing will most definitely be needed. The evenings are cold, and few places other than expensive hotels are heated. Warm clothes are also needed in the Himalayan foothills and if you will be visiting any of the hill stations found throughout the country.

It is not acceptable for women to wear skimpy shorts or short skirts. A bra should always be worn, and a long-sleeved blouse is better than a tight T-shirt. There are good social reasons for dressing modestly, as Indian women do. Breaking the rules just increases harassment (for them as well as for you) and cheapens the already low image of Western women.

Comfortable footwear is essential. Shoes must be removed in many places, so laces are a nuisance. Chappals, the local sandals, are cheap and come in many styles. Western-style sandals are available for those who find the toe loop uncomfortable or must wear socks. Leather soles are less tiring on the feet than plastic ones.

You are expected to remove shoes before entering any temple or mosque, and also many tombs. Overshoes are provided at a few places, or you may be permitted to keep your socks on. As long as the ground is dry there is no health risk in going barefoot. Shoe custodians at the entrance are tipped around 25np (less than 1p or a cent) per pair. Don't worry if there is no custodian, shoes outside shrines seem to be sacrosanct. In Sikh gurudwaras, mosques, and the holier Muslim shrines both men and women are required to cover their heads and be modestly dressed. Belts, camera cases and other leather items are barred from Jain and certain Hindu temples.

A hat is very useful; it keeps your hair clean in the invariably dusty atmosphere and the sun out of your eyes.

Check the quality carefully when buying clothes in India. Blemishes in cloth are common, and some garments fall apart after a few days' wear. Much of the fashion clothing in the cheap shops of Delhi and Bombay is in fact export reject.

As little as ten years ago the experienced eye could place an Indian woman pretty accurately by the way she dressed, but in recent years the Punjabi trouser suit has become a high-fashion garment acceptable to women of all religions and castes. The designs are stunning, and many Western women take to this practical clothing. It is neither clever nor comfortable to wear a sari.

In most places where you stay a local dhobi will launder and press your clothes well and quickly. Prices are low, but the process is none too gentle and buttons soon suffer. Always agree prices and delivery in advance.

Cameras. Everywhere you look in India there is a good photo opportunity, so come prepared! Modern SLRs are less bulky, but for most purposes you will do just as well with a compact automatic with zoom. If you do opt for an SLR an 80–200mm zoom, or a 135mm telephoto, is essential for getting natural, unposed close-ups. Such shots have to be taken quickly, so autofocus is ideal.

Whenever possible fit a skylight 1A or a UV filter to each lens. Apart from cutting through haze they will protect the lens from dust and dirt. With an SLR you will find a polarising filter very useful. Use a special brush to remove dust from lens and filter and take lens tissues and cleaning fluid with you and use them regularly. Cleaning a lens or filter with your handkerchief will quickly ruin it.

Colour print film is readily available. Colour slide film is harder to find and often of dubious age and quality. You are allowed to import 25 rolls, so buy film at discount before you leave home; in Britain at least it will be cheaper than duty-free. Manufacturers advise you not to carry around exposed colour films for long in the Indian climate, though we have never had any problems. Processing in India is not yet universally good, and it is preferable to send Kodachrome home in batches. Many of the best shots, in shops and narrow streets, are not well lit, so 200ASA (24din) or faster film is useful. Never pack your films in your baggage and insist on having your camera bag physically checked rather than X-rayed at airports.

Communications

TELEPHONE

The telephone system within India has improved to the extent that it is now worth listing hotel phone numbers. Overseas calls to and from major cities are not too bad (there is direct dialling) but are very chancy elsewhere. Trying to call reverse charge (collect) complicates matters greatly. Most larger post offices offer a telex service.

International calls from India. Experienced travellers will tell you of boring hours waiting at inaccessible telephone exchanges for an overseas connection, and of screaming your head off and trying to listen over the static if you eventually got through. No more. Just look for a booth with an STD sign and make the call yourself, checking the cost on a digital read-out. Prices might be slightly cheaper at official telecommunications offices, more expensive in hotels.

International codes:

UK	00 44
USA	00 1
Canada	00 1
Australia	00 61
New Zealand	00 64
South Africa	00 27

Calling India from abroad. All Indian cities can be dialled direct from abroad. The code for India is 91 preceded by the international access code of the country you are calling from.

Fax. Fax agencies are available all over India, often the same places as STD phones.

TELEGRAMS

Telegrams are a useful stand-by, especially if you cannot contact a remote place on the phone. They are fairly reliable, but you should always confirm in writing.

MAIL

The postal service in India is pretty good, at least for overseas mail to and from the main cities; elsewhere within the country it can be slow and erratic. Use aerograms when writing, they're inexpensive and most reliable. When sending anything with stamps on, save would-be sinners from temptation by having every single one franked in front of you. This is not insulting to postal staff, Indians do just the same. The author neglected this simple precaution once in Jodhpur, and his daughter did not get her birthday card.

Parcels. Sending parcels is a bit of a pain as they have to be securely sewn up in cloth. Insurance requires the parcel to be sealed along the seams with wax. At the post office you fill in three declaration forms; glue one to the parcel, sew on another one, and hand the third over the counter. Many shops will pack the goods for you, but stand over them while they do it. Otherwise you can often find people to do the job outside major post offices, or a small tailor will do the sewing. Always demand a receipt for the parcel.

Poste restante. Mail can be sent to you at any post office in India addressed thus:

> JD LEAK
> Poste Restante
> GPO
> Any Town
> India

The name and address must be printed clearly and, to avoid confusion, use initials rather than first names or have the surname underlined, and leave out titles such as 'Mr'. In India, as in other places, given names often come after the family name, so you can't blame clerks for misfiling. If mail you expect is not filed under your surname initial try that of your given name, or even all the mail they hold. It's not their alphabet, after all. Always take your passport as identity.

Mail addressed to Poste Restante, Delhi rather than New Delhi will end up at the Old Delhi GPO near Kashmiri Gate, rather than at the Foreign Post Office on Bhai Vir Singh Marg (Market Road) — most inconvenient. Letters are held for two months in Delhi and one month in most other places. If you are about to leave town, you can ask one post office to forward mail to another (free of charge). Sometimes it works, sometimes it doesn't.

MEDIA

Newspapers. A wide range of newspapers and magazines in English is published all over India. The newspapers have improved a lot over the last few years, though they mostly still carry little foreign news. The Bofors kickback scandal of the eighties, which purportedly involved Rajiv Gandhi, was the turning point for the Indian press. Papers hitherto content to recycle government press releases suddenly discovered investigative journalism and began running long, well researched articles. The best English-language papers include the *Asian Age*, the *Indian Express*, the *Independent* and the *Calcutta Telegraph*; several other less lively titles are also available nationally.

Magazines. Some of the news magazines, notably *Frontline* and *Gentleman*, are extremely good. *India Today* has become a morass of tedious political reportage, and the once prestigious *Illustrated Weekly of India* has failed to keep up with the times. The emergence of the new middle class is mirrored in a sudden growth in the market for women's and special interest magazines. As with the rest of the English-language press these can give you useful insights into the Indian way of life.

The India Magazine is a high-quality monthly about the people and culture of India. Subscription details from *The India Magazine*, Wadia Building, 17/19 Dalal Street, Bombay 400 001. Currently US$52 (around £30) to Europe or US$56 (around £34) to America or Australia by airmail. The Tata publication *Marg*, also available overseas on subscription, is superb. Details from Marg Publications, Army and Navy Building, 148 MG Road, Bombay 400 001, or from Tata offices abroad.

English and American papers a day or two old can be found in British Council and USIA libraries. They are now also on sale (but expensive) in Delhi, where you can read yesterday's *Daily Telegraph* for free at the Tourist Camp. The Asian editions of *Time* and *Newsweek* are sold in larger towns, and *The Economist* reaches Delhi quicker than it does Cumbria, England.

Radio. The government radio is All India Radio. It broadcasts regular news bulletins in English, and the cricket test match commentators have unbelievably plummy accents. A better bet might be the BBC World Service, which, as elsewhere in the world, can be found on various short-wave frequencies; try 11.96MHz, 15.31MHz, 15.56MHz or 17.79MHz — which is best will depend on the time of day and where you are in the country. Further information on frequencies is available from the BBC Transmission Planning Unit in London (Tel 0171-257 2685).

Television. Until recently all television was in the hands of the government-run Doordarshan, and pretty turgid it was too, despite a few good documentaries. Satellite and cable have now arrived in a big way and, with the exception of the BBC World Service (found on the Star TV network), dispense the usual sort of garbage. At least it has made Doordarshan brighten itself up a bit.

India is a big country, and unless you can afford to fly everywhere you will spend a lot of time in trains and buses. Some people find this a bore, but it really is an essential part of the Indian experience.

PLANNING

To plan or not to plan? It depends on a number of factors, notably the time at your disposal and your attitude towards being unable to do what you want when you want. In short, if you have little time (or little patience) you need a fully planned itinerary with everything booked in advance.

This imposition of Western standards, however, is not the way to meet India. You need to give yourself more time and the flexibility that goes with it. Read as many guide books as you like, but you will always hear of new ideas and new adventures once you have arrived in India.

This book concentrates on major tourist attractions. India has hundreds of towns — and even villages — that have an interesting temple, monument or fort. Like journalists, writers of travel books love a scoop, the shangri-la missed by everyone else. The sad truth is that most, if not all, of these places are hard to reach, disappointing when you get there, and totally lacking in amenities.

Few people, however, have the time to get far off the beaten track. We strongly feel that it is better to see a few places thoroughly, and enjoy them, than to spend too much time travelling. India away from the air routes and mainline railways is a slow and tiring country in which to travel. The effort sometimes has its rewards, but only if you have plenty of time.

Maps. Maps and guides produced in the West attract flak from the Indian authorities because of their depiction of India's borders. Guide books and atlases are regularly impounded for getting it wrong. The trouble is that they cannot decide where the borders really are. They are certain, however, that they are not the cease-fire lines with the Pakistanis and Chinese that constitute the de facto borders. Now that Kashmir is effectively off limits these disputes have no practical effect on travellers.

The best map for general use is Bartholomew's *Indian Subcontinent* at a scale of 1:4,000,000.

Festivals. Before you go or as soon as you arrive find out from a tourist office whether any festivals are due. If necessary tailor your itinerary around them, as the major ones are always worth seeing.

Stars. To help you in itinerary planning many sights have been graded with one, two, or three stars to indicate what, in our opinion, is most worth seeing. A few places are awarded a ° suggesting that they are absolute duds. Others are not graded at all. These are mostly special interest items, and you will have to decide for yourself about these.

We have tried to be consistent, but there are stars and stars. Do not expect three stars in Gwalior to be the same as three stars in Delhi or Agra.

Safety valves. However friendly and helpful the Indians are (and very few fault them) their country is a wearing one in which to travel. Luckily, scattered around the edges are little enclaves, usually ethnically or culturally distinct, which provide an escape. The main requirements are (relative) quiet, lack of hassles, and good cheap, more or less Western food. These places, in the same order as they are covered in the book, are Dharamsala, Manali, Pushkar, Diu, Goa, Kovalam, Mahabalipuram, Pondicherry, Puri, and Darjeeling. In addition, and bang in the middle, is Khajuraho. Kathmandu, though not covered in this book, is in the same category.

FLYING

Until recently India had only two scheduled internal carriers, Indian Airlines and Vayudoot. State-owned Indian Airlines served the main routes, with some help from Air India, and Vayudoot the more remote places. Vayudoot was a political football for most of its life and is little lamented. Indian Airlines was a typical state monopoly, overstaffed, inefficient, and totally uncaring of the needs of its customers.

Recent deregulation has seen the formation of several private sector airlines, including ModiLuft (abetted by the German carrier Lufthansa) and Jet Airways. Further growth is likely, and the situation will remain fluid. More seats and price competition is a big improvement even if making reservations is less convenient. The networks are extensive and fares low by European standards.

Reservations. Demand on all routes is high, and making reservations in India is still time-consuming. Foreigners may get preferential treatment, but unless you have time on your hands it is best to leave the whole thing to a local travel agent or your hotel. There will quite possibly be a 'service charge', which should be agreed in advance. You may hate being tied to a fixed itinerary, but it is no good visiting India and expecting just to pick up flights. For a short visit make all the reservations in advance through your own travel agent or the local Air India office.

Having got your reservation do not be late at the airport or slow onto the aircraft. Seat allocations are rare, and they may have overbooked! And no show means no refund.

Schedules for the various airlines are available through Government of India tourist offices abroad. Major travel agents abroad have this information and will make reservations for you.

Fares. Indian Airlines fares on sample sectors are:

Delhi–Agra	$35 (£21)	Delhi–Varanasi	$90 (£54)
Delhi–Bombay	$130 (£78)	Madras–Bombay	$123 (£74)
Delhi–Calcutta	$151 (£90.5)	Madras–Calcutta	$172 (£103)
Delhi–Gwalior	$47 (£28)	Khajuraho–Agra	$53 (£32)
Delhi–Khajuraho	$71 (£42.5)	Varanasi–Khajuraho	$54 (£32.5)

Fares on other airlines are comparable. Although fixed and quoted in US dollars, fares may be paid in any foreign currency. The old trick of paying the lower rupee fare by presenting a bank receipt has been stopped.

Anyone under the age of 30 is entitled to a 25% discount on internal fares. A 'Discover India' ticket, which allows 21 days' unlimited travel on Indian Airlines, costs $500 (no under-30 discount).

RAILWAYS

India has the largest rail network in the world, over 62,000km of track, and new lines are still being built. Indian Railways runs 7800 passenger services daily. Eleven million people travel by train every day, too many of them, it sometimes seems, with the same destination as yourself. The railway is the best inexpensive way of getting around India, and it is here that you will really come into contact with the Indian way of life — and bureaucracy.

It is an immensely exciting way to travel. The moving scene from a train window tells you more about India than any guided tour or museum. The stately progress of even the fastest trains matches the easy tempo of Indian rural life. No visit to India is complete without at least a short train journey.

Indian Railways' operations are complicated by having two major gauges. In the former British India broad gauge (1.68m/5ft 6in) is standard, and in the old princely states one-metre gauge (3ft 3in). A major programme of converting important metre-

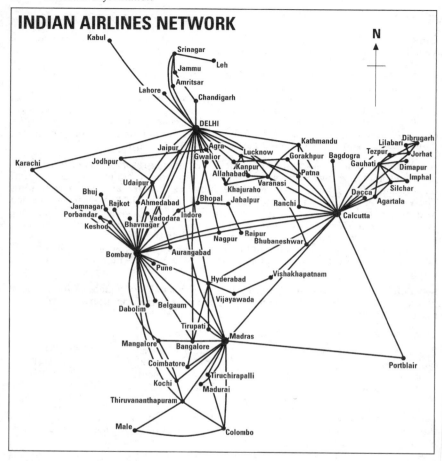

INDIAN AIRLINES NETWORK

gauge lines to broad-gauge is being undertaken, and is still causing a certain amount of disruption. Two different narrow gauges are by no means restricted to the mountain railways.

Route planning. The regional railways publish cheap timetables of all their services, and this information is collected together in *Newman's Indian Bradshaw*, which is available from Wheeler's bookstall on (Old) Delhi station or from Wm Dawson and Sons Ltd, Cannon House, Folkestone, Kent. Although a great diversion on a long journey this is bulky and inconvenient to use. Better is *Trains at a Glance*, which details all the major mail and express trains (not locals) and costs only a few rupees at large stations. Stanfords (12–14 Long Acre, London WC2E 9LP) usually has this in stock, as do General Sales Agents abroad; see under Indrail Passes. Thomas Cook's *Overseas Timetable* also lists mail and express trains; better travel agents have this. Whichever timetable you use always double-check the actual departure time at the station or reservation office, as it is liable to be advanced. This is why precise times are not quoted in this book.

Classes. For passengers, it's a case of 'you pays your money (though not too much), and you takes your choice', as there are many classes and sub-classes. At rock-bottom is **unreserved second class** — wooden seats and, more often than not, a degree of crowding beyond description. Doors on Indian trains open inwards, though because of the press inside second class they usually don't open at all, so throw your pack through a window and then follow it. Not for nothing is it the only class without barred windows.

Reserved second class is usually in sleeper coaches, and here there are two sub-classes. In 'two-tier' (which is rare now) there is a padded berth above the seating. The disadvantage here is that people come and go during the night creating disturbance and presenting a security risk. 'Three-tier' coaches provide sleeper-only accommodation from 9pm–6am and all-reserved seating during the day. In theory at least the attendant locks the doors between stations and keeps out undesirables. 'Three-tier' has been updated by installing slightly padded seats and berths. A closed compartment reserved for ladies is sometimes found in these coaches. These get very mixed reports, many of them centring on screaming children.

(Non-air-conditioned) first class is far more comfortable, though still basic by Western standards; it offers separate compartments, well padded seats and berths, and above all space. Compartments have two or four berths and carry three or six passengers during the day.

Air-conditioned chair car is only half the first-class fare but far from comfortable for overnight journeys. It is normally available on the Shatabdi Expresses and other express services.

A new class, **air-conditioned three-tier**, is now being introduced, priced between air-conditioned chair and first class; this has open-plan carriages with six-berth cubicles (separated by curtains).

Available on an increasing number of trains, and best value for money of all, is **air-conditioned two-tier**. For a slightly higher fare than non-air-conditioned first class you get all the advantages of air-conditioning and only marginally less space and privacy (four-berth, curtain-separated cubicles). The plan is that air-conditioned two-tier should eventually replace first class compartments, which railway buffs would think a shame; one appreciates ending a journey not covered in dust and grime (which is what you are really paying for in air-conditioned), but resents the loss of contact with the outside world.

Air-conditioned first class (A/C) is luxurious, clean and quiet, though it hermetically seals you off from the real India. This is the highest standard available, present on very few trains, and passengers are provided with attendant services.

Which class do you choose? To an extent the decisions are made for you. Except on the Taj Express (Delhi–Agra), Pink City Express (Delhi–Jaipur) and a few other superfast trains, such as the Shatabdi Expresses, it is not possible to make reservations in any class for short journeys, usually defined as less than 320km/200 miles. This means travelling by day and either taking a chance on unreserved second class or paying for first class. The conductor will usually find seats for second class Indrail Pass holders even without a reservation, and you will be extremely unlucky not to find a seat in first class. The compartments actually seat eight in comfort, and few passengers object to this.

Reservations. Rail travel in India is rarely a simple matter of going to the station and buying a ticket. Trains are always full, and Indians try to make their reservations months in advance. Fortunately Indian Railways now has an extremely efficient computerised booking system on its main routes. In major tourist centres special offices help foreigners make reservations at short notice; more details under 'Connections' for each place. Given sufficient time Thomas Cook can make all your reservations in advance of your trip to India.

Off the beaten track you have to go to the station and find the correct booking window for your train; in larger stations first class and second class reservations will

	AC 1st Class	1st Class *AC 2 tier/* *AC chair*	2nd Class
VALIDITY			
7 days	$300	$150	$80
15 days	$370	$185	$90
21 days	$440	$220	$100
30 days	$550	$275	$125
60 days	$800	$400	$185
90 days	$1060	$530	$235

be entirely separate. Usually there is an indicator showing whether accommodation is available. Otherwise barge your way to the front and ask; the queues move slowly and it's no good waiting hours for a 'no'. If accommodation is available get a requisition form, fill it in, and join the queue.

It is, however, almost inevitable that your train will be full, so go to the enquiry window and utter the magic formula 'tourist quota'. On many trains seats are set aside for tourists and you will have to find whoever allocates them. It may be the Reservations Supervisor or it may be someone in an office several kilometres away. If this ploy fails try the Divisional Superintendent, or the Commercial Manager... or anybody. There are always quotas from which you can scrounge a couple of seats, railway staff are invariably helpful, and polite persistence always pays in the end.

Allow at least half a day and a lot of nervous energy for making reservations. Try to keep calm. If all else fails, you could always just hop on the train and hope that Rs20 (around 40p/65 cents) bakshish to the conductor will produce a berth — this sometimes works.

Tickets. Fares are very low. To travel the 1400km from Delhi to Bombay costs only Rs263 (around £5.25/$8.75) in a second-class sleeper, Rs537 (around £10.75/$18) in air-conditioned chair car, Rs965 (£19/$32.25) in first class, Rs1239 (£25/$41) in air-conditioned two-tier sleeper, or Rs2202 (£44/$73.50) in first-class air-conditioned. Small extra charges are made for reservations, bedding in air-conditioned two-tier, and travel on 'superfast' trains. The Rajdhani Express (no second class) has its own fare structure about 30% over these figures, though this does include meals. No student discounts are given on any fares.

Indian trains may be cheap but they are also slow, and it is important to select the right train before trying to make a reservation. To return to our Delhi–Bombay example, the Jammu Tawi Express takes a little over 20 hours, the Paschim Express 23 hours, and the Dehra Dun Express 31½ hours. The Rajdhani takes only just over 16 hours, but you pay dearly for the speed. Running mostly on less important lines are 'Fast' Passenger trains, which average about 25kph, and the even slower Passenger and Mixed trains. Janata (People's) expresses are second class only and usually slow; luckily they seem to have gone out of fashion.

The problem lies in actually getting a ticket. A special window may sell current day tickets, but the queue is likely to be long.

The alternative, if time is short, is to board the train and pay the ticket examiner when he comes round. Obviously you are not meant to do this, but you are unlikely to meet with any serious complaint.

Indrail Pass. One answer is the Indrail Pass, which entitles you to unlimited travel within the specified period. Costs in US dollars are indicated in the above table.

None of the surcharges or the reservation fee are payable for pass holders. You also receive preferential treatment in making reservations. The Indrail Pass used to be worth the money even if you did not get the full value of the fares. Now, however, prices have gone up faster than the cost of individual tickets. Planning an itinerary in advance you can use the distance and fare tables in *Trains at a Glance* to see whether the pass will be good value for you.

General Sales Agents abroad for the Indrail Pass, and who also usually sell *Trains at a Glance*, are:

UK
SD Enterprises, 103 Wembley Park Drive, Wembley HA9 8HG
Tel 0181-903 3411 Fax 0181-903 0392

USA
Hariworld Travels, 30 Rockefeller Plaza, 21 North Mezzanine, New York, NY 10112
Tel 212-957-3000

Canada
Hariworld Travel, 1 Financial Place, 1 Adelaide Street East, Toronto, Ontario M5C 2V8
Tel 416-366-2000

Australia
Adventure World, PO Box 480, North Sydney, NSW 2059
Tel 02-9956 7766

South Africa
MK Bobby Naidoo Travel, PO Box 2878, Durban, 4001
Tel 031-309 4710

Facilities. Restaurant cars are rare — in fact the author has only ever seen one, on the Taj Express. On other trains the attendants take orders for meals to be served in the coaches. The food is very reasonable, and big efforts are being made to improve quality. All but the fastest long-distance trains make leisurely stops every couple of hours that allow you to buy food and drink in the stations.

For the enthusiast. You don't have to be a railway fanatic to enjoy the Indian Railways system, though the author has met people who visit India for no other reason. One of the great joys is the sheer variety. In a few days you can travel on broad gauge (1.68m/5ft 6in), metre gauge (3ft 3in), and two narrow gauges (0.61m/2ft, and 0.76m/2ft 6in), and behind steam, diesel and electric locomotives. Also on offer are diesel rail cars and a cable-hauled mountain tramway that rises to 2500m. Steam has been mostly superseded on the main lines; the country metre gauge lines of Rajasthan are the best place in the north of India to see steam at work, though it is being rapidly phased out.

Going north from Delhi you can travel on the broad gauge line through Chandigarh to Kalka, and change there on to the narrow gauge mountain railway to Simla, a pleasant hill station and the hot weather capital of India during the Raj. From there you have to travel by road to Jogindernagar (this is where the tramway is), which is the terminus of a narrow gauge line to Pathankot. This is a beautiful run along the Himalayan foothills. Pathankot is on the broad gauge line from Jammu back to Delhi.

To the south of Delhi three narrow gauge lines run out into the countryside from Dholpur and Gwalior. For the moment at least the Dholpur line still uses steam traction. These are quite different from the mountain lines, being sophisticated light railways. These lines can be visited on the way from Agra to Khajuraho.

Taking photographs of trains involves getting a permit from Rail Bhavan in New Delhi. You have to specify all the stations where you want to photograph; the permit also allows access to sheds and workshops. Contact, in the first instance, the Deputy

Director of Public Relations who will send you along to the appropriate office. This takes time, of course, but you will find everyone very friendly and helpful. Despite the regulations, however, you may find that taking a few pictures at a station will not create too many problems, and may even go unnoticed.

BUS

If there is a road on the map someone is bound to run a bus along it. Like the trains, standards vary. At the bottom of the heap local buses are decrepit boneshakers, and unless you board at the point of origin, your chances of getting a seat are slim. Rarely can you reserve a seat, and the best ploy is to ignore the scrummage round the door and heave your shoulder bag or whatever (one item per person) through a window onto a vacant seat. Other passengers will respect this and people already on the bus will usually help. If there are two of you, one can look after this while the other gets your gear onto the roof and chains it down. Express buses are just the same but make fewer stops. Deluxe buses, which run on relatively few routes, allow advance booking and are slightly more comfortable but can still be desperately short of leg room for a long ride. Overnight buses are best avoided.

For shorter journeys buses are generally faster than trains. Locals cost about the same as the second-class train fare, deluxe twice that, i.e. half the first-class train fare.

Major cities are connected by so-called super deluxe buses, but as these are built on the same antiquated lorry chassis as all the others high standards of ride and silence should not be expected. Always check before booking whether the bus has a video system; you can be sure that it will be belting out Hindi movies at ear-splitting volume for the whole journey. Equally, beware of seats in the very front or over the rear wheels, which have even less leg-room than others, and in the back where you'll be bounced around like a yo-yo. On top of all that something in the Indian gastric system does not agree with buses, and there is always someone vomitting on the floor.

To add to these joys are constant vibration, rattling windows and hairy overtaking manoeuvres. Most travellers, including the author, prefer to stick to the trains and takes a bus only when there is no alternative.

HITCHING

Hitching, as such, is virtually unknown in India. There is little private car traffic between cities and, given the indifference to lower forms of life (e.g. non-car owners), your chances of a lift are low. Most lorries do carry passengers, but the drivers expect payment of roughly half the bus fare. Cabs, though large, are usually crowded, and you will probably end up on top, which is hot and dusty. This mode of transport is unsuitable for women, whether they are escorted by a man or not.

LOCAL TRANSPORT

There are many forms of in-town transport apart from buses. They vary in type and design from place to place, but you will not have to travel far to encounter the following.

Cycle rickshaws. The infamous 'Indian helicopter' is common everywhere except Bombay and Calcutta. Never metered, the fare should be about Re1 per km in small places, rather higher in the cities. There is no harm in settling on a tourist price of Rs5 (around 10p/16 cents) per km, but certainly no more.

Scooter rickshaws. These are two-passenger three-wheelers based on scooter components. Like taxis they are usually black and yellow. Driving style and manoeuvrability are terrifying. In many places they are metered (same conditions as taxis), but drivers can be very reluctant to use the meter. Average fare is around Rs5 (around 10p/16 cents) per km.

Taxis. Almost always black with a yellow roof. Most are metered, and drivers are not usually too difficult about using the meter. Because of ever-rising fuel costs it is difficult constantly to uprate meters, and the driver will probably ask more than is indicated. He should however, have a printed card with the revised fares. There is often a supplement at night and a small charge may be made for baggage. In Bombay the meter measures distance rather than cost and (again) the fare is read from a card. If the taxi is unmetered or the meter 'broken' a fare of Rs10 (around 20p/33 cents) per km is average.

Car hire. Until recently there was no self-drive hire in India, something few people regretted once they had seen the standard of driving. In all larger towns and tourist venues you can hire a car with a driver through the local tourist office. Prices range from Rs10 per km for a standard car to Rs15 per km for an air-conditioned one. If you use one of these cars on a point-to-point basis you have to pay for the return journey at the full rate. Your hotel may offer to arrange car hire for you; always compare their price with what the tourist office quotes.

Tempos. These operate like Turkish dolmus taxis on fixed routes. The most common pattern is a strange German-designed two-stroke three-wheeler. In parts of Gujarat they are based on motorbikes, and in Delhi splendid devices built on old Harley-Davidsons, presumably despatch bikes left over from the Second World War. Fares are fixed and low, e.g. Rs2.50 from Connaught Place to Chandni Chowk in Old Delhi.

Tongas. Tongas are two-wheeled carriages drawn by scarecrow horses, and often in a frightening state of decrepitude. A full tonga should cost each passenger 50–75np per km (under 3p/5 cents a mile).

Rickshaws. The man-pulled rickshaw is encountered only in Calcutta and one or two hill stations. By the time you read this they will probably have been banished from central Calcutta. A lot of rubbish is spoken about the indignity inflicted on the puller. Work is scarce in India and they are happy to be earning, so why not patronise them? Tourist price should be between Re1 and Rs2 per km (under 7p/10 cents a mile) though they will always ask for more.

A word about fares in unmetered conveyances: all the other guides tell you to settle the fare before getting in, but this gives the driver a big advantage, if only in that he can refuse to take you. The alternative requires a bit of nerve, but once you get used to distances and prices you can just jump in and pay the appropriate fare at your destination. The driver will probably register discontent over the amount you offer. Take no notice of his moaning unless he actually has tears in his eyes, in which case it can be assumed that you have underpaid him.

Bicycles. In most places apart from the big cities the best, though possibly not the safest, way of getting around is by bicycle. It's faster and less tiring than walking and, unlike a bus, you can stop whenever something catches your fancy.

Bikes can usually be hired from bicycle shops. Rates start at about 50np per hour and can be anything from Rs3 to Rs6 per day. These bikes are rarely young, and it is a good idea to see if the brakes work before you leave the shop. Most come with a carrier, which is useful for your camera bag; take a strap or elastic cord to secure it. Service is cheap: 50np to pump up a tyre, Rs2 to repair a puncture.

If you think it worth it you can buy a bike; a new 'sit-up-and-beg' model complete with bell, carrier, and lock will set you back less than Rs750 (around £15/$25). A basic mountain bike (fixed speed) costs Rs1150 (£23/$38) and a ten-speed racer Rs1600 (£32/$53). Purists will sneer at these bikes, but they are strong (the racer weighs

28kg), will stand up to rough roads, and spares are readily available. Take your own bags.

For long journeys you put the bike on top of the bus or in the luggage van of the train; the charge is about half the passenger fare. There is something very pleasing in being able to cycle out of stations past all the squabbling rickshaw-wallahs. Things depreciate slowly in India and you can recover most of your outlay by selling before you leave.

GUIDED TOURS

Guided tours are organised by the tourist authorities in most major places. These are usually very good value, but the quality varies from place to place. The main problem is trying to pack too many places into one tour, and a new drawback is the dreaded video bus. More information in each section.

DRIVING

For those with the experience of driving overland from Europe India will not be too frightening. Shipping in a vehicle you will have to be extremely careful until you are used to the anarchic conditions on the roads.

Driving is nominally on the left. All the main roads are surfaced but tend to be rough. They are narrow and cluttered with ox-carts, pedestrians, buses, and lorries. Whatever the law may say right of way belongs to the larger vehicle. Indian drivers have no judgement of space and time, cyclists never look where they are going, tail-lights rarely work, and pedestrians are plain suicidal. Very powerful horns (European air horns are the minimum) are essential and must be used freely. Indian drivers never look in their mirrors, even if they have them.

Petrol is rather cheaper than in England, Rs20 (40p/65 cents) per litre (but rising fast), diesel is around Rs9 (18p/30 cents). Petrol stations can be few and far between so don't run low. Jerricans are a wise precaution especially as distribution is erratic.

Driving at night is preferable in some ways as the ox carts and other slow traffic is off the road, but you need really good long-range lights, if only to force oncoming traffic to dip theirs. You will be lucky to average much over 50kph by day, a bit more at night, and less in the mountains. Signposting is poor and good maps hard to find.

SELF-DRIVE CAR HIRE

Budget and Hertz have recently started self-drive car hire. As an idea of costs a Maruti saloon (the equivalent of a Suzuki Swift) is Rs500 (around £10/$16.50) per day for 3–6 days or Rs3200 (£64/$105) per week both with unlimited mileage. A returnable insurance deposit of Rs1000 (£20/$33) is levied, and foreigners must have a valid International Driving Licence. Minimum age is 21. Larger Indian vehicles are also available. Leaving the car other than where you hired it will cost Rs2 (4p/7 cents) per kilometre for its return. Further details from Budget, Hertz or Government of India tourist offices.

As implied in the preceding section driving in India is not always enjoyable. You need to choose carefully where to use a hire car or, indeed, to travel by road at all. Major trunk roads should be avoided; all are single carriageways and carry very heavy traffic. Most of that traffic is driven in a lunatic fashion. The road from Ahmedabad down to Bombay has the worst accident rate in the world, a statistic in which alcohol plays a large part. Other trunk roads are little better.

In contrast travelling from Goa up to Hampi, Badami, and Bijapur would be delightful. Even so you should not get the idea that any trust whatsoever should be placed in any other road user. An Indian lorry driver who finds his vehicle going a little faster than the one in front will simply pull out to overtake, regardless of anything coming the other way.

BUYING A VEHICLE IN INDIA

An increasingly popular way of getting around India is buying a motorbike, usually an Enfield 350. Greater production, of cars as well as bikes, has led to a more active second-hand market, though there are still no used bike and car dealers in the Western sense. Watch for the brokers' advertisements in the press and ask around garages and accessory shops. In Delhi start at the tourist car garages on Janpath, and in Bombay in the Pasta Lanes area. The best car to go for is an Ambassador; it uses more fuel than a Maruti, but is safer, more reliable, and better suited to long distances on Indian roads. Expect to pay Rs10,000 for an old Enfield, up to Rs25,000 for a two-year-old example, and Rs45,000 or Rs85,000 for an Ambassador of similar vintage. Documentation is surprisingly simple, but do make sure you get everything, especially the chit that allows you to sell the vehicle in a state other than where you bought it.

The Indians are great travellers in their own country, and it follows that there is plenty of accommodation in most of the places you are likely to go. In all but the smallest towns there will be at least one hotel and quite likely a bungalow of some kind.

HOTELS

Hotels vary widely in quality and price, the two often not related. There are luxury hotels in the cities and tourist places; these are of reasonably high standard, and cheap in Western terms (Rs1000–2000 double; £20–40/$33–66), but outside the scope of this book. Below this are many medium-priced hotels in the range Rs50–100 (£1–2/$1.65–3.30) single and Rs100–200 (£2–4/$3.30–6.60) double; some of these are remarkable value for money, others no better than much cheaper places. Outside the big cities you should have no difficulty finding a reasonably clean and comfortable room for Rs65 (£1.30/$2.15) single, Rs100 (£2/$3.30) double, sometimes a little less.

All lower-priced hotel rooms are a bit spartan by Western standards, though all but the very cheapest have a private 'bathroom' for each room. For a people that makes such a fetish of bodily cleanliness Indian bathing facilities can be remarkably primitive. At the bottom of the scale you can find yourself crouching on the floor in a dark, dank hole pouring cupfuls of water over yourself. Hot water, if asked for, will be brought in buckets. Toilets are of the 'hole in the floor' variety, which, for hygienic reasons, most visitors quickly come to prefer. Spending Rs100 (£2/$3.30) or more you can expect running hot water, towels, soap, and so on. Toilet paper is rarely provided (but easily found in shops). In common with most of the Middle East Indian practice is to use water and the left hand, rather than paper. The new middle class is apparently converting to the use of toilet paper. The effect on already overtaxed sewage systems does not bear thinking about.

The following abbreviations are used in the accommodation listings in this book:

SR — single room; DR — double room; SWB — single with bathroom; DWB — double with bathroom; A/C — air-conditioned.

BUNGALOWS

As a legacy of the time when Indian and British officials would go on tour there are **bungalows** scattered all over India. Most common are the Dak (Post) bungalows, which are very cheap (as little as Rs10 (20p/33 cents) single) and usually clean. Most state tourist corporations have tourist bungalows, though over the last few years most have been renamed as hotels. Prices have gone up and nothing much else has changed. They vary considerably in quality from state to state, but are usually comfortable and very good value; many have dormitories. Organisations such as the Public Works Department (PWD), Archaeological Survey and Irrigation Department all have bungalows available to the public if not required for official use. In most cases you are supposed to have a permit from some official or another, but a little bakshish to the chowkidar (who will probably pocket the room rate anyway) will solve such problems. You are most unlikely to be allowed to stay in Circuit Houses, which are reserved for judges and senior officials. Although the less expensive Indian hotels are improving, as a rule bungalows are a better bet than hotels. They tend to be quieter and the staff are more used to foreigners. The word 'bungalow' can be misleading; many are indistinguishable from hotels, others can be like a dilapidated village cricket pavilion.

RETIRING ROOMS

Most railway stations have **retiring rooms** as well as waiting rooms. Retiring rooms are comfortable and invariably spotless bedrooms and dormitories, the snag with the latter being that people come and go during the night and that lights are rarely turned out. Typical prices are Rs10–20 (20–40p/33–66 cents) for a dormitory bed and Rs50–100 (£1–2/$1.65–3.30) for a double room with bath. You must be in possession of an onward ticket or Indrail Pass to use the retiring rooms. You can also try to sleep (for free) in the waiting rooms. In large stations there are separate rooms for A/C, first class, second class sleeper, and ladies; elsewhere all the 'upper class' passengers are lumped together. Obviously security is a problem, and it is unwise to place any reliance on the attendants. Most waiting rooms provide toilets and showers at no cost.

YOUTH HOSTELS

Youth hostels are not very numerous in India, and tend to be too far from town centres for convenience. They are, however, very cheap and do not insist on membership. A few are covered in this book, and a full list is available from your national YHA.

DHARAMSALAS AND GURUDWARAS

In many places very basic accommodation is available free in dharamsalas (pilgrim accommodation) and gurudwaras (Sikh temples), and in the latter you will also get free food. These are religious establishments and cater mainly for pilgrims. Do not use them unless you are prepared to observe their rules, which usually involve not smoking or drinking and, in many cases, not eating non-vegetarian food. You should also make a reasonable donation at least to cover the cost of what you have had.

CAMPING

India has few recognised camp sites, no great disadvantage when hotels are so cheap.

On the other hand a tent is a useful stand-by when all the hotels are full; tourist and Public Works Department bungalows and certain other establishments allow camping in their compounds. Rough camping in the Himalayas attracts no attention, but is not recommended elsewhere. The place may seem quiet enough on arrival, but you will attract a crowd in no time at all.

Eating and Drinking

As you would expect in an area as large as Europe the food varies a lot as you travel around India. Because of Hindu dietary laws (many people are not supposed to eat any flesh, let alone beef) you will usually have a choice between vegetarian and non-vegetarian food; and vegetarian is just that, no eggs or animal fat. Another marked difference is between the areas where wheat and rice are the staples.

In the north there is Mughal and Persian influence, with plenty of meat and interesting rice dishes like pulao and biryani. Food tends to be spicy rather than hot, especially in Kashmir where yoghurt is often added. The south, along with Gujarat, is mainly vegetarian and the basis of any meal is rice, mountains of it. There are many ingenious ways of preparation, but the result is always the same, unappetising in both appearance and taste and of dubious nutritive value.

RESTAURANTS

There has in the past been no tradition of dining out for pleasure in India. Quite apart from caste reasons most Indians take the view that the best food is cooked by their mother or wife (often true), and eat out purely through necessity. There is also the financial aspect — the vast majority simply cannot afford the better restaurants.

In many of the places where you will eat, either through lack of alternatives or for reasons of cost, the food will be of a dismally low standard. The problem lies in the low quality of some ingredients (particularly meat) and the low esteem in which cooks are held. In fact, it is a lot easier to find good Indian food in England (often cheaper too, in real terms). Hand in hand with quality is nutrition. It is very hard to get either a balanced diet or the calorie count you need. Many people stop eating meat in India and wonder why they have no energy; if you do this you must substitute by eating lots of eggs and dhal, which are rich in protein (as are peanuts). Vegetables are usually cooked to death, so if you don't want to chance the salads, you must eat plenty of fruit.

Fruit and vegetables are plentiful and taste better than the high-yield strains from Western farms. Because cow-dung is used as fuel human manure is common, and it follows that if you want to eat unpeeled fruit it must be thoroughly soaked in strongly chlorinated or iodinised water. The prepared fruit and vegetables sold on many stalls will have been washed in unpurified water, and may have been lying around long enough to collect other contamination.

Most menus offer dahi, or curd, which is fresh natural yoghurt. This is a good accompaniment to many dishes, and the bacteria in it will soothe a troubled stomach. It is also more effective than water for cooling you down after a very hot dish. A banana can also help.

You will find Western ('continental') and Chinese dishes on many menus, but the standard is generally very disappointing except in a few expensive hotels and restaurants. The Kwality chain of restaurants can be relied upon for good food at reasonable prices. When Indians travel they like to eat the food they are used to rather than the local stuff. This means that you can find a Punjabi restaurant in most towns and they are a safe bet for solid, nutritious food. Sikh lorry drivers have the knack of finding good places; look to see where they eat. Railway station restaurants are a useful stand-by.

SNACKS

The Indians are great eaters between meals, and a huge range of snacks is on offer to cater for this taste. These are usually available in the better restaurants, but most people buy from street vendors. Samosas are the Indian equivalent of the Cornish pasty, and there are many kinds of pakora (fritter) and so on. Kebabs are not as common in India as the Middle East. Hygiene may worry you; the best rule is to go for freshly fried food rather than things that have been kept warm.

Beware of greasy bus-stand snacks, particularly those ingested by women passengers that tend to reappear along a bumpy road. The incredible thing is the way they stoke up again at the next stop. And then are sick again.

Sweets. Traditional Indian confectionery is incredibly sweet. Some, such as barfi and jalebi, are delicious in small quantities. Give them a try with your tea or coffee. Manufactured sweets are good, and there is Cadbury's chocolate. Smarties addicts have only to ask for Gems, and a 5 Star is a fair substitute for a Mars bar.

Ice cream. Kwality (same people as the restaurants) ice cream is good and safe to eat, which is more than can be said for some other brands. In New Delhi and Bombay there are now American-style ice cream parlours, of which some (e.g. Nirula's) are excellent. Traditional Indian ice-cream, kulfi, is made from reduced milk and is very rich.

DRINKING

Fluid intake is essential to health in a hot country like India. The first thing an Indian does when he sits down in a restaurant or snack bar is down a large tumbler of water. You will often feel like doing the same but be fearful of the results.

Soft drinks

Water. Contrary to common belief the water in many cities and towns is filtered, chlorinated, and safe to drink, but this is certainly not true everywhere. Bottled water is now quite readily available, usually costing Rs10–15 (20–30p/33–50 cents) per litre. How genuine some of this is or where it comes from is open to conjecture. One sometimes suspects that someone is making the plastic caps (easy enough) and that the bottles are filled from the nearest tap. The most common brand is Bisleri, which is safe though you must always check that the seal on the bottle has not been tampered with. The only brand that actually tastes like mineral water is Golden Eagle, certainly more palatable than their beer. Travelling off the beaten track you still need either a small filter of the kind sold by outdoor shops or purifying tablets. A water bottle is very useful on long journeys.

Tea and coffee. Tea is a universal drink and more or less safe (water has to be boiled at least ten minutes to be totally safe). It will always be prepared with milk and sugar (sweeter in the north) unless you specify otherwise. The first words of Hindi most visitors learn are *chini nay*, no sugar. Indian coffee, with a distinctive caramelly flavour is good when strong enough. It is common in the south, but in the north you will get mostly instant coffee. Look out for Indian Coffee Houses, which also serve good cheap snacks.

Other drinks. Major brands of soft drinks (which are very sweet) are safe, but some local ones and soda water are no better than the water they are made from. Green coconuts are often on sale and the juice of these is cool and refreshing. Another excellent cold drink is lassi, which is churned curd flavoured with sugar, salt, or rose-water. Be wary of ice; freezing does not kill bugs.

Alcohol in India

There is a strong sentiment against alcohol in India. The problem stems from the way it is used. Social drinking is catching on only slowly. Those Indians who partake of alcohol drink spirits at the rate we drink beer and with the sole intention of getting plastered. Be wary of accepting invitations to drink unless you want to end up the same way. By the same token saying that you visit your local pub or bar two or three times a week could well be understood to mean that you get falling-down drunk each time.

The availability of alcohol around India is in a state of flux. Gujarat always maintained total prohibition while other states relaxed the rules in varying degrees. There are various 'dry days' when liquor shops are closed, and in many states there are few places outside expensive tourist hotels where you can enjoy a drink with your meal.

Recent popular agitation, mostly from women's groups, has led to the reintroduction of prohibition in Andhra Pradesh and Haryana. Other states may follow, and the election of a Bharatiya Janata Party (BJP) government would accelerate the trend.

Imported liquor is extremely expensive, and wine is found only in the most expensive hotels.

Indian wine, produced near Bombay and in Andhra Pradesh, is slowly improving with French help. The brands readily available, usually Golconda, tend still to be very heavy and sweet. Bosca is a better bet. An absolutely excellent méthode champenoise (called Marquise de Pompadour in India and Omar Khayyam in the West!) is now made in Maharashtra. A similar product from Goa may be worth a try.

Beer (all lager) is now available in most places and no longer seen merely as a drink for cissies. Dozens of brands are on sale; these notes are from our last trip: Golden Eagle still undrinkable; Vazir excellent, mid-strength; London Pilsner — draught horrible, bottled OK; Khajuraho said to be undrinkable; San Peter — excellent lunchtime drink, light, really tastes like beer; German Orange Gold one of the better strong beers, not too sweet; Black Knight strong, OK; Shivalik OK but no more; Solan No 1 better than Golden Eagle; Dansberg (Sikkim) boring; Sun Lager OK but does not live up to first taste; Godfather good; Haywards 5000 Super Strong Beer, label says 'Not exceeding 7.5% VV', but it can't miss by much; Kingfisher is found all over India and always a good bet; made in several breweries, Bangalore is reckoned to be the best.

Prices vary considerably from state to state. The same beer can cost as little as Rs25 (50p/80 cents) in Goa and Rs50 or more in Kerala. And more than that, of course, in a smart hotel.

Hard stuff. Liquor stores are usually called Wine Shop or English Wine Shop. They sell neither wine nor anything made in England. The term refers to the sale of Indian-Made Foreign Liquor, IMFL for short, and includes whisky, gin, rum and brandy. Some of the more expensive whiskies, such as McDowells and Diplomat, are quite drinkable but still induce a hangover of heroic proportions. The brandy is vile, Old Monk Rum thought-provoking, and the gin excellent. Try the gin with Limca or fresh lime and soda, and bring your own angostura if you like it pink. Do not make the mistake of thinking that Kashmir apple brandy may be like calvados — it isn't. There are also some regional drinks you may like to try: in Goa there is feni, and in various parts of the south toddy, which is fermented coconut sap. In many places you will find country liquor, which is strong and can usually be trusted not to blind you.

Hygiene is not a strong point in India (or most other places) and you will not have much fun if you worry about everything you eat and drink. Just enjoy yourself and trust in the miracles of modern medicine.

SMOKES AND PAAN

India is the fourth largest producer of tobacco in the world, and a major exporter. Foreign cigarettes are not readily obtainable, but Indian ones are dirt cheap and, it is said, not bad. Poorer people smoke bidis, which are inferior tobacco rolled up in a jungle leaf and tied with thread. They are much cheaper than cigarettes, taste disgusting and are even more of a health hazard. Cigars, made in the south and not readily available outside large cities in the north, are cheap and good. Pipe tobacco is hard to find.

Pavements and walls all over India are splattered red. This is not the aftermath of some horrific accident, but the result of paan chewing. Paan, sold in smart shops as well as at tens of thousands of wayside stalls, is crushed areca nut wrapped in betel leaf. The additional ingredients, which usually include lime paste, are a matter of choice, but the result is a very good and cooling digestif after a meal and also mildly narcotic. The most successful paan-wallas guard their formulae closely and can become very wealthy men. Long-term use plays havoc with the teeth, but once in a while does no harm. Mint or spearmint are probably the best bet for Westerners. If you don't want to try the real thing, you can buy paan-flavoured Polo mints instead.

MUSEUMS AND ART GALLERIES

India has hundreds and hundreds of museums. These range from a modern high-tech display as good as any in the world to the moth-eaten collection of an eccentric, long-dead maharaja. Both varieties have their fascination, and the best are described under the relevant sections in this guide. As a rule captioning is in English but very skimpy.

Beware of 'art galleries'. Apart from the few official ones described in this book, the rest are commercial undertakings selling reproductions where you can expect a hard sell.

THE GREAT OUTDOORS

Flora and fauna. Increases in population and the consequent need for land have had dire effects on wildlife, and schemes have had to be launched to save the once common tiger and crocodile from extinction. There are now many national parks and sanctuaries, which should provide a haven for the Asian lion, gaur (Indian bison), rhinoceros, and wild elephant. In the mountains, and more truly wild, are ibex, markhor, Kashmir stag, and even, for the chosen few, the snow leopard.

It requires effort, patience, and luck to see any of these animals, but everywhere outside the cities you will be aware of spectacular bird life. A glance out of the train window anywhere in the northern plains could show you peacocks, egrets, an adjutant stork, and dozens of bright parakeets. Every little pool has a kingfisher, and racket-tailed drongoes perch on the wires beside the track. In the foothills of the Himalayas you see birds every colour of the rainbow. The author had taken little interest in bird-watching before visiting India, but never ventures into the country now without binoculars and one of Salim Ali's excellent (and cheap) handbooks. These are available from good bookshops in all the major cities.

Vegetation in India is very varied and follows roughly the geographical divisions already mentioned. In the foothills of the western Himalayas is a temperate zone with mainly coniferous forests and, above this, silver birch and silver fir reach almost to 5000m. There is a similar temperate zone around Darjeeling but with more deciduous trees (oaks, maples, etc.) and also evergreens like the rhododendron. In many areas a carpet of alpine flowers covers the ground in spring (April to June according to altitude). Even further east are the rain forests of Assam.

There is very little room for wild vegetation on the intensively farmed northern plains, and the uninhabited parts of the Deccan support mainly scrub jungle though there is some mixed deciduous forest, for example around Periyar. The southern coastal plains are heavily populated and apart from pockets of hardwood forest, there are mainly cash-cropping palm trees. The Indians are great gardeners and you will rarely be far from colourful and highly scented blooms.

Wildlife parks and reserves. India's wildlife reserves are in a state of crisis. Grazing encroachment is destroying the natural habitats, and park staff are prevented by political interference from doing anything, even if they feel so inclined. Major animals are under threat from poachers and, again, it seems that nothing much is being done. The parks are worth visiting to get an idea of India's rapidly vanishing natural state, but your chances of seeing big game are remote.

RECREATION

India is not all temples, forts, and museums. There are great opportunities for sport and adventure all over the country. Facilities may be sparse by Western standards, but think of it as part of the adventure.

Sport and adventure

Mention sport in India and the older generation automatically thinks of shooting. Conservation needs have pretty well put an end to this, but there is still plenty of good **fishing**. Streams are stocked with trout in the Himalayan foothills, the Nilgiri Hills of the south, and one or two other places, and there is coarse fishing in many lakes and rivers. Some rivers have big mahseer, a superb fighting fish. Conditions are often primitive, and you need to take all your own tackle. Unless you are after mahseer you can have a lot of fun with just a telescopic spinning rod and cheap reel. Local tourist offices will provide full details, but you can expect to pay only Rs10 or so (around 20p/33 cents) for a day's trout fishing.

Mountaineers will find plenty of scope in the Indian Himalayas, though the troubles in Kashmir have reduced the freedom to wander. When you are planning remember also that some areas, especially in Ladakh, are not open to foreigners and that you need permission to tackle major peaks. The Mountaineering Institute and Allied Sports, Manali, offers basic and advanced 28-day mountaineering courses at very reasonable all-inclusive prices. **Rock climbing** is possible all over India.

Skiing was most extensively developed at Gulmarg in Kashmir, but political trouble has put that effectively out of bounds. The main resort is now Auli in northern Uttar Pradesh. Simple facilities also exist at Kufri, Narkanda, and Solang Nullah (certainly very basic at the last-named) in Himachal Pradesh. Kufri is near Simla and has a Winter Sports Club where you can hire equipment. The Mountaineering Institute and Allied Sports, Manali, runs basic (21 days) and advanced (28 days) ski courses that sound a real bargain. Remember Indian bureaucracy and book these courses well in advance. The winter sports season in India is usually 15 December to 15 March.

Trekking routes in the Western Himalayas are easily the equal of those in Nepal and often in much wilder and less inhabited country. The tourism departments of both Jammu and Kashmir and Himachal Pradesh publish booklets that detail some trekking routes, and can also supply passable (1:25,000) maps, though these cover only a limited area. The Survey of India (office next to the Central Cottage Industries Emporium, Janpath, New Delhi) maps the whole of India at 1:50,000 or 1:63,360. The catch is that you need Ministry of Defence permission to buy any maps of border and coastal areas. These are, of course, precisely the ones you need for trekking. In the UK, Stanfords (see page 58) can supply cheap reprints of US military maps, which are hard to read but better than nothing. Contact L'Astrolabe, 46 Rue de Provence, 75009 Paris, France and Artou, 8 Rue de Rive, 1204 Geneva, Switzerland for details of their stocks. Because of the attitude towards security it is best to keep any such maps out of sight.

When arranging trekking always compare whatever price you are quoted with the government-fixed rates for porters, pack ponies, and so on (available at tourist offices). Take any promises to provide down sleeping bags, clothing or proper boots with a pinch of salt unless you actually see them. Unlike Kathmandu such equipment is not normally obtainable on hire in India.

West Coast Manufacturers and Traders, 92-UB Jawahar Nagar, Delhi 110007 sell a wide range of good inexpensive mountaineering and trekking equipment. You can now get a limited range of dehydrated foods in India, but many items including disposable gas cylinders are unobtainable, and if you are planning a serious expedition you will need to bring everything with you.

Rafting is organised on the Beas River during May and June by Himalayan Adventure Pte Ltd, The Mall, Manali (Tel 2182). The season on the Upper Ganga (Uttarakhand) is October to mid-December and February to April; contact Himalayan River Runners, 188A Jor Bagh, New Delhi (Tel 615736).

Other ideas. There are many **golf courses** in India, including some of the highest and prettiest in the world. Delhi is the main centre for **gliding**, and tremendously long cross-country flights are possible. **Hang-gliding** and **ballooning** are also growing in popularity.

Beaches

The good news is that India has thousands of miles of beautiful beaches. The bad news is that as soon as you stray from the established resorts you find that either there are no amenities at all or, if the place is populated, the beach is used as a latrine. Despite the growing popularity of Goa, Kovalam, and Mahabalipuram it is still possible to find peace, good food, and a beer at reasonable prices nearby.

Swimming pools

India is not well endowed with swimming pools. There are virtually no public pools, and the only opportunity for a swim is at a tourist hotel in a large city. Rates vary widely, some having risen so high that it is wise to phone first.

Entertainment

The best entertainment in India is free: street life, the view from the train window, and just people-watching. Yet many visitors plug in a personal stereo and immerse themselves in a book. Why come to one of the most interesting and entertaining countries in the world and not make the most of it?

CINEMA AND THEATRE

India has the largest **cinema** industry in the world, producing some eight hundred feature films a year. Until recently television reached only a tiny urban minority, and the cinema constituted the sole form of entertainment for the masses. The producers give them what they want — escapism. The typical Bollywood 'formula' movie has a facile plot, songs, dances, fights, a car chase and, most importantly, a happy ending.

While the majority of films are in Hindi they are also made in the other important languages. The industry is centred mainly on Bombay (for Hindi films), Madras, Calcutta, and Bangalore. Of the tremendous output only a dozen or so productions a year can claim any artistic merit, and these films are rarely a commercial success. It is a peculiar medium and well worth seeing. Don't worry about the language barrier, there is no difficulty understanding the action.

At one point it looked as if the cinema industry would be eclipsed by the rapid rise in television viewing, especially satellite television. The response of the producers, oddly enough, has been not more escapism but less. A new wave of social realism films is proving very popular with cinema-goers, so we can expect interesting developments.

Theatre in the Western sense is not a common art form in India (except perhaps in Bengal) and, of course, there are language problems for visitors. Folk theatre along religious lines, such as the Ram Lila, is very popular. These performances take place at the time of major festivals, and in larger towns can be quite spectacular.

MUSIC AND DANCE

The Indian tradition of dance and music is the oldest in the world, stretching back 3000 years. Little is written down, and continuity comes from the guru (teacher) passing on his knowledge to the chela (pupil) over many years. Thus a musician can trace his technique back for centuries. Indian dance and music were embraced and embellished by the less strict of the Muslim rulers.

Classical music. The north and south of India each provide a major form of classical music, Hindustani and Karnatak. Indian music is so different that it is best enjoyed with reference to Western music.

The structure is simpler than Western music in that there are no chords, harmony or bars. Indian music adds ten microtones to the Western scale of 12 tones, making a scale of 22 tones. All the music derives from 36 traditional melodies (ragas), and while the structure may be simpler than Western music, the scales and rhythm are the very opposite. The scope for variation and improvisation are limitless. Even watching Ravi Shankar, the sitar player once described by George Harrison as the greatest musician in the world, you sometimes wonder whether he himself knows where a piece will start and finish.

Except for well bred girls learning the veena, music in India is a job for professionals and not amateurs. The mark of a cultured man was to be a good critical listener rather than a second-rate player. These days audience behaviour at concerts can be a bit of a shock to Westerners used to reverential silence.

Popular music. Mainly though you will hear, or have your ears assaulted by, Hindi film music. Much of the success of a film depends on its tunes, and the 'playback singers' who record the songs the stars mime to are popular artists in their own right.

Classical dance. The essential thing to grasp about Indian classical dance is that it all stems from religious ritual. Its purpose is not to entertain, but to guide and educate. There are two main classical styles, Bharata Natyam (southern) and Kathak (northern).

These dances are stylised and deliberate, and the dancers spend many years learning their skills. Every dance tells a story, and every movement has a specific meaning. The music that accompanies the dance simply provides a rhythm for the dancer, who is solely responsible for interpreting the story. Manipuri dancing from Bengal is freer in style.

Performances are frequent, both in the major hotels and in public auditoria. Less frequently seen in the north is Kathakali, the dance-mime of Kerala. This is one of the world's outstanding performing arts and definitely not to be missed if the opportunity arises.

Folk music and dance. Local folk dancing can quickly become too much of a good thing, unless you happen to catch the Gujarati one where the man dances with a fire pot on his head. The performances put on in tourist hotels are pretty sterile. To appreciate Indian folk music and dance you need to be sitting on a charpoy in the open air in a village.

NIGHTLIFE

India does not pander to the tourist looking for a swinging holiday, and night-life is virtually non-existent. Lets hope it stays that way.

SPECTATOR SPORTS

Amongst spectator sports **horse racing** is popular in Delhi, Calcutta, Bombay, Bangalore, and Ootacamund; **polo** can be seen occasionally and, of course, there are test matches during the winter **cricket** season. Field sport enthusiasts will be intrigued to hear that the Kadir Cup is still contested. **Kabbadi** is a Punjabi game likened to rugby without a ball. A robust game, it developed from military training for youngsters. **Football** is growing rapidly in popularity.

Details of all these activities can be obtained from Government of India tourist offices.

OFFBEAT INDIA

This book covers most of the mainstream attractions in India. Some of these are unusual enough; a temple full of rats, for instance, and lakes with floating islands are hardly commonplace. Many other spectacles, often of a truly folk nature, have their appeal for minority interests.

Bullfighting takes place in two forms. In Goa bulls and buffaloes are pitted against one another (and a lot of money can change hands on the result), and in Tamil Nadu humans take on the beasts (see Madurai).

Bullock and buffalo racing are popular in Kerala and Karnataka, again in two styles. Bullocks have a surprising turn of speed when drawing a light cart on a good surface. These days bullocks are bred specially for racing, and successful animals fetch up to Rs50,000 (around £1000/$1650). Water buffalo are raced, mainly in Karnataka, down a straight wet muddy course. The driver stands on a board behind and scores points for the height of the wake he raises.

Kalari. Again in Kerala (see Thiruvananthapuram) you can watch a display of kalaripayattu, arguably the world's prototype martial art predating karate and all the others, and including the use of an awesome four-metre-long sword.

Cemeteries. The British, along with the many other nationalities who tried to colonise, evangelise, or simply make money in India, left their poignant memorials all over the country. These cemeteries are decaying rapidly, but still full of interest and history. Track down a copy of *Two Monsoons* by Theon Wilkinson for a fascinating guide.

Motor racing and motorcycle racing keep a fairly low profile for social reasons, but are surprisingly popular. The main car event is the All-India Grand Prix in February or March on a new purpose-built circuit near Madras. Other meetings take place on airfields near Bombay and Calcutta. A new formula for Maruti-powered single-seaters provides Formula Ford-style close racing, and the sight of thirty Ambassadors door-handling their way round a corner is not to be missed.

Vintage cars. Several thousand vintage cars, many unique, survived the dispersals of the maharajas' stables in the seventies. Rallies are held in Delhi and Bombay, perhaps elsewhere also. Major collections are held in Bombay and Indore; we do not quote names and addresses as these are private, but the real enthusiast will have little trouble making contact with the owners.

Fun transport. Esoteric forms of public transport include Delhi rickshaws based on Harley-Davidson frames (although no longer with the original engines), a vertiginous cable-hauled tramway (see Jogindernagar), the chairlift at Rajgir, and a number of steam-hauled narrow gauge railways. Bridge building has seen many ferries superceded in the last ten years, but we bet there is still an old steamboat working somewhere. Depending on the season you should be able to hitch a ride on one of the dhows that ply the trade routes between Gujarat and Kerala.

Firewalking can be seen at times in Tamil Nadu, and on Hassan bus-stand the author saw (well, *thought* he saw) a fakir push a sharpened bicycle spoke in through one cheek and out through the other. However there is no doubt that some of these people can create illusions in the minds of those prepared to see them — which was, of course, the basis of the Indian rope trick.

And where else in the world would you see a Shitole Restaurant?

FESTIVALS

India is a country of many festivals and public holidays, which are an essential part of the way of life. As elsewhere in the world, these mostly have a religious basis.

Problems can arise during Holi (see below), and in fact events at most of these festivals can easily get out of hand. Processions are often routed provocatively past rival places of worship, and anyone who has been in a football crowd knows how quickly the mood of a mob can change. Have fun but always keep your wits about you and an eye on the exit.

Hindu festivals

Holi, followed mainly in northern India, is a spring fertility festival marked by the throwing and squirting of brightly coloured dyes, not a time to be out in smart clothes. In many places Holi has degenerated into drunkenness and over-exuberance verging on thuggery. Sensible Indians, especially women, keep well out of the way until at least midday when everyone goes home to clean up.

Dussehra (September/October), also known as Durga Puja, honours Durga or Devi on the day that her husband Shiva slew a buffalo-headed demon. Probably the most popular of all Hindu festivals.

Diwali (October/November) is the festival of light. Vishnu, who had killed a giant on this day, was greeted by Lakshmi and other women bearing lamps. Fairy lights or, more traditionally, little earthenware oil lamps line all the houses and temples. Once a quieter and more reflective affair than other Hindu festivals, that bane of Indians enjoying themselves, amplified music, is now as obtrusive as at other festivities.

Muslim festivals

Bakr-Id commemorates Abraham's would-be sacrifice of Ishmael. **Muharram** marks the martyrdom of Hassan and Hussain, descendants of Muhammed, and is observed mainly by the Shias. Tazias (replica tombs) are paraded, and the biggest show is in Lucknow. Self-flagellation is discouraged these days, but I have seen drummers work their hands into a bloody mess. The end of **Ramadan**, the month of fasting observed throughout the Muslim world, is marked in India by **Id-ul-fitr,** a joyous occasion of feasting and new beginnings.

Other religious festivals

The Buddhists celebrate **Buddha Jayanti** (May/June) as the date on which Buddha was born, achieved enlightenment, and died. The Christian festivals of **Good Friday** and **Christmas Day** are public holidays. Goa and Bombay are the best places for Christmas, though Sikhs sometimes provide hospitality as it coincides with the birthday of one of their gurus.

Secular festivals

Three secular festivals are **Republic Day** (26 January), **Independence Day** (15 August), and **Gandhi's Birthday** (2 October). The most important of these is Republic Day, celebrated all over the country and marked by a spectacular parade in Delhi. Many other festivals of a more local nature take place throughout the year, and a number of these are mentioned in the text. These are often more spontaneous and enjoyable than the larger events.

More enterprising tourist authorities, notably Rajasthan, use special festivals to promote tourism. The Jaisalmer Desert Festival is one example, and the Jaipur Elephant Festival in April is an attempt to extend the season. These sometimes start off well and later degenerate into over-commercialised tourist traps.

Dates and details. Government of India tourist offices produce a list each year giving the dates of the major festivals. Hindu festivals occur in the same period each year, the exact date depending on the phase of the moon. Muslim ones are based on a calendar of 354 days and in time take place in any season of the year; dates for

Ramadan are December 31 (1997), December 20 (1998) and December 11 (1999). Precise dates of local festivals are better checked with the state tourist organisation. Festivities often spread over several days either side of the official date, and you can miss a lot arriving on the specified date.

Opening hours. The usual hours for Indian shops are 10am–5pm or 6pm, often a bit later in tourist areas. Almost all shops shut on Sunday, but in towns and cities their place is taken by lively street markets.

Shopping. India is a paradise for souvenir hunters. Every part of the country has its special handicrafts, and everywhere there are beautiful textiles.

Most non-tourist shops will sell to you at the same price as the locals, and fruit vendors and so on rarely up their prices by much. Nobody wants to be done, but it is hardly worth arguing over a few paise. Where you do have to be careful is in the tourist shops. Salesmen are extremely persistent and charge what the market will stand. Get an idea of prices in one of the many government stores; you should be able to buy for substantially less elsewhere. Check the quality of every item very carefully; many things are spoiled by careless finishing and lack of quality control.

Be extremely cautious in the case of high-cost items unless you are an expert. Many of the gems on offer are fake or of low quality, and silver has a funny habit of turning green after a while. Carpets are usually cheaper for a given quality in London or New York. All sorts of rubbishy furs are dyed and sold as expensive ones. Bone is sold as ivory, and ivory 'antiqued' by boiling in tea. To test apply a lighted match; bone will char, ivory will not. Leaving aside any considerations about the welfare of elephants, however, bear in mind that you are likely to find it very difficult to import ivory into your home country. Be dubious of handmade items; salesmen know that 'handmade' is a magic word for Westerners, and use it accordingly.

When you have been unable to price something first, look at the material content and guess how long it would have taken to make. Materials and labour are cheap, but shops will often multiply their cost price ten or even twenty times. When you are going to bid think of a number and halve it, always speak to your companion in a language other than English, and remember the walk-away trick. You can afford to be tough; no-one in India sells at a loss.

Never go shopping with a hotelier, guide, houseboat man or taxi driver; do not buy where you are staying, and do not tell the shopkeeper the name of your hotel or houseboat. That way he has no commission (commonly 20%, sometimes a lot more) to pay, and you can hit him harder on price. The great thing is to take your time and wear the man down. It's all a game really. Finally, if the vendor smiles or offers you tea after agreeing a price you're paying too much.

Indian tradesmen have a very bad reputation as regards despatching goods that have been paid for, and you can expect absolutely no help from either tourist or legal authorities. Remember, too, that even a 10% deposit can be a lot of money in Indian terms. When you buy something you cannot carry away yourself have the vendor pack it (this should be part of the deal) and stand over him while he does it. Then accompany him to the post office or airfreight office and obtain the proper receipt. Paying by credit card means that the card company will chase the vendor if necessary and, in Britain at least, they have to reimburse you if the goods do not arrive.

Health and Hygiene

Many people are put off visiting India by health worries. In fact, during the main tourist season (October to March) India is a healthy place, and a few simple precautions will keep you out of trouble. If you have any particular worries read *Travellers' Health: How to Stay Healthy Abroad* by Richard Dawood (Oxford University Press).

NATURAL HAZARDS

Heat. The heat can easily lead to dehydration in those unaccustomed to it. Exhaustion, accompanied by thirst and sometimes nausea, are the result. The cure is simply to rest, take salt tablets, and drink copiously. Dehydration is avoided by drinking enough in the first place. A good rule is that the body needs four litres of fluid a day at 20°C, five litres at 30°C, and six litres at 40°C. Coloured urine is an indication of insufficient fluid intake, though this does not work if you are using iodine as a water purifier. It is often difficult to get the fluids you need; see the section on food and drink. If things go further than this, with body temperature apparently out of control, get into a cold shower or bath and seek medical advice.

Sun. There was a time when the children and soldiers of the Raj were punished for going out without a hat to protect them from sunstroke. It now seems that the damage was done not by the sun's rays but dehydration. In the cities the air is so thick with smoke and dust that most of the UV is filtered out, and there is little risk of burning. This is certainly not the case elsewhere, and the usual precautions should be taken. Sun screen creams are not readily available in India, and very expensive when they are.

Insects. Mosquito nets are usually provided in areas where mosquitoes are a real pest. Otherwise burn a coil under the bed (wrecks the throat but you sleep) or use one of the electric devices cheaply available in India. It is not much use taking your own net as there is rarely anything to hang it on.

In cheap or dirty lodgings beware of bed bugs. Little black spots on the bed frame or bedding are the warning. Apply a lighted match to the joints and wait for something like a squashed ladybird to emerge. If it does, find somewhere else to stay.

Snakes. Unless you go traipsing around fields the only snake you are likely to see is a snake charmer's cobra. Many people in the country do die of snake bite every year, mostly during the monsoon when the snakes are washed out of their usual lairs.

DISEASES AND OTHER HEALTH HAZARDS

Inoculations. There are no official vaccination requirements for India unless you arrive from an area where yellow fever is endemic. However inoculations for meningitis, typhoid and hepatitis A are recommended. A cholera jab (which is not very effective anyway) may be needed if you plan to travel north from Rishikesh into the pilgrimage area of Uttarakhand. You need an official card as proof of inoculation and the doctor's signature will have to be validated, so get this done well before departure.

TABT protects against typhoid, paratyphoid and, more usefully, tetanus. Polio is a risk in India and, even if you have nothing else, a booster is a wise precaution.

Malaria is present throughout India except in high-altitude regions, and it is essential to take precautions. Evidence of chloroquine-resistant malarial strains exists, so make sure your doctor has the latest information on the most effective preventative tablets available. The current favourite is a combination of both daily and weekly pills. Treatment must start well before you set out for India and continue for the specified period after leaving the country. A new weekly drug that was supposed to deal with chloroquine-resistance, mefloquine (Lariam), has proved to have very unpleasant side effects on some people.

Gastric problems. Follow carefully the advice in the food and drink section, and you stand an excellent chance of having no health problems at all. It has to be admitted, however, that diarrhoea is not unknown in India; not for nothing have generations of travellers dreaded Delhi belly. This can strike simply because the bacteria in your stomach and intestines that aid digestion are unused to the bacteria in Indian food. There is not necessarily anything wrong with the food, it is just different.

For a simple attack of diarrhoea the first and most important thing is to go on a very strict diet. Fat in any form (including milk) is completely out, and so are fruit juices, fresh fruit and vegetables, cold drinks and ice cream. All the things, in fact, that you might expect to soothe a troubled tum. Take two Lomotil every four hours and, if you can, stick to plain boiled rice and curd (sets like concrete), and drink hot black tea (sugar is okay). If this has not worked after three days at most, or if you are passing blood, go to a doctor and have tests done. Indian doctors are mostly very competent; they know the local bugs and how to deal with them.

The alternative is a bit naughty, because you are supposed to take antibiotics as a full course, but useful when you are on the move. Carry with you Flagyl or Oxytetracycline, which can be bought at any pharmacy in India without a prescription. Take one pill at the first sign of trouble, perhaps one more later, and hope for the best. The author has found this method effective, and it has been recommended by a doctor.

Severe diarrhoea, at its extreme in cholera, is a killer because of dehydration. If you are unable to keep down the necessary liquids it is worth knowing that a small amount of opium can save your life by stopping dehydration. It does not however, kill the bugs that are causing the trouble; it is strictly for emergencies.

Whatever the severity of diarrhoea, it is essential to replace the fluids and salts that you are losing; drink plenty of water and take rehydration salts (ideally bought before you left for India).

Hepatitis. Probably the worst thing you can get is viral hepatitis (hepatitis B). It comes from impure water, dirty utensils, lack of hygiene and joints shared with carriers. Apart from making your skin and eyes yellow, it is a debilitating disease that can cause permanent liver damage and recur over a period of years. Western medicine has no real answer to it; relief has been reported from using Ayurvedic medication. Ayurveda is the ancient Indian medical system based on natural ingredients. The risk is highest during the hot weather, and Nepal is worse than India. You must be extra careful if you go trekking; there are many carriers, and sanitation is simply unknown up in the mountains.

Controversy surrounds the effectiveness of gamma globulin against hepatitis A. It does seem that the protection, if it works at all, is short-lived and may well leave you more susceptible to the disease when it wears off. Ask your doctor what he thinks. The Havrix vaccine is more expensive but highly effective, and can provide protection for 10 years.

Rabies is a serious problem in India. If you are bitten or even have a scratch licked by a dog, cat, monkey or bat it is essential to have a rabies shot. This is not as unpleasant as it used to be, and better than dying — there is no cure for rabies. The moral is simple: give all animals a very wide berth.

AIDS. Contrary to what the government claims, AIDS has a dangerous hold in India. A large percentage of prostitutes and their clients — people such as lorry drivers — are HIV positive, especially in the larger cities. Take all the usual precautions.

MEDICAL TREATMENT

As noted above Indian doctors are mostly well trained and understand their local bugs. Many have their own laboratories for doing tests.

In theory, at least, free medical care and hospitals are available but, away from the big cities, expect conditions to be extremely basic. The best bet is always a mission hospital or a teaching hospital. Hotels and tourist offices are the best sources of information. You must have medical insurance to cover private treatment and repatriation, and expect to pay for drugs and treatment as you go along.

Dental care is extremely poor; head for one of the big four cities and get advice from your high commission or consulate.

Pharmacies. All but the smallest towns have well stocked pharmacies that provide sound advice on what to take. Your hotel or a doctor will advise which are open late or on Sundays. Most drugs are very cheap and sold without a prescription. If drugs appear not to be working as quickly as they should, try the same thing from a different source or an alternative; adulterated and counterfeit drugs are not unknown, and it is also worth checking the sell-by date of any drugs you buy before you hand over the cash.

EVERYDAY HEALTH

Cuts, grazes, and insect bites can easily become infected by dirt and flies. Apply a mild antiseptic cream and keep the area scrupulously clean until the skin is completely healed.

Women's health. It is advisable to bring your own tampons. Check with your doctor before having inoculations during pregnancy.

Toilets in India are mostly of the hole in the floor variety, a big advantage in a country where few things get regular maintenance. Public toilets are unknown. In desperation try a hotel, restaurant or offices. About the only good thing about Indian toilets is the bottom-washing tap, which can be a real boon for hot tired feet.

This may all sound a bit daunting, but don't worry, the vast majority of people have no trouble at all. Just be sensible. While the author's approach to hygiene may seem a bit casual, India is the only place in the world where he has ever had to take a laxative.

INSURANCE

It is absolutely essential that, before you leave home, you take out insurance to cover medical expenses, repatriation, and baggage and belongings. Consider carefully the cost of replacing all your gear and add something for souvenirs and other acquisitions. If you plan to go trekking make absolutely sure that helicopter evacuation is covered.

Crime and Safety

India is a safe country for the foreign visitor. Take simple precautions and you can reduce the risk of theft almost to zero.

The black market. Gone are the days when the backpacker could spin out his time in India by selling his belongings. Improved consumer goods production and wholesale smuggling have killed that game. The only things readily saleable at a profit are foreign liquor and cigarettes. Take a litre bottle of Johnny Walker Red Label and 200 English (not American) cigarettes, preferably ones with flashy packs. The easiest place to sell these is outside the airport bus office in Janpath, New Delhi; the men there pay cash and don't mess about. If you are travelling from Nepal, it is worth knowing that you can fly from Kathmandu to Patna and make up part of the extra cost of the air ticket by selling duty-free tobacco and alcohol. The price in a smallish place like Patna may well be better than in the big cities.

Do not deal with unofficial money changers unless you have a black belt in karate and can run in two directions at once. Do not hand over money to anybody until you are quite convinced that you have got what you are paying for.

Crime against visitors. The only crime specifically aimed at foreigners is theft on the busy train routes between Delhi, Varanasi, Agra, and Jaipur and a few other places. The main target is hand baggage, which is most likely to contain cameras, passports, and travellers' cheques. The stations are more of a risk than the trains themselves. Especially beware, if your companion has gone for tea or whatever, of someone rushing up saying they need help. It's a hundred to one they don't, and it's just a ruse to throw you off guard.

How to avoid robbery. You've probably heard all sorts of horror stories about cunning oriental thieves, but theft is not really a major problem in India. Hardly a person who has been robbed has anyone but themselves to blame. Mostly it is the result of stupidity or sheer carelessness. Wherever in the world you are, most thieves are opportunists rather than professionals; they are easily deterred, and if you make things at all hard for them they will go and pick on someone else. In places like Goa, Pushkar, and Manali there is more risk of being robbed by a broke Westerner than by one of the locals.

Your most important belongings are your passport and travellers' cheques. There is only one place for these and that is next to your body. Money belts are useless outside clothing and very uncomfortable under it. The best thing is a purse hung round the neck and worn under the shirt. This should be unobtrusive and carry the valuables on the front of your body. Never use a belt pouch or bum bag.

Have a button-down pocket in your shirt or the front of your trousers in which to carry only the amount of cash (say Rs200 — around £4/$6.50) you need for the day. It is bad security, not to mention unkind, to flash a wad of Rs100 notes in front of people who have to live on next to nothing. Keep the rest of your cash in the purse or money belt.

Take a padlock and chain with you. They will secure your baggage on a bus or train, and the lock will close your hotel room more securely than the one supplied by the hotel. When you have to put your pack on top of a bus (don't if you can help it) take all your valuables into the bus with you. Standing on a bus or in a crowded place put your bag on the floor between your feet; that way no-one can delve into it or slice it open.

Be very wary of letting anybody handle your watch or camera. Do not leave your camera or other valuables in a hotel room; if you don't want to take them with you, have them locked in the hotel safe and obtain a receipt. Check carefully when you get the things back.

Reporting a crime. In the event of a crime you must get the police to make a written record, 'file an FIR' (First Information Report) to use the jargon. You will need a copy of this for any insurance claim or to replace your passport or travellers' cheques. Indian police are well used to fraudulent reports of theft, and you can expect them to be sceptical to say the least. Western women are probably quite safe, but it is still better for a man to accompany them to a police station.

Violence. Reading Indian newspapers you realise that India is a pretty violent country. Unlike more urbanised countries this is mostly rural violence and, like rural violence elsewhere, caused by disputes over zan, zar and zamin — women, gold and land. The risk of violence to foreigners is minute.

Police. India has many different police forces, and they wear a bewildering array of uniforms. To clear up the main cause of confusion: anyone in khaki is a policeman, while the army wears jungle green. The army is only involved in law enforcement when things have got totally out of hand. If they are on the streets you shouldn't be.

The Indians do not much like their police, seeing them as corrupt and heavy-handed. The officers, distinguished by their better uniforms and caps instead of berets, usually speak English and are helpful to foreigners.

Drugs. There is little to say about dope beyond the fact that it is illegal. The possession and discreet use of small amounts is unlikely to get you into much trouble, but can be used as an excuse for a shakedown. Police behaviour is getting out of hand in certain places; appropriate warnings are given in the text.

Photography. Do not take photographs of anything — including bridges, dams and trains — that may in any way be considered to be of strategic importance. You risk having your film and camera confiscated, and being locked up.

Children. Apart from the obvious problems with food and dehydration children cope well with northern India in the cool weather. The heat and humidity of the south are more difficult. You will find that children open many social contacts — and get spoiled rotten.

Travellers with disabilities. India is not a good country for disabled travellers. Blind or partially sighted travellers will find the streets lethal, and there is little or no provision for wheelchairs. Worst of all, in the land of karma, understanding and sympathy are rare.

Electrical equipment. Supply is nominally 220V at 50Hz but, given a chronic shortage of generating capacity, voltage is often much lower (too often 220V lower).

Youth and student concessions. Indian Airlines gives a 25% discount for anyone under 30, and that's about it. This is a consequence of there being too many forged student cards in the past.

Complaints. All state-owned establishments have a complaints book. They must work; the only time I demanded the book (in Palitana, Gujarat) they got into a terrible state.

Time. Indian Standard Time (IST), which covers the whole country, is 5½ hours ahead of GMT. There is no daylight saving; why bother, when most people's lives are ruled by the rising and setting of the sun?

Weights and measures. The metric system is in universal use.

TOURIST INFORMATION

India takes tourism seriously, as much for its 'home tourists' as for foreign visitors. Most of the tourist offices are very good and dish out lots of useful information. The staff can sometimes seem unnervingly off-hand; they aren't, it seems to be the Indian way of efficiency. It does help though to know exactly what you want.

Tourist offices abroad. The Government of India maintains tourist offices in major cities around the world, and these can provide most mainstream information:

UK
7 Cork Street, London W1X 2AB
Tel 0171-437 3677 Fax 0171-494 1048

USA
30 Rockefeller Plaza, Room 15, North Mezzanine, New York, NY 10020
Tel 212-586-4901 Fax 212-582-3274

230 North Michigan Avenue, Chicago, IL 60601
Tel 312-236-6899

3550 Wilshire Bvd, Suite 204, Los Angeles, CA 90010
Tel 213-380-8855 Fax 213-380-6111

Canada
60 Bloor Street, West Suite No 1003, Toronto, M4W 3B8
Tel 416-962-3787 Fax 416-962-6279

Australia
Carlton Centre, 55 Elizabeth Street, Sydney, NSW 2000
Tel 02-9232 1600 Fax 02-9223 3003

Tourist offices in India. The Government of India runs offices in the main centres. In addition each state has its own organisation with local offices and, usually, one in Delhi as well. These can often provide more detailed information on local events and the less frequented places.

Tourist handouts come on two levels, the glossy brochures intended to lure you to the area, and then the hard facts. The latter take the form of booklets, which are usually very good. Most are dated on the back; check this before placing any reliance on prices and other variable data.

EMBASSIES, HIGH COMMISSIONS AND CONSULATES IN INDIA

UK
British High Commission
50 Shantipath, Chanakyapuri, New Delhi
Tel 687 2161 Fax 687 2882

USA
United States Embassy
Shantipath, Chanakyapuri, New Delhi
Tel 600 651

Canada
Canadian High Commission
7/8 Shantipath, Chanakyapuri, New Delhi
Tel 687 6500 Fax 687 6579

Australia
Australian High Commission
1/50G Shantipath, Chanakyapuri, New Delhi
Tel 688 8232 Fax 688 5088

New Zealand
New Zealand High Commission
50N Nyaya Marg, Chanakyapuri, New Delhi
Tel 688 3170 Fax 687 2317

Chanakya, in case you were wondering, was minister and diplomat to the Maurayan
king Chandragupta, a forebear of Ashoka. An acknowledged master of statecraft, he
is the alleged author of a famous work on the subject.

Delhi

India Gate
New Delhi

Delhi is the capital of India and the most important arrival point for foreign visitors. At the time of independence Delhi was a quiet British and Muslim city with a population of around 500,000. As a result of partition many Muslims left, and there was a huge influx of Punjabis, mostly Sikhs, who had been forced to leave their homes and wealth in what became Pakistan. Naturally enterprising and very hard working, they have made Delhi their city. The population is now 10 million and, like the Punjabis, it's a bit brash and raucous. Happily, again under Punjabi influence, it has a lively and welcoming air. Certainly a better place to arrive in India than Bombay, which can be a bit of a culture shock.

History

Delhi is strategically located at the crossroads of northern India and, despite official moves to other places, has always been at the centre of events. Lacking any natural defences it has long been the target of invaders from the north-west. The Muslims, in the shape of the Pathans, first took it in 1192, it was raided by Tamurlane (or Timur) the Mongol in 1398, Sher Shah (an Afghan) deposed Humayun for a time, and the Persian Nadir Shah despoiled it in 1739. From then until the British took it from the Marathas in 1803 it was a story of constant decline and destruction. Despite heavy fighting during the Mutiny and the deposing of the last Mughal emperor in 1857, the British made little mark on Delhi until they decided to establish New Delhi as their capital. With Independence this proved a fortuitous move as it would have been unthinkable for Indians to govern the country from one of the coastal cities.

The ancient cities of Delhi

The earliest known city at Delhi was Indraprastha on the site now occupied by the Purana Qila. The ruins of Lal Kot and Rai Pithora, north of the Qutb Minar, are the only remains above ground of the pre-Muslim period. Some walls remain but there is little of real interest, and the same can be said of the early Muslim settlements of Siri (1304) and Jahanpanah (1325).

Predating these, however, is the group of buildings known collectively as the **Qutb Minar*****, though strictly this name applies only to the graceful 73m-high tower. Built around 1200 of finely carved red sandstone and white marble it served a dual function as victory memorial and minaret. The mosque at the base was the first in India and used materials from 27 demolished Hindu and Jain temples; the sculpture on these was concealed by plaster. Take a good look at the arched screen that fronted the now demolished prayer hall. The intricate carving on the outer arches is quite different from that on the central five, which belonged to the original small mosque. Thirty years after it was first built Altamish added these arches and a cloister to enclose a larger courtyard. The **Alai Darwaza**, the huge gateway on the south side of the courtyard, was built by Alai-ud-Din in 1300, when he further extended the courtyard. The same man planned a tower twice as high as the Qutb Minar. This project lapsed with his death, and the base, 26m high, still stands to the north of the main enclosure.

In the first courtyard is the iron pillar beloved of sensationalist writers like von Daniken. There is no mystery about its history because inscriptions on it record that it was made in AD300–400, and brought to Delhi from Bihar around 1050. It has not rusted for the simple reason that it is very pure wrought iron, a material within the capabilities of contemporary technology, but impressive for all that. The Qutb Minar complex is the author's favourite place in Delhi, more deserving of your time than the Red Fort. The earlier you arrive the more peaceful it is.

The earliest city remains worth a look are **Tughlakabad** (1321). The massive walls of the city and fortress are intact, and the tomb of its builder Ghiyasuddin Tughlak (died 1325) stands near the main gate. The town was cursed by a holy man who accused the king of poaching workers he had employed to dig a tank, and never occupied after Tughlak's death.

After the failure of the move to Daulatabad (see page 273), the city of **Firozabad*** was founded by and named after Firozshah Tughlak in 1354. This is pretty battered as it has been used as a supply of stone for later developments, and all that remains is the citadel, now better known as Firozshah Kotla. Its Jama Masjid superseded that at the Qutb Minar, and an Ashoka Pillar with its various inscriptions stands on a tall building. The pillar was brought the 200km from Ambala by Firozshah Tughlak, the founder.

Two hundred years later Sher Shah and Humayun, who fought each other for the throne, both had a hand in building the **Purana Qila**** (Old Fort). The high walls are almost intact, and inside are the lovely mosque of Sher Shah and the octagonal Sher Manzil. Take care! Humayun, who used this building as a library, died after a fall on the steps, not surprising as they are dangerously steep. Excavations near the Sher Manzil uncovered successive layers of building starting from the time of the

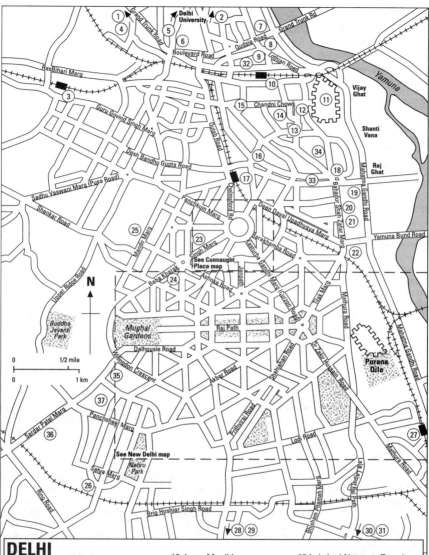

DELHI

1 Shalimar Bagh
2 Coronation Durbar Site
3 Sarai Rohilla Railway Station
4 Roshanara Bagh
5 Hindu Rao Hospital and Ashoka Pillar
6 Mutiny Memorial
7 Qudsia Bagh (Tourist Camp)
8 Kashmiri Gate ISBT (Bus Terminal)
9 Kashmiri Gate
10 Old Delhi Railway Station
11 Red Fort
12 Jain Temple

13 Jama Masjid
14 Sunehri Masjid
15 Fatehpuri Mosque
16 Ajmeri Gate
17 New Delhi Railway Station
18 Delhi Gate
19 Gandhi National Museum
20 Feroz Shah Kotla
21 International Dolls Museum
22 Hans Bhavan (Foreigners' Registration Office)
23 Poste Restante
24 Post Office

25 Lakshmi Narayan Temple
26 Rail Transport Museum
27 Nizamuddin Railway Station
28 Hauz Khas
29 Qutab Minar Complex
30 Tughlaqabad
31 Tomb of Ghiyas-ud-din
32 Tera Hotel
33 Tourist Camp
34 Moti Mahal Restaurant
35 Diplomat Hotel
36 Maurya Sheraton Hotel
37 Youth Hostel

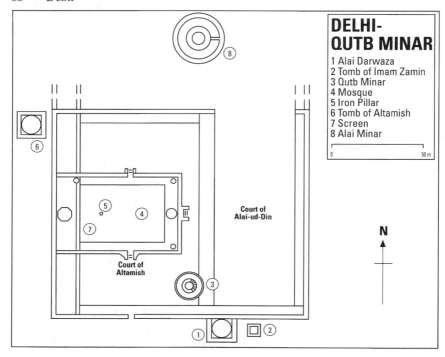

**DELHI-
QUTB MINAR**
1 Alai Darwaza
2 Tomb of Imam Zamin
3 Qutb Minar
4 Mosque
5 Iron Pillar
6 Tomb of Altamish
7 Screen
8 Alai Minar

0   50 m

Court of
Alai-ud-Din

Court of
Altamish

N

Maurayan Empire in the third century BC. The excavated area has deteriorated to
the point where you cannot really see anything; most of the finds are in the museum
just inside the main gate.

Old Delhi

Delhi lost importance for a time under the Mughals as Akbar, Jehangir, and
Shahjahan preferred Fatehpur Sikri, Lahore, and Agra for their capitals. In 1639,
however, Shahjahan began construction of the city popularly known now as **Old
Delhi**, more properly Shahjahanabad. This, popularly referred to as the seventh Delhi
(more like the 14th in actual fact), was a walled city of which the Red Fort was both
citadel and palace. Several of the city gates and fragments of the wall still survive.

The **Red Fort***, a colossal structure 2km around, was built between 1639 and
1648. You enter through the Lahore Gate, to which the outer reinforcement was
added by Aurangzeb. The long shopping arcade you pass through is still fulfilling its
original purpose; noblewomen used to play here at being shopkeepers for the women
of the royal family confined in purdah. Emerging into the open again you come upon
a large gateway (the wall to either side has gone) of which the upper floor was used
by musicians to welcome distinguished arrivals. Passing through this you are faced by
the **Diwan-i-Am** (Hall of Public Audience) where the emperor could meet his
subjects. The inlaid panels were originally made by Austin of Bordeaux, a Frenchman
who worked on the Taj Mahal. Looted during the Mutiny they were restored in 1909
by the viceroy Lord Curzon. Behind is the **Rang Mahal** (Palace of Colours), which
once had a silver-gilt ceiling and was the empress's quarters. Just north of here along

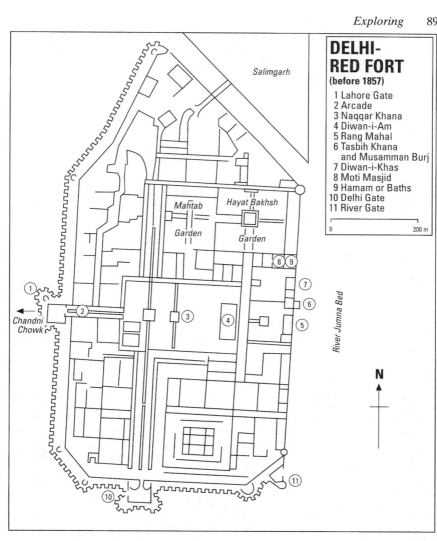

**DELHI-
RED FORT**
(before 1857)

Salimgarh

1 Lahore Gate
2 Arcade
3 Naqqar Khana
4 Diwan-i-Am
5 Rang Mahal
6 Tasbih Khana
  and Musamman Burj
7 Diwan-i-Khas
8 Moti Masjid
9 Hamam or Baths
10 Delhi Gate
11 River Gate

0   200 m

Mahtab   Hayat Bakhsh

Garden   Garden

Chandni
Chowk

River Jumna Bed

N

the wall are the **private apartments** with some fine marble tracery screens. Next is the **Diwan-i-Khas** (Hall of Private Audience), which is where the fabulous Peacock Throne stood. Like the Rang Mahal the ceiling was once of silver, but it takes a little effort now to conjure up the splendour that inspired the Persian inscription: 'If on earth there be a paradise of bliss/It is this, it is this, it is this.'

North again are the **Hamam**, or baths, and the **Moti Masjid** (Pearl Mosque). Shahjahan was not a particularly devout Muslim and neglected to build a mosque in the fort, making do with a meditation room in his quarters. This was not good enough for Aurangzeb who added this lovely little mosque. The emperors visited the Jama Masjid only on Fridays. Behind here is a **formal garden** with pavilions. The reason the east wall of the fort is so low, incidentally, is that the River Yamuna used to flow right underneath it. There is a **Sound and Light Show** most evenings (except during the monsoon), which is cheap and very well done. Warm clothing or insect repellent is needed, according to the season. Information and tickets at the fort or the Government of India Tourist Office. The Red Fort is obviously worth seeing, but its general condition is worse than that of its counterpart in Agra. Time is better spent at the Qutb Minar.

The **Jama Masjid***** is the largest mosque in India, its courtyard 100m square. It is altogether a very imposing building with two 40m-high minarets, all built in red sandstone with detailing in white marble. You can climb one of the minarets (small charge plus camera fee) from the south entrance. In the north-east corner of the courtyard is a collection of relics of the Prophet Mohammed including a hair of his beard (bakshish expected).

Near the beginning of Chandni Chowk is a **Digambar Jain**** temple, as usual richly decorated inside, and attached to it a birds' hospital. **Chandni Chowk***** is the commercial centre of Shahjahanabad. The name means Silver Street, and seems to have derived from the water channel that once ran down the centre, rather than from the silversmiths who still frequent part of it. On the left as you go down Chandni Chowk is the **Sisganj Gurudwara**, which marks the spot where Guru Tegh Bahadur was put to death by Aurangzeb in 1675. Almost next door are the gilded domes of the **Sonehri Masjid**. The end of Chandni Chowk is marked by the **Fatehpuri Masjid**. Around the back of this people with a sweet tooth (you need one in India) will enjoy crystallised fruit; there are also many, many varieties of pickle. Chandni Chowk is India in the raw; incredibly crowded, it is a noisy, smelly, gaudy assault on the senses. You can easily spend a day wandering around this fascinating area, but be careful, it is one of very few places in India where you really have to watch out for pick-pockets and thieves.

New Delhi

Although Delhi was a popular capital for land invaders the British were a sea-faring race and preferred to rule India from the three centres of Bombay, Madras, and Calcutta. However it was announced in 1911 that a move was to be made to Delhi, and Sir Edwin Lutyens and Sir Herbert Baker laid out a new city in the space between Shahjahanabad and the older cities to the south. **New Delhi** is a planned city on a grand scale with the main avenue 350m wide and more than 3km long. The new streets were aligned with existing features so you will find a view of the Jama Masjid or Purana Qila along a modern road. Construction was delayed by the First World War, and it was 1931 before the government officially moved in.

The great east-west avenue is **Rajpath** culminating in **Rashtrapati Bhavan***** (the president's residence, originally built for the viceroy). This is a cosy little 54-bedroom detached house with a 330-acre back garden. The garden is open only during February, the house sometimes by request. Flanking Rashtrapati Bhavan are the **Secretariat** buildings, which house a few of India's army of bureaucrats. Nearby is the circular **Sansad Bhavan****, the houses of parliament; your embassy or high commission can provide a permit to visit. A long way down Rajpath is **India Gate*****, a 42m-high triumphal arch that is also a memorial to India's dead of the First World War. A few snake charmers always hang around here. On both sides of Rajpath are quiet and elegant residential areas where you could feel a million miles from Chandni Chowk. Not far from here, adjoining the Purana Qila, is the **zoo**, which contrives, despite its vast area, to have far too many neurotic animals in tiny cages. Worth visiting to see the white tigers, though.

The commercial centre of New Delhi is **Connaught Place**** built around a circular garden and fountain. Shady arcades make window-shopping pleasant, but one is tempted to think how much better the place would look without all the tattily

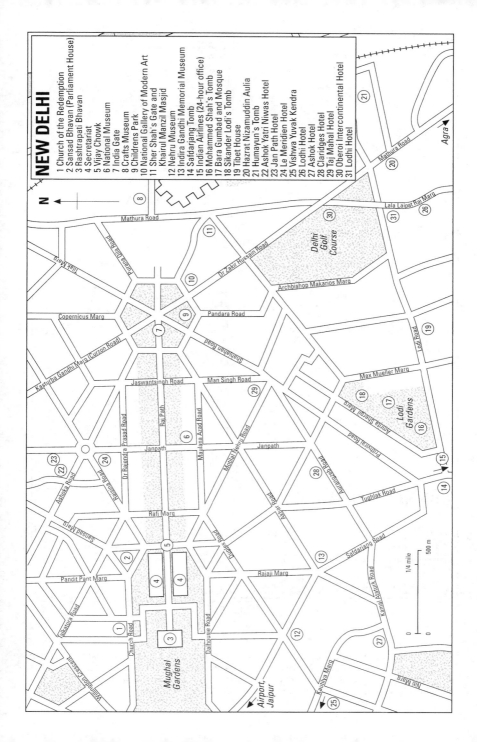

NEW DELHI

1 Church of the Redemption
2 Sansad Bhavan (Parliament House)
3 Rashtrapati Bhavan
4 Secretariat
5 Vijay Chowk
6 National Museum
7 India Gate
8 Crafts Museum
9 Childrens Park
10 National Gallery of Modern Art
11 Sher Shah's Gate and Khairul Manzil Masjid
12 Nehru Museum
13 Indira Gandhi Memorial Museum
14 Safdarjang Tomb
15 Indian Airlines (24-hour office)
16 Mohammed Shah's Tomb
17 Bara Gumbad and Mosque
18 Sikander Lodi's Tomb
19 Tibet House
20 Hazrat Nizamuddin Aulia
21 Humayun's Tomb
22 Ashok Yatri Niwas Hotel
23 Jan Path Hotel
24 Le Meridien Hotel
25 Vishwa Yuvak Kendra
26 Lodhi Hotel
27 Ashok Hotel
28 Claridges Hotel
29 Taj Mahal Hotel
30 Oberoi Intercontinental Hotel
31 Lodhi Hotel

N

Mughal Gardens

Delhi Golf Course

Lodi Gardens

Airport, Jaipur

Agra

0   1/4 mile
0   500 m

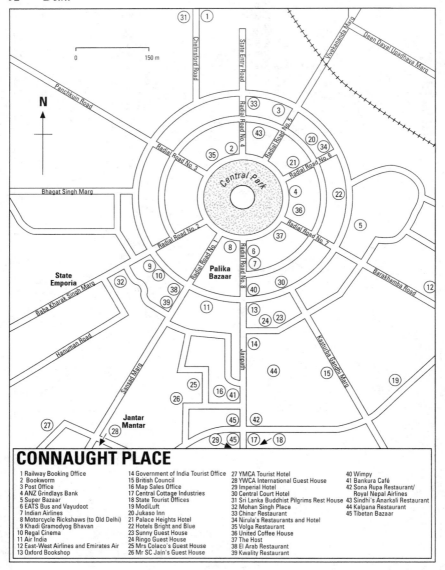

CONNAUGHT PLACE

1 Railway Booking Office	14 Government of India Tourist Office	27 YMCA Tourist Hotel	40 Wimpy
2 Bookworm	15 British Council	28 YWCA International Guest House	41 Bankura Café
3 Post Office	16 Map Sales Office	29 Imperial Hotel	42 Sona Rupa Restaurant/
4 ANZ Grindlays Bank	17 Central Cottage Industries	30 Central Court Hotel	Royal Nepal Airlines
5 Super Bazaar	18 State Tourist Offices	31 Sri Lanka Buddhist Pilgrims Rest House	43 Sindhi's Anarkali Restaurant
6 EATS Bus and Vayudoot	19 ModiLuft	32 Mohan Singh Place	44 Kalpana Restaurant
7 Indian Airlines	20 Jukaso Inn	33 Chinar Restaurant	45 Tibetan Bazaar
8 Motorcycle Rickshaws (to Old Delhi)	21 Palace Heights Hotel	34 Nirula's Restaurants and Hotel	
9 Khadi Gramodyog Bhavan	22 Hotels Bright and Blue	35 Volga Restaurant	
10 Regal Cinema	23 Sunny Guest House	36 United Coffee House	
11 Air India	24 Ringo Guest House	37 The Host	
12 East-West Airlines and Emirates Air	25 Mrs Colaco's Guest House	38 El Arab Restaurant	
13 Oxford Bookshop	26 Mr SC Jain's Guest House	39 Kwality Restaurant	

enclosed balconies, sign boards, and air conditioners. A short distance down Parliament Street (Sansad Marg) is the **Jantar Mantar****, one of Jai Singh II's observatories. The masonry instruments here may appear crude but in fact gave extremely accurate data about heavenly bodies.

Tombs and gardens

In part of southern Delhi you can trace the development of the Mughal garden tomb leading to the Taj Mahal — and its ultimate eclipse. There are four tombs in the landscaped **Lodi Gardens**** (which are also a good place for some peace and quiet). Note the mixture of styles; you can see Hindu brackets and Afghan sloping buttresses on the same building. Some also display the remains of ceramic tile decoration, a feature commonly found in Middle Eastern Islamic architecture. Attached to the **Bara Gumbad** is a small mosque with superb plaster decoration in the form of calligraphy. The latest tomb, that of Sikander Lodi (died 1517) introduces the idea of the walled garden.

Humayun's tomb*** (1560) is a great advance over the Lodi tombs. Although built mainly of red sandstone it has marble decoration and is clearly the direct predecessor of the Taj. You can see several other slightly earlier tombs in this area including that of Isa Khan, which also has a small mosque. At the other end of a long straight road is an interesting contrast. The **tomb of Safdarjung*** (prime minister to a late Mughal emperor) was built in 1753–4, the last of its kind. The proportions are fine, but the detail is fussy and workmanship crude compared with earlier tombs. The marble and sandstone cladding was taken from the tomb of Khan-i-Khanan a short distance from Humayun's Tomb.

Near Humayun's tomb is **Hazrat Nizamuddin Aulia****, the tomb of the saint who quarrelled with Tughlak Shah. There is some very fine marble tracery in the several tombs and a richly decorated mosque.

The one remaining place to see is **Rajghat****, the site of Mahatma Gandhi's cremation. This is now marked by a slab of black marble and enclosed by walls bearing inscriptions of his writings in many languages. Rajghat is something rare in India, impressive without being pompous or impersonal. The **Gandhi Darshan** and **Gandhi Museum**, both just over the road, are good.

Museums and art galleries

National Museum (Janpath just south of Rajpath) has a bit of everything. 10am–5pm, closed Mondays.

National Museum of Modern Art (near India Gate) is of especial interest for the work of the Tagore school. 10am–5pm, closed Mondays.

Air Force Museum (1.5km from Palam Airport) has a good collection of aircraft and ephemera. 10am–1.30pm, closed Tuesdays.

National Philatelic Museum (Post Office HQ, Parliament Street) has a vast and well displayed collection of Indian and foreign stamps. 10.30am–1.30pm, and 2–5pm, closed Sundays.

Rail Transport Museum, Chanakyapuri, traces railway development in India. A fine collection of locomotives and rolling stock. 10.30am–5.30pm (July–March), 8.30–11.30am, and 4–7.30pm (April–June), closed Mondays.

Tibet House (near Lodi Gardens) displays Tibetan art and artefacts and has a shop selling clothes, carpets, etc. 9.30am–1pm, and 2–6pm, closed Mondays.

Shopping

Delhi is the place for shopping. It has the best selection of goods from all over India, often at lower prices than in the place of origin. The main shopping area is around Connaught Place and down Janpath. On the corner of Connaught Place and Janpath is the underground **Palika Bazaar**; prices tend to be higher here because of high rents but you may feel that the air conditioning makes up for that. On the corner of Connaught Circus and Baba Kharak Singh Marg is **Khadi Gramodyog Bhavan** selling first-class handloom materials and clothes at rock-bottom prices. On the right down Baba Kharak Singh Marg are the various **state emporia** offering their local specialities, mostly missed by visitors but good value. A mouthwatering selection from all over the country can be seen in the **Central Cottage Industry Emporium** on Janpath; prices are fixed and goods guaranteed. Further down Janpath outside the Hotel Imperial is a **Tibetan bazaar,** again with fixed prices (unless you buy in bulk) and fair dealing. A lively evening bazaar takes place at the foot of the Indianoil Building on Janpath.

For wholesale deals on clothing try Main Bazaar in **Paharganj,** opposite New Delhi station. The **Super Bazaar** on Connaught Circus is of more use to locals but worth a look if you have time. All the shops in Delhi shut on Sunday, but street markets operate near the Indianoil Building and along Chandni Chowk in Old Delhi, and there is the **Red Fort flea market,** a huge jumble sale.

Festivals

India's Republic Day is January 26 and this is marked by a tremendous parade down Rajpath. The military units display a standard of turnout and drill to match any army in the world; there are camel cavalry, elephants, folk dancers, and more pipe bands than they have in Scotland. This is a great show, and you must not miss it if you are in India at the time. Grandstand seats are available through the Government of India Tourist Office. Two nights later retreat is beaten outside Rashtrapati Bhavan, and the government buildings are illuminated, again superb.

Practical Information *i* The Government of India Tourist Office at 88 Janpath has information on the whole country; there is also one at Palam Airport. Delhi Tourism is at N Block, Connaught Place and at both railway stations. Both organise guided tours, which are good value and very convenient given how spread out Delhi is. A museum tour and day trip to Agra can also be booked from the Janpath office.

Many of the **state governments** have tourist offices in Delhi. Those of Haryana, Himachal Pradesh, Jammu and Kashmir, Rajasthan, and Uttar Pradesh are in Chanderlok Building, 36 Janpath. Others are in the state emporia premises on Baba Kharak Singh Marg. Sikkim is at 15 Barakhamba Road.

Local transport. In New Delhi there are metered taxis and scooter-rickshaws; always insist on the meter being used. Cycle rickshaws are not allowed into New Delhi. The most convenient way of getting from New Delhi to Old Delhi is by Harley-Davidson auto-rickshaw (tempo); these run from a stand in front of Palika Bazaar (the underground market) past the Tourist Camp to the Fountain area of Chandni Chowk (fare Rs2.50; around 5p/8 cents) and will drop you off near the Jama Masjid or Red Fort. Fountain is about 750m from Delhi Station. There is a regular tonga service from just outside New Delhi Station to the north side of Connaught Circus (Re1).

The **bus service** is cheap, comprehensive, and crowded; you can get a guide book (Rs2) from Delhi Transport Corporation at Scindia House (corner of Janpath and Connaught Circus). A few useful routes are:

51   Delhi Station–Tourist Camp–Janpath–National Museum–Safdarjung's Tomb
230   Regal–Delhi Station–ISBT
502   Delhi Station–Red Fort–Firozeshah Kotla–India Gate–Safdarjung's Tomb–Qutb Minar
40   Regal–India Gate–Lodi Colony (for Lodi Gardens and tombs)
630   Regal–Chanakyapuri–Rail Museum
101   Regal–Red Fort–ISBT
780   Super Bazaar–Chanakyapuri–Rail Museum–Palam Airport
530   Nehru Marg–Scindia House–National Museum–Safdarjung's Tomb–Qutb Minar
21   Red Fort–Firozeshah Kotla–India Gate–Lodi Colony

420   Super Bazaar–India Gate–Purana Qila–Lajpat Nagar–Tughlakabad
417   Lajpat Nagar–Qutb Minar
Regal is the area around the junction of Connaught Place and Baba Kharak Singh
Marg; bus stops are scattered so check you have the right one. Connaught Circus is
the outermost ring of Connaught Place.

Arrival and departure

Flying. Palam Airport for all flights. Bus service (Rs16; 32p/53 cents) run by EATS
from office on Janpath near Connaught Place; tickets into town available inside
airport departures building. There is also a local bus (780), which parks coyly about
200m from the arrivals hall past the control tower, much cheaper but slower and
inconvenient if you have baggage. Indian Airline reservations at their office at
Kanchenjunga Building, Barakhamba Road.

Rail. There are main railway stations at both Delhi and New Delhi. Metre gauge
trains for Rajasthan and Gujarat leave only from Delhi but most broad gauge trains
call at both stations. A few trains (broad gauge only) leave from Hazrat Nizamuddin
station near Humayun's Tomb. **Reservations** for all destinations are now made at
New Delhi station upstairs from the main concourse. Very quick and efficient
compared with the old days; always take the passports of every person for whom you
are making reservations.
   Long-distance buses leave from the Inter-State Bus Terminus (ISBT) near
Kashmiri Gate north of the Red Fort. Advance booking is possible there for most
destinations. Agents for many independent bus companies are located around
Connaught Place.

Connaught Place and around:
   Hotel Imperial, Janpath. Tel 332 5332. SWB A/C
Rs2200 (around £44/$73) DWB A/C Rs2400. Rest
(2). Bar (2). Originally *the* hotel of New Delhi.
Splendid, spacious rooms, old-fashioned in the
very best way. Good atmosphere with a lot of old retainers who take a real pride in
the place. Lovely garden with terrace restaurant and bar. Swimming pool (open to
non-residents for Rs120 for a full day). Tennis court. Way outside the budget price
range, but more worthy of a splurge than certain highly touted palace hotels.
   Nirula's Hotel, L Block, Connaught Circus. Tel 332 2419. SWB A/C Rs850 (£17/$28)
DWB A/C Rs1100, plus 10% SC. Rest (see below). Bar (2). Rooms better than many
at much higher prices. A totally professional operation.
   Central Court, N Block, Connaught Circus. Tel 331 5013. SR A/C Rs450 (£9/$15)
SWB A/C Rs550 DR A/C Rs575 DWB A/C Rs790. Rest (3). Clean, but very plain
considering prices. Quieter than most.
   YWCA International Guest House, Parliament Street. Tel 311 561. SWB A/C Rs300
(£6/$10) DWB A/C Rs500 plus 10% SC. Rest. Very friendly.
   Ashok Yatri Niwas, corner of Ashoka Road and Janpath. Tel 332 4511. SWB Rs250
DWB Rs350. Rest (24hr self-service). Bar. Ashok Group's (ITDC) stab at an
economy hotel, though the prices keep going up. Excellent value for money but, as
usual, they are over-economising on maintenance.
   YMCA Tourist Hostel, Jai Singh Road. Tel 311 915. SR Rs250 SWB A/C Rs460 DR
Rs430 DWB A/C Rs775 plus 5% SC (including breakfast). Rest.
   YWCA, Ashoka Road. Tel 310 133. SWB Rs400 DWB Rs750 (all including
breakfast) plus 5% SC. Plain but clean and comfortable. No restrictions on men.
   Palace Heights, D Block, Connaught Circus. Tel 352 1369. SR Rs170 DR Rs275
DWB A/C Rs500. Breakfast, tea, etc. in room or on balcony. Hot water in bucket.
Plain but clean. Rather noisy.
   Hotel Bright, M Block, Connaught Circus. Tel 332 0444. SR Rs110 DR Rs150 SWB

Rs250 DWB Rs300 plus 10% SC. Rest. A bit primitive. High prices supposed to be justified by incipient renovation.

Hotel Blue, M Block, Connaught Circus. Tel 332 2222. SR Rs60/80 DR Rs110 SWB Rs110 DWB Rs150. Room service food. Basic. In the same building as Bright, opposite Super Bazaar.

Sunny Guest House, Tolstoy Lane. Tel 331 2909. SR Rs90 DR Rs140 DWB Rs200/250 Dorm Rs60. Breakfast.

Ringo Guest House, Tolstoy Lane. Tel 331 0605. SR Rs160 DR Rs185 DWB Rs275 Dorm Rs60. With the Sunny two old established and popular places.

Colaco Guest House, Janpath Lane. Tel 332 8758. SR Rs125 DR Rs150 Dorm Rs65. Some pretty rude things have been written about this establishment, but the author still enjoys staying here, not least for the hot showers in winter. Dear old Mother Colaco died a few years ago, but the business is continued by her son Mario.

There are several other inexpensive places in Janpath Lane and Tolstoy Lane.

In Paharganj (near New Delhi station):

Vivek Hotel, Main Bazaar. Tel 777 7062. SR Rs80 SWB Rs120 DR Rs120 DWB Rs190 DWB A/C Rs345. Rest (Ind/Chi).

Vishal Hotel, Main Bazaar. Tel 753 2079. SWB Rs130 DWB Rs180. Rest. Very popular over the years. 99% Western clientele so you should be spared the dawn chorus of phantom gobbers.

Venus Hotel, Main Bazaar. Tel 526 256. SR Rs80 DR Rs120 SWB Rs120 DWB Rs180.

All these places are down the same street more or less opposite New Delhi station. They are within walking distance, and you may get a reduction if the hotelier does not have to pay commission to a rickshaw-wallah. There are many other cheap hotels in this area. Avoid the Hotel Anand where travellers report having drugs planted on them for a bust. In fact, judged by the number of stories one hears about this kind of thing, it may be best to avoid Paharganj altogether. Certainly do not buy or possess any dope there.

Sri Lanka Buddhist Pilgrims Rest House, Chelmsford Road. DR Rs50 (£1/$1.65). Rest. Actually between Connaught Place and Paharganj. Food reported to be good.

In Old Delhi:

Tera Hotel, Kashmiri Gate. Tel 252 1581. SWB Rs100 DWB Rs140 SWB A/C Rs140/160 DWB A/C Rs180/210. Rest. Clean and comfortable, convenient for Old Delhi station. Turn left out of station, walk 100m, cross railway by footbridge, straight on at end of bridge, then first right, 100m down on right.

Tourist Camp, Nehru Marg. Tel 278 929. SR Rs24/32 DR Rs36/48 Dorm Rs18. Rest. Camping. Parking. Located between Delhi and New Delhi on the tempo route from Chandni Chowk to Connaught Place. The overland buses and trucks usually park here.

Tourist Camp, Kashmiri Gate. Tel 252 3121. Similar to the above. Just across the road from the Interstate Bus Terminal (ISBT), convenient for late arrivals or early departures. Adjacent to the pleasant Qudsia Gardens.

In South Delhi:

Most of the top-class hotels are in this area on the way to the airport. Rooms are generally Rs2500 (£50/$83) or more and outside the scope of this book.

Hotel Diplomat, 9 Sardar Patel Road (Diplomatic Enclave). Tel 301 0204. SWB A/C Rs1100 DWB A/C Rs1600. Rest. Bar. Smaller hotel with good atmosphere.

Lodhi Hotel, Lala Lajpat Rai Marg (near Nizamuddin). Tel 362 422. SWB A/C Rs1000 DWB A/C Rs1350. Rest. Bar. Spacious, comfortable rooms with separate dressing rooms. Good value for money.

Vishwa Yuvak Kendra (International Youth Centre), Circular Road, Chanakyapuri

(Diplomatic Enclave). Tel 301 3631. SR Rs218 DR Rs284 SWB Rs268 DWB Rs338 Dorm Rs50 plus 10% SC, plus Rs10 membership fee (30 days). Note that prices are 20–25% lower on second and subsequent days and include breakfast (not dorm). Rest.

Near the VYK is a *Youth Hostel*. Tel 301 6285. Rs25 (members only) for a dorm bed.

Retiring rooms are available at Palam Airport.

Important note. As in other cities the influx of foreign businessmen has caused hotel prices to rocket. Cheaper places are less affected, but be prepared to pay more than listed here.

Eating and Drinking

Connaught Place and around:

Imperial Hotel, Janpath. *Tavern Restaurant and Bar.* Exp (around Rs250 per head). Ind/Chi/Cont. Large and interesting menu. You can see the chefs at work, thankfully behind glass. *Garden Party Restaurant and Cocktail Bar.* Exp (from Rs30 (60p/$1) for snacks, meals Rs50 (£1/$1.65) upwards, beer Rs60 (£1.20/$2)). Meals and snacks, including a selection of traditional Anglo-Indian dishes. You can sit out on the lawn surrounded by trees and flowers. Uniformed bearers and even a well fed black cat prowl. Danger! this lifestyle could be habit-forming.

Janpath Hotel. Buffet lunch and dinner Rs100, à la carte Rs60–100. Coffee shop snacks around Rs25, meals Rs50.

Nirula's Hotel, L Block, Connaught Circus. *Pot-Pourri.* Exp. A/C. Bar. Pizzas and burgers, but the best value is the self-serve salad bar, as much as you can eat for Rs72. Beer is Rs57.50 and wine even more. You can tell this place is patronised by foreigners — not only is paper provided in the toilet, but it is padlocked! Also a *Chinese restaurant, fast food bar*, and excellent *ice cream parlour* on the premises.

Kwality, Parliament Street. Exp (around Rs80–100 per head). Ind/Chi/Cont. Excellent Indian food, professional service. Trattoria decor, the best of a very good chain.

Al-Arab, corner of Connaught Circus and Parliament Street. Exp. Lebanese. Rs110 for as much as you can eat of eight well prepared dishes plus dessert. Very good value despite the apparently high price. A rare treat for meat-eaters.

Degchi, below Al-Arab. Mod/Exp. Lunch and supper buffet of top-quality home-style Indian cooking. Also a few Chi/Cont dishes. Prices from Rs22.50 up to Rs30 for as much as you can eat. Easily best value breakfast around — juice, proper fried breakfast, butter toast, and tea or coffee for Rs25. Functional decor. Music might annoy some, but not excessive. Pleasant service. A degchi, incidentally, is a pot-bellied cooking pot and the origin of the English word dixie.

Chinar, K Block, Connaught Place. Mod/Exp. A/C. Intimate atmosphere. Recommended for north Indian food.

Bankura, Janpath (adjacent to Central Cottage Industries Emporium). Cheap/ Mod. Snacks and varied lunch menu. Good ambience, though can be cold in winter. Popular with locals who like their food and know a bargain.

Sona Rupa, Janpath. Cheap/Mod. South Indian self-serve buffet; excellent value if you like the food. The sit-down restaurant is upstairs.

Kalpana, Tolstoy Lane. Cheap/Mod. Punjabi and a few south Indian specialities. Popular breakfast haunt.

Wimpy, Janpath. Cheap/Mod. The author wouldn't be seen dead in one in England, but these lamburgers are really rather good. Nice too to see young Indians behaving like youngsters everywhere else and enjoying themselves.

Sindhi's Anarkali, back of C Block, Connaught Place. Cheap. Good for kebabs.

The following places (along with many food stalls) are all in *Mohan Singh Place*, an indoor market on Baba Kharak Singh Marg, all good if you can accept the grisly state of the building:

Indian Coffee House, Top Floor. Cheap. South Indian food, mainly snacks and breakfast. Open-air roof terrace. Real coffee (ask for it strong) for less than the price of instant!

Dinesh Fruit Mart, Mezzanine. Milk shakes, fruit juices, and excellent fruit salad with whipped cream for Rs15.

Tee-Pee-O, Basement. Cheap/Mod. Punjabi.

Biryani Corner, Basement. Cheap/Mod. Punjabi. Both these places do good kebabs and, in winter, excellent fish. Try the pomfret, a flat fish brought up from Bombay.

Around Connaught Place are the *United Coffee House* (elegant) and *Volga* (1930s stark). Expect to pay Rs75–125 and receive very good food and service. In Pusa Marg, behind Super Bazaar, is *Mogul Mahal*, which is supposed to be a lot better than *Moti Mahal*. A stall on the corner of Janpath and Janpath Lane, next to Annapurna Store, has good snacks including passable chocolate eclairs. Watch out for the kites; a whoosh past your right ear and the food's gone!

In Paharganj (near New Delhi station):

Metropolis, Main Bazaar. Cheap/Exp. Vast menu covering almost every cuisine you can think of. Not bad at all, ideal for an India-jaded palate.

In Old Delhi:

Needo, Chandni Chowk (near Fountain). Mod/Exp. Ind.

Flora, Urdu Bazaar (almost opposite south steps of Jama Masjid). Exp (approximately Rs50 per head). A/C. Mughlai food, excellent.

Moti Mahal, Netaji Subhash Marg. Exp. Mughlai food. Live traditional music. You dine in the open air in warm weather, in a marquee in winter. Good again after a bad patch. On tempo route from Connaught Place to Chandni Chowk.

In South Delhi:

Lodhi Woodlands, Lodhi Hotel. Mod/Exp. Famous south Indian vegetarian restaurant, reckoned to be the best in Delhi. Also a non-vegetarian restaurant and coffee shop.

Qutb (ITDC), at Qutb Minar. Mod/Exp. Convenient for a snack or a full meal.

Most of the major hotels have 24-hour coffee shops. *Madhuban* at Akbar Hotel is nearest the airport, and *Open House* (Janpath Hotel) nearest the city centre.

Only in the major hotels can you enjoy a beer with your meal.

The Western Himalayas

Temple at Naggar

Jammu and Kashmir — Punjab — Himachal Pradesh — Northern Uttar Pradesh

India's northern border, as defined by the Himalayas, is more than just political. In the past the mountains have prevented invasion except through the western passes, and the difficulty of crossing them may well have influenced Indian introspection and desire for self-sufficiency. The Himalayas also have a crucial effect on climate as, without them, the cold air of Tibet and Siberia would make the temperature range of northern India even more extreme. Their contribution to the water supply, the key to food production, is even more important. Great snow-fed rivers — the Ganges, Indus, Brahmaputra, and Yamuna — water huge areas of the northern plains even when the monsoon fails. In addition water vapour in warm air condenses over the foothills and falls as rain.

Population density throughout this area is relatively low, beggars are rare and, in Kashmir at least, one used to see a reasonable degree of prosperity. Both Kashmir and Himachal Pradesh are famous for their fruit and nuts, which are sent all over India. Potatoes have become a major cash crop in the Kullu valley, and the same area produces things such as celery and parsley, never seen in the markets, for the five-star

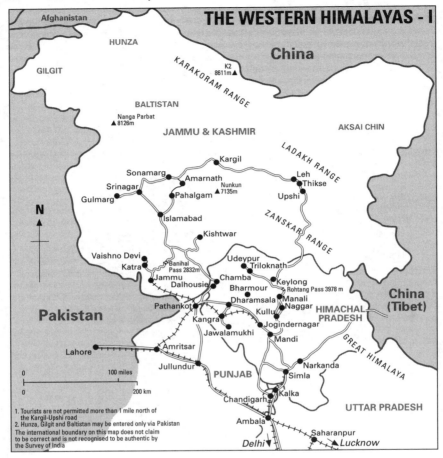

THE WESTERN HIMALAYAS - I

Afghanistan

HUNZA

China

GILGIT

KARAKORAM RANGE   K2 8611m▲

BALTISTAN

Nanga Parbat ▲8126m

JAMMU & KASHMIR

AKSAI CHIN

LADAKH RANGE

Kargil

Sonamarg   Amarnath   Nunkun ▲7135m   Leh   Thikse
Srinagar
Gulmarg   Pahalgam   Upshi

N

Islamabad

ZANSKAR RANGE

Kishtwar

Vaishno Devi   Udeypur
Katra   Banihal Pass 2832m   Triloknath
Jammu   Chamba   Keylong
Dalhousie   Bharmour   Rohtang Pass 3978 m
Pathankot   Dharamsala   Manali   China (Tibet)
Kullu   Naggar
Pakistan   Kangra   HIMACHAL PRADESH
Jawalamukhi   Jogindernagar
Lahore   Mandi
Amritsar   GREAT HIMALAYA
0   100 miles
Jullundur   Narkanda
0   200 km   PUNJAB   Simla

1. Tourists are not permitted more than 1 mile north of the Kargil-Upshi road
2. Hunza, Gilgit and Baltistan may be entered only via Pakistan
The international boundary on this map does not claim to be correct and is not recognised to be authentic by the Survey of India

Chandigarh   Kalka

UTTAR PRADESH

Ambala

Delhi▼   Saharanpur   ▲Lucknow

hotels. Pampore, just outside Srinagar, is second only to Spain in production of saffron — trying to buy it unadulterated is another matter.

Handicrafts. Kashmir is probably the richest state in India for souvenirs. Best known and best value are the papier-mâché boxes and knick-knacks. The wood carving, mostly in walnut, can be of high quality but is rarely to Western taste. Kashmir shawls are known all over the world and range from a Rs200 (around £4/$6.50) machine one (they'll say it's handmade) to Rs5000 (£100/$165) or more for a genuine pashmina, which is made from the soft throat and belly wool of goats. These are works of art and the price is justified by the tremendous amount of labour required; a whole family may work all winter to produce just one shawl.

Oriental carpets in many patterns and qualities are made in Srinagar. It is interesting to visit one of the factories, but read the item on 'Buying' before you do so. It is also worth bearing in mind that too many carpet factories are dependent on child labour. You would be naive to believe that jewellery is as described. Buying furs just encourages the already uncontrolled slaughter of wildlife. Suede and leather can be good buys. Buddhist artefacts, both antique and repro, are available wherever there is a Tibetan community. Distinctively patterned shawls are produced in the Kullu valley.

The troubles in the state have caused Kashmiri merchants to concentrate their sales efforts on India's other tourist resorts, and they have brought with them their extremely dubious business ethic. These people have a very bad reputation for misrepresenting their stock and for not despatching goods that have been paid for. In neither case can you expect any help at all from tourist or legal authorities in India. The best way of avoiding trouble is to pay by credit card, as the card company (in Britain at least) has to reimburse you if things go wrong. Otherwise, if you buy something you cannot carry away yourself, have the vendor pack it (this should be part of the deal), stand over him while he does it, and go with him to the post office. Make sure that all the stamps are cancelled and that you have the proper receipt.

Climate. Srinagar is at its best from March to October, though July and August can be oppressively humid; it is cold and damp in winter. Simla is higher, and colder in winter. Places like Pahalgam, Gulmarg and Manali are under several feet of snow from December to March, and temperatures in Ladakh can fall to −40°C. Remember that this is a mountain area; the local weather can change dangerously quickly. Do not go high-level trekking or on the mountains unless you are properly equipped.

N.B. Because of the troubles in Kashmir outlined below it has not been possible to update the section on Jammu and Kashmir. **We strongly advise you against visiting Jammu and Kashmir** (this includes Zanskar, which has lately also become unsafe) except for Ladakh, and include the information solely for the record. The only people who will tell you it is safe are those who hope to make money out of you, or worse.

JAMMU AND KASHMIR

Maps published in India (and this book) show the theoretical, in the Indian view, border of Kashmir, and not the de facto one. At the time of Independence in 1947 India's princes were given the choice of joining India or Pakistan, or becoming independent. This was not an easy decision in Kashmir, the largest of all princely states, where a Hindu maharaja ruled a predominantly Muslim population. His vacillation led to a revolt in some areas, followed by an invasion of Pakistani tribesmen, and eventually the Pakistani army. At that time road and rail links from India were almost non-existent, but an improvised airlift enabled the Indian army to stage an epic defence of Srinagar. Despite this and further fighting in 1966, much of the western part of Kashmir and the northern districts of Hunza, Gilgit, and Baltistan have remained occupied by Pakistan.

The United Nations directed long ago that a plebiscite be held in both parts of Kashmir, but no satisfactory format could be devised and the idea lapsed into permanent abeyance. Despite the Kashmiris' obvious kinship with Pakistan the non-fanatics had a shrewd idea as to which side their bread was buttered and frequently played the Pakistan card to get preferential treatment from Delhi. Latterly, however, fundamentalist groups were encouraged by politicians in the central government for their own short-term advantage. As in Punjab these movements soon got out of hand, and at the time of writing Kashmir is in a state of armed insurrection. The Indian army just about controls things, but newspaper stories of 6000 Pakistani-armed and trained guerillas waiting for the snow to melt so that they can cross over to take up the fight does not bode well for the future. Foreigners have been taken hostage, and at least one has been tortured and murdered in cold blood.

The appeal of Kashmir for the Mughal emperors and later ruling classes of Englishmen and Indians is understandable. Less privileged travellers tended to find it a hassle from beginning to end. My advice has always been to visit Pahalgam and Ladakh and spend the rest of the time in Himachal Pradesh instead. Read about Srinagar and the houseboats to see why. The only people who will encourage you to go there at present are those who stand to make money out of you; you are permitted to visit (though advised not to) but can expect to be a prisoner on your houseboat. Shortage of tourist earnings has simply increased the hassles and pressures. Banks, hotels, restaurants, and most other amenities are closed.

To the north-east of Kashmir is an area called Aksai Chin. India claims this as her territory on the rather tenuous grounds that a 19th century British survey showed it as part of India; subsequent surveys omitted it. The discovery in 1961 that China had built a road across Aksai Chin led India to send in troops. The Chinese, who felt their position in Tibet threatened, attacked them (in Arunachal Pradesh as well) and inflicted a crushing defeat. Today a much better equipped and mountain-trained Indian army deploys a large part of its strength along the cease-fire lines of Kashmir.

JAMMU

Most people rush through Jammu on the way to Srinagar, but it is an interesting place and worth a day. The centre of the old town, still quite medieval, has quaint streets and markets and many temples. The two **Raghunath Temples** are dedicated to Rama, while the **Ranbireswar Temple** displays its Shiva allegiance in the form of thousands of lingams, some of crystal.

The **Dogra Art Gallery** in Gandhi Bhavan has a good collection of miniature paintings in local styles, also some archaeological finds. The **Amar Singh Palace**, designed like a chateau by a Frenchman and just outside town, is now a museum. The River Tawi, which it overlooks, is famous for mahseer fishing.

Jammu is a good place to buy textiles. A myriad of small shops offers everything, including cheap silk and, unlike some places, the shopkeepers are fair in their dealings with foreigners. The government shop has lots of home-spun khadi clothes.

Information. Jammu and Kashmir Tourism at Tourist Reception Centre.

Arrival and departure. Airport (7km). Indian Airlines office at Tourist Reception Centre.

Trains from Delhi (12½hrs), Bombay (32hrs), Amritsar via Pathankot or Jullundur, Lucknow (14hrs), etc. Trains from Delhi run overnight, but only the 4645 Shalimar Express arrives in time for a bus connection direct to Srinagar. These buses leave from the railway station, and you have the choice of four different classes. Other Srinagar buses run from the Tourist Reception Centre, and locals from the main bus-stand. Tempos connect all these points.

Accommodation
Tourist Reception Centre (3km from station, 1km from bus-stand). Rest. A bit tatty.
Retiring rooms at station (and another Tourist Reception Centre) and many cheap hotels in town; all the ones the author has seen pretty horrible and/or noisy.

VAISHNO DEVI

An interesting excursion can be made from Jammu to the **holy cave** of Vaishno Devi. A switchback hill path with tremendous views climbs the 14km/9 miles from the village of Katra to the cave. The most devout will do the whole journey bare-foot; no need for you to follow suit, but do enter into the spirit of things and greet your fellow-pilgrims with a cheery cry of 'Jai Mataji' ('Hail Mother of God'). This pilgrimage has been much cleaned up in recent years and, as in other places, a new access road apparently provides a short cut to the summit. One might take the view that if you are going to do a pilgrimage you may as well do it properly and enjoy the walk. So start from Katra.

The shrine is deep in a cave that is also the source of a stream, and access is uncommonly ordered. An official used to take foreigners by the back way to the holy of holies, which obviated queuing up to the knees in cold water for several hours. The shrine is claustrophobic, but find a quiet corner to watch proceedings, and particularly the amount of money changing hands. This now benefits local charities instead of just going into the pockets of the priests. Major pilgrimages take place in March/April and September/October, but you can go any time.

Arrival and departure. Bus to Katra (2hrs) from central bus-stand in Jammu, then walk.

Accommodation. Tourist Bungalow at Katra. Dharamsalas at top of hill, accommodation free, blankets for hire.

Eating and drinking. Refreshment stalls along path, simple vegetarian meals at top of hill.

SRINAGAR

It is very hard to write objectively about Srinagar. It is too easy to feel that you are being hustled all day long, and rapacious cab drivers whose meters never work, and merchants who do not mail the goods you have paid for do not help. You may want to stay on a houseboat for only a couple of nights to say you've done it and then head off to somewhere quiet like Pahalgam or Ladakh. Away from the tourist areas, however, there is another and much more pleasing aspect.

Srinagar is a city of water. Apart from the River Jhelum, which divides it in two, there are lakes and canals, and the old quarters, seen from land or water, are very picturesque. Many people live on **houseboats** on the smaller waterways. These were the inspiration for the tourist boats on the lakes, which were devised originally by ingenious Englishmen wanting to escape the heat of the plains. Like other non-Kashmiris they were not allowed by the maharaja to purchase land or property, and this was a convenient loophole.

A raised bank, **the Bund**, along the river Jhelum makes a pleasant walk. Shikaras run across the river from here to the **museum**. The collection is vast and varied, certainly worth seeing despite poor captioning and shambolic arrangement. The building itself is interesting, being a former royal palace, and has a quiet, colourful garden.

In the old part of town the **Jama Masjid** (take a tempo from Lal Chowk) is built mainly of wood with huge deodar pine pillars. The current building, dating from 1674, is at least the fourth on this site, earlier ones having burned down. There is a good view from the roof if you can disregard the fact that the ever-present pigeons spread an unpleasant lung disease. Not too far away, on the river bank is the **Shah Hamadam Mosque**. Richly decorated, the interior of this pagoda is not open to infidels (you can peep through the door), though you should be able to visit a pretty prayer room on the river side. You may find that the odd stone will fly your way, but you should walk around this area, the architecture and local scenes are fascinating. Many people, especially women, are camera-shy, so be circumspect.

You can get a marvellous view of the whole city by climbing **Shankaracharya Hill** (known to the Muslims as Solomon's Throne). A road runs up from The Boulevard (taxi if you must); the best route on foot is up a narrow path from behind the bus-stand between Dal Gate and the Tourist Reception Centre. The hill is surmounted by an 18th century Hindu temple and, now, a television mast.

You will, no doubt, be startled to learn that not only did Jesus live and raise a family in Kashmir, but that He is buried in Srinagar. His simple tomb is near the Rozabal mosque. A Faber-Kaiser has written a book called *Jesus Died in Kashmir* (you should find it in local bookshops), which, if less than entirely convincing, puts up a lot of interesting ideas.

Actually, most visitors to Srinagar are content just to relax (or try to) on their houseboats and take the occasional shikara ride round the lakes. Kashmir was the Mughal emperors' summer playground, and they have left four famous **gardens** around Dal Lake. Bus tours run from the Tourist Office, or you could cycle. The Shalimar Bagh, the largest, is accessible by shikara, and a **sound and light show** is held here on summer evenings; details and tickets from the Tourist Office.

Handicrafts. Don't bother with the Government Emporium in Srinagar; it sells tacky goods at fancy prices. Visit the shop of Suffering Moses on the Bund to see just how good papier-mâché can be. His prices are high but so is the quality. A special Foreign Post Office near Zero Bridge in Srinagar deals with export parcels (poste restante and normal services are at the GPO on The Bund). An Air India air-freight office is near the Broadway Hotel.

Practical Information *i*

Tourist office (poor) in Tourist Reception Centre. Several conducted tours available. Houseboat and hotel booking offices are also located here, but you will do much better negotiating for yourself. The office of the trekking and mountain-eering department is in the Tourist Reception Centre.

Arrival and departure. Airport (12km); bus from airport to Tourist Reception Centre (if the taxi-wallahs haven't bribed the bus driver to disappear). Indian Airlines office at the Tourist Reception Centre. Flights from Delhi, Jammu, Amritsar, and Leh.

Buses (several different classes) from Tourist Reception Centre to Jammu and Leh, and luxury buses to Pahalgam, Sonamarg, and Gulmarg. You can get to Pahalgam and Gulmarg much more cheaply from the Batmaloo main bus-stand on the far side of town than from the Tourist Reception Centre; almost any bus going west down Hotel Road will take you there. Reserve a seat by buying your ticket in advance. In the Lal Chowk area are several private companies running services to obscure places like Kishtwar.

Accommodation

Tourist Reception Centre. Rest. Rooms passable, dorms infested with bugs last time the author saw them. Convenient, all tourist buses stop and set off from here.

Hotels. Medium-priced hotels along The Boulevard past Dal Gate. Cheap ones near Zero Bridge, a short walk from the Tourist Reception Centre.

Houseboats. There are boats on the various lakes and waterways all around Srinagar, and they range from floating palaces 40m long to tiny and decrepit ones. Nearby will always be another boat that is home to the family and kitchen for both them and the guests.

The river and canal boats have the great advantage of easy access at all times (shikara fares tend to multiply ten-fold at night), but most suffer from traffic noise. For real peace have a look at Nagin Lake, which is some way out of town, though the backwaters of Dal Lake are pretty quiet and less inconvenient.

Buses from Jammu and Leh arrive at the Tourist Reception Centre in the evening and it is no joke to be surrounded by a horde of screaming houseboat men when you are too tired to think. Ideally, one would stay the night in the Tourist Reception Centre (but see above) and hunt for a boat in the morning. Failing this the best thing is to turn left as you walk out of the Tourist Reception Centre and carry straight on until you reach The Bund along the River Jhelum. Turn right here and you will find houseboats moored along the bank below. Some of these are very nice, and you may be happy to stay there (they are certainly the most convenient), otherwise leave your kit there in the morning and go looking at your leisure. There is no point in recommending specific boats as space on them is so limited.

All boats are graded (deluxe, and A–D) by the tourist authorities, and there is a published tariff, but this is grossly inflated and quite meaningless. Actual prices are entirely negotiable and depend on many factors including meals (how many, vegetarian or non-vegetarian), number of tourists in town, your apparent gullibility, and probably the mood of the houseboat man's wife (no doubt about who wears the trousers here). In practical terms, outside peak tourist times you might get dinner (vegetarian), bed, and breakfast for around 60% of those figures. Shop around and bargain hard.

Transport on the lakes is by shikara, a cross between a punt and a canoe. Check that the price you agree for the houseboat includes trips from the boat to the shore and back. This being Kashmir it may be as well to agree how many a day and how late. Official prices for taxi shikaras (and excursions) are posted at the main landing stages. The rough shikaras run by the kids should be half the price of the fancy ones.

Especially on Lake Dal you will be plagued by salesmen invading your privacy. Unfortunately the only way to stop this is to be thoroughly offensive to the first man and chase him off without even looking at his goods. The word will soon get around and you will be left alone. Until, that is, the houseboat man realises he is not going to earn any commission (up to 40% of sales) and tries to raise your rent. Great place, Srinagar.

Eating and drinking

Shahenshah Hotel, The Boulevard. Mod/Exp. Ind. Kashmiri specialities. Dine outside in summer in beautiful garden. Live Kashmiri music. Highly recommended.

Yaar's, Residency Road. Cheap. Ind. Quiet and intimate.

A little *patisserie* near Dal Gate is run by a German woman, and *Ahdoo's* on The Bund is famous for its cream cakes and biryani.

Further Afield

Srinagar to Pahalgam

At **Avantipur** and **Martand** (both on the road from Srinagar to Pahalgam) are the remains of Hindu temples that show strong Greek influence. At **Aishmuqam** on the same road is a large mosque built on the site of a Buddhist monastery, another place connected with the Jesus of Kashmiri legend.

South of **Islamabad** (Anantnag), also on this road are Achabal, Verinag, and Kokernag all with gardens and springs. There is a Tourist Bungalow at Achabal.

PAHALGAM

Pahalgam is a lovely place to get away from the heat and hurly-burly of Srinagar. Before the troubles it had become a popular resort for Indians and could be crowded in June and July. At 2100m/6888ft Pahalgam is at the confluence of two rivers and surrounded by pineclad mountains. This is a good base for trekking and fishing, and you can live here very cheaply.

Walking 23km/14 miles up the West Liddar valley brings you to **Liddarwat** (stop halfway at Aru, if you wish) and from here you can make day trips to Tarsar and Marsar Lakes and the Kolahoi Glacier. The chowkidar at the Public Works Department Bungalow may sell you rice and dhal, but you will need to take all other supplies. There are excellent camp sites, and wood and water are readily available. Less ambitious walkers will find plenty to enjoy around Pahalgam, especially the hour's stroll up to **Baisaran**, a large pine-girt meadow with a stream, and an ideal picnic spot.

Pahalgam is the start of the annual pilgrimage to the **holy cave of Amarnath** (3962m/12,995ft), which shelters a large ice lingam. Elaborate preparations are made for the main event in July/August. Obviously the 47km/29 miles walk can be done at other times though this will mean having to carry your own food. There are various kinds of accommodation along the way.

Information. Tourist office near bus-stand.

Arrival and departure. Pahalgam is 98km/61 miles from Srinagar, an ordinary bus from Batmaloo bus-stand takes 3½hrs. Tourist buses from the Tourist Reception Centre in Srinagar are much faster and more comfortable, but stop at Avantipur and Anantnag (Islamabad) temples *en route*.

Accommodation. It is hard to imagine visiting this beautiful place again in the near future. Favourite backpacker places used to be *Windrush House*, and *Aksa Lodge* and *Bentes Lodge*, quietly located over the river from town.

Aru Public Works Department Bungalow. Very cheap and extremely basic. Chowkidar may provide simple meals. Tea stall nearby. Book in advance at PWD office in Pahalgam. Camping near bungalow and possibility of accommodation in village.

Liddarwat Public Works Department Bungalow. Cheap and extremely basic. Chowkidar may provide simple meals. Book at PWD office in Pahalgam. Beautiful campsite nearby, plenty of wood and water.

GULMARG

Gulmarg (Meadow of Flowers) is an old-established hill resort at 2700m/8856ft, which can be visited at any time of the year, though the weather tends to be unpredictable. The **ski resort** operates from December to March, and equipment hire is cheap. Once the snow has melted Gulmarg boasts what may be the highest **golf course** in the world. There is some splendid walking; the 11km circular path gives superb views all over the Kashmir Valley as far as Srinagar and the 8000m/26,240ft peak of Nanga Parbat to the north. At **Barbareshi** (5km/3 miles) is the tomb of a Muslim saint that has become a place of pilgrimage for Hindus, Muslims, and Sikhs alike. **Khilanmarg** (4km/2.5 miles) is another meadow ideal for a picnic and, for more serious walkers, there is icy **Alpather Lake** 13km/8 miles away.

Information. Tourist Office at golf clubhouse.

Arrival and departure. Gulmarg is 38km/24miles from Srinagar, excursion bus (2hrs) from Tourist Reception Centre in Srinagar. Local buses stop at Tangmarg leaving you a stiff walk up, or a pony ride.

SONAMARG

The village at Sonamarg (Meadow of Gold) is little more than a collection of tin shacks, but the surroundings are splendid. The drive up from Srinagar ranks with the best in the world; fertile farmland, snowcapped peaks, misty-blue forests, waterfalls, and nomadic herdsmen are all here. Sonamarg makes a good trekking base (as long as you take all supplies with you). Amarnath is only 13km/8 miles (all uphill) from nearby Baltal.

Arrival and departure. On Leh-Srinagar road, tourist and local buses, day trip from Tourist Reception Centre in Srinagar.

Accommodation. Glacier Hotel is very basic, the Rest House just out of town is more expensive and probably better.

LADAKH

Ladakh is a world of its own, known as the Moonland for its arid, treeless landscape or the Dreamland from the monasteries perched like fairy castles on rocky crags. The remote location accounts for both these characteristics. High mountain ranges prevent rain and snowfall, and also outside influence. For centuries an independent kingdom owing allegiance to Tibet, Ladakh was opened to tourism only twenty years ago. It is still largely unspoiled in its Buddhist peacefulness and, despite a bleakness akin to a Middle Eastern desert, a beautiful place.

History

The Tibetans are great chroniclers, so we have a pretty accurate picture of Ladakh's history. It is thought that the first inhabitants were Indians, and their descendants, the Mons, still live here though they are little regarded by the rest of the population. The Tibetans arrived from the north-east around the sixth century AD. At this time they were still adherents of the old Bon-po religion, which was gradually supplanted by Buddhism.

Buddhism reached Tibet in the seventh century, and violent resistance to it led to the break-up of the kingdom in 842. In 900 a descendant of the first Tibetan kings founded the kingdom of Ngari, which, on his death, was split between his three sons, one of whom inherited Ladakh.

In the 15th century Takbumde ruled over Upper Ladakh from capitals in Shey and Leh while Lower Ladakh was ruled from Basgo by Takpabum. Takbumde built the Red Temple of Leh; he was visited by emissaries of Tsong Khapa, founder of the Gelupa order, and restored Spituk as the first monastery of this reformed order.

It was under the Basgo dynasty that the kingdom was unified. In effect the grandson of Takpabum, Bhagan, deposed the sovereign of Leh. However the country was exposed to attacks from Kashmir, Muslim for a century, which conquered Baltistan. It fell to Tashi Namgyal, son of Bhagan, to assure the survival of Ladakh, the kings of which bore the name Namgyal from then on.

Tashi Namgyal (1500–1535) built the fort of Leh, Namgyal Tsemo, and the Gonkhang, or temple of the tutelary deities. The second part of his reign was marked by a Turco-Mongol invasion, a holy war against the Buddhist unbelievers by the Khan of Kashgar. His general, Mirza Haidar, invaded Tibet, then withdrew to Ladakh, and executed Tashi Namgyal. The Turco-Mongols finished by regaining Kashmir, leaving behind them the usual trail of ruin.

Not content with repulsing new attacks from Kashmir, Tsewang Namgyal (1535–1575) nephew of Tashi, retook part of Baltistan and expanded his kingdom to the east. At Basgo he built a temple to Maitreya; a mural there depicts him with his two brothers. The younger, Jamyang Namgyal, was unable to prevent the invasion of Ali Mir, king of Baltistan, whose daughter he had to marry.

From this union with a Balti princess came the most celebrated king of Ladakh, Senge Namgyal (1575–1620). Fifteen years campaigning saw the conquest of neighbouring states, but this made him more vulnerable to the attacks of the Mongols. Under their general Gushri Khan they championed the cause of the 15th Dalai Lama who was determined to be master of a reunified Tibet. Senge Namgyal was proud of fighting his way to the gates of Lhasa, but his victories cost Ladakh dear.

He destroyed the independent buffer states around him at precisely the moment that the Mughal empire under Jahangir was exerting a growing pressure to the west, having conquered Kashmir and Baltistan.

Apart from his warlike activities Senge Namgyal was a great builder. He built the palace of Leh and the monasteries of Hemis, Stakna, and Chemre dedicated to the Dugpa-Kagyupa order, which thus arrived in Ladakh with royal patronage.

For 20 years Deldan Namgyal (1620–1640), the son of Senge, held the empire together with the help of his brothers. He paid lip service to the Mughal's pretensions of suzerainty, limiting himself to the marking out of a mosque at Leh in 1645. He erected to the memory of his father the great Buddha at Shey and dedicated a temple to Avalokiteswara at Leh.

It was Delek Namgyal (1640–1680) who suffered the disastrous consequences of his grandfather's political short sight. The empire disintegrated under the impact of the armies of the Dalai Lama who took a dim view of the ties between the kings of Ladakh and the Dugpa-Kagyupa order and its most eminent representative, Ngawang Namgyal, founder of the Bhutanese theocracy (Bhutan still mainly follows this sect). At this point the sovereign of united Tibet tried to reconquer Bhutan, and the intervention of Delek had the sole result of an immediate invasion by the Tibeto-Mongol army, which advanced as far as Basgo. They were held there for three years unable to take the fortress until the arrival of Mughal troops to whom Delek had called for help. The army of the Dalai Lama was routed (1647), but Ladakh lost on two counts; territory was lost to Tibet for good, while the king had to adopt Islam (momentarily at any rate) and pay an annual tribute to Kashmir.

Despite this Ladakh preserved its independence until the 18th century while maintaining close commercial and religious ties with Tibet. With the collapse of the Mughal empire the last great invasion of Ladakh came from the Hindu state of Jammu. Zorawar Singh with 5000 men crossed the Bhotkol Pass and exiled the king to Stok. Ladakh was absorbed into first Jammu and Kashmir, then the British Raj, and finally independent India.

Buddhism in Ladakh

The monasteries (or gompas) are the main point of interest in Ladakh where the people follow the Tibetan form of Buddhism. Much hedged about by demons and Hindu reversions, the art is intriguing and colourful.

The Buddhism followed in Ladakh and Tibet is a Yogo-tantric form that absorbed many beliefs from the original Bon-po religion of Tibet. The followers of this tradition are called the Red Hats. In the 15th century a reforming monk founded the Gelugpa (Virtuous Order) sect. These were the first Yellow Hats, though in time other reform sects also became known as that. The Dalai Lama always comes from this sect. Just like other baddies the adherents of Bon-po were called Black Hats.

Belief in Maitreya, the Buddha to come, is fundamental, and his statues and paintings are seen all over Ladakh. Vairocana, seen in Red Hat monasteries, is their concept of an immaculate meditating Buddha.

LEH

The capital of Ladakh (3500m/11,480ft) has one main street and a warren of alleys to the houses that climb up the hillside towards the towering palace and monastery. The palace is ruined and the monastery virtually deserted these days, but you get a marvellous view from up there.

Palace

The remains of the palace dominate the town of Leh. Built around 1600, when the king of Leh ruled much of western Tibet, the palace is a little earlier than the Potala in Lhasa, which it rather resembles. This is a large building, 60m long and very nearly as high. Rising above all the neighbouring buildings it is at once a huge fortress and a fine piece of architecture. Because of its present tragic state of dilapidation it is hard to see the true grandeur of this building. The real importance of the palace is the light it throws on the culture of the mountain people and the way they developed an architecture to suit this harsh terrain.

Above the palace stands the Temple of Namgyal Tsemo (height of victory) built during the reign of Tashi Namgyal (1500–1532). The palace itself, properly called the Lechen Palkhar, was built by Senge Namgyal (1590–1635). According to tradition his father intended to build a palace high above Leh, but the exact choice of site fell to Senge Namgyal who selected a granite outcrop shaped like the head of an elephant. The work took less than three years and, as happened elsewhere, the head mason had his right hand cut off to prevent him repeating his masterpiece.

During the Dogra war in 1836 the palace was besieged and the stupa to the south-west partially destroyed. The royal family fled to Stok, to the south of Leh, where their descendents still live. Thus the palace lost its purpose and was never repaired. It was this war and the resulting disruption of the social order that reduced the palace and its splendours to an incomplete ruin. Its once colourful and imposing social and religious functions disappeared almost completely. Today the palace is used only for the New Year festival in January/February. Monks are invited from different monasteries in turn to carry out the rites that guarantee health and prosperity. This festival is the great social and religious event of the year for the people of Leh.

The palace was part of a series of buildings on the ridge of Namgyal Tsemo. This extends for several kilometres, and the buildings, in a more or less severe state of dilapidation, include the fortress dating from around 1520 built by Tashi Namgyal, and the Gon-khang, Temple of the Divine Guardians built by the same king, red in colour, and containing an image of Makhala with six arms. Below is a temple of Maitreya. Along the ridge you can see the ruins of several watchtowers mostly built before the reign of Tashi Namgyal. On the southern slope of the ridge and close to the palace is a stupa; above that is a temple dedicated to Padmasambhava, the Red Hat who first brought Buddhism to Ladakh. On the same flank anchored in the rock below the palace are two stables and the new monastery, the Soma Gompa, a building of two storeys with a vast courtyard in front, dedicated to Chakyamuni.

On the south-west flank are two more temples dating from the early 15th century, one to Avalokiteswara, the other to Maitreya. Behind the palace near a group of houses called Chubi are the spring and reservoir that supplied the palace's water.

The construction of the palace shows clearly the traditional methods and skills of the artisans of Ladakh. In every respect this is a perfect expression of Tibetan architecture, and of course the location is superb. Following the traditions of Tibetan builders there are always nine distinct levels. Again following tradition the upper part is reserved for noble use: royal apartments, state rooms, throne room, and two temples. The lower floors are for staff, shops, and stables.

In the middle of the building, at fourth floor level, the main courtyard (Kataog chemno), looking out to the south, is around 40m above ground level. It formed the centre of the cultural and religious life of the royal family.

The construction methods are influenced by the precarious location, using heavy masonry with foundations and transverse walls that support the southern front. These walls are around 1.75m thick at the base, reducing to 0.5m where the stone gives way to brick. The arrangement of the windows and their proportions are characteristic of Tibetan architecture. At the bottom of the palace they are narrow slits, partly for structural reasons and partly for defence and also because the rooms are mainly stores. On the higher levels the rooms become larger and are used as state rooms and lodgings, so the need for light increases and with that the size of the windows. The size of the windows evolves in inverse proportion to the thickness of the walls. Inside the walls have been plastered with a layer of mud; the more important rooms have received a layer of fine clay. The noble rooms have been decorated in water colour, usually a pale yellow. The main rooms are embellished by murals.

Until recently there was a risk that the palace would fall into total ruin, but an ambitious programme of restoration is now being undertaken. A new museum in the palace should help bring new life to this splendid building.

Practical Information

Tourist office in the Dak Bungalow in the centre of town.

Arrival and departure. Airport (4km). Indian Airlines flights from Srinagar, Delhi (daily), and Chandigarh (once weekly). Indian Airlines office (Tel 2276) in town centre. In winter the flights from Srinagar are the only means of travel to Ladakh. Weather conditions can cause cancellation or delay at any time of year.

The Srinagar-Leh road is open usually from early May to late October; it is not infrequently blocked by landslides and unseasonal snow. Buses from the Tourist Reception Centre in Srinagar (various classes) take two days, making an overnight stop in Kargil. Jeeps and taxis do the trip in one day and are very expensive; try bargaining. The Manali-Leh road now carries limited civilian traffic, but is open only July–September. A local bus service covers all the places you are likely to want to visit.

Health note. Leh is at 3500m/11,480ft. The air is thin and the sun intense. Do not run about too much until you have acclimatised, which takes several days. However brown you are, be extremely cautious of the sun, both on your skin and on your head. Keep up your fluid intake. You risk making yourself extremely ill if you ignore this advice. Altitude sickness should not be a problem, but if you do find yourself experiencing breathing difficulties, severe headaches, and particularly water retention get medical help without delay.

Accommodation (STD Code 01982)

Khangri Hotel, near diesel generator. Tel 2251. SWB Rs500 (around £10/$16.50) DWB Rs600 (£12/$20). Rest. Bar. Nice place, the only snag being the aforementioned generator.

Lungse-Jung, near Dreamland. SWB Rs200 DWB Rs300. A nice place with lashings of hot water. The nearby *Ibex* is similarly priced.

In the lowest price bracket you can get a room for Rs50–100 (£1–2/$1.60–3.30) and a dorm bed around Rs25 (50p/80 cents). Popular places include *Moonland Guest House*, *Palace View Guest House*, *Dreamland*, and *Palace View Kidar Hotel*, which does good cheap meals in a traditional Ladakhi kitchen. Equally traditional is the earth latrine. Lots more at this price in the town centre and a short walk away.

Rather further out, say a twenty minute walk, is the *Otsal Guest House* in a rural setting by a stream, highly recommended. Several others in this area.

Eating and drinking

Dreamland Hotel. Cheap/Mod. Tibetan. Superb food, great atmosphere. The first proper restaurant in Leh and still going strong.

German Bakery. Fort Road. Cakes, coffee, and bread. Great.

Many small cheap restaurants are either unnamed or called 'Tibetan Hotal' (sic).

THE MONASTERIES OF THE LADAKH VALLEY

Apart from their obvious religious significance the monasteries reflect the local concern about land tenure, and also an approach to birth control. Because of the lack of rainfall arable land is restricted to the river valleys, and the potential output of food is obviously low. Thus, not only must the population be kept stable, but farms must not be split into uneconomically small units. For centuries it has been the tradition that the eldest son inherits all his father's land and responsibility for the family, and that the second son becomes a monk. Younger sons usually work on the family land; they rarely marry but may enjoy the fruits of a polyandrous marriage (though only when big brother is away!). Outside influences are starting to erode these traditions.

Mulbekh

Approaching Ladakh on the Srinagar–Leh road Mulbekh is your first sight of a Tibetan monastery, and probably a sense of wonder at just how they stick the buildings to the hillside. The temple houses eight deities probably of Bon-po origin. An old Dard fortress also occupies the site. A little further on, the great rock sculpture of Maitreya, more than 7m/23ft high, dates probably from the eighth century. These days Mulbekh is a Buddhist island in Muslim territory.

Arrival and departure. Mulbekh is on the far side of the Fatu La pass (4094m) and a good 150km from Leh, an interesting place to stop on the way through but an awfully long way for an excursion.

Accommodation. Basic hotels.

Lamayuru

One reaches Lamayuru by a track leaving the Srinagar–Leh road a little after leaving the Fatu-La. The monastery buildings climb up a hill overlooking a stunning countryside surrounded by spiky rocks coloured a fantastic ochre yellow.

In times of old, according to legend, a great lake occupied the floor of the valley. Then a disciple of Ananda (faithful companion of Buddha) settled on an island and prophesied the building of a monastery. Throwing grains of barley as an offering to the spirits his faith made a breach that emptied the waters of the lake.

In the tenth century the great Indian sage Naropa meditated for several years in a cave. Then came Rinchen Sangpo to whom is attributed the building of 108 (a holy number) of monasteries. Lamayuru is one of these. It comprises five buildings; one of them, the Sengesang, is the present monastery though little remains of the others. For the following 600 years Lamayuru held to the Kadampa order.

However at the end of the 16th century the king Jamyang Namgyal was suffering from incurable leprosy inflicted by a spirit injured during the construction of an irrigation canal near Hemis. Following a prophecy a lama of the Digungpa order was sent for, who meditated in a cave on Mount Kailash; the king recovered and offered him Lamayuru monastery in thanks. With the monastery went certain rights, notably that of sanctuary. The monastery is known as Tharpa Liong (Place of Freedom), and criminals were safe in a radius of one mile. Several other monasteries are subsidiary to Lamayuru of which the Superior — an incarnation of Togden Rinpoche — ranks after only Hemis in importance.

The temple of Sengesang, the oldest, contains a fine stucco of Vairocana seated on a throne of lions and surmounted by a Garuda and makaras. In one side chapel stand the images of three guardian deities of which Mahakal guards a stupa. In the main temple is a cavity, called the cave of Naropa, holding clay statues of Naropa, Marpa, and Milarepa, the three main teachers of the Kagyupa tradition. Others represent the founder Danmatsang and Digungpa teachers.

Accommodation. Basic hotels and a government rest house.

Thikse

This architectural fantasy covers a small hill from top to bottom. Tsong Khapa had prophesied the founding of a monastery in this place and it was done by the nephew of one of his disciples. At present some 24 monks reside here.

The Dukhang Karpo (White Temple), halfway up, is most worthy of notice. Above, a temple of Maitreya has a series of statuettes representing lamas. Over the main temple a veranda has murals of the 24 mahasiddhas.

The main interest at Thikse is its location. The view from above is superb, and the buildings themselves perfectly sum up the Ladakhi form of Tibetan architecture. Seen against a clear blue sky Thikse Gompa is one of the great sights of India.

Hemis

Hemis is the largest monastery in Ladakh. It was founded in 1602 by Tagtsangrepa, a Bhutanese monk of the Dugpa-Kagyupa order who was brought here by King Senge Namgyal. The monastery has stayed with this order ever since, and 1200 monks are attached to it. For several years Hemis was deprived of its Superior as he was taken prisoner by the Chinese while studying in Lhasa. A new incarnation of the founder Dugpa Tamche Khyenpo was accordingly found to take over.

The murals in Hemis are in Tibetan style. In the courtyard are represented in a naive but refreshing style the 24 mahasiddhas or Indian tantric masters of whom the founder had a vision. Of the two principal temples the Tsogkhang is the more interesting; it contains a beautiful Buddha statue and several stupas covered with silver, gold and semi-precious stones. The Lhakhang Nyima (Old Temple) is distinguished by the quality of its murals. One of the small temples on the roof contains a statue of Tagtsangrepa, and a large gold and silver stupa contains his relics. Right at the end of the roof, in the Zabkhang (Elegant Room), are assembled some Kashmiri bronzes and statues of eminent Dugpa-Kagyupa lamas. Finally, visitors lucky enough to attend the festival for the year of the monkey (next in 2004) will see unrolled the huge thanka, embroidered and decorated with pearls, showing Padmasambhava in his eight forms.

PUNJAB

PATHANKOT

As observed from the window of a bus Pathankot looks like a place to hurry through. It is.

Information. Himachal Pradesh Tourism office (Tel 316) is opposite the railway station.

Arrival and departure. On Delhi (10½hrs)–Jammu (2½hrs) railway line. Also a line to Amritsar. Narrow gauge railway to Kangra (5hrs) for Dharamsala and to Jogindernagar (10hrs), a really beautiful run. Buses for Chamba (6hrs) and Dharamsala (3½hrs) may be available from the railway station, otherwise the bus-stand (400m from station); turn left from station, along main street. Rickshaw-wallahs will, of course, tell you that the bus-stand is much further away.

HIMACHAL PRADESH

Himachal Pradesh grew to its present shape in 1966 when parts of Punjab including Simla were transferred to the existing mountain districts. Although the Pahari-speaking locals predominate there were Rajput, Sikh and Dogra states in the foothills, and their influence remains. Another distinct group are the Gaddis, nomadic herdsmen analogous to the Gujjars of Kashmir. They have flocks of their own, and also take on other peoples' as spring starts them on the gradual climb to the summer pastures in the mountains. Himachal Pradesh is quite as beautiful as Kashmir and infinitely more relaxed and welcoming. The only really bad news about Himachal is that Golden Eagle is brewed there, and is often the only beer available.

CHAMBA

Himachal Pradesh is an attractive state, but Chamba is almost in a class of its own; its people are lively and friendly and the women exceptionally beautiful. It is also a trekking base, with routes to Kishtwar in Kashmir, and Dharamsala, Zanskar and Manali (all via Bharmour). Mahseer fishing in the Ravi is good, though the water looks like café au lait in March; licences are available from the Fisheries Officer in Chamba.

Chamba was the capital of a Rajput state founded in 920AD and, it is said, ruled by the same dynasty right up to the time of independence. It was incorporated in the Sikh empire from 1810 to 1846, and was again part of Punjab from 1947 until the expansion of Himachal Pradesh in 1966. Chamba is at 926m/3037ft so can be visited all year round, but is pretty hot from June to September.

Chamba is the most peculiar place, not at all what you expect to find in a remote Himalayan valley. Seen from across the river or the Chaugan (as the maidan is called here), it looks remarkably like a northern Italian town. Instead of campaniles, however, you have the spires of a **group of temples***, some dating back to the tenth century. These are quite unusual, consisting in the main of just the spire over the shrine, and having only a vestigial porch. The wood and slate porches you see are, of course, much later additions. The oddest feature is the two little octagonal roofs on each making them a cross between the standard North Indian sikhara style and the pagodas to be seen in the Kullu Valley. The temples are dedicated to various local deities, and you can tell whether these are attributes of Shiva or Vishnu by, respectively, the Nandi or Garuda in front and the trident or chakra on top.

Nearer to the Ravi River, by the red gate, is the **Hari Rai Temple*** (ninth century), similar to the others and having a superb bronze image. Several other small temples overlook the town and river, and are worth the climb for the views.

Chamba and the other local states of Kangra and Basohli were famous for their distinctive styles of miniature painting. The **Bhuri Singh Museum**** (10am–5pm, closed Monday) has a superb collection and is much better than most local museums (and a lot of the big ones too). Bhuri Singh was the raja who founded the collection in 1908.

Chamba and the Chaugan are perched a good 100m/328ft above the raging River Ravi, the Iravati of legend and one of the five rivers of the Punjab. The town is an important commercial centre for both the local hill people and the nomadic Gaddi herdsmen, and fairs and their attendant folk dancing and music are frequent. The main events are the Sui-ka-Mela, a six-day fair in late April, and the Minjar fair in August, which is a fertility rite of the Gaddis before the onset of the monsoon.

Information. Tourist Office at Hotel Irawati, about 150m from bus-stand.

Arrival and departure. Bus from Dharamsala (10½hrs) or Pathankot (6hrs), both skirt Dalhousie.

Accommodation (STD Code 018992)

Hotel Irawati, near bus-stand. Tel 2671. DWB Rs300–500 (around £6–10/$10–16.50). Rest (very good). Beer — if Golden Eagle deserves to be called that. Clean and comfortable.

Hotel Champak, next to Irawati. Tel 2774. DR from Rs100 (£2/$3.30) Dorm Rs45 (90p/$1.50). Both these places are run by Himachal Tourism.

Hotel Akhand Chandi. Tel 2371. Part of the old palace, used to be a very nice place to stay; see if it has reopened after a fire.

Janata Hotel is cheaper but noisy.

Eating and drinking
  Café Ravi View overlooks the Chaugan and river.

EXCURSIONS FROM CHAMBA

Dalhousie sounds like just another hill station, but the walk to it from Chamba is very fine; stay overnight at Khajjiar.

Travelling 70km up the River Ravi from Chamba you find **Bharmour**, the old capital of Chamba state, with many temples.

You can also get a bus from Chamba to Saluni and on through the Bhandal Valley to **Bhadawah**. An annual pilgrimage goes from here to **Kaplash Lake** at 4400m. The scenery is very striking. In summer it should be possible to get a bus or truck from Bhadawah through to Kishtwar (saffron growing and sapphire mines) in Kashmir, whence there is a bus service to Srinagar or Jammu — but take advice on security first.

KANGRA

Kangra was famed for the once fabulously rich **Devi Vajresri Temple**. Plundered many times it was finally destroyed in the earthquake that devastated this area in 1905. Now rebuilt it is of minimal interest.

The **Nagarkot** fort stands high above the junction of two rivers. First built by the Rajputs, it was taken by Mahmud of Ghazni in 1099. Other Muslims followed, then the Sikhs, until eventually in 1775 the Rajputs staged a comeback. This is a superb defensive position but, while the outer walls are mainly intact, all the interior buildings and temples were wrecked by the earthquake. Not wildly exciting but a nice place for a picnic with distant views of the mountains. A forlorn British cemetery stands near the entrance. The marble plaques have been taken from many of the monuments for grinding spices on.

Arrival and departure. Train from Pathankot or Jogindernagar. Walk down the steps from the station into the valley, cross the bridge, and wait for a bus at the toll point. You should be able to get one straight to Dharamsala (1hr), otherwise change at the bus-stand in the town centre. The fort is a short walk from the toll point, the town 3km/2 miles. Most bus services to Dharamsala pass through Kangra.

DHARAMSALA

The name covers two quite distinct places. Dharamsala itself, often referred to as Lower Dharamsala, is of little interest although a new **Museum of Kangra Art** has opened recently.

Tibet in exile

McLeodganj***, which is 500m/1640ft higher at 1850m/6068ft, is a very different matter. This mainly Tibetan village is the home in exile of the Dalai Lama and a large number of his followers, both monks and lay people. It is impossible not to like the cheerful and placid Tibetans, and there are reminders of their unswerving Buddhist faith all around. In the centre of the village is a large **chorten** and beside it a **huge prayer wheel**. Walk down the black-top road from the end of the bazaar, past the Dalai Lama's palace, and branch left onto a rough path. This will take you on a **devotional walk** garlanded with prayer flags and bordered with inscribed stones. Buddhists always walk clockwise round stupas and mani walls and the like, so this is the wrong way round. We suggest it because you will meet more people walking along telling their rosaries and twirling prayer wheels. You are welcome to attend prayer meetings at the **monastery** adjoining the palace, and the drumming and chanting can make this a powerful, emotional experience.

Mountain strolls

There are many good **day walks** around McLeodganj. A higher road parallel to the main one to Dharamsala will take you to Dal Lake (more of a muddy pond) and on to Nadi village (3km/2 miles) from where there is a marvellous view of the Dhauladar Mountains. A path runs from here to the Shiva shrine on the way to Triund (see below). Returning from Nadi walk down to Forsythganj and back along the main road to the **Church of St John in the Wilderness**. Anyone who has any doubts about the sacrifices the British made in India should read some of the tombstones here. Whole families were carried off in a few days by disease, and the 1905 earthquake claimed many victims. Just on the town side of the church is the old camel trail down to Dharamsala. On this, as on any walk through the woods here, you will see many beautiful birds. Another route down to Dharamsala is to bear left at the end of the bazaar. Halfway down is the **Tibetan Central Secretariat**, which contains a museum and library. This is the place to find out about studying Tibetan Buddhism. Courses are run in McLeodganj in summer and occasionally in Bodhgaya in winter. Interesting, but less pleasant as a walk than it used to be now that taxis use it as a short cut.

Bhagsunath is a pleasant stroll. Continue through the **temple** compound to the slate mines, and follow the stream up to the Shiva Café. To make a different return follow the water pipe round the hill and then descend through the paddies to Bhagsunath village.

Serious walking

More ambitious walkers can set off up the road from the bus-stand towards **Triund**, a high pasture used by nomadic herdsmen called Gaddis. Turn left past the Mountaineering Institute and you come to Dharamkot village. The path to the left of the school goes straight up to a Shiva shrine on the col above Bhagsunath Temple. The pack trail to the left follows a gentler and longer route to the same place. From the shrine you have an exhilarating high-level walk to Triund at nearly 3000m/9840ft. Allow 3½–4 hours for the walk up, half that to return. There are superb views of the mountains and plains, better earlier in the day, and a rest house if you want to stay. Gaddi huts and caves can also be used when the rightful owners are not in residence. Staying up here allows you to explore the route towards Laka Got, another pasture (3350m/10,988ft), and the Indrahar Pass at 4320m/14,197ft. It is just about possible to return by heading south along the ridge from Triund, but very hard to pick up a good path down to Bhagsunath. The trick is to go much further along the ridge than you might think and then aim for one of the inhabited villages — not the first two you see below, which are only seasonal and have no proper paths down.

How long the peacefulness of Triund will last is anyone's guess; some Delhiwala plans to build a hotel up here. The foundation stone for the planned cable car to Triund stands right next to Dharamkot School. A lot of land at this bottom end has apparently been promised for a complex as well as on the ridge. This plan will probably result in the population of the village being dispossessed. India is dotted with the forlorn foundation stones of abandoned projects. We can only pray.

Dharamsala is also a base for serious treks. Yeti Trekking (Tel 2887), a short walk up from the bus-stand, do short routes at Rs500 (around £10/$16.65) per day inclusive of everything but transport to the start point and Rs625 (around £12.50/$20.85) for longer routes (over the pass). You need your own sleeping bag and pack. Before May one is limited to 2500m/8200ft. Manali takes 12 or 18 days, Leh 40 days via Keylong and the Rohtang Pass. This is much more adventure-trekking than in Nepal, using Gaddi caves on the shorter routes.

McLeodganj is one of the most relaxed and pleasant places in India. Several yoga ashrams are based here, and there are frequent lectures and courses on many subjects including Bon-po, the ancient religion of Tibet. Good food, too.

Practical Information

Tourist Office in Kotwali Bazaar, Lower Dharamsala.

Arrival and departure. Airport at Gaggal, 13km/8 miles from Dharamsala.

Buses to Dharamsala from Kangra (1hr), Chandigarh, Pathankot (3½hrs), Jogindernagar (4hrs), Mandi, and Chamba (10½hrs) or Dalhousie. All these buses terminate in Dharamsala, and there is a regular bus service from there to McLeodganj. To catch the train to Jogindernagar or Pathankot take a bus through Kangra and have the conductor drop you off at the station road on top of the hill. The train ride to Jogindernagar is very beautiful and, though slower, is definitely preferable to the bus. For travel towards Dharamsala by train, read the Kangra section. Train reservations from Pathankot to Delhi can be made at the bus-stand in Lower Dharamsala (10am–1pm only).

Accommodation (STD Code 01892)
In lower Dharamsala:
Hotel Dhauladhar (Kotwali Bazaar, above bus-stand). Tel 2256. Rest. Bar. Similar prices to Bhagsu (see below), which is also run by Himachal Tourism. Good place. Steps lead up from the end of the bus-stand platform to the Dhauladhar and the bazaar where the other cheaper hotels are.

Two cheap hotels, including *Sun 'n' Snow*, are downhill from the Dhauladhar and several more are uphill.

In McLeodganj:
Hotel Bhagsu. Tel 3191. SWB/DWB Rs400–700 (£8–14/$13–23) 3-bed cottage Rs950. Rest. Bar. Well run. Quiet, small garden, superb views.

Hotel Tibet, Bhagsunath Road. Tel 22587. Has a wide range of rooms from Rs350 up. Rest (excellent). Bar (the author's wife says the best in India). Large comfortable rooms. No longer cheap, but fabulous people and simply a nice place to stay.

Hotel Green, Bhagsunath Road. Tel 2526. SR Rs35 (70p/$1.15) DR Rs60 DWB Rs100/120. Rest. Clean and very popular over the years.

Hotel Kokonor, Bhagsunath Road. Tel 2311. DR Rs75 3R Rs100. Rest.

Hotel Kailash, main bazaar. DR Rs80 3R Rs120 Dorm Rs30. Rest (see below).

Om Guest House, below bazaar. SR Rs40 DR Rs80. Rest. Roof terrace. A lot of Westerners stay here but a bit far out, man.

Kalsang Tsomo International Guest House, just down from PO. Tel 2476. DR Rs95 DWB Rs160. Rest. Nice people.

Lots more small places. AJ Thapa, who runs Yeti Trekking, has pleasant accommodation at his home just above the bus-stand, spacious garden. It is also possible to rent rooms and cottages around McLeodganj, some in very quiet beautiful places.

Eating and drinking
Hotel Tibet. Mod/Exp. Ind/Chi/Jap/Tibetan. Bar. Best in town.
Kailash Hotel. Cheap/Mod. Hippy international. Lively scene.

Rising Horizon has pies, quiches, and sourdough bread. Apple pie and custard a real treat after a few months in India.

Excursions from Dharamsala

Jawalamukhi, which means 'flaming goddess', has one of India's more unusual temples. Instead of an image, a burning jet of natural gas that issues from the ground represents the deity. The white marble temple is pretty with its gold domes, and well located on a wooded hillside. Don't go along expecting something like the flare on an oil rig, the flame is about as dramatic as a bunsen burner.

Arrival and departure. Bus from Dharamsala (3hrs), Kangra (2hrs), or Jawalamukhi Road (1hr), the last two named being on the Pathankot–Jogindernagar narrow gauge railway.

Nadaun, 10km from Jawalamukhi, has good mahseer fishing and, according to Himachal Pradesh Tourism, a quiet picturesque rest house. **Andretta** (13km from Palampur) has an art gallery devoted to Sobha Singh, a sort of Indian romanticist, who lived there. At **Masrur** (40km from Dharamsala) are rock-cut temples similar in style to Ellora.

JOGINDERNAGAR

Jogindernagar is notable for its hydro-electric plant, one of the first built in India. Water for the turbines comes from the River Uhl in the adjoining valley, and passes through a tunnel several kilometres long before running down the penstocks (the big pipes you can see on the mountainside) to the powerhouse. All this was originally constructed in the 1920s under the direction of a British military engineer and has since been extended with Hungarian help. Local engineers were incredulous that the name of Colonel Batty is unknown in Britain. Apparently many of the older houses around Barot have a photo of him, and local children mention him in their prayers in school each morning.

The story goes that when the flow of water through the tunnel was cut off in 1980 for inspection and extension work his ghost appeared to an engineer in the powerhouse demanding to know the reason for the silence. When told of the inspection it replied "Why do they need to make an inspection? I certified this work for 100 years, and it will last 100 years."

Jolly interesting, but so what? The point is that to facilitate construction a cable-hauled **trolleyway** was built over the mountain ridge between the two valleys and, for enthusiasts of esoteric transport, this is not to be missed. The ride, which will not be enjoyed by those of nervous disposition, takes 3½ hours, reaches 2500m/8200ft with a maximum gradient of 48°, and provides splendid views. It really is the next best thing to a helicopter, and every mountain should have one. Even better there is no charge, though you must get permission from the Resident Engineer (walk 2.5km/1.5 miles up the railway line from Jogindernagar station and ask for his office), and sign a blood chit (they call it an Indemnity Bond) to the effect that if you are killed or maimed it is entirely your own fault and nothing whatsoever to do with the Punjab State Electricity Board. You can usually return the same day, but read about Barot, where the trolleyway terminates.

Arrival and departure. Terminus of narrow gauge railway line from Pathankot (10hrs). Read the note about the railway in the section on Dharamsala. Buses from Mandi and Dharamsala (4hrs). Bus-stand and railway station are 50m apart. Trolleyway starts beside powerhouse, 2.5km from station.

Accommodation

Tourist Bungalow, about 1.5km from station. Tel 2. SWB/DWB Rs200/300 (around

£4/6, $6.50/10). Rest (good). Bar. Clean rooms, good views, nice staff; what more can you ask for?

Also *PWD Bungalow* (500m from bus-stand) and *Tourist Hotel* adjacent to bus-stand, which was terrible when last seen. Punjab State Electricity Board has a *Guest House* in superb location at top of trolleyway (2434m/7984ft up); ask Executive Engineer.

BAROT

Barot is the village where the waters of the River Uhl are harnessed for the Jogindernagar power station. Apart from the necessary headworks the Uhl Valley is quite unspoiled; probably the most peaceful and beautiful place to be so accessible.

There is excellent **trout fishing** in the river; fast water above the headworks and a couple of deep pools below if you follow the path down the right bank for about 4km. The lower reservoir holds large fish though they are hard to catch. Permits (Rs10 per day) from the trout hatchery, spinning permitted. Non-fishermen will get just as much enjoyment from the scenery and observing the local way of life.

The bazaar in Barot is rudimentary; bring any food you will want for picnics.

Arrival and departure. Bus or trolleyway (3½hrs) to Jogindernagar, also bus to Mandi (4hrs). Alternatively, walk to Katrain on the Kullu–Manali road (4–5 days) crossing the Bherianga Pass at 4140m; you will need a tent and all supplies.

Accommodation. The Punjab State Electricity Board has two rest houses here, check when you arrange to travel on the trolleyway. The chowkidar at the lower one is a keen fisherman and an excellent cook. The Public Works Department Rest House (Log Cabin) is about 1km from the bottom of the trolleyway and near to the trout farm.

Eating and drinking. Very simple food in the bazaar, best to eat at the rest house.

MANDI

Mandi is a convenient place to break the long journey to Kullu or Manali. As yet little spoiled by development, it is a pleasant market town (*mandi* means market) on the old trade route between India and Ladakh. The atmosphere is quiet and unhurried and, unlike so many Indian towns, it is a joy to wander about. A sunken garden in the centre of town is overlooked by the old palace buildings, and many of the old shops and houses around have fronts of carved wood. Note the distinctive way the local Sikhs tie their turbans; at one time the boundaries of the Punjab extended well into these hills. The author discovered in one of the local gun shops that muzzle-loaders are still manufactured in India, though progress being what it is, these are percussion cap devices rather than flintlock. Shame.

Information. Tourist Office at Hotel Mandan (formerly the Tourist Lodge) above bus-stand or at Café Shiraz in town centre.

Arrival and departure. All buses to Kullu (3hrs) and Manali (5hrs) from Delhi (16hrs), Simla (6hrs), Chandigarh (11hrs), Dharamsala (6hrs), etc. pass through Mandi.

Accommodation

Raj Mahal Hotel, town centre. Tel 22 401. Not too expensive (around Rs150; about £3/$5). Rest. Bar. Maharaja's old palace. Very comfortable, decor and art not to be missed.

Hotel Mandan (formerly Tourist Lodge), above bus-stand. Tel 22 123. DWB Rs300 plus 8% Dorm Rs45. Rest. Bar (both good). They've knocked down the old block, which had views over the town; maybe the new one will be as good.

Eating and drinking. Café Shiraz (town centre). Cheap. Mainly only snacks, but would you believe — sausage, egg, and chips? Other cheap places in the town centre.

Cheaper hotels around the main square.

Around Mandi

Rewalsar Lake is popular with pilgrims and famous for its floating islands. A much smaller lake near **Kataula** (bus or walk from Mandi) also has one of these islands and an ancient temple in a spectacular setting.

KULLU VALLEY

KULLU

Unlike the Kullu Valley as a whole, Kullu town is a nondescript sort of place worth visiting only at the time of the Dussehra festival in October/November. This is when the images from many other temples in the Kullu Valley are taken to pay homage to the chief deity Ragunath who normally resides in a temple on the hill above Dhalpur. A huge fair is held on the Maidan, and the gods are taken out in procession with their temple bands and the raja, all very lively, noisy, and colourful.

Information. Tourist Office behind the taxi stand at the north end of the Maidan.

Arrival and departure. Airport at Bhunter (10km south of Kullu) served by Jagson (Tel 65 286).

Kullu is on the main road from Mandi to Manali, and all buses pass through. For Dussehra, or a place to stay, get off the bus at Dhalpur (where the Maidan is), 2km south of Akhara bazaar, where the main bus-stand is located.

Accommodation (STD Code 01902)

Hotel Sarvari (Tourist Bungalow), Maidan. Tel 2471. DWB Rs400 (£8/$13) plus 8%. Dorm Rs50 (£1/$1.65). Rest. Bar. Comfortable old-fashioned rooms, delightful gardens, and quiet; best bet in Kullu.

Hotels on the Maidan, such as *Fancy Guest House*, and others nearby are much quieter than those in bazaar near bus-stand.

Eating and drinking. Café at the tourist office on the Maidan.

NAGGAR

Naggar is an attractive village roughly half-way between Kullu and Manali, but on the other side of the valley from the main road. Naggar was for many years the home of Nicholas Roerich, a Russian artist and indologist, whose family had once ruled Finland. This extraordinary man designed ballet sets for Diaghilev, wrote the libretto for Stravinsky's *Rite of Spring*, and became the guru of a large and prosperous American cult. He left Russia at the time of the revolution in 1917 and eventually settled in Kullu. His house, The Hall, had been built high up above the valley for a British officer. Now the **Roerich Museum**** (9am–1pm and 2–5pm, Sundays noon–1pm and 2–5pm), its collection is mainly mountainscapes, a small sample of his prolific output. The work is, as you might expect, quite mystical. The colour effects may look odd, but in fact capture well the tricks that light can play in the mountains.

Naggar Castle (so-called) is going on for 500 years old. Originally the residence of the local ruler before he moved his capital to Kullu, the stone used in its construction came from an old fort on the other side of the river. In the castle is a small temple containing a stone slab carried here by bees from a cliff above Vashisht, where you can see the mark it left. A small museum of local artefacts is also housed here. Best of all the castle is now a reasonably priced hotel, its balconies commanding views along the Kullu Valley. This is one of the most unusual and attractive places to stay in India.

Naggar allows you to see all four styles of temple architecture followed in the Kullu Valley: stone sikhara (imported from the plains); tower with wooden chalet on top; chalet on its own; and pagoda. The best stone example is the small **Gaurishankar Temple** below the castle, much prettier than the larger one near Poonam Lodge. Beside the road to the Roerich Museum are a newly rebuilt pagoda and a miniature chalet, one of several in the village.

Naggar village is quite unspoiled and makes a quiet yet civilised place to stay. A popular (and very steep) walk is the 7km from Naggar to the Chanderkhani Pass at 3660m. The other side of the pass is Malana with its famous Jamlu Temple.

Arrival and departure. Regular buses along the left bank of the Beas from Manali and Kullu, slower and much more attractive than the main road on the right bank. A road links Naggar to Patli Kuhl on the Kullu–Manali road near Katrain, and is short-cutted by a path following the stream. Better walked down than up.

Accommodation
Castle Hotel, Naggar. Tel 7 (reservations). DR Rs125 (around £2.50/$4.15) 4R (actually two doubles) Rs200 DWB Rs250 Dorm Rs45 (90p/$1.50). Rest. Book there or at tourist office in Kullu. Beautiful old building with fabulous views. One of the great hotel experiences of India — simpler, of course, but far more cachet than the Lake Palace in Udaipur, which every package tourist has been to.
Poonam Lodge, Naggar. Tel 12. SR Rs75 DR Rs150 DWB Rs200. Rest. Well fitted out and spotless. Food is excellent. Beware of the huge apple strudel, order one between two!

MANALI

Manali, at 1800m, is the highest town in the Kullu Valley. It is quite a cosmopolitan place with Tibetans, Gaddis (nomadic herdsmen), wealthy Indian tourists, and resident freaks all mixing with the amiable locals. Colourful street vendors sell saffron, musk, and amber. This is not the sort of hard amber pipe stems are made of; amongst its other interesting properties this aromatic substance is supposed to be an aphrodisiac. The book all these men carry about their goods makes entertaining reading.

A wooden pagoda

Above the town is the **Hadimba Devi Temple**, built in 1555 and typical of the local pagoda style. The story goes that the craftsman who did the wood-carving had his right hand cut off by the local ruler to prevent him repeating his masterpiece. Unwisely, perhaps, he trained his left hand and produced an even finer temple at Chamba. His employer there took no chances and chopped his head off as soon as he had finished the job. The temple is a lot more attractive outside, especially the carved wooden porch, than in. In fact all there is inside is a large stone slab. You are also likely to encounter people who think they gain favour in the eyes of the Almighty by chopping the heads off chickens. While this temple is similar to others in the Kullu Valley, Penelope

Chetwode linked the design to that of some Scandinavian churches and mentions the discovery of Norse artefacts in the area.

Sit on the terrace and watch the behaviour of Indian tourists. They pay no attention to the near-unique architecture; just rush inside, hand over some money, get a little holy water, and rush off to the next place on the list.

Old Manali

Manali bazaar is a recent development, and you should walk up to **Old Manali** to see how the local people really live. The forest that holds the **aviary** and pinetarium (!) continues all the way to the bridge and is a far more pleasant walk than the road. Note the composite construction of the traditional village buildings. The layers of timber between the stone give protection against the earth tremors common in this area. As in Switzerland, which has a similar climate, the animals live downstairs and the humans above. Old Manali is more properly known as Manaligarh, from the **old fort** that dominated the village. Much of this has been plundered for building material, and a small chalet temple preserves fragments of old sculpture. Another similar temple is on the hill behind the fort. Good views. Much, much higher up the hill is another fort.

Walking trips

Two good **walks** can be made from Old Manali. Manaslu Nalla is the stream below the village, and about two hours walk up the valley is a good camping place and, a little past that, some Gaddi shelters if you have no tent. Another half-hour on, after a bit of a scramble, a meadow opens out above the path. Climb a little way up here for a marvellous view in both directions. The path goes further before eventually petering out.

Alternatively find the Manu Temple and continue uphill from there looking for a path heading up the Beas valley. Although a bit vague in places you can find a way through plantations and little clearings before dropping down to the big village over the river from Bahang on the main road.

Returning to Manali bazaar from Old Manali turn uphill when you reach the main road and, just past Hamto Cottage, you will find an unusual **memorial** to Harold Banon, one of the Indo-Irish family that popularised Manali as a hill resort. Like his three brothers he fought in the First World War, and was killed in France. The Latin inscription translates roughly as: 'A soldier who far away from here died before his time but for his country. I will rise again.' You're on your own with the Tibetan.

The Tibetan settlement is on the outskirts of town and, despite the obvious poverty, boasts the usual giant prayer wheel and Buddha. A little further on is a brightly decorated monastery. Another good **walk** is to climb up above this monastery and then find a path running along on the level between the paddies and orchards. You can go as far as you like down the valley passing through little villages, and either return on a different level or descend to the road and go back along the stream. If you choose the latter you will come into town through the reserve forest. We found a peculiar plant there like a bright red corn-on-the-cob.

Local and tourist buses run up to the **Rohtang Pass** (3978m), or you can even walk; this is about 26km on foot and 52km by road. On the way you pass through Vashisht and Kothi (see below).

Manali is no longer a quiet little place, but peace and tranquillity can be found, and having a good shopping centre nearby is handy. Have a look in Tibet Emporium, next to the PO, which has beautiful clothes and an excellent range of books on Tibet, the Himalayas, and religion. The surroundings and the friendliness of the local people add to the charm of the place.

Practical Information

i

Information. Tourist Office 100m up from bus-stand. Various tours and details of government-owned accommodation. Maps on sale.

Arrival and departure. Airport at Bhunter, see under Kullu. Buses from Simla (occasional luxury bus, ask at the Tourist Office), Chandigarh, Dharamsala, Jogindernagar, etc. You can break the long journeys in Mandi. Local buses run over the Rohtang Pass (May–September only) to Keylong and Udeypur in Lahaul and Spiti, and also to Leh in Ladakh.

Accommodation

John Banon's Guest House, Manali Orchards. Tel 2335. SWB Rs250 (£5/$8.30) DWB Rs475. Rest. Bar. The original place to stay in Manali and still the best. Run by the Indo-Irish family that did so much to popularise Manali. Old world charm and comfort.

Sunshine Guest House, next to Banon Guest House. Tel 2320. DWB Rs275 up. Rest (cheap/mod). Nice garden and a superb view down the valley. Lovely old building — the author would not mind this as a home.

Anand Sunder. DWB Rs275 (Rs175 off season). Modern building surrounded, for the moment, by apple orchards.

Greenland Guest House. DWB Rs210 (Rs155 off season). Rest. Bucket of hot water.

Awasthi Cottage. SR Rs35 DR Rs70 DWB Rs140. Pleasant and knowledgeable proprietor. Basic, but what do you expect at this price?

Scenic Cottage, Dhungri village, above Hadimba Temple. DR Rs60 or Rs400 for ten days. Very basic but some rooms have fireplaces where you can cook. Quiet, super views.

Now that central Manali has become so much busier Westerners who want peace, and are prepared to put up with fairly basic conditions, mostly stay in Old Manali or up Manaslu Nulla where there is plenty of accommodation, some located right by the stream. The *Youth Hostel* is over the bridge and a short way along the road to Vashisht.

Manali is responding to the explosion in 'home tourism' by putting up dozens of hotels in the apple orchards that once surrounded the town. Not quite as bad as it sounds, and certainly makes it easier to find a room. Prices around Rs200 (£4/$6.50; Rs100 off season). Every hotel should display its officially approved prices, and off season prices should be much lower.

Eating and drinking

Mount View, Main Street. Cheap/Mod. Chi/Jap/Tibetan. Excellent food, good atmosphere, and great crack.

Mona Lisa, near bus-stand. Cheap/Mod. Ind/Chi/Cont. Good.

Trish's, Vashisht Road. Cheap. Trish, a Yorkshirewoman who has lived in Manali for many years, does good cakes, salads, quiches, and so on.

Many more restaurants in all price brackets, and a couple of good bakers, around town. Things change fast in Manali, have a good look around.

Between Kullu and Manali is the *Himalayan Safari campsite*, about 5km north of Katrain; a little suspension bridge leads over the river to it.

Further Afield

Vashisht

Vashisht is a picturesque village with superb views along the valley. It is best known for its health-giving hot sulphur baths. The **tourist baths** cost Rs10–20 (around 20–40p/33–66 cents) and offer privacy.

The free **public baths** (separate units for men and women) are much more fun because they function as a social centre for the village. The greyness of the water comes from the minerals, not dirt. Because they are used by the saddhus men can get away with skinny dipping, but women are expected to wear knickers or a swimsuit. The **temple** in the same compound as the baths is typical of the local chalet style. The odd thing is the way the older small temple has been enclosed by a much larger new one in the same style. Note the tree trunk used as a capstone on the roof.

The nearby **Rama Temple** consists of an old stone sikhara with a porch in the local style added in front. One of the figures carved on the doors represents Rama. Inside is an additional shrine dedicated to Shiva but with a statue of Hanuman, Rama's helper.

Vashisht is not quite as quiet as Old Manali, but has more facilities like cafés and hence is a popular place to stay.

Arrival and departure. Bus or walk from Manali. A signposted short cut leads from the road up to the tourist baths.

Accommodation. *Moonlight Café* has basic rooms at Rs40/80. *Freedom Café* DR Rs50, mattress but no blankets. Good view, no toilet!

SOLANG NULLAH

The Himachal Pradesh Mountaineering Institute has a well equipped hut here beside a large meadow with splendid views. A short **ski-tow** has been installed, and slapdash development is doing nothing for the tranquillity and beauty of the place. It is still, however, a good base for day walks. There is **trout fishing** in the nearby River Beas; permits from the Tourist Office in Manali. Given the flow at most times of the year and the lure-snagging submerged wood the only way you are likely to catch anything is with a worm and a large lump of lead. Kindly do not tell anyone it was our idea.

Arrival and departure. Bus from Manali to Palchan. From the top end of the village take the road signposted to the Rohtang Tunnel (under construction), cross River Beas and walk 2km.

Accommodation

Mountaineering Institute Hut. Civilised dormitory accommodation with foam mattresses, proper latrines, etc. Book at Mountaineering Institute in Manali. Small hotels, chai stalls, and simple restaurants (also chang) nearby.

KOTHI

When the snow melts at Solang Nullah skiing and the snowline tours move on to the slopes above this small village. The skiing is a bit of a joke really; you are pushed uphill on a sledge for a run all of 100m long. Much better to walk up the road from Kothi village towards the Rohtang Pass for 2km and then branch left on to the old packhorse trail. You can follow this as far as time and the snow permit. In spring there are dozens of waterfalls, alpine flowers, butterflies — and total peace and quiet.

Arrival and departure. Bus from Manali.

ELSEWHERE IN THE KULLU VALLEY

Manikaran (bus from Kullu) has hot springs and temples. There are many interesting places a little off the beaten track in the Kullu Valley; get a copy of Penelope Chetwode's book *Kullu: The End of the Habitable World*. You can travel over the Rohtang Pass to Lahaul (you need a permit for Spiti) and visit Keylong — described as a 'barbaric jewel'. There are major temples at Triloknath and Udeypur and also

Buddhist monasteries. Lahaul promises to be as different and as interesting as Ladakh.

SIMLA

Simla is one of the more bizarre leftovers of the British Raj. Before Independence the whole Government of India, complete with files and red tape, used to come up here in April to escape the heat of Calcutta and Delhi. Hill stations like Simla played an important social role during the Raj. Many British officials were stationed in remote areas and for eleven months of the year were cut off from agreeable company. Leave in Simla was not only an escape from the grim realities of India, but also a chance to renew old friendships and angle for new postings. Indians still like it for a break from the heat; its attractions for Western travellers today are harder to define.

The main street, **The Mall**, still resembles a small English town of the 1920s (one that has not been painted since then). There are stockbroker Tudor houses, and the whole town is dominated by a Gothic church and a mock Scottish castle. Simla straggles over several hills and ridges, and climbing **Jakkoo Hill** (2440m) from the path beside the church you can get a good view of the whole place. There is little special to see apart from the **State Museum** (10am–1.30pm and 2–5pm, closed Monday), but you can easily spend a couple of days here. Women travellers like Simla as it is so hassle-free. The main streets are closed to traffic, and a promenade is still the favourite pastime, though you can always amuse yourself with a game of snooker (ask directions to the snooker hall) or by browsing in the second-hand bookshops on The Mall.

Information. Tourist Office at junction of Mall and Ridge.

Arrival and departure. Train from Delhi (15½hrs) or Chandigarh (9hrs) with a change at Kalka to narrow gauge line. The rail motor service is more expensive (unless you have an Indrail Pass) than first class on a regular train, but worth it for the all-round visibility. Tourist and regular buses from Delhi, Chandigarh, Kullu, Manali, etc.

Accommodation (STD Code 0177)
Hotel Dreamland, The Mall. Tel 77377. SWB/DWB Rs250 (around £5/$8.35).
Hotel Dalziel, The Mall. Tel 2691. SWB/DWB Rs200–300 (less 30–40% off season). Modern baths and geezers, it says on the card.
Hotel Snow View, Jakhu. Tel 3244. SWB/DWB Rs150–250 (less 25–35% off season).
Several more hotels, also the *YMCA*, in the same price bracket past the Dreamland and above Christ Church. Accommodation, if you can find it, is very expensive from May to September.

Eating and drinking
Ashiana, The Ridge. Mod/Exp. Bar. Comfortable, good food, and a great place to watch the (very colourful) world go by.
Alfa, The Mall. Mod. Ind/Chi/Cont. Large portions of good food, well served. Some unusual dishes. Highly recommended.
Cheaper restaurants in the lower bazaar.

DAYS OUT FROM SIMLA

Between Dehra Dun and Simla is **Renuka Lake**, which looks really beautiful. The spectacular **Bhimkali Temple** at Sarahan nearby once claimed human sacrifices, and between the two there is a 'Fossil Park'. Still in the Simla area **Manau** and **Hotkoti** have unusual temples.

NORTHERN UTTAR PRADESH

Uttarakhand is the mountainous part of Uttar Pradesh between Himachal Pradesh and Nepal. Many rivers have their sources here, and this has long made it a target for pilgrims. An unfortunate side-effect of this is that tourist facilities are primitive or non-existent — pilgrims will put up with any discomfort. The temples are interesting and the scenery grand, but you will not enjoy Uttarakhand unless you are prepared to rough it. Accommodation is hard to find, non-vegetarian food more so, and alcohol unobtainable. Stock up in Haridwar or Rishikesh if you plan to trek or camp; the bazaars thereafter are very limited. All the temples are at high altitude and open only from the beginning of May to mid-October.

HARIDWAR

Haridwar, known by various other names in the past, is one of the oldest pilgrimage towns in India as it marks the place where the Ganges leaves the mountains for the plains. It attracts many holy men and pilgrims, and the huge Kumbh Mela festival is held here every twelve years. The **bathing ghats**, especially Hari-ki-Pauri with its footprint of Vishnu and clock tower, are very popular. Safety chains hang under the

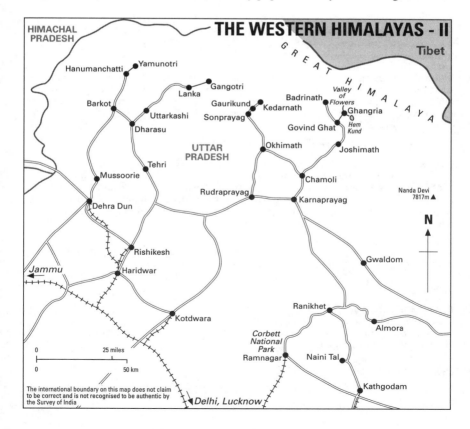

footbridge at Hari-ki-Pauri to protect bathers from the current. Indeed it is hard to relate the clean, cold, fast-flowing stream here to the turbid flood at Varanasi. A broad esplanade along the river has many open air restaurants and tea stalls as well as temples.

Pilgrims traditionally visit the hilltop **Mansa Devi Temple**, which overlooks the town. A new cablecar helps the weight-disadvantaged. The nearby **Beauty Point** gives an even better view.

A nice place Haridwar, in the cool weather anyway, but photography is actively discouraged in most areas.

Information. For tourist office turn left out of station, about 750m.

Arrival and departure. Railway from Delhi (5¼hrs), Varanasi (18hrs), Lucknow (10hrs), Rishikesh (1hr). The bus-stand is adjacent to the railway station, though most services into the mountains leave from Rishikesh.

Accommodation (STD Code 0133)
Tourist Bungalow, Belwala (1.5km from station). Tel 426 379. SWB Rs175 (£3.50/$5.80) DWB Rs200 Dorm Rs40 (80p/$1.30). Rest. Quiet riverside location away from town.

Many other cheaper hotels in Station Road near station and bus-stand.

RISHIKESH

Rishikesh, which means the abode of the saint, is the gateway to the great river source pilgrimages of the Himalayas. Sages would often winter here before starting their arduous journeys in the spring. The many yoga and meditation ashrams are a natural result of this, and Rishikesh is popular with both Indian and Western seekers after truth. The headquarters of the Divine Life Society is here, as is the ashram of Maharishi Mahesh Yogi (formerly the Beatles' guru), though this used at one time not to accept foreigners. Many of the ashrams and an extraordinarily ugly 13-storey temple are on the other side of the river from town and connected to it by the fine **Laxmanjhoola suspension bridge**. Otherwise Rishikesh is simply the base for exploring Uttarakhand.

Information. Tourist office on Railway Station Road.

Arrival and departure. Train or bus from Haridwar (1hr). Buses for Uttarakhand do not leave from the bus-stand, you must find the ticket office of the Tehri Garhwal Motor Owners Union near the bridge between Rishikesh proper and Muni-Ki-Reti (the area around the Tourist Bungalow). Another bus company is based in a side-street nearby. Always book in advance and check before travelling whether a cholera jab is required.

Accommodation (STD Code 01364)
Inderlok Hotel, Railway Road. Tel 30555. SWB Rs300 (£6/$10) DWB Rs400 SWB A/C Rs400 DWB A/C Rs600. Rest. The best in town.
Tourist Bungalow, Muni-Ki-Reti. Tel 30373. SWB/DWB Rs150/290. Rest. Quiet location.

Eating and drinking
Indrani, Inderlok Hotel. Ind/Chi/Cont. Mod/Exp.
Numerous lodges and dharamsalas. Total prohibition on alcohol and non-vegetarian food in Rishikesh.

JOSHIMATH

Joshimath is an overnight stay on the way from Rishikesh to Badrinath and the Valley of Flowers. A pleasant little town with a useful bazaar.

Arrival and departure. Joshimath is 10½hrs from Rishikesh by bus. Buses on to Govind Ghat, Badrinath and Auli.

Accommodation. *Tourist Rest House* (Tel 01389 2118) with dorm, *Public Works Department Bungalow*, and hotels.

AULI

Auli is India's best equipped ski resort with some good long runs. The season is January to March with a festival over the first weekend in March. Courses are run, and equipment can be hired.

Arrival and departure. Bus from Joshimath (8km).

Accommodation. *Tourist Rest House* (Tel 013712 2236) or in Joshimath.

GOVIND GHAT

Govind Ghat (1828m), on the Joshimath–Badrinath road, is the base for the walk to Ghangria from where you can explore Hem Kund and the Valley of Flowers.

Arrival and departure. Bus to Govind Ghat from Joshimath or Badrinath.

Accommodation
   Gurudwara. Free accommodation (on the floor) and (also free) huge helpings of first-class vegetarian food. Make a donation.

GHANGRIA

Ghangria is a small settlement and bazaar at 3048m that forms the base for treks to the Valley of Flowers and Hem Kund.

Arrival and departure. From Govind Ghat walk or take a pony (porters are also available) 15km/9.5 miles to Ghangria. Tea shops on the way.

Accommodation.
   Tourist Rest House. DR Rs80 DWB Rs165. Also a *Forest Bungalow* and the *gurudwara*.

Eating and drinking. Tea shops serve basic food, and limited stores are available.

HEM KUND

The Sikhs, as a rule, do not believe in pilgrimages to lakes and rivers. The lake of **Hem Kund** at 4330m, however, has been associated with the tenth Guru, Govind Singh. A new gurudwara on the lakeside marks where Govind Singh meditated in an earlier life, surrounded by seven snowy peaks. Building the gurudwara took many years because the season is so short and all the materials had to be manhandled up there. Enter into the spirit of things with a holy dip in the lake. Considerately, they break the ice for you, and hot, sweet tea (free) afterwards aids recovery.

Arrival and departure. Hem Kund is a 5km walk (and a climb of 1300m) from Ghangria. You will see portly Sikh women being carried up in chairs on the backs of porters.

THE VALLEY OF FLOWERS

From the hamlet of Ghangria you can walk the 4km to the start of the beautiful 10km-long **Valley of Flowers**. The best time to visit is July and August when the famous alpine blooms are at their best, though this is also the wet season. Access to the valley has been limited at times for ecological reasons.

Accommodation. None. Camping is banned in the valley to protect the fragile ecology, so you must return to Ghangria overnight.

BADRINATH

The story goes that Vishnu was in his favourite pose reclining on the sea-serpent Shesha having his feet massaged by Laxmi when a holy man came along and suggested he was going soft. Deeply hurt he sent Laxmi off and headed for the hills. There he found a place where badri, or wild berries, abounded, and he meditated for several years, sustained by the fruit. When Laxmi eventually tracked him down she addressed him as Badrinath, Lord of the Berries.

The confluence of the Rishi Ganga and Alakhnanda rivers is another reason for Badrinath's sanctity. The pretty, brightly painted **temple** stands near this and a hot spring. In the time of Ashoka the temple became a Buddhist shrine (it still looks like one) and was not restored to Hinduism until a thousand years later. The similarity of the image in this temple to a Buddha is explained by the belief that Buddha was the ninth avatar, or incarnation of Vishnu on earth. The temple is open from May to mid-November.

Visible beyond Badrinath is the snow-capped peak of Nilkanth (6596m), literally 'blue throat', one of the forms of Shiva. It may be possible to walk to Vasudhara Falls (122m high) and Satopanth Lake (25km away), though going anywhere beyond Badrinath is tricky because of the closeness of the border with Tibet.

Arrival and departure. Bus from Joshimath (2½hrs).

Accommodation

Hotel Deolok. Tel Chamoli 12. DR Rs70 DWB Rs140. A fair selection of other hotels.

BADRINATH TO KEDARNATH

Kedarnath is only 40km from Badrinath as the lammergeier flies but separated from it by the great Himalayas range, so there is no short trekking or pilgrim route. The normal bus route via Karnaprayag and Rudraprayag is 243km. It may be possible to get a truck from Chamoli to Okhimath, which is a huge short cut and possibly more interesting. This route is certainly much hillier and has better views than the main road, which follows the river valleys. This section (about 42km) should also make a good walk; it is a pilgrim route so there is accommodation (including PWD Bungalows at Mandal and Dogalbitta) and food along the way.

A lammergeier, incidentally, is a bearded vulture, the only attractive member of this rather repulsive family. They are carrion eaters and famous for their trick of breaking bones by carrying them to a great height and then dropping them onto rocks so they can get at the marrow inside. The author watched one of these huge birds (up to 3m/10ft wingspan) in Kashmir for half an hour as he searched the hillsides for food, and he did not beat his wings once, relying entirely on thermals and updraughts.

KEDARNATH

Set at over 3500m/11,480ft and surrounded by snow-capped mountains is the **Temple of Sri Kedarnath**, once a place of refuge for Shiva. The Mahabharata relates how, after killing their kinsmen, the Pandavas set out for Varanasi to seek absolution from

Shiva. Unwilling to do this Shiva fled to Uttarakhand and, when the Pandavas followed him, changed into a bull. Detected by the giant Bhim Shiva sank into the ground, but not quickly enough. Bhim grasped his hump, and Shiva, impressed by their tenacity, forgave the brothers their sins and instructed them to venerate his hump.

The **temple** is said to have been built by the Pandavas, but is in the order of 800 or 1000 years old. The structure is of large slabs of carefully trimmed stone, quite an achievement at this altitude. The form is unlike most Hindu temples and has quite a Greek classical look. In the inner hall is a conical rock shaped like a bull's hump and worshipped as an emblem of Shiva. The temple is one of the twelve jyotirlingas, most sacred Shiva shrines.

Visible from Kedarnath are the 400m/1300ft-high Mandakini Falls. Shankaracharya, the eighth-century sage credited with restoring India to Hinduism after the Buddhist period, finished his mission in Kedarnath. His memorial can be seen, and also the Mahapanth where pilgrims would take a short cut to eternity by jumping off. Basukital is a pretty little lake 5km from Kedarnath.

Arrival and departure. Bus to Sonprayag from Rishikesh or Joshimath (via Rudraprayag), bus or jeep from Sonprayag to Gaurikund (you could also walk the 7km), and then walk 13km (climbing 1600m) to Kedarnath.

Accommodation
Tourist Rest House, DR Rs70 Dorm Rs35. Otherwise very difficult. There is some government-owned accommodation on the path into the village and also behind the temple, but you will probably end up on someone's floor.

GANGOTRI

The Ganges is the holiest river in India, and its source is thus an important place of pilgrimage. The village of Gangotri is 3140m high and surrounded by giant deodars. The temple of the Goddess Ganga was built in the early 19th century by the Gurkha general Amar Singh Thapa, when Nepal still ruled this area. The actual source is reckoned to be at Gaumukh (Cow's mouth), an ice cave at the foot of the Gangotri Glacier. This is 1100m and a 14km walk above Gangotri village.

Arrival and departure. Bus from Rishikesh (12hrs), from Badrinath and Kedarnath change in Rudraprayag.

Accommodation
Tourist Rest House. DR Rs70 DWB Rs140 Dorm Rs35.

YAMUNOTRI

Yamunotri, the source of the Yamuna (Delhi's river), is held to be a frozen lake at 4421m. Access to this is difficult, so the temple is a little lower down. The temple is built right under a rugged cliff at the head of a long flight of steps. Pilgrims cook their food in hot springs and offer it to the goddess before eating it themselves.

Arrival and departure. Bus from Rishikesh (10hrs); buses take several different routes, the one via Dehra Dun and Mussoorie is most attractive, and you could break the journey in Mussoorie. Bus to Gangotri (9hrs). Buses terminate at Hanumanchatti, and you walk the remaining 11km to Yamunotri.

Accommodation. *Tourist Rest House* at Jankichatti, halfway between Hanumanchatti and Yamunotri. *Dharamsalas* at Yamunotri.

NAINI TAL

At an altitude of 1938m Naini Tal is the leading hill station in eastern Uttarakhand. Its two bazaars are at opposite ends of the lake, which is its main asset and is famous for sailing. The highest hill above the town is **Naina Peak** (otherwise Chaina Peak, 2611m). This is a pleasant walk from Talli Tal Bazaar via Snow View (2270m), or you can take the **cable car** direct from The Mall to Snow View. Good views of the Himalayas on a clear day, but not the sort of exciting ridge walk you might expect from below.

Actually the best thing about Naini Tal is the **Boat House Club**, whose rambling premises on the lake shore enshrine Raj nostalgia and a cosy bar. Yachts are available, and membership costs Rs200 for three days or Rs300 for a week, a bargain. We are told that winds on the lake are tricky; shouldn't disturb anyone used to Windermere in the English Lake District, which, in a grander way, Naini Tal rather resembles.

Though of obvious interest to sailing enthusiasts Naini Tal is probably too busy and expensive to appeal to many other travellers.

Arrival and departure. Train from Lucknow (11hrs) to Haldwani; there is apparently a direct train from Delhi, but it is not in the author's timetable. Kathgodam is a bit closer to Naini Tal, but bus connections from Haldwani are better. A taxi from Kathgodam costs about Rs100; taking this route watch out for roadside strawberry sellers. Bus to Delhi (6hrs). Bus to Karnaprayag *en route* for Badrinath and Kedarnath.

Accommodation (STD Code 05942)

Hotel Evelyn, The Mall. Tel 2457. SWB/DWB Rs175–350 (£3.50–7/$5.80–11.60). Off-season prices. We were so annoyed at being charged extra for blankets that we forgot to check high-season prices.

Hotel Everest, The Mall. Tel 2453. SWB/DWB Rs100–750 (Rs100–400 off season). Clean and modern. Three beds in each room for the price of two.

Hotel Elphinstone, The Mall. Tel 2534. SWB Rs200 (Rs80 off season) DWB Rs400 (Rs250 off season). Rest (Ind/Cont). Bay windows in all rooms.

Asoka Hotel and Savoy Hotel, Tallital (near PO). Tel 2180/2721. SR Rs50 DR Rs60 SWB Rs80/100 DWB Rs150. Rest. Rooms a bit dim but clean. Convenient for busstand.

Tourist Reception Centre, Sukhatal. Tel 2374. DWB Rs150 (Rs75 off season) Dorm Rs20 (Rs10 off season). Rest. Quite a way out of town but quiet.

Youth Hostel, Sukhatal. Tel 2353. Dorm Rs12/22, also some double rooms. Near and similar to Tourist Reception Centre.

Eating and drinking

Unusually for a hill station the restaurants in Naini Tal are pretty poor, and too often expensive as well. The small places in Mallital are better value than those on The Mall. *Negi* does good kebabs. Best is a man in the bazaar on the far side of The Flats who does excellent noodles for a few rupees.

Naini Tal Boat House Club, The Mall. Rest. Bar. The real reason for coming to Naini Tal. Delightful, relaxed, old-fashioned bar-lounge, or you can enjoy your drink on the terrace beside the lake. Sailing. Billiards. Table tennis. Membership Rs205 (around £4/$6.80) for three days or Rs305 for seven days for a couple. Children are not allowed in bar or lounge. Apparently no specific dress code, but you should keep the flag flying, don't y'know?

Near Naini Tal

To the east near Naini Tal are **Almora** and **Ranikhet**, two more hill stations. In this area are many lakes good for fishing and bird-watching, and also a lot of smaller resorts. Bus operators in Naini Tal run tours visiting some of these places.

On the fringe of Uttarakhand is **Corbett National Park**, named after one of the most famous hunters of man-eating tigers. Despite this reputation he was a great conservationist who limited his shooting to absolute necessity.

The Northern Plains

Taj Mahal, Agra

Punjab and Haryana — Southern Uttar Pradesh — Bihar — West Bengal

The northern plains, comprising the states Punjab, Haryana, Uttar Pradesh, Bihar and West Bengal, sweep across India from Pakistan to Bangladesh, bordered on the north by the Himalayas and to the south by the hills of Madhya Pradesh leading to the Deccan. The area is, in effect, the Ganges basin, and this rich farmland, sometimes called India's granary, supports 40% of the population on only one-fifth of the land area. Nearly half of India's 600,000 or so villages are found here. Except for southern Bihar the whole area is as flat as a pancake; the Yamuna (in union with the Ganges) travels 1600km from Delhi to the Bay of Bengal falling only 200m on the way. This is nevertheless a beautiful landscape (except in the hot weather anyway), very green and with plenty of trees. It may seem to change little as you look out of the train window, but there is always something new to see.

Socially, the central part of this area, Haryana, Uttar Pradesh, Bihar and part of Madhya Pradesh, constitutes the 'Hindi Heartland' of India, sometimes called the cow belt.

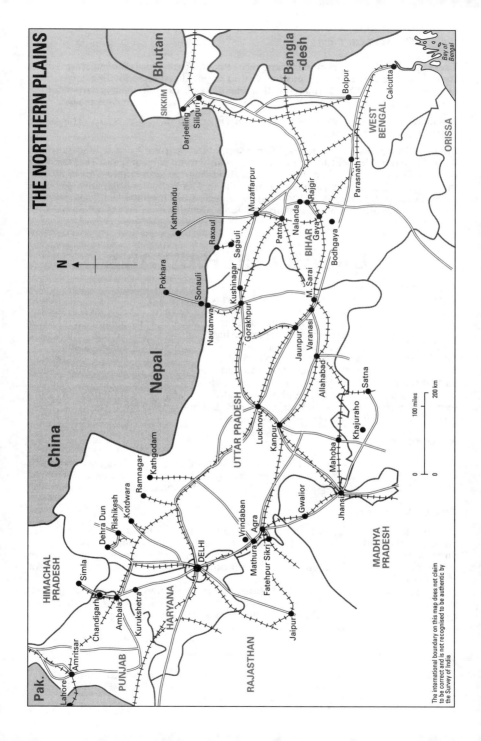

THE NORTHERN PLAINS

The international boundary on this map does not claim to be correct and is not recognised to be authentic by the Survey of India

Language. Hindi is the dominant language. Punjabi is not far removed from Hindi. Before Independence it was mostly written in the Persian script like Urdu; now Gurmukhi, a script like Devanagri with a line on top, is used. Bengali is harder for the Hindi speaker to understand; it has its own script like an angular Devanagri.

Handicrafts. The two notable places are Agra for inlaid stone boxes and Varanasi for spectacular silks, especially brocades.

Climate. The climate is extreme. Inland temperatures from April to mid-June are 40–45°C, and in May and June you can expect little relief even at night. The best time is November to March when the sky is clear and daytime temperatures around 20°C, though they fall almost to freezing at night in December and January. Even in Calcutta temperatures below 10°C can be expected in December and January. The monsoon generally reaches Delhi around June 20 and lasts nearly three months.

PUNJAB AND HARYANA

The Punjab has been much reduced in size of late. In 1947 The Indo-Pakistan border was drawn through it, and in 1966 it lost half its remaining territory to form the Hindi-speaking state of Haryana, and more to Himachal Pradesh. This has meant that the Sikhs are now in a majority in the state, and the results are pretty obvious. It is visibly the most productive and prosperous part of India, and you will see more tractors in rural Punjab than in all the rest of the country. The name Punjab means 'Land of the Five Rivers' but only two of these, the Sutlej and Beas, greatly affect the present Punjab. The Chenab and Jhelum flow through Pakistan, and the Ravi forms a short part of the border between the Indian and Pakistani Punjabs.

Basically one of the smaller and poorer states Haryana has benefited greatly from recent irrigation and hydro-electric schemes. Despite producing a surplus of food grains it is still better known for stock raising.

AMRITSAR

Amritsar, the centre of the Sikh religion, was founded in 1577 by Ram Das, the fourth of the ten Sikh gurus. The site was donated by Akbar and centred on a holy tank; *amrit* is the nectar of the gods, and *sar* or *sarovar* is a tank or lake.

The Golden Temple

Around the tank has grown up the Sikhs' holiest shrine, the Darbar Sahib, better known as the **Golden Temple***. The bridge between Hinduism and Islam which Sikhism set out to create is symbolised by the foundation stone, laid by a Sufi (Muslim) mystic, and the four gates indicating openness to all four castes of Hinduism.

The main shrine in the tank, the **Harmandir**, was built by Guru Arjun, Ram Das' successor. The white marble temple acquired its gilt copper cladding, and hence its name, in 1802 courtesy of Maharaja Ranjit Singh, the man who founded the secular Sikh state. The original of the Sikh holy book, the Granth Sahib, is kept here, and priests maintain a continuous reading from later copies of the work. The atmosphere in this delightful building belies the extraordinary bloodshed and destruction it has witnessed over the years.

The tank is surrounded by a broad Jaipur marble pavement, offices, and lodgings for visitors, mostly the different Sikh communities. The **Akal Takht** (Eternal Throne), facing the bridge to the Harmandir, was constructed by Hargobind, Guru Arjun's son and the sixth guru. Razed to the ground when the temple was desecrated by Afghans in 1761, it was rebuilt and the upper three storeys added by Ranjit Singh. This is the council hall of Sikh elders.

The essential **langar**, the communal kitchen and canteen, and the **Guru ka Bagh**, temple garden, are adjacent to the main compound.

Massacre in the Jallianwalla Bagh

Until the making of the film *Gandhi* the massacre in **Jallianwalla Bagh** had become a half-forgotten, albeit disgraceful, event. Briefly, in 1919 Indian Army troops under the command of General Dyer opened fire on a banned political meeting protesting the arrest of Mahatma Gandhi. The toll was 379 killed and more than 1200 wounded; small by the standards of other colonial powers, but quite exceptional in British India. There is little doubt that Dyer was looking for an excuse to 'teach the agitators a lesson', though anyone who has seen even a small Indian crowd start to get out of hand might wonder at the portrayal of the incident in the film. Whatever, the event was a turning point in the freedom struggle.

The troubles in Punjab

So much for ancient history; the last ten years have been just as sanguinary. Agitation for a separate Sikh state goes back to the time of independence when Sikhs realised the danger of their interests being ignored in a Hindu India. The problem simmered until 1977 when Mrs Gandhi lost the general election, and the Akali Dal (a Sikh party) took over the state government of Punjab. As part of his campaign of destabilising governments allied to the Janata, his mother's opponents in Delhi, Sanjay Gandhi promoted the cause of Jarnail Singh Bhindranwale, an itinerant fundamentalist preacher. Playing on Sikh fears of being re-absorbed into the Hindu mainstream in the same way as the Buddhists, Bhindranwale fomented violence against first nonconformist Sikhs and then Hindus in Punjab. Soon the puppet was pulling the strings, and well armed and highly motivated guerillas simply outgunned the local police. The Pakistani government denies that it or its army arms the Sikh militants (or for that matter Kashmiri separatists), but Pakistan is awash with arms as a result of the war in Afghanistan and its own unrest in Sind and Baluchistan.

At its peak the conflict caused an average of 25 deaths every day. As elsewhere, criminal elements took advantage of the breakdown in law and order, and perhaps a third of those deaths resulted from inter-gang feuding and general thuggery. The Indian Army and many paramilitary police units now more or less contain the violence. The influence of the separatists is widespread, however. At their behest all the media refer to them as militants rather than terrorists. Journalists who refused to toe the line were killed. In the last couple of years things have settled down enough for elections to be held, so hopefully Punjab will gradually return to normality.

Despite all this Amritsar remains a friendly and hassle-free place. Nevertheless, one does feel that over the centuries it has seen more than its share of bloodshed, and the graphic illustrations in the Golden Temple give the impression of revelling in it.

Nearby

Tarn Taran is 24km south of Amritsar. The gurudwara here, beside a beautiful tank, is older than the Golden Temple. Lepers may be cured by swimming across the tank.

Information. Tourist office opposite railway station. *Amritsar: Mrs Gandhi's Last Battle* by Mark Tully and Satish Jacob (Cape) provides the best background to the Punjab problem.

Arrival and departure. Airport, internal flights and also from Kabul by Ariana. Indian Airlines (Tel 225 321) office on The Mall.

By rail from Lahore in Pakistan (3½hrs), Delhi (10½hrs, only 8hrs by Paschim A/C Express but no 2nd class), Jammu (5¼hrs), change in Pathankot. Also a line to Tarn Taran.

Accommodation. Cheap hotels in the area opposite the station. For something better try Hotel Airlines (Tel 0183 64848) in the same area. After many years of refusing to take Westerners the Golden Temple is again providing free accommodation. The rules are simple: no smoking, no drinking, no drugs, no display of affection whatsoever. Break the rules and we'll be banned again. You *must* make a fair donation.

Eating and drinking. *Kwality* on Mall Road. Free meals in the Golden Temple, but again you must make a donation.

SOUTHERN UTTAR PRADESH

Uttar Pradesh is by far the most populous state (139 million) despite being smaller than Madhya Pradesh, Rajasthan, or Maharashtra. Less than 5% of the population works in factories, and the farmland is extensively irrigated — over 12,000km of canals and 300,000 pumped tubewells. As in most of the area the land produces two crops a year, rabi (which means spring harvest and comprises mostly wheat and peas) before the monsoon, and kharif (the autumn harvest of rice and maize) after it. Sugar cane is an important cash crop.

MATHURA

Mathura (Muttra) is a place of religious associations. One of the Jain tirthankas was born here, Buddha visited, and subsequently there were many Buddhist monasteries.

Mainly, however, it is known as the **birthplace of Krishna**. The eighth incarnation of Vishnu is in many ways the most popular of all Hindu deities, not least for his earthy sense of humour and identification with rural folk. Although a prince Krishna was born in captivity, and the cell (open all day) is preserved. Two florid modern temples (open 6–10am and 4.30–8pm) also stand here. The original Katra Keshav Deo temple was demolished by Firozshah Tughlaq (14th century), and again by Sikander Lodi (15th–16th century). Jehangir allowed the Maharaja of Orchha to rebuild it, only for it to be finally destroyed in the time of Aurangzeb. The site of the original temple, behind the present temple compound, is occupied by the triple-domed **Idgah Mosque** built by one of Aurangzeb's governors. Now that the fundamentalists have got their way at Ayodhya this is likely to be the next target.

The holiest place in Mathura is the **bathing ghats**. The square tower by the river commemorates the sati of a Jaipur maharaja's wife.

Mathura was the centre of a school of sculpture. In the **Museum of Archaeology** (closed Monday) you can trace the development from Indo-Hellenic to a purely Indian style. Some of the early statues would pass as Greek. For all this Mathura is just one more sprawling, dusty, noisy Indian town.

Information. Tourist office at bus-stand.

Arrival and departure. On New Delhi (2hrs)–Bombay CT (22hrs) line, also Agra (1hr). Metre gauge line to Lucknow (11hrs). Buses from Delhi or Agra.

Accommodation. The *International Guest House* near the Krishna temple is cheap and good. Overlooking the river is *Hotel Agra*, DWB around Rs200 (around £4/$6.50).

VRINDABAN

Like nearby Mathura, Vrindaban is associated with Krishna for it was here that he stole the Gopis' (milkmaids) clothes while they bathed, an event depicted in paintings, reliefs, and murals all over India.

As you walk into town from the bus-stand a large red sandstone temple, the **Govind Dev****, stands on the left. From the outside you would never mistake this for anything other than a Hindu temple, but inside the cruciform plan and vaulted roof (most unusual) are more like a church. The lotus motif in the centre is carved from a single stone and once had a diamond pendant. Beside the door of the present shrine is a relief showing Krishna lifting the mountain at nearby Goverdhan to shelter villagers from the rain. At the bottom of the left doorpost is Krishna with Radha, and above that scenes from his life. The temple used to be much taller than now, the upper levels and tower having been demolished in the time of Aurangzeb, and you can still get a splendid view from the roof if you can find the man with the key. Around the back you can see where the original shrine (demolished when the other damage was done) has been replaced by a four-pillared pavilion.

The **Rangji Temple** opposite is an insipid 19th century copy of a south Indian temple. Like most temples in the south it is closed to foreigners; the view from the Rajput-style gateway suffices. Some odd animated puppets perform here, and in a shed outside is a Krishna chariot with horses straight from a fairground roundabout.

Round the back of the Rangji is the **Glass Temple** with thousands of little convex mirrors, very pretty. Of a modern design the marble temple of **Shah Behari** is also worth seeing. There are dozens more temples (most closed 11am–5pm) and many fine secular buildings, some of the latter hospices where Hindu widows gain shelter in return for singing the praises of Krishna.

The **ghats** are of little interest; the river has retreated, and the buildings are dilapidated.

Vrindaban is a nice, quiet place to wander around, and there always seems to be something interesting going on. On our last visit we saw a naked saddhu riding pillion on a policeman's Enfield; was he being arrested or just getting a lift? Not far away a sari-clad woman rode a motorcycle on a wall of death.

Arrival and departure. Bus or tempo from Mathura. On Mathura–Lucknow metre gauge railway line.

Accommodation. ISKCON, the International Centre for Krishna Consciousness, is based in Vrindaban and their guest house (Tel 0565 442 478) is the best place to stay. The restaurant is said to produce the best chips in India.

AGRA

Agra is, of course, the City of the Taj Mahal, and because of this the many other superb monuments tend to be rushed, if not overlooked altogether. The Red Fort, for instance, is more interesting and its palace buildings better preserved and more attractive than those in Delhi. The Taj Mahal is described last because it is the latest Mughal building in Agra, and is better not seen first. Take your time; Agra can not be seen in a day.

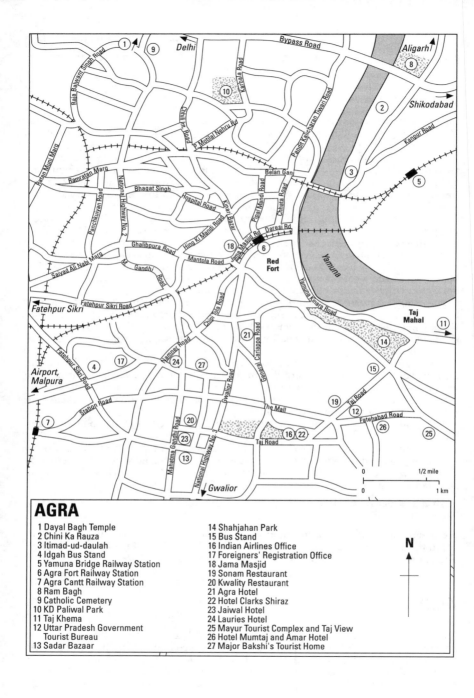

AGRA

1 Dayal Bagh Temple
2 Chini Ka Rauza
3 Itimad-ud-daulah
4 Idgah Bus Stand
5 Yamuna Bridge Railway Station
6 Agra Fort Railway Station
7 Agra Cantt Railway Station
8 Ram Bagh
9 Catholic Cemetery
10 KD Paliwal Park
11 Taj Khema
12 Uttar Pradesh Government
   Tourist Bureau
13 Sadar Bazaar

14 Shahjahan Park
15 Bus Stand
16 Indian Airlines Office
17 Foreigners' Registration Office
18 Jama Masjid
19 Sonam Restaurant
20 Kwality Restaurant
21 Agra Hotel
22 Hotel Clarks Shiraz
23 Jaiwal Hotel
24 Lauries Hotel
25 Mayur Tourist Complex and Taj View
26 Hotel Mumtaj and Amar Hotel
27 Major Bakshi's Tourist Home

N

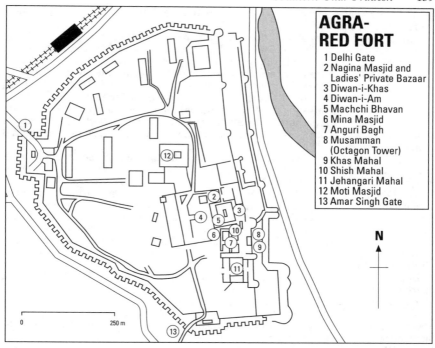

**AGRA-
RED FORT**
1 Delhi Gate
2 Nagina Masjid and
  Ladies' Private Bazaar
3 Diwan-i-Khas
4 Diwan-i-Am
5 Machchi Bhavan
6 Mina Masjid
7 Anguri Bagh
8 Musamman
  (Octagon Tower)
9 Khas Mahal
10 Shish Mahal
11 Jehangari Mahal
12 Moti Masjid
13 Amar Singh Gate

N

History

Agra is a town of ancient foundation, its first significance probably being as a border town when Aryan expansion was still limited by the River Yamuna. As such it would have been an important market, a tradition it has maintained ever since.

The Rajputs are known to have had a fort here, but Agra's documented history starts in 1504 when Sikander Lodi moved his capital from Delhi. However the Mughals in the form of Babur took it in 1526 so Agra can be said to be a Mughal city, for long periods the capital of their empire.

The city's decline began in 1658 when Aurangzeb, after locking up his father Shahjahan in the Red Fort, left for his campaigns in the Deccan. His successors ruled a contracting and impoverished empire from Delhi. Agra was captured in 1761 by the Jats of Bharatpur who were forced out by the Marathas of Gwalior in 1764. The Mughals recaptured it in 1773, and the Marathas staged a comeback in 1785. Every time the place was looted and further damaged. Finally in 1803 the British took Agra for its strategic position; from there they could keep an eye on the Mughals whom they still allowed to rule over Delhi, the Jats in Bharatpur, and the various Maratha powers based on Pune, Gwalior, and Indore. The fort was besieged in a half-hearted fashion during the Mutiny, but since then Agra has peaceably carried on what it does best, trading and making money.

The Red Fort

The **Red Fort***** was built by Akbar over the ten years from 1564 on the site of the earlier Rajput and Lodi structures. The fort and palaces symbolised

Akbar's consolidation of Mughal power in India; until then he had had no base worthy of an emperor.

The entrance is through the **Amar Singh Gate**, the outer defence wall and gate probably added by Shahjahan. The walls bear the marks of English cannonballs, and the drawbridge mechanism is still in place.

In Mughal times the public entrance was through the Delhi Gate on the west of the fort. From there one passed through a bazaar like that in the Delhi Red Fort, coming out at the Diwan-i-Am. To see things in the right order walk straight ahead as far as you can go. The **Moti Masjid** (Pearl Mosque) was built by Shahjahan after completion of the Taj Mahal and is reputed to be the largest mosque in the world lined totally in white marble. For a variety of reasons you are unlikely to see any more than the red sandstone exterior.

On the left as you leave the Moti Masjid is the **purdah bazaar** where women merchants could sell to the ladies of the court. This is overlooked by the empress' marble balcony and the Nagina Masjid.

The **Diwan-i-Am**, of red sandstone covered with chunam, dates from the reign of Shahjahan. His throne was set in the inlaid alcove, flanked by jali screens for the ladies, and his vizier occupied the marble dais in front. A silver rail marked out the space for high-ranking officials. Unlike the Delhi Red Fort the square in front of the Diwan-i-Am is more or less intact. JR Colvin, whose tomb stands in front of the Diwan-i-Am, was governor of the province and died while the fort was under siege during the Mutiny.

Behind the Diwan-i-Am is the **Machchi Bhavan** (Fish Palace). The Jats took the marble tanks and waterways in which goldfish swam. In one corner is the triple-domed **Nagina Masjid**, the ladies' mosque. Akbar brought the large **gates** between this garden and the purdah bazaar as a trophy from Chittaurgarh. The black marble **throne** on the terrace belonged to Prince Salim, later Jehangir; the crack is said to have been caused by a Jat sitting on it.

The **Diwan-i-Khas** is again the work of Shahjahan, built in 1637. This white marble pavilion with early inlay work was the emperor's meeting place with ministers and foreign ambassadors. The round hole in one of the arches was caused by a cannonball. Behind here is the **Mina Masjid**, probably the smallest mosque in the world, having space for only 18 worshippers, and probably closed as well.

Steps lead down to the private palace. The **Musamman** (Octagon), the name having been corrupted as Saman Burj (Prisoner's Tower) and Yasmin Burj (Jasmine Tower), was built around 1620 for Nur Jahan and later used by her niece Mumtaz Mahal. This delightful, though rather battered, suite of rooms later became Shahjahan's prison and was where he died in 1666. The **Khas Mahal** was a private palace divided from the rest of the zenana by a marble partition. The central pavilion (which may have been the pattern for the Diwan-i-Khas in Delhi's Red Fort) was a reception room where the emperor could meet his daughters and the other women of the court. A small section of the ceiling was restored a hundred years ago. The two gold-roofed pavilions are popularly believed to have been the homes of Jahanara and Roshanara, Shahjahan's two daughters. Niches in the wall were for the ladies' jewellery, the access too small for a man's hand.

In front of the Khas Mahal the **Anguri Bagh** (Grape Garden) had stone pergolas for vines. The **Shish Mahal** (Mirror Palace) was a beautifully inlaid Turkish bath, and other underground rooms provided a cool retreat from Agra's searing summer heat. Shahjahan's private apartments are nearby, but the murals have been destroyed and they are of little interest. Return to the main path and walk round to the front of the Jehangiri Mahal.

Despite its name the **Jehangari Mahal** was probably built by Akbar. It is interesting in that its design predates the development of a purely Mughal style. The entrance is angled to slow down any assault and leads into a large courtyard. Note the elaborate stone cutting, especially the chajja brackets. The roof of the hall on the left is supported by serpent-shaped beams, and some of the wall painting survives in the room straight ahead. The huge **stone basin** on the lawn in front was apparently a wedding present from Jehangir to Nur Jahan; what she was supposed to do with it is anyone's guess.

All that remains of the **Akbari Mahal**, further south, are some rooms along the wall of the fort. The rest of the palace surrounded a large central courtyard, but now there are only low hedges to indicate the walls. Near here are some of the magazines and ammunition hoists installed by the British. A long gun ramp leads from here up onto the ramparts which students of military architecture will find very interesting.

Few visitors pay much attention to the exterior of the Red Fort, which is a shame, especially as it set the pattern for its successor in Delhi in having a facing of dressed stone on its exterior walls. Flanking the River Yamuna is an outer defence wall, and a moat completed the defences on the other three sides. The gardens around are pleasant, and the gate defences repay some study. This was a much more serious fort than the Delhi one. Follow the wall up to the Delhi Gate, where military buffs will find a tiny piece of history, and on to the Jama Masjid.

The old town

The **Jama Masjid*** faces the Delhi Gate and was built by Shahjahan in the name of his daughter Jahanara. The inscription on the central arch recounts that construction of Agra's main mosque began in 1644, the same year as its counterpart in Delhi. This is a more modest design, but still very pleasing. The three domes are of red sandstone having a herringbone inlay of white marble. The cloisters on either side have rows of domed kiosks on top and are still used as a madrasa. The mimbar (pulpit) has a picture of the front elevation of the building. The floor is mostly in a chequered design of red and yellow sandstone to denote the prayer spaces. The two side chambers were for ladies, that on the right having an inlaid marble floor. Whitewash is splashed all over the space supposedly used by Jahanara. The Jama Masjid was meant to be seen from further away than is now possible, the view blocked by the railway and other new buildings.

A trip over the Yamuna

The best way of crossing the river is the combined road/rail Strachey Bridge. Note the steel gates with loopholes. Alternatively the walkway of the rail bridge to the south gives the best views of the fort.

The **Tomb of Itimad-ud-Daulah*****, called The Baby Taj by rickshaw-wallahs, represents an important step in the development of the Taj Mahal. It was the first tomb completely covered with marble having extensive inlay. The tomb is that of Mirza Ghiyas Beg and his wife. He was the father of Mehr-un-Nissa who married Prince Salim (later Jehangir) and became known as Nur Jahan (Light of the World). As emperor Jehangir spent most of his reign in an alcohol and opium-induced haze. Nur Jahan took over the affairs of state aided by her father who, as the effective prime minister, became known as the Itimad-ud-Daulah, or Confidence of the State. After his death in 1622 Nur Jahan built this tomb for him and her mother. An old legend relates that the queen intended to build it entirely of silver. Jehangir's tomb near Lahore (now in Pakistan), also built by Nur Jahan, is essentially the same design.

The decoration is commonly referred to as inlay, but in fact there are two quite different kinds of work. The hexagonal and other geometrical patterns represent traditional Indian and Persian work, more akin to mosaic. Smaller sections show the beginnings of the floral designs that reached fruition on the Taj Mahal. The inspiration for this may have come from Italy where it is known as pietra dura. The two tombstones on the lower level are similar in size and design, which is unusual.

The roof pavilion is built entirely of marble with all inlaid decoration. The floor of this pavilion is quite different from those on the lower levels, being in a free-flowing naturalistic form. Although this tomb is mainly Saracenic in style, the roof is Bengali in shape. The brackets outside this pavilion are also Hindu in form — and richly inlaid. Much of the inlay is done in a yellow sedimentary rock from Jaisalmer in Rajasthan. Also buried within the tomb is Asaf Khan, Nur Jahan's brother and father of Mumtaz Mahal, the lady of the Taj. The tomb is set in an attractive garden, and the gatehouse is worth some attention.

The road from the Itimad-ud-Daulah north towards the new bridge passes the **Chini-ka-Rauza***, the burial place of Afzal Khan, a Persian who was a minister of Shahjahan. The name translates as China Tomb, as the enamelled exterior resembled porcelain, and enough of this remains to indicate its former splendour. Some of the painted decoration inside also remains. Outside steps lead up to a gallery, and from the roof there is access to the void between the two domes, giving a unique view of this important structural feature.

Babur records in his diary creating a garden in India, and the **Ram Bagh** was long believed to have been it. Legend further related that this was Babur's temporary resting place before his body was taken to Kabul for burial. It now seems much more likely that Babur's garden was actually located in Dholpur 56 kilometres away. The Ram Bagh may still be the oldest extant Mughal garden in India, but is in poor condition now. Since a Muslim is unlikely to have named a garden after Rama the original form was more likely Aram Bagh (Pleasure Garden).

Crossing back over the river by the new bridge you have a chance to see how the Taj Mahal was built. Slowly taking shape is the **Samadh of Soamiji Maharaj****. Soamiji Maharaj was born in 1818, started the Radhasoami Faith in 1861, and was its leading light up to his death in 1878. The foundation stone of this monument, or samadh, was laid in 1904. The design, best appreciated by seeing the model, is for an ornate domed building about 60m high. The samadh embraces many styles, both Western and Indian. Built entirely of white marble, the quality of some of the carving is amazing. The inlay work rivals any to be seen elsewhere in India.

The **Catholic Cemetery** is intriguing. Many Jesuits are interred in the Martyrs' Chapel which was originally the tomb of an Armenian merchant; also buried here is an Armenian bishop (1615). The oldest English grave is that of John Mildenhall who left London in 1599, arrived in India in 1603, and met Akbar. He was lucky in being a Catholic. The East India Company employed only Protestants, and the Jesuits, who controlled this cemetery, saw to it that such heretics were buried in unconsecrated ground. The largest tomb, a miniature Taj in red sandstone, commemorates John William Hessing, 'late a colonel in the service of Maharaja Daulat Rao Scindia'. Veroneo, a Venetian jeweller sometimes wrongly cited as architect of the Taj Mahal, lies here too.

The Taj Mahal

Edward Lear, the limerick man, wrote, 'descriptions of this wonderfully lovely place are simply silly, as no words can describe it at all.' He's right, so we'll just give you the facts and let you see for yourself.

The quiet **Shahjahan Gardens** almost link the Red Fort and the Taj Mahal, a pleasant and relaxing walk. The **conservatory** in the gardens is worth a visit, and every now and then the domes of the Taj peek enticingly through the trees. Outside the gardens is a **rose garden** and, over the road, an unusual thatched cottage. Strolling through these gardens is the perfect approach to the Taj Mahal.

History. The story of the Taj Mahal is like a Bollywood epic. Prince Khurram fell for Mumtaz Mahal, the beautiful daughter of his father Jehangir's prime minister. He was made by his father to marry a Persian princess for reasons of state, but bided his time. Five years passed before he could marry his true love. Then in 1629, only three years after Khurram's accession as the emperor Shahjahan, Mumtaz died bearing their 14th

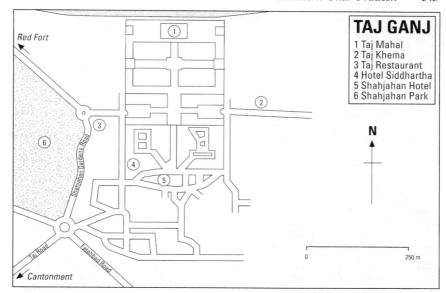

child. In his grief Shahjahan raised over her grave the most famous building in the world.

Design and building. The architect of the Taj Mahal is not known, there being no historical evidence for the various names bandied about. The inspiration presumably came from Shahjahan himself. Ustad Ahmed Lahori, who built the Red Fort in Delhi, was certainly involved and, in a project of this size, the rest was probably down to teamwork.

Looking at earlier Mughal tombs it can be seen that there are no new elements at the Taj Mahal. The general shape is very like Humayun's tomb, marble cladding appeared on the tomb of Itimad-ud-Daula, and even the minarets were tried out on the gate of Akbar's tomb. The genius lay in the way they were combined.

Construction began in 1631 and took 22 years. The sandstone came from Fatehpur Sikri, the marble from Jaipur, and semi-precious stones from a wide area. Craftsmen travelled great distances, and 20,000 people toiled to complete the tomb. And they were all paid a fair wage, no slave labour was used.

It is not easy to approach the most highly acclaimed building in the world for the first time. You need a clear mind; walking through the Shahjahan Gardens helps. Don't be like the wretched tourists who march straight up the central path to the shrine. Use the gardens to take your time, sit down if you like, and view calmly.

A teardrop on the face of time. Shahjahan's own description of the Taj Mahal is appropriate to a building that inspires awe and arouses strong emotions. The biggest surprise is the sheer size. The white marble plinth is 5.5m high, and the finial on top of the dome 70m above that. The minarets are 41m high. Inside the great height and subdued light produce a cathedral-like aura. Your chances of enjoying it in silence are slight. Despite the apparent height the dome above is only half as high as the outer one, there being a large void between the two.

As in all these tombs the occupants are buried, in accordance with Muslim law, seven feet underground. The actual graves are in a vault, once lined with gold. This has been closed in recent years for security reasons. On the higher level there is a replica of each tombstone so that no-one shall walk over the graves. The superbly inlaid marble screen round the upper tombstones replaces a gold one which Aurangzeb had to liquidate to fund his military campaigns. Mumtaz Mahal's tombstone is in the centre of the building, while Shahjahan's is offset and actually overlaps part of the floor design. This suggests that Shahjahan did not intend to have himself buried here. Old reports say that he planned a black marble counterpart for himself across the river, the two to be linked by a bridge. Alarmed at the further depletion of his inheritance Aurangzeb locked up his father in the Red Fort and, seven years later (in 1666), buried him in the Taj beside his beloved Mumtaz.

Although the detailing on the tomb is superb it is the overall effect that really counts, and it is extraordinary how such a huge building seems almost to float. The appearance varies with the light, so be prepared to make several visits. For four days either side of the full moon the Taj is open until midnight (security permitting), and this is a sight not to be missed.

To the west of the Taj Mahal is a red sandstone **mosque** for the use of the emperor and his court. Matching it on the other side of the terrace is its jawab, or mirror, whose sole function is symmetry. The Taj Mahal is meant to be seen balanced between these two buildings, impossible today because of unplanned tree growth. A small, interesting **museum** occupies the west wall pavilion.

The environs. Everyone is too excited to notice the **main gate** on the way in, so have a good look as you leave; this is a superb piece of work in its own right. Several other tombs and mosques are dotted round the Taj Mahal. The roof of the **Fatehpuri Masjid**, beside the Taj Restaurant, provides a good view. In the lane outside the east wall is another small **mosque**, perhaps older than the Taj Mahal, with a quiet garden. The urban area to the south, now known as Taj Ganj, was formerly Mumtazabad and the greatest international market in northern India.

Air pollution from an oil refinery at Mathura has in recent years been a threat to the Taj Mahal. India's fledgling environmental movement is having some success here, and the Supreme Court has amazed everybody by coming out on their side.

The best way to close this section is to quote again from Lear's *Indian Journal*: 'Henceforth, let the inhabitants of the world be divided into two classes — them as has seen the Taj Mahal; and them as hasn't.' Truly one of the wonders of the world.

Practical Information

Government of India Tourist Office at 191 The Mall. A guided tour of the Taj Mahal, the Red Fort, and Fatehpur Sikri leaves Agra Cantonment station at 10.30am (after arrival of the Taj Express); three classes of bus. Other, more comprehensive, tours start at 7.30am and pick up passengers from the station, Government of India Tourist Office, and the Tourist Bungalow in Raja-ki-Mandi.

Local transport. Agra has a good town bus service. Useful routes as follows: 7 — Agra Cantonment station to Taj Mahal; 21 — Taj Mahal–Red Fort–Mosque/Agra Fort station–Sikandra; 28 — Taj Mahal–Tomb of Itimad-ud-Daula. The rickshaw-wallahs are too used to easy pickings and can be a real pain. If they take you into shops insist on a reduction in the fare because they get an introductory fee whether you buy anything or not.

Shopping note. Agra shopkeepers and their touts are an absolute menace. Expect a hard sell in any shop you enter, and real unpleasantness if you fail to make a purchase. Beware especially of the friendly types who offer you a smoke. Except for the stone knick-knacks sold by street vendors there is nothing, repeat nothing, in Agra that you cannot buy cheaper or with less hassle in Delhi. Heard the one about the man who paid an Agra gem dealer £700 for some stones? He was given the name of a jeweller near where he lived who would, he was assured, give him a good profit on them. Needless to say this was the first the jeweller had heard about it, but he valued the stones anyway. They were worth £34.

Arrival and departure. Airport (9km from centre). Indian Airlines office (Tel 360 948) at Hotel Clarks Shiraz on Taj Road.

On Delhi (3hrs)–Bombay VT (25½hrs) line. Metre gauge line from Jaipur to Agra Fort (8½hrs) and many other connections. India's two fastest trains, the Shatabdi (1¼hrs) and Taj (2¾hrs) Expresses, run from New Delhi each morning and return in the evening.

Bus services from Idgah bus-stand to all the obvious places.

Accommodation

The STD code for Agra is 0562.

Clarks Shiraz, 5 Taj Road. Tel 361 421 Fax 361 620. SWB Rs1200 (around £24/$40) DWB Rs2400 (view of Taj and Red Fort). Rest (2). Bar. Coffee shop open till midnight. Rooftop bar and à la carte restaurant (around Rs200–250 for full meal excluding drinks), marvellous views. Swimming pool. Superb menu, especially if you can get a party together; how about a whole sheep?

Taj View, Fatehabad Road. Tel 361 171 Fax 361 179. SWB $135 (£81) DWB $145. Rest (Ind/Chi/Cont). Bar. 24-hour coffee shop. Health club and sauna. Taj views from north-facing rooms, others are cheaper.

Mayur Tourist Complex, Fatehabad Road. Tel 360 302. SWB Rs400 SWB A/C Rs500 DWB Rs550 DWB A/C Rs750. Rest. Bar. Rooms located in separate cottages in large garden. Good atmosphere and value for money.

Jaiwal Hotel, Taj Road (Sadar Bazaar). Tel 363 716. SWB A/C Rs200 DWB A/C Rs300. Rest (very good). Bar. OK, but most rooms open onto central well, so rather noisy and light.

Hotel Amar, Fatehabad Road. Tel 360 696. SWB A/C Rs700 DWB A/C Rs900. Rest (A/C). Bar. Comfortable and nicely furnished. Swimming pool.

Hotel Ratandeep, Fatehabad Road. Tel 360 027. SWB Rs350 DWB Rs500. Rest. Good middle-of-the-road place. Rooms nicer than hall and stairs might suggest.

Lauries Hotel, Mahatma Gandhi Road. Tel 364 536. SWB Rs325 DWB Rs450. Rest. Bar. Spacious rooms, reasonably quiet. Seems to have fallen on hard times, which is a shame as it has considerable charm. Swimming pool. Camping in grounds.

Major Bakshi Tourist Home, Ajmer Road (roughly behind GPO). Tel 363 716. SWB Rs150 DWB Rs250. Meals if ordered in advance. Paying-guest accommodation in the home of a very hospitable Sikh family. Take no notice of what rickshaw-wallahs say about this and Mrs Framjee's place — they get no commission at either.

Taj Khema Hotel, 100m outside Eastern Gate, Taj Mahal. Tel 360 140. SR Rs100 (£2/$3.30) SWB Rs150 DR Rs125 DWB Rs175. Rest. Bar. Open-air barbecue. Camping. Good view of Taj from large gardens. All rooms air-cooled. Little used, but very good.

Agra Hotel, General Cariappa Road. Tel 363 331. SWB Rs125 DWB Rs175 Suite A/C Rs475. Rest. Beer. Hot water. Big old house set in gardens. Reasonably quiet, near Red Fort.

Hotel Sidharth, Western Gate, Taj Mahal. Tel 264 711. SWB Rs80 DWB Rs100. Clean and comfortable. Garden.

Hotel Shahjahan, Southern Gate, Taj Mahal. SR Rs35 DR Rs45 DWB Rs80/100 Dorm Rs10 (around 20p/33 cents). Rest (usually good). Famous old hippy hang-out which has its ups and downs. Interesting people. Again, don't listen to rickshaw-wallahs.

A very popular cheap place of old, the *Jaggi* (Sadar Bazaar) has deteriorated a lot of late. It may be worth trying *Hotel Tourist*, The Mall (1km from Agra Cantonment station) or hunting around in Tajganj; *Mumtaz Mahal* is another old favourite here.

Camping and parking at the *Highway Inn*, Fatehabad, and the inconvenient *Tourist Bungalow* in Raja-ki-Mandi.

Eating and Drinking

Kwality, Sadar Bazaar. Mod/Exp. Ind/Chi/Cont. You can get a good meal, with soft drink, for around Rs90 (£1.80/$3), though it is possible to spend a lot more.

Taj, Western Gate of Taj Mahal. Mod/Exp. Ind/Cont. Bar. An ITDC establishment, pleasant and convenient.

Sonam, 51 Taj Road. Mod/Exp. Ind/Chi/Cont. Good food in nice old building, once home of British Commander-in-Chief.

Also several very cheap restaurants in Tajganj, of which *New Star Dhaba* (close to Hotel Shahjahan) is probably best.

SIKANDRA

Sikander is the Indian form of Alexander, and Sikandra the site of a city founded by Sikander Lodi, one of the last sultans of Delhi before the Mughal take-over. Nothing much remains of the city, and the only point of interest is the **Tomb of Akbar***** (open sunrise to sunset). This is a very strange building. Looking at first the Lodi tombs, then Humayun's (both in Delhi), and finally the Itimad-ud-Daula you can see the line of development which led to the Taj Mahal. Yet Akbar's tomb owes little to these. It is known that Akbar was responsible for the general design himself, and it is conjectured that he borrowed the form of a Buddhist structure (like the Panch Mahal at Fatehpur Sikri) to symbolise his ecumenism. Jehangir finished the job, and it is to him that we owe the white marble top storey and, more importantly, the main gate with its four minarets.

Akbar was buried in a solid gold coffin, but that was looted by the Jats in 1761 and his remains scattered. The white marble cenotaph on the top level is engraved with the 99 names of God. Legend has it (on no very sound grounds) that the Koh-i-Noor diamond once occupied the small marble pillar near the cenotaph.

Take some time to look around the gardens, the waterworks, and the pavilions which bisect the walls. And watch out for the monkeys.

Just to the east outside the main gate is a small beautifully decorated building. Worth a quick look, it is not obvious whether it was a house or a tomb. A little further along the main road is **Maryam's Tomb**. This baradari, or pavilion, was built in 1495 by Sikander Lodi and became the tomb of Mariam uz Zamani in the following century. Despite the popular belief that she was a Christian, this wife of Akbar was actually a Hindu.

Arrival and departure. Sikandra is 12km from Agra. Bus from Idgah bus-stand, auto-rickshaw, or an interesting but far from peaceful cycle ride.

FATEHPUR SIKRI

Fatehpur Sikri is the best preserved and most impressive of India's ghost towns. After making do for 40 years with hand-me-downs this was the first purpose-built Mughal capital of India, a symbol that they intended to stay rather than return to their Central Asian fastness like so many previous invaders.

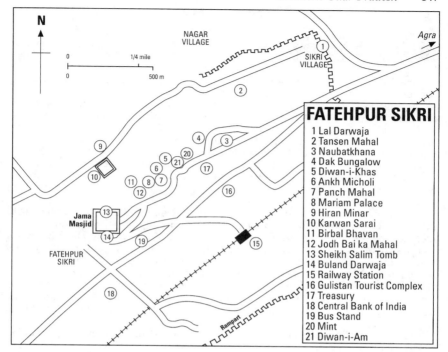

History

In 1568, despite consolidating the Mughal empire, Akbar was a worried man because he had no male heir. Then, a Sufi holy man based at Sikri predicted he would have three sons. Taking no chances Akbar sent his pregnant queen to stay with the holy man, and the following year Prince Salim, later Jehangir, was born. On the strength of this Akbar decided to build a new capital there, and a city was rapidly constructed in the traditional red sandstone.

Ensconced in his own creation Akbar could indulge the beliefs which made him a truly great man. For a start he removed all the penalties earlier Muslim rulers had applied to Hindus, and gave them equal opportunity at his court. He took much interest in other religions and philosophies, and welcomed all priests and holy men; it was only the bigoted, notably his own mullahs, who really annoyed him. Eventually he synthesised his own eclectic religion, Din-i-Ilahi (Divine Faith), with himself as spiritual leader. Some of his close followers converted, but the grip of orthodoxy, whether Muslim or Hindu, prevented any mass conversions.

Only 16 years after its completion Fatehpur Sikri was abandoned. The reason usually given is failure of the water supply, but political pressures played a larger part. The only major threat to the Mughal empire came from Afghanistan, and Akbar needed to be in Lahore to contain that.

Fatehpur Sikri's isolation has proved its best protection, but it must be borne in mind that the town is not at all as it was built. Few of the hundreds of buildings outside the palace have survived, and others have been altered by later users. The romantic nature of the city has led to misleading names and purposes being attached to many of the buildings.

The Jama Masjid

The **Jama Masjid***** is the most important building of Fatehpur Sikri. Its south gate, the **Buland Darwaza**, was not part of the original design, having been finished in 1575, some three years after the mosque as a whole. It commemorates one of Akbar's campaigns in Gujarat and also symbolises the confidence of a man who finally felt secure in his own realm.

The Buland Darwaza is huge (54m high) and this posed great difficulties for the architect. Imagine how dull a rectangular structure with just the entrance in the centre would have looked; that is the reason for the chamfered sides, the subsidiary arches and, above all, the detailing on the main face. Take away those three panels of buff sandstone above the arch, or the white border of the red sandstone spandrels, or the rosettes, and you substantially degrade the appearance of the whole. The panels of script are verses from the Koran, superbly drawn by one of Shaikh Salim's disciples. Beside the steps is a deep well which villagers dive into to entertain visitors.

Many horseshoes are nailed to the gates, perhaps pleas for Shaikh Salim's help with sick animals. On either side of the inner arch are inscriptions, the one on the right recording a visit by Akbar in 1601 after his conquest of the Deccan. The other reads 'Isa [Jesus], on whom be peace, said: The world is a bridge, pass over it, but build no house upon it. He who hopes for an hour may hope for eternity. The world endures but an hour, spend it in devotion. The rest is unseen.' The Kashmiris and the Ahmadiyya Muslim sect believe that Jesus survived crucifixion and died in Srinagar (see page 103). This quotation comes from a collection of his sayings. The attendants may let you climb the gateway for a view of the city and especially of the walls to the south.

The Jama Masjid itself was begun in 1567, and construction took five years. The courtyard is considerably larger than that of the Jama Masjid in Delhi. The prayer hall consists of three domed chambers with Hindu-pillared corridors decorated by tile inlay and painting.

After his death in 1572 Sheikh Salim was buried close to his favourite place of meditation, a common practice in Sufism. The beautiful **dargah**, or tomb, was altered in the time of Jehangir by adding the outer screens and the marble paving of the dais. The marble cladding of the dome and the pavement in front date from the latter part of the 19th century.

The structure of the tomb chamber is of red sandstone, covered with chunam and painted all over with flowers. Above the inner door are the 99 names of God, and of the Prophet and the four caliphs. The tomb itself is covered by an ebony canopy supported on four pillars, all covered by a mosaic of mother-of-pearl. The white marble screens are very delicate and probably the finest to be seen in India. The marble tracery extends even to the infill of the serpentine chajja brackets.

Belief in Sheikh Salim's power to help childless couples lives on. Each thread on the screens of the inner chamber represents a prayer for a child. At least as many Hindu women (in saris) as Muslim (tight trouser suits) visit the tomb and they all offer the same prasad, an offering of flowers and sweets, as in a Hindu temple. Some of the silk scarves have been brought from Mecca, others are the plain white ones traditional to Tibetan Buddhism. In fact, practice here is a fusion of Islamic, Hindu, and Buddhist beliefs. Visitors even make a point of walking around the tomb clockwise, as they would at a Buddhist memorial stupa.

The **Jamaat Khana** (known as the Tomb of Islam Khan) was a monastery for Sheikh Salim's disciples. It was open to all the sects of Islam, and later also to Hindu yogis and Parsi and Jesuit priests. The various tombs belong to Shaikh Hajji Husain, who controlled the Jamaat Khana, the sons and sons-in-law of Shaikh Salim, and of Islam Khan, a descendent of the Shaikh, who is buried under a wooden canopy.

Behind the Dargah and the Jamaat Khana is the north cloister, which became the **zenana rauza**, or women's tomb. This was originally a meeting place for the sama, a trance-inducing music and dance performance of the kind which gave rise to the expression 'whirling dervish'. Return now to the Buland Darwaza to pick up your shoes and exit by the Badshahi Darwaza (Royal Gate); this is the entrance used by Akbar on the way from his palace for prayers.

The palace approach

Head now for the Diwan-i-Am, noting on the left a large pile of rubble. This is thought to have been the **Ibadat Khana** (House of Worship) associated with Akbar's own religion. Further on you pass through the remains of a courtyard with, on the right, the **Daftar Khana** (Record Office). Although illiterate, Akbar had a huge library and commissioned translations of many religious and philosophical works which would then be read to him. The work was done here, and a direct access to the back of the Diwan-i-Khas opposite was provided.

Below the Diwan-i-Am is the public approach to the palace. The **Chahar Suk** (known as Naubat Khana) is a walled courtyard with four gates. The east and west gates (over the road) are Saracenic in style and the other two Hindu. A naubat khana is the same as a nakkar khana, and musicians would play for distinguished guests.

Shops which constituted the palace market lined the road, and the niches in the back held the official price list. The **Mint** was more probably the imperial workshops which would have produced, amongst other things, jewellery and embroidery. Over the road from the Mint is the so-called **Treasury**, more probably the house of a noble.

The **Diwan-i-Am**** is a spacious open court. A single-storeyed cloister with a deep chajja runs all round; most of the enclosures in the palace had similar cloisters. The Diwan-i-Am, like all the palace and haram buildings, has a north–south axis to align it with the Jama Masjid. The imperial throne was set in a balcony flanked by red sandstone jali screens. The room behind the balcony leads into the main palace.

Akbar's palace

From the Diwan-i-Am you enter a large open space originally subdivided. The garden was separated from the courtyard ahead of you by a wall, and another cut off the treasury buildings to the right. In the courtyard is a **pachisi board**. There is no evidence for the old legend of slave girls being used as pieces, nor is the game anything like chess. In fact, with dice and four counters per player, it sounds more like ludo.

In the Mughal empire there was no distinction between state finances and those of the emperor himself, so it is no surprise to find the Treasury in the palace compound. One of the main buildings is known as the **Ankh Michauli**** (meaning 'blind man's bluff'), which is, of course, irrelevant. The monsters carved on the cross-beams inside are seen elsewhere as guardians of treasure. The doors were of stone, and stone slabs closed the recesses to form storage bins for gold and silver coins. Outside is a **kiosk** (called the 'astrologer's seat'), probably occupied by a treasurer. The torana brackets are of Jain design.

The other extant part of the Treasury (a separate store once existed for copper coins) is the **Jewel House*****. The exterior suggests a conventional two-storeyed building, yet inside one finds a huge void with a central pillar surmounted by a platform connected by gangways to each corner. The shaft of the pillar is superbly carved, and a capital formed by numerous brackets supports the platform. Descriptions of Akbar sitting on a high platform while courtiers and holy men argued below caused this building to be confused with the Diwan-i-Khas and Ibadat Khana. As with most other buildings at Fatehpur Sikri the argument over name and function continues. The Jewel House and Treasury were provided with a separate entrance from the Diwan-i-Am for officials who did not merit entry to the palace proper.

Heading back over the pachisi court is the **Abdar Khana** (Water Store), a larder for drinking water and food, and certainly not the girls' school it is often called.

The **Anup Talao** (Peerless Pool) is a pool with a central throne. Beside it is a pavilion known as the **Turkish Sultana's House****, though no royal women would have been allowed in this relatively public part of the palace. This delightful building is ornately carved in geometrical and floral designs. The dadoes have animal (all defaced) and floral themes. The lattice work above was used for storage. Mirrors may have been inset, and some of the flowers have recesses for semi-precious stones. The design on the ceiling is just like those still used on Kashmiri houseboats.

Beside the tank is the **Diwan-i-Khas*** comprising two ground-floor rooms with a few traces of the painted decoration remaining. A raised platform in the inner chamber formed Akbar's throne, and it was here that Akbar had his first discussions with Jesuits who later had high hopes of converting him to Christianity.

Up on the roof is the **Khilwatkada-i-Khas** (loosely interpreted as 'Akbar's den'). The interior has lovely painted decoration and Persian inscriptions in gold. For once the popular name **Khwabgah** (Dream Chamber) got it more or less right, though Akbar could walk over the roof from here to the haram.

The Haram Sara

The rest of the palace comprises the Haram Sara, or women's palace, more commonly called a zenana in India. Only the emperor and his closest male relatives had access, and security was tight.

The **Panch Mahal***** is the building which best symbolises the cultural fusion Akbar so valued. The idea of a summer palace designed to take advantage of the slightest breeze is Persian, but this building combines Indian decorative themes with a Buddhist structural form. The ground floor has 84 columns, an auspicious number as it is the product of seven (the number of planets known at that time) and twelve (the signs of the zodiac). More interesting are the 56 first-floor columns of Hindu design, all different. The five storeys (panch means five) are progressively smaller and culminate in a kiosk. Jali screens may have made the Panch Mahal less open than it appears at present, and in the hot weather cooling grass mats would have hung over the apertures.

Akbar's mother was known as Maryam Makani (on a par with Mary), **Maryam's House** being her part of the Haram Sara. Known as the Sunahra Makan (Golden House) it was once richly gilded and painted.

The largest building in the zenana is known as Jodh Bai's Palace. Actually the **Principal Haram Sara**** it provided accommodation for most of Akbar's 300 wives. Jodh Bai, a Rajput princess, married Prince Salim in 1585, by which time the palace ascribed to her had been in existence for a dozen years. The entrance is flanked by a guard house, and a closed viaduct on top of a wall ran from the Diwan-i-Khas to here. The entrance hall is purely Hindu in style, and across the courtyard is a matching building which functioned as a shrine for the many Hindu women. The style of this is similar to the Khajuraho temples. Behind the north pavilion is the beautifully screened balcony of the Hawa Mahal (Wind Palace) overlooking the zenana garden. The roof above this is of corrugated blue ceramic tiles.

To the north of Jodh Bai's Palace is the small **zenana garden**. In the corner nearest the house is a bath in the form of a small tank with a central pillar and roof. It was of course walled, like the garden as a whole. In the opposite corner is the **Nagina Masjid** (Jewel or Ladies' Mosque), a simple building whose appearance has not been improved by whitewash.

Birbal, a Hindu, was one of the 'Nine Gems' of Akbar's court and a close confidant of the emperor. Akbar had a house built for him, but it could not have been in the palace. **Birbal's House**** is in fact another component of the Haram Sara, probably occupied by Akbar's two senior wives. The odd ground plan and interior arrangement make sense when you think of it as two self-contained apartments. Each balcony, for instance, is invisible from the other unit. Much of the wall area is delicately carved in predominantly Hindu designs.

Backing on to the Principal Haram Sara are two **stable** blocks. As with so many of these appellations the idea of noisy smelly stables and their male grooms so close to the Haram is laughable. The larger of the two, the 'elephant stables' is simply quarters for women of lower rank and serving maids. The 'camel stables' was a store. You can exit from the south end of the stables or take a path from near 'Birbal's House' down to the Hathi Pol.

Other buildings

A path leads north from the Badshahi entrance of the mosque, and in a compound just behind the mosque are the **houses of Faizi and Abul Fazl**. These two brothers, favourite courtiers of Akbar, may later have lived in these houses, but Akbar had them built so his young princes could be close to Shaikh Salim. They are well preserved examples of small-scale Mughal domestic architecture.

The path passes through the remains of a hamam and goes on down to the **Hathi Pol**, which was the emperor's entrance to the haram and palace. Outside this are the remains of two stone elephants which must originally have been about 3m high. Past here on the left is the Samam Burj, a keep, further the caravan serai, and eventually the **Hiran Minar*** (Deer Tower). Deer were kept beside the lake, and miniature paintings show such towers used for shooting, though there is no evidence to connect the two here. The outside is adorned by stone elephant tusks, mostly now broken, which are set in alternating octagons and stars of white inlay. If you have any energy left you can climb this, taking care on the irregular steps.

The octagonal structure on the left as you ascend the path is a well with underground chambers. Man-powered windlasses and bucket chains formed the first of five stages in raising water to the palace. These detours are of minor interest and not recommended if you are already hot and tired.

Practical Information *i*

The ASI produces an excellent guide book on sale here and at Sikandra and the Taj Mahal.

Arrival and departure. Bus from Idgah bus-stand in Agra (the railway is much slower). The bus-stand in Fatehpur Sikri is near the Jama Masjid. Conducted tours leave from Agra Cantonment station shortly after the arrival of the Taj Express, tickets being sold on the train. Bus onwards to Bharatpur or Jaipur, the railway does not connect conveniently with either of these places.

Accommodation (STD Code 05619)

Gulistan Tourist Complex, between station and Jama Masjid. Tel 2490. Rest. Bar. DWB Rs200–425 (around £4–8.50/$6.50–14). An efficient and pleasant UP Tourism place.

Maurya Rest House, near Buland Darwaza. Tel 2348. Rest (veg). Rs40–120 (80p–£2.40/$1.35–4). Comfortable and friendly.

Archaeological Survey Rest House, near Diwan-i-Am. Very cheap. Book in advance at Archaeological Survey of India, 22 The Mall, Agra, or you will have to wait until 6.30pm to find out if you have a room.

Several other cheap lodges and restaurants in the bazaar below the Buland Darwaza.

LUCKNOW

Lucknow is today the capital of Uttar Pradesh, the most populous state in the union. Perhaps named after Lakshman, brother of Rama, it later became capital of Oudh (or Awadh). This Mughal province was ruled by nawabs who asserted their independence of Delhi from 1707 onwards. These rulers were Shia Muslims, and Lucknow remains the main centre in the north of this sect (Bombay is in the south). Lucknow has always been famous for its arts, notably Urdu poetry, and courtly manners. The ornate and flowery style of many of the buildings is not to everyone's taste, but they are great fun. A period of decadence and misrule began in the 19th century culminating in the deposing of the last nawab in 1856, one of the direct causes of the Indian Mutiny. Despite the modernising of the city Lucknow has preserved its charm, and it remains a stylish and relaxed place to visit.

An epic stand

As a result of Clive's machinations the ruler of Oudh was a British puppet from the late 18th century onwards. British officials were posted to keep an eye on the nawab, and the latter was obliged to build a grand residency for them. When the Great Mutiny of the Bengal Army broke out in June 1857 the British barricaded themselves in their cantonments and residencies all over northern India. Some of these held out until British and loyal Indian troops arrived from Punjab, Bombay, and Madras. Others, like nearby Kanpur (Cawnpore) were overrun or surrendered and the defenders slaughtered.

The 3000 people trapped in the **Lucknow Residency**** (half were Indians, and half of those troops) expected to be able to survive for a few weeks. In fact, despite the much greater numbers and matériel of the besiegers, they held out until 25 September 1857, when a relief column fought its way in. By this time less than 1000 of the defenders were still alive. The siege resumed, until on 17 November a stronger force arrived to cover a withdrawal. It was March of the following year before Lucknow was finally recaptured. Like so many of their other military cock-ups Lucknow became a symbol of British pluck and determination, and as a mark of this the Union Flag flew over the ruins of the Residency night and day until Independence. The poignant ruins are open sunrise to sunset, last entry to the Model Room (a diorama of the military positions) being at 4.30pm.

To mark the hundredth anniversary of the Mutiny (First War of Independence being the preferred term these days) a **Martyrs' Memorial** was constructed nearby on the banks of the River Gomti. Such a memorial was certainly needed for balance, but this somehow lacks the required dignity.

Old Lucknow

The heart of Lucknow, however, is around the older area of Chowk. Here you can see the best examples of the florid Oudh style of architecture. The **Bara Imambara***** is one of the oddest buildings in India. Constructed in 1784 as a famine-relief project, it covers the modest tomb of its builder Asaf-ud-daula (nawab 1775–97). The vaulted hall is one of the largest of its kind in the world. Behind it is the **Bhulbhulaiyan**, a labyrinth. Note the quaint restrictions on access to this. To one side is a large mosque (closed to non-Muslims), and to the other a deep baoli, or well, in a cloister.

Opposite the gatehouse of the Bara Imambara is **Laxman Tila**, the site of the original Rajput town of Lakhimpur, now crowned by the **Alamgir Mosque**.

Nearby is the **Rumi Darwaza****. The gates of Indian cities are often named after the town they lead to. This name translates literally as Rome Gate, which refers not to Rome itself but to Byzantium. By the time this gate was built Constantinople (now

Istanbul) had been in the hands of the Turks for 300 years, and yet the tradition of the Eastern Roman Empire lingered on. Whether it is really a replica of one of Byzantium's gates is another matter. To the author's wife it looked uncommonly like a ham studded with cloves; funny how after a few months in India one's fantasies all centre on food.

Walk through the gate and head for the **Clock Tower**, at 67m the highest in India. Next to this is the **Art Gallery*** housed in a baradari of Muhammed Ali Shah (nawab 1837–42). Upstairs are portraits of most of the nawabs and kings of Oudh, and on the ground-floor level you can see saris being embroidered, a traditional Muslim art in Lucknow. Nearby is the **Satkhanda** which, as the *sat* in the name implies, was intended to be a seven-storeyed watchtower. Four floors had been completed by the time of the death of Muhammed Ali Shah, and that was where it remained.

Over the road the **Chhota Imambara**** (Small or Hussainabad Imambara) is the tomb of Muhammed Ali Shah and his mother. The approach is beside a long tank flanked on one side by a mosque and on the other by a clumsy model of the Taj Mahal. The domes of both these buildings are finished off with replicas of the crown of Oudh. The interior of the tomb is actually more like a palace, and a rather jolly one at that. Most enjoyable. An imambara, incidentally, is the place to which the tazias (replicas of Caliph Husain's tomb) are carried during Muharram, which is why you see them lying around these buildings. The **Jama Masjid** is also in this area but, like many Shia shrines, closed to non-Muslims.

The **Shahnajaf Imambara**** is the tomb of Ghazi-ud-din Haidar (nawab 1814–1827) and his wives. It takes its name from the city near Baghdad where Caliph Ali was murdered, a key place for the Shias. There appears to be a riverside walk between here and the Martyrs' Memorial, which could be pleasant on a cool day.

The **Museum** is in the grounds of the depressing **Zoo**.

Kim's school

On the outskirts of Lucknow is **Constantia Palace****, one of the most peculiar buildings in India, and a match for anything the nawabs built. Claude Martin (1735–1800) was a French soldier of fortune, first in Pondicherry, and later in the service of the nawabs before joining the army of the British East India Company. Having amassed a considerable fortune he set out to build an appropriate house for himself. Martin died before it was complete, but endowed it as La Martinière School. Originally for Anglo-Indian children, this is where Kim was educated.

Practical Information *i* Uttar Pradesh Government tourist office on Station Road near railway station, also information at station and Hotel Gomti. Daily conducted tour from Hotel Gomti (Rs60). The ten-day Lucknow Festival in February is original, mainly cultural (including qwwali singing), and also a lot of fun events. The best books on the Mutiny are *A Season in Hell* by Michael Edwardes and *The Great Indian Mutiny* by Christopher Hibbert.

Shopping. Lucknow is famous for its perfumes and embroidery.

Local transport. Most places in the city are connected by six-seater auto rickshaws (tempos), and this is the best way of getting around. Local people will always help you find the right one.

Arrival and departure. Airport (14km), bus from Hotel Clarks Avadh, 8 MG Marg. Indian Airlines office (Tel 240 927) at Hotel Clarks Avadh, flights to Delhi, Bombay, Patna, and Calcutta. Sahara also flies to Delhi.

On the Delhi (8hrs)–Varanasi (5hrs) railway line, also from Puri via Varanasi (28hrs), and Agra Cantonment (9hrs), noting that the metre gauge line from Agra

Fort takes 14½hrs. Metre gauge line to Gorakhpur (5hrs) for Sonauli entry to Nepal. The station is in two separate but adjacent parts, Northern Railway (broad gauge lines) and North-Eastern Railway (metre gauge lines).

Buses to Delhi (12hrs), Agra, Gorakhpur (7hrs), Sonauli (11hrs), and Varanasi (9hrs) from Kaisarbagh bus station (2.5km from station).

Accommodation

Carlton Hotel, Shahnajaf Road. Tel 244 021. Rs350–850 (£7–17/$12–28). Rest (eat in or out, buffet lunch or dinner Rs160). Bar. Nice old house in lovely gardens. Seems well run, despite the upper-class twit reception staff.

Hotel Gomti (formerly Tourist Bungalow), Sapru Marg. Tel 232 291. Rs250–650 Dorm Rs50 (£1/$1.65). Rest (good). Bar. Entrance like a five-star hotel and good large rooms. Outdoor bar and restaurant. A good place to stay. Consider the likelihood of a power cut before getting in the lift.

Capoor Hotel, Hazratganj. Tel 243 958. Rs180–250. Rest (see below). Bar.

Hotel Ramakrishna, Ashok Marg (near Gomti). Tel 262 653. Rs125–170. Hot water in doubles. Rest. Not bad at all.

Some slightly cheaper hotels near the station, e.g. *Mohan Hotel* and *Bengali Lodge*, and more in the slightly quieter Hazratganj (the main shopping area).

Eating and drinking

Capoor's, Hazratganj. A/C. Mod/Exp. Ind/Chi/Cont. Very good but, as usual, the Western food is never quite what you expect. Best to stick with Mughlai food.

Kwality, Hazratganj. A/C. Mod/Exp. Ind/Chi. As reliable as usual.

Lots more restaurants in Hazratganj. A group of interesting and inexpensive-looking restaurants stands near Clarks Hotel, including an open-air tandoori and a Chinese.

Lucknow is famous for its cuisine, with a strong Mughal influence. The best inexpensive way to sample this is the many excellent street stalls.

VARANASI

Varanasi (Benares) is the holiest city of the Hindus, although before Brahma made a ten-horse sacrifice at Dasaswamedh Ghat it was surpassed by Allahabad. Now more than a million pilgrims a year visit, the most dedicated making a six-day, 58km circuit of the city on foot. Anyone, regardless of creed, who dies within this area achieves nirvana, freedom from the cycle of death and rebirth. Hence many old and infirm people come here for their last days. There are old-established places for these people, similar to hospices, where the accent is on spiritual rather than physical care.

Along the holy Ganges

Most of the action in Varanasi takes place on the **Ghats***. These are steep flights of stone steps which run down from the town to the river over a distance of 5km. Many were built by, and bear the names of, India's princely rulers. The majority are bathing ghats, and there are five in particular which the pilgrim should visit in a prescribed order, having a holy dip at each. The best introduction to the ghats is a boat trip over their full length, which costs about Rs15 per hour. Afterwards walk the most interesting section; the atmosphere has to be experienced to be believed, and a boat is too distant. You must make a visit at sunrise which, apart from being beautiful, is of special significance for the worshippers.

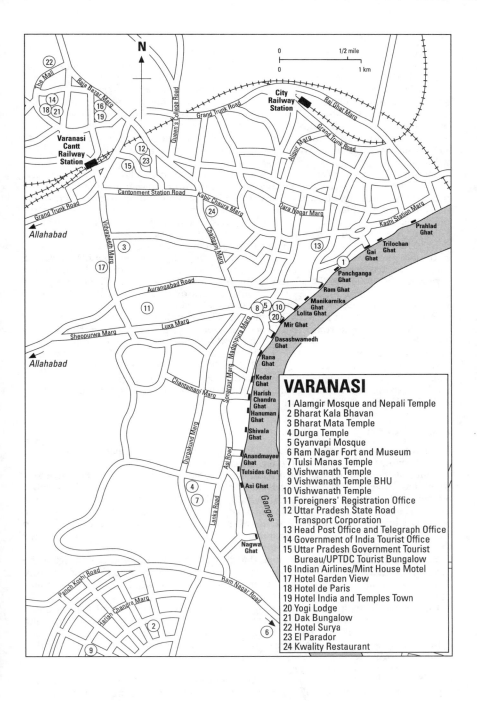

N

0   1/2 mile
0   1 km

(22) The Mall
(14) (16)
(18) (21) (19)
Raja Bazar Marg
Queen's College Road
Grand Trunk Road
City Railway Station
Rai Ghat Marg
Grand Trunk Road
Alapur Marg

Varanasi Cantt Railway Station
(12) (23)
(15)
Cantonment Station Road
Kabir Chaura Marg
Chaitganj Marg
Dara Nagar Marg
Kashi Station Marg

Grand Trunk Road
Allahabad
(24)
(3)
(17)
Aurangabad Road
(13)
(1)
Prahlad Ghat
Trilochan Ghat
Gai Ghat
Panchganga Ghat
Ram Ghat

(11)
Luxa Marg
Vidyapeeth Marg
Sheopurwa Marg
Allahabad

(8) (5) (10)
(20)
Manikarnika Ghat
Lolita Ghat
Mir Ghat
Dasashwamedh Ghat

Chantamani Marg
Sonarpur Marg
Madanpura Marg
Rana Ghat
Kedar Ghat
Harish Chandra Ghat
Hanuman Ghat

Durgakund Marg
Asi Road
Shivala Ghat
Anandmayee Ghat
Tulsidas Ghat
Asi Ghat

(4)
(7)
Lanka Road

Ganges

Nagwa Ghat

Panch Koshi Road
Harish Chandra Marg
(2)
Ram Nagar Road
(6)

(9)

VARANASI

1 Alamgir Mosque and Nepali Temple
2 Bharat Kala Bhavan
3 Bharat Mata Temple
4 Durga Temple
5 Gyanvapi Mosque
6 Ram Nagar Fort and Museum
7 Tulsi Manas Temple
8 Vishwanath Temple
9 Vishwanath Temple BHU
10 Vishwanath Temple
11 Foreigners' Registration Office
12 Uttar Pradesh State Road
    Transport Corporation
13 Head Post Office and Telegraph Office
14 Government of India Tourist Office
15 Uttar Pradesh Government Tourist
    Bureau/UPTDC Tourist Bungalow
16 Indian Airlines/Mint House Motel
17 Hotel Garden View
18 Hotel de Paris
19 Hotel India and Temples Town
20 Yogi Lodge
21 Dak Bungalow
22 Hotel Surya
23 El Parador
24 Kwality Restaurant

Start at **Dasaswamedh Ghat**, which means ten (das) horse (aswa) sacrifice (medh), and is one of the busiest. The square building is the Sitala Temple. This name can be transcribed as Shitole, and you may even see a Shitole Restaurant! Even less appetising when you know that Sitala is the goddess of smallpox. The large building above **Man Mandir Ghat** is a palace of the Maharaja of Jaipur. The tigers on the roof next door signify the house of the harijan who runs the burning ghats, a very wealthy man. Above Lalita Ghat the **Nepali Temple*** is renowned for its erotic carvings. These are intended to keep away the goddess of lightning, who is supposed to be rather straight-laced! Look up as you walk along for the flood marks on the walls, and you will realise why the ghats are so high.

Jalsain is the main burning ghat where cremations are carried out around the clock. You will be in very serious trouble if you are caught photographing the cremations; there is little problem elsewhere. Next is the holiest of all, **Manikarnika Ghat**, where the cockeyed temple is dedicated to Durga. Devotees swim down to this in the monsoon; sometimes they come back, sometimes they don't. Above **Panchganga Ghat** is the **Alamgir Mosque**, one of two built by Aurangzeb on the bases of demolished temples and using material from them. This is worth a visit for the view of the city and the river from the roof. Return to Jalsain Ghat and take B Bishwanath Singh Lane. This leads eventually to the **Great Mosque of Aurangzeb***, known as the Gyanvapi Mosque from the adjacent Well of Knowledge. Walk round the back to see the remains of the temple. As with similar places ownership is contested between Hindus and Muslims, and armed police constantly stand guard.

Popularly called the **Golden Temple** the Vishwanath Temple is the most sacred shrine of Shiva, the patron deity of Varanasi. Oddly the gold plating for the roofs was given by the Sikh Maharaja Ranjit Singh. Although closed to non-Hindus vantage points provide a view inside (for a little bakshish). High above Man Mandir Ghat, and giving a good view of the river and ghats is the **Observatory*** of Jai Singh, much smaller than those in Delhi and Jaipur but no less interesting. The crowds drawn by the big festivals make it almost impossible to move on the ghats, so hire a boat (up to Rs30 per hour at such times).

Around town

The modern **Bharat Mata** (Mother India) temple is one of few open to non-Hindus; a relief map of India replaces the usual image.

South of the main part of town is the large campus of Benares Hindu University, which has an **art gallery*** (Bharat Kala Bhavan) and the **New Vishwanath Temple***, a lovely building endowed by the Birla industrial family. On the way you will pass the **Durga Temple**, better known as the Monkey Temple for reasons which will become obvious. Close to this is the **Tulsi Manas Mandir***, which commemorates the man who translated the Ramayana into Hindi from Sanskrit. Murals and animated puppets tell the story.

Further south, and the other side of the river (the dry season pontoon bridge is the best way of getting there) is **Ramnagar Fort****, palace of the Maharaja of Benares. There is some interesting stuff in the museum, and the peace and quiet comes as a real relief.

Enthusiasts of such things will enjoy the old **cemetery*** on Maqbul Alam Road.

Some people find Varanasi quite overpowering, others reckon it more pleasant and easier to cope with than Agra or Jaipur. It certainly is not the quiet place one might expect from its religious significance, and despite the frequent reminders of death it is bursting with life.

Practical Information *i* Government of India Tourist Office near the Tourist Dak Bungalow in the cantonment. They run guided tours of the city including a sunrise river trip, and also to Sarnath and Ramnagar (the latter is sometimes missed because of traffic jams on the main bridge). Uttar Pradesh Tourism at the station and the Tourist Bungalow (not Tourist Dak Bungalow). The best book is *Benares: City of Light* by Diana L Eck.

Arrival and departure. Airport at Babatpur (22km), flights from Kathmandu as well as internal. Airport bus, but it is little more expensive for four people to share a taxi. Indian Airlines office (Tel 64146/66116) has moved from the Mint House to opposite the Hotel de Paris in the cantonment.

Trains from Delhi (13hrs), Calcutta (12hrs) (noting that several Delhi–Calcutta trains stop at Mughal Sarai rather than Varanasi), and Patna (5½hrs). From Muzaffarpur a train to Mughal Sarai takes 8hrs, and you have to take a bus or share a taxi the remaining 17km/10 miles to Varanasi. Allow a good two hours to get to Mughal Sarai station because of jams on the bridge. Full details about getting to and from Khajuraho in that section. Paul Travels, near the Tourist Bungalow, run a daily bus direct to Pokhara and Kathmandu, fares from Rs175.

The long-distance bus-stand is near the station. Local buses, which can be used to get to Sarnath or Ramnagar, are terrible; departures from Godowlia.

Accommodation (STD Code 0542)

Hotel de Paris, The Mall. Tel 46601. SWB A/C Rs550 (£11/$18) DWB A/C Rs760. Rest (3). Bar. Colonial building with large rooms and attractive shady garden. Swimming pool planned. Adjacent to Government of India tourist office.

Hotel India, 59 Patel Nagar. Tel 43309. SWB Rs175 DWB Rs250 SWB A/C Rs300 DWB A/C Rs400. Rest (Ambar). Bar. Very good smaller hotel. Nice little garden, reasonably quiet.

Hotel Temples Town, Patel Nagar. Tel 46582. SWB Rs95 DWB Rs145. Breakfast available.

Tourist Dak Bungalow, The Mall. Tel 42182. SWB Rs100 DWB Rs150–250. Rest (Ind/Chi/Cont). Camping. Parking. Large compound, used by overland buses and lorries.

Hotel Surya, The Mall. Tel 385 930. SWB Rs150 DWB Rs200 SWB A/C Rs275 DWB A/C Rs300. Rest (Ind/Chi/Cont). Simple but very clean and quiet. Hot water and mosquito nets in all rooms. Beautiful spacious garden backed by old palace of King of Nepal.

Tourist Bungalow, Parade Kothi. Tel 43413. SWB Rs100/150 (around £2–3/$3.30–5) DWB Rs125/200 Dorm Rs20. Rest. Bar. A bit dingy. We have heard strange (and unsubstantiated) stories about this place, which suggest it is not wise to drink tea with strangers.

Mint House Motel, Nadesar. Tel 43819. SWB Rs80 DWB Rs160. Rest (Western food). Parking. A very old building, still belonging to the maharaja. Many of the more expensive rooms are huge. The proprietor is an interesting man; he used to run the maharaja's guest house.

Hotel Garden View, Vidyapath Road, Sigra. Tel 360 859. SR Rs50 SWB Rs135 DWB Rs175. Rest. Comfortable, pleasant garden. Give them a ring and they'll pick you up anywhere in town. No more hassles with rickshaw-wallas, and they give 10% discount to anyone using this guide!

Yogi Lodge, Kalika Ghat. Tel 322 588. SR Rs60 (£1.20/$2) DR Rs85 3R Rs45 Dorm Rs20. Rest. Basic (to put it mildly) but friendly. Hot showers. Right in the thick of it near the Golden Temple. Do not confuse with New Yogi, Jogi and Yogesh Lodges!

The *Hotel Overlander* is no more, the *YMCA* no longer provides accommodation, and it is said, rightly or wrongly, that *Hotel Blue Star*, *Tandoon House* and *Bharat Rest House* are best avoided. The really intrepid can try the *houseboats* on the river.

Warning. An organised gang of rickshaw-wallahs at the railway station will try to take you to one of five hotels (Park Villa, New Imperial, Chandra, Satyam, or Varuna)

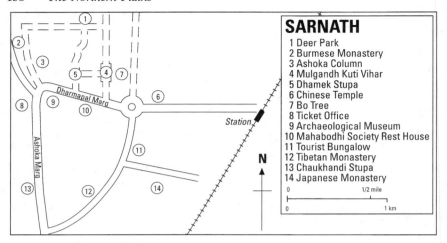

SARNATH

1 Deer Park
2 Burmese Monastery
3 Ashoka Column
4 Mulgandh Kuti Vihar
5 Dhamek Stupa
6 Chinese Temple
7 Bo Tree
8 Ticket Office
9 Archaeological Museum
10 Mahabodhi Society Rest House
11 Tourist Bungalow
12 Tibetan Monastery
13 Chaukhandi Stupa
14 Japanese Monastery

where you will be grossly overcharged. Beware especially of Park Villa, which has no name outside and where they might take you instead of the Garden View.

Eating and drinking

Pretty desperate. Three Chinese, *Winfa* in Lohurabir and those near each of the Tourist Bungalows, are nothing special. People have enthused about *The Aces*, Godowlia, but it does not impress us. Even the *Kwality* is a dud, probably the only one in the chain. The *Sindhi Restaurant*, near Lalita Cinema, Belupur, which we have not tried, is supposed to be good.

El Parador, Chetganj (near Hotel Basant). Tel 64552. Italian/Greek/ Mexican. Claims waffles and maple syrup, brown bread, tacos, and so on. The chef apparently worked in embassies in Delhi.

The restaurants of the *Varanasi Ashok* and *Clarks Varanasi* hotels (both in the cantonment) are excellent and not outrageously expensive (say Rs150–200 per head) for the quality of food and service.

See also Sarnath.

SARNATH

Siddhartha, a prince from Lumbini in nearby Nepal, put himself through six years of austerity in his search for enlightenment. This failed, so he broke his fast and meditated for seven days under a pipal tree at Bodhgaya. There, in 528BC, he became the Buddha, the Enlightened One. Walking to Sarnath he met with his fellow ascetics and preached his first sermon to them in a nature reserve of the local king. A monastery was soon founded, and much expanded in the time of Ashoka, 300 years later. Sarnath was at its height in the fourth to sixth centuries AD, but in decline by AD800 as Indian Buddhism was reabsorbed into the Hindu mainstream. It remained a place of learning until it was destroyed by the Muslims in 1194.

The first monument you see is the **Chaukhandi**, a Mughal tower built in 1588 on top of what appeared until recently to be a small grassy hill. Excavation has now shown it to be a brick stupa. Good view from the top.

Pride of place in the **Museum**** goes to a magnificent lion capital from the Ashoka column. This is the state emblem of modern India. Other sculptures cover the whole period of Sarnath's use.

In a large garden, known still as the **Deer Park*****, is the huge **Dhamek Stupa** which marks where Buddha preached his first sermon. Built initially by Ashoka it was later enlarged in several stages. The stone cladding of the base is adorned by unfinished carving of the Gupta period (fourth or fifth century AD), and this final stage may never have been completed at all.

As you take the path from the Dhamek Stupa to the Main Shrine you are walking literally in the Buddha's footsteps; he strode up and down here as he taught his disciples. The thick walls of the **Main Shrine**, marking where Buddha meditated, used to support a superstructure 61m/200ft high. To one side of this is part of the **monolithic stone railing** once on top of the **Dharmarajika Stupa**. This 30m/98ft-high stupa was first built by Ashoka to house relics of the Buddha, and much enlarged later. The stupa was destroyed in the 18th century for its building materials, its base standing to the south of the Main Shrine. Nearby is a part of the **Ashoka Pillar**, once 15m high, which once supported the lion capital.

North of the Main Shrine are the remains of the **monasteries**, the oldest dating from the time of Ashoka. Note the moulded bricks, and also the tunnel under Monument II which no-one has explained.

Nearby are modern Jain and Buddhist temples. The latter, the **Mulgandha Kuti Vihar**, has murals by a Japanese artist depicting events in Buddha's life. Close to this is a **pipal tree**, bedecked by prayer flags, which is a direct descendant of the one under which Buddha achieved enlightenment.

Various Buddhist communities have built their temples in the village. The Chinese has a beautiful marble image, and the Tibetan captures some of the atmosphere of a Ladakhi monastery. Sarnath is best avoided at weekends when crowds and cassette players shatter the calm.

Arrival and departure. Sarnath is 11km north of Varanasi. Bus (terrible) from Godowlia or rickshaw. If you can get four or five people together take a taxi.

Accommodation
Tourist Bungalow. Tel 42515. SWB Rs60/125 DWB Rs75/150 Dorm Rs20. Rest. Very disappointing; scruffy and uncomfortable, and on a cramped site next to a noisy school.

GORAKHPUR

This squalid town was formerly a British army recruiting and training base for Gurkha soldiers. Much to the disgust of Indian politicians its use continued for some time after Independence before transfer to a new base in Nepal. It remains, unfortunately, a stepping stone on the overland route to Pokhara in Nepal.

Information. Tourist offices at station and on Park Road.

Arrival and departure. Train to Lucknow (5hrs), Varanasi (7hrs), and New Jalpaiguri for Darjeeling (17hrs). Change here for Nautanwa (3hrs) *en route* for Sonauli on Nepal border, but faster by bus or share taxi/jeep. Bus-stand is 300m down street opposite station; share taxis near bus-stand.

Accommodation
Hotel Amber, 1km from station. Tel 0551 338 331. Rs70–300 (air-cooled). Rest (room service). Clean and comfortable, but noisy.
Railway retiring rooms are most convenient for station, and *Standard Hotel* is nearby.

Eating and drinking
Bobio's, next to Hotel Amber. A/C. Ind. Mod. Better food and service than in many more prepossessing towns.

SONAULI

The Nepalese border crossing nearest to Pokhara, much quieter and more relaxed than the Raxaul/Birganj crossing for Kathmandu.

Arrival and departure. The rail terminus of Nautanwa is 10km from Sonauli and connects only with Gorakhpur; slower than the bus. Bus to Gorakhpur (3hrs) for rail connections, also share jeeps and taxis, faster but no less uncomfortable. It is possible to get 16 people in a jeep. Direct buses to Varanasi (305km, 9hrs) or Lucknow (12hrs).

Bus to Pokhara (10hrs, best views from the right side of the bus as you travel to Sonauli), also to Kathmandu (12hrs). The fastest buses (Saja) run from Bhairawa, 4km from Sonauli. The views on both these runs are tremendous, so it is obviously silly to take a night bus.

Here, as in Gorakhpur, buy tickets for yourself from the official sources, not from touts.

Accommodation

Uttar Pradesh Tourism runs the *Hotel Niranjana* (Tel 4901). Rest. Very reasonable. Also small lodges, mostly on the Nepalese side of the border; *Mamata Lodge* is cheap and adequate, good restaurant, too. At least one hotel at Nautanwa.

LUMBINI (Nepal)

Lumbini is the birth place of the Lord Buddha, which one would expect to have made it an important place of pilgrimage over the centuries. In fact, mainly because of its location in the inaccessible and unhealthy Terai, few people visited it, and there was little more than a garden and a few minor temples to see. The Japanese Buddhists, the richest and most influential community, now plan to change all this and develop the area as a kind of Buddhist theme park.

Information. Although only 22km from the border a Nepalese visa is essential for visiting Lumbini; this is available on the frontier at Sonauli.

Arrival and departure. Bus from Sonauli or Bhairawa (1hr).

POKHARA (Nepal)

The most important town in western Nepal is not in itself especially interesting. It is, however, a good place for a break from travelling. One can relax in small inexpensive lodges around Phewa Lake and enjoy the sub-tropical vegetation and wonderful views of Macchupuchhare, the Fishtail Mountain, often confused with Annapurna. Pokhara is also an ideal trekking base. Unlike the Indian mountain areas of Himachal Pradesh and Uttarakhand the climate is mild and pleasant in winter.

Arrival and departure. Bus from Sonauli (10hrs) and Kathmandu (12hrs).

KUSHINAGAR

The Buddha died and was cremated here. It is an easy detour on the way to Nepal though of limited interest. The **Mahaparinirvana Temple** has a 6m/20ft long statue of the reclining Buddha dating from the fifth century AD, though the fad for dressing such images makes it impossible to see anything but the head. Nearby is another large statue and a small **museum**. The **Ramabhar Stupa** 2km away marks the cremation site. There are extensive remains of monastic buildings and several modern temples.

Information. Tourist office between main road and Traveller's Lodge.

Arrival and departure. Bus (1½hrs) or share taxi from Gorakhpur, which is on the railway line to Nautanwa near the Nepalese border.

Accommodation

Pathik Niwas (Travellers Lodge). SWB Rs75/125 DWB Rs100/150 SWB A/C Rs175 DWB A/C Rs225 Dorm Rs20. Rest.

Accommodation in dharamsalas for a few rupees a night, ask at tourist office.

BIHAR

Bihar is regarded by enlightened Indians as the most backward and violent of the major states. Like eastern Uttar Pradesh it is run by feudal landlords (thakkurs) entirely for their own benefit. Land law reforms, particularly the size of holding allowed for individuals and families, are strongly resisted, and attempts by landless labourers and untouchables to enforce them cause much bloodshed. The police side with the landlords because they are the same caste, and nothing that Delhi says or does makes any difference. There was an appalling incident back in the 1980s when the police in Bhagalpur took to blinding criminals. This was bad enough, but who was to say that the 'criminals' were not ordinary people demanding their rights?

In the past Bihar played an important part in Indian history, religion, and culture. It is strongly associated with Buddha, and both Mahavira (founder of Jainism) and Ashoka were born and lived there. The first republic in the world (sixth century BC) was based in Vaishali, and Ashoka ruled his great empire from Pataliputra. Bihar has a great deal of heavy industry, mostly based on its extensive mineral deposits, and is also a major producer of rice.

BIRGANJ (Nepal)

Birganj is the Nepalese town across the border from Raxaul. Another place to hurry through.

Arrival and departure. Bus from Kathmandu (12hrs). Rickshaw over the border from Raxaul (Rs20).

Accommodation. *Hotel Diyalo*, by bus-stand, is the best. Many other hotels cheaper than this, some a lot better than others for the same price. See also Raxaul.

RAXAUL

Raxaul is the Indian border town on the road route to Kathmandu. Like this area as a whole it is a poor and grubby place.

Arrival and departure. Train services much improved lately, direct to Calcutta (19hrs), Varanasi (12½hrs) and Delhi (29hrs). Bus to Patna (5hrs).

Accommodation. Best bet are the retiring rooms at the station, otherwise various grubby lodges. See also Birganj.

PATNA

Patna is now merely the capital of Bihar but, under Ashoka, it was the centre of an empire stretching as far as Afghanistan. The excavated site of Pataliputra, the old city, is at Kumrahar (5km/3 miles from the station, take a tempo) though this is barely distinguishable from any other hole in the ground.

Arabic and Persian scholars know Patna for the **Khuda Baksh Oriental Library**, which will also appeal to calligraphers, but there is little on display, and you really need to know what you are looking for. All the other guides enthuse about the **Golghar***, a hemispherical granary capable of holding 137,000 tonnes. It was built in 1786 by Warren Hastings to obviate famine, but rarely used until recently. Spiral steps lead up the outside to the filling aperture. At least the top provides a good view of the Ganges.

Patna Museum* is very proud of its 200-million-year-old fossil tree. A large collection of Tibetan Buddhist thankas (one finely embroidered) and other artefacts is more interesting. A Krupp garrison artillery piece sits outside; needless to say no-one knows where it came from.

Patna is just a place to pass through on the way to or from Nepal. You can kill a bit of time at the Golghar and the museum, but it has nothing else at all to offer. It has a menacing atmosphere and is, moreover, notorious for its thieves; watch your gear extra-closely here, especially on the station.

Information. Tourist Office in railway station, head office in Fraser Road. Conducted tours possible but unlikely.

Arrival and departure. Airport only 4km from station, as easy to take a rickshaw as the Indian Airlines bus. Indian Airlines (Tel 226 433) on Gandhi Maidan near Golghar. Flights to Delhi, Calcutta, Lucknow, Varanasi, and Kathmandu.

On one of the main Delhi (15¼hrs)–Calcutta (8¾hrs) lines. Also Varanasi (4hrs), or go to Mughal Sarai and bus or share taxi from there. One express a day to Gaya, always late and crowded. Don't even think about the passenger trains. Raxaul, on the border with Nepal, takes all day by train, better by bus. Note that there are two stations; you want Patna Junction.

The bus-stand is close to the station. Routes to Muzaffarpur (*en route* for Raxaul), direct to Raxaul, and also Nalanda and Rajgir. Himalayan Tours and Travels, New Market do an all-in package to Kathmandu (Rs185–235 depending on accommodation); booking through tourist offices. Travel Bureau at the Hotel Rajasthan offers a similar deal.

Accommodation

Hotel Samrat International, Fraser Road. Tel 220 560. SWB Rs350 (around £7/$11.65) DWB Rs450 SWB A/C Rs600 DWB A/C Rs700. Rest. Bar. Modern, well kept.

Rajasthan Hotel, Fraser Road. Tel 225 102. SWB/DWB Rs250/325. Rest A/C (veg, good). Standard Indian hotel.

Tourist Bhavan (Tourist Bungalow), 1km from station. SWB/DWB Rs175 (£3.50/$5.80) Dorm Rs60 (£1.20/$2).

Park(er) Hotel, Fraser Road. SR Rs45 DR Rs55 SWB Rs80 DWB Rs100. Basic.

Eating and drinking

Ashoka, Fraser Road. Ind non-veg. Mod. Bar. Dingy, but food good.

All these hotels and restaurants are within walking distance of the station, Fraser Road is straight ahead.

Around Patna

Vaishali, near Muzaffarpur, has an Ashoka pillar and also the remains of many stupas and temples at Vaishali. A Tourist Bungalow and Public Works Department Bungalow provide accommodation.

Sonepur, just over the river from Patna, has probably the largest livestock fair in the world every October/November. This is the place to buy your second-hand elephant. Best to stay in Patna.

GAYA

Gaya is an important pilgrimage place for Hindus. The most important of the many temples is the **Vishnupad** (Vishnu's footprint) where pilgrims make offerings to ensure the peace of departed relatives. The temple is closed to non-Hindus, and the town itself is horrible, no more than a gateway to Bodhgaya and Rajgir.

Information. Tourist Office in railway station.

Arrival and departure. On Delhi (16½hrs)–Calcutta (7hrs) line, not the main one, you have to pick your trains. See also Patna.

Hard though it may be to believe, the private bus-stand is even dirtier and more fly-blown than the rest of town. Luckily buses and auto-rickshaws for Bodhgaya (Rs5 share, one to yourself costs Rs35–40) leave from elsewhere; cycle rickshaw from station to here Rs3.

Accommodation (STD Code 0631)

Hotel Siddhartha International, Station Road. Tel 21254. SWB Rs325 DWB Rs450 SWB A/C Rs625 DWB A/C Rs800. Rest (very good). Bar. Modern hotel, well kept, comfortable rooms.

Ajatsatru, Station Road (directly opposite station). Tel 21514. SWB Rs90 DWB Rs150. Rest. Basic and reasonably clean. Ask for a room at the back for quietness.

Satkar Hotel. SR Rs50 DR Rs80 SWB Rs70 DWB Rs100. Clean rooms, don't let the entrance put you off.

BODHGAYA

Bodhgaya is one of the four most important Buddhist places of pilgrimage as Buddha achieved enlightenment here in about 528BC. The **Mahabodhi Temple*** marks the site of the Bodhi tree (actually a peepul or fig; bodhi means enlightenment) under which Buddha sat and meditated. On the right, as you enter the compound through a torana, is an old temple with a standing figure of Buddha and a library of Tibetan books. The original temple, built by Ashoka, forms a base for the present structure which dates from the second century AD. Inside is a large gilded image of Buddha, and very little else, none of the fine carving you might expect. The pyramidal spire rises 50m/164ft, but despite the good atmosphere the temple is a disappointment aesthetically, probably because of crude restoration by Burmese Buddhists in the last century. The sunken courtyard with its many stupas is more pleasing. The tree festooned with flags grew from a cutting of one at Annuradhapura in Sri Lanka, itself grown from the original tree. The rather tatty stone railing around the temple is a copy, most of the original having been removed to various museums.

Many Buddhist communities have built **temples***, monasteries, and rest houses at Bodhgaya in recent years, and these are well worth seeing. Most notable is a 25m/82ft-high **statue**** of a seated Buddha in meditation pose built by the Japanese. **Meditation courses** are run during the winter.

It is hard to sum up Bodhgaya. It is certainly a quiet and pleasant place to visit, but whether it justifies the effort and time involved in getting there must be a personal decision.

Information. Tourist office near bus-stand.

Arrival and departure. See under Gaya.

Accommodation

Tourist Bungalow No 1. Dorm Rs35.

Tourist Bungalow No 2. SWB Rs140 DWB Rs200 SWB A/C Rs250 DWB A/C Rs275 Dorm Rs50; plus 7% tax (except dorm). Rest (advance order). Both now called *Hotel Buddha Vihar*. In quiet location.

The *Travellers Lodge* is now the *Hotel Bodhgaya Ashok* (expensive). You can try the rest houses belonging to each community, though if one is full they all are. Mosquito nets needed most of the year. Luckily it is only a short rickshaw or bus ride to Gaya.

RAJGIR

Rajgir is visited mainly for its association with Buddha, and is also significant historically.

On a hilltop 6km/4 miles from the village is the huge **Shanti Stupa**** and a **temple*** built by Japanese Buddhists. The dazzling white stupa with gold images of Buddha and immaculate Japanese gardens are all a bit un-Indian in character; a **chair lift** takes you up there. A short walk from the lower end of the chair lift is **Gridhrakuta**, reputedly the Buddha's favourite place of meditation. Do not walk down to here from the stupa or anywhere else in the hills, there are bandits about.

The whole of the valley you pass through on the way back to Rajgir was once the town of **Rajagriha**, the sixth-century BC capital of a north Indian empire. The outer fortification followed the ridge of the hills all around. At Suraj Kund in the entrance to the valley are temples with **hot springs and baths**, and also the start of the path to **Saptarpani Cave** where a conference was held after the Great Demise (of Buddha). Strange place for a conference but an interesting view of the land pattern. Between Suraj Kund and the village are the ruins of **New Rajagriha**, rather later and more complete.

Between Gaya and Rajgir are the **Barabar Hills** and Caves, the 'Marabar' of EM Forster's *A Passage to India*.

Information. This whole area is covered in detail by one of the Archaeological Survey of India's excellent and inexpensive guide books; note that some of the details on the map are out of date. Tourist office near the hot springs; ASI guide sold here.

Arrival and departure. Train (unbelievably slow) or bus from Patna. Bus from Gaya. The last time the author tried this he fought his way on to the bus, then sat for 45 minutes in a puddle of sweat, deafened by the video, while the crew had a punch-up with two would-be passengers. Eventually they just disappeared altogether, and he gave up. Pity, he really enjoyed Nalanda and Rajgir on previous visits.

Accommodation. Two *Tourist Bungalows*, rooms and dorm beds in No 1, which also has a restaurant of sorts, dorm only (Rs45) in No 2. *Triptee's Hotel*, around Rs200, is the nicest place to stay.

Also cheap (mostly) accommodation in temples and rest houses, though the *Burmese* was dirty and expensive when last visited. We have heard of a smarter place, the *Hotel Centaur Hokke*, though this sounds a bit Japanese, which probably means high prices.

Eating and drinking. *Triptee's Hotel*. Cheap/Mod. The only real restaurant in town.

NALANDA

Nalanda has the ruins, excellently tended, of a huge **Buddhist monastic university**. Founded in the fifth century AD, it was in decline by the ninth (as was Buddhism in India generally) and sacked by Muslims in the 12th century. These remains are far more impressive than those at Sarnath. The **museum** is nearby.

The great thing about a place like this is that it gets you out of town and into the real India. Wander up to the **memorial** to Hieun Tsang (he was a seventh-century Chinese monk to whose record of his travels we owe much of our knowledge of Buddhism) and into the village to see the tank and temple. Above all use the opportunity to observe the way of life; it can have changed little since the university's heyday.

Despite their lack of amenities Nalanda and Rajgir are much underrated, not least for the peace and quiet.

Information. Tourist office. ASI booklet available.

Arrival and departure. On Patna–Rajgir railway line. Bus from Rajgir.

Accommodation. *PWD Rest House*, but most people choose to stay in Rajgir.

SOUTHERN BIHAR

Southern Bihar is virgin territory as far as foreign visitors are concerned. The area comprises mainly the hilly, forested Chotanagpur Plateau, the main centre being Ranchi. The countryside is attractive and home to a large number of aboriginal people, 'Scheduled Tribes' in Indian bureaucrat-speak. *A Goddess in the Stones* by Norman Lewis is an excellent account of a visit to this area.

At **Parasnath** is a hilltop group of Jain temples second only to Palitana in importance. **Netarhat** is a hill station at 1127m (*Tourist and Public Works Department Bungalows*), and there are wildlife sanctuaries at **Hazaribagh** and **Palamau National Park**, both holding tigers (*Tourist Lodge* and several *Forest Rest Houses*).

Information. Bihar Tourism has plenty of information on these places; one hopes only that transport arrangements are better than in the north of the state. One guesses that this is a place for the tough and resourceful.

WEST BENGAL

Like The Punjab, Bengal was divided in 1947 between India and Pakistan causing inevitable population transfers, and the bloodshed that went with them. The upheavals leading to and following the creation of Bangladesh in 1971 caused a further exodus, and the repercussions of both these events still cause great problems. Apart from the human tragedy, partition cut off the jute mills of Calcutta from most of their raw materials in what was then East Pakistan.

Bengalis are the most volatile of Indians, and it was Ram Mohan Roy (1770–1833), Ramakrishna (1834–1886), the leader of a Hindu revival, and his disciple Vivekananda who laid the base of Indian nationalism. SC Bose (you will find streets bearing his name all over India) became a hero for forming the Indian National Army to fight the Allies in Burma during the Second World War, but he seems to have been more trouble to the Japanese than the British. Bengal is also the intellectual heart of India, and has produced poets, painters, dramatists and film makers of international repute.

In recent years nationalism has turned to radicalism, and the state now has a communist government. Hopes of a popular revolution, however, have quickly evaporated in the usual venality and corruption of Indian politics.

CALCUTTA

The very mention of Calcutta, Kipling's 'city of dreadful night', fills many travellers with horror. Ten years ago one could write, 'if it is worse than any other Indian city it is only a matter of degree, and things have been (superficially) improved lately by clearing most of the street-dwellers out of the centre'. Now it is hard to make any excuses for the place at all. Calcutta is a dying city, a complete contrast with Bombay

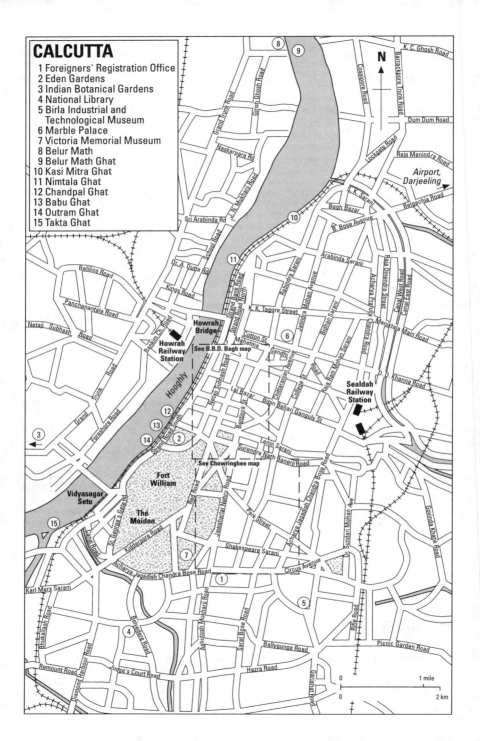

where, despite the slums and other problems, you can feel hope and energy in the air. Here nothing works properly, and the people are clearly resigned to the fact that it never will. You see few smiling faces in Calcutta.

And yet Calcuttans defend their city as if it were still an intellectual powerhouse and a good place to live and work. A few years ago there were furious protests about the filming of an already emasculated version of *City of Joy*, which is seen as defamatory of the city and its population. Bengalis seem too bound up with past glories to recognise the present appalling reality. If, incidentally, some loquacious Bengali intellectual has a go at you about that city of dreadful night epithet you can point out that it was originally the title of a poem by James Thomson (1834–1882). He was writing about London.

When a beggar approaches you in Bombay you *suspect* that he has made a conscious decision to beg, knowing that he will earn more that way than by taking one of the readily available jobs. Here you *know* that it is the only alternative to starvation — a tangible expression of the general air of desperation. For all this, Calcutta is a historic city and rivalled only by Bombay for places of interest. Of course if you go poking around in the bastees you are going to see slums and deprivation as bad as any on Earth. But why go? You will not be welcome, especially with a camera, and how could you help matters?

History

Calcutta, like Bombay and Madras, was founded by the English as a trading post. After various problems with local rulers a permanent factory (as warehouses were called) and fort were in being by 1700. In 1756 the Nawab of Murshidabad took Calcutta and there followed the Black Hole incident, now regarded as of highly dubious provenance. It was this act that brought Clive north from Madras and began a chain of events culminating in the British assumption of political power in India. By 1774 Calcutta was effectively the capital of British India, a position it held until 1911 when the move to Delhi was announced. For many years thereafter Calcutta, like Bombay, remained of greater commercial importance than the new capital. Now business is moving away and there is little new investment.

Chowringhee and the Maidan

For the visitor the centre of Calcutta is **Chowringhee**, bordered by the **Maidan**, a broad green park originally cleared to give the guns of **Fort William** a clear field of fire. The fort is still used by the army and difficult to visit; a shame as there are few examples of British military architecture of this period.

South of the Maidan is the **Victoria Memorial**** (10am–4pm in winter, 10am–5pm in summer, closed Monday). This white marble edifice houses a splendid art gallery and museum of British imperial history; note how a few Mughal touches have crept into the otherwise Western design. Just over the road is the **racecourse** where you can get a good idea how the other half lives in Calcutta. Not far away is the **zoo***, much better than most in India and boasting some white tigers. The grounds are quiet and there is an air-conditioned restaurant which makes a good place for lunch. Further south from here is the **Kali Temple** at Kalighat, which some reckon to be the source of the city's name.

The **Academy of Fine Arts Gallery** (open 3–8pm) is notable for its collection of Tagore paintings, and puts on frequent special shows. **St Paul's Cathedral*** (open 9am–noon and 3–6pm) is a large Gothic building completed in 1847. A painting inside shows it in its early form with a slender spire, and the memorial tablets make fascinating reading. The **Birla Planetarium** is next door; this being India astrology is combined with astronomy.

Back up Chowringhee Road is the **Indian Museum** which you are going to love or

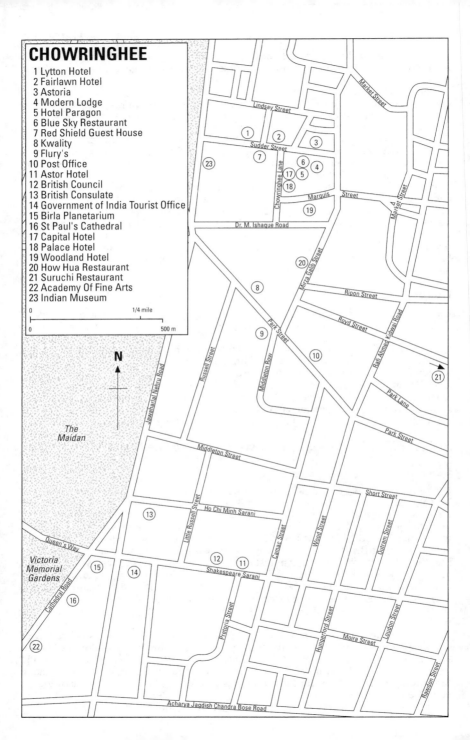

CHOWRINGHEE

1 Lytton Hotel
2 Fairlawn Hotel
3 Astoria
4 Modern Lodge
5 Hotel Paragon
6 Blue Sky Restaurant
7 Red Shield Guest House
8 Kwality
9 Flury's
10 Post Office
11 British Council
12 British Consulate
13 British Consulate
14 Government of India Tourist Office
15 Birla Planetarium
16 St Paul's Cathedral
17 Capital Hotel
18 Palace Hotel
19 Woodland Hotel
20 How Hua Restaurant
21 Suruchi Restaurant
22 Academy Of Fine Arts
23 Indian Museum

0   1/4 mile

0   500 m

N

The
Maidan

Victoria
Memorial
Gardens

hate. A real Victorian establishment, a start has finally been made on rearranging its vast collection. A short distance away **New Market** is the place for handicrafts and souvenir shopping, if you can put up with the blandishments of the 'boys', the freelance touts angling for commissions.

Old Calcutta

At the northern end of the Maidan is the **Ochterlony Monument***, named after the man who defeated Nepal in 1814–16. Now sometimes called the Shahid Minar (Martyrs' Tower), you can climb this (it is 46m high) for the view; apply at Lal Bazaar police station for a permit. The tower is open only during the middle two weeks of the month. You ask them why.

This is the edge of Calcutta's business area, the oldest part of town. **St John's Church**** was the first in Calcutta and once the cathedral. It has some fine memorials including one to Job Charnock, the Englishman who founded Calcutta, and the visitors' book makes fascinating reading.

The site of the first Fort William is now occupied by the **General Post Office**. The fort lock-up was known as the Black Hole; captives were herded into this when the fort was captured in 1757, and a certain number died of suffocation. Brass strips marking the fort walls could still be seen in the 1970s, but they are now gone, and the memorial has been removed to St John's churchyard. Just as well really, the incident was hugely exaggerated. Over the road is **BBD Bagh** (Dalhousie Square) and the vast **Writers' Building**, which housed the clerks of the East India Company, and now houses those of the local government.

Hard to find, but worth the effort, is the **Marble Palace***** which has a remarkable private art collection including works by Rubens and Reynolds; a permit to visit must be obtained from the Government of India Tourist Office.

Calcutta has a lot of interesting architecture from the imperial days. **Raj Bhavan** (the governor's residence and formerly known as Government House) is modelled on Keddlestone Hall in Derbyshire, England, the **High Courts** on the Staadhaus at Ypres in Belgium, and **Belvedere House**, now the National Library, is classical, like the **Town Hall**.

Over the Hooghly

The **Howrah Bridge** must have seemed pretty impressive when it was built (1943) but it looks rather ordinary now and is notable only for the tide of humanity constantly flowing across it. You are not allowed to photograph the bridge, but no-one will object to you buying a picture postcard of it! Unless you count Howrah station as a tourist attraction or really want to visit the bastees the only thing to see on the far side of the river is the **Botanical Gardens**, which claim to have the largest banyan tree in the world. Despite losing its central trunk it has kept growing and now covers an area of over 10,000 sq m. Take a ferry from Chandpal Ghat to Shivpur to avoid the jams on Howrah Bridge.

Practical Information *i*   Government of India Tourist Office at 4 Shakespeare Sarani. Various guided tours and details of cultural events.

Geoffrey Moorhouse's *Calcutta* is fascinating; *The Black Hole* by Iris Macfarlane (Allen and Unwin) debunks most of the myth about this infamous incident.

Local transport. Calcutta's Metro operates 8am–8pm with a train every 12 minutes between Esplanade and Tollygunge stations. Fares Re1/1.50 — and it's spotless! The tram depot is at the northern end of the Maidan. No 12A runs from Howrah through the depot to Sudder Street; Nos 12, 14 and 17 from Sealdah to the depot; Nos 12, 20 and 26 from Sealdah to Howrah; Nos 24, 29, 30, and 32 all run from the depot past

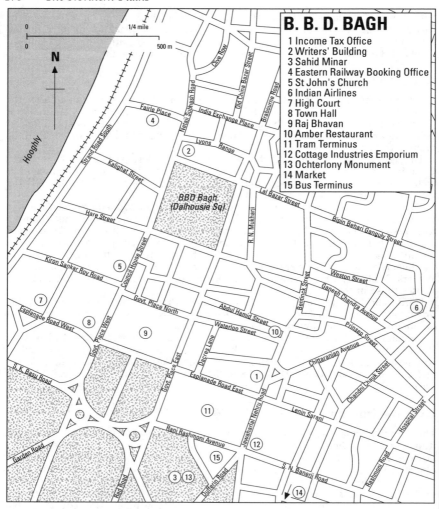

B. B. D. BAGH

1 Income Tax Office
2 Writers' Building
3 Sahid Minar
4 Eastern Railway Booking Office
5 St John's Church
6 Indian Airlines
7 High Court
8 Town Hall
9 Raj Bhavan
10 Amber Restaurant
11 Tram Terminus
12 Cottage Industries Emporium
13 Ochterlony Monument
14 Market
15 Bus Terminus

Sudder Street to the Victoria Memorial area. Nos 31 and 35 run to Ekbalpur for the zoo and Nepalese consulate. No 30 travels via Fairlie Place for the railway booking offices.

Ordinary buses are impossibly crowded. Try the minibuses which are much faster and more comfortable. For the Botanical Gardens take a tram to Howrah and then a No 55 or 55A bus.

Taxis are quite cheap and the drivers mostly good about using the meter. Add 50% if the meter starts on Rs6; if it starts on Rs8 it indicates the correct fare.

Arrival and departure. International and domestic airport at Dum Dum (12km), a name notorious the world over for the soft-nose (not explosive) bullets first produced in the ordnance factory there. Indian Airlines office (Tel 263 390) at 39 Chittaranjan Avenue.

Train from Madras (25hrs), Bhubaneswar (6hrs), Puri (8¼hrs), Varanasi (14½hrs), Muzaffarpur for Nepal (14½hrs), Delhi (24hrs or 16¾hrs by Rajdhani Express), Patna (10hrs), Darjeeling (18½hrs) change at New Jalpaiguri. Note that there are two major stations, Howrah and Sealdah, and two separate booking offices. South-Eastern Railway is on the Esplanade near the tram depot, that of the Eastern Railway is on Strand Road; you can save a lot of time by going straight to the Centralised Foreign Tourist Office in Fairlie Place (9am–4pm Mon–Sat, 9am–2pm Sunday and holidays, closed for lunch 1–1.30pm). Payment in foreign currency or rupees with an encashment certificate.

Accommodation (STD Code 033)

All of the following are in the Chowringhee area behind the Indian Museum:

Fairlawn Hotel, 13/A Sudder Street. Tel 245 1510 Fax 244 1835. SWB A/C $35 (£21) DWB A/C $50, both full board, less for bed and breakfast. Rest. Bar. A traditional English country guest house in the midst of Calcutta's turmoil. Bedrooms chintzily comfortable. Super staff. Have afternoon tea or a beer in the plant-bedecked courtyard. The English food is supposed to be good, lunch Rs75 dinner Rs85, non-residents must order in advance.

Lytton Hotel, 14 Sudder Street. Tel 249 1872. SWB A/C Rs900 DWB A/C Rs1100. Rest (2) A/C. Bar A/C.

Astoria Hotel, 6/2/3 Sudder Street. Tel 244 9679. SWB/DWB A/C Rs550. Breakfast.

Shilton Hotel, Sudder Street. Tel 245 1512. SWB Rs150 DWB Rs225.

Hilson Hotel, 4 Sudder Street. Tel 244 5283. SR Rs80 DWB Rs150.

Capital Guest House, 11B Chowringhee Lane. Tel 245 0598. SWB Rs100 (£2/$3.35) DWB Rs170 SWB A/C Rs250 DWB A/C Rs300. Small rooms but vastly preferable to most others in this price bracket.

Woodland Guest House, just off Marco Street opposite end of Stuart Lane. DR Rs190 DWB Rs260. Clean and well kept.

Modern Lodge, 1 Stuart Lane. Tel 244 4960. DR Rs70 DWB Rs150 Dorm Rs40 (all include breakfast). Not bad at all, well kept. Don't rely on there being a dorm, it may be converted into rooms.

Paragon, 2 Stuart Lane. Tel 244 2445. SR Rs80 DR Rs105 DWB Rs150 Dorm Rs45.

Hotel Palace, 13 Chowringhee Lane. Tel 244 6214. SWB Rs110 DWB Rs150.

Hotel Maria, 5-1 Sudder Street. Tel 245 0860. SR Rs90 DR Rs150 Dorm Rs40.

Red Shield Hostel, 2 Sudder Street. Tel 245 0599. DR Rs80/120 DWB Rs150 Dorm Rs20/30.

Tourist Inn, Sudder Street, appears to be a rather desperate place.

Eating and drinking

How Hua, Mirza Ghalib Street. Chi. Mod/Exp. Real Chinese food. Most dishes Rs25–35. Chimney soup superb — a meal in itself. Special dishes (advance order) include duck, pigeon and suckling pig.

Blue Sky, Sudder Street. Cheap/Mod. Old established hippy haven. Good food, lassi, and curd.

Gipsy, Mirza Ghalib Street. Punjabi/Chi/Kebabs. Cheap/Mod.

The New Market (bakers and food stalls inside), Sudder Street and Mirza Ghalib Street area has many restaurants and food shops; worth a good look round. Smarter and mostly more expensive restaurants on Park Street. Other cheaper Chinese restaurants near to How Hua. The *Ambar* on Waterloo Street (behind the tram terminal) is often said to have the best north Indian food in Cal, and the *Astor Hotel*, Shakespeare Sarani, has an excellent restaurant and beer at Rs45. One of very few places where you can try the interesting Bengali cuisine (no Bengali believes anyone can cook as well as his wife or mother) is *Suruchi*, 89 Elliott Road (continuation of Royd Street and roughly parallel to Park Street).

Central India

Detail from Temple, Khajuraho

Madhya Pradesh

Historically the name Central India has a great ring to it. For centuries it was an adventure playground for empire builders, a place where dynasties and cultures clashed. Marathas and Mughals, Rajputs and the British fought for the main prize, and the dogs of war — Pindaris, dacoits and Thugs — grew fat on the pickings. Fortunes were made and lost, often through foul treachery, and magnificent forts and palaces were built. The Central India Horse, still one of the Indian Army's crack cavalry regiments, rode out in splendid uniforms, and big game abounded.

MADHYA PRADESH

Madhya Pradesh is the largest state in India; its 443,000 sq km make it half as large again as Uttar Pradesh or Maharashtra, and not much smaller than France. The population is over 66 million, thinly spread compared with most of India.

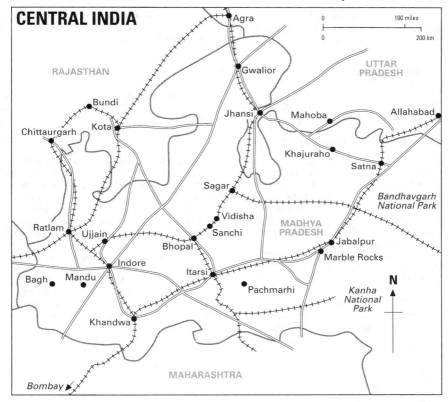

Most of the land is a plateau around 500m/1640ft above sea level crested by the Vindhaya (north of the Narmada valley) and Satpura (to the south) hills, though these rise to little over 1300m/4264ft. There is little industry, and the vast majority of the population lives on the land, about a third of which is still forested. Much of the countryside is very beautiful, especially along the road from Jhansi to Khajuraho and around Pachmarhi. The hills and forests make a welcome contrast with the flatness of the northern plains.

Madhya Pradesh is the crossroads between north India and south India, a link between the northern plains and the Deccan. Culturally it belongs to the north, most of the population speaking various dialects of Hindi, and geographically to the south. Its position means that it has always been on the traditional route of conquest from north to south, and was caught in the middle when the Marathas expanded north from their base in Pune.

From the visitor's viewpoint Madhya Pradesh's attractions are spread out and involve a lot of travelling. Khajuraho and Sanchi, however, are two of the most important religious sites in India, and places like Gwalior and Indore are much underrated. Madhya Pradesh may be classified as a backward state in terms of literacy and infant mortality but, unlike Bihar, this is not obvious to the traveller, and the state is an attractive and interesting place to visit.

Handicrafts. Nothing of especial note though, as elsewhere in India, there are lovely, locally made textiles. These are mostly produced on power looms rather than hand ones, but many are owned by small operators so there is great individuality in the products. Rough silk is produced from a species of wild silk worm and handloomed.

Climate. Like the rest of northern India, Madhya Pradesh is at its best from October to March, though the winter evenings can be chilly. The hot season (April–June) can be very hot and dry indeed, and erratic monsoon rains are a real problem. Madhya Pradesh is best avoided during a good monsoon (July–September) when communications can be chaotic.

THE MARATHAS IN CENTRAL INDIA

For the 300 years from 1660 up to Independence the history of this area was bound up with the exploits of the Marathas. In the 18th century four great families, Gaekwar of Baroda, Holkar of Indore, Scindia of Gwalior, and Bhonsle of Nagpur established their states here. Although theoretically part of the Maratha confederacy based on Poona they soon asserted their independence. The states all suffered the same chronic instability as other Maratha fiefs. What could have been a united Hindu empire succeeding the Mughals (and quite possibly keeping out the British) degenerated into bloody anarchy.

At the height of their power these northern Maratha families controlled Delhi, including the Mughal emperor, and much of Rajasthan. Their weakness stemmed from their fiscal methods which, like Shivaji's, were based on plunder, and on the structure of the state which depended entirely on the strength and character of the man at the top. Their infighting and their tolerance of anarchic groups like the Pindaris and Thugs (see page 180) created instability on the borders of British India, and made it only a matter of time before the British moved against them. Like so many other invaders the British found a disunited opposition which they picked off one at a time in a series of wars between 1775 and 1819. Bound by treaty to the British crown the Maratha families continued to rule their states, mostly very well, until 1947.

GWALIOR

Gwalior has one of the great forts of northern India and many other places of interest. Its position on the railway from Bombay to Delhi and on the road between Agra and Khajuraho makes it easy to visit, yet most people race through, their eyes firmly fixed on the Taj Mahal or Khajuraho's so-called erotic temples. Break your journey and give Gwalior a chance.

History

Gwalior's strategic position led to a typically troubled history. Probably founded in the sixth century AD, it was for a time part of the Chandella kingdom based on Khajuraho. For many centuries after that it alternated between Rajput and Muslim control, the latter sometimes from Mandu, more often the Delhi sultans or the Mughals. The Mughals held Gwalior for 200 years until the Marathas took it in 1754, lost it to the Jats, who lost it to the Marathas, who lost it to the British, who gave it back to the Jats, who lost it to the Marathas (the Scindia family this time) in 1784, who lost it to the British in 1804, who gave it back to Scindia the following year. That's just fifty years of Gwalior's history, and we can assume that these transactions were mostly not of a friendly nature. After the Mutiny the British decided to garrison Gwalior so they swapped it for Jhansi. Finally in 1886 they decided they preferred Jhansi after all, so the army moved back there, and Gwalior reverted to the Maharaja.

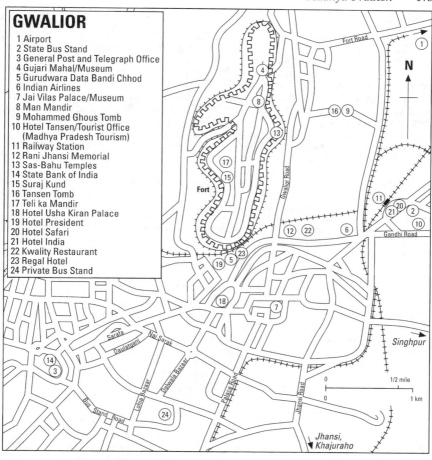

GWALIOR

1 Airport
2 State Bus Stand
3 General Post and Telegraph Office
4 Gujari Mahal/Museum
5 Gurudwara Data Bandi Chhod
6 Indian Airlines
7 Jai Vilas Palace/Museum
8 Man Mandir
9 Mohammed Ghous Tomb
10 Hotel Tansen/Tourist Office
   (Madhya Pradesh Tourism)
11 Railway Station
12 Rani Jhansi Memorial
13 Sas-Bahu Temples
14 State Bank of India
15 Suraj Kund
16 Tansen Tomb
17 Teli ka Mandir
18 Hotel Usha Kiran Palace
19 Hotel President
20 Hotel Safari
21 Hotel India
22 Kwality Restaurant
23 Regal Hotel
24 Private Bus Stand

The Scindia family ruled right up to Independence, and proved a pretty enlightened lot.

The old town

A short distance from the eastern entrance to the fort is a large Muslim graveyard. The most imposing structure is the **Tomb of Muhammad Ghaus***, a Muslim saint and guru of Akbar. The old custodian claims to be a direct descendant. Tansen was a famous singer and one of the 'Nine Gems' (or favourites) of Akbar's court. His simple tomb is in front of that of Muhammad Ghaus (Jabalpur also claims to have his tomb, incidentally). One of the trees nearby is a tamarind; legend has it that singers who chew its leaves will acquire a voice as good as Tansen's. The leaves taste awful.

Nearer the gate of the fort, the **Jama Masjid*** is a nicely proportioned building worth a quick look.

The fort

Gwalior is dominated by a hill nearly 3km/2miles long rising sheer above the plain. Varying in width from 200m to 800m this natural defensive position is enhanced by dizzying walls. Roughly parallel to it is the similarly flat-topped hill of Hanuman.

The original approach to the **Fort*** is the elephant ramp to the north-east, spanned by five (once six) great gates. The first two gates are the Alamgiri (outer, and later) and the Hindola. Looking closely at the latter you can still see the rows of ducks which adorn it, though most of the colour has now gone, and two squirrels. On the right inside the Hindola Gate is the Gujari Mahal, the palace built by Man Singh for Mriganaya ('Doe-eyed'), his dancing-girl wife from the Gujar tribe. This now houses the **Archaeological Museum**** (closed Monday). In addition to all the statuary there are copies of the frescoes in the Bagh caves. Note all the elephants above the entrance.

Walking up the rough road towards the fort, and through the Ganesh Gate, you come to a small white temple and the **Cave of Gwalipa***, a sage who lent his name to the town. Just by this temple are steps leading to the north-eastern group of **Jain statues**°. On the opposite side of the road, and below, is a defensive outwork called, confusingly, the Kabutar Khana or pigeon house. Where the road takes a hairpin to the right is the rock-cut **Chatarbhuj Mandir** (temple of the four-armed), sacred to Vishnu. Inscriptions date it to the ninth century, like the road and the walls. The remaining two gates are the Lakshman and Hathiyar, the latter named from the large stone elephant which once stood here.

The **Chit Mandir***** (Painted Palace) of Man Singh (1486–1516), Gwalior's greatest Rajput ruler, is the first and finest of the secular buildings in the fort. Observe the bands of ceramic decoration; now imagine them in their original brightness and the whole structure, cupolas and all, covered in brilliant white chunam. Before the Mughals started building this was almost certainly the finest palace in northern India. The interior displays more ceramics and finely carved sandstone. The lower levels were cool rooms for the summer; later used by the Mughals as a state prison they witnessed some pretty foul deeds. Four newer **palaces** and the **jauhar tank** lie north of the Chit Mandir, but are of limited interest. Military architecture buffs will find things of interest in this area, and there is a fine view straight down into the town.

Heading south from the Chit Mandir, note the British magazine, then take the left fork in the road and follow the line of the walls. Over to the right are the round towers and walls of the **Bale Qila**, an inner fort built by the Marathas. This and the southern part of the plateau are occupied by a public (i.e. private) school. Up on the main wall are two old cannon, and then comes the **Sasbahu-ka-Mandir****, a pair of temples. 'Sas' means mother-in-law, and 'bahu' daughter-in-law; an Indian daughter-in-law is still pretty much a slave to her husband's mother, and the temples gained this nickname from their proximity. The larger temple had a tall spire, and may have been Jain despite the Vishnu figures over the door. The smaller temple has lost its shrine. Both were built in the 11th century and show similarities of style to the temples of Khajuraho. The Muslims damaged these temples, and it's said that British squaddies in the 19th century used the figures for target practice. A good view along the walls from here.

Nearby rise the white domes of a new **gurudwara** built over the spot where Har Gobind Singh (the sixth Sikh guru) and 52 Hindu princes were released from prison by Jehangir. This is your only hope for a drink if no-one is selling them at the Chit Mandir. Just to the west is the **Teli-ka-mandir**** owes its odd appearance (for this part of India) to Dravidian influence. It is probably the oldest (eighth century) building on the hill. The Garuda over the door indicates allegiance to Vishnu, but the temple is now dedicated to Shiva. The name translates literally as 'oil merchant's temple', but is more likely a corruption of Telangana (i.e. Telugu or from Andhra Pradesh).

Suraj Kund is the pool where Gwalipa cured Suraj Sen, the Rajput founder of Gwalior, of leprosy. The temple here is dedicated to Surya, the sun god.

Giant statues

Head north again towards the telecommunications tower and take the path down into the ravine, where you will find many Jain **monolithic statues*** (15th century) including one of Adinath 17m/56ft high. The bar in front of the naughty bits probably signifies chastity. There are lots of these sculptures about, the other main group being on the south-east flank of the fort, but these are the most accessible. It is possible to continue down the valley to the outer defences and walk into town from there (not much chance of a rickshaw). The railway signals controlled traffic when this was a single-track road.

The new town

Down on the level again the **Jai Vilas Palace**** is a huge building in rag-bag Italian style which is now a museum (closed Monday). The palace (19th century) was designed, built, and equipped by Sir Michael Filose, whose Italian adventurer forebears had become courtiers of Scindia. The collection is eclectic (to say the least) and now rather tatty but still fascinating. Pride of place goes to the huge darbar hall. The carpet is said to be the largest one-piece one in the world and had to be woven in place. The crystal chandeliers come from Vienna and, again, are said to be the largest ever. They tested the ability of the roof to support them by marching a dozen elephants over it for several days! The maharajas were railway nuts (and still are, the present one sometime Minister of Railways) and you may be able to see the silver train which carried the cigars and liqueurs round the dinner table. Despite the 200 rooms the maharaja soon tired of the European style and had the Motimahal — a more Indian palace — built, this time with 900 smaller rooms.

The **Kala Mandika** is a small art gallery which puts on occasional shows and has a permanent collection.

The two **narrow gauge railways** (2ft gauge) which run out into the country from Gwalior are now all diesel. A steam locomotive is preserved in front of the narrow gauge offices, and a small **museum** has been set up. Old wagons and railcars are also kept. Two other railways (2½ft gauge) operate from Dholpur, 65km/41 miles north of Gwalior on the way to Agra, and may still be steam-hauled.

Practical Information *i*	Tourist office at Motel Tansen near station. *Princess* by Vijayaraje Scindia (the Dowager Maharani) and Manohar Malgonkar (Century, but cheap editions available in India) is a fascinating insight into the lives of the princes.

Arrival and departure. Airport (5km/3 miles). Indian Airlines (Tel 23045) on Maharani Lakshmi Bai (MLB) Road near station.

On New Delhi (5hrs)–Bombay VT (23¾hrs) railway line (not to be confused with the line to Bombay Central which takes a different route); Agra (2hrs), Jhansi (2hrs) on same line. See also under Khajuraho.

Buses to Agra, Jhansi, and Shivpuri. Bus-stand is close to the railway station (the private bus-stand is miles away in Lashkar). Tempos connect all major places within the town.

Accommodation (STD Code 0751)

Motel Tansen (Tourist Bungalow), 500m from station. Tel 340 370. SWB Rs225 DWB Rs275. Rest (very good). Bar (pleasant). An excellent place to stay.

Hotel President, Maharani Laxmi Bai Road, Lashkar (1.5km/1 mile from station).

Tel 24673. SWB Rs225 DWB Rs250 (air-cooled). Rest. Bar. Good food. Roof terrace. Rooms at back are quiet.

Regal Hotel, Maharani Laxmi Bai Road (1.75km/1 mile from station). Tel 22599. SR Rs75 (£1.50/$2.50) DR Rs100 SWB Rs120 DWB Rs210. Rest. Bar. Very good food. Again, make sure you get a room at the back. Good value for money, but being charged extra for bedding is always annoying.

Hotel India, adjacent to station. Tel 341 983. SWB Rs85–100 DWB Rs120–140.

Hotel Safari, Station Road. Tel 24638. SR Rs75 DR Rs120 Dorm Rs30.

Opposite the India is the *Ashok*, cheaper but horrible. The *Retiring Rooms* on the station have dorm beds.

A popular place in Lashkar is *Gujri Mahal* (Tel 23942).

Eating and drinking

Kwality, MLB Road. Mod/Exp. Excellent. With the nearby President and Regal Hotels eating out is a real pleasure in Gwalior.

Indian Coffee House, at Hotel India. Cheap. South Indian vegetarian and snacks. Other cheap places near the station.

SHIVPURI

Shivpuri, at an altitude of 400m, was the summer centre of Gwalior's government. Little cooler, but much healthier than the city in the hot weather.

Madhav Rao Scindia (Maharaja of Gwalior 1886–1925) and his mother Maharani Sakhya Raja Scindia were cremated here, and their memorial **chhattris** are set in a fine formal garden 2km from the town centre. The maharaja's, built in 1926 of white marble in Rajput style, has inlay work to match the tomb of Itmad-ud-Daulah in Agra — and there is total peace.

The **Madhav National Park** (4km/2.5 miles further along the same road from the town centre) has tigers, panthers, bears, and many other species; all you are likely to see are deer. The rest house in the park is in the old sailing club buildings on a large lake. Now, perhaps out of deference to the crocodiles, there are only pedaloes. Sightseeing is by jeep (capacity eight people), and you can fish in the lake.

Arrival and departure. Bus from Gwalior (3hrs) or Jhansi (3½hrs). A broad gauge railway line to Gwalior has replaced the narrow gauge line, still shown on some maps, which was dismantled many years ago.

Accommodation (STD Code 07492)

Chinkara Motel, Agra–Bombay Road. Tel 2297. SWB Rs180 DWB Rs240 SWB A/C Rs295 DWB A/C Rs325. Rest.

Cheaper hotels and restaurants in same street. Madhya Pradesh Tourism have a *Tourist Village* at Bhadaiya Kund, near the chhattris (DWB from Rs250), and the *Forest Rest House* by the lake is reasonable.

JHANSI

Jhansi is actually in Uttar Pradesh. The convoluted border is a hangover from the Raj when Jhansi was part of United Provinces (the part of British India which became Uttar Pradesh), and the surrounding areas were princely states. Because it lies between Gwalior and Khajuraho we'll deal with it here.

Jhansi was founded by the Marathas in 1734 in succession to Orchha which they had conquered. They ruled until 1803 when the British made it a protectorate leaving the Raja in nominal charge.

Jhansi was one of the major flashpoints of the Mutiny in 1857. As had happened in many other states in the preceding thirty years, the British took over Jhansi when the Raja died without an heir, disregarding the Hindu custom of adopting an heir. This was just part of a process of Westernisation which Indians felt to threaten their faiths and way of life. The Raja's widow, Rani Lakshmi Bhai, was unsurprisingly disgruntled despite a generous pension. Taking advantage of the outbreak of the Mutiny in Meerut and Delhi she led her Afghan bodyguard in a slaughter of the British garrison. She later escaped from Jhansi fort when British forces stormed it and made her way to Gwalior. There she died, sword in hand, leading her troops in a sortie from the fort.

The old British part of the town is a typical cantonment, wide streets, trees, and lots of space. This is pleasant enough, but of minimal interest. The **fort** was heavily altered in the 19th century and is of note only for the views from the top. The **museum** is the all-too-familiar collection of battered statuary.

Information. Uttar Pradesh and Madhya Pradesh tourist offices on railway station.

Arrival and departure. On New Delhi (7hrs)–Bombay VT (21¾hrs) railway line (not the line to Bombay Central); Agra (4hrs), Gwalior (2hrs) on same line.

The railway station and bus-stand are 3km/2 miles apart; tempos run a regular service. The route between Gwalior, Jhansi, and Khajuraho is covered fully under Khajuraho.

Accommodation (STD Code 0517)

Jhansi Hotel, Shastri Marg (Tel 441 360) is a traditional hangover from the Raj, rooms from Rs350. Uttar Pradesh Tourism's *Hotel Veerangana*, Shivpuri Road (Tel 442402) is cheaper, doubles Rs100 up, and has dorm beds; both are a Rs10 rickshaw ride from the station or bus-stand.

ORCHHA

Orchha, in a wild riverside setting between Khajuraho and Jhansi, has a profusion of palaces and temples. The city was founded in the 1520s when the Bundelas established their capital on an island in the River Betwa. Following rajas expanded the state, the most successful being Birsingh Deo who built forts and palaces all over his realm. Towards the end of Akbar's reign he ingratiated himself with Prince Salim, later Jehangir, by murdering Abul Fazl, a historian and great favourite at Akbar's court; an unfair end for the man who had persuaded Akbar to treat the Hindus better than any previous Muslim ruler. Akbar's army devastated the state, but Birsingh escaped and was restored a few years later when Jehangir came to the throne. He finally came unstuck when he backed the wrong side in the next succession struggle in 1627.

Later Bundela princes distinguished themselves in the armies of Shahjahan and Aurangzeb. The anarchy of the 18th century prompted a move to the more defensible Tikamgarh (95km/59 miles south of Orchha), and Orchha has been deserted ever since.

The fine buildings include the **Jehangiri Mahal**, gratefully named after Jehangir, and the **Raj Mahal** with its murals. The **Lakshminarayan temple** also has murals. Now that Khajuraho has become more popular Orchha is a good place to relax.

Information. Cassette guided tours from Hotel Sheesh Mahal.

Arrival and departure. Orchha is 18km/11 miles from Jhansi, buses and tempos run regularly from the main bus-stand in Jhansi.

Accommodation. Madhya Pradesh Tourism run both *Hotel Sheesh Mahal* (Tel 224), which is part of one of the old palaces, and *Betwa Cottages*; prices from Rs200 up, bookable through Madhya Pradesh Tourism offices elsewhere. *Hotel Mansarovar* is cheaper and good, *Palkhi Mahal* equally cheap and much more atmospheric.

Eating and drinking. Restaurants at the hotels, and the cheap rooftop *Betwa Tarang*.

BUNDELKHAND

Bundelkhand was an area of small Rajput states including Orchha, Chhattarpur, and Panna spreading east from Jhansi. This was traditionally a lawless area, and continued to give the British Political Agent (who dealt with relations between the government of India and the states) plenty to do right up to the end of the Raj.

Thugs, dacoits, and other baddies

When the Mysore War ended in 1799 and the Maratha Wars in 1819 the British were able to assess the war-torn dominion they found, more or less by accident, under their control. One of the first things they realised was that huge numbers of travellers, sometimes in excess of 10,000 a year, were going missing. The finger was soon pointed at the cult of Thuggee whose members, the **Thugs**, were devotees of the destructive goddess Kali. Kali demands sacrifice, and as part of their method of robbery the Thugs strangled their victims with a cloth normally worn around the waist. They were highly organised, both in reconnaissance and concealment of bodies, and very persistent. A group of Thugs might travel with their victims for several days before finding a suitable place for the murders. One of the strangest aspects of the cult, never really explained, was that many members were Muslims.

Thuggee had been established for centuries, affecting both north and south India, but the anarchy following the collapse of the Mughal empire saw a huge increase in the Thugs' activities. Groups of up to 150 Thugs could tackle even large numbers of travellers banded together for safety. The gangs had the protection of local princes who exacted a percentage of the take. William Sleeman (1788–1856) was appointed to deal with the problem and, by a combination of good intelligence and rough justice, had more or less eliminated Thuggee by 1840. Part of his method was to set up training schools where the Thugs could learn a trade, one of which was at Jabalpur. A huge carpet woven by retired Thugs is still in the Waterloo Chamber in Windsor Castle, England.

Sleeman wrote his own account of the suppression of Thuggee: *Rambles and Recollections of an Indian Official*. Philip Meadows Taylor, a contemporary of Sleeman, wrote the novel *Confessions of a Thug* and, more recently, John Masters based *The Deceivers* around the cult.

The suppression of Thuggee did not end the problem of hereditary castes of robbers or **dacoits**. As late as 1911 the government of India passed the Criminal Tribes Act to intern and attempt to retrain some of an estimated four million outlaws. One of these camps was at Nowgong, on the road from Jhansi to Khajuraho. Indian newspapers carry frequent reports of dacoities — legally a dacoity is robbery with violence or menaces committed by a group of five or more — still often carried out by rural gangs invading the suburbs. Many dacoits are based in the Chambal Ravines area between Agra and Gwalior and make the headlines by holding up trains and buses. As with the Naxalites, landlords and big business are popular targets, and a Robin Hood element sometimes shares the proceeds with poverty-stricken local villagers.

Reading reports of dacoities you will come across the word 'encounter', meaning a firefight between dacoits and police. Police casualties rarely occur, and these are in fact often summary executions of dacoits betrayed for reward. Ambitious dacoits can become quite celebrated, and at election time local politicians try to arrange surrenders which give them publicity and the dacoit a chance of survival. The most celebrated dacoit of recent years has been Phoolan Devi, a woman who set out to avenge her rape by a group of higher-caste men. This involved slaughtering all the men in the village responsible. Promised safe conduct to jail she surrendered in front of TV cameras. As often happens in the slow-moving Indian legal system she spent 11 years in jail awaiting trial. Eventually freed on bail, her exploits are immortalised in the film *Bandit Queen*.

The **Pindaris** were bands of marauders who plundered their way across southern and central India and Rajputana. They had their origin in the armies of Bijapur and Golconda which dispersed after defeat by the Mughals. The leaders were Muslims but, over time, they attracted recruits from all the dregs of society. They created havoc, one historian describing them as 'pestilence after famine'. Eventually there were several bands of up to 10,000 men each, destroying everything in their path. They even made incursions into British territory, and in 1817 the British felt they had to act. They assembled an army of 43,000 in the north and another of 70,000 in the south and crushed the Pindaris between them. Some of the Maratha princes were obstructive, which provided the excuse for finally sorting them out, and the states of Rajputana were also brought under British protection. After hundreds of years of plunder and rapine the rule of peace and justice descended on Central India. Small wonder that the British were tolerated, if not exactly welcomed, for so long.

KHAJURAHO

Khajuraho must be the most pleasant and relaxed of India's major tourist attractions, having the great merit of being a small quiet village miles from anywhere, though by the same token, getting there can be arduous. The western temples and their garden may well rank second only to the Taj Mahal as India's best sight. And for much of the day you have the place to yourself.

Once the capital of the Chandella Rajput state of Bundelkhand, Khajuraho was a substantial city built mainly between AD950 and 1150. Soon, however, the Muslims were becoming a serious threat, and attention was switched to the more defensible site of Mahoba. As was to happen elsewhere later the various local Rajput kingdoms failed to unite in a common front against the invader, and Khajuraho fell in 1203. Nothing remains now but 22 temples (there were once 85) and their world-famous erotic sculpture.

Many theories have been put forward for the significance of these energetic carvings. The simplest suggestion is that they were advertising for the temple dancers, who also functioned as prostitutes. Other explanations range from tantric cults to flights of psychology that would leave Freud breathless.

Exploring

The western temples

The **western group of temples***, surrounded by quiet and beautiful gardens, is best known. Outside the garden is the **Matangeswara Temple**, earlier in date (AD900) than those inside. Note, as elsewhere, how bits and pieces from ruined temples have been used to rebuild the steps. Unlike most Indian temples all these are built on tall plinths, rather than hidden away behind walls. The plain interior has a huge lingam. This is the only temple still used for worship, and it is interesting to find a quiet corner to watch proceedings. This is a Shiva temple, but when Khajuraho was built Vishnu was the dominant deity. Referring to the description of Vishnu's incarnations (see page 34) will explain much of the imagery on the later temples.

Inside the garden the **Lakshmana Temple** (AD950) is a fine example of the mature Khajuraho style. The outer porch is the *ardha-mandapa* — note the musicians on the torana brackets — and the inner one the *mandapa*. The main hall, the *maha-mandapa*, has a raised portion for the temple dancers, the devadasis. The *garba-griha*, or shrine, is below the *sikhara* (spire). The passage behind the shrine makes this a *sandhara* temple; earlier ones without this feature are said to be *nirandhara*.

The bracket figures in the ceiling are superb, and lower down you can see two slabs for cracking the coconuts brought as offerings; drains take the milk outside. Note the

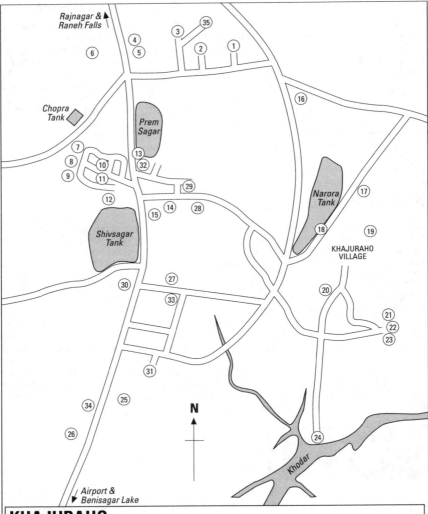

KHAJURAHO

1 Hotel Payal	14 Old Bus Stand (Bike Hire)	28 Jain Lodge
2 Camp Site	15 Archaeological Museum	29 New Bharat Lodge
3 Rahil Janta Hotel	16 Excavations	and Bupta Hotel
4 Tourist Bungalow	17 Vamana Temple	30 Hotel Sunset View
5 Circuit House	18 Brahma Temple	31 Hotel Jass Oberoi
6 Khajuraho Ashok Hotel	19 Javari Temple	32 Raja's
7 Chitragupta Temple	20 Ghantai Temple	33 Bus Stand
8 Devi Jagadambi Temple	21 Adinath Temple	34 Indian Airlines and Modiluft
9 Kandariya Mahadeo Temple	22 Parsvanath Temple	35 Tourist Village
10 Vishwanath Temple	23 Shanti Nath Temple	
11 Parvati Temple	24 Duladeo Temple	
12 Matangeswara Temple	25 Hotel Chandela	
13 Government of India	26 Clark's Bundela Hotel	
Tourist Office	27 Cheap Restaurants	

sculpture around the doorway of the garba-griha depicting the various incarnations of Vishnu, and round to the left the gruesome one of Krishna sucking dry a witch sent to kill him with poisoned milk. Outside don't get so engrossed in the mithuna (loving couples) that you miss the rest of the decoration. There is so much to see: dancers, soldiers, hunters, elephants, and even, on the plinth, a bit of animal husbandry. This is a *panchayata* (five shrine) temple and the only one here with all four corner shrines surviving. On one of them an artist is depicted at work, perhaps the architect of the temple.

The small Lakshmi or **Devi Temple** was an adjunct to the Lakshmana and cannot definitely be ascribed to either of these goddesses.

The **Varaha Shrine** is the oldest in the garden. The large boar, another of Vishnu's incarnations, is covered with small deities. Only the feet remain of a statue of Prithvi, the Vedic earth goddess.

The **Kandariya-Mahadeva Temple** is later (AD1025–1050) and more ornate than the Lakshmana; this is the ultimate in north Indian temple architecture. Dedicated to Shiva (note the conch shells in the steps) it has three bands of stunning sculpture on the outside. As you enter note the bracket figures in the doorways; those inside, if the thieves have left any, are even finer. Clustered around the 30m/98ft-high spire are 84 smaller sikharas.

The **Jagadambi Temple** is of the simpler nirandhara pattern. It was presumably originally a Vishnu temple, but is now dedicated to Shakti, the cosmic energy central to Tantric beliefs. The exterior sculpture is as good as any.

The **Chitragupta Temple** is very similar to the Jagadambi, though currently dedicated to Surya, the Vedic sun god. The image in the garba-griha shows him standing in a chariot drawn by seven horses, each symbolising a colour of the rainbow. On the outside is an eleven-headed Vishnu showing all his incarnations.

The **Vishvanatha Temple** is a Shiva temple and, as usual, a nandi faces the entrance. Like the boar this is a superb piece of sculpture.

The small temple nearby is supposedly dedicated to Parvati, Shiva's wife, but the figure in the centre of the lintel is of Vishnu.

The **Chausath-Yogini Temple** ('64 female ascetics'), behind the village tank, is a crude granite structure more like a fort. There is a cell for each of the yoginis plus one for Kali. This is a wonderful place to watch the sunset and the 'cow-dust hour', that magic time as man and beast head home and the cooking fires are lit.

The **museum** opposite the western group has some very fine sculpture. The entry ticket for the western group gets you in here too. The lions at the door come from the Vishvanatha Temple. The best way to appreciate Khajuraho is to take the lecture tour of the western group and then spend plenty of time wandering about on your own.

The eastern temples

Of the **eastern group of temples**** the tiny **Brahma Temple** beside the tank is really a Vishnu one, the four-faced lingam of Brahma being a late installation.

The **Vamana Temple** is of the simpler layout with no internal passage around the sanctuary despite its late date (AD1075). Vamana is Vishnu's dwarf incarnation. The chaitya carvings on the spire are a Buddhist throwback.

The **Javeri Temple** is very similar to the Vamana, but notable for the vertical accentuation of its lines. Both these temples have suffered severe mutilation at the hands of Muslim invaders (and present-day local robbers), but their pastoral settings more than make up for this. From here you can see the walled group of Jain temples near the old village, and take a pleasant walk through the fields to them.

The **Santinatha Temple** is a modern construction using old materials. The design of a courtyard surrounded by a cloister is unlike anything else at Khajuraho, but typically Jain, just like Sravana-Belgola in fact. Despite the name the main image is of Adinatha. Note the pictures of other Jain holy places and the fossil fern in the paving outside the door.

The **Parsvanath Temple** is contemporary with the Lakshmana and very similar in style. There is little indication on the outside that this is a Jain temple, but inside is a large black image of Parsvanath (the last tirthanka before Mahavira) with a nine-hooded cobra and many other smaller images.

The small **Adinatha Temple** is very like the Vamana, though the porch has been reconstructed recently. The external sculpture is among the best at Khajuraho, though again you have to look inside for a Jain identity.

These Jain temples have been lovingly restored over the years and protected from the recent vandalism that has afflicted the Hindu ones. The new **museum** is just outside the temple compound.

All that remains of the Hindu **Ghantai Temple** is the mandapa and shrine doorway; it probably looked like the Parsvanath. A ghanta is a bell, and the temple is named for the carvings on the pillars, though a new fence makes access difficult.

The southern temples

The **Duladeo Temple***, one of two in the so-called southern group, was among the last built (1100–1150) and gives the impression of having been put up in a hurry. Note particularly how the sculpture is in much lower relief than on other temples and how some of the interior carvings do not line up. This is nevertheless lighter and airier than the older temples.

It is possible to ford the river below the Duladeo Temple to reach the **Chaturbhuja Temple****. Despite its small size and inferior external sculpture this houses the most attractive image in Khajuraho, of Dakshinamurti, Shiva in his role of universal teacher. Returning by the main road takes you past the abode of a hospitable Shiva devotee usually ready to spend some time with you and share a chillum.

Excursions

Khajuraho is not just temples; the countryside around is beautiful and interesting. **Raneh Falls** are in a spectacular rocky ravine 20km/13 miles from Khajuraho. Cycle in cool weather, or bus to Chandranagar, then walk 2km. Superb camping place at end of road 7–8km further on; deep pools with shoals of fish, turtles, gaurial, and otters.

Panna National Park, along the River Ken, is one of the largest in India. The owner of the Raja Restaurant (see below) has a tree house here; ask for more information.

Rajgarh is an old palace of the Maharajas of Chhattarpur. The buildings are not well kept, but the location on a wooded hillside with extensive views is grand. A good place for one of the Raja Restaurant's packed lunches and a couple of bottles of beer. A jeep costs Rs200, or take a Panna bus then walk a hot 2km from the main road.

Practical Information

Government of India Tourist Office opposite western group. Lecture tours from here twice a day (Rs5), check times, they vary according to season. A very detailed Archaeological Survey of India guide book is sold at the museum.

Local transport. Hire a bike to see Khajuraho, or even walk if the weather is cool enough. The rickshaws will rush you around, and give you no chance to get the feel of rural India.

Arrival and departure. Airport (5km), definitely the easiest way if you can afford it. Flights from Delhi, Agra, Varanasi, and Bhubaneswar. Indian Airlines at Hotel

Temple (Tel 2035), but due to move to new office near bus-stand. ModiLuft also plans flights to Khajuraho. Taxi from airport to town, Rs10 up.

Train from Varanasi to Satna, rickshaw or tonga to bus-stand (3km), then bus (4hrs). Train timings on this route change constantly, but there is usually a train three or four days a week which leaves Varanasi early enough to connect with a bus straight on to Khajuraho. Going towards Varanasi sometimes involves staying overnight in Satna because of train timings. Alternatively, bus to Mahoba and pick up the night train to Varanasi; this runs from Gwalior and Jhansi so you should be able to make an advance booking there before travelling to Khajuraho.

Buses to Agra (one daily, 11½hrs), also calls at Gwalior, and Jhansi (several daily, 5hrs). Frequent trains from Jhansi (station 4km from bus-stand, tempo service) to Gwalior, Agra, Delhi, and Sanchi. India's fastest train, the Shatabdi Express, does the 410km/256 miles from Jhansi to Delhi in 4½hrs, others take up to 9hrs.

Buses from Jhansi station to Khajuraho in the morning, after that from the bus-stand, but the last leaves little after midday. You have several options if you miss it: stay in Jhansi (worst idea), go out to Orchha and return in the morning for the bus (best), or catch an afternoon bus to Chhattarpur and either stay there or take a jeep (Rs250) on to Khajuraho.

Accommodation (STD Code 076 861)
Hotel Payal. Tel 2076. SWB Rs225 DWB Rs275. Rest. Bar. Nicely appointed with comfortable rooms, private verandahs, and gardens.

Hotel Sunset View. Tel 2077. SR Rs60 DR Rs80 SWB Rs125 DWB Rs150 SWB A/C Rs250 DWB A/C Rs300 Dorm Rs20. Rest. Ganesh Gautam, the owner, is a fund of knowledge.

Rahil Hotel. Tel 2062. SWB Rs130 (£2.60/$4.35) DWB Rs150 Dorm Rs30 plus 10% SC. Rest (good). Nicely kept. Very pleasant and helpful staff.

Jain Lodge. Tel 2052. SR Rs50 DR Rs70 SWB Rs80 DWB Rs100 4WB Rs105. Rest (veg). Clean and spacious rooms, running hot showers. Family run, and it shows.

Gupta Hotel, opposite old bus-stand. SWB Rs60 DWB Rs80/100. Rest. Rooms air-cooled and hot water included.

Tourist Village. Tel 2128. SWB/DWB Rs150. Rest (basic). Accommodation consists of suites in local-style cottages. Quietest, most interesting, and best value for money.

Tourist Bungalow. Tel 2064. DR Rs225 4R Rs300. Rest. Nice gardens, in same compound as Circuit House.

New Bharat and *Apsara* are adjacent to the Gupta and similarly priced.

Campsite near Hotel Payal. If you want to stay in Khajuraho for some time (and it is well worth it) ask about a room in the village, around Rs50 per week.

Eating and drinking
Raja, opposite temple compound. Mod. Ind/Cont. Open-air. Under the control of the Swiss owner and back to its previous high standard. Rösti? Of course!

Madras Coffee House. Cheap. Vegetarian plus eggs.

Gupta and the other hotels have cheap restaurants.

Near Khajuraho
Ken River Lodge, Panna Wildlife Park, 26km/16 miles from Khajuraho. Good fishing including mahseer.

MAHOBA

Mahoba really only gets a mention because it is on an alternative route to Khajuraho from Jhansi and Varanasi. It is, however, a town of very ancient foundation, and the Chandela Rajputs did a lot of building here before concentrating their efforts on Khajuraho. The main relics are several large artificial lakes, a wealth of temples, and Jain monoliths.

Arrival and departure. On little-used railway line from Jhansi (4hrs) to Varanasi (13hrs). Bus (2½hrs) from Khajuraho. Train times are rarely convenient.

Accommodation. Inexpensive Uttar Pradesh Tourism *Tourist Bungalow.*

SATNA

Satna is just a place where you change transport between Varanasi and Khajuraho. The **Chachai Falls** on the River Bihad (100km/63 miles away, bus via Rewa) are 130m/426ft high and well worth a look.

Information. Tourist office at railway station.

Arrival and departure. See under Khajuraho above. Bus-stand and station are 3km apart, rickshaw Rs10.

Accommodation. The best bet is Madhya Pradesh Tourism's *Hotel Barhut* (Tel 07672 5471) in the Rs175–300 bracket; *Hotel India,* near the bus-stand is half the price.

BANDHAVGARH NATIONAL PARK

Bandhavgarh National Park is reckoned to be one of the most reliable places to see tigers, especially as the weather gets hotter (April to June). The scenery is grand and dominated by the 14th century fort which gives the area its name. Jeeps can be hired morning and evening to get around the 450 sq km reserve. The Park is closed from the beginning of July to the end of October.

The Maharaja of Rewa confirmed old legends by finding the first true white tiger (as opposed to an albino) here in 1951. Descendants of these rare beasts can be seen in Delhi and Calcutta Zoos.

Arrival and departure. Access to the park is by the village of Tala, where accommodation and transport are concentrated. The nearest station is Umaria (30km/19 miles) which is on the Katni–Bilaspur line. The Sarnath Express gets from Satna (on the route between Khajuraho and Benares) to Umaria in 2½hrs. The one through-train daily from Jabalpur takes 5hrs to do the 150km/94 miles, otherwise you have to change at Katni Junction. Bus from Satna (4hrs), maybe also from Jabalpur.

Accommodation
White Tiger Forest Lodge, Tala. Tel 308. SWB Rs250 DWB Rs300 DWB A/C Rs450. Rest. Bar. Good location by the river. Book through Madhya Pradesh Tourism.

Cheaper accommodation is available in the village.

JABALPUR

Historically Jabalpur was the centre of Gondwana. This was the land of the Gonds, an aboriginal people of negroid origin. They worshipped deities based on cholera and smallpox long before these were incorporated in the Hindu pantheon. Gondwana passed through many hands including Huns, Muslims, and the Gonds themselves. In 1564, when it was one of the few surviving Rajput states outside Rajasthan, one of Akbar's generals captured it. The Marathas took it in 1789, and it was wrested from them by the British 20 years later.

Once the Thugs, who were mostly based in the region, had been subdued Jabalpur lapsed again into obscurity until the coming of the railway. It then became an important centre for the British for no much better reason than that it is roughly halfway between Bombay and Calcutta and has a slightly more pleasant climate than anywhere else on the railway line. A large army base and defence-related industry grew up here.

Jabalpur is a pleasant enough place with extensive bazaars, but of limited interest for the traveller. It is, however, a useful base for visiting Kanha National Park and Marble Rocks.

Practical Information

Information. Tourist office on railway station. Reservations made for Madhya Pradesh Tourism accommodation.

Arrival and departure. On the Jalgaon (10hrs)–Satna (3hrs)–Varanasi (9½hrs) line. Jalgaon is the station for the Ajanta and Ellora caves; if you miss the direct train change at Bhusaval. Direct train from Bhopal (5½hrs), otherwise change at Itarsi.

Long-distance buses to Khajuraho (11hrs), Varanasi, Bhopal and others, but the trains are a better bet. Buses for Bandhavgarh and Kanha National Parks, see those sections for details.

Accommodation (STD Code 0761)

Madhya Pradesh Tourism's *Hotel Kalchuri* (Tel 321 491) is a short walk from the station, rooms Rs250–300 and a good restaurant. *Jackson's Hotel* (Tel 323 412) nearby is run down but fun and half the price. Really cheap places near the bus-stand (*Hotel Mayur*) and in the bazaar.

Eating and drinking. *Indian Coffee House* near bus-stand.

Further Afield

Marble Rocks

Here the Narmada river flows through a spectacular gorge of white and pink magnesian limestone. The cliffs are not in fact very high (32m/105ft) but most attractive. The regular boat trips are very reasonable, but do not run during and just after the monsoon (usually July to October). The gorge is closed by the **Dhuandhar** (Smoke Cascade), a fine waterfall.

The Narmada is as sacred as other rivers, and the **Madanpur Temple** stands above the lower end of the gorge. This, like the more basic one at Khajuraho, is dedicated to the Chaunsath Yogini, the 64 female ascetics who attend Shiva. The statues survive but are badly mutilated.

Marble Rocks is best avoided at weekends and full-moon time.

Arrival and departure. Marble Rocks is 23km/14 miles from central Jabalpur. Tempo from the stand near the museum in Jabalpur to the Motel Marble Rocks. Cycling is possible, and has the advantage of letting you potter around, but the main road is busy. Follow the signs for Bhedaghat; you can also detour to the **Madan Mahal**, a hilltop fort built in the 12th century by the Gond kings (good views).

Accommodation. Madhya Pradesh Tourism's *Motel Marble Rocks* (Tel 0761 83424), around Rs250, is good (restaurant too) but must be booked in advance.

Eating and drinking. Cheap restaurants in village.

Kanha National Park

This is one of the largest nature reserves in India (1945 sq km) and probably the one with the best facilities. Chances of seeing tigers are good, especially late in the season (May and June).

Despite serious poaching and highly optimistic estimates of numbers in other parks Kanha seems to be a great success. The number of tigers has doubled to around 100.

Panther, sambhar, cheetal, gaur (bison), black buck, barking deer and swamp deer can all be seen.

The countryside is most attractive, but temperatures are extreme; expect 40°C/104°F and more in May and June and freezing cold in December and January.

Information. Kisli and Kanha are centres inside the park; the two entrances are Mukki and Khatia, most facilities provided at the latter. Excellent visitor centres at Khatia, Kanha, and Mukki. All open 7–10.30am and 4–6pm. Nightly film show at Khatia.

Arrival and departure. Two morning buses from Jabalpur to Kisli (6hrs) pass through Khatia.

Local transport. Transport in the park is by jeep and costs Rs400–500 (£8–10/$13.35–16.65) per session, to which you have to add the small entry charge and guide fee. Six people can cram into a jeep, four is the comfortable limit. Entry times vary slightly through the year, but the park is closed in the middle part of the day, and no traffic movement is allowed at night.

Accommodation. All the following places are run by Madhya Pradesh Tourism. Reservations more than five days in advance must be made at Madhya Pradesh Tourism offices in Bhopal (Gangotri, TT Nagar, Tel 0755 554 340), Bombay (World Trade Centre, Colaba, Tel 022 218 4860), Calcutta (Chitrakoot Bldg, 230 AJC Bose Road, Tel 033 247 8543), or New Delhi (Kanishka Shopping Plaza, Ashok Road, Tel 011 332 1187). A 50% deposit is required. After that you have to deal direct with the unit, though the Madhya Pradesh Tourism office on Jabalpur station (Tel 0761 322 111) will tell you what is available.

Jungle Camp, Khatia. DWB Rs200 full board (vegetarian). 3km from Kisli, but plenty of transport.

Tourist Hostel, Kisli. Dorm Rs150 full board (vegetarian).

Baghira Log Huts, Kisli. Rest. Bar. DWB A/C Rs350. Because both this and the Tourist Hostel are inside the park boundary you must check in before 6.30pm; any later and you cannot enter the park.

Kanha Safari Lodge, Mukki. Rest. Bar. Rs300, more for A/C. Good place, and open all through year. Often has space when others are full, but hard to get to on public transport.

Inexpensive private accommodation, such as *Machan Complex*, at Khatia. Several other privately owned places, such as *Indian Adventures* and *Kipling Camp* get good reports, but prices are almost in the five-star hotel bracket.

PACHMARHI

Pachmarhi, at 1067m/3500ft, is the hill resort of Madhya Pradesh. The climate in summer is hardly bracing, but certainly fresher than the plains. In winter temperatures drop to zero. Surrounded by the rugged Satpura hills and forest Pachmarhi offers grand scenery and good walking. Some of the numerous waterfalls have pools safe for swimming. The Lansdowne golf course is one of the oldest in India, and equipment can be hired.

Pachmari is also a place of pilgrimage. The Mahadeo Shrine and its deep cave have been holy places for centuries. Mahadeo is a form of Shiva, and large numbers of holy men congregate for Shivaratri (February/March). Chauragarh is a hilltop Shiva shrine well worth the walk. Many other cave shrines are dotted around, some with ancient paintings.

Arrival and departure. Bus from Bhopal (7hrs). Bus or share jeep (2hrs) from Pipariya which is on the Bombay (16hrs)–Varanasi (12hrs)–Calcutta (24hrs) railway line.

Accommodation. Most accommodation is controlled by Madhya Pradesh Tourism, and it's best to consult them on availability before going. Cheap dormitory beds at the *Youth Centre.*

SANCHI

Sanchi is easily the best of the various Buddhist sites in India. It is readily accessible, peaceful, and displays every major form of Buddhist architecture. Unlike most of these holy places Buddha himself never visited Sanchi. Its sanctity stems from Ashoka's wife Devi, who came from nearby Vidisha and established a monastery (third century BC) for their son Mahendra, the man who took Buddhism to Ceylon (now Sri Lanka). Its use as a holy place continued over a period of 1500 years. From the 12th century AD Sanchi lay deserted, protected from Muslim and other invaders by its remoteness and the jungle which soon grew over it. Sanchi was rediscovered in 1818 by British soldiers on mopping-up operations after the war against Pindari freebooters. Amateur archaeologists soon more or less destroyed the stupas in their quest for relics. Exactly the same thing was happening in Britain at the time as so-called antiquarians dug up and despoiled prehistoric burial chambers. Restoration was carried out between 1883 and 1919, but much material and information has been lost for ever.

 The **museum**** (10am–5pm, closed Friday) has many relics, including fine statuary, excavated from the site. Buy a ticket for the hilltop here, head up the road, and take the steps off to the right.

The Great Stupa

Stupas are basically mounds, usually covered with brick or stone. They serve two purposes, either housing relics or being simply memorials of devotion. The hilltop at Sanchi is surrounded by pleasant, wooded country and crowned by three major stupas and many other remains.

Stupa 1 (the **Great Stupa**) was first built by Ashoka in the third century BC. Somehow it sustained damage not long after, and when rebuilt in the following century emerged twice its original size, 37m/121ft in diameter and 16m/52ft to the top of the dome. The original brick core was covered by layers of stone with a concrete cladding to which, at some later date, a layer of plaster was added. The terrace for pilgrims to walk around was built at the time of the rebuilding. The wooden railings of the terrace were replaced by stone ones of similar design, and the superb toranas, or gateways, added in the first century BC. The Buddhas, in the dhyana or meditation position, facing the entrances were installed in the fifth century AD. A quarter of the stupa was hacked away in the last century by clumsy excavation and restored in the 1920s.

The outstanding feature of the stupa is the carvings on the toranas. These were done over a longish period of time, and probably to start with by men more used to working in wood, so the style does vary. In the early days Buddha was never depicted as a person, being symbolised by his footprint, an empty throne, or the bo tree under which he achieved enlightenment; later panels, when Buddhism was changing from a monastic order to a popular religion, depict him more conventionally. All the toranas were surmounted by the wheel of the law, and the carvings depict scenes from the Jataka Tales (about Buddha's previous incarnations), the life of Buddha, and the history of Buddhism, Ashoka also making an appearance.

North torana. The outer face of the right pillar shows an empty chariot and a riderless horse suggesting the excursions on which Buddha first encountered human suffering and decided to renounce his easy life. The centre lintel on the inner face shows the temptation by Mara and his daughters. The style of carving is deeper and more developed on this, the latest of the toranas. Like the east torana the pillars have elephant capitals, in this case with sockets for ivory tusks.

East torana. The outer face of the centre lintel depicts Buddha leaving his home Kapilavastu in strip cartoon form; the riderless horse and groom with umbrella pass through the city gate, travel on, and finally horse and groom return while Buddha's footprints continue the journey. Below that Ashoka visits the bodhi tree. On the left pillar Buddha, pictured as a throne, walks on the River Nairanjana.

South torana. The outer face of the lower lintel depicts the siege of Kushinagar, an event in Ashoka's attempt to collect and redistribute the relics of Buddha. This is the oldest of the toranas.

West torana. The four trees and three stupas on the outer face of the top lintel depict Buddha's seven incarnations. Below that a wheel of the law represents enlightenment. The bottom lintel shows the Jataka Tale in which Buddha is born as the six-tusked elephant Chhadanta. One of his two wives feels neglected and, reborn in human form, arranges a hunt in which Chhadanta is killed. His tusks are cut off, and she dies of remorse at the sight of them.

By the south torana are the remains of an **Ashoka column** once 13m/42ft high. This weighed 40 tonnes and was brought from near Benares by river. The four-lion capital, similar to that at Sarnath, is in the museum. The remains of many more pillars can be seen.

More stupas

When originally built **stupa 3** was plastered over, and moulded onto this were garlands around the dome. These were brightly painted and gold leafed. The stupa was opened in the 19th century and found to contain relics of two of Buddha's first five disciples, which ranks it only just below stupa 1. The remains were taken to London and, on their return in 1953, housed in the rather ugly modern monastery.

Some stupas had a votive function rather than being memorials. A well-off Buddhist would build one according to his pocket, in the same way as a Christian endowed a church or chapel, in the hope of spiritual advancement. Many of these small monuments stand around.

Other hilltop monuments

Many other monasteries, temples, and small stupas are scattered over the hilltop. **Temple 18** (seventh century AD but on the site of an older building) is identical in layout to a rock-cut chapel. You can see the inner plan with the pillars, and the semicircular wall at the end where the stupa stood. The solid outer wall formed an aisle round the whole nave and apse. This chapel had a tiled roof.

Temple 17 dates from the Gupta period (fifth century AD). This is an attractive little building showing clear Greek influence, having probably been built by Bactrian craftsmen.

Temple 45 is a late building (ninth or tenth century AD) on the foundations of an earlier one and within the quadrangle of a much older monastery. It once had a Hindu style sikhara of which only the rubble infill remains. The imagery is also Hindu, and thus this temple symbolises the end of Buddhism in India by its reabsorption into Hinduism.

Keep an eye on the vultures using the updraughts and thermals from the hill. The moment one sees a potential meal and dives down to take a closer look, his neighbours, who always watch him as well as the ground below, head over. Then their neighbours arrive, and in no time you have a hundred birds milling noisily around. As likely as not it was a false alarm, so they circle effortlessly gaining altitude before heading back to their regular stations. Vultures may be ungainly and gruesome on the ground, but on the wing you can't help admiring them.

The monastery

Below the hilltop is **monastery 51**, following the usual pattern of a courtyard surrounded by the monks' cells. This may have been a two-storeyed structure. A verandah, presumably covered, ran between the cells and the courtyard. A huge **stone bowl** for offerings, now broken, lies nearby.

Lower down the hill is the rather plain **stupa 2** (second century BC), its position reflecting the lesser importance of the ten holy men whose remains were enshrined here. Although much of the sculpture is of a later date it includes the oldest (by a long way) known representation of a horseman using stirrups. The path continues down the hill to return to the museum.

For some reason Sanchi is rarely visited by Westerners. It has, however, a quiet charm, and is one of few places where you find real peace.

Practical Information The monuments are all numbered as noted above. Excellent guide book and map (Rs5) available from museum; gives a complete explanation of all the scenes on the toranas.

Arrival and departure. On Delhi (10½hrs)–Bombay (12½hrs) line. Note that not all trains stop at Sanchi. First-class passengers can ask the guard or conductor to stop the train specially; otherwise get off at Vidisha (10km/6 miles away) and bus. Also bus from Bhopal (1½hrs), make sure you get the direct bus.

Accommodation (STD Code 07592)

Travellers Lodge (500m from station). Tel 81223. SWB Rs225 DWB Rs275 SWB A/C Rs260 DWB A/C Rs290. Rest. Bar.

Tourist Cafeteria. Tel 81243. SWB Rs175 DWB Rs225. Rest. Bar. Both these places are well run by Madhya Pradesh Tourism. Good food, too.

Sanchi Rest House (behind Cafeteria). No-one in when we called and looks very run down.

Buddhist Guest House (50m from station). Cheap, basic, and none too clean.

Railway Retiring Rooms, clean and convenient but not a good idea. Heavy trains rumble and hoot their way through Sanchi all night, and the further you are from the line the better you will sleep.

Excursions Sanchi is such a quiet and pleasant place to stay that it is worth using it as a base for visiting other places of interest.

Vidisha

Vidisha was a large and ancient city by the fifth century BC. Under the Mauryas, and before he became emperor, Ashoka was governor. Here he met his wife Devi who is credited with converting him to Buddhism. The few remains, including what is perhaps the oldest Brahmanical temple in India, are of little interest. The **museum** may merit a quick look on the way to Udaygiri.

Arrival and departure. The modern town of Vidisha (10km from Sanchi) is on the main Delhi–Bombay railway line. The fastest trains do not stop there, check carefully. Buses run from Sanchi, and it is possible to cycle.

Udaygiri

The 29 cave temples at Udaygiri, dating from the Gupta period (fourth and fifth century AD), are amongst the most elaborate of their kind. The best houses a huge Varaha image. Udaygiri means Sunrise Hill.

Arrival and departure. 4km/2½ miles from Vidisha. Tonga and scooter-rickshaw wallahs see few Westerners and charge accordingly; better to hire a bike.

Heliodorus pillar

Heliodorus, a Greek, was the ambassador of the Indo-Greek king of Taxila (near Rawalpindi in Pakistan) to the court of Vidisha. To mark his conversion to Hinduism in 90BC he erected a superb Indo-Hellenic pillar. This finely carved monolith is an odd cultural mix; there is Greek influence (bead moulding and honeysuckle), Buddhist motifs (the geese), and an inscription telling of the conversion of Heliodorus to the worship of Vasudeva, an early form of Vishnu. As you might expect the pillar was once surmounted by a Garuda.

Arrival and departure. After visiting the Udaygiri caves turn left onto the main road again and go 1km further. The pillar is known locally as Khambha Baba.

Gyraspur

Two groups of finely carved pillars are all that remain of tenth century Hindu temples. Impressive, but a long way to go.

Arrival and departure. Gyraspur is 41km/25 miles from Sanchi. Bus from Vidisha.

BHOPAL

Bhopal is the capital of Madhya Pradesh. It supposedly takes its name from Raja Bhoj who settled here in the 11th century and constructed several dams or pals. The present city was founded by the Afghan Dost Muhammed Khan. He had been posted to Bhairsia as governor and took advantage of the disorder after Aurangzeb's death in 1707 to carve out his own state. As the 18th century progressed Bhopal became a Muslim island in Maratha territory and had to fight hard for survival. Between 1837 and 1926 Bhopal was ruled by three remarkable women, unusual anywhere in India and quite exceptional in a Muslim state. Despite maintaining purdah the Begums instituted a liberal and socially advanced regime. Bhopal is not of great interest, most people visiting only on the way to Sanchi or Indore.

The main monuments are three 19th century mosques. The **Taj-ul-Masjid**, built by Shahjahan Begum (1868–1901) but never quite finished, is the largest mosque in India. The others are the **Jama Masjid**, built by Qudsia Begum (1837) and the **Moti Masjid**, a florid copy of Delhi's Jama Masjid.

The larger of Bhopal's two lakes provides boating and yachting. Bhopal is home to a Birla-endowed **Lakshmi Narayan Temple**. Situated on Arera Hill this is worth visiting for the views over the city and lakes. The **museum** is nearby.

Sadly, no description of Bhopal is complete without some reference to the Union Carbide disaster. On 3 December 1984 a large quantity of lethal gas escaped from the Union Carbide plant. At least 2500 people died instantly, and another 5000 or more have died since. The health of much of the population of Bhopal has been irreversibly affected. Union Carbide eventually settled for the paltry sum of $470 million, little of which, even now, has got through to the people who need it.

Information. Tourist office on railway station.

Arrival and departure. Airport (10km/6 miles). Indian Airlines office in TT Nagar

(Tel 550480). On main line from Delhi (13hrs) to Bombay Victoria Terminus (15hrs). Full details on getting to Sanchi, Indore, etc. in those sections.

Accommodation. *Hotel Ranjeet,* Hamidia Road (500m from station, exit from rear). Tel 0755 75211. Around Rs100. Rest (good). Bar. Other hotels, some cheaper, along the same road.

INDORE

Indore was the seat of the Holkars, a Maratha family who established their state in 1733. Socially advanced, they laid out a pleasant city which found prosperity in textiles.

Indore today is mostly visited only on the way to Mandu, but the **Hukumchand Jain Temple**** (Kanch Mandir) should be seen. Here the peculiar Jain art form is taken to the extreme. Every square inch of the interior is covered with little pieces of mirror, mother-of-pearl, and coloured glass. As in other Jain temples their holy places are illustrated: the panel numbered 12 is Sravana Belgola, 16 Girnar Hill, and 30 Bayapur where Mahavira gave up life in a lotus pool to achieve nirvana. More unusual are those on morality: 37–46 are on the theme of crime and punishment, 40 on theft and its consequences, 44 on gambling, and 36 on self-indulgence (and a bit of self-abuse too!). The ceiling panels in front of the shrine show how Mahavira (just like Buddha) conquered various temptations, most obviously by the dancing girls.

The **museum°** is pretty depressing. The best sculpture has been taken to Bhopal, and no attempt has been made to fill the gaping holes in the displays. A few curiosities remain, one a small panel of a woman being taken from behind as she washes up. There are also three or four Jaina figures that, if they are not sitting on snakes, have erections. If you don't find this amusing give the museum a miss.

Students of modern architecture might be tempted to find the **Manik Bagh Palace**, built in the 1930s in Art Deco-Modernist style by Eckart Muthesius. This is now government offices, and the fixtures and furniture (which are the only things that make such buildings interesting) have been dispersed.

Indore, with some justification, claims to produce the best kulfi, a very rich ice cream, in India. A nice place, Indore.

Information. Tourist office at the Tourist Bungalow which is 500m from the station.

Arrival and departure. Airport 10km/6 miles from centre. Indian Airlines (Tel 431 595) on Dr Rosen Singh Bandari Marg in the new part of town. Damania (Tel 433 922) flies to Bombay.

By rail from Bhopal (7¼hrs) or Khandwar (5½hrs), both on Bombay–Delhi line, also Jaipur (15hrs), Chittaurgarh (10¾hrs), and Bombay (14hrs).

Private bus companies in the station approach operate to Bombay, Pune, Gwalior, Udaipur, and Jaipur, but most are video services.

Accommodation (STD Code 0731)

Indotels Manor House, Bombay–Agra Road. Tel 537 301. DWB A/C Rs425–575 plus 10% tax. Rest (see below). Bar. 24-hour coffee shop. Swimming pool. Quieter than the address suggests.

Tourist Bungalow, behind Ravindra Natyagraha, 500m from station. Tel 38888. SWB A/C Rs200 DWB A/C Rs250 plus taxes (includes early morning tea and breakfast). Rooms clean and comfortable and the mice are quite friendly.

Ashoka Hotel, opposite Sarwate bus-stand. Tel 465 991. SWB Rs90 DWB Rs125. Rest (room service). TV. OK.

Many other places in the area between the station and bus-stand, but Indore is not a cheap place to stay, so try the retiring rooms at the station first.

Eating and drinking

Three Seasons, Indotels Manor House. Ind/Chi/Cont. Bar. Superb buffet lunch Rs85. Dinner à la carte.

Apsara, in front of Tourist Bungalow. Ind/Chi veg. Mod. Good as long as you eat Indian food. Spring rolls are edible if you tell them to lay off the chillies.

Volga, MG Road. Indian veg. Cheap/Mod. Good range of snacks, shakes and fruit juices. Very good all-in three-course lunch or dinner for Rs45, though you can eat à la carte for less.

MANDU

Mandu was the capital of the Hindu kingdom of Malwa until captured by the Muslims in 1305. A hundred years later its ruler declared his independence of the Delhi sultans, and a period of intense construction started. Despite various upheavals this lasted until Akbar's takeover in 1561. Known as Shadiabad, the City of Joy, Shahjahan enthused over its climate, location, and fine buildings. Now its silent ruins are scattered over a fortified plateau of 40 sq km. The area is especially green and beautiful after the rains, but you must see Mandu in its own light. Do not expect to find something as well preserved as the later Fatehpur Sikri.

The city buildings

In the present-day village of Mandu is the **Great Mosque***** (1454), supposedly modelled on that in Damascus. The imposing entrance hall has a single dome matching that in the centre of the prayer hall opposite. Note the blue enamel in the niches and running round the drum below the dome. The arches here are in fact corbelled and not true arches, most easily seen from the Ashrafi Mahal over the road.

The prayer hall has three large domes and many smaller ones. The mihrab is of polished black stone and white marble, the outer band of which has marvellous inscriptions of verses from the Koran. Hindu touches appear in the carving of the other white marble elements of this. Other mihrabs of the same basic design line the west wall, each surrounded by Hindu-style carving. The mimbar is again in Hindu patterns, diamond shapes, chajja brackets, and so on. Sockets indicate that it once had a banister. The raised floors at either end of the hall were secluded places for women worshippers.

The king did not use the main entrance, unlike the Jama Masjid in Delhi where he was just about the only person who did. In the north wall, near the ladies' section, is the king's private entrance with a domed porch outside. A simpler entrance further along the same wall was used by members of the court. Note how women of the royal family could use the king's entrance and go straight upstairs unseen by the congregation. A triple-bay cloister with many, many small domes, parts of which are still intact, ran right round the 80m/262ft square courtyard. This mosque is a typically plain Afghan building, but one of the most imposing in India.

Behind the mosque is the **Tomb of Hoshang Shah***** who died in 1435. This is a nicely proportioned single-domed white marble building. Very plain both inside and out, it has just one line of black marble and a couple of rows of blue tiles at the base of the dome. It has been said that this tomb was studied by Shahjahan's architects before they designed the Taj Mahal, but this is not true. A tiny inscription to the right of the door tells how the visit was made in 1659, by which time the Taj Mahal was complete. Shahjahan himself, however, was familiar with the tomb from visits here in his youth, so it may well have had an influence on the Taj Mahal.

The hall on the west side of the tomb enclosure is called the **dharamsala**, probably not because it was ever used as such, but because of the Hindu-pattern columns and

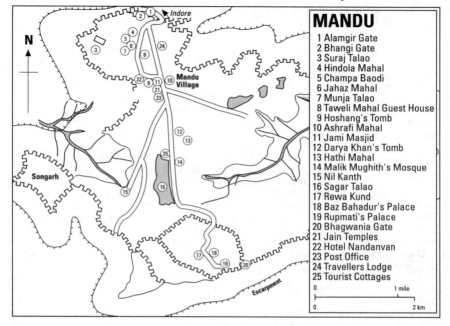

MANDU

1 Alamgir Gate
2 Bhangi Gate
3 Suraj Talao
4 Hindola Mahal
5 Champa Baodi
6 Jahaz Mahal
7 Munja Talao
8 Taweli Mahal Guest House
9 Hoshang's Tomb
10 Ashrafi Mahal
11 Jami Masjid
12 Darya Khan's Tomb
13 Hathi Mahal
14 Malik Mughith's Mosque
15 Nil Kanth
16 Sagar Talao
17 Rewa Kund
18 Baz Bahadur's Palace
19 Rupmati's Palace
20 Bhagwania Gate
21 Jain Temples
22 Hotel Nandanvan
23 Post Office
24 Travellers Lodge
25 Tourist Cottages

post and lintel construction. It is from here that you are most aware of the plainness of the Jama Masjid. This is nothing uncommon for a mosque, and it makes you all the more conscious of the success of the design of the Jama Masjid in Delhi, which looks as good from the outside as the inside.

Over the road from the Jama Masjid is the building known as the **Ashrafi-Mahal***, a spurious later name equating its beauty to that of a gold coin. This was originally a religious college (madrasa) dating from the reign of Mahmud Khalji (1436–1469). As built it enclosed a quadrangle, but only one side remains, this containing cells for novices. On the left corner as you face it is the base of a victory tower, once seven storeys (perhaps 50m/164ft or more) high. This was added by Mahmud Khalji to commemorate his victory over Raja Khumba of Mewar (Chittaurgarh), and the same man later filled in the courtyard of the madrasa to make the foundation for his own marble tomb. The steps in front and the porch were added to form the entrance, and the dome lined up with both main domes of the Jama Masjid and that of Hoshang Shah's tomb. Look across from the remains of the tomb to the entrance of the Jama Masjid, imagine something half as large again and you will get a rough idea of the size of this tomb. The tomb was covered in white, yellow, and black marble, the fragments on the terrace mostly Hindu in design and contrasting oddly with the Islamic inscriptions around the arches. The cenotaph has disappeared leaving only the yellow marble base. Like other buildings at Mandu these were shoddily built and quickly collapsed.

The palace enclave

The main palace buildings are a short walk from the village. The **Jahaz Mahal**** (Ship Palace) is so-called because it appears to float on the lakes on either side of it. It was almost certainly built in the reign of Ghiyath-ud-Din (1469–1500) as a haramsara, or women's palace. This devout and kindly man is said to have had a haram of 1500 women, 500 of them Turkis dressed as men and armed with bows, another 500 Abyssinian women with matchlock muskets. At the age of eighty, still going strong, he was poisoned by his son Nasir-ud-Din. Jehangir writes in his memoirs that he kicked Nasir-ud-Din's tomb (serious stuff in the Muslim world), then, considering that a bit mild, had his remains dug up and thrown in the Narmada river.

The white marble around the doorway was covered with a layer of plaster and then painted, traces can be seen on the higher levels. The interior was given the same treatment, again a little survives. At the northern end of the roof terrace is a tank and beside it one of those curly water channels you see here and there in India. A lift took water from the tank at the southern end of the palace up to roof level where it ran along a channel to the pool on the roof and from there to a lower one. Running water cools the air and soothes the nerves in a hot climate. Traces of blue and yellow tiling can be made out on the pavilion and colonnade. As elsewhere it is hard to imagine how bright and colourful these buildings once were.

Behind the Jahaz Mahal is the Munja Talao (Camphor Lake), and beside it the Shahini Mahal with underground summer chambers around a deep well, the Champa Baoli. In the lake facing the Jahaz Mahal are the remains of the water pavilion, a colonnaded building partly faced with white marble, the rest plastered. Not much is left, but this was perhaps the finest building in Mandu.

The nearby **Hindola Mahal*** has massive sloping buttresses making it resemble an Indian swing chair (hindola). The severity of its design seems to be a reaction to the frivolity of the slightly earlier Jahaz Mahal. This T-shaped building was probably an audience hall with the crossbar of the T a later addition. The neatness of the exterior stonework suggests that it was left unplastered. Note the coloured tiles set in one or two of the merlons. About halfway up the buttresses are marks indicating that some sort of decoration was applied. The roof of the extension shows how that of the main hall was done in vaulted stone. It was the outward thrust of this huge weight that required not only walls 2.7m/9ft thick but the buttresses as well.

Also in this area are several deep wells, some with cool underground chambers for summer use.

Further Afield

Heading through Mandu village to the south the road passes a compound containing several **Jain temples**, mostly modern but very attractive.

Darya Khan's Tomb. Darya Khan was a nobleman at the court of Mahmud II (1510–1526), so this is a late building in Mandu terms. The tomb is surrounded by a cloister and, on three sides, a moat. The exterior is red sandstone, and traces of enamelling can still be seen. The central tombstone has inlay work. Steps lead up from the interior to the roof.

The Hathi Mahal (Elephant Palace) gets its nickname from the hefty columns of its central element, probably a baradari or pavilion. When it later became a tomb the mosque and a counterpart on the other side were added, aesthetically rather too close.

The **Palace of Baz Bahadur*** is named after Mandu's last king, but an inscription over the doorway says it was built in 1508, well before his accession. This is of limited interest except perhaps for the view from the roof pavilions. The same is true of the **Palace of Rupamati*** on top of the hill, though the view here is quite something as it is perched on the very edge of the plateau.

The **Nil-Kanth Mahal*** was presumably built on the site of a Shiva shrine. Nil-Kanth means blue throat and refers to the story of Shiva saving the world by drinking an otherwise lethal poison. This pleasure palace, just below the level of the plateau, was Jehangir's favourite place in Mandu, and earlier his father Akbar had added inscriptions extolling his conquests in the Deccan. Four centuries after it was built the Nil-Kanth has again become a Shiva shrine.

Many other buildings, mostly in the austere Afghan style, are scattered over the plateau, and this is a rewarding and wonderfully peaceful place to relax from travelling for a few days.

Malwa, Marwar, Mewar, and Merwara

These names cause constant confusion. For the record, **Malwa** was the state centred on Mandu, **Marwar** corresponded with the later state of Jodhpur, **Mewar** was centred on first Chitor and later Udaipur, and **Merwara** was a small state in the Aravalli Hills bordering Ajmer.

Practical Information

Archaeological Survey Office and small museum at the Taveli Mahal (1km from bus-stand), map and guide book (Rs4) available — excellent, but don't trust the scale on the map. The one tempo runs out to Baz Bahadur Palace, but it's best to hire a bike to get around.

Arrival and departure. Bus from Indore (3½hrs direct or 4½hrs with a change in Dhar). For Ujjain or Bhopal change in Indore. Check bus schedules very carefully. We had to pay Rs450 for a jeep back to Indore when the bus we expected failed to materialise. The only day trip from Indore (Rs60) is operated by Vijayent Travels on Tagore Road. This runs on Sunday and probably involves suffering a video.

Accommodation (STD Code 07292)
   Tourist Cottages, Roopmati Road. Tel 63235. DWB Rs225/275 DWB A/C Rs495. Rest. Bar. A lakeside cluster of cottages which has replaced the old Tourist Bungalow. The restaurant was rebuilt recently.
   Travellers Lodge. Tel 63221. SWB Rs225 DWB Rs275 plus 5%. Rest. Neat and well kept. Best to make a reservation for these two places at the tourist office in Indore.
   Taveli Mahal Rest House. Tel 63225. DWB Rs100. Huge, comfortable rooms in old palace. Operated by the ASI and often occupied by their staff.
   Hotel Nandanvan, between tomb of Hoshang Shah and Taveli Mahal. SR/DR Rs145 (£2.90/$4.80). Rest (basic). Local flavour, but a lot of money for what it is.
   The *Tourist Rest House* opposite the Jama Masjid is basic but cheap.

Eating and drinking. Simple but good vegetarian restaurants in the bazaar. Good non-vegetarian food at the Travellers Lodge.

BAGH CAVES

The **Bagh Caves** are rock-cut Buddhist monasteries contemporary with Ajanta and having the remains of wall paintings. By all accounts they have deteriorated to the point where a visit is pointless. Copies of some of the paintings can be seen in the archaeological museum in Gwalior.

Arrival and departure. The caves are 158km/99 miles from Indore. Bus to Bagh village, which is 7km/4.5 miles from the caves.

Accommodation. *PWD Rest House* or *Archaeological Survey of India Rest House.*

UJJAIN

Ujjain is one of the seven holiest cities in India and venue of the Kumbh Mela every 12 years, the next being due in 2004. The city was the capital of Malwa under first Hindus and then Muslims until Mandu took its place. Malwa was conquered by Akbar in 1562 and held by the Mughals until 1732 when the Marathas took over.

Ujjain was the capital of the Scindia rajas until they moved to Gwalior in 1810. The long period of Muslim rule took its toll on the old temples, and the ones to be seen today date from the 18th and 19th centuries.

The most important temple is the **Mahakaleswar**, dedicated to Shiva and one of the 12 jyotirlingas. Like other religious centres Ujjain is built on a river, the Shipri, and most worship takes place on the **ghats** along it, notably Ram Ghat.

Ujjain was an ancient seat of learning and, as Indian astronomers developed their craft here, it was regarded as the prime meridian, like Greenwich today. Later, Maharaja Jai Singh II of Jaipur was governor here for the Mughals, and he erected one of his five observatories. This **observatory**, while smaller than those in Jaipur and Delhi, follows the same principles.

Ujjain is a pleasant enough place but, outside festival times, of limited interest to the Western traveller.

Information. Madhya Pradesh Tourism at Hotel Shipra (see below).

Arrival and departure. Trains from Indore (1½hrs), Ahmedabad (9hrs), Bombay 12¼hrs), and Delhi (17hrs). Buses from Indore (1½hrs) and Bhopal (4hrs).

Accommodation (STD Code 0734)

Lots of choice in the Rs75–150 bracket near the station, mostly good, *Hotel Ajay* (Tel 50856) recommended. Madhya Pradesh Tourism's *Hotel Shipra* (Tel 51495) is 1km from station and very good (Rs250–300). Dorm beds (Rs30) at Madhya Pradesh Tourism's *Yatri Niwas* (Tel 51498) 2km from centre, also some rooms.

Western India

Hawa Mahal, Jaipur

Rajasthan — Gujarat

RAJASTHAN

Rajasthan is the modern state covering most of the old Rajputana, the home of the martial Rajputs. Much of the state is given over to the Thar Desert, reclamation being made difficult by the salt which irrigation brings to the surface. As in so many other desert lands the people of Rajasthan are colourful and friendly, the women wearing lots of jewellery and swirling skirts in bright colours, and the men intricately wound turbans. Rajputana was a centre of resistance against the various Muslim invaders, and every town and fort can tell a story of heroism and chivalry. The Mughals paid

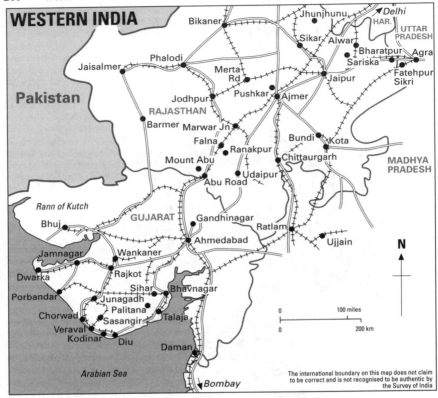

WESTERN INDIA

Bikaner · Jhunjhunu · Delhi · HAR. · UTTAR PRADESH · Sikar · Alwar · Bharatpur · Agra · Sariska · Phalodi · Jaisalmer · Merta Rd · Jaipur · Fatehpur Sikri · Jodhpur · Pushkar · Ajmer · Pakistan · RAJASTHAN · Barmer · Marwar Jn · Falna · Bundi · Kota · Ranakpur · Mount Abu · Chittaurgarh · MADHYA PRADESH · Abu Road · Udaipur · Rann of Kutch · GUJARAT · Gandhinagar · Bhuj · Ratlam · Ahmedabad · Ujjain · Jamnagar · Wankaner · N · Dwarka · Rajkot · Sihar · Bhavnagar · Porbandar · Junagadh · Palitana · Chorwad · Sasangir · Talaja · Veraval · Kodinar · Diu · Daman · Arabian Sea · Bombay

0   100 miles
0   200 km

The international boundary on this map does not claim to be correct and is not recognised to be authentic by the Survey of India

tribute to the Rajputs by employing them as generals and taking Rajput princesses as wives. Many Mughal emperors had Hindu mothers.

Handicrafts. Rajasthan, especially Jaipur, is famous for gems, jewellery, and block-printed fabrics. Large paintings on cloth, and small ones on ivory are seen in many places.

Climate. November–February is most comfortable, though evenings can be chilly. Temperatures can be very (and even unbearably) high in May and June, prior to the monsoon, but drop sharply from mid-September.

ALWAR

You'll probably only come here on the way to Sariska, but it's a pleasantly quiet town worth a quick look. Alwar was a latecomer among the princely states of Rajasthan, Pratap Singh declaring his independence of Jaipur only in 1771.

The **City Palace**** has an excellent museum and art collection (closed Friday). Among the paintings is a series of portraits of the Mughal emperors and their families and courtiers. Some of the erotic ones are amusing; no surprise that the man on the tiger skin has turned blue! The manuscript library is world-renowned. The armoury includes a suit of medieval European-style armour worn in battle by a maharaja as late as the 1800s and some very interesting sporting guns. The one with a copper ball underneath is an air weapon. These guns were very powerful, almost silent, and much faster to reload than an ordinary musket. In fact the Austrian army was equipped with them for a time.

Behind the palace is a large tank, now in rather a mess, and the red sandstone and white marble **chhattri of Bakhtawar Singh***, successor of Pratap Singh. This is overlooked by the hilltop fort, which you need permission from the police to visit. Interesting **jewellery bazaar** (including enamel work) as you leave the palace on the way to the station.

The **Purjan Vihar*** (Company Garden) is a large conservatory set below ground level, and its complex sprinkler system keeps it always cool and green.

The large domed **tomb of Fateh Jang**, a minister of Shahjahan, near the station is quite well preserved, but is kept locked. A pity, the chhattri on top of the dome promises a good view.

Information. Tourist office over the road from the Company Garden.

Arrival and departure. On Delhi (2½hrs)–Jaipur (2½hrs) rail route. Also buses but not on the main Delhi–Jaipur road.

Accommodation. Most people stay at Sariska (see below). Another possibility if you have transport is the *Lake Palace Tourist Bungalow* (Tel 0144 22991) at Siliserh (13km). Its lakeside position is supposedly very attractive. The lake is said to provide good fishing.

Two inexpensive hotels in town are the *Tourist* and *Ashok*, both in Manu Marg not far from the bus-stand. Also a *PWD Rest House* near the station.

Eating and drinking. Nothing much in the way of restaurants, best to bring a packed lunch. The restaurant of the Tourist Bungalow at Sariska is good, though slow at weekends. No reports about that at Siliserh.

SARISKA

This **wildlife sanctuary****, one of the Project Tiger reserves, covers nearly 400 sq km of the Aravalli Hills and is an ideal place to spend a few days away from Delhi. There is no village at Sariska, just the Tourist Bungalow and a hunting lodge of the Maharaja of Alwar, now a hotel. Apart from tigers Sariska holds different species of deer, wild cats, porcupines, and blue bull (nilgai). Bird life is abundant and you can walk for miles through the scrub jungle outside the park and see more animals than people.

For a variety of reasons the chances of seeing a tiger are at present small. Big changes are planned at Sariska, however, which should improve matters. The first step is to open up new tracks to reach other parts of the sanctuary; there are potentially spectacular viewpoints. The aim is also to develop tourism at several lakes in the area which attract migratory birds. This will give visitors something to do in the middle of the day when there is no chance of seeing a tiger.

The down side is that the cost of accommodation at Sariska and transport in the park has risen to levels beyond many budget travellers. Jeep hire is Rs250 per session, plus Rs100 for it to enter the park, plus Rs25 per person, and plus Rs10 per still camera. The total is split by as many people as use the jeep — expensive if there are only two of you. The photographic hides are no longer used as it was impossible to supervise them, and thoughtless people disturbed the wildlife. Sariska tends to be crowded at weekends.

There have been reports lately that the tiger population is far below the official figure and still declining fast. The reason is poaching to meet the demand for tiger bones in China where they are used in patent medicines.

Information. Forest Office near the Tourist Bungalow, the officer is knowledgeable and helpful.

Arrival and departure. Train or bus to Alwar (from Delhi 2½hrs, Jaipur 2½hrs), tonga or rickshaw to bus-stand, bus to Sariska (35km, 1½hrs).

Accommodation (STD Code 0144)
Hotel Sariska Palace. Tel 41322. SWB A/C Rs1050 DWB A/C Rs1300. Rest. Bar. This former palace of the Maharaja of Alwar is very grand in a rather old-fashioned (and slightly threadbare) way. Immaculate gardens, lawns, and tennis court. Meals for non-residents.
Tiger Den Tourist Bungalow. Tel 41342. SWB Rs200/300 DWB Rs250/400 Dorm Rs40. Rest. Bar (both cheerless). Surrounded by attractive garden (eat out if you wish), and absolutely quiet. Very good Indian food, Continental also offered, and service to match. Comfortable and well furnished within its price range, but likely to be busy at weekends when the catering can be shambolic. Some years ago a local played the fiddle as we dined here. There were bells on the bow and, if you shut your eyes, you would have sworn it was Hungarian gipsy music. After all, it has been suggested that the Romanies came from Rajasthan.
The *Forest Rest House* is not available.

BHARATPUR

The **Keoladeo Ghana National Park***** is India's premier bird sanctuary. Even if you aren't a keen bird-watcher it's exciting to watch large storks catching catfish and juggling them into position to swallow, or to see sleepy-looking owls cuddling up to one another. The Ghana is a great marsh that attracts a hundred species of migratory bird to add to the indigenous hundred or so. Early in the century it was formed by damming a stream to make a duck shoot. Huge bags were taken, sometimes thousands in a day, but now any form of hunting is banned.
The sanctuary consists of large areas of low-lying ground which flood after heavy rain. Islands dot the lagoons, and raised dykes with trees and bushes for cover provide human access. The best season to visit is from October to the end of January. The indigenous water birds, including storks, ibises, and herons nest between October and December. In December many species of migratory water bird, among them the very rare Siberian crane, begin to arrive. By March much of the water and most of the birds have gone. The best time of day is just after dawn when the large birds are feeding. In the lightly forested parkland between the bird sanctuary and the main road can be seen deer, nilgai, and hyenas.
The most satisfactory way of making a visit is to take one of the licenced rickshaw-wallahs, who know the English names of all the birds and where to find them. Alternatively, take a rickshaw just to the end of the road (where the **shooting monument** must be seen) and walk from there. Boat trips can be taken from Shanti Kutir, and a bicycle is a pleasant way of covering a lot of ground during the day.
A wildlife **film show** is put on at Shanti Kutir every evening from October to the end of February. It is held out of doors, which means that in winter warm clothing is required and, at any other time, copious amounts of mosquito repellent. Staying at the Tourist Bungalow you will have to walk back in the dark afterwards. Don't worry, the road is straight and the stars should be bright. There were marvellous sound effects when we last did this: someone playing a bugle, a temple bell ringing, and a wedding band belting out a raucous tune.
Bharatpur itself has had a typically turbulent history, having become in 1733 the capital of a small Jat state. The Jats are an agriculturist caste who successfully turned their hands to soldiering. They held Agra for a number of years and even launched an attack on Delhi. They were eventually subdued by the British in 1826 but retained their separate identity as a princely state. In the town is the **Lohagarh** (Steel Fort) containing palace buildings and a museum.

Information. Rajasthan Tourism at the Tourist Bungalow.

Arrival and departure. Bharatpur is on the metre gauge line between Jaipur (4hrs) and Agra Fort (1hr) and on the Western Railway route from Bombay to Delhi.

Several buses pass through Bharatpur daily on their journey between Agra and Jaipur. Deluxe buses do not usually make a stop at Bharatpur. They do, however, pass the Tourist Bungalow and it should not be difficult to persuade the driver to stop. Since you will have to pay the full fare it only makes sense to do this when travelling from Jaipur. Express buses stop at the bus-stand in the town. The real problem with bus travel comes when you leave Bharatpur because your chances of getting a seat are remote. You can enquire about reservations at the bus-stand, but the place is a bit of a shambles.

Rickshaw-wallahs at the bus-stand have a trick of agreeing to take you to the Tourist Bungalow for about the right fare. They would, in fact, take you to the Circuit House (where you are not allowed to stay), then by a circuitous route to the Tourist Bungalow where they would demand a grossly inflated fee. If this happens ignore their bleating, pay the agreed amount, and retire inside quickly.

Accommodation (STD Code 05644)

Forest Rest House (Shanti Kutir), Ghana National Park (adjacent to Forest Lodge). Tel 2265. SWB/DWB Rs400. Rooms large and plain, but comfortable enough. Advance booking essential.

Sarus Tourist Bungalow, Agra Road (approximately 5km from station, 2km from bus-stand, 500m from entrance to park). Tel 23700. SWB Rs250 DWB Rs300 SWB A/C Rs450 DWB A/C Rs550 Dorm Rs40. Rest. Bar. After years of complaints this place must have a new manager. Friendly welcome, good food, and much improved service. Check the room is not damp before accepting it.

Bambino Guest House, 100m from Tourist Bungalow. SWB Rs120 DWB Rs150 Tents S Rs45 D Rs75. Rest (Cheap/Mod, Chi/Ind).

Hotel Eagle's Nest, 100m from Tourist Bungalow. SWB/DWB Rs350 Dec/Jan, Rs250 other times. Rest.

Tourist Camp, 200m from Tourist Bungalow. Tents with toilet and tap. The man here starts talking in telephone numbers, but if it's not busy you may get in for Rs50.

All places except Shanti Kutir are on the main road and tend to be noisy. They are on the edge of town as you come from Fatehpur Sikri, and on the route of Agra–Jaipur deluxe buses.

JAIPUR

The Pink City has entranced visitors for two centuries and has, rather fancifully, been compared with Paris and Venice. Until the early 18th century the capital of Dhundar state had been at Amber. Maharaja Jai Singh II came to the throne in 1699 and restored the fortunes of the state after a bad patch. Using this new-found prosperity he planned a new capital to be named after himself.

History

Jaipur, begun in 1727, emerged as a planned city surrounded by high walls with seven gates. The city is in nine blocks, and its main axis, Tripolia Bazaar, followed a slight ridge, which is why it is not truly east–west. In the same way Nahargarh hill prevented the obvious three-by-three layout, and the ninth block had be tacked onto the south-eastern corner. Oddly enough, given its popular image, Jaipur did not start life as a pink city; initially it was white and later, when Jai Singh found this too glaring, each quarter was painted a different colour. The pink came only around 1850 when the place was restored by the then maharaja.

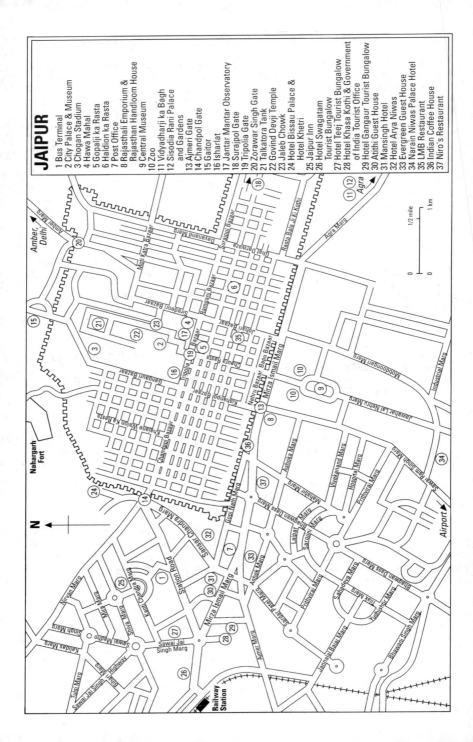

JAIPUR

1 Bus Terminal
2 City Palace & Museum
3 Chogan Stadium
4 Hawa Mahal
5 Gopalji ka Rasta
6 Haldion ka Rasta
7 Post Office
8 Rajasthali Emporium &
  Rajasthan Handloom House
9 Central Museum
10 Zoo
11 Vidyadharji ka Bagh
12 Sisodia Rani Palace
   and Gardens
13 Ajmeri Gate
14 Chandpol Gate
15 Gaitor
16 Isharlat
17 Jantar Mantar Observatory
18 Surajpol Gate
19 Tripolia Gate
20 Zorawar Singh Gate
21 Talkatora Tank
22 Govind Devji Temple
23 Jaleb Chowk
24 Hotel Bissau Palace &
   Hotel Khetri
25 Jaipur Inn
26 Hotel Swagatam
   Tourist Bungalow
27 Hotel Teej Tourist Bungalow
28 Hotel Khasa Kothi & Government
   of India Tourist Office
29 Hotel Gangaur Tourist Bungalow
30 Atithi Guest House
31 Mansingh Hotel
32 Hotel Arya Niwas
33 Evergreen Guest House
34 Narain Niwas Palace Hotel
35 LMB Restaurant
36 Indian Coffee House
37 Niro's Restaurant

Exploring

The Pink City

The City Palace**** (9.30am–4.45pm every day) of Jai Singh II and its gardens occupy two of the city's nine blocks. The ceremonial entry to the palace passes through seven gates, beginning with the **Sireh Deorhi**, which faces the rising sun. The second gate is the **Nakkar-Khana-ka-Darwaza** (Drum House Gate) with its musicians' gallery. Passing through you enter **Jaleb Chowk**, the parade ground of the maharaja's guards, now taken over by law courts. Directly across Jaleb Chowk is the elaborately painted third gateway with its studded brass doors. Inside it is possible to see a further painted gateway where the route made a left turn to approach the Hall of Public Audience. From here detour to the public entrance.

Enter the palace compound through the **Gainda-ki-Deorhi** (Rhinoceros Gate: one used to be kept here). Ignore the buildings here for the moment and go through the **Sarhad-ki-Deorhi** (Boundary Gate) flanked by two marble elephants, and turn sharp right.

The **Saba Newas** (Hall of Public Audience) now houses the **Art Gallery** and manuscript collection. This large hall was originally open on three sides, and the maharaja and his ministers sat on the central platform with the plaintiffs around them, on the floor and outside. The huge carpets which covered the floors had seen earlier service at Amber. Above are the jali screens of the zenana balcony.

A large collection of manuscript books includes some miniatures. Apart from Persian translations of the Ramayana and Mahabharata most are in Sanskrit and some are finely illuminated. Note the book of tables associated with the use of the Jayprakash instrument in the observatory. In addition to the bound volumes you will see several books in the older form of narrow, separate leaves, some on paper, some on palm leaf. The paintings, mostly miniatures, represent several different schools. Among them is one of the Madonna and Child, not unique, but very rare. Most amusing is Departure of the Lover.

The **Serbata** (Hall of Private Audience) is a square-pillared hall raised above the level of the courtyard on a plinth. Originally open on all sides, the corners were later enclosed. The two large silver pots were made for Madho Singh II to carry a supply of Ganges water on his trips to Europe, notably for the coronation of Edward VII in 1902. The pink paint on this building is supposed to be the authentic shade.

A passage on the west side leads to **Pritam Niwas Chowk**, the courtyard between the Gunijan Khana (now the armoury) and the Chandra Mahal, the main palace building. Two of the four splendid doors of this courtyard are painted in peacock designs. One of the others has above it a marble insert of Ganesh, and the adjacent one has Shiva, identified by his trident and the Ganges flowing from the matted locks of his hair. Note how frequently the sun is represented.

The **Chandra Mahal** (Moon Palace), the main palace building, has seven floors built at different times by different maharajas. The styles vary and the overall effect is one of great exuberance. Now that the Rambagh Palace is a hotel the maharaja and his family have moved back to the City Palace, and only part of the ground floor of the Chandra Mahal is open to the public.

In the centre of a pleasant tree-lined courtyard is the **Mubarak Mahal** built by Madho Singh II around 1900 as a guest house. The marble facings, balconies, and decoration of this delightful building simulate a wooden structure. The upper floor of the Mubarak Mahal now houses the textile section of the **museum**, along with some musical instruments. The textiles include local block-printed work, and also brocades, muslins, and others from all over India. There are some very impressive royal costumes. It is just possible to see through the windows here into the reception hall below. Note how the marble panels below these windows and the stones inlaid in them are translucent. A good view can be obtained from the balcony around this level, including the back of the Hawa Mahal and, if no-one is looking, you can nip up on the roof to take photos.

In the north-western corner of this courtyard is the entrance to the **armoury** (Sileh Khana) section of the museum. This occupies the Gunijan Khana, quarters once used by the royal dancing girls and musicians, and the decorated ceilings, one inlaid with mirrors, date from this time. On the stairs on the way up is a painting of a military parade that gives an idea of how smart the town was in its heyday.

Persian and Indian armourers brought such great skill to bear on their products that they become art objects. A collection of swords, including ones presented by Jehangir and Shahjahan, is of great historical value. Most impressive is the 5kg broadsword of Raja Man Singh I; he must have been a very big man to use that single-handed. The large blunderbuss-like weapons on the walls are swivel guns which could be fired from an elephant howdah, or even a camel saddle. One final thing to note is the Jaipur-made handguns; despite resembling a modern automatic they are percussion cap muzzle-loaders.

The City Palace has a delightfully serene atmosphere that belies the hurly-burly outside. Take your time.

The **Observatory***** (open 9am–4.30pm) was built at the same time as the City Palace. Astrology has always played an important part in Indian life and, like many of the princes, Jai Singh was an expert. Realising that the data relating to the movements of the heavenly bodies were inaccurate, he set out to correct them. In the most important of his five observatories the construction of large, carefully aligned masonry instruments permitted very precise observation despite the crude appearance. The biggest instrument is a sundial with a 30m-high gnomon, and accurate to within a few seconds. These instruments work on the precise time for Jaipur's longitude; this has to be corrected to Indian Standard Time. Early morning light is best for photography, but the starkness of midday presents a surreal scene.

Return now to Jaleb Chowk, take the north exit, and look to the left for an archway which leads to the **Govind Devji Temple***. The story goes that the building was intended as a residence for Jai Singh II during construction of the City Palace. One night he was thrown out of his bed, and a vision told him that this was the abode of Krishna. The maharaja moved out, and an image of Krishna from Amber was installed. Puja here is a lively performance, several during the day. From the temple you can see the private part of the palace gardens and the verandah of the Chandra Mahal. Behind the temple is the lower part of the palace gardens, running all the way down to Talkatora Lake.

The **Hawa Mahal***** (Palace of the Winds), whose ornate facade seems to owe more to patisserie than architecture, is Jaipur's best-known building. Yet it was built in 1799, long after the main part of the city. The entrance is round the back; the interior is of little interest, but there is a great view from the top. Its function was mainly as an ornate grandstand for the ladies of the court to watch festivities without being seen. It has been unkindly suggested that the name referred to vapid feminine gossip. On the opposite side of the road steps lead up to a roof from where you can take photographs.

From Tripolia Bazaar you glimpse the **Ishwar Lath***, a tower of victory. Known to the locals as Swarga Suli, 'the minaret that pierces heaven', the name also has a more gruesome significance as the stake on which criminals were impaled. Beware of the **Nawab Saheb Ki Haveli**° where you have to pay for a view you can achieve for free at the Hawa Mahal.

A walk in the bazaars

Despite traffic pollution Jaipur's streets are still best seen on foot. The following **walk**** also covers some of the best **shopping areas**.

Start at Niro's Restaurant and walk along Mirza Ismail Road to Ajmeri Gate. Very

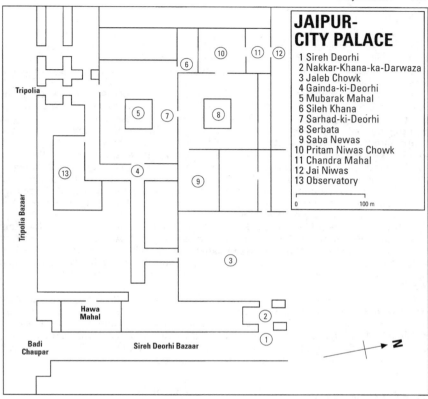

JAIPUR-
CITY PALACE

1 Sireh Deorhi
2 Nakkar-Khana-ka-Darwaza
3 Jaleb Chowk
4 Gainda-ki-Deorhi
5 Mubarak Mahal
6 Sileh Khana
7 Sarhad-ki-Deorhi
8 Serbata
9 Saba Newas
10 Pritam Niwas Chowk
11 Chandra Mahal
12 Jai Niwas
13 Observatory

good shops along here, expensive but honest, also the Rajasthan Government's Handicrafts Emporium and Handloom House. Enter the Pink City through Ajmeri Gate and turn right along Nehru Bazaar. Continue along Bapu Bazaar and turn left into Johari (Jewellers') Bazaar; the best jewellers' shops are in fact in side-lanes, Haldiyon-ka-Rasta and Gopalji-ka-Rasta. Read the warning in the Agra section about buying stones. At 167 Johari Bazaar a rhythmic thumping will lead you to two men making the silver leaf you see on the more expensive sweets; they get Rs2 per sheet. Don't peel it off if you try these sweets, it's supposed to be good for the digestion. Johari Bazaar joins Tripolia Bazaar at Badi Chaupar. Continuing straight ahead down Siredeori Bazaar you will find several antique shops.

In the south-west corner of Badi Chaupar are shops selling wedding outfits, and these continue in a colourful covered bazaar behind this area. Access from Johari Bazaar. Now head down Tripolia Bazaar on the south side. Between shops 349 and 350 is Maniharon-ka-Rasta where bangles and other souvenirs are made from lac (a by-product of bugs), colourful and cheap. Between shops 359 and 360 is Khajane Walone-ka-Rasta, the sculptors quarter. You can either continue to the end of this lane and turn right and left to come out near Niro's, or return to Tripolia Bazaar and walk to Chandpol for a rickshaw. Tripolia Bazaar itself, especially near Badi Chaupar, is best in late afternoon and early evening. Allow plenty of time for this walk, and do not be afraid to explore the maze of alleys off the main streets.

The new city

The **Central Museum*** (closed Friday) was designed by Indian architects working with Sir Swinton Jacob, the State Engineer, and draws heavily on local themes. The building was planned from the start as a museum but also had a further function as a Durbar Hall (look in the centre to see this). Locals dubbed it the Ajib Khana, or House of Wonders.

The ground floor was remodelled in the mid-sixties as a folk museum. It covers the various communities of Rajasthan, and their customs and costumes. Of particular interest is the display on the Gadiya-Lohar, those nomads whose women you see working on roads and building sites all over northern India. Local handicrafts are well represented: the blue and white pottery of Jaipur, the much more elaborate gold, red, and black of Bikaner, and some nice examples of enamel work. Upstairs is the mish-mash all too familiar in Victorian-Indian museums. This is really quite fun if you have the time, but you can learn more about India and its people in an hour on the ground floor than from any number of books. Just by the exit are four copies of the murals in the Buddhist cave temples at Ajanta, useful in view of the poor condition of the originals, and the difficulty of getting there.

Between the Albert Hall and the Pink City, on either side of the street, are the Ram Niwas gardens where the **Zoo** and its aviary are located. Adjacent to the eastern section of the zoo is the **Ravindra Rangmanch Theatre** which incorporates a **modern art gallery**. There is a permanent exhibition (pleasant if not startlingly original) and occasional special shows. The academy exhibition in Jaipur is in the first two weeks of April.

Further south, close to the prominent Moti Doongri hill, is the new **Lakshmi Narayan Temple***. Like its namesake in Delhi this fine structure, clad entirely in white marble, is endowed by the Birla family. The relief left of the main door inside depicts Krishna and Arjuna in their chariot. Looking round the outside the figures on the bases of the pillars are of course mainly Hindu. A few though are Christian and you can also see Confucius and Minerva, the Roman goddess of wisdom.

Excursions

Gaitor and a walk in the hills

Gaitor**, at the foot of the hill which dominates Jaipur, is the cremation place of the maharajas. The three interconnecting compounds hold a white marble chhattri for each maharaja. The one opposite the entrance commemorates Madho Singh II (1888–1923); a frieze on the upper level shows a Dussehra procession leaving the City Palace, passing the Hawa Mahal, the town hall, and other landmarks on its way back to the palace. The oldest chhattri, of Jai Singh II, is in the final compound.

Walking up the battlemented wall to the right of the entrance to Gaitor (as you face it) brings you to **Ganeshgarh***. This small white fort, on the axis of the City Palace and Jawaharlal Nehru Marg in the new town, enshrines a Ganesh temple. The main reason for coming up here is, of course, the superb view of the city. The peace and space are a welcome bonus.

The path continues uphill past Ganeshgarh to a TV antenna that you pass on your left; if in doubt follow the water pipe. You come out on the Amber–Nahargarh road at the **Charan Mandir**. The temple will probably be locked, so you won't see Krishna's footprints, but the adjoining fort and high watchtower are older and more interesting anyway.

From here the **Nahargarh*** (Tiger Fort) is clearly visible. This is contemporary with Jaipur itself, though taking its present form as late as 1902. The royal apartments are deteriorating rapidly, but the view is tremendous and you can get a cold beer or meal. A steep path leads back down to the city. As an alternative you could walk from the city up to Nahargarh, along the road to Jaigarh, and down to Amber, catching a bus or tempo back from there.

More peace and quiet

Head east down Tripolia Bazaar (the local elephants are kept towards the end), out through Suraj Pol (Sun Gate), and over the main road to a chai shop where bikes can be left. Then walk up the zig-zag path to the **Surya Temple*** dedicated to the sun (significant here as the maharajas trace their descent from the sun). The temple was built in the 18th century by a Jain who was Jai Singh II's ambassador to the Mughal court. From here you can see the whole city and the ridge to the north with Nahargarh at one end and Jaigarh at the other. As with Nahargarh (or any other vantage point in India) it is best to do this early in the day before dust and haze obscure the view.

From the nearby dharamsala you can walk on down to the deep gorge of **Galta**. A bathing tank on the way down has some quaint instructions on a marble plaque. At the bottom are two unusual matching temples of Gopalji and Rama. The best view of these is from the **cave of Sri Krishna Das Payahariji**, a hermit who lived on nothing but milk.

A short distance out of town on the Agra road is the **Vidyaharji-ka-Bagh***, a pleasant garden named after Jai Singh II's architect. Note the painted decoration simulating raised plasterwork. Somewhat further is the **Sisodia Rani-ka-Bagh***, a garden and small palace built for Jai Singh II's favourite wife (a princess of the Sisodia clan of Udaipur). The zig-zag path up to the Jain temple looks quite a challenge. Turning off the main road to the left leads to Galta, passing on the way a **Hanuman Temple** where the local monkeys are fed at 4pm every day. The snag with making a circular tour is getting a bike over the ridge, but cycling back from Sisodia Rani-ka-Bagh is no joke either.

Practical Information ℹ️

Shopping. Jaipur is a great place for souvenir hunting, and following the walk described above will show you most of what is available. Block-printed fabrics are the best buy; the top place is Anokhi in the new town, the cheapest are the street traders around the City Palace. Handloom Haveli near the Mansingh Hotel is worth a look. Paintings on ivory, paper, and cloth are popular, but don't believe any stories about them being old. Children will pester you in the streets to visit their artist brothers. Most are just commission agents, but it is possible to find genuine artists and buy at reasonable prices. Traditional blue and white pottery is very attractive. If you do want to buy gems the Rajasthan government runs a testing laboratory, but we repeat that any stories about selling for a profit in the West are moonshine.

Information. Government of India Tourist Office at Rajasthan State Hotel, and Rajasthan Tourist Bureau at railway station — both have maps. Guided tours available but not recommended — this is not a place to rush.

Stalls outside the City Palace sell a good booklet explaining all the instruments in the observatory.

A Princess Remembers by Gayatri Devi, the dowager Maharani of Jaipur, is fascinating. A good insight into the rotten world of Indian politics, and thought-provoking on the problems of a Western-minded woman in a polygamous household.

Arrival and departure. Airport (16 km). Indian Airlines office (Tel 514 407) on Tonk Road; flights to Delhi, Bombay, and Udaipur.

On Delhi (6½hrs)–Ahmedabad (15½hrs) metre gauge line, or from Agra Fort (7½hrs). The broad gauge Shatabdi Express, which has replaced the old Pink City

Express, leaves from New Delhi early in the morning and returns in the evening (4¼hrs each way).

Rajasthan Roadways bus-stand on Station Road. Services to Delhi (including private operators), Agra, and everywhere else in Rajasthan.

The rickshaw drivers are especially tiresome here, very persistent and always hassling over fares. Though Jaipur is less flat than some places a bike is definitely the best way to get around.

 Many of Jaipur's hotels are a tourist attraction in their own right, and you don't have to be a millionaire to stay in a palace. Jaipur's STD code is 0141.

Hotel Khasa Khoti (Rajasthan State Hotel), Mirza Ismail Road. Tel 375 151. SWB Rs575 DWB Rs695 Suite Rs1500. Rest (a bit basic). Bar. Huge, quiet, tree-studded lawns. Swimming pool. That peculiar mixture of the grand and the slightly tatty that one becomes so used to in India.

Hotel Narain Niwas, Narain Singh Road. Tel 563 448. SWB Rs650 DWB Rs875 plus 10% SC. Rest (residents only). No liquor. Incredible Indo-Victorian splendour. A palace filled with furniture (including a huge four-poster bed) bought from the East India Company when it was wound up, muskets, bric-a-brac, and sporting trophies. Possibly not as comfortable as more modern places, but has to be seen to be believed. See also Kanota.

Hotel Bissau Palace, outside Chandpol. Tel 317 628. SWB Rs500 DWB Rs650. Rest (residents only). Bar. Not as quiet as the Khetri, but much more interesting inside with weapons and tigers' heads on the walls. A delightful place. The approach from Chandpol (same as for Khetri) is, shall we say, picturesque. Do not let that deter you.

Gangaur Tourist Bungalow, MI Road (500m from station). Tel 371 641. SWB Rs200 DWB Rs250 SWB A/C Rs400 DWB A/C Rs500. Rest. Bar. 24-hour Coffee Shop (all A/C). Very pleasant, if a little noisy.

Teej Tourist Bungalow, Sawai Jai Singh Road (500m from station). Tel 374 373. SWB Rs250 DWB Rs350 SWB A/C Rs400 DWB A/C Rs550. Rest. Bar.

Hotel Khetri House, outside Chandpol. Tel 369 183. SWB Rs290 (£5.80/$9.65) DWB Rs380 Suite Rs550. Rest (residents only). Bar. Just outside a bastion of the city walls and overlooked by the Nahargarh Fort. Absolutely quiet, large gardens. Former palace of a tributary raja, all in 1920s style. There is even a piano in one of the huge suites.

Swagatam Tourist Bungalow, off Station Road (200m from station). Tel 310 595. SWB Rs100/200 DWB Rs200/300 Dorm Rs40. Rest (simple). Not the quietest of places, but by no means unpleasant.

Jaipur Inn, Shiv Marg (1.5km from station). Tel 316 157. SR/DR Rs80/120 SWB Rs250 DWB Rs300 Dorm Rs40. Rest. Camping. Parking. Excellent hot buffet supper Rs35. Quiet location, very well run by W/Cdr Bhargava. Rightly popular.

Atithi Guest House, 1 Park House Scheme. Tel 378 679. SWB Rs225/325 DWB Rs250/350. Rest (veg). Spotless, friendly family-run place despite insalubrious surroundings.

Hotel Arya Niwas, behind Amber Cinema, Sansar Chandra Road. Tel 372 456. SWB Rs150/350 DWB Rs250/450. Rest (self-service, very good). One of the neatest and cleanest hotels in this price range. Spotless kitchen.

Hotel Kantichandra Palace, off Station Road. Tel 367 560. SR Rs95 DR Rs145 SWB Rs150 DWB Rs225. Rest (basic). An old palace with a nice garden but very run down. Same approach as Golden Inn.

Golden Inn, Vivek Nagar. Tel 374 005. SR Rs95 DR Rs140 SWB Rs125 DWB Rs195. Rest (rooftop or room service). Family run. Turn right out of bus-stand, then first right.

Golden Hotel, Kanti Nagar. Tel 366 606. SR Rs95 DR Rs140 SWB Rs125 DWB Rs195. Rest (room service only). Under same ownership as Golden Inn and recommended. Reasonably quiet. Free homoeopathic medicine if you need it. Turn right out of bus-stand, third right (at Hotel Swapnika), and first left.

Evergreen Lodge, MI Road. We mention this place in recognition of its fame, and not as any sort of recommendation.

Rooms in the older establishments can vary a lot in size and quality; ask to see others if you do not like the first you are shown.

Eating and Drinking

Rambagh Palace Hotel, Bhawani Singh Marg. Tel 521 241. Exp (Rs250–350 per head, could spend a lot more). Ind/Cont. Magnificent dining room, food and service to match. Have a drink in the Polo Bar or on the terrace beforehand and enjoy the unique atmosphere. Well worth saving for, and a far better place to spend the money than the Lake Palace.

Rooftop Restaurant, Mansingh Hotel. Exp (similar to Rambagh). Reputed to be the best Indian food in town — and the view!

Copper Chimney (formerly Kwality), MI Road. Exp (Rs120–180 per head; £2.40–3.60/$4–6). Ind/Chi (including Szechuan). Attractive and imaginative decor. Good food and service — recommended. Some street maps still show this as Kwality (and sometimes in the wrong place); it is actually almost opposite the GPO.

LMB, Johari Bazaar. Mod/Exp. Ind (vegetarian only). The authors are, on the whole, no enthusiasts of vegetarian food, but always have at least one buffet lunch here when in Jaipur. Top-class food and excellent value for money.

Natraj, MI Road. Mod/Exp. Ind (vegetarian only). Very clean and handy for tea and a snack when shopping. Huge range of Indian sweets and pastries.

Niro's, close to Natraj, is similar in price to Copper Chimney and equally good.

Moti Mahal, MI Road (near Copper Chimney). Cheap/Mod. Ind. Recommended.

Shri Jai Ambey Pavitra Bhojnalaya, near bus-stand. Cheap. Ind veg. Eat in or out, latter lively if rather noisy. Very good food for the price.

Many small, cheap restaurants (some very good) in Nehru Bazaar and on the south side of Chandpol Bazaar.

AMBER AND JAIGARH FORT

Outside the old city's Zorawar Gate a group of **chhattris** behind a high wall marks the cremation place of the ranis. On the other side of the road is a number of workshops producing **block-printed fabrics**. The process is well worth seeing, but do not buy here. Bus tours have forced up prices, and you will do much better with the street traders (if only because their stock is the seconds).

Further out you pass the **Jal Mahal**, a water palace and shooting lodge most attractive from a distance.

Passing through Ghati Darwaza, part of the outer defences of Amber, you see Maota Lake and Amber Palace; get off the bus or tempo here and walk the rest of the way to enjoy the view. Cross the dam — the gardens and pavilions here provided accommodation for high-ranking Muslims on the pilgrimage to Ajmer — and join the steep path up to the palace entrance.

Amber Palace

Amber Palace***, the capital of the state of Dhundar, was built in two main stages. The newer part, where you are now, is the work of Jai Singh I (1622–1667). The older

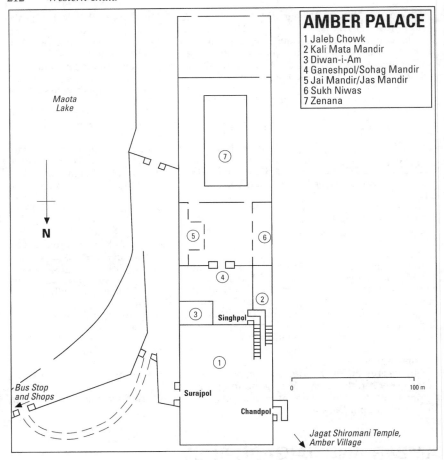

AMBER PALACE
1 Jaleb Chowk
2 Kali Mata Mandir
3 Diwan-i-Am
4 Ganeshpol/Sohag Mandir
5 Jai Mandir/Jas Mandir
6 Sukh Niwas
7 Zenana

Maota Lake

N

Bus Stop and Shops

Surajpol

Singhpol

Chandpol

Jagat Shiromani Temple, Amber Village

0   100 m

zenana palace (missed by most visitors) dates to the reign of Man Singh I (1589–1615). **Jaleb Chowk** is entered by Surajpol (Sun Gate), and was the quarters of the royal guards. Try an elephant ride here, much cheaper than riding one up from the village. The terrace of the restaurant gives a view of other palaces and temples in the old city.

In one corner is the **Shila Devi Temple**, dedicated to Kali whose gruesome pictures decorate the silver doors. More like a white marble mosque inside, the temple was completely rebuilt to this form earlier this century. The temple is closed noon–4pm, and photography is banned. Beside the temple, steps lead up to Singhpol (Lion Gate).

The first courtyard is dominated by the **Diwan-i-Am**, a superb building on Mughal lines. Too superb, perhaps, for Jehangir became jealous, and the columns had to be camouflaged with plaster. The zenana screens round the roof gallery which rather spoil the proportions are a 19th century addition, as is the closed room at the back.

Ganeshpol separates the public part of the palace from the private. Note the jali screens allowing the royal women to watch proceedings in the Diwan-i-Am, and the image of Ganesh above the gate. Inside is a small formal garden and, on the left, the **Jai Mandir** (Jai's Palace) which functioned as a hall of private audience. It is also known as the Shish Mahal which means Mirror Palace, as the suite of three rooms is brilliantly decorated with tiny mirrors, coloured glass, and carved plaster. Wait for the custodians to open one of the side rooms for a group, these are even prettier. Facing this over the garden is the **Sukh Niwas** (Hall of Pleasure), a summer palace cooled by a cascade of water combined with air vents. The water was raised from the lakes by a series of Persian wheels.

At a higher level the upper part of Ganeshpol is the **Sohag Mandir**, richly decorated. Above the Jai Mandir is the **Jas Mandir** (Hall of Glory). The terrace in front of these marble rooms was used for moonlit durbars and music recitals. The windows overlook the lake and the Mohan Bari, a formal garden. From here you can enter the palace of Man Singh I, which became the zenana (women's palace) when the new palace was built. This is a rabbit warren of passages and tiny rooms. Interesting but, for some indefinable reason, slightly depressing.

Jaigarh Fort

Dominating Amber, and probably older, is **Jaigarh****. This fort has its own set of palace buildings and also the workshops where the fabled Jaipur artillery was cast and machined. The most dramatic product is the Jai Vana, a 50-tonne behemoth that fired an 11 inch-cannonball 35km. At the other end of the scale Rs10 will allow you to fire a miniature cannon. The best thing though is the views; note how the outer defence walls followed the hills around. You can walk up to Jaigarh or take a jeep from Jaleb Chowk, expensive but open to negotiation.

Amber village

Leaving Jaleb Chowk by Chandpol (Moon Gate) you can walk down to the **Jagat Shiromani Temple**. Purely Rajput in style this enshrines images of Krishna and Radha and, behind them, Vishnu and Lakshmi. The mixture of stone is unusual in a temple, and some of the sculpture is very fine. The cobbled street below leads to the bus-stand in the village.

Allow plenty of time for Amber. It is not hard to spend a whole day here; enjoy the more popular buildings between the lemming groups, and find peace in the quieter places.

Arrival and departure. Bus or tempo from outside the Hawa Mahal, also a pleasant cycle ride. Returning it is easier to board a bus in Amber village than at the tourist bazaar. Just after Ghati Darwaza, as you return to Jaipur, a road on the right leads up to Jaigarh and Nahargarh.

AJMER

Ajmer was something of an oddity in Rajasthan in that it was under direct British control instead of being a princely state. The Mughals established this practice, partly because of Ajmer's strategic position, and partly because of its religious significance for Muslims.

Sufism, a mystical offshoot of Islam, fitted well into the eclectic Indian religious scene, and a succession of Chishti saints is still held in high regard. The first of these was Khwaja Muin-ud-din Chishti, who came to Ajmer from Persia in 1166. His tomb, known as the **Dargah****, is of white marble with painted decoration and has doors and rails of silver. Non-Muslims may enter as long as they are properly dressed and their heads covered. As in all these places it is best to ignore the attendants hassling you and find a quiet corner to watch proceedings. A donation, Rs5 is quite enough, is expected. In the same compound are a white marble mosque built by Shahjahan, an older one by Akbar (who especially revered Muin-ud-din and came on pilgrimage regularly), and a tank partly hewn from the bedrock.

Actually the most interesting things here are the two **huge cooking pots** just inside the entrance. The larger of these holds 120 maunds, an ancient measure of weight which, just to confuse everybody, varied around India, being here 40kg/88lbs. Rich Muslim pilgrims pay Rs40,000 for sackfuls of rice, ghee, sugar, almonds, raisins and spices to be cooked for the benefit of local families.

A short distance uphill from the Dargah is the **Adhai-din-ka-Jhonpra**** (mosque of two and a half days), owing its name to the legend that it was built in that time. The mosque was first built in 1153 on the site of a Jain college using the material from demolished temples. Each of the slender carved pillars is in fact three Hindu and Jain ones superimposed. The seven-arched (not true arches) screen in front was added by Qutb-ud-din in around 1200. This is notable for its fine Islamic inscriptions and for being in far better condition than the same man's very similar mosque at the Qutb Minar in Delhi.

The **Government Museum** (10am–4.30pm, closed Friday) is the usual crummy offering, run by people who couldn't care less. It is of interest solely for being located in Akbar's fortified palace.

In the Jain **Nasiyan Mandir***** (or Red Temple) is an amazing feat of model-making. This miniature golden Disneyworld depicts (with the help of English captions) the Jain conception of the universe and the five main events (conception, birth, penance, enlightenment, and salvation) in the life of Adinath, the first tirthankar or Jain guru. The temple itself is richly decorated even by Jain standards. Not to be missed.

Away from the busy main streets Ajmer has a good, relatively quiet atmosphere. Walking between the places described and then down Nalla Bazaar to the station is a real pleasure.

Information. Tourist office at Khadim Hotel (Tourist Bungalow). Make sure you get the tourist officer and not a freelance guide who hangs about here. The Jain temple is fully described in a book (Rs4) available here.

Arrival and departure. On Delhi Sarai Rohilla (9¾hrs)–Jaipur (3¼hrs)–Ahmedabad (13hrs) line, but the new broad gauge service from New Delhi takes 6½hrs. Also Udaipur (8hrs) and Chittaurgarh (4hrs). State and private buses to all the likely places. Station and bus-stand are about 2km apart. For Pushkar see below.

Accommodation (STD Code 0145)
Khadim Tourist Bungalow, 200m from bus-stand. Tel 52490. SWB Rs150 DWB Rs200 SWB A/C Rs300 DWB A/C Rs400 Dorm Rs40. Rest. Bar.
Nagpal Tourist Hotel, near station. SWB Rs90 DWB Rs150 plus 5% SC. Breakfast. Clean but noisy.
Sirtaj Tourist Hotel nearby is similar.

Eating and drinking
Honeydew, next to Nagpal Tourist Hotel. Mod. Ind/Cont. Very good.
Other hotels and restaurants in area opposite station.

PUSHKAR

Only 11km/7 miles from the Muslim centre of Ajmer is the holiest lake of the Hindus. Pushkar Lake, surrounded by hills, has been a major place of pilgrimage for at least 2000 years. In the sixties it became firmly established as a hippy haven, and some of the old atmosphere lingers on.

The many temples are relatively recent, as a result of destruction during Aurangzeb's time. Among them is one (some say the only) **Brahma Temple****. Apart from the novelty this is of interest only for the silver coins of the Raj period set in many of the memorial stones. The silver tortoise represents Vishnu's second incarnation. Over the inside of the gateway is a goose, Brahma's vehicle like Shiva's Nandi.

The **ghats** are different from those in Varanasi in that you cannot readily walk along them, and that the only people who will welcome your presence are renegade priests hoping to perform an expensive puja. This makes about as much sense as an English vicar forcing communion on a Hindu visitor to his church, and then demanding money with menaces. We met a woman, new to India, who had been intimidated into paying Rs500 to one of these wretches.

No matter. Except during major festivals Pushkar is a quiet, calm place where you can live very cheaply and relax. The most important festival is **Pushkar Mela** at the time of the October/November full moon when as many as 200,000 pilgrims come here to bathe. Perhaps of more interest is the concurrent camel and cattle fair. Roll up! roll up! and see the camel races.

Information. Tourist office at the Tourist Bungalow. Any Rajasthan or Government of India tourist office will have the precise date of Pushkar Mela.

Arrival and departure. Bus or share jeep from Ajmer. Ignore the rickshaw-wallahs at Ajmer station, walk outside and turn right, only 150m down on the left you will find a bus which runs to the east side of Pushkar, most convenient for the Tourist Bungalow and Pushkar Palace. Avoid the private Studebaker buses which could have a serious effect on your life expectancy. Buses from the main bus-stand in Ajmer run to the main bus-stand in Pushkar (on the north side of town), convenient for the White House. The trip out to Pushkar would be an interesting but strenuous bike ride.

Accommodation (STD Code 014581)

Hotel Pushkar Palace. Tel 3401. SR Rs60 (£1.20/$2) DR Rs100 SWB Rs250 DWB Rs350 SWB A/C Rs600 DWB A/C Rs750. Rest (veg, good, excellent buffet for Rs60). Best location right on the lake. Some double rooms cramped; ask for a move after the first night and, if you want to sleep, for a room well away from the noisy reception office.

Hotel Sarovar (Tourist Bungalow). Tel 2040. SR Rs75 DR Rs100 SWB Rs100 DWB Rs150 SWB A/C Rs200 DWB A/C Rs250. Rest (veg, good). Combination of old palace on lake shore and modern block. Lovely garden, well kept rooms, some overlooking the lake, some the hills.

White House, Pushkar Sarovar. Tel 2147. SR Rs50 DR Rs100 DWB Rs150. Rest (rooftop). Good setting near hills. Convenient for Marwar bus-stand. Really nice people and a bargain at these prices.

Bharatpur Palace, near lake. SR Rs50 DR Rs70–140. Clean. Good views.

Payal Guest House, Municipality Sadar Bazaar. Tel 2163. SR Rs30 DR Rs50 DWB Rs85. Rest (breakfast). Good value.

Krishna Guest House, Krishna temple. Tel 91. SR Rs40 DR Rs60 SWB Rs60 DWB Rs110. Rest. Nice little garden.

Evergreen, near bus-stand. SR Rs30 DR Rs60 DWB Rs80. Not seen, but reportedly good.

Eating and drinking

Shiva. Ind/Cont. Cheap/Mod. Best value in Pushkar. Open air. Buffet dinner (Rs25) includes curries, pasta, salad, and chips all freshly prepared.

Sanjay Rooftop. Ind/Cont. Cheap/Mod. Distant views of lake. Famous for its humus and falafel. Poster for breakfast says 'Get stuffed for Rs25', and you can too.

Many others, all with their ardent supporters. We reckon the *Swagatam* produced the worst soup we have had in our lives, and the fermenting tomato sauce was the nearest thing to alcohol in Pushkar. You are unlikely to find eggs, never mind meat or alcohol, in this holy place.

Lots of hotels being built, worth looking around. *Peacock Hotel*, a little out of town from Ajmer bus-stand, gets good reports. Rajasthan Tourism puts up a tent city during Pushkar Mela, advance booking essential.

SHEKHAWATI

Shekhawati was a federation of small prosperous Rajput states centred on Sikar, 100km/62 miles north-west of Jaipur. As elsewhere in Rajasthan and Gujarat the wealthy built themselves fine houses, or havelis; unlike most other places many of these are adorned by murals.

Pilani is home to the Birla Institute of Science and Technology, so it is no surprise to find an unusual white temple here. The Sharda Mandir enshrines not only great Indians like Gandhi and Tagore, but also scientists, including Pasteur, Fleming, Edison, and Marie Curie.

Shekhawati is one of those places which greatly appeal to some people and which others (the majority) find do not justify the difficulty and expense of travel.

Information. *Shekhawati* by Islay Cooper may still be available.

BIKANER

Like Jaisalmer, Bikaner owes its importance to its position on the caravan routes from the Middle East and Africa to northern India. The present city was founded in 1488 by Rao Bikaji, a kinsman of the founder of Jodhpur, though settlement goes back a lot earlier than that.

The one real reason for visiting Bikaner is the **Junagarh*****, meaning Old Fort (10am–4.30pm). Entry Rs20, plus Rs25 for a still camera. Built mainly by Raja Rai Singh (1571–1611) this has arguably the most beautiful palace apartments in India; equally important, given the rough state of most such places, they are almost perfectly preserved. The entrance is through four gates. The second, the Daulat Prole, has many sati memorials, and two life-size elephants stand guard at the Suraj Prole. Inside that is a little gold-leafed statue of Ganesh, the elephant-headed god. In the first courtyard are elaborate staircases and balconies.

A tank of white Carrara marble stands in the inner courtyard, off which lead the cloud-painted Monsoon Palace and a throne room resplendent in maroon and gold. The private apartments are equally attractive; gold, coloured glass, and mirrors. A really unusual feature is the blue-tiled roof pavilion. The original punkah still hangs from the ceiling with its painting of Radha and Krishna dancing, and the walls are covered with mirrors and tiles cut from various blue and white dinner services. See how many you can spot!

A large Darbar Hall of white marble and red sandstone was added in this century. Among the reliefs is one of Krishna putting the gopis' clothes in a tree. The various First World War trophies, including a roughly restored biplane (DH4 or DH9 perhaps), date from Maharaja Ganga Singh's representing India at war conferences and the subsequent Versailles Settlement.

The **Shri Sadul Museum** (10am–5pm, closed Wednesday) at the Lallgarh Palace Hotel has a huge collection of ephemera connected with the maharajas. Unless you are in to big-game hunting or the social history of endangered human species it is of limited interest. The **Ganga Golden Jubilee Museum** (10am–5pm, closed Friday) may be better, but it is liable to be closed.

Bikaner is famous above all for its camels. Camel-mounted Bikaneri soldiers have fought as far away as Somaliland and China, and their descendants still participate in ceremonial parades in Delhi. At a more practical level they help the Border Security Force patrol the desert border with Pakistan. The government **camel breeding farm**

(3–5pm only) seeks to improve the breed, but provides zero information on its aims and methods. This is presumably a security measure — photography is banned too. The main attraction is the babies, which look cuddly in an ugly sort of way.

At **Deshnok** (30km) is a temple where rats are revered while awaiting reincarnation as bards. This is an expensive and/or uncomfortable place to reach; the time is better spent in the palace.

Information. Tourist office at Dhola Maru Hotel (Tourist Bungalow). Desert Tours, behind the GPO, are preparing a book on Bikaner and arrange camel trekking.

Arrival and departure. Two night trains from Jaipur (10hrs for the express), Sawai Madhopur (14hrs), Jodhpur (7hrs), and Delhi (10½hrs). Also buses, including one to Jaisalmer (10hrs). This is an uncomfortable ride, but at least seats can be reserved. Hire a bike to get around, the rickshaw and tonga drivers are rapacious.

Accommodation (STD Code 0151)

Hotel Dhola Maru (Tourist Bungalow). Tel 28621. SWB Rs110/200 DWB Rs150/250 SWB A/C Rs350 DWB A/C Rs400 Dorm Rs40. Rest. Bar.

Deluxe Hotel, Station Road. Tel 23292. SWB Rs85 DWB Rs105. Rest (snacks).

Green Hotel, Station Road. Tel 23396. SR Rs45 SWB Rs75 DR Rs70 DWB Rs100 4WB Rs150, plus Rs10 in summer for cooler. Bedding Rs3 in winter. Rest. Snacks and cold drinks. Next to Deluxe, walk out of station and turn right.

Eating and drinking

Amber. Cheap/Mod. Good in every respect. Name in Devanagri only, but it's the smart one opposite Green Hotel.

JAISALMER

Marooned in the middle of the Thar Desert Jaisalmer is a dream in stone. It's not so long ago that only a couple of dozen foreigners were in Jaisalmer at any one time. Things have changed, but it is still a good place to unwind; it's small and unhurried (by Indian standards) and you can spend hours (or days) happily wandering about the quiet streets and alleys. Definitely one of the top places in India.

History

Jaisalmer was once the most important oasis on the desert caravan routes. It was the capital of the Bhatti Rajputs who trace their descent from Krishna. Their previous capital was Lodurva but, as elsewhere, the need for better defences led to the choice of a hilltop site, hence in 1156 the move to Jaisal Meru (the hill of Jaisal). The legend is, of course, more exciting: Krishna came here after the battle of Kurukshetra (as related in the Mahabharata) to perform a sacrifice. Afterwards he prophesied that one of his descendants would build the capital of a great state here. To make this possible he changed an unreliable brackish well into a perennial source of sweet water.

The rise and fall of Jaisalmer's fortunes has been entirely a matter of geography. Its wealth came mainly from taxes on caravans. Merchants and traders migrated here because of the desert security and, as usual in peaceful and prosperous places, the arts flourished. The most notable legacy of this period are temples and havelis (mansions) built of the local yellow sandstone, the facades, balconies, and screens of which are intricately carved.

The downfall began with the development of ports, notably Bombay, and of railways, both of which bypassed Jaisalmer. Rapacious ministers in the 19th century made matters worse; the wealthy emigrated, and Jaisalmer, once a city of 35,000, was

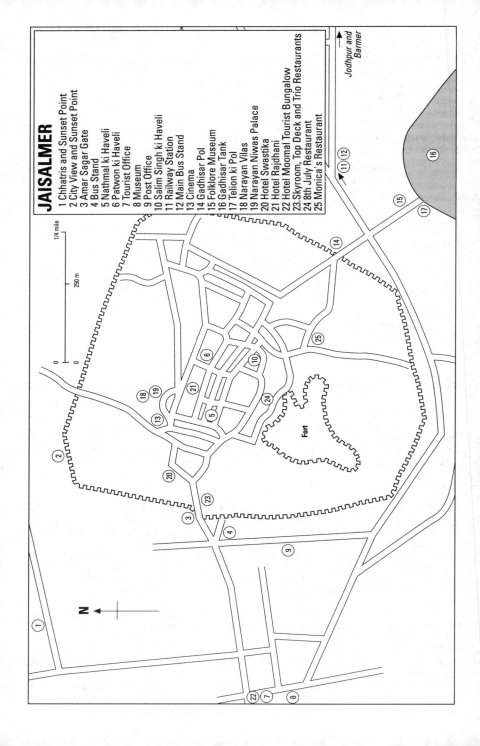

JAISALMER

1 Chhatris and Sunset Point
2 City View and Sunset Point
3 Amar Sagar Gate
4 Bus Stand
5 Nathmal ki Haveli
6 Patwon ki Haveli
7 Tourist Office
8 Museum
9 Post Office
10 Salim Singh ki Haveli
11 Railway Station
12 Main Bus Stand
13 Cinema
14 Gadhisar Pol
15 Folklore Museum
16 Gadhisar Tank
17 Telion ki Pol
18 Narayan Vilas
19 Narayan Niwas Palace
20 Hotel Swastika
21 Hotel Rajdhani
22 Hotel Moomal Tourist Bungalow
23 Skyroom, Top Deck and Trio Restaurants
24 8th July Restaurant
25 Monica's Restaurant

Jodhpur and Barmer

Fort

1/4 mile

250 m

N

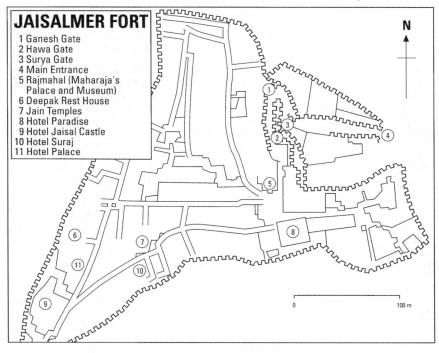

JAISALMER FORT

1 Ganesh Gate
2 Hawa Gate
3 Surya Gate
4 Main Entrance
5 Rajmahal (Maharaja's Palace and Museum)
6 Deepak Rest House
7 Jain Temples
8 Hotel Paradise
9 Hotel Jaisal Castle
10 Hotel Suraj
11 Hotel Palace

N

0 _____ 100 m

reduced to a population of only 4000. Partition and the nearby border with Pakistan have given Jaisalmer a new importance. Recent development as a tourist centre (not to mention smuggling over the border) has restored some slight measure of prosperity.

Exploring

The fort

All Jaisalmer, and the desert for many miles around, is dominated by the fort on Trikuta Hill, the oldest part of the city. The approach winds uphill through strong defences (and overhung by part of the palace) and then opens out into a square. On one side is the **Rajmahal*****, or royal palace. The marble throne on the steps was used for the public audiences of the maharawal (the local title for maharaja).

The palace developed over a long period of time, but most dates from around 1844. The Dancing Hall has a marble floor, some unpolished sections still stamped 'Produce of Italy' (in English!): odd in a country renowned for its marble! The yellow Jaisalmer stone in the central motif contains sea shells; this stone has been used in many other buildings in northern India, notably the Itimad-ud-Daulah in Agra. The Indian tiles which form the dadoes were installed about 25 years ago. The maharawal's little balcony is beside the dance floor. In the corners of the room are panels of niches, above these is a narrow slot from which water cascaded.

The maharawal's salon beside the dancing hall has blue and white tiles from Calcutta about 75 years old. Most of these tiles could have come from anywhere, but at the tops of the pillars are some which are obviously Indian. Ever seen lino on a ceiling before? Rings presumably supported a throne or punkahs. Traces of the original painted decoration remain on the balcony outside this room. This gives a vertiginous view over the lively scene in the square. The maharawal's dining hall has also been tiled; the painted decoration which this conceals can be seen in the balconies.

The maharani's sleeping chamber is beautifully decorated with floral designs in red, blue and gold. The murals depict Jaipur, Ajmer, and Jodhpur; Jaisalmer appears in the background of a boar hunt. One of the mirrored panels has a hole in it. Looking on the other side of this you will find a wooden roller, on the other side of the stairs are two more, and a final one in a wooden door. These led the punkah cord outside the building, so that the poor old punkah-wallah out in the hot sun ran no risk of glimpsing the ladies. The roof of the palace provides the best view of Jaisalmer.

Commerce and tolerance brought many Jains to Jaisalmer. They prospered, and, like wealthy merchants in Europe, endowed places of worship. A group of seven ornate **Jain temples***** (open until midday) dating from the 16th century represents their hopes of salvation. To the right of the main group is the **Parasnath Temple**. The maha-mandapa is supported by eight superb columns each with makara-toranas, and the 'dome' has bracket figures and a long stalactite in the centre now disfigured by a bizarre light fitting. The **Shambunath Temple**, which leads off the Parasnath, has the most marvellous bracket figures of musicians and dancers in the roof of the maha-mandapa. Below this is the **treasury**, or Ghyan Bhandar (Well of Knowledge), which holds manuscripts dating back to the 11th century. It also has several miniature images of Jina, one of emerald set in gold, others in sandalwood and ivory. Opening hours are very limited; check before looking at the temples.

Steps lead up from the porch of the Parasnath Temple to the **Shantinath Temple**, the shrine of which is in the upper part of the spire of the **Kuntunath Temple** below. The image here is of gold. Note the panels with many, many Jinas on either side of the shrine door and the kittenish lions.

Another set of steps leads down from that terrace to the lower level which has a white marble **image of Chandraprabhu**, identified by the crescent moon on the base. This temple is most unusual for having a gallery round the mandapa. The frieze on this below the balustrade has musicians and exuberant dancers. The bracket figures comprise an amorous couple on the upper section, below is Ganesh in a multi-armed form, perhaps dancing. This temple has shrines at three different levels, one above the other. Niches above this suggest that a fourth level of images may have been planned.

Finally comes the **Rishabdev Temple**, the exterior of which is adorned by Hindu deities as are many of the pillars in front of it. Note the image of Ganesh and the mouse. The yellow sandstone Jaina figures behind the temple owe their polish to a mixture of sandalwood paste and saffron. The exclusion of leather articles in all the temples is strictly enforced, and photography is banned.

As in the new town below half the fun is just wandering about exploring on your own. Have a look at the ramparts, still surmounted by guns and piles of stones to be dropped on attackers. The main wall with its 90-odd semicircular bastions was added around the beginning of the 17th century. A walk round the ramparts would be nice, but modern sanitation has yet to reach many homes.

The lower town

Stability in the 18th century encouraged expansion of the city below the fortress, and this was subsequently surrounded by a wall with fine gates and many bastions. This, in its slightly different way, is just as pleasant a place to stroll around as the fort.

The palace in the fort was superseded by the **Badal Vilas Palace** just inside Amar Sagar Pole, the west gate of the city. This is still occupied by the maharawal and his family and normally closed, but the outside is worth a look. The palace dates from the late 19th century and is as ornate as any earlier building. Even the underneath of the chajjas is carved in foliage patterns. It is said that the palace was built (like most others in the town) by Muslim craftsmen who gave their labour free. Their price was the resemblance of the tower to a tazia, the representation of the tombs of Hassan and Hussain, carried in Moharram processions.

The havelis

Wealthy merchants and courtiers emulated the king, some might say surpassed him, by building ornately carved havelis, or mansions. Just off the main street a late-19th-century diwan, Nathmal, built the **Nathmalji-ki-Haveli*****. The astounding exterior repays careful study; there are many motifs you would not expect on so traditional-looking a building. The two halves, left and right, were carved separately by two brothers, hence the variations. The upper levels have the appearance of a later addition; the stone is a different colour, and the workmanship not a patch on the lower levels. Stone elephants stand at each end of the terrace, and the steps are guarded by sepoy sentinels with fixed bayonets.

The house is still occupied by the extended family of descendants of Nathmal. One of the main halls is open, and the original decoration has been well preserved. The most striking feature is the balcony which curves over, and the balustrade of which is made from only four pieces of stone, one for each side. The longer side must be close to 5m long, and every screen is a different pattern. There are murals and also miniatures set in the wall behind glass, a once common practice which has survived in few other places. On the balcony over the inner well are two Rajput dwarapalas.

Turn right out of the Nathmalji-ki-Haveli and follow the street down to a T-junction, turn right, follow the road round at the end and you come to the **Patuon-ki-Haveli*****. A patwa or patuon is a brocade merchant, and this mansion was built for the five sons of one such. They must have been a talented family; four became diwans or high officials in other Rajput states. The house is in five separate but adjoining parts, the idea being to combine privacy (something, you will have noticed, held in scant regard elsewhere in India) with collective security.

The most interesting part of this haveli fronts onto not the main street but an alleyway through an arch. The view as you pass through the arch takes the breath away. Balconies cascade like a frozen waterfall (you won't find much purple prose in the author's books, but Jaisalmer does tax one's descriptive powers). House 1 is derelict and plain inside, but worth exploring for the views from balconies and roof. House 2 is closed. House 3 is now an antique shop (with a very interesting stock). One of the ceilings has fallen in because of the depredations of termites, a common problem. Upstairs on the first-floor level is the house temple, beautifully carved with makara-toranas and wonderfully painted. House 4 is closed. Access to House 5 is limited to the ground floor but, because the ceiling has collapsed, you can see murals in the first-floor rooms. Restoration has now started, so things will change.

Salim Singh, diwan in the early 19th century, was a nasty piece of work whose greed virtually bankrupted the state. Wounded by an adversary, his wife finished him off by poison. His ambition is symbolised by **Salim Singh Haveli*****, a structure almost as high as the fort. The lower parts of this tower are relatively plain, all the decorative effort having gone into the Moti Mahal (Pearl Palace) at the top. The haveli is closed; properties opposite provide access for viewing on varying conditions.

Outside Gadisar Pol is the attractive **Gadisar*** (or Garisar) tank; wild birds, chhattris, memorials, some pleasure palaces in the lake, and temples (all closed in the afternoon). The lovely gateway is the Telion Ki Pol. Telion, a famous courtesan, built it at the beginning of the 19th century and promptly ran into trouble with the royal family who objected to passing under a gate built by a harlot. Demolition was threatened but, taking the advice of a crafty Brahmin, Telion added a shrine to

Satyanarayan (Krishna in his form as god of truth) whose sanctity preserved it. Gadisar is a good place for some peace and quiet — as long as you can elude the over-friendly kids.

Nearby is the **Jaisalmer Folklore Museum**** (open 9am–noon and 3–6pm, Rs5 and worth it). This excellent little museum is the work of a local man Nand Kishore Sharma. It has a broad collection of all the folk arts of western Rajasthan and, wonder of wonders, lots of information in the form of well written captions. The earth bank beside the museum gives one of the best views of the fort.

In contrast, the **Government Museum** next to the Tourist Bungalow (9am–4.30pm, closed Friday) is of minimal interest.

Excursions

Oases and sand dunes

Several excursions can be made from Jaisalmer. If it's not too hot hire a bike (or a horse if you can find one) and head out of town on the Sam road, fork right after 3km and you soon come to **Amar Sagar** oasis. In a good year the rainfall around Jaisalmer might be 30cm (less than half that in Jaipur, itself hardly well watered); for five years in the eighties no rain fell at all. So the sagar, or tank, is likely to be dry. The Jain temple the other side of it is finely carved and being extensively restored, though the new work is nothing like the quality of the old. The tank was constructed in 1740 and named after Amar Singh who defended Jaisalmer from a Bikaneri attack. The once fine gardens below the dam now grow nothing more exciting than spinach. A deep well is worked by an ox-powered water lift of interest for the automatic means of emptying.

A further 11km along this road is **Lodurva**, the capital before Jaisalmer was built. Little remains, though the Jain temples have been rebuilt recently. Leave Amar Sagar village the way you entered and turn left. Turn left again at a T-junction heading towards six antenna towers, then take the right in front of the military camp.

Bada Bagh* (or Bara Bagh) is the cremation place of the royal family and, as usual, there is a commemorative chhattri for each ruler. The earlier memorials are built on a Hindu post and lintel pattern with a pyramidal top. Later ones are more Mughal in style with true arches and domes. A higher mortality rate among the latter seems to indicate that the old way is best. Each has a stone in the centre bearing a representation of the prince on horseback. Chhattri No 8 also shows three women, wives who have committed sati. No 39, judged by the crudeness of the workmanship, is the most recent. The last maharawal died in 1983, and a cenotaph has yet to be built.

Continuing along the main road for 3km past the Amar Sagar turn takes you to **Mool Sagar**, another oasis similar to Amar Sagar. A lot further (share jeep or bus) is **Sam**, the nearest sand dunes to Jaisalmer. Pretty commercialised, but a good place to try a short camel ride or watch the desert sunset. Peaceful simple accommodation available, ask at the tourist office in Jaisalmer.

Camel safaris

Many visitors come to Jaisalmer to make a camel safari in the Thar Desert. While Jaisalmer people are too polite and relaxed to indulge in the hard sell you will find pressure from operators to book with them and also a certain amount of disinformation. The first thing to understand is that the camel is the most uncomfortable form of transport in the world. Before committing yourself to a long trek take a bus or jeep out to Sam and arrange a two-hour ride to see how you find it. Extrapolate the aches and pains over so many days, and throw in cold nights, sleeping on the ground, and basic food. Right, you're in for a great experience.

But first the complications. A lot of trouble has been caused over the last few years by fierce price competition between the operators. Too many visitors went for these very cheap treks and then complained that they did not meet expectations. To get around this the Jaisalmer Hoteliers' Association laid down certain rules and fixed a minimum rate, currently Rs200 per person per day. This price assures you of a camel for each person and separate camels for baggage and camel drivers. The rules state very clearly that drivers are allowed to ride with male tourists but not female. Remember this is a *minimum* rate. Do not allow anyone to pressure you into an agreement until you have spoken to travellers who have already made their trek. Agree precisely with the operator your route and what you are getting for your money, and then check everything, especially water and blankets, before departure.

The snag with starting your trek from Jaisalmer is that you spend the first two or three days in very ordinary scrubby country before reaching the real desert. You do the same on the return journey, so maybe only two days out of seven are spent in truly wild country. On a short trek you simply will not see the real thing at all. The answer is to catch a bus out to **Khuri** and actually start the trek in the desert. Everyone in Jaisalmer will tell you that the people in Khuri are crooks, their camels are no good, and so on. From all we have heard they are super people and offer easily the best trekking and best value for money. Check at the tourist office or Collectorate (near Tourist Bungalow) whether a **permit** is required to travel to Khuri, easily obtained if necessary.

Practical Information i

Festivals. The Desert Festival (January–February) offers folk performing arts, camel races, and all the fun of the fair, but is reportedly now mainly an event for package tourists. A similar, less commercialised, event takes place at Nagaur (see page 227).

Information. Tourist office at Tourist Bungalow. Open 8am–noon and 3–6pm. Tourist quota for trains, also book buses to Jodhpur. *Jaisalmer: The Golden City* by NK Sharma (the man who runs the Folklore Museum) is good, though women may take issue with some of his pronouncements.

Arrival and departure. Airport, bus from Tourist Bungalow. Jagson office (Tel 52392) at the same place.

By train (8hrs) from Jodhpur; day and night trains. The station is well out of town; a taxi costs Rs15, some hotels provide free transport. Tourist quota reservations from the Tourist Bungalow.

State and private buses from Bikaner (an unpleasant 10hrs) and Jodhpur (5½hrs). The main bus-stand is near Gadisar, but most buses will drop you at Amar Sagar Pole which is more convenient for most hotels and the Tourist Bungalow.

Accommodation (STD Code 02992)
In the fort:
Hotel Jaisal Castle, fort. Tel 52362. SWB Rs500 DWB Rs650. Rest (barbecue Rs150 per head). Bar. Good location and atmosphere, and most people feel this justifies the price. Bedrooms are very simple, offering little more than the view. Advance booking essential.
Hotel Paradise, opposite palace, fort. Tel 52674. SR Rs45 DR Rs85 DWB Rs225–400 Dorm Rs25. Breakfast.
Deepak Rest House, behind Jain temple, Fort. Tel 52665. DR Rs50/80 DWB Rs90/110 Dorm Rs15. Rest. Tremendous views. Best value in fort.

Around town:
Moomal Tourist Bungalow, outside Amar Sagar Gate. Tel 52392. SWB Rs200/250 (£4–5/$6.65–8.35) DWB Rs200/250 SWB A/C Rs500 DWB A/C Rs550 Dorm Rs40. Rest. Bar. Lowest room prices are for Rajasthani-style huts, fun and excellent value.

Royal Palace, Amar Singh Gate. SR Rs50 DR Rs100/120 DWB Rs250. Not bad at all and handy for late arrivals.

Hotel Swastika, Chainpura Street, Amar Sagar Gate. Tel 52483. SR Rs60 DR Rs90 SWB Rs100 DWB Rs125 Dorm Rs30. Free morning tea and transport to the station. Don't let the name put you off, a friendly place.

Hotel Rajdhani, near Patuon-ki-Haveli. Tel 52746. SWB Rs100 DWB Rs125. Rest (on roof). Good view of fort, highly recommended.

Eating and drinking

Narayan Niwas Palace. Interesting old building, super bar with fires near every table, good place for a drink. Set dinner Rs220, fine if you are sick of Indian food. Nice place to stay, too, but outside our price bracket.

Trio, Amar Sagar Gate. Ind/Chi/Cont. Mod/Exp. Large portions of excellent food, around Rs80 per head. Local music.

Sky Room, near and similar in character to Trio. Very good food. Live music and folk dancer. Warm clothing needed on winter evenings.

8th July, main street. Ind/Chi. Cheap/Mod. Roof-top good for Chinese food.

Monica's, below fort gate. Cheap/Mod. Good for a snack but a bit grubby.

JODHPUR

Jodhpur is a town of little charm despite having the most impressive fort in Rajasthan. The state of Marwar (the name can be translated as 'Land of Death') was the largest state in Rajputana. The Rathore family, which claims descent from Rama, first ruled in Kanauj near Kanpur. Losing that to the Muslims in the 12th century, one branch of the family moved to Rajasthan and established a small state. They slowly built up their holdings and took Mandor at the beginning of the 15th century. The need for a more defensible base saw the move to Jodhpur fort 50 years later. Marwar reached its height under Rao Maldeo (1532–1569) when its territories stretched as far as Sind, now in Pakistan.

And yes, jodhpurs do come from here. The story goes that the secret of how to cut them was known only to the maharaja and his personal tailor but, on a trip to Europe, all his baggage went astray. Thus the maharaja had to reveal all to an English tailor and soon everybody was wearing them.

The fort

The **Meherangarh Fort***** (9am–5pm every day) was founded in 1459 by Rao Jodha (hence the name of the town) and much added to by later princes. This massive pile, rising sheer from its rock, dominates the old town and now houses a fascinating and well organised museum. The inscriptions on the rocks on the approach to the fort are extracts from the Ramayana. This is a popular morning walk, so people can refresh their minds as they exercise their bodies. The quotations are changed every 15 days to obviate boredom.

The **Jai Pol** (Victory Gate) and outer wall were added in 1809 to strengthen the fort and commemorate beating off an attack by Jaipur. The actual gates were looted from Ahmedabad some 70 years before. **Lakhna Pol**, at the time the outer gate, still bears the marks of Jaipur cannon balls. **Loha Pol** (Iron Gate) is the same age as the fort and has sati marks on both sides. A drummer and musicians over **Suraj Pol**, which is the entrance to the palace complex, perpetuate its use as a Naqqar Khana.

The white marble throne in **Sringar Chauki** was the coronation place of the maharajas. In the **Palki Khana** (Palanquin Room) is a most ornate glass-domed palanquin, which needed 12 men to carry it. Another oddity is what appears to be a

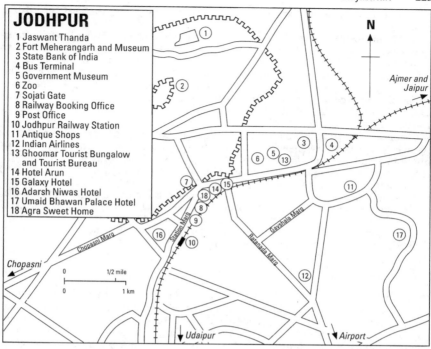

JODHPUR
1 Jaswant Thanda
2 Fort Meherangarh and Museum
3 State Bank of India
4 Bus Terminal
5 Government Museum
6 Zoo
7 Sojati Gate
8 Railway Booking Office
9 Post Office
10 Jodhpur Railway Station
11 Antique Shops
12 Indian Airlines
13 Ghoomar Tourist Bungalow
   and Tourist Bureau
14 Hotel Arun
15 Galaxy Hotel
16 Adarsh Niwas Hotel
17 Umaid Bhawan Palace Hotel
18 Agra Sweet Home

London sedan chair with side handles rather than poles. The stands for the palanquins are decorated with the flags and coats of arms of the princely states of Rajputana.

On one side of the **Khabka Mahal** is the throne room or office of the prime minister, and in the room opposite, which functioned as a cabinet room, is a painting by the German artist Müller who also worked at Jaipur. Both rooms are finished in fine white chunam.

The **Jhanki Mahal**, which you might translate as Peeping Palace, gave the women of the household a view over the courtyards below. It now houses a collection of royal cradles.

The **Moti Mahal** (Pearl Palace) is a fine room with a mirrored ceiling. The gold throne was presented to Jaswant Singh (1638–1678) by Shahjahan. The lesser thrones have the names of the small states, each under its own feudal lord, which constituted Jodhpur. On the back wall are five niches, once curtained, where five ranis could sit and listen to if not watch proceedings. The Moti Mahal opens off the Zenana Baodi which is the courtyard of the ladies' palace.

The **Sardar Vilas** displays local craftsmanship. **Umaid Vilas** is now the art gallery, mostly miniatures of the Jodhpur school. Note the very strange cartoon in case 22 of Breughelish appearance.

The **Takhat Vilas** was the maharaja's bedchamber up to 1873. The wooden ceiling of this splendid room is lacquered in the Kathiawar style of Gujarat (one of the maharanis came from there). This is one of the few places where the original punkah is still in place.

Outside the gallery of musical instruments some of the jali screens are cut at an angle to give a view downwards. Looking from this gallery towards the Umaid Bhavan Palace a section of the city wall can be seen climbing over a hill and, in front of that, a rock pinnacle surmounted by a Ganesh temple. The wall was once 20km around.

The **Phul Mahal** (Flower Palace), a hall of private audience, is the finest room in the palace. The ceiling is of carved gilt wood adorned by portraits of former maharajas. At the bottom of the stairs from here is a glass case holding two locks. The smaller one, for the treasury, has four keys all of which were required to open it. The other, weighing 17kg and having three keys, was for the main gate of the fort.

The **Daulat Khana** houses another part of the art collection and an ornate tent captured from the Mughals. The **Maan Vilas** has one of the finest displays of arms in Rajasthan.

Uphill from the palace a part of the ramparts is accessible. Most of the artillery on show is rather ordinary English field guns, though others come from Abhai Singh's celebrated raid on Ahmedabad. Down the slope towards the white Shiva temple is a bronze mortar of Islamic design, presumably also from there.

Facing the main entrance of the fort is the **Jaswant Thada***, a cremation memorial to Jaswant Singh II (1873–1895). The main memorial is built entirely of white marble, some panels translucent despite their considerable thickness. The two shell-shaped memorials behind railings mark the cremation places of two famous polo players, younger sons of a former maharaja, though what they are meant to signify is anybody's guess. The best **view of the fort** is from here.

The town

Between Sojati Gate and the fort are colourful **bazaars** that other writers enthuse about. However they are fiendishly noisy, and people can be strangely unhelpful (and the children an absolute pain). Jodhpur is the fort; if you want to stroll around pleasant bazaars do it in Udaipur or Ajmer. In recent years Jodhpur has become a major **antiques** dealing centre. Western dealers know this, so there are no great bargains to be had, and it is easy to lose money on a deal. Abani Handicrafts, near the Tourist Bungalow, are said to be trustworthy; they certainly have an interesting stock.

The **Umaid Gardens** house the **Government Museum** (10am–4.30pm, closed Friday). Unless you are into Second World War aircraft recognition models, this may well be the least informative and least interesting museum in India. Quite a distinction really. Nearby is the zoo with extensive **aviaries**.

The colossal **Umaid Bhavan**** was the last major palace built by an Indian prince. Now a five-star hotel only the **museum** (9am–5pm, Rs10) is open to casual visitors.

| **Practical Information** *i* | Rajasthan Tourism at Tourist Bungalow. Maps and conducted tours available. Good booklet available at the fort. |

Arrival and departure. Airport (4km), Indian Airlines office (Tel 28600) on Airport Road.

Rail from Jaisalmer (8hrs), Bikaner (5hrs), Delhi Sarai Rohilla (10½hrs), and Ahmedabad (9hrs).

Bus to most other places in Rajasthan. Comfortable bus from Tourist Bungalow to Jaisalmer. Two bus companies in the same street as Hotel Adarsh Niwas run services to Delhi, Ahmedabad and Udaipur.

Accommodation (STD Code 0291)

Hotel Adarsh Niwas, Station Road. Tel 26936. SWB Rs350 DWB Rs400 SWB A/C Rs500 DWB A/C Rs600. Rest (see below). Snack bar. If you want a bit of comfort after the desert this is the place.

Ghoomar Tourist Bungalow, 2km from station, past Sojati Gate. Tel 44010. SWB

Rs150/300 DWB Rs200/350 SWB A/C Rs400 DWB A/C Rs500 Dorm Rs40. Rest. Bar. Well run. Try for a room at the back, much quieter.

Hotel Arun, outside Sojati Gate. Tel 20238. SWB Rs125 (£2.50/$4.15) DWB Rs195 Dorm Rs20–35. Really good at the price, even in the dorm you get towels and free tea in the morning.

Galaxy Hotel, over bridge. Tel 20796. SR Rs60 DR Rs80 SWB Rs90/120 DWB Rs150/250. OK for one night, nothing like as good as the Arun.

More cheap hotels in area opposite station, mostly not very good.

Eating and drinking

Kalinga, Adarsh Niwas Hotel. Mod/Exp. Ind/Chi/Cont. Very good.

Snack Bar, Adarsh Niwas Hotel. Cheap. Snacks are mostly big enough for a meal. Recommended.

Agra Sweet Home, Sojati Gate. Cheap. Snacks, huge range of sweets, and coffee.

Many inexpensive eating places opposite station. For Sojati Gate turn right out of station, 1km.

Excursions

Mandore

After the dust and noise of town the **Mandore Gardens**** (bus from stand near Sojati Gate) are a haven of peace and lush greenery. Mandore was the capital of Marwar before the building of Jodhpur in 1459. Nothing much remains of the city, but grand memorials, some more like temples, mark the cremation places of the earlier maharajas. There are fountains, and a temple dedicated to every god in the Hindu pantheon, all 330 million of them. That many images would be a tall order even in India, so you find 16 large, brightly coloured monolithic statues representing major deities and folk heroes. The gardens are at their best in late afternoon and early evening when peacocks and desert birds fly in to roost. A bazaar and restaurants stand outside the gate.

Nagaur

The annual livestock fair at Nagaur (January–February) attracts 80,000 people and 200,000 cattle and camels. Also a large spice market, and still much less commercialised than the Jaisalmer Desert Festival.

Arrival and departure. Bus from Bikaner or Jodhpur, train from Bikaner or Merta Road on Jaipur–Jodhpur line.

Accommodation. Rajasthan Tourism arranges tented accommodation.

Sodawas

Sodawas, on the road between Jodhpur and Udaipur, is a typical Rajasthan village, set in a rugged landscape. The castle is now a guest house, and this should be a good way of seeing something of rural life in this very traditional and largely unproductive area. Explore the countryside by horse safari, Rs200–250 per day (must be better than a camel).

Information. From tourist office in Tourist Bungalow at Jodhpur or from RS Ashia at the Bhartiya Lok Kala Mandal (Folk Museum) in Udaipur.

Arrival and departure. Buses between Jodhpur (90km/56 miles) and Udaipur (170km/106 miles).

Accommodation. Sodawas Castle, Sodawas, District Pali, Rajasthan. Rs250 full board. Looks super. Promises folk music and dancing in evenings. The one report we have is not unalloyed praise.

MOUNT ABU

When you've had enough of the dust and heat of Rajasthan and Gujarat head for Mount Abu, a lush green plateau rising 1000m/3280ft above the torrid plains. Abu is a popular though quiet honeymoon resort. Most visitors, Indian and Western, are content just to stroll around, stuff themselves with good food (and alcohol after dry Gujarat), and visit some superb nearby temples.

The main attraction of Mount Abu is really that it is still quiet; few people bring their own transport. Warm clothing is required in winter; the lake actually froze over a few years back.

 **Around town**

The attractive (though artificial) **Nakki Lake** is surrounded by palm trees and the gracious summer retreats of Rajasthan's former princes, a sort of Rajput Riviera. The lake area somehow has a very English look, even the sunset colours being like the fells of Cumbria. The road from the lake to the bazaar is reminiscent of an up-market version of the English resort of Blackpool, though that sounds like a contradiction in terms. On the south shore of the lake several hermitages have been built in clefts in the rock near the Raghunathji Temple.

Close to the lake are several **view points** over the plains. The most popular is Sunset Point, usually infested by noisy trippers. In the evening it's best to turn right off the road before Sunset Point and follow Baylay's Walk. The peace will be complete and the sunset pure magic (take a torch). There are good walks in the hills on the north side of the lake; take the road to Honeymoon Point and climb up from there.

Below Honeymoon Point is Anadra village. The zig-zag path is 10km/6 miles long, and Abu's milk supply comes this way. It takes the porters 5hrs with their headloads, arriving a little before midday, and they earn Rs13 per trip. This was the only access to Abu before the road was constructed, and elephants carried all the marble for the Delwara temples up this way.

Delwara temples

The **Delwara Jain temples***** (noon–6pm only) are a pleasant walk or short bus ride from town. Built in white marble these are one of the great tourist sights of India; the quality of the carving is outstanding and the profusion mind-boggling. The **Vimal Vasahi** was built in 1032, like the others later, by a minister to the ruler of Gujarat. The temple is dedicated to Adinath, the first tirthanka or Jain guru. In the main hall in front of the shrine the bracket figures are of musicians and dancers, and in the dome are the 16 Vidhyadevis, the goddesses of knowledge. Each of these has her own symbol, and you can make out a chakra, a thunderbolt, a sword, and what looks very like a hand grenade. Look closely at the carving around the shrine doorway, many of the figures are completely hollowed out behind. Some unusual satyr-like figures here.

In the cloister surrounding the main shrine the ceiling carvings of cell 20 are outstanding. The corner shrine predates the rest of the temple and contains some very old sculpture. The ceiling in front of cell 32 (which is actually No 29, just to confuse you) is a relief of Krishna subduing a snake-tailed demon. The elephant shrine in front of the temple (AD1147) had been completely dismantled for restoration when last seen.

The **Luna Vasahi**, also known as the Tejpal Temple, was begun in 1320. The lotus carvings in the main dome of the Rang Mandap and in the smaller sections in front of the shrine are even finer than in the Vimal Temple, probably in fact the finest stone carving to be seen on a building anywhere. The best of all is around the door of the shrine and on either side of it. Above the side shrines are Jain figures surrounded by miniature temples with tiny columns and toranas.

In front of shrine 9 you can see sailing boats and a representation of Girnar Hill. At the back of the temple and concealed by a screen wall are ten marble elephants. In cell 44 are the Jain chaubisi (chaubis is 24), 72 tirthankas comprising the 24 of the past, the 24 of the present, and the 24 to come, which dates back to the 16th century. This appears to be made all of the same stone, but the central figure has been coloured a rich brown by many applications of sandalwood and saffron paste. Cell 50 has a remarkable ceiling with the effect of looking down into a deep pool of water.

The **Pitthalkar Temple** is of little interest. The cloister apparently once ran right round it. There is little carving in this temple, and traces of the painted decoration can still be seen. The **Khatara Temple** has fine sculpture round the shrine, some of it erotic.

Entry to the temples is free, though there is a charge for cameras, and photography of the images is banned.

More temples and great views

Further out are the **Achalgarh temples**, better situated but crude in comparison with Delwara. The **Shiva Temple** has two blue elephants outside and a huge brass Nandi in the compound. Inside the yoni is completely covered with leaves and flowers. In the socket for the lingam is one of Shiva's toes, and the water used to anoint it goes straight down the bottomless hole. Behind this are two tiny images of crystal set in gold, transparent when the light is behind them, but blue when lit from the front.

Near this temple is a tank dating from about 900AD. Legend has it that this was filled with ghee, and that every night three buffaloes came to drink it. The king, Adi Pal, took exception to this and shot them all. He and the buffaloes, immortalised in stone, still stand beside the tank.

The **Adinath Temple***, brightly painted, is another Jain edifice. On the walls are the usual pictures of Jain holy places; that on the left of the door as you enter is Mount Abu with a train at Abu Road station at the bottom. The shrine is four-sided, displaying a large gold image, the other three images visible only from outside. There are another four images on the upper level, the main one of Parsvanath. Quite a good view from here, but of limited interest really. The path continues up past the temples to a fort, as the 'garh' in the name suggests. You're on your own.

The highest point on Mount Abu is **Guru Shikar*** (1700m/5576ft) which, despite defilement by radar antennae and an observatory, gives panoramic views of Abu and the plains. Beneath an oddly shaped rock is a hermitage.

Religion

Mount Abu is the headquarters of the Brahma Kumaris, which purports to be some sort of universal religion. One tends to be suspicious of organisations that (a) are so well endowed, and (b) lay on events called 'Universal Transformation Conference' and the like. Visit their centre near the Polo Ground and see what you think.

Practical Information The tourist office opposite the bus-stand is not much help; tours and nothing much else. The only merit of the Rs30 conducted bus tour is that it takes you up Guru Shikar. Take the morning tour, drop off after Guru Shikar to have a look at the Achalgarh temples, and then make your own way back for plenty of time at Delwara. A good booklet on the Delwara temples is available at the ticket office there.

Arrival and departure. Train to Abu Road, on Delhi Sarai Rohilla (14½hrs)–

Ahmedabad (5hrs) line, also Jodhpur (7hrs), Jaipur (11½hrs), then bus or share jeep. Train reservations in Mount Abu at the foot of the road to the Tourist Bungalow.

Bus from Jodhpur, Udaipur, etc. There is no convenient bus to Ranakpur; you can get to Sadri (7hrs), but then have to find transport for the 7km/4.5 miles to Ranakpur. The alternative of a train from Abu Road to Falna and then a bus (40km/25 miles) is probably even worse.

Accommodation (STD Code 0297)

Bikaner Palace, Delwara Road. Tel 3121. DWB Rs750 Suite D Rs900 (less 30% off-season). Rest. Bar. Former summer home of the Maharaja of Bikaner. Huge Victorian rooms, nice gardens, and tennis courts.

Sunset Palace, Bharatpur Kothi. Tel 3214. DWB A/C Rs500 Suite A/C Rs1000 (less 40% off-season). Rest (Ind/Chi, good). Bar. Bedrooms individually decorated, carved wood furniture in some, red and gold lacquer in others. Formerly house of the Maharaja of Bharatpur. Good views.

Connaught House. Tel 3439. DWB Rs800 (Rs400 new rooms only). Rest. Old rooms very attractive but have no view. New rooms light and very comfortable with lovely views. A real bargain off-season and a delightful place to stay.

Mount Hotel. Tel 3150. DWB Rs300 (Rs200) 3WB Rs390 (Rs300). Rest. Looks like a village cricket pavilion. Perhaps expensive for what it is, charming lady owner.

Shikhar Tourist Bungalow. Tel 3129. SWB Rs125/250 (£2.50–5/$4.15–8.30) DWB Rs175/300 Dorm Rs30. Rest. Bar. Lower-priced rooms best value, all have hot water and are clean. Modern concrete building, but better than the dingy boxes in town.

Tourist Guest House, below Tourist Bungalow. Tel 3200. DWB Rs90. Rest (breakfast and snacks). Nice garden and super manager.

Shri Ravjikaka Guest House. The octagonal building on top of the hill. Primitive, but super views. Closed when we called in winter, but included for old time's sake, a double was Rs6 when the author last stayed there.

Hotel Kesar Palace may be worth a look, closed when we called. Other fine old houses may be converted into hotels. Jaipur House, for instance, has been a hotel and may re-open as one.

The hotel selection may seem a bit top-heavy costwise, and when it's really busy prices can be even higher. The point is that there are real bargains off-season (mid-November to mid-March excluding Christmas and New Year), and this is a good place to spend a little extra. Sharing a concrete box with exuberant Gujarati honeymooners is not the best way of enjoying Mount Abu. Food is cheap and you can save on that.

Eating and drinking

Handi, Hilltone Hotel. Ind/Chi/Cont. Exp. Very wide menu and reportedly good food.

Sher e Punjab, Vegetable Market. Punjabi non-veg. Cheap/Mod. A favourite for many years.

Veena, Polo Ground. Gujarati veg. Cheap/Mod. Very good. If you get blasted out by horrible music try the similar *Chandra Vilas* at other end of the row. Equally good food and no chillies. Lots, lots more restaurants of all kinds.

UDAIPUR

Udaipur is the author's favourite city in India (though only by a short head from Mysore) and one of the nicest anywhere. There are many fine buildings, but it is above all a city of lakes and gardens. Like any other Indian city, parts of Udaipur are noisy and suffer severe air pollution. Much of the old walled city, however, is delightful to stroll around.

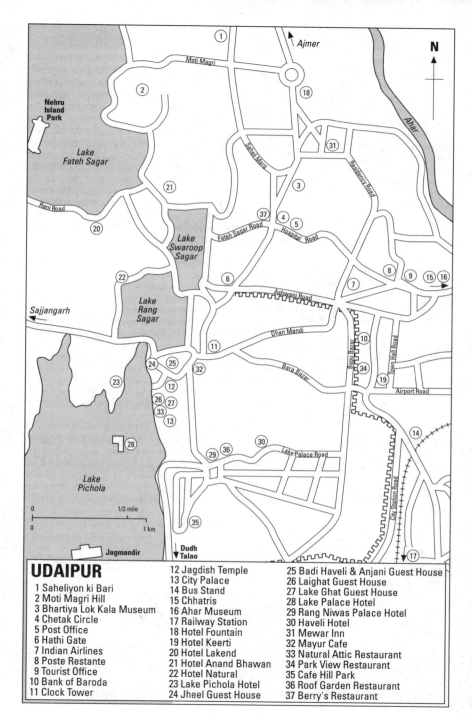

UDAIPUR

1 Saheliyon ki Bari
2 Moti Magri Hill
3 Bhartiya Lok Kala Museum
4 Chetak Circle
5 Post Office
6 Hathi Gate
7 Indian Airlines
8 Poste Restante
9 Tourist Office
10 Bank of Baroda
11 Clock Tower
12 Jagdish Temple
13 City Palace
14 Bus Stand
15 Chhatris
16 Ahar Museum
17 Railway Station
18 Hotel Fountain
19 Hotel Keerti
20 Hotel Lakend
21 Hotel Anand Bhawan
22 Hotel Natural
23 Lake Pichola Hotel
24 Jheel Guest House
25 Badi Haveli & Anjani Guest House
26 Laighat Guest House
27 Lake Ghat Guest House
28 Lake Palace Hotel
29 Rang Niwas Palace Hotel
30 Haveli Hotel
31 Mewar Inn
32 Mayur Cafe
33 Natural Attic Restaurant
34 Park View Restaurant
35 Cafe Hill Park
36 Roof Garden Restaurant
37 Berry's Restaurant

History

It is often said that Udaipur owes its founding to the third sack of Chittaur in 1568, but this is only partly true. In fact Maharana Udai Singh had realised the untenability of Chittaur in the face of an expansionist Mughal empire and had made advance preparations to move the capital of Mewar. His successor Pratap Singh was actually driven out of Udaipur after the Battle of Haldighati (1576), but continued a guerilla war. Amar Singh, who followed him, eventually paid tribute to Jehangir, on his own terms and long after the other Rajput princes had capitulated. A fragile prosperity, and with it much building, ensued. This ended, as did so much else, with the arrival on the scene of Aurangzeb. Udaipur had to be abandoned again, and all the temples were destroyed. This time Mewari guerilla tactics paid off, but the victory was hardly to the advantage of Udaipur. A century of chaos involving war with neighbouring states, Pindari freebooters, and the Marathas resulted in depopulation and impoverishment. Finally a treaty with the British in 1817 brought peace. The first British agent, incidentally, was Colonel James Tod, to whose monumental *Annals and Antiquities of Rajasthan* we owe so much of our knowledge of Rajput legend and history.

 **Exploring**

The City Palace

Udaipur's outstanding monument is the **City Palace***** (open 9.30am–4.30pm). Built on a ridge so as to command both the town and Lake Picchola this is a maze of small rooms, made light and ethereal by mirrors and coloured glass. The first gate on the approach to the palace is the **Bari Pol** (Great Gate). Inside are eight **torans**, stone arches under which the maharanas were weighed against gold and silver coins for distribution to the populace. The **Tripolia Pol** (Triple Gate) opens on to a broad terrace with raised semi-circular beds for the palace elephants which could be tethered to the pierced stones. Above the entrance to the Mardana (Men's Palace) are the arms of Udaipur, a bit fake as the heraldic concept is purely European. On the left inside is the **Durbar Hall**, now an emporium.

Entrance to the inner palace is through **Ganesh Dauri**, dominated by an image of Ganesh surrounded by tiles and coloured glass set in plaster. Above is a very Rajput-looking sun. Steps lead up to **Raja Angun** (or Rai Anjun, royal courtyard), the oldest part of the palace (around 1571). On the east of this courtyard is the **Neeka-ki-Chaupa** which was the jewel room. In the **Haldighati Kaksh** is a large painting depicting the battle of Haldighati. On the left can be seen Pratap Singh making his getaway on the faithful Chetak pursued by Mughal horsemen, and finally the death of Chetak.

Steps lead up from Raja Angun to the **Chandra Mahal** (Moon Palace) which overlooks the lake. The pillars and ceiling of the first hall are covered in chunam. The early maharanas were crowned on the marble throne, at which time the basin in the floor was filled with coins. The floor inlay of yellow Jaisalmer stone displays seashells.

Next up is the **Amar Vilas** built by Amar Singh II in the early 18th century; this is also called Bari Mahal, meaning Garden Palace. Apparently a roof garden, it is actually based on solid ground, a small hilltop over which the rest of the palace is built. The pool in the centre is surrounded by huge slabs of white marble. On the north side is a durbar hall, and in it an aerial view of the maharana conducting a durbar. Interesting details can be picked out including the marble balustrade which once enclosed the garden. Looking down from the durbar hall a low wall can be seen; elephant fights used to take place over this and a picture shows one of these events. On the Tripolia Gate is the Hawa Mahal (Wind Palace) from which the maharana watched the fights. Also looking out from here a frieze around the palace can be seen depicting elephants in various activities.

From here the domestic part of the palace is entered. The **Kanch-ki-Burj** is a domed chamber completely lined in mirrors and coloured glass, even the floor being mirror. The room opposite, **Chitram-ki-Burj**, has murals (early 19th century) showing events in and around the City Palace.

The **Badi Chatur Shali** (Great China Palace) of Sangram Singh II (1711–1734) has blue and gold Chinese tiles and, inset, some Dutch ones of biblical scenes. In a pavilion on one side of this court are three views of the Madan Vilas, a monsoon palace, which seems to be the same as Sajjangar. Spelling and dialect variations make names confusing in Udaipur. They never did get round to building the tower.

Steps lead down to the **Moti Mahal** (Pearl Palace), another mirrored room with coloured glass windows looking out over the city. More steps go down to the **Surya Chaupar** and **Surya Gokhra** (Sun Court and Sun Lodge). Here is the back of the bronze sun visible on the outside of the palace. On the wall is another fine Rajput sun, and below dadoes of moulded plaster elaborately painted. Among the scenes are lion hunting and an artist at work. Next to this is an odd tableau of women dressed in local style but with angels' wings. Worth a close look, many unusual scenes.

This brings you down to **Mor Chowk** (Peacock Court) with its magnificent glass and mirror work done in the late 19th century, 250 years after the courtyard was built. Note the elaborate balcony in the centre of the long wall; near it can be seen the remains of the enamel work which was the original decoration and would have covered large areas. Off this is the **Manak Mahal** (Ruby Palace). This suite of mirrored rooms — note the use of glass paperweights in the walls — was used by the princesses to watch festivities in Mor Chauk. Strict purdah was enforced on the royal women of Udaipur (and their female visitors) until after the time of independence. The inner doors are now mounted in the porch. And so back to the Raja Angun. Down the steps is a small **armoury**.

The **Government Museum** (10am–4.30pm, closed Friday) is worth a brief look, partly for the superb collection of miniature paintings and partly for the views over the lake.

Many people miss the Queens' Palace or **Zenana**, and the exhibits here are in fact a bit of a jumble but very interesting. It also has the best views over the lake. The Salters weighing machine which superseded the torans went up to 33 stone (210kg); the maharanas were big men! The art gallery in the upper storeys includes many hunting scenes.

Around town

In the approach to the City Palace is the **Jagdish Temple**** built by Jagat Singh in 1628–1653. One of the most important Vishnu temples in northern India, its position and size (which is not obvious from the street below) symbolise Rajput defiance of the Muslim invader. The brass Garuda in the entrance has a decidedly Chinese aspect. This is a traditional panchayata (five-shrine) temple, and the four corner shrines are dedicated to Ganesh (south-east), Surya (south-west), Shakti (north-west), and Shiva (north-east). Round the pedestal are five bands of sculpture; elephants, horses and horsemen, dancers and musicians, and apsaras. Here and there the elephants are fighting with lions and crocodiles or with one another. On the base of the spire are a further two bands of sculpture in high relief. The many pigeons are attracted, like the squirrels, by the offerings of corn made by pilgrims. Inside, the central black image is of Jagdish or Jagganath, Vishnu in his form of Lord of the Universe. The figure to the right is Krishna. Bracket figures in the dome are hard to see because of the bird screens. Much of the interior sculpture has been obscured by multiple applications of whitewash which is now being cleaned off.

In the street between the Jagdish Temple and the Clock Tower is the Jain **Shital Nath Temple** marked by a profusion of white spires. This is said to have been started at the same time as the royal palaces in 1567. There are altogether 36 Jain temples in

Udaipur, and the head of the monastic order was held in high regard by the maharanas. The interior is in modern painted and mirrored idiom, worth seeing, especially if you are not going to visit any other examples of this genre. The large number of Hindu deities shown in addition to all the Jain ones is unusual. The representations of Jain holy hills, including Shatrunjaya in next-door Gujarat, are more typical.

The **Folk Museum**** (Bhartiya Lok Kala Mandal, 9am–5.45pm) is excellent. Apart from features on Indian tribals and their art it is the home of a world-renowned puppet troupe, and frequent short demonstrations of string and glove puppets are given. Longer displays take place in the evenings. RS Ashia (the director), a charming and knowledgeable man, will arrange for you to see the puppets being made. The museum is getting a little run down now, but is not to be missed.

Lakes and gardens

Udaipur is above all a city of lakes and gardens. The city owes its existence to the adequate and fairly reliable rainfall, unique in Rajasthan. The lakes developed from the need to store this invaluable commodity. The most important is **Lake Picchola***** which was begun in the 14th century by a banjara (grain dealer) and finished by Udai Singh in advance of the fall of Chittaur.

Two artificial islands stand in the lake. The nearer one is the Jag Niwas, now better known as the Lake Palace Hotel; the other the Jag Mandir. The Lake Palace Hotel runs evening boat trips round the lake; casual visitors to the hotel, except for dinner, are not encouraged.

The **Jag Niwas** was built as a summer palace in the 18th century by Jagat Singh II, but much added to and altered over the years. Probably the second most familiar image of tourist India it has played a large part in popularising Udaipur.

The **Jag Mandir** was begun by Jagat Singh I (17th century), with most of the work done nearly a century later by Sangram Singh II. The island consists mainly of a courtyard with palace buildings on the south side, arcaded around and with an open pavilion in front. Behind that, beside a large pool is a grey marble throne. Facing out over the north side of the island are eight elephants with their trunks raised in welcome. A circular apartment has a floor of black and white marble, and walls inlaid with semi-precious stones like those at Agra but with Hindu designs of birds and flowers. Fergusson, the father of archaeology in India, thought the buildings on these islands the finest in India — and superior to anything in Europe. The Jag Mandir provided a refuge for Prince Khurram, later Shahjahan, when he was in revolt against his father Jehangir, and again for British people during the Mutiny.

Walk or cycle down from the Jagdish Temple to the lake, and follow the ghats along past small temples to **Chandpol** (Moon Gate). Cross the bridge and turn left, first along the ghats, then down a narrow street aiming for a ghat by a group of temples. From here you get the best views of the City Palace and the lake. Return to the city and follow the banks of **Rang Sagar** to Hathipol (Elephant Gate). On the way you pass Rajasthan Armoury which makes replica antique firearms. Keeping to the bank of **Swaroop Sagar** is a bit trickier as the road peters out into a footpath. Carry on one way or another until you reach **Fateh Sagar**, another large lake. The Nehru Park island was built in the 1960s on the foundations of a palace whose construction was halted by the Second World War.

Walk up through attractive gardens to the equestrian **statue of Maharana Pratap***** which overlooks Fateh Sagar. Superb views. Below the statue are the ruins of **Moti Magri**, the royal palace before the City Palace was built, and below that a viewing platform over the lake. A different descent leads through a kind of Japanese garden. Retrieve your bike and continue to the dam, turn right downhill and left at the bottom.

The **Sahelion-Ki-Bari***** (Garden of the Maids of Honour) is the best of Udaipur's many gardens. It was first built by Sangram Singh II (18th century) as a place where he could meet the ladies of the zenana informally. Devastated by a collapse of the Fateh Sagar dam they were rebuilt by Fateh Singh (19th century). The extensive gardens surround a walled, white-marble pool with hundreds of fountains. A black stone pavilion in each corner contrasts with the white marble; note the pigeons on them. This is one of the most entrancing places in India; wait for some peace and quiet between the tour groups and absorb the atmosphere. In the absence of other visitors you may have to buy a ticket for the fountains yourself. Most visitors, luckily, miss the rest of the gardens behind the walled section, another haven of peace. A large fountain has lions at the base and pelicans above, and probably a real kingfisher on top if you wait a little.

Rather than cycle back up the steep hill continue along the road past the gardens and turn left at the crossroads to return to the dam of Fateh Sagar. The **temple** on the conical hill is dedicated to the goddess Neemuch Mata, and plays a central part in a festival which takes place during the monsoon. The view scarcely justifies the climb. Continue right round Fateh Sagar back to the city; you can be pretty sure of seeing a pied kingfisher on the way.

Back in town, the **Sajjan Niwas Gardens** are attractive, but noisy and the worst place in Udaipur for being hassled by kids.

The **Hill Park** is far more pleasant, and even going no further than the café you have good views over Lake Picchola and the city. This is the start of a **pleasant stroll****; from the café aim first for the pink folly and then either go straight up to the wall or follow the easier path to the square **fort of Eklingarh**. In the days when few people had watches midday and midnight guns were fired from this fort. Continue along the wall past a Muslim shrine to the bastion where the wall turns downhill; super views on all sides. Follow the wall down over the gate in the valley and descend at the first modern building. Take the road past the waterworks, with a reassuringly strong smell of chlorine, to Dudh Talao and back to the café.

Prominent on a hill to the west of the city is **Sajjangarh**, a small palace used during the monsoon. From Chandpol the road forks right through the municipal rubbish dump (just like Chamundi Hill in Mysore). A rickshaw costs Rs60, but only one in perfect condition will get up the hill, most will cook the engine halfway leaving you with a long hot walk. Forget about bicycles. The palace itself is closed as it houses a police radio station, and badly vandalised anyway. The views are extensive and surprisingly green, but whether this justifies the time and expense is another matter. A **deer safari park** at the foot of the hill was closed when we last passed by.

Allow plenty of time for Udaipur. Cycle round the lakes and gardens, wander through the bazaars and try to absorb a little of the atmosphere. The ghats are colourful and interesting, but don't go blundering about with your camera — Rajasthani women are none too coy when bathing but that does not mean that they like being photographed in the nude.

Excursions

Ahar (or Ahad) predates both Chittaur and Udaipur as the capital of Mewar and functioned as a reserve capital and place of refuge when things got too hot at Chittaur. All that is left to see are the cremation memorials of 19 maharanas and their wives and families. In a quiet wooded location one of the two largest memorials is to Amar Singh I who died in 1620. That in the tank is perhaps that of Gandharva Sen, a brother of the king of Ujjain. Ahar is said to be founded on the site of Tambavati, a Harappan settlement, and excavations have revealed habitation dating back to 1750BC. The four old Jain temples are nearly 1000 years old. The small **museum** nearby is of limited interest.

Eklingji temple and lake are 21km/13 miles from Udaipur (bus). Set in a rocky valley the temple (open 10.30am–12.30pm and 5.30–7.30pm) is associated with Bappu

Rawal, founder of Chittaur, and still a regular place of worship for the Maharana of Udaipur.

Practical Information *i*

Tourist office at Tourist Bungalow. The tour of Eklingji, Haldighati, and Nathdwara is easily the best way of getting there.

Arrival and departure. Airport (25km), take a taxi Rs140. Indian Airlines (Tel 410999) at Delhi Gate near Tourist Bungalow.

By rail direct from Ahmedabad (9¼hrs) or Delhi (17hrs), but see Chittaur, and Agra (via Jaipur 12¾hrs), Ajmer (8½hrs), Chittaur (3¾hrs).

Bus from Mount Abu and all the obvious places.

Rickshaw-wallahs commonly get 50% of the first night's rent at your hotel and 35% in shops. It is, of course, you who pay this.

Accommodation (STD Code 0294)

Lake Picchola Hotel, outside Chandpol. Tel 529 387. DWB A/C Rs600. Rest. Bar. Modern building comfortably fitted-out in traditional style.

Anand Bhavan, Fateh Sagar Road. Tel 523 247. SWB Rs450 DWB Rs550. Rest. Bar. Hilltop location giving views over Rang Sagar and Fateh Sagar. Beautifully kept and a bargain. More expensive rooms upstairs have better view and modern bathrooms.

Hotel Lakend, Fateh Sagar. Tel 523 841. Rest. Bar. Quiet place with rooms in Rs350–450 bracket. Have a camping ground nearby.

Hotel Fountain, 2 Sukhadia Circle. Tel 526 646. SWB Rs225 DWB Rs275. Rest.

Rangniwas Palace, Lake Palace Road. Tel 523 891. SR Rs150 DR Rs200 SWB Rs250 DWB Rs350 Dorm Rs35. Rest. Bar. Swimming pool. Professional management, well kept, getting better and better.

Lal Ghat Guest House, near Jagdish Temple. Tel 525 301. SR Rs75 DR Rs100 DWB Rs200 Dorm Rs40. Self-catering. Very clean and excellent dorm. The owner plans a guest house in the fort at Chittaurgarh.

Jagat Niwas, Lalghat. DR Rs85 DWB Rs125–275. Rest. Super place with courtyard overlooking lake. Even the shared bathrooms have hot water. *One of the very best budget hotels in India.*

Badi Haveli, Jagdish Chowk. Tel 523 500. SR/DR Rs100 DWB Rs180. Rest. A rambling old place with a good view from the roof. Clean, don't be put off by the entrance.

Jheel Guest House, 56 Gangor Road. Tel 28321. SR/DR Rs100 (£2/$3.35) SWB/DWB Rs200. Rest (breakfast and snacks). Nice old house with roof terrace and views over Lake Picchola. If you've ever had fantasies about bedrooms and mirrors check room No 1!

Lake Ghat Guest House, Lalghat. DWB Rs100–150 and cheaper rooms. Rest (see below). Bar. Discount if you turn up on foot.

Mewar Inn, 42 Residency Road. Tel 522 090. SR Rs28 DR Rs37 DWB Rs80. Rest (veg and eggs). Friendly people, would be good value at twice the price.

Natural, 55 Rangsagar. Tel 527 879. DWB Rs75/120. Rest. Many rooms with view over Rang Sagar. Could do with a lick of paint but good value.

Hotel Keerti, Airport Road. Tel 523 639. SWB Rs40–80 DWB Rs60–100 Dorm Rs10. Rest (veg). Bit grubby but very friendly. A real oldie.

Rickshaw-wallahs are becoming a real pain here, most unwilling to take you somewhere which does not pay commission.

Eating and drinking

Lake Palace Hotel. Non-residents can have only a buffet dinner, which cost Rs450 the last time we tried it and was poor value for money. The food was not especially good and the room (not the main restaurant) definitely ordinary.

Parkview, Town Hall Road. Exp. Ind/Chi. Dimly lit, good food.

Berry's, Chetak Circle. Ind/Chi. Mod/Exp. An old travellers' favourite for a treat.

Lake Ghat Guest House. Ind/Chi. Mod/Exp. Bar. Arguably the best food in town. The chef trained with the Taj Group and it shows.

Roof Garden Café, Lake Palace Road. Ind. Mod/Exp. Bar. Relaxed open-air restaurant with view of City Palace.

Natural Attic. Ind/Cont. Cheap/Mod. Superb breakfasts, so much few people need lunch afterwards.

Four Seasons. Ind/Chi. Cheap/Mod. Hard to account for the popularity of this place. The staff give the impression of running it just for the opportunity of picking up Western girls. Beware especially of offers of bhang lassi — or any other kind of lassi which they might slip bhang into.

Restaurant Mayur Café, City Palace Road. Ind veg. Cheap/Mod.

Ground Café, near Rooftop, gets good reports.

To try something different go into a cheap restaurant and order dhal barti; it's the usual vegetarian stuff but with small wholemeal bread rolls and ghee instead of chapatis. Idlis can also be worth trying in Rajasthan; unlike the bland rice cakes of the south they are made of suji, which looks like cous-cous, and is much more palatable.

Outside Udaipur

Pratap Country Inn, Titadhia Village. Tel 583 138. DWB Rs200–600. Rest. Bar. In a rural area well out of town, free transport from Keerti. Swimming pool, free horse-riding in mornings, and good walks. Basic, but makes a good break from Indian towns and hassles.

RANAKPUR

The **Adishwar Temple***, in a valley of the Aravalli Hills, is astonishing. Dedicated to Adinath and built over 65 years from 1367 onwards, it is perhaps the largest single temple (as opposed to complex) in India. The structure is supported by 1444 columns, all different, and is much the same size as a medieval cathedral. Indeed its great height and airiness give it more the feeling of a cathedral than the usual dark and claustrophobic temple. Likers of darkness and claustrophobia (and sticky humidity) can explore the vaults where the images were hidden from Muslim iconoclasts. The quality of carving in the white marble interior does not match that of the Mount Abu temples, but the scale easily compensates. An elegant building in a superb setting, and not to be missed.

Nearby are small Parsvanath and Neminath temples, both with black marble images. The **Surya Temple***, dedicated to the sun god, is more interesting outside than in. A band of prancing horses encircles it, and the little balconies are reminiscent of those at Khajuraho.

The temples are open noon–5pm, and photography (not of the images) is permitted.

Arrival and departure. Bus from Mount Abu to Sadri (7hrs) which is 7km/4.5 miles from Ranakpur, or from Udaipur (3½hrs). It is possible to break the bus journey between Udaipur and Jodhpur at Ranakpur, the interval is sufficient for temple-visiting, but why rush something so good? The comfortable way is for four or five people to share a taxi from Udaipur (Rs400–450). Train to Falna on Jaipur–Ahmedabad line, then bus.

Accommodation

Shilpi Tourist Bungalow. Tel 26. SWB Rs125 DWB Rs150 SWB A/C Rs200 DWB A/C Rs250 Dorm Rs40. Rest. A quiet and pleasant way of breaking a long journey.

Dharamsala at the temple provides accommodation and a very good inexpensive vegetarian thali.

CHITTAUR

Chittaur (or Chitor) is the quintessence of Rajasthan. The fort, which covers the whole of a 5km/3 miles-long hill 150m/492ft above the plains, is the largest in India and has witnessed acts of chivalry unrivalled anywhere in the world.

History

Chittaur owes its name to Chitrang who laid claim to it in the seventh century and founded Chitrakot. A hundred years later it was taken by Bappa Rawal, a direct ancestor of the present Maharana of Udaipur. This continuity is most unusual in the complex and bloody history of Rajasthan and was achieved in the face of constant warfare, as often against Rajput neighbours as Muslim invaders. In time it became the capital of the state of Mewar, the rulers of which were always the most unyielding opponents of the Muslims. Three times this cost them dear and the fort was sacked. In 1303 Sultan Ala-ud-din of Delhi took it, in 1535 Bahadur Shah of Gujarat, and finally in 1567 the Mughal emperor Akbar.

On each occasion when the siege was about to succeed jauhar was performed. The women preserved their honour in ritual suicide by fire, and the men charged out in their orange wedding robes for one last desperate battle against the invaders. The cost of honour was high; on each occasion the city was sacked and tens of thousands of Rajputs lost their lives. After the third jauhar Maharana Udai Singh decided enough was enough and transferred his capital to the less accessible Udaipur. Nor was that quite the end of the story. In 1792 the army of Scindia of Gwalior had to dislodge a rebel from Chittaurgarh, and used the same southern line of attack as Ala-ud-din and Akbar.

The fort approach

The modern town at the foot of the hill is of no interest. Seeing **Chittaurgarh fort***** properly requires a full day. The winding approach has **seven gates**, and is well worth the mile walk. Between the second gate, Bhairon Pol, and the third, Hanuman Pol, are the two chhattris of (first) Kalla and (second) Jaimal who died in the defence of 1567 against Akbar, and also a modern memorial to the pair. On a slab outside Hanuman Pol is a group of memorial stones, one of two women and a couple of others to man and wife. The gates themselves have anti-elephant spikes.

Next up is Ganesh Pol with, predictably enough, a Ganesh shrine outside it. Lakshman Pol has a row of upside-down ducks and a Hanuman relief from which some of the layers of silver leaf and vermilion have been picked off. As on many other shrines this builds up over the years and obscures all detail. The sculptures on the outside of Ram Pol, the main gate, are interesting. At the bottom are elephants. Above are horses mostly caparisoned in what looks like European medieval fashion, and above that a band of assorted figures, soldiers, horsemen, musicians, and the occasional copulating couple. Note, too, the four-legged (three now) goose. Standing memorial stones have the sun and moon at the top.

The palace area

Just inside Rampol is the memorial to Patta, another hero of Akbar's siege. Heading south is the **Naulakha Bhandar** (nine-lakh store), a circular tower used as a treasury. The **Sringar Chauri**, a delightfully ornate Jain temple (15th century) nearby, is unusual because it was at one time built over by the wall of the inner citadel, now cleared away. It has two entrances and inside a free-standing pavilion, which presumably housed a four-faced figure. The **Topkhana** (artillery park), down the wall beside the Sringar Chauri, has only one gun of interest, a huge bronze one.

Behind the wall is the **Palace of Rana Kumbha** (1433–1468), the basis of which is perhaps a hundred years older. A ramp leads up to a stables-like cloister, the kiosk outside having been a musicians' gallery. Over to the left on the east side is where offerings were made to Surya at sunrise — the section done in smooth grey stone. When the palace was built the main approach to the fort was the Surya Gate to the east. So the Tripolia Gate, aligned to it, was the main entrance of the palace, and inside it is a courtyard used as a diwan-i-am. It is said that the king and (highly unlikely) queen occupied the two balconies. Beside the Tripolia Gate is the domed elephant stable. Above the main buildings are a couple of curly domed kiosks, very rare in India. Recent excavation has cleared huge cellars where the jauhar of 1303 is supposed to have taken place, unlikely in view of the lack of air.

The imposing **Kumbha-Shyam Temple** was built around the same time as the palace, though on a much older base, and dedicated to Vishnu in his Varaha (boar) incarnation. In front of the temple is a black Garuda with a realistic cobra under his clasped hands. One of the reliefs shows Vishnu reclining on a cobra, but above him emerging from his side is another figure, Buddha perhaps. The lowest frieze on the base belongs to the earlier temple. The **Mirabhai Temple**, named after a mystical poetess, in the same compound is now disfigured by cardboard cartoon cutouts and taped devotional music. The entrance to the compound is adorned by what appears to be a large Jaina figure.

Over on the fort wall is the **Jata Shankar Temple** dedicated to Shiva; better preserved than most it still has the bracket figures in the mandapa. These are undamaged and in the top of the dome is carving in the Mount Abu style.

The Tower of Victory

Follow the wall down to the next group of buildings, the first of which is the **North Jauhar Gate**. This marked the limit of the Kumbha Palace, the Mirabhai Temple having been in the palace compound. The gate leads into the **Mahasati Sthal**, the cremation place of the ranas, and most probably of the three jauhars as well. Many memorial and sati stones can be seen. Leave the Mahasati Sthal by the east gate. On one side of this is the grotesque figure of Chamundi, the goddess of hunger, with a scorpion on her belly, and on the other are two male figures putting on garlands of skulls.

The **Jai Stambha** (Tower of Victory) is unarguably one of the top five architectural achievements in India. Built 1440–1448 to commemorate Kumbha's defeat of Mahmud Khilji of Mandu its nine storeys (34m/112ft) are covered inside and out with statues of Hindu deities in all their many forms. In a dead end on the second level is Adharinareshwar, a half male and half female form of Shiva. Elsewhere are Harihara, half Shiva and half Vishnu and, very unusual, Hariharpati which combines Brahma, Shiva, and Vishnu in one image. At the top of one of the screens is a carving in the shape of a tree with birds and animals in it very like the Muslim tree of life depicted on carpets. The end of the steps is on the level below the top — for the intrepid only!

Back in the Mahasati Sthal is the **Samiddeshwar Temple**. The main frieze, which comprises almost entirely elephants, includes an odd scene of an ox cart being rammed from behind by an elephant and someone flying out of the front. Inside an extra eight pillars in the mandapa now support the roof; some of the capitals above the original pillars have also had to be replaced. Behind the lingam is an attractive Shiva Trimurti. The two inscriptions on black stone on either side of the main doors tell the story of the building of the temple (1150, though the foundation is undoubtedly older) and its restoration (1428). The lion-like animal over the shrine is

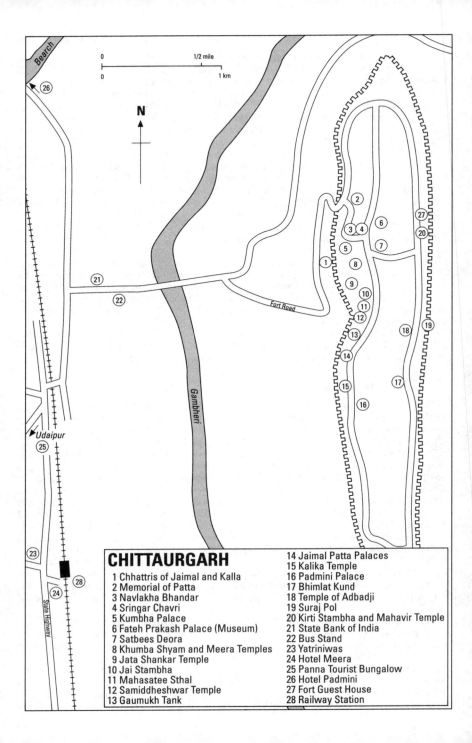

CHITTAURGARH

1 Chhattris of Jaimal and Kalla
2 Memorial of Patta
3 Navlakha Bhandar
4 Sringar Chavri
5 Kumbha Palace
6 Fateh Prakash Palace (Museum)
7 Satbees Deora
8 Khumba Shyam and Meera Temples
9 Jata Shankar Temple
10 Jai Stambha
11 Mahasatee Sthal
12 Samiddheshwar Temple
13 Gaumukh Tank
14 Jaimal Patta Palaces
15 Kalika Temple
16 Padmini Palace
17 Bhimlat Kund
18 Temple of Adbadji
19 Suraj Pol
20 Kirti Stambha and Mahavir Temple
21 State Bank of India
22 Bus Stand
23 Yatriniwas
24 Hotel Meera
25 Panna Tourist Bungalow
26 Hotel Padmini
27 Fort Guest House
28 Railway Station

a yali, a beast mentioned in the Rig-Veda which is vegetarian and a guardian of all other animals.

The third (southern) gate of Mahasati Sthal leads down to the **Gaumukh Tank**. A permanent spring runs out through the Gaumukh (cow's head); this is inside a pavilion and usually half submerged. The blue paint on many of the houses below does not signify occupation by brahmins, that applies only in Jodhpur. Follow the wall as far as the ruined **Jaimal-Patta Palace** and cross over to the road. Behind the building with the domed tower is a small Muslim graveyard with the tomb of a 'nine-yard saint'.

The **Kali Temple** is the oldest building on the hill, dating in part from the eighth century. Reliefs on the outside include the churning of the primeval ocean on the back of the turtle. On the outer wall of the shrine are images of Surya, one of him sitting in his chariot with seven horses in front, and also an extremely rare one of a horse-headed god. Under the tree in front are several lions, Kali's vehicle, and also tridents left by pilgrims. The original dedication of this temple to Surya is evidenced by more than just the sculptures; it lacks the forbidding atmosphere of a true Kali temple.

Padmini's Palace

The **Padmini Palace** is the setting of a legend both romantic and tragic. It is related that Ala-ud-din Khilji, the Sultan of Delhi, became infatuated by Padmini, wife of the rana's uncle, and laid siege to the fort to claim her in marriage. Eventually he agreed to be bought off by a glimpse of her face, though because of purdah this could not be direct. The room of the palace which projects into the tank is circular inside and has four mirrors in its domed ceiling. The steps of the water pavilion, supposedly the women's summer retreat, can be seen through the one over the door and this is reputedly how Padmini revealed herself to Ala-ud-din. Rajput soldiers with swords drawn stood either side and behind him to make sure he did not turn round for a direct view. A nice story, but it seems unlikely that the queen would have strayed so far from purdah in the main palace. Ala-ud-din reneged on the deal and renewed the siege, leading to the first jauhar and sack in 1303.

The southern part of the fort is occupied by a deer park and inaccessible, so take the short cut over to the eastern road. The **Bhimlat Kund** is a tank supposedly dug by Bhim, the hero of the Mahabharata. Many sati stones stand by the tank.

The **Temple of Adabadji** (1483) has another three-faced image of Shiva; more unusual is the external sculpture of a woman seated on a camel and writing a letter!

Outside **Surajpol** (Sun Gate) is the earlier approach to the fort, also with seven gates. On a low ridge is a shooting tower — perhaps the one Akbar built to mark the centre of his camp and from which he directed his siege.

The Tower of Fame

The **Kirti Stambha** (Tower of Fame) was built in the 13th century by a rich Jain merchant in honour of Adinath, the first tirthanka. The seven storeys rise to 23m/75ft and enclose a narrow staircase. At the very top is deep stone-cutting and pendant figures very similar to that at Mount Abu. The round sockets in each lotus bud would have held pendants. It does seem odd that these two towers appear to be the only ones of their kind, but the author has seen nothing similar elsewhere in India. The **Mahavira Temple** nearby, dedicated to the founder of Jainism, is later and made up from bits and pieces of older temples.

The remains in the north of the fort are of little interest. The **Sat Bees Deora** (27 shrines) temple is contemporary with those on Mount Abu and broadly similar in style. The proportions are pleasing and the carvings intricate. One might expect the cloister to extend right round it, but it stops half way. Instead, on a raised platform is a nearly matching pair of temples facing east towards Surya Pol. All the temples have been heavily restored since 1942.

The **Government Museum** (open 10am–4.30pm) in Fateh Prakash Palace (20th century) is very boring, even worse than Indore in that there is nothing to laugh at!

Annular channels can be seen in many parts of the fort. These were used with a circular stone on a radial beam for grinding and mixing mortar; one near the Sringar Chauri is still used. An identical device was used in Normandy and Jersey for crushing cider apples, which seems far more sensible.

Practical Information *i* Tourist office at Yatriniwas (formerly Janata Avas Grah) near station. Morning and afternoon tours of fort from here and Tourist Bungalow if sufficient demand; sometimes conducted by a guide who lives near Ram Pol and knows his stuff. Take the morning tour, if available, and spend the rest of the day at the places which most interest you. Food and refreshment in the fort are very limited.

Arrival and departure. Train from Udaipur (3½hrs), Jaipur (7½hrs), Ajmer (4hrs), and Ratlam (4½hrs) on Bombay Central–Delhi line. This is a quicker way from Bombay than Ahmedabad–Udaipur, and has the very considerable advantage of avoiding Ahmedabad. One passenger train daily on the new broad gauge line from Chittaurgarh to Kota, also on Bombay Central–Delhi line.

Bus from Udaipur, Bundi, etc. Bus-stand is 2km from station and hotels. Auto-rickshaw Rs10–15 from station to top of hill for two, only Rs3/4 if sharing with a full load. Not much fun getting it up there, but a bike would be ideal around the fort.

Accommodation (STD Code 01472)

Hotel Padmini, Chandeniya Road. Tel 41718. SWB A/C Rs550 DWB A/C Rs650 plus 6% tax. Rest. Bar. Very clean, perhaps a little quieter than places in town.

Hotel Meera, near station. Tel 41266. SWB Rs150 DWB Rs200 SWB A/C Rs350 DWB A/C Rs450. Rest (veg). Clean but tends to be noisy.

Panna Tourist Bungalow. Tel 41238. SWB Rs80 (£1.60/$2.65) DWB Rs125 SWB A/C Rs350 DWB A/C Rs450 Dorm Rs40. Rest. Bar. The staff here are absolutely first class, which more than makes up for the tatty state of the building. Very good cook. We recommend the soup and roast chicken, a very welcome break from curry.

Yatriniwas, near station. Tel 41238. Recently refurbished and still some inexpensive rooms. Rest. Bar. Menu looks interesting.

Fort Guest House, fort. Rest (veg). Very reasonable. We saw this place while it was still at the planning stage. If everything works out it will provide simple accommodation in a super, quiet location. No alcohol or non-veg food as it is within temple precincts.

BUNDI

Bundi was the capital of a princely state founded in 1342. Always isolated it is still pleasantly off the tourist trail. The town is situated in a valley of the Aravalli Hills and the palace climbs up the hillside like a Ladakhi monastery.

Around town

The best way of getting round town is on foot. Start by finding the Punjab Hotel; behind here is the **Rani-Ki-Bari**, a step well with carvings and the remains of wall paintings. Return to the street, continue in the original direction until you reach a main road; turn right and follow this round the hill. This gives an excellent view of the palace and brings you to the **Naval Sagar** tank. The temple in this is dedicated to Varuna, the god of the winds. Walk round the three sides of the tank and look for the steep ramp leading up to the palace. Find the chowkidar before you climb all the way up.

The palace, the **Chattar Mahal***** (Palace of Towers), was started in the 16th century and much extended in the 18th. It is famous for its murals in the Bundi school of Rajput painting. The murals date from the 18th century, and on one side are the usual religious scenes of Krishna: stealing the gopis' clothes, dancing with Radha, and lifting Mount Govardhan with his little finger. Elsewhere you will see the palace itself and also other scenes around town. Because of a legal dispute access to the palace is problematic. Since the palace is the main reason for visiting Bundi it is wise to check before travelling.

You have to get police permission to climb up to the **Taragarh** (Star Fort) behind the palace as they have a radio station there. Make your way back through the colourful and traffic-free streets; this is no place to hurry as everywhere has something of interest to see.

Out of town

Next hire a bike and get directions to the **Jait Sagar**, an attractive lake just outside town. Follow the shore of the lake (this is a beautiful and interesting ride) until you come to a couple of chai shops and ask there to be pointed towards the **Shikar Burj***, a hunting lodge with a pretty tank, a Shiva temple and extensive gardens. One of the ruling princes abdicated his throne and retired here as a holy man. A few hundred metres before the chai shops you passed the **Sar Bagh**, the cremation place of the princes. The garden has 66 chhattris, some of them with fine carving. The author was advised that it's worth continuing 7km/4.5 miles on this road to see the **Rameswaram Palace**. Also near to town is the **Phool Mahal**, the modern palace still used by the maharaja, and apparently decorated with murals done in the 1940s by Italian prisoners of war.

Bundi is delightful. It's a very colourful and friendly sort of place though few people speak English. It must be said that most of the places described are pretty knocked about, but if more people visit perhaps repairs will be carried out.

Information. Rajasthan Tourism at the Circuit House.

Arrival and departure. Bus from Ajmer or Chittaur. 40km/25 miles away (bus) is Kota on the Delhi–Bombay railway.

Accommodation
Sukh Mahal Rest House, Jait Sagar tank. Not cheap, but will appeal to Kipling fans, as he stayed here (in acute discomfort).
Other possibilities are the *Hotel Bundi Tourist Palace* and a rather basic *dharamsala*. Tourist Bungalow.

Eating and drinking. *Diamond Hotel* and *KN Singh Restaurant*.

RANTHAMBOR

The Ranthambor National Park should be the leading tiger reserve in India. The reason it isn't is a depressing combination of poaching, official connivance, and fudging the figures. As elsewhere in India tiger numbers are little more than half the official statistics, and still falling fast. Unless something is done urgently the tiger is likely to be extinct in India in ten years. The Nepalese, with far fewer resources, have completely stopped poaching in the Chitwan Park by deploying 500 troops with orders to shoot poachers. The problem soon ceased.

Ranthambor is set in very attractive country, covering 400 sq km/156 sq miles of undulating dry deciduous jungle. There is an old fort and many crumbling monuments. Jeeps and trucks run on set routes in the reserve; a seat in a truck costs

Rs60, and a jeep is Rs500 which can be shared by up to six people, though four is much more comfortable. Entry fees and camera charges are on top.

Ranthambor is a beautiful place, and there is a lot of wildlife. As at Sariska, however, prices are going up and your chances of seeing a tiger are going down.

Information. Project Tiger office in Sawai Madhopur, where you book for jeeps or truck.

Arrival and departure. Sawai Madhopur is on the main Bombay Central (16½hrs)–Delhi (6¾hrs) line. Jaipur is only 3¼hrs, so this is a good way of getting from Bombay to Rajasthan without having to go through Ahmedabad.

Accommodation. Best bet are the Rajasthan Tourism places if only because they have fixed prices. The *Kamdhenu Tourist Bungalow* (Tel 20334) has dorm beds at Rs30 and rooms from Rs250 (£5/$8.35). *Castle Jhoomar Baori* (Tel 20495) is an old royal shooting lodge in great scenery, rooms around Rs400; this is a much more rewarding sort of place for the budget traveller to have a splurge than a palace hotel in a town. You get comfort and peace and quiet.

GUJARAT

Gujarat was taken over by the Rajputs after the collapse of the Gupta empire (seventh century AD) and ruled by them until their eviction by the Muslims a century or two later. The state is very varied, from the desolate salt flats of the Rann of Kutch to the rich farmlands of Saurashtra, almost matching the Punjab in prosperity. Progressive in some ways it is still a stronghold of the dowry system, and wife-burning is distressingly common. Most Gujaratis are vegetarian, and while food can be outstanding in the home it is pretty dreadful in most restaurants. Strict prohibition is in force in Gujarat; what else in Gandhi's home state?

Gujarat is an old centre of civilisation; there are Harappan remains contemporary with Mohenjo Daro, and Romans and Greeks came to trade in the silks which are still famous.

In Gujarat there is lacquered wooden furniture, the mirror-decorated items wrongly associated with Rajasthan, and fine wood and ivory carvings. In Saurashtra beadwork decorates belts, necklaces and wall hangings.

AHMEDABAD

Whoever christened Ahmedabad the Manchester of India on account of its cotton mills was being charitable, although Mancunians might say libellous. The emperor Jehangir was nearer the mark with 'Gardabad', the City of Dust. Ahmedabad is still dusty, and now suffers gross traffic and noise pollution as well. Getting around on foot or by bus is purgatory, so be prepared to fork out for scooter rickshaws.

Mosques and shaking minarets

Ahmedabad's fascination lies in the blend of architectural styles, the pre-Mughal Muslim rulers having used Hindu craftsmen and designs in their mosques and tombs. The **Jama Masjid*** is Hindu in both style and structure, the hall supported by 260 Hindu pillars. Inside the central arch are two finely fluted pillars much higher than all the others, and under the main dome is a gallery. A similar arrangement is used in the adjacent bays and, even more unusual, these pillars support makara-toranas. The main mihrab is relatively plain while the others, which would pass as

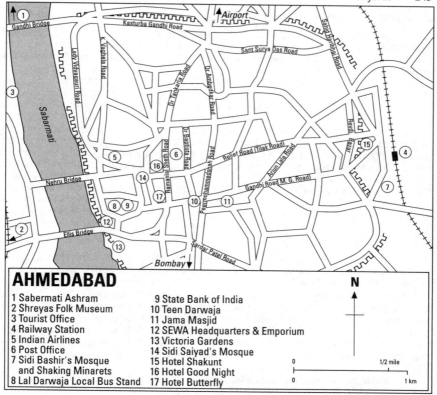

AHMEDABAD

1 Sabermati Ashram
2 Shreyas Folk Museum
3 Tourist Office
4 Railway Station
5 Indian Airlines
6 Post Office
7 Sidi Bashir's Mosque
   and Shaking Minarets
8 Lal Darwaja Local Bus Stand

9 State Bank of India
10 Teen Darwaja
11 Jama Masjid
12 SEWA Headquarters & Emporium
13 Victoria Gardens
14 Sidi Saiyad's Mosque
15 Hotel Shakunt
16 Hotel Good Night
17 Hotel Butterfly

N

0   1/2 mile

0   1 km

entrances to a Jain or Hindu shrine, are very ornate. To one side is the raised screened portion for women in purdah. Outside the eastern entrance is the **tomb of Ahmed Shah I** if you can be bothered to take your shoes off again. The street on the south side of the Jama Masjid is a lively bazaar, and a huge covered market occupies what looks like another mosque.

The **Sidi Sayyid Masjid*** is a fine little mosque despite having lost its minarets, like most mosques in Ahmedabad. The main interest is the superb tracery in the back wall of the mosque, especially two wonderful trees.

Several of the mosques of Ahmedabad were built with shaking minarets. The two towers are connected only by their very solid base, yet when one is shaken the other moves also. Despite pulling one apart engineers failed to discover the secret, and the thing would not work when they reassembled it. So the mystery remains, but the idea is protection from earthquakes rather than the amusement of tourists.

The best-known surviving **shaking minarets** are those of the Sidi Bashir Masjid, a short walk from the station. You cannot see them moving, but can appreciate the wealth of Hindu-style decoration on both the pedestal and the three balconies of the minarets themselves. These were once covered with a layer of plaster and presumably painted; a little green can be seen on top of one of the minarets. Facing the minarets is a substantial domed tomb, the sides unfortunately filled by unsightly concrete blocks. The dozens more mosques and temples around town are of decidedly limited interest.

Superb museums

For all its horrors Ahmedabad has two of the best museums in India. The **Shreyas Folk Museum**** (Tuesday–Saturday 3–6pm, Sunday 10am–noon and 3–6pm) is absolutely excellent. Large display on tribal dress and crafts, mostly with very informative captions. Buses 41 and 34/3 or 34/4.

Part of the **Calico Museum***** (10.15am–12.30pm and 2.45–5pm, closed Wednesday) is located in a beautiful 90-year-old house, and centres on Islamic calligraphy. The second part of the collection is in a traditional haveli with marvellous wood carvings similar to those which once adorned most of the buildings in Ahmedabad. The exterior is stunning, intricately carved in Burmese teak and painted with murals including a train. The collection of textiles, including the tent of a Mughal emperor, is beyond description. Simply magnificent. Tours start at 10.15am and 2.45pm, which may sound a bit regimented, but in fact are not too rushed and the guides really know what they are talking about. Serious students (who can prove it) can spend as long as they wish and use the copious documentation on all the exhibits. The two houses are set in superb gardens of great interest to botanists. This is arguably the best museum in India. Photography is permitted of the exterior of the haveli, but banned inside.

Freedom fighters

Above all, of course, Ahmedabad is associated with Mahatma Gandhi. He lived here for 15 years (martyrdom in itself), founding the **Sabarmati Ashram****, and left in 1930 on his march against the salt tax. The ashram still functions as a handicraft centre and as a memorial, the latter in the form of a photographic display on Gandhi's life. The ashram gives you an idea of the absolute simplicity of the man's lifestyle (belying his very considerable abilities as a political manipulator) and the reactions he inspired in leading Western thinkers. It's a shame to see him idolised in a way he would obviously have hated; and to see India, now independent, hijacked by the unscrupulous self-seekers who run it today. A *son et lumiere* in English takes place on Sunday, Wednesday, and Friday at 10.30pm.

The **Sardar Patel National Memorial** would be worth visiting if any of the captions were in English. In fact they are in Hindi, a language not read by half of India's literates, and by no foreign visitors. Patel, frequently forgotten these days, was the third member of the triumvirate which secured India's freedom. The iron man of Congress, his death in 1950 robbed the party leadership, which meant the too nice Nehru, of the brutish pragmatism which the country needed, and from the lack of which it is still suffering. Not without a sense of humour, he was once rebuked for smoking a cigar when Congress was boycotting foreign goods; he replied 'I'm burning foreign goods, what's wrong with that?'

Flying kites

Ahmedabad is famous for **kite-flying**, and a major festival takes place in mid-January when thousands of kites are flown from the rooftops. This is a competitive sport; the strings are coated with ground glass to cut free your opponent's kite. This string is called dhor, and in alleyways you will see plain string being coated with maasa paste, a mixture of rice, colour, and ground glass. Specialist kite-flyers from all over the world come to participate in a concurrent display. Ahmedabad Municipal Corporation has a **kite museum**.

Practical Information *i* Tourism Corporation of Gujarat is down a lane beside the Ahmedabad Industrial Corporation in HK House. Helpful people, and a good map of Gujarat (Rs10). Ahmedabad Corporation at Town Hall and station, the latter rarely open.

City sightseeing from Lal Darwaja bus-stand daily. Don't expect too much of a guided tour when the guide is too busy pointing out the police court to mention a beautiful pair of minarets on the other side of the road.

Arrival and departure. Airport. Indian Airlines (Tel 353 333) on Tilak Road near Nehru Bridge. Jet Airways (Tel 467 886) also has flights to Bombay.

Major rail junction. Metre gauge trains from Delhi (19hrs) via Ajmer and Abu Road; also from Jodhpur (9hrs). Broad gauge from Bombay (7½hrs). Reservations in a new building adjacent to the station. Open 8am–1.30pm and 2–8pm, but closes 4.30pm on Sunday. Best to go straight to the supervisor at Counter 29 who should deal with things for you.

Bus-stands at Lal Darwaja (local) and Gita Mandir (interstate).

Accommodation (STD Code 079)

Shakunt, opposite station. Tel 344 615. SWB Rs180/219 DWB Rs206/243. Phone and TV in all rooms.

Hotel Goodnight, opposite Sidi Sayyid Mosque. Tel 351 997. DWB Rs250 (£5/$8.35) DWB A/C Rs325. Rest (excellent). New and very professional, easily the best value in Ahmedabad.

Hotel Butterfly. SWB Rs85 DWB Rs180 DWB A/C Rs256. Tiny rooms but clean and well kept.

Hotel Garden, Khadia Char Rasta. Tel 340 764. SWB Rs79 DWB Rs91/110. About as cheap as there is, but dingy and none too clean.

Ahmedabad is not a cheap place to stay; try the retiring rooms at the station first.

Eating and drinking

Hotel Goodnight. Ind/Chi. Mod/Exp. Highly recommended.

Kwality, Tilak (Relief) Road. Ind. Mod/Exp. Good food, zero atmosphere.

Vishalla, opposite Vasana Toll Naka, Vasana. Tel 403 357. Gujarati vegetarian. Rs72 for as much superb food as you can eat, as long as you can sit cross-legged anyway. Traditional village setting with folk music, dancing, and puppets. Also a fascinating museum, but not a cheap night out when you add in Rs70–80 for a rickshaw.

PALITANA

Were it not in the middle of nowhere Palitana would probably rank a lot higher on the tourist trail. The attraction is the nearby **holy mountain***** of Shatrunjaya and its crown of Jain temples. Take a tonga (Rs4–5) to the foot of the hill and start walking; in 2½km/1½ miles you climb more than 400m/1300ft and many, many steps. Photography (exterior only) is free but you must get a permit at the Anandji Kalyani Pedhi on the way to the hill. You may also be able to arrange here to see the fabulous temple jewels.

The two hilltops are completely covered by the 863 temples. Construction has spread over 900 years and covers every aspect of Jain architecture. None is as intricate as Delwara (see Mount Abu), and because of Muslim destruction all date from after 1600, but the colossal scale and extensive views make up for that. The holiest temple is that of Sri Adishwara, the first tirthanka, which is superbly decorated. Look for a green flag flying nearby; here is a lone Muslim shrine where barren women of all religions offer miniature cradles and pray for a child.

Arrival and departure. Train from Ahmedabad via Sihor (10hrs) or Bhavnagar. Bus from Ahmedabad, Bhavnagar, or Una/Kodinar for Diu.

Accommodation (STD Code 02848)

Hotel Toran Sumeru. Tel 2327. DWB Rs300 (£6/$10) DWB A/C Rs400 Dorm Rs35. Rest. Gujarat Tourism strikes again. Dirty rooms, lousy food, TV at full volume for the benefit of the staff, and a water pump that keeps you awake half (if not all) the night.

Hotel Shravak (Tel 2428) appears to have closed down.

TALAJA

You have to change buses here between Palitana and Una (for Diu). A group of **Jain temples** occupies a hilltop on the outskirts of town.

Arrival and departure. On Bhavnagar–Una bus route and Bhavnagar–Mahuva narrow gauge railway line (very slow).

Accommodation. Reputedly a government guest house here.

DIU

Diu was the smallest of the Portuguese seafaring enclaves taken over in 1961. Unlike Goa, which is now a fully fledged state, Daman and Diu are still administered by the union government in Delhi. The territory consists of an island 11km/7 miles by 3km/2 miles with the town of Diu at the eastern end and also the village of Goghla on the mainland opposite.

Diu town has kept something of its continental flavour; much of the architecture is Iberian, the houses are brightly painted, and the narrow streets clean and traffic-free. What's more, several little bars around the square sell beer, feni, and locally made spirits.

The **Fort**** (7am–noon and 2–5pm) resisted siege by the Arabs in 1545, and again in 1670. The fort was used in the past as a prison, and in the entrance is a complaints box labelled 'Sub-Jail Diu'; we bet it never did anyone any good! A bronze statue of Vasco da Gama stands in the courtyard. The walls of the citadel, on which the black-and-white lighthouse is situated, appear to have been damaged by shell fire from the sea.

What resembles a chapel right in the middle of the fort was actually a magazine and is now a museum. It contains many Portuguese tombstones and other inscribed stones including Hindu and Arabic ones, and also one that appears to be Armenian or perhaps Coptic dated 1538. Four wooden pillars come from the chapel in the fort. In a compound opposite are half a dozen field guns, British 4½-inch QF howitzers of First World War vintage. For some strange reason one has an inscription on the breach in Cyrillic characters, and the safety catch on top is marked in Portuguese as well as Cyrillic! Most of the old guns in the fort are of cast iron or bronze, but on top of the bastion over the entrance causeway is one made on the earlier principle of bars wrapped with wrought iron. Fishermen work their nets on the banks around the mid-channel fort at low tide. Two shells hit this, probably aimed at the slot cut in the side for a machine gun.

Eleven churches, of which five remain, once stood on Diu. Most of the figures from these are collected in **Our Lady of the Immaculate Conception*** (known locally as St Paul's), built in 1601. The usual splendid wood carving adorns the pulpit and the screen behind the altar. The beasts on two wooden gargoyles projecting in front of the side altars have a very Hindu look. This is the main place of worship on the island, though the priest does visit the others to keep them alive. 37 Christian families still live on Diu, a lot of Goans who used to work here having moved back in 1987 when Goa became a state. Attached to the church is the former Professed House of the Jesuits, now a school. One of the other two large churches in Diu town is now a hospital and the other a sports centre.

As a resort Diu is pleasantly like the Goa of ten years ago. Much of the southern coast of the island is one long deserted beach, and the rocky sections are a delight for the beachcomber. The only facilities are at **Nagoa Beach***** where there is one hotel and one bar and restaurant. Simple huts can be rented very reasonably.

Vanakbara, a smelly, fly-blown fishing port at the western end of the island is worth avoiding.

Don't expect too much of Diu. Although the kids no longer call out 'Hippy, hippy' after any Westerner not wearing a suit, it is still a quiet little backwater. You can find everything you need for a comfortable and peaceful stay, but there is little choice.

Arrival and departure. Airport, East-West (agent Oceanic Travels, Tel 2180) flies to Bombay. If you have any illusions about Indian non-violence check out the bombed and bullet-scarred terminal and radio station. The Indians blockaded Diu and the other Portuguese possessions in the 1950s, so the airport was Diu's link with the outside world, and the nearest to Portugal. When India decided to take the enclaves by force in 1961 it became the first target. Have you noticed the Indians' passion for labelling everything? When they filled the craters in the runway in 1961 they marked each one with the weight of the bomb and the name of the pilot who dropped it!

Direct bus from Veraval at 9.30am. If you miss that you have to go to Una (2hrs). At Una bus-stand times of buses to Diu are posted in English; they run every two hours or so from 6am–8pm and take 45 minutes. Now the bridge is complete there is no need to take the ferry from Goghla though this still operates. Check under Palitana for details of getting there.

Delvada station is only 5km/3 miles or so from Goghla, on the Una road. One train daily to Veraval, another to Sasangir and Jungadh, very slow but you see more than you can from a bus.

Bicycles can be hired in the town, and this is easily the best way of getting around.

Accommodation (STD Code 028758)

Public Works Department Guest House, Fort Road. Tel 2476. DWB Rs100/250. Rest. Bar. Comfortable and peaceful.

Hotel Alishan, Sea Shore Fort Road. Tel 2340. DR Rs75 DWB Rs100/150. Rest (veg/non-veg).

Apana Guest House, Sea Shore Fort Road. Tel 2992. DR Rs60 DWB Rs80–125. Rest. Clean.

Hotel Prince, Main Bazaar. Tel 2265. DWB Rs75/100. Rest. Bar. Basic and clean.

Hotel Sanman, Fort Road. Tel 2273. DWB Rs80. Nice old colonial house. Perhaps a restaurant by now, but owners are Jains so no meat or alcohol.

Hotel Mozambique. Tel 2223. DR Rs80 (£1.60/$2.65) DWB Rs120. Rest. Looks alright outside, but try the others first.

Hotel Krishna, Fish Market. Tel 2213. DR Rs70. Rest. Bar. Basic, but pleasant manager and a good place to stay. Reportedly good food but for residents only.

Circuit House, near PWD Guest House, may be opening up to non-official visitors. Good location, worth checking.

Eating and drinking

DeePee, Main Square. Ind/Chi veg. Seems to be the in place, can't think why.

Jagat Bar, Main Square. Ind/Goan. Best fish, prawns, and chips in town, the author's choice; sat and watched the local drinking habits and saw three men polish off a full bottle of whisky in seven minutes! Then they presumably drove off in their buses and lorries.

At Jallandhar Beach

Tourist Cottages. Tel 2424. DWB Rs225 DWB A/C Rs350. Rest. Bar. Super location, the best place to stay.

Jay Shankar Restaurant. Cheap/Mod. Excellent.

At Nagoa Beach
Ganga Sagar Guest House. Tel 2249. DR Rs70 (£1.40/$2.35) upwards. Rest (good).
Bar. Quiet location right on the beach. More relaxed than in the past, a good
place.
Oasis Camping Site, next to Ganga Sagar, has expensive tents in the winter
season.
Mombasa, adjacent to Ganga Sagar. Cheap. Goan seafood. Bar.
It used to be possible to rent primitive huts from the fishermen, but this has now
been banned.

KODINAR

Kodinar is a place you'll visit only if you make a mess of your bus schedules, but it's
a nice little old town, and a local doctor and his wife gave the author the best birthday
feast he's ever had.

Arrival and departure. On bus route between Diu and Veraval, sometimes necessary
to change here.

Accommodation. Best bet probably the *Government Rest House*; failing that try the
very basic *Somnath Guest House*. And hope Dr Solanki hears you are in town and
invites you round for conversation and some superb home cooking.

VERAVAL

Veraval was once a major port for the pilgrimage to Mecca. It is now a busy
commercial port and claims to be the biggest fishing harbour in India. Traditional
wooden dhows up to 350 tonnes capacity are built here; they carry salt and limestone
as far as the Persian Gulf, and return with dates.
   The main interest, however, is not Veraval itself but at Somnath Patan 5km away.
The **Somnath Temple** is one of the twelve most sacred Shiva shrines (jyotirlingas) in
the country. The temple has been destroyed seven times, with some of history's more
celebrated vandals like Mahomed of Ghazni and Aurangzeb getting in on the act.
Each time it has been rebuilt, and the current reconstruction (begun in 1950) is
nearing completion.
   The base of the sikhara and mandapa still have many flat slabs of stone that will
eventually be sculpted; you can see where a few have been roughed out already. The
temple has been extended by adding a further mandapa, which is now more or less
complete. The lingam in the sanctum has a silver head and face of Shiva, and behind
that is a seven-headed cobra. A huge receptacle-cum-safe accepts what they call
'secret offerings'. Indulgences are sold here, the only instance of this the author
knows in Hinduism. They cost Rs10,000 for ten years and seem to apply to the future
rather than being retrospective, quite a marketing ploy. The temple drums and bells
play for the start of prayers at 7am, noon and 7pm.
   Fragments from the old temple are kept in the compound. This temple is certainly
very big, and in a fine location right on the seashore but, that said, it has very little
going for it. Opposite the entrance is a statue of Sardar Patel who led the
rebuilding.
   The **Prabhas Patan Museum** (8.30am–12.15pm and 2.30–6.15pm, closed Wednesday
and 2nd and 4th Saturdays) is in an old mosque made from bits of Hindu temples, and
of as much interest in itself as for its contents, which is not much. The old town is
much nicer than the new, but Veraval as a whole bears a striking resemblance to the
grimmer sort of housing project, and there is nowhere decent to stay or eat.

Arrival and departure. Bus from most places, see Sasangir and Diu. Terminus of a
tortuous railway line.

Accommodation
Hotel Satkar, opposite bus-stand. Tel 20120. Rooms Rs75–125 (£1.50–2.50/$2.50–4.15) or Rs250–350 A/C. Noisy and not as clean as one is entitled to expect for the price. Better than the Tourist Bungalow, which is not saying much.

Toran Tourist Bungalow, College Road. Tel 20488. DWB Rs150/200. This place has had no maintenance nor, it seems, been cleaned since last visited 12 years ago. The staff cannot be bothered to cook, and a noisy chemical plant behind will keep you awake all night.

If you have to stay in this truly awful place the *Sri Somnath Guest House* and *Hotel Mayur* near the Somnath temple may be better and cheaper than places in Veraval.

Eating and drinking *New Apsara*. Cheap. Vegetarian plus fish. Pretty grim but there seems to be nothing better.

CHORWAD

A town 30km/19 miles west of Veraval with a beach resort a further 4km/2.5 miles away. The resort is centred on the summer palace of the Nawabs of Junagadh, now a hotel. The beach is pretty good and, as usual, deserted; not so usual is the fact that it is clean and shows signs of surf. You can fish off the rocks or should be able to go out with the local fishermen.

Arrival and departure. Occasional direct bus from Veraval.

Accommodation. *Palace Beach Resort.* Tel 0287 688 557. DWB Rs200–500. Rest. We haven't seen this since it was upgraded. Its location is good, but would you trust Gujarat Tourism to get anything else right?

SASANGIR

The Asiatic lion was once common enough for Ashoka to choose it as the emblem of his empire — a symbol perpetuated by the republic. That any survive, however, is due to Lord Curzon who declined an invitation to hunt them and persuaded the Nawab of Junagadh to set up the **Gir Forest Reserve**. Despite the constant pressure for cattle-grazing it still exists. About 200 lions live in the 1500 sq km and, while not as tame as those in a safari park, you stand an excellent chance of seeing them at close quarters (far more so than tiger). There are also the usual varieties of deer, bear, pig, nilgai and chinkara, the only gazelle in India.

Transport round the sanctuary leaves from the Reception Centre in the grounds of the Forestry Lodge at 7am and 4pm. A jeep costs Rs5 per kilometre, and they normally do 30–40km in the 2½ or 3-hour duration of the trip. A very short way into the reserve a cheetah sat quietly by the track and watched our jeep pass. People who have stayed in the Irrigation Inspection Bungalow at the dam 10km away reported having to shoo the lions off the verandah!

Between the station and the Forestry Lodge is a **Crocodile Rearing Centre** where hundreds of crocodiles are raised from eggs to a size large enough for release. Beautifully kept and with a couple of creeper-covered arbours.

You will probably see people around here of obviously negroid origin; one theory is that they are descendants of a former Nawab's bodyguard.

Sasangir is a very pleasant place to spend two or three days while you wait to see the lions. Very quiet, and the Forestry Lodge has a lovely garden.

Arrival and departure. Direct by rail from Veraval, or from Junagadh, change at Vivasadar. Direct bus from Veraval or Junagadh, perhaps a share taxi from the latter.

Accommodation
Lion Safari Lodge. Tel 21. DWB Rs350 Dorm Rs30. Rest. Far better than other Gujarat Tourism places. Good food, caters for non-residents but all must order in advance.
Forestry Lodge. DWB Rs150 (£3/$5) Suite Rs400. Rest (breakfast and lunch only). Comfortable, clean, and with a delightful garden. The suites are not good value as the extra money buys you a dressing room and extra bathroom rather than a sitting room.
Cheap eateries over the road from the Forestry Lodge.

JUNAGADH

Junagadh was the capital of a Muslim state whose rulers embellished it with many fine buildings. The last Nawab, another prince who preferred his dogs to his fellow man, decamped to Pakistan at Independence, and the town has been quietly decaying ever since.

A hilltop pilgrimage

These days Junagadh is visited (if at all) for **Girnar Hill*****, an important place of pilgrimage. The hill (a range of hills, really) towers over the town and has several major Jain temples and Hindu shrines of less importance. Buses run to the foot of the hill from the small bus-stand in town. It is, however, worth walking out of the Wagheshwari Gate to see the **Ashoka Stone** with its various inscriptions; you could even do things properly and walk the pilgrim route all the way, there's a lot to see.

According to local lore 10,000 steps lead to the top, very nearly 1000m/3280ft up. Emerging from the forest on the lower slopes vultures nest and roost on the bare rock faces. One of the little wayside shrines depicts the Hindu trinity, Brahma, Vishnu, and Shiva on a cow. It is unusual to see the three together in this way. Just above is Kali wearing a necklace of skulls and standing on a man's head. Must be a feminist.

Roughly two-thirds of the way up is Deva Kota, the group of Jain temples. The **Neminath Temple** is the largest and most important, but on the other side of the path is the unusual Vastupal or **Mallinath Temple**. The black image is of Mallinath, the ninth tirthanka. The dome in front of the shrine has the usual bracket figures, dancers above and musicians below. The unique feature of this temple, however, is in the side chapels. Each has a representation of one of the Jains' holy hills, Maru and Parasnath. Both are stepped and capped by four-faced images. The marble coolness of this temple is a real boon after the hot climb. These temples, dating from the 12th century AD, have been much altered since, not least in their mosaic domes.

On the first peak is the Hindu **Amba Mata Temple** which is a place of pilgrimage for newly-weds. This is actually a Devi temple and in rather a mess, not least because of the holy men who live and cook in it. The lion in the mandapa is the vehicle of Devi and unusual in having one foot on a globe. This was the emblem of the nawab, and may have been borrowed from elsewhere. The peak past the Amba Mata Temple is the abode of a couple of Shiva devotees; there are two shrines and a red-painted rock with a forest of tridents left here by pilgrims. On one of the bushes by the path are bangles and strips of cloth torn from saris. The furthest peak also has a shrine, splendid views all round. Cold drinks are available at intervals all the way up and snacks at the top.

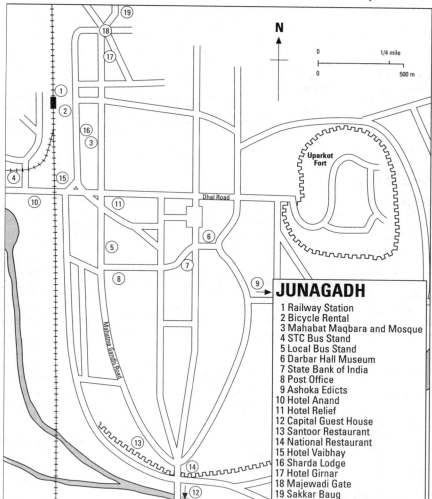

The fort

Junagadh means Old Fort and refers to the **Uparkot**** which dominates the town. Entering through a strong gate you find a large Egyptian cannon left behind by the Arabs who besieged Diu. This is enclosed in a cage which makes it impossible to photograph while failing in its purpose of preventing people from scratching their names on it... and gives the painters an excuse for splashing it with paint. Like so many others in this area the **Jama Masjid** is made from elements of Hindu temples. The mihrabs, complete with the bells and chains on the columns, must have been shrine doorways. This was a triple-domed building (perhaps not true domes), though these have collapsed. The 'arches' in some of the bays have no structural function, the aim seems to have been to make it look a bit more like a mosque.

The bases and capitals of the columns in the **Buddhist cave temple** were obviously very ornate, with swags and vases, but all cut from very soft stone and badly eroded by water running through the roof. The cave was never completed. The **Adi-Chadi Vav** consists of a deep gorge with steps cut down to a circular well. A seat on the ramparts nearby allows you to relax and contemplate Girnar Hill. You can congratulate yourself on having climbed it or have second thoughts about doing it tomorrow. Coming here after Rajasthan or Kutch everything looks very green and lush compared with the desert.

The **Naughan** well is even deeper than the Adi-Chadi. Cut out of solid rock the steps zig-zag their way down into what feels like the bowels of the Earth. Nearby is a small cave cut as a Buddhist shrine and now dedicated to Shiva. In the south-western corner of the fort, between the playground and a reservoir, is a huge bronze cannon called Kadanal, far more impressive than the first one.

Around town

The town itself is quite interesting. The **Darbar Hall Museum**** (9am–12.15pm and 3–6pm, closed Wednesday and 2nd and 4th Saturdays) is a must, a real monument to expensive bad taste (fun!). A photo on one of the columns shows how the hall used to look in its heyday with the original ceiling and when the columns and walls were properly decorated. Apart from the silver furniture the best feature is the huge number of chandeliers in multi-coloured glass. At each corner of the throne dais are bases for silver posts which supported a canopy. A picture entitled 'Judgment of Jehangir' depicts that emperor on the peacock throne. This looks splendid, but the picture's historical veracity is called into question by the knowledge that the throne was built later than this for his son Shahjahan! The portrait gallery is rather jolly for the period photographs. Note the one of the magnificently moustachioed petty prince posing like a 1920s matinee idol.

Next to the gaily painted mosque are some fine **mausolea** in a sort of rococo Saracenic style.

The **Museum** (9am–12.30pm and 2.45–6.15pm, closed Wednesday) has quite a good collection, especially of miniature paintings and silverware, but there is minimal information in English. Like the Darbar Hall it is most interesting for the amazing variety of chandeliers. The **zoo**, in the same park (the Sakkar Baug), has Asian lions if you are unlucky at Sasangir.

Practical Information *i*

Gujarat Tourism office at Hotel Girnar, of limited use.

Arrival and departure. Airport at Keshod (47km/ 29.5 miles). On Veraval (1¾hrs)–Ahmedabad (13hrs) rail line.

Buses from Rajkot, Veraval, Porbandar, Dwarkar, and Ahmedabad, also deluxe (night) bus from Ahmedabad. Share taxis run on fixed routes. Try either outside the bus-stand or at the road junction by the level crossing close to the Hotel Anand. Mostly big old American cars.

Accommodation (STD Code 0285)

Hotel Girnar, Majwadi Darwaza. Tel 21201. Rest (veg/non-veg). SWB Rs225 DWB Rs350 SWB A/C Rs350 DWB A/C Rs475. Shabby but spacious rooms. May be worth the money just for the quiet location.

Hotel Relief, Chittakhana Chauk. Tel 20280. SR Rs75 SWB Rs100 DWB Rs150. Rest (small portions, not cheap). This is one of those places where prices and quality have gone in opposite directions following a good write-up in a travel guide. Beware of flexible pricing.

Hotel Anand, bus-stand road. Tel 22657. DR Rs110 DWB Rs165 DWB A/C Rs360.

Clean and well looked after, best value in Junagadh. A bit noisy, but so is the rest of India.

Hotel Vaibhav, bus-stand road. Tel 21070. SR Rs60 (£1.20/$2) DWB Rs75 DWB A/C Rs146. Rest. Management planning renovation, it certainly needs it.

Sharda Lodge, railway station road. SR Rs60 DR Rs100 Dorm Rs25. Rest (unlimited thali Rs14). Basic but clean.

Capital Guest House, Kalwa Chauk, is very cheap and was fine on a previous visit.

Eating and drinking

Santoor, MG Road near Kalwa Chowk. Cheap/Mod. Veg. Probably the only smart restaurant in town, highly recommended.

National, Kalwa Chowk. Ind. Cheap/Mod. Very basic but meat if you want it.

Hotel Vaibhav. Cheap. Veg.

BHUJ

This remote corner of India — Bhuj is as far west as Kabul — is a place on its own. Culturally cut off from the rest of India, physically as well when the monsoon floods the Great Rann of Kutch, Kutch has produced a population of hardy, independent-minded seafarers. These sailors brought back both ideas and goods which were seized upon by the rulers; strong men who provided an enlightened rule within a feudal framework.

The Ranns of Kutch are barren salt flats, home only to the Indian wild ass and breeding ground for flamingoes, pelicans, and avocets. Small communities earn a precarious living on the fringes either stock-raising or from handicrafts. This is the true home of the mirror embroidery erroneously attributed to Rajasthan. The main centre is Bhuj, a colourful little town surrounded by scrub desert.

Exploring

The palace

The heart of the old walled town is the palace compound. As you enter notice the dwarapala (doorkeeper) in European dress including tricorne hat. The **Old Palace*****, known as the Aina Mahal (Mirror Palace), is quite astonishing, not as ornate as some but delightful. You enter through a summer palace with an island throne surrounded by water and fountains and with a roof like that of a palace in Kerala. Brass and glass candle-holders and hanging lanterns provide a subdued light, and the fountains relieve the ferocious heat of a Kutchi summer. Behind this the maharao's bed chamber is surrounded by mirrors (hence the name) and the walls dotted with semi-precious stones. The floor tiles were made in Bhuj by Ram Singh, a Kathiawari who, as the result of a shipwreck, spent 16 years in Holland and picked up all sorts of skills. The same man produced part of the large collection of china, porcelain, and clocks. The rest, including Hogarth prints, is the mixture that makes these Indian palaces so entertaining.

A pair of superb ivory-inlaid doors led through from the maharao's quarters to the zenana palace; they are 275 years old and in perfect condition. The large settees in the old darbar hall must have been made for the new one, as must some of the ormolu-backed chairs. The later maharaos must have had many interests; the collection includes a couple of steam-powered model trains, telescopes, and even a static-electricity generator. The curator can show you the catalogue of the London scientific supplier from which these were bought.

The **new palace** is the Prag Mahal built for Maharao Pragmal (1860–1876). The style is Victorian Etruscan, and it was actually built in part by Italian artisans. Much of this is now used as government offices, but the huge darbar hall and clock tower are open. In the darbar hall, as well as downstairs, the more subdued colours — the

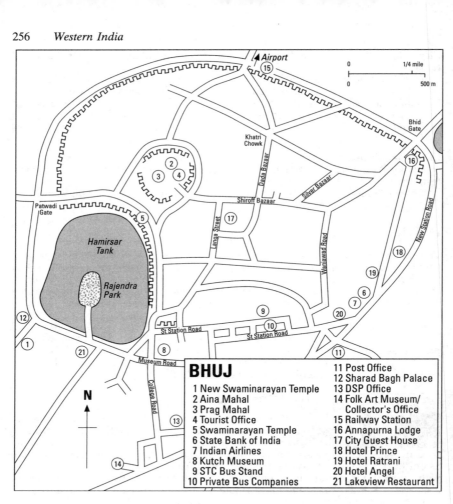

BHUJ

1 New Swaminarayan Temple
2 Aina Mahal
3 Prag Mahal
4 Tourist Office
5 Swaminarayan Temple
6 State Bank of India
7 Indian Airlines
8 Kutch Museum
9 STC Bus Stand
10 Private Bus Companies
11 Post Office
12 Sharad Bagh Palace
13 DSP Office
14 Folk Art Museum/
   Collector's Office
15 Railway Station
16 Annapurna Lodge
17 City Guest House
18 Hotel Prince
19 Hotel Ratrani
20 Hotel Angel
21 Lakeview Restaurant

rather dull red, cream and yellow — are preferable to the pastels one expects in an Indian palace of this period. The campanile has a set of five bells cast in London. Unfortunately these are just a chime for the clock, and that is not working at present. The big bell could reputedly be heard 60km away.

Around town

Outside the walled palace enclosure is the **Swaminarayan Temple***. Exuberantly decorated places of worship are not uncommon in India, but this does seem to go a little over the top. The same complex includes both the Narayan temple and a Jain one. Over the road is a ladies' temple where only women can officiate; most unusual.

The same road runs past several more small temples to a gate marking the limit of the walled city. Outside is the **Kutch Museum** (9am–noon and 3–6pm, closed Wednesday), the oldest in Gujarat. In contrast to the palace museum this is distinctly ordinary. A fine collection of model dhows testifies to the fame of the seamen of Kutch, yet not a word of description appears in English.

Follow the lake shore past the swimming pool and island park to the recently completed **New Swaminarayan Temple***. This has a mosaic dome like some at Junagadh, and inside are friezes in white marble. The **Sharad Bagh Palace**, a little further on, was occupied by the maharao up to his death in 1991. It has now been opened as a museum.

Because of the proximity of the border with Pakistan there is a large military presence locally. This, and income from seafarers, are the main reasons why Bhuj is such a prosperous little town, and not the spurious prosperity of tourism. Perversely this prosperity is causing some very fine old buildings to be replaced by concrete blocks. The military presence is a drawback too; many places are closed, and you have to be careful where you point a camera. Bhuj is a friendly place; even the horse and donkey-cart men whack the cart rather than the animals with their sticks.

Practical Information *i*

Tourist information at the Palace Museum (9am–noon and 3–6pm, closed Saturday), which also has interesting books on the area and information on handicrafts. This office is not state-run, and doesn't it show!

Arrival and departure. Airport (5km), flights from Bombay via Jamnagar. Indian Airlines office (Tel 21433) on Station Road near Hotel Anam.

The direct train from Ahmedabad (16hrs) is only a metre gauge Fast Passenger and travels 491km/307 miles via Palanpur. The 300km/188 miles on broad gauge from Ahmedabad to Gandhidam takes only six hours, and a bus does the remaining 60km/38 miles in an hour or two.

Buses to Ahmedabad and Jaisalmer (two days via Barmer). Several private bus companies outside the bus-stand offer deluxe services to Ahmedabad, and to Rajkot (4½hrs) on the way to Saurashtra.

Accommodation

Hotel Prince, Station Road. Tel 20370. SWB Rs225 (£4.50/$7.50) DWB Rs250 SWB A/C Rs410 DWB A/C Rs460. Rest (see below). Breakfast in room. First-class value for money.

Anam Guest House, Station Road. Tel 21390. SWB Rs135 DWB Rs250 DWB A/C Rs500. Rest (Gujarati thali Rs20).

Ratrani Hotel, New Station Road. Tel 22388. SWB Rs34/50 DWB Rs50/68. Rest (Gujarati thali Rs10). More expensive rooms have showers and hot water. Not bad at all; wallpaper (wallpaper!) peeling off in deluxe rooms but clean enough.

City Guest House, Langa Street. Tel 21067. SR Rs45 DR Rs65 Dorm Rs30. Basic but OK, and pleasantly in centre of bazaar.

Eating and drinking

Hotel Prince. Ind/Chi veg/non-veg. Mod/Exp. Excellent food and service.

Hotel Angel. South Indian and Punjabi vegetarian. Cheap/Mod. Offensive music.

KD Resorts by the lake, opposite the causeway to the island, has a veg rest, swimming pool, and perhaps by now bedrooms. *Annapurna* reported as OK place to stay and having good food.

Excursions

Out in the Rann of Kutch **Hodaka** is an attractive spotlessly clean village of harijans, entirely dependent on handicrafts, mainly embroidery work and slippers. You have to bargain but prices are very reasonable. Most of the stuff is new, a few items old. Sweets will make you very popular in these villages.

Dhordo is a Muslim community of the Mutwa caste. Mention of caste among Muslims may seem anomalous, but Islam in India has evolved its own castes. These even fall into four groups, just as the Hindu ones do. A very self-contained community of herdsmen, they settled here in 1947 preferring India to Pakistan. The ruler of Kutch used his popularity to ensure the safety of all minorities. A healthy lot, they say that if a man dies at eighty he dies young! Some families trace their ancestry back to Arabia, having come to Kutch via Sind. Great horsemen and breeders, they certainly look after their animals. The usual embroidered items are made, and they will also embroider little mirrors onto your own clothing. The women prefer not to be photographed.

Like other villages this does have a bus service, though a day trip may not be possible. The headman will provide accommodation for a night or two, but this hospitality must not be abused.

Lodiya produces turned and carved wooden items as well as embroidery. These include bottles which would be good for salad oil and the like. Lodiya is a long way out, adding 50km/31 miles to the round trip, and scarcely justifies the cost.

Passes. Because the Pakistan border is so close a pass is needed to travel out from Bhuj to the villages and the Rann. Start at the Magistrate's office; a little time-consuming, but free.

Arrival and departure. As mentioned above these villages do have bus services, though these mostly involve overnight stays. A taxi allows you to visit all three villages in one day. Reckon about 200km at Rs3 per kilometre, not so bad if you can get a few people together. Rohit Gajjour of Shakti Travels, opposite Prince Hotel, is a good driver and guide.

BARODA

Baroda (officially Vadodara), between Bombay and Ahmedabad, was the capital of a major Maratha princely state (more information in the preceding chapter). Little visited by Westerners, Baroda is a pleasant, well kept city.

The **Vadodara Museum** incorporates an art gallery with a good collection of Indian miniature paintings. A miniature railway runs round the park in which the museum stands. Works by major European artists can be seen in the **Maharaja Fateh Singh Museum**.

One hour up the railway line towards Ahmedabad is Nadiad, the centre of a network of **narrow gauge railway lines**.

Information. The tourist office is across the road from the station, to the left, and upstairs.

Arrival and departure. On the main line from Bombay CT (5hrs) to Ahmedabad (7hrs) and Delhi via Kota.

Accommodation. Cheap hotels near station, the *Ambassador* (Tel 0265 327 653) costs around Rs300 and is much better. *Kwality* restaurant also in this area.

South-Western India

The Backwaters, Kerala

Maharashtra — Karnataka — Goa — Kerala

The northern two states in this area, Maharashtra and Karnataka, are divided into two distinct parts by the Western Ghat hills: the fertile and densely populated coastal plain and the much drier Deccan.

The main languages are Marathi in Maharashtra, an Indo-Aryan language related to Hindi and using the same Devanagri script; Kannada in Karnataka and Malayalam in Kerala, both Dravidian and with distinctive scripts; and Konkani is spoken in Goa.

Handicrafts. Mysore is famous for ivory and sandalwood carvings, Bangalore for silks. You will find snake and crocodile skin products in many places, though there are now restrictions on exporting these.

Climate. November–March is the most pleasant time, with late December and January the best of all for visiting Goa. The monsoon from early June to August is at its heaviest here. Temperatures in the hot weather are not as high as in the north, although humidity is extreme near the coast. You can usually rely on a cooling breeze

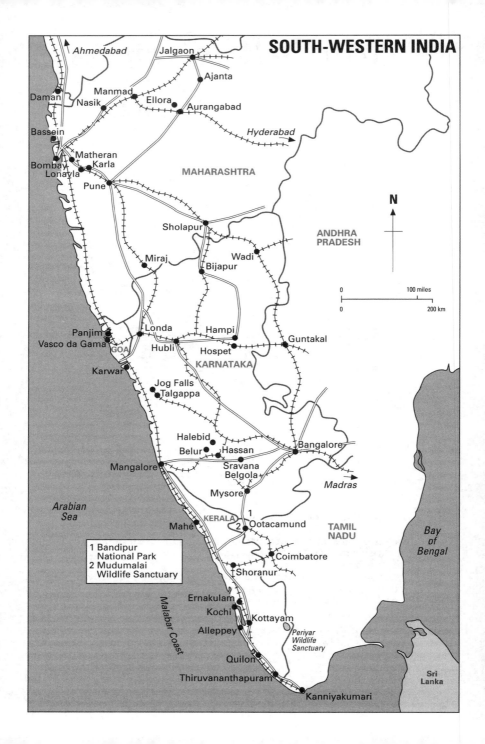

in the coastal areas. Inland Mysore and Bijapur have pleasant climates with relatively low rainfall.

MAHARASHTRA

Maharashtra is the home of the Marathas (the Indian army still uses the old form Mahratta), another of India's martial communities who, like the Rajputs, spent much of their time in conflict with invading Muslims. After the eclipse of the Mughals they built a substantial empire before being finally subdued by the British early in the 19th century. Best known of the Maratha leaders was Shivaji (died 1680), who managed to form a confederation of Hindu states and challenge effectively Mughal power in the latter part of the 17th century. He is often regarded as India's first great nationalist leader.

Despite all the industry around Bombay 70% of the population still works on the land. Tobacco and cotton are important crops, and offshore drilling for oil, though initially hampered by a reluctance to admit foreign investment, is now showing good results.

BOMBAY

The largest and most cosmopolitan of India's cities presents two faces. One is shown by the wealthy entrepreneurial elite with its very Western lifestyle; the other stems from Bombay being an indisputably Indian city with all that that implies. Spending most of your time in Colaba you will be unaware of the appalling slums that stretch ever further up the peninsula. The magnetic attraction of the city for the rural poor, and their determination to make a decent living for themselves, has made Bombay the powerhouse of India. The spending power of those who have clawed their way up the ladder fuels the local economy and ensures the further growth of Bombay's prosperity. This is a very different state of affairs from the dreadful mess that Calcutta is in. Downtown Bombay is a vibrant place, but expensive by Indian standards. If only one could afford to spend more time here!

Bombay is, of course, no longer Bombay. In May 1995 the BJP and Shiv Sena government of Maharashtra (a highly nationalistic coalition), elected a few weeks before, renamed Bombay Mumbai. The last time they did this, in 1981, they put up big signs at the Gateway of India proclaiming Mumbai, but nobody took any notice. The fact that it is only Mumbai in Marathi, the Hindi version being Bambai, does not commend the change to innately conservative Indians. Mumba Devi has for centuries been the presiding deity of Bombay, a strange figure with no mouth.

History

The English were already well established in India (to the north in Surat, and in Madras) when Bombay came into their possession as part of the dowry of Catherine of Braganza, the Portuguese bride of Charles II. Not much of a prize it seemed, for at the time it was a malarial swamp inhabited only by fishermen. Charles leased the place to the East India Company in 1668 (for the princely sum of £10 a year!), and its history since then has been one of constant land reclamation and growth. Its prosperity grew rapidly to surpass Madras and Calcutta, a process greatly aided by Jain, Parsee, and Baghdadi Jewish entrepreneurs. It is the financial and commercial centre of India and visibly the richest of the five big cities. It has moreover a great deal of interest for the visitor and a friendly, if frenetic, atmosphere.

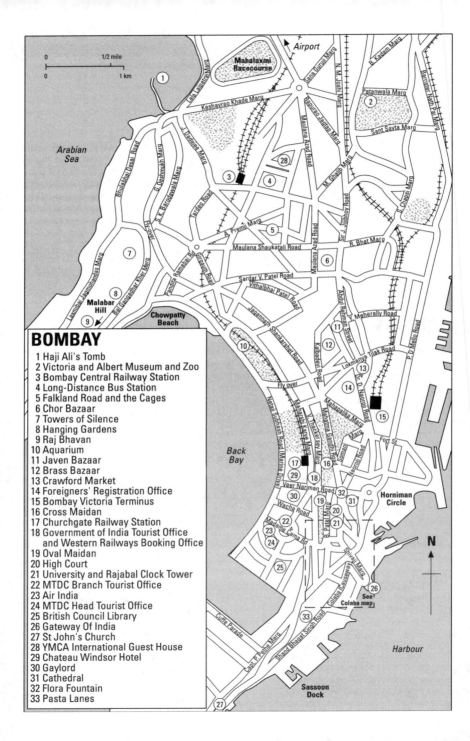

BOMBAY

1 Haji Ali's Tomb
2 Victoria and Albert Museum and Zoo
3 Bombay Central Railway Station
4 Long-Distance Bus Station
5 Falkland Road and the Cages
6 Chor Bazaar
7 Towers of Silence
8 Hanging Gardens
9 Raj Bhavan
10 Aquarium
11 Javen Bazaar
12 Brass Bazaar
13 Crawford Market
14 Foreigners' Registration Office
15 Bombay Victoria Terminus
16 Cross Maidan
17 Churchgate Railway Station
18 Government of India Tourist Office
    and Western Railways Booking Office
19 Oval Maidan
20 High Court
21 University and Rajabal Clock Tower
22 MTDC Branch Tourist Office
23 Air India
24 MTDC Head Tourist Office
25 British Council Library
26 Gateway Of India
27 St John's Church
28 YMCA International Guest House
29 Chateau Windsor Hotel
30 Gaylord
31 Cathedral
32 Flora Fountain
33 Pasta Lanes

Exploring

Downtown

Most people choose to stay in Colaba, and many of the places of interest are within easy reach of here. Bombay has one of the largest natural harbours in the world, and Apollo Bunder was the landing place of the famous. The **Gateway of India****, a huge arch, was built to commemorate the arrival of George V in 1911 for his Coronation durbar in Delhi. It is not, as many people will tell you, the arch through which the king passed; that was a temporary structure of wood and plaster. The permanent item, in Gujarati style, came later.

Statues of Shivaji, the great Maratha leader, and Swami Vivekananda, proponent of the universal gospel, are nearby. This area is a lively and popular evening promenade. The new Taj Hotel, adjoining the old, makes one wonder what Shahjahan might have achieved with stressed concrete.

A short distance from the Gateway of India is the **Prince of Wales Museum***** (10.30am–6pm, closed Monday; Rs2, free Tuesday), which was founded on George V's earlier visit in 1905. The ground floor has been reorganised to great effect. Instead of the previous jumble there are high-quality displays concentrating on Indian and related art, well lit and with a good deal of information. The collection of Sir Ratan Tata, doyen of the Parsee industrial family, is now banished to the top floor; lots of good stuff but minimal information. There is a fine selection of arms and armour, and a first-class natural history section.

Next door is the **Jehangir Art Gallery***** which puts on frequent shows, some of extremely high standard. A roof gallery provides a view of the animated street scene. Lunch in the excellent garden restaurant is a good opportunity to meet young Indian professionals. An impromptu art show sometimes takes place on the railings outside. Over the road is the Sassoon Institute. The Sassoons were Baghdadi Jews who, before establishing themselves as English country gentlemen, handled more of Bombay's commerce than everyone else put together.

The classical style of the **Town Hall**, on Horniman Circle, makes a nice change from Gothic revival; it now houses the Asiatic Society.

Around Churchgate Station at lunchtime you will see something unique to Bombay. Over 120,000 cooked lunches are delivered to office workers every day by dabbawallahs who carry them around in long trays precariously balanced on their heads. This service costs about Rs12 per month.

Heading south down Colaba Causeway on the right is the Pasta Lane area, like London mews before they were renovated and brought up-market. There are all sorts of interesting machinery, including vintage cars in the garages here. Further down on the left is Sassoon Dock, now a fishing harbour. The southernmost part of Colaba is a military area and inaccessible, but **St John's Church**, better known as the Afghan Church, can be visited. This is a more attractive building than the cathedral but, despite the Afghan connection, has less interesting memorials. The bookrests on the seats have notches to hold rifles, a legacy of the Mutiny when unarmed soldiers were slaughtered in church.

Now, prepare yourself for a long and interesting walk. From the Prince of Wales Museum head north along Mahatma Gandhi Road. Not far on the left is **Bombay University**, behind which is the Rajabai clock tower housing the library. This is built in Victorian Gothic and 79m high (not open to the public). The University Hall next door, in French 15th century style, was founded by Sir Cowasjee Readymoney, an oriental Lombard perhaps. Continue north beside the Oval (Pope Paul) Maidan as far as the early English Gothic buildings of the High Court, and return to Gandhi Road. You will come out at Flora Fountain (now Hutatma Chowk), the old business centre of the city.

The **Cathedral of St Thomas****, between Flora Fountain and Horniman Circle, is nothing special architecturally but has many, many superb memorials to the men who

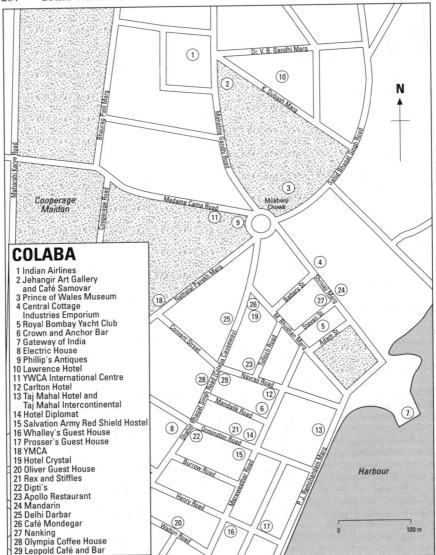

COLABA

1 Indian Airlines
2 Jehangir Art Gallery
  and Café Samovar
3 Prince of Wales Museum
4 Central Cottage
  Industries Emporium
5 Royal Bombay Yacht Club
6 Crown and Anchor Bar
7 Gateway of India
8 Electric House
9 Phillip's Antiques
10 Lawrence Hotel
11 YWCA International Centre
12 Carlton Hotel
13 Taj Mahal Hotel and
   Taj Mahal Intercontinental
14 Hotel Diplomat
15 Salvation Army Red Shield Hostel
16 Whalley's Guest House
17 Prosser's Guest House
18 YMCA
19 Hotel Crystal
20 Oliver Guest House
21 Rex and Stiffles
22 Dipti's
23 Apollo Restaurant
24 Mandarin
25 Delhi Darbar
26 Café Mondegar
27 Nanking
28 Olympia Coffee House
29 Leopold Café and Bar

created British India. A lot of history; pathos too, many proving the dictum that two monsoons were the span of a man's life in Bombay.

Return to Flora Fountain and branch off right up Dr Dadabhai Naoroji Road. The best shops are here and in Gandhi Road, and this leads via a lively street market (much smuggled merchandise) to **Victoria Terminus**. Surely the most striking railway station ever built, it is in Italian Gothic and saw India's first train service as early as 1853. This is now officially Chhatrapati Shivaji Terminus, named after the great

Maratha warlord. Just over the road is another Gothic building housing Bombay Municipal Corporation. Further on is **Crawford Market**** offering foodstuffs, cage birds, souvenirs, aquarium fish, and much more.

Bazaar Bombay

The moment you cross the road to Adbul Rahman Street all Western influence vanishes in the maze of narrow streets. There are hundreds of goldsmiths and jewellers in this area offering high-quality goods very different from the usual tourist tat. Watch out on the left for another covered market, the Javeri Bazaar. Carry on through this fascinating quarter aiming for Patthe Bapuro Marg (still better known as **Falkland Road**). Along here is Bombay's notorious red-light area, with seemingly countless scantily dressed women looking for business, and more inside in the infamous cages. Employ a large minder if you want to take photographs around here. A short detour brings you to **Chor Bazaar**, the thieves' market, which is centred on Mutton Street between Grant Road (Maulana Shaukatali Road) and Sardar Patel Road. This is an antique and junk market, lots of good stuff though mostly repro these days. Eventually you come out at Central Terminus and can take a bus back to Colaba or a train to Churchgate Station. Have a beer in Leopold's, you've earned it.

Further Afield

The energetic can take another walk down Mme Cama Road past the Institute of Science and through the high-rise offices to Back Bay near Nariman Point. From here Marine Drive follows the coast round to the excellent **Aquarium****. This is a long and shadeless walk just as well seen from the top of one of Bombay's red double-decked buses. Believe it or not, there is a fish and chip shop behind the Aquarium! A bit further on is **Chowpatty Beach** with hundreds of bhel puri vendors and masseurs, best in the early evening. Not far from here is the Royal Opera House. You are now coming to Malabar Hill where the rich live, and where a quite modest flat costs a million — in pounds sterling. You can walk up to the **Hanging Gardens**. They are nothing special, but the view across Back Bay is. Enjoy it and a refreshing drink on the terrace of Naaz Restaurant. Don't bother to go along to the five Parsi **Towers of Silence**, there is nothing to see.

Out to the north-west are the **racecourse** and the **Haji Ali Mosque** where, on an island with a causeway to the mainland, there is the tomb of a Muslim saint. New construction has spoiled its pretty silhouette against the sunset, but it's worth seeing.

The **Victoria and Albert Museum**** (10.30am–5pm, closed Wednesday) has an excellent display downstairs on the development of Bombay; many old photos and watercolours and, wonder of wonders, they are quite well captioned. Model soldiers in the multifarious uniforms of the Indian army and ship models add interest. By the museum entrance is the breech of a huge gun of peculiar design. Statues of British worthies, removed from various parts of town, are in a small garden beside the museum; these are in a pretty beat-up state and of no great interest anyway. In the grounds is the **Zoo** (10.30am–5pm, closed Wed). The zoo is averagely horrible, but the gardens are well kept and best seen as such. In the gardens there are more statues and that other symbol of colonialism, a Maxim gun. To quote Belloc's *The Modern Traveller*: 'Whatever happens we have got/The Maxim Gun, and they have not.' Take a suburban train from Victoria Terminus to Byculla, cross over the bridge to the main exit, go straight ahead under the flyover and turn left, about 300m.

Bollywood

Bombay is the centre of India's prolific **film industry**, probably the largest in the world. The Government of India Tourist Office will arrange a visit to a set for you, but if you hang around the Red Shield Hostel in Merewether Road (Tel 241 824) at breakfast time you stand a fair chance of a day's work as an extra. Pay is Rs40–50 (80p–£1/$1.35–1.65) plus overtime and fares. The stars, who are very popular figures, ham outrageously and plots tend towards the implausible, but some of the sets are superb. The author spent a happy day in a huge revolving restaurant that actually went round.

Across the harbour

Across the harbour on **Elephanta Island**** are several cave temples, the main one with some splendid sculptures. The caves are dedicated to Shiva, and the sculpture of Shiva Trimurti (three-headed to depict his aspects as creator, protector, and destroyer) alone justifies the journey. Take a boat from Gateway of India (Rs25 or Rs40 return) noting that the cheaper ones tend to be slow and unreliable. Conducted tours from the ticket office at the top of the steps every half hour from 10.30am–2.30pm, only for holders of Rs40 tickets. Higher up on the island are two British coastal defence guns of 7.5-inch calibre that covered the harbour. A restaurant by the jetty has passable food, beer, and cold drinks. Elephanta is definitely to be avoided at weekends.

Shopping

The various markets in the old part of town have been mentioned already. Most Western style shops are on Colaba Causeway, Shivaji Marg (fixed-price **Cottage Industries Emporium** here), and up Mahatma Gandhi Marg and Naoroji Marg on the way to Victoria Terminus. This is also one long street market. **Phillips Antiques** on Regal Circle is a wonderful place for a browse, as is **The New and Secondhand Bookshop**, 526 Kalbadevi Road (near Metro Cinema), which has a huge stock. More chaotic than Michael Moon's second-hand bookshop, and even more fun! The pharmacy at the Taj Hotel sells sun screen, lip salve, and so on. A funny little shop stands next door but one to Rex/Stiffles Hotels. Worth a look around, they also buy surplus backpacks, etc.

Practical *i*	Government of India Tourist Office facing side
Information	entrance of Churchgate Station, also at airport and

Practical Information *i*   Government of India Tourist Office facing side entrance of Churchgate Station, also at airport and Taj Intercontinental Hotel. They publish a programme of the many **dance performances and concerts** in the city.

Maharashtra Tourism offices at the main rail stations, Central Terminus and Victoria Terminus, and Madame Cama Road (head office; Tel 202 6713). The various city and suburban tours are too rushed to be enjoyable, but the Maharashtra Tourism Development Corporation (MTDC) has some interesting offers. For Rs500–600 you can do a rock-climbing course or a five/six-day jungle safari inclusive of equipment, board and lodging. Pretty basic, one would guess, but excellent value for money. Should also be a good way to meet educated young Indians socially. MTDC hires out tents, backpacks, and other camping equipment if you prefer to make your own way. They also run a deluxe bus to Aurangabad for Ellora and promote **special events** each month ranging from a vintage car rally to cultural performances.

The best book on the history of Bombay is *City of Gold* by Gillian Tindall (Temple Smith). Students of architecture will appreciate *Bombay: The Cities Within* by Sharada Dwivedi and Rahul Mehrotra (India Book House Pvt). This is expensive, but very good, and especially strong on Bombay's wealth of Art Deco buildings.

Local transport

Taxis. There are no cycle rickshaws or scooters in downtown Bombay, only taxis which are quite reasonable (and the drivers usually very good about using the meters).

Bombay Electricity Supply and Transport (BEST) run an extensive and efficient **bus service** which is not too crowded outside rush hours. They publish a guide to these services which incorporates an excellent city map. Ltd (Limited) buses make fewer stops. Popular routes, all from Prince of Wales Museum/Electricity House area (Colaba) are:

70/124 to Bombay Central Terminus
1/1 Ltd/7/103/124 to Bombay Victoria Terminus
124/132/133 to Haji Ali
70/126/132/133 to Churchgate Station
1/1 Ltd/3/6 Ltd to Victoria Gardens
70/124 to racecourse
103/107/123 to Chowpatty
For Goa ferry 1/1 Ltd/3/103/124 to Crawford Market, then 41 to ferry wharf (much easier by taxi).

Other routes include:
42/48 Bombay Central Terminus to ferry wharf
106 Churchgate to Hanging Gardens
123 Churchgate to Aquarium

Suburban trains run from Churchgate to Bombay Central Terminus, Dadar, and Mahalaxmi for racecourse; from Bombay Victoria Terminus to Byculla for Victoria Gardens, on to Dadar, and Neral Junction for Matheran. The Indrail Pass is valid on these services, and there are first class compartments. Main line tickets into Bombay Central Terminus include the trip down to Churchgate.

It's a bit pricey (so bargain hard) but fun to hire a victoria (horse and carriage) in the evening.

Arrival and departure

Air. International (Sahar) and domestic (Santa Cruz) terminals at same airport but quite separate. Bombay is served by many international airlines which have their own offices or representatives in town, details from tourist offices.

Indian Airlines flights all over India. The Indian Airlines office (Tel 202 3031) is on MG Road, but due at some point to move back to its usual base on Nariman Point.

Other domestic airlines (some serving only one or two destinations) include East-West (Tel 643 6678), Jet Airways on Madame Cama Road (Tel 285 5788), and Damania (Tel 610 2545). With the proliferation of airlines it is easier to deal through a travel agent than direct; always check fares though.

The airport terminals are difficult to reach on public transport; best to take the **airline bus** from the Air India/Indian Airlines building on Nariman Point: international (1 hour) Rs27, domestic (45 minutes) Rs20, but allow twice these times morning and evening. Returning to town the bus will drop passengers in Colaba. Official stalls at the airports will fix you up with a black and yellow **taxi** at a fair price (around Rs180; £3.60/$6); beware of stalls offering much more expensive hire cars or 'tourist taxis'.

Trains. Western Railway from Bombay Central Terminus (CT) to Delhi (Rajdhani Express 16¼hrs, others 23hrs or more); Ahmedabad (8hrs) to connect with metre gauge for Rajasthan and Gujarat; Jammu (32hrs). Central Railway from Bombay Victoria Terminus (VT), now officially Mumbai CST, to Delhi (27½hrs); Calcutta

(32½hrs); Secunderabad (14½hrs) for Hyderabad; Madras (31hrs, but from Dadar 24hrs); Vasco da Gama (24hrs) for Goa, change at Miraj.

Tourist quota reservations for Western Railway departures from CT at ground floor of Government of India Tourist Office opposite side entrance of Churchgate Station. Tourist quota reservations for VT departures, from window 22 in the computerised booking centre at VT, can only be made within 24hrs of departure time except for Indrail Pass holders. A few trains also leave from Dadar, check carefully.

Buses. Interstate bus terminal is near Bombay CT.

Ferry. There's a ferry to Goa again but it's Rs1000 (£20/$33)! Still a jetfoil that takes five hours must be better than the old luggers that took 20 and left you savaged by bugs, even if it cost only Rs35 (70p/$1.15). Another disadvantage is that it has to sail so far out to avoid the dhows that you can't see anything. Contact Damania (Tel 610 2525) for bookings.

Arriving in Bombay from abroad

Customs at Bombay Airport, even in Green Channel, is a good introduction to Indian bureaucracy. Your baggage has to be X-rayed (and probably searched) and a chit signed and stamped. Change money before leaving the arrivals hall. One person can do this while another deals with the baggage. Just outside the hall are stalls for booking the airport bus into town and tourist taxis (Rs350 upwards; £7/$11.65). These are more comfortable than the black and yellow cabs, but the latter are only half the price. Book a black and yellow cab at a stall just outside the building; **do not** get into a cab without doing so beforehand. Watch your baggage like a hawk, although this is not always easy when you are tired and distracted.

Leaving Bombay for abroad

See above for transport to the airport, and allow plenty of time. Pay the Rs300 (£6/$10) departure tax before attempting to check in.

Accommodation The influx of foreign businessmen is forcing up hotel prices in Bombay at a furious pace. Expect to pay even more than shown here. The STD code for Bombay is 022.

Colaba/Gateway of India area:

Hotel Diplomat, Merewether Road. Tel 202 1661. SWB A/C Rs700 (£14/$23.35) DWB A/C Rs900. Rest. Bar. Comfortable. May seem overpriced for what it is, but so is everywhere else in Bombay.

Whalley's Guest House, Merewether Road. Tel 221 802. SR Rs300 DR Rs400 DWB Rs600. Most rooms light and airy.

YWCA International Centre, Madame Cama Road. Tel 202 5053. SWB Rs300 DWB Rs585. Prices include morning tea, breakfast, and buffet dinner. Couples accepted, but not men on their own. Very good but little chance of getting in without a reservation.

Hotel Crystal, Colaba Causeway opposite Delhi Durbar. Tel 202 0673. SR Rs250 DR Rs350 DWB Rs650. Not for claustrophobes, but you'll see far worse.

Carlton Hotel, Merewether Road. Tel 202 0642. SR Rs150 (£3/$5) DR Rs250. Better than it used to be.

Stiffles Hotel and *Rex Hotel*, Ormiston Road. Tel 202 1518. There is a threat to upgrade both these old favourites (they share a building). The only thing to go up will be the prices, if we know anything about it.

Prosser Boarding House, Henry Road. Tel 241 715. SR Rs200 DR Rs300.

Red Shield Hostel (Salvation Army), Merewether Road. Tel 241 824. DWB Rs300 (full-board) DWB A/C Rs400 (full-board) Dorm Rs70 (bed and breakfast)/Rs100 (full-board). Easily the best value for money in Bombay, consequently hard to get in. Beds are allocated at 10am, but usually you need to be in the queue long before that.

Hotel Sampsons, Strand Road, said to be excellent value, around DWB Rs450.

Lawrence Hotel, Dubhash Marg, behind PoW Museum. Tel 243 618. SR Rs125 DR Rs250.

Also a *YMCA*, Parikh (Wodehouse) Road. Tel 202 0079.

Avoid *Suba Guest House* on Battery Street.

Churchgate/Marine Drive area:

Chateau Windsor Guest House, 86 Veer Nariman Road. Tel 204 3376. SR Rs575 DR Rs700 DWB Rs950 plus 10% tax and 5% SC. Highly rated by travellers.

Near Central Terminus:

YMCA International House, YMCA Road (500m from station). Tel 370 0601. Nice rooms but not cheap; Rs300 (£6/$10) or more.

Eating and Drinking

Colaba/Gateway of India area:

Nanking, Shivaji Marg. Chi. Exp. See Mandarin.

Mandarin, Shivaji Marg. Chi. Exp. Both these places are excellent. Except for a few places in Calcutta and very expensive hotel restaurants this is the only really authentic Chinese food in India.

Samovar, in Jahangir Art Gallery (open 10.30am–5.30pm). Cheap/Mod. Beer. Lively garden restaurant with friendly atmosphere. Good place for conversation with well educated young Indians. Good food, too. Highly recommended.

Olympia Coffee House, Colaba Causeway. Very cheap but good food (non-veg) in traditional Muslim restaurant. Do not expect to take your time at the table.

Appollo, Navroji Road. Ind. Cheap.

Leopold's Café, Colaba Causeway. Ind/Chi/Cont. Cheap/Mod. Bar. Large portions of excellent food. Fresh juices. The kind of marvellous 'colonial' place you would expect to find all over India, but don't because the English always preferred their clubs. Enjoy a cold beer and watch the world go by.

Dipti's, Ormiston Road, is just a hole in the wall, but has been famous for years for its fruit juices and lassi.

Many, many more restaurants of all kinds in this area including quite good Western fast food.

Churchgate/Marine Drive area:

Gaylord, Churchgate Street (near station). Smart *Terrace* for snacks (Rs40–80) and drinks (lassi Rs16 and beer Rs34). A/C restaurant inside. Exp. Ind/Cont. Bar. Most dishes Rs65–85, lobster Rs220.

Further afield:

The following three restaurants are off the tourist trail and frequented by not-so-rich Bombay-wallahs who take their food seriously:

Noor Mohammedi Hotel, Bhendi Bazaar. Excellent cheap Muslim food including delicacies not to be found elsewhere.

Friends Union Joshi Club, 381/A Kalbadevi Road (opposite Khad Bazaar) is reputed to do the biggest and best thali in the world (Rs20 plus Rs7 for dessert). Both this and Noor Mohammedi in Muslim part of town north of Crawford Market.

Brost Hyderabadi, SV Road, Bandra. Excellent Deccani Muslim food at Mod/Exp (just) prices, but is best known for its Kentucky Fried Chicken (Rs45). Most of the way to the airport, probably only makes sense if you are staying in Juhu (eccentric) or catching a late flight.

 **Excursions**

NORTH OF BOMBAY

Karnala

This small bird sanctuary is home to rare residents and attracts many winter migrants. Over 150 species have been spotted here.

Arrival and departure. By bus (70km) from Bombay. Nearest station is Panvel (12km) on line from Bombay VT.

Accommodation. Forest Rest Houses to be booked through the Forest Office in Thana.

Bassein

Bassein (now Vasai) was the richest of the Portuguese settlements in India. Already in decline it was plundered by the Marathas in 1739, and taken over by the British in 1780. The fort is intact and there are the ruins of many churches, but the local fishing village may well be of more interest.

The village of Sopara, near Vasai Road station, has been identified with the Biblical Ophir.

Arrival and departure. Vasai Road (the nearest station) is 1¼ hours from Bombay Central on the main line to Delhi. Expresses do not stop, only slow passenger trains. Share scooter rickshaws run from station to fort.

Accommodation. A basic government rest house.

Nasik

Nasik is a major pilgrimage town reputed to have 2000 temples. The Godavari river is the holiest in southern India, and the great **Kumbh Mela** festival takes place here every 12 years.

Arrival and departure. Nasik Road station (8km from the city) is on the Bombay VT (4hrs)–Delhi railway.

Accommodation. Wide range of hotels.

SOUTH OF BOMBAY

Maharashtra Tourism is developing a number of **beach resorts**, some of them around old sea forts of the Shivaji era. One of these is **Murud**, from which you can visit the island fort and palace of Janjira. Janjira was the fief of the Sidis, a Muslim dynasty whose piratical activities were a thorn in the flesh of Shivaji and just about everyone else. They held off the Marathas and occupied the palace until just a few years ago. The beach is good and deserted.

Information. Full details from the MTDC office on Madame Cama Road in Bombay.

Arrival and departure. Bus from main bus-stand near Bombay Central Terminus.

Accommodation. *Murud Beach Resort.* Tel 278. Rest. Simple but adequate.

The Konkan Railway. As long ago as 1880 a railway was planned down the west coast of India to link Bombay with Mangalore. The difficult terrain, especially the numerous creeks and mountain ridges, put the project beyond existing technology and finance. The project was revived in the 1960s but interest soon waned, and no more than 100km of track was laid. In the mid-80s it was decided to have a serious

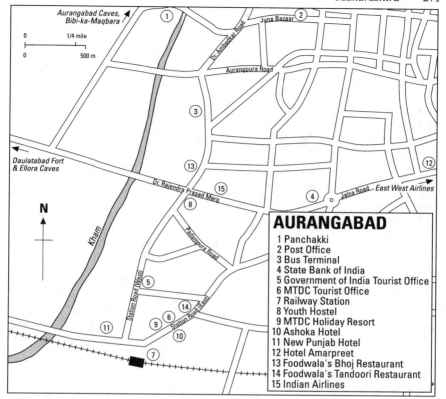

AURANGABAD

1 Panchakki
2 Post Office
3 Bus Terminal
4 State Bank of India
5 Government of India Tourist Office
6 MTDC Tourist Office
7 Railway Station
8 Youth Hostel
9 MTDC Holiday Resort
10 Ashoka Hotel
11 New Punjab Hotel
12 Hotel Amarpreet
13 Foodwala's Bhoj Restaurant
14 Foodwala's Tandoori Restaurant
15 Indian Airlines

go at filling the remaining 760km gap. A development corporation, independent of the railway ministry, was set up, and the $800 million financing, a quarter put up by the states the railway serves, was arranged. This was a huge project — well over 2000 bridges had to be built — and was done entirely out of Indian resources. Some novel ideas were adopted; all the bridge sections, for instance, are standardised. 11% of the line is in tunnels, another novelty as there are few other tunnels on Indian railways.

The line should be completely open by the time this book is published and will greatly reduce travel times, especially from Bombay to Goa. Fares will be 40% higher than elsewhere on Indian Railways to recoup the huge investment.

AURANGABAD

Aurangabad is a useful base for exploring the Ajanta and Ellora caves; it derives its name from Aurangzeb who made his capital here during his efforts to subjugate the South. The town itself is pleasant if rather uninteresting (and peculiarly spread out), but a couple of places on the outskirts are worth seeing.

The **panchakki*** (water mill) was the ashram of Chishti Sufis who provided a place of refuge for orphans, fakirs, and other destitutes. The millstones, driven by an iron-bladed turbine below, ground wheat and generated income for these people. The water comes from 6km away in an underground channel, a form of supply common in Afghanistan, very rare in India. The water also feeds a cascade, and the niches below this would have held lamps behind coloured glass. Behind the mosque is the dargah, an attractive late Mughal building containing two tombs, one of Aurangzeb's guru and the other of his nephew, both Chishti saints from Bokhara in what was formerly Soviet Uzbekistan.

Between the panchakki and the Bibi-ka-Maqbara you pass a section of the old **city walls.**

Oddly enough, given his attitude to Shahjahan's expenditure on the Taj Mahal, Aurangzeb allowed his son Azam Shah to raise a great tomb for his mother the Begum Rabia Durani, Aurangzeb's first wife. The **Bibi-ka-Maqbara***** was built in 1660 and, unlike the Taj, an inscription in the gateway gives the name of the architect as well as the precise cost.

The gatehouse was painted in simulation of the inlay work on earlier tombs. The herringbone pattern in red and white on the minarets forming the corners is like that on the gatehouse of the Taj. The design of the tomb is clumsy by comparison with the Taj Mahal, and construction was done on the cheap, mostly of brick and ordinary stone covered with chunam. This is nevertheless a most imposing building with some very fine detailing, especially the marble screen around the grave. The design is unusual in that the crypt is open rather than having a roof and a replica tombstone above. The grave with its earth top is now, as in so many places, covered with brightly coloured shrouds. This tomb thus obeys the letter rather than the spirit of the injunction that there should be nothing but earth over a Muslim grave.

This tomb is unique in having two mosques, one on the platform and the other where you would expect to find it in the western wall of the garden. The latter is worth a look, more of the decoration having survived. The mosque on the platform must have been an afterthought; it is very unsightly, and the platform has had to be buttressed to support it.

In the traffic circle in front of the gatehouse is a number of tombs. Most are Muslim, but in a square enclosure are some Christian ones, mainly of soldiers in the army of the East India Company and also one in the service of the Nizam of Hyderabad. Bengal NI on one of the stones means Bengal Native Infantry, that is one of the regiments of Indian soldiers raised by the British East India Company.

The nine small **cave temples** are of minimal interest, especially as Ellora is so close, though the boddhisatva in Cave 7 is absolutely marvellous.

Information. Government of India Tourist Office (Tel 31217) 300m from station. Conducted tours of Ellora including Daulatabad and Khuldabad, and also Ajanta.

Ajanta, Ellora and Aurangabad: An Appreciation by TV Pathy, available locally, is very detailed.

Arrival and departure. Airport (10km from city). On Indian Airlines Bombay–Udaipur–Jaipur–Delhi route. Indian Airlines office on Dr Rajendra Prasad Road (Tel 24864). East-West Airlines (Tel 29990) flies to Bombay.

By rail from Manmad (2¾hrs) which is on Bombay VT (5¾hrs)–Delhi (18hrs) line.

Deluxe bus from Bombay operated by MTDC from their office on Madame Cama Road; they also do a three-day package (from Rs1210; around £24/$40) that sounds a bit like an assault course. Bus from Jalgaon, also on Bombay VT (8¾hrs)–Delhi (15½hrs) line; see Ajanta. Buses to Ellora, which call at Daulatabad and Khuldabad. Bus-stand is 2.5km from station, bus, tonga (Rs3), or auto-rickshaw between the two.

The stall of the Ajanta Meter Taxi Union outside the bus-stand offers Ellora sight-seeing for five people at Rs250 (£5/$8.35); that allows 5hrs after which Rs20 per hour is added. Also Ajanta Rs450, Paitan Rs250, and Pune Rs600 for five seats. They will get a group together; you pay pro rata for your seat.

Accommodation (STD Code 02432)

Hotel Amarpreet, Nehru Marg. Tel 24615. SWB Rs375 DWB Rs425 SWB A/C Rs425 DWB A/C Rs525. Rest (excellent). Bar. 24-hour coffee shop.

MTDC Holiday Resort, Station Road. Tel 34259. SWB/DWB Rs200. Rest (Kailash). Bar. Spacious clean rooms, nice garden.

New Punjab Hotel, Station Road. Tel 26391. DR Rs80 DWB Rs250 DWB A/C Rs350. Rest. Bar.

Ashoka Hotel, Station Road. DR Rs85 DWB Rs110.

Youth Hostel, Station Road. Tel 29801. Dorm Rs20 for members and student card holders, otherwise Rs30. Bedding and mosquito nets.

Eating and drinking

Kailash, Holiday Resort. Ind/Chi. Mod/Exp. Very good.

Foodwala's Tandoori, Station Road. Mughal/Deccani. Mod/Exp.

Foodwala's Bhoj, Dr Ambedkar Road. Ind. Veg. Mod. Both these restaurants are excellent.

Cheap restaurants near the station.

Excursions  Daulatabad

In 1338, long before Aurangabad was founded, Muhammed Tughlaq, one of the Delhi sultans, decided to make his capital at **Daulatabad***. The idea found no favour with his subjects, many thousands of whom died on the way from Delhi. Tughlaq eventually lost interest, and more died on the march back to Delhi. Since limited use by the Mughals, the place has been deserted.

The entry to the fort through multiple walls and barbicans indicates the strength of its defences. The slopes of the hill were carved away to make it even more formidable.

The **Chand Minar**, a 65m (213ft) high minaret, was built in 1435 to celebrate the capture of the place by another Muslim king. Not as pretty as the Qutb Minar but near enough as high, and you're allowed to climb all the way to the top.

The **mosque** opposite is an odd combination. The main hall is constructed on the usual Hindu pillar and lintel system, and most bays are roofed in the traditional fashion by overlapping layers of stone, yet in the centre is a proper dome. The central mihrab, which probably started as the doorway to a temple sanctum, has reverted to a Hindu shrine. Note the diamond and chequer design on the lintels; there is a similar piece in the steps up to the minar.

The **Chini Mahal**, or China Palace, on the way up, is so-named from its blue and white tiling. The circular bastion nearby has a magnificent bronze gun on top. Passing through a passage hewn from solid rock, you enter a courtyard. This was gated, and the doorway leading up is one of the earlier Hindu parts of the fort (ignore the long flight of steps up, this is modern and forms the exit). Above the foot of the steps inside is a port from which boiling oil and the like could be poured on invaders. At the top of the steps is part of the iron shutters on top of which a large fire was lit to exhaust all air from the tunnel. Give one of the torch men his few rupees, and he'll explain all the intricacies of this unique defensive system.

At the top of the hill are Mughal pavilions and a citadel surmounted by another huge cannon. Note the reservoirs here and elsewhere.

Arrival and departure. Daulatabad is 15km/9.5 miles from Aurangabad on the bus route to Ellora.

Accommodation. None.

Khuldabad

Khuldabad (The Heavenly Abode) is a walled village which has long attracted holy men. In one corner of the courtyard of a domed tomb is the **grave of Aurangzeb***. No hypocrite, his tomb is modest in the extreme and open to the elements. Even the marble screen around the tomb is a modern addition, put there by one of the Nizams of Hyderabad. The domed tomb, which belongs to a saint from Shiraz in Iran, is worth a quick look. The chain hanging over the cenotaph is of ostrich eggs, and in one corner is a complete Koran in minute writing on a sheet of paper little bigger than A4. An enclosure in an adjacent corner to Aurangzeb's has three tombstones, those of Azam Shah who built the Bibi-ka-Maqbara, his wife, and another saint.

Arrival and departure. 26km/16 miles from Aurangabad and 4km/2.5 miles from Ellora. The bus-stand at Khuldabad is a good kilometre out of town, but some tempos still pass through. Not all Aurangabad–Ellora buses call at the bus-stand; if necessary get off at the T-junction.

Accommodation. *Government Rest House.*

Eating and drinking. Extremely limited.

Pitalkhora

The 13 Buddhist cave temples here are the oldest in India (2nd century BC to second century AD). Some of the murals have survived.

Arrival and departure. Bus or share taxi (78km/49 miles) from Aurangabad.

Accommodation. *Government Rest House,* contact Executive Engineer in Aurangabad.

ELLORA

Ellora has the largest collection of cave temples in India, unmatched for beauty or scale. An alliance with the Guptas introduced the dominant local dynasty in the sixth century, the Chalukyas of Badami, to the wonders of India's Golden Age. They and the succeeding Rashtrakutas used this vision to the full at Ajanta and Ellora. At the latter 34 temples were excavated from the soft stone of the Sahyadri Hills.

The Buddhist cave temples

Start at the southern end with the **Buddhist caves*** and work your way north, this way you see things roughly in chronological order. The first 12 caves are Buddhist in two forms. The viharas are monasteries with living cells and the one chaitya is a chapel. All were constructed between AD550 and AD750.

Cave 1 is a very simple monastery with seven completed cells and one incomplete. Apparently the only pillars were three in front which have disappeared. **Cave 2** is one of the latest of the Buddhist monasteries dateable to the mid-eighth century AD, and the similarity of the pillars to those of Elephanta is obvious. The usual cells at the sides are replaced by galleries each with a number of seated Buddhas. The figures on either side of the shrine are boddhisatvas. **Caves 3 and 4** are incomplete, and the front of 4 has collapsed. The remaining pillars exhibit the beginning of the carving process.

Cave 5 is very large and was probably intended as a meeting place for all the monks, perhaps as a place of instruction or even as a dining hall. Looking closely at the pillars you can see the various stages of carving; some have been marked out, some roughly cut, and others are more or less complete. Buddha is in the dharmashankra mutra (teaching posture).

Cave 6 is very fine despite most of the front portion having collapsed. On the left of the shrine is a boddhisatva with a small image of the seated Buddha in his fancy hair-do. On the right side wall is a figure variously identified as Mayuri or Saraswati, respectively the Buddhist and Hindu goddesses of learning. To the left of the main figure is a peacock fanning its tail and, below that, what appears to be a typist at work. The main figure and the subsidiary ones in the shrine are very fine indeed. Cells lead off the two side chapels.

A passageway runs from Cave 6 to Cave 9. The facade above this has a number of chaitya symbols like the Greek capital omega, below that is a frieze of seated Buddhas. **Cave 7** is a very plain vihara hall and cells. **Cave 8** is the only vihara at Ellora having an ambulatory around the shrine.

Cave 10 is the only chaitya or chapel cave at Ellora. The arch is typical of a late chaitya; instead of the pure omega shape there are three openings below and a small window above. The interior is dominated by a grand statue of Buddha in front of the huge dagoba (dome). Small images of Buddha continue round the back of the dagoba, which is much more complicated than usual. A frieze of figures runs above the pillars. Steps lead up to the gallery. The frieze running around the gallery consists of loving couples, and each of the roof ribs appears to be supported by a naga figure hooded by cobras. The doorway to the left of the main entrance has a design like a Greek key cut round the top half of it, and in the centre of the lintel is something like a double Staffordshire knot, possibly unique in India.

Caves 11 and 12 are more impressive for their size than anything else. The Hindu caves were already under construction, and there seems to have been an effort to match their scale. Cave 11 has a fine sanctuary on the first floor level and a very large hall at the top. Steps lead up from the right-hand side of the ground floor gallery of Cave 12 past a side chapel with a huge lotus carved in the ceiling. The monks must have been going soft when this cave was cut; the cells have a stone bed and pillow instead of just a plain floor. The top floor is very impressive; the figure in the sanctuary is being restored at present. On either side of that are half a dozen female figures wearing haloes and nothing much else, though they appear to have a brahminical thread from left shoulder to waist. Rows and rows of Buddhas adorn the walls on either side of the shrine ante-chamber. The top floor of 12 is a magnificent hall by any standards; imagine how it looked when all the figures were painted. In a few places are remains of the ceiling plaster and faint traces of the painted designs.

Cave 13 is a small store room.

The Hindu cave temples

North of here are the **Hindu caves*****, construction of which started around AD600 and was continued until AD875. All these caves are dedicated to Shiva, and it follows that most of the figures in them are different forms of him, though avatars of Vishnu also appear. In **Cave 14** the first figure on the left as you enter is Durga, who has her foot on a lion. The trident in her hand is a common symbol of Shiva. The halo has carried over from the Buddhist caves and can be seen behind Durga's head. Similarly chaityas appear on the pilasters separating this from the following panels. Next but one to Durga is the Varaha (boar) avatar of Vishnu. The shrine, from which the lingam is missing, is flanked by figures of the goddesses Ganga and Yamuna. Two figures have umbrellas over them, another Buddhist convention. To the right of the shrine is a panel of the seven mother goddesses (Saptamatrikas) with their children. With them is Ganesh and also Kala and Kali, the male and female forms of death. The emblem of each goddess — dog, boar, elephant, and so on — is on the pedestal below. Moving towards the front other panels show a multi-headed Ravanna shaking Mount Kailash. Then comes Shiva dancing, followed by Shiva and Parvati playing dice over the figure of a Brahma bull, and finally one of Parvati killing a buffalo demon which is also being attacked by a lion.

Cave 15 has superb sculpture on the first-floor level. Starting from the left you have Shiva spearing a demon, then an absolutely astonishing one of him dancing. The way the sculptor has captured the sense of rhythm is matched only by South Indian bronzes of this subject. Shiva and Parvati are seen first playing dice then at their marriage. Hard to see in the corner is a multi-armed and multi-headed Ravanna shaking Mount Kailash. On the facing walls of the shrine ante-chamber are figures of Ganesh and his brother Kartikkeya the god of war (both sons of Shiva and Parvati). To the right of the shrine ante-chamber Shiva can be seen emerging from a lingam. On one side of him is the four-headed Brahma and on the other Vishnu, both paying homage to him, according with the dominant status of Shiva when these caves were cut. Sculptures down the right-hand wall depict various aspects of Shiva and stories of Krishna. Most obvious is the Varaha avatar, also Narasimha (the man-lion). On the pillars and ceiling on this side are remains of plaster and painting. The mandapa in the courtyard is clearly a precursor of the Kailasha Temple next door, the sculpture on top best seen from the upper level. Two elephants flank the steps. This cave may well have started out as a Buddhist one; it is certainly very similar in pattern to Caves 11 and 12, it contains Buddhist figures, and chaitya symbols are on the mandapa.

A temple carved from solid rock

Everything at Ellora is surpassed by the **Kailasha Temple*****. Imagine starting to carve down into solid rock fashioning the outside of a large and ornate temple as you go, and then hollowing out the interior. Quite a large area around the temple had also to be cleared, this time leaving behind pillars and two elephants. In addition complex caves were cut in the rock faces around the temple. All this involved the removal of about 200,000 tonnes of material over a 30-year period, all done by hand. It really is impossible to give a detailed description of this place. The thing is to spend plenty of time here and have a good look round while we point out a few details which will help you to understand and enjoy it.

Facing the entrance is Gajalaxmi (the goddess of wealth) sitting on a lotus in a pond, elephants pouring water over her in devotion. This symbolises the prosperity and stability necessary for the undertaking of a project of this magnitude. But entering the Kailasha Temple for the first time forget about this book for a moment (and the screaming hordes) and either walk slowly around or find a quiet corner to contemplate the scale of the structure. It is hard to accept that it was simply carved out of the hillside.

The main shrine has a yoni-lingam and in the ceiling above it a finely carved lotus. The yoni around the lingam functioned as a basin for the water used to wash it, and a drain leads outside to another basin. Outside the style of the tower over the main shrine is Dravidian, and this is mirrored by the five subsidiary shrines around and behind it. A certain amount of the incised and painted plaster has survived on the walls and ceilings. A fragment in the porch seems to have depicted Shiva dancing — a pair of legs can be made out, and also the head of an elephant. Under the bridge linking the main part of the temple and the mandapa are two great sculptures, one of Shiva killing an elephant demon, and the other of him in contemplative pose as Mahayogi.

On the north side of the enclosure is the Lankesvara Hall, which constitutes a cave temple in itself, and despite being overshadowed by the Kailasha is probably the finest in India. Loving couples adorn the balustrade around the hall. This hall contains the finest carving and sculpture of any cave temple, best of all being Shiva dancing to the right of the shrine. Anywhere else this temple would be a wonder in its own right, here it is just a rather minor ancillary to the Kailasha. Two rather casual-looking gods either side of the Nandi look as if they have just put in a hard stint rock-cutting.

A cloister and attendant sculpture are cut in the rock face behind the temple. An unusual subject in the northern section is a lingam surrounded by nine heads; these are the spares of Ravanna, seen sitting below, who has cut them off as an offering to Shiva. In the centre of the eastern wall is a trio of figures representing Shiva (hands together in namaste), Vishnu, and the four-headed Brahma, rarely depicted together in this way despite constituting the Hindu trinity. On the south side is the demon king Ravanna attempting to lift a lingam, and next to that Narasimha, the man-lion incarnation of Vishnu tearing someone open. After that Vishnu reclines on a serpent, Krishna lifts the mountain at Goverdhan, and finally comes Annapurna, the goddess of food, whose name graces dingy restaurants all over India.

At the foot of the steps leading down from the south cloister is a huge carving, now rather eroded, of a multi-armed Ravanna shaking the holy mountain of Kailasha. Shiva, whose retreat it is, applies the pressure of just one toe, crushing him and locking him in forever. To the left of this are eight bands of frieze representing the Ramayana epic in which Hanuman plays a prominent role. The corresponding scenes on the other side of the plinth depict events in the life of Krishna and the Mahabharata.

Climb the steps to the left of the Kailasha Temple for an overall view. Apart from giving a better idea of the scale, this also reveals a lot of detail invisible from ground level.

More Hindu caves

Cave 17 is notable only for the fine sculpture of Ganesh apparently tucking in to a bowl of cherries. **Caves 18, 19, and 20** are incomplete.

Cave 21 has some of the finest sculpture of all. In front of it is a screen wall with pillars and bracket figures. In the side chapel to the right on entry the main scene is of the seven elegantly coiffed Saptamatrikas with their children flanked on the left by Shiva and on the right by Ganesh. The panel to the left is Shiva dancing and to the right a gruesome one of Kali and Kala. In the side chapel opposite is the wedding of Shiva and Parvati with the guests carrying presents. In the shrine antechamber Ravanna shakes Kailasha. On the right of the antechamber is a marvellous deep relief of Shiva and Parvati playing dice and, as the story goes, squabbling over who is winning. A maidservant fans them. The dwarapalas beside the door of the shrine and the detailing around it are worth study.

Cave 22 is of no interest. **Cave 23**, above Cave 24, has several small shrines, one with a polished lingam and on the wall behind a trimurti, the Hindu trinity. **Cave 24** comprises a small Shiva shrine and is of no interest. The same applies to the unnumbered caves above Cave 24.

Follow the lower of the two paths from Cave 24, taking care on the slippery wet rocks. **Cave 25** is large and plain. The only interest is the ceiling in front of the sanctum which depicts the seven-horse chariot of Surya the sun god. **Caves 26 and 27** are of no interest. **Cave 28** is tiny and spectacularly located behind a waterfall. Inside the front wall is an eight-armed Durga.

Cave 29 is the most ambitious apart from Kailasha. In effect this is a halfway house between a conventional cave temple and one separated from the parent rock like the Kailasha. The openings on either side are a move towards the latter. The sculpture follows the usual forms, and you will recognise the scenes from earlier descriptions. The sculpture around the shrine is large but somehow lacks the finesse of that in other temples.

The Jain cave temples

The **Jain caves**** (AD800–1000) are as complexly carved as one would expect. **Cave**

31 is very small and really only an adjunct to **Cave 32**, which borrows a lot of ideas from the Kailasha temple. In the courtyard are a Dravidian-style temple with a four-faced Mahavira, a pillar again with a four-faced Jain figure, and an elephant. The main hall at the lower level is unfinished and stinks of bats. The floor above is a very different matter indeed. Climbing the steep stairs the figure on an elephant is Matunga, the Jain god of wealth; facing that Sidaika the goddess of generosity sits on a lion. These figures are not as well preserved as smaller ones of the same subjects in one of the side chapels on the ground floor.

Quite a bit of the ceiling painting has survived in the porch above these two figures. To the right of the shrine is Gomateswara, the figure depicted at Sravana-Belgola. Vines twine around his legs, a common Jain symbol, also a scorpion and at his feet a deer. The matching figure is Parsvanatha shaded by cobras. At the feet of the female to the left are what appear to be two mermaids. The figure in the sanctum is Mahavira. Take a good look at the door surrounds which have traces of painting and rich decoration. The ceiling of the hall has a colossal lotus. In the side chapels just below this level quite a lot of ceiling painting has survived in front of the sanctum, faded but clearly discernible. From the other side chapel a passage leads to **Cave 33**, which is in most respects similar to 32. Substantial traces of ceiling painting survive in the main hall at first-floor level and wall paintings as well. Not that that discourages the locals from scratching their names on it. The lower hall is badly eroded. From a side chapel of Cave 33 a passage leads to **Cave 34**.

Steps beside 31 lead up to a small and unfinished temple, and the path continues to Cave 30 which is called Chhota Kailasha (Little Kailash) by the locals. This is of interest only because it is unfinished, allowing the successive stages of cutting to be seen.

Also at Ellora is the **Grishneshwar Temple**, one of 12 jyotirlingas, or most sacred Shiva shrines.

Practical Information *i*

Avoid Ajanta and Ellora at weekends and public holidays.

Arrival and departure. Bus, taxi, or tempo from Aurangabad (29km/18 miles). Buses from Ellora to Aurangabad are very erratic. Watch out for tempos (green or blue Matadors) or jeeps as an alternative, and do not spurn the offer of a lift in the back of a lorry!

Accommodation
Hotel Kailash. Tel 02347 41063. Rest. Bar. Range of good accommodation from cheap to expensive.
Vijay's Rock Art Gallery and Restaurant. Basic easy-going place.

Eating and drinking. Maharashtra Tourism has a good inexpensive restaurant and bar, and there are even cheaper places by the bus-stand.

AJANTA

The 29 Buddhist cave temples at Ajanta were forgotten for many centuries until a British hunting party by chance found them in 1819. At the time of discovery their murals were in a fine state of preservation, but remain now in only four caves. To prevent further deterioration illumination is low and flash photography is banned. Entry to these caves — Nos 1, 2, 16 and 17 — is limited to guided groups.

The paintings in **Cave 1** date from the sixth or seventh century AD. Most are in such poor condition, and the lighting is so dim, that even with a guide it is next to impossible to make out what they represent. Three concurrent commentaries echo around, and all you get is a headache.

Cave 2 (mid-seventh century AD) is slightly better, notably the ceilings in front of the sanctum. There are also extensive remains of painting in the porch where you can at least see it properly.

Cave 9 is a small chaitya with a little painting, otherwise quite plain. **Cave 10** is a much larger chaitya with a huge dagoba. A certain amount of painting from the second century BC is now protected behind glass — pity they didn't put it up before the Indians scratched their names on it.

Cave 12 is monastic, an open hall with just chaitya symbols around the walls and stone beds in the cells. Elephants flank the stairs up to the gallery leading to the rest of the cave.

Cave 16 has only fragments of painting. **Cave 17** is probably the best preserved of the lot which is not saying much.

Cave 19 (fifth century AD) is a small chaitya with an ornate dagoba. The ribbed roof imitates wooden beams. Fine columns, interesting images above them, and a good frieze above that. On the pair of pillars in front of the shrine are the feet of the dwarapalas. The exterior is very attractive, having yakshas on either side of the window and fine figures of Buddha flanking the door. On the left as you face it is a very fine sculpture of the Nagaraja with cobra hood.

Cave 23 is notable only for the quality of the lotus medallions on one of the pilasters. Inside is a lovely relief of a galloping horse. Though incomplete the hall obviously would have been large and shows the method of excavation.

Cave 26 is the largest of the chaityas. The porch has disappeared, but the wealth of statuary makes up for that. Inside on the left is a marvellous figure of the ailing Buddha attended by grieving disciples. The panel next to this shows the temptation of Buddha by Mara. Buddha sits under a bo tree, and below him are Mara's daughters in seductive poses. Mara, seated on an elephant in the top left corner, directs operations and all around the main figure is a host of demons and temptations. Mara appears again in the bottom right corner looking pretty fed up because his ruse has failed. The pillars and the entablature above them are well carved.

From the path below the caves you can walk up the valley through a small forest park where light refreshments are available. Cross the footbridge and turn right for a view of the pool and waterfall at the head of the valley. The path on this side of the river leads back to the car park, though there is no bridge. No problem as long as the water is low. A vantage point high above here gives the best view of the valley and caves.

Although Ajanta is always mentioned in the same breath as Ellora it is questionable whether it is worth visiting. The location is grand with the temple and monastery caves in a sweeping cliff over the river, but the few remaining murals scarcely justify the considerable effort of getting there. Otherwise there is nothing you cannot see better and more easily at Ellora.

Information. Avoid Ajanta and Ellora at weekends and public holidays.

Arrival and departure. From Jalgaon on Delhi (20hrs)–Bombay VT (7½hrs) line. From Jalgaon station (where there is a tourist information counter on the platform) take a scooter rickshaw from station to bus-stand, and then bus to caves (2hrs). Bus from Aurangabad to Ajanta (2½hrs). The caves are 4km from the main road, make sure your bus calls at the caves or you will have to walk.

See under Aurangabad for conducted tours and taxis.

Accommodation

Travellers Lodge (MTDC), at bus-stand by caves. Tel 426. SR Rs100 DR Rs150. Rest now run by Foodwala of Aurangabad and better than it was, but far from wonderful. Beer.

Forest Rest House (800m from caves). Quiet and well located.

MTDC Holiday Resort, Fardapur (5km from caves, regular buses). Tel 430. Rest. Bar. Dorm. Good place.

Jalgaon

Jalgaon is simply a staging post on the way to or from Ajanta and Ellora.

Information. Tourist information on the railway station.

Arrival and departure. On Delhi (20hrs)–Bombay VT (7½hrs) and Bombay VT–Calcutta (30hrs) lines. Also Ahmedabad (10hrs) and Hyderabad (26¼hrs). From Khandwa Junction (3hrs) on the way to Delhi a metre gauge line runs north to Indore, then Chittaurgarh and the rest of Rajasthan.

Buses to Ajanta (2hrs) and Aurangabad (4½hrs). Tonga or scooter rickshaw between station and bus-stand.

Accommodation

Hotel Plaza, Station Road (100m from station). Tel 24854. SWB Rs100 DWB Rs150.

Hotel Tourist Resort, 300m from station. Tel 25192. Rest. SWB Rs135 DWB Rs175.

Eating and drinking

Hotel Anjali, near station. Gujarati veg. Cheap/Mod. Bar.

Excursions

BOMBAY TO THE DECCAN

The railway line from Bombay up the Western Ghats is quite spectacular. The line snakes around deep ravines and wooded hills with a gradient of up to 1:37. At one point you can see an old reversing station, used before the present easier alignment was made. This was the first line in India to be electrified, way back in the 1920s. Even if you are not calling at any points *en route* arrange to make this journey in daylight.

Matheran

Matheran is a pleasant wooded hill resort within easy reach of Bombay; it is a good place to spend those frustrating days waiting for your plane. Very peaceful, there are no cars, only horses and man-pulled rickshaws, and half the fun is in getting there. While there is now a road up to Matheran the narrow gauge railway, which takes two hours to travel 20km and climbs nearly 800m in the process, is less nerve-wracking and lets you enjoy the tremendous views. One of the odd Koppel and Orenstein steam locos (the front and rear axles floated to cope with the tight curves) is preserved in Matheran station.

Horses are an expensive way of getting around and, unless you are very lucky, tottering old wrecks reluctant to depart from their usual route. Better just to walk round the perimeter path. There seems to be a good ridge walk south from Garbutt Point, and certainly a path along the first half-mile or so, which is a fairly wide plateau. Quite how you would get from the other end to Neral or vice versa is another matter. We are told that this should not be attempted solo or by women on their own — natives can be unfriendly.

Avoid Matheran at weekends and check before visiting that it is not holiday or festival time, otherwise you may find the place very crowded and noisy these days, and all the hotels full. A further risk is the threat to extend the road in to the town, supposedly for the benefit of hefty Gujarati matrons. You can guess what that will mean.

Information. Tourist office opposite Matheran station. A small toll is collected on arrival.

Arrival and departure. Suburban train from Bombay VT to Neral Junction (1¾hrs) then as above, but check connections or you may have a long wait. A few Pune-bound expresses also stop at Neral, otherwise you must change at Karjat. No steam anymore, sadly, but for Rs54 per head (minimum total Rs432) you can charter a 14-seater railcar like a small 1930s bus; three days' notice required. The narrow gauge line up to Matheran does not operate during the monsoon. The road stops 2.5km/1.5 miles from the town centre.

Accommodation (STD Code 021483)

Royal Hotel. Tel 247 or Bombay 386 8840 (reservations). SWB Rs200 (Rs400) DWB Rs400 (Rs800) plus taxes, all prices full board. Rest (veg). Bar. Very obliging staff.

Divadkar Hotel. Tel 223. SWB Rs90 upwards (Rs130) DWB Rs110/150 (Rs150/180). Rest. Bar. Good value. Turn right out of station, 50m.

Hope Hall Hotel, MG Road. Tel 253. SWB/DWB Rs60/75 (£1.20–1.50/$2–2.50) (Rs110). Basic but pleasant family atmosphere. Check out 7am!

Bombay View Hotel, 2.5km from station. Tel 279. Nice and quiet.

Khan's Hotel, MG Road, 300m from station. Tel 240. Rest. DR Rs85 (Rs225) but the semi-subterranean rooms are primitive.

Higher prices in brackets apply ten days either side of Diwali and Christmas, also several other holidays. Main season is from 15 April to 15 June when prices can be even higher. Increased leisure and the proximity of Bombay guarantee prices will rise further. Most places offer only full-board terms in season, which is no joke as this is primarily a Gujarati resort and serves food to suit them. The few places open during the monsoon are very cheap.

Eating and drinking

Relax Inn, Bazaar. Mod. Menu includes North Indian non-veg dishes.

Khan's, Bazaar. Cheap/Mod. Indian non-veg. Pleasant terrace overlooking The Mall.

Many more restaurants and shops selling chikki (local toffee), honey and fudge.

Karla

Karla has the largest and best preserved **Buddhist cave temple***** in India and is within convenient distance of Bombay if you have no time to visit Ajanta and Ellora. Dating from the second century AD this chaitya has some marvellous sculpture, both in the porch and on the pillars that separate the nave from the side aisles. The dagoba (like a small stupa) still has the remains of a wooden umbrella, and wooden ribs can be seen in the roof. Outside is a lion pillar, later and more Indian in style than the Ashoka column at Sarnath. There is a number of vihara, or monastery, caves in the same rock face, and a gaudy Hindu temple which attracts many red-powder-throwing pilgrims. Take no notice of the attendant who tries to charge for photography. Like Elephanta this is a place to avoid at weekends.

Over the valley (about a 3km walk) are the **Bhaja Caves**, later and inferior and, above them, a couple of old forts. Roughly 5km further are the **Bedsa Caves**.

Information. Tourist office in forecourt of Lonavla station.

Arrival and departure. Train to Lonavla on Bombay (2hrs)–Pune (1hr) line, the ride from Bombay is spectacular, then bus to foot of hill. Bus-stand is 500m from station, straight ahead. If no direct bus take one to Karla village and walk 1.5km, or use a scooter rickshaw (about Rs20 one way).

Accommodation. There is no accommodation at Karla caves. Lonavla is a hill resort, so plenty of accommodation in the town. Also a Maharashtra government *Holiday Resort* about 3km from Karla caves.

PUNE

Poona, as it used to be called, has a more pleasant climate than the coast and used to be seat of the Bombay government during the monsoon. An important place in its own right, Pune is also a dormitory town for Bombay and has imported some of its lively and trendy atmosphere.

Its history is interesting as it was the seat of the Peshwas, the hereditary leaders of the Maratha Confederacy established by Shivaji. The anarchy created by the Marathas, not only in their own area but as far away as Rajasthan and Delhi, eventually caused the British to move against them. A great battle was fought at nearby Kirkee in 1817, and the British took possession of Poona. Kirkee subsequently became a major base for the Bombay Presidency's army, and remains one for the Indian army.

Pune has two interesting museums. The **Raja Dinkar Kelkar Museum** (8.30am–12.30pm and 3–6pm daily) is the collection of a noted Marathi poet, and quite as eclectic as that of the more eccentric maharajas. Entry for non-Indians is Rs50. The **Tribal Museum** (10am–5pm daily) is devoted to the tribal communities of Maharashtra.

Mahatma Gandhi and his wife Kasturba were interned in Poona from 1942 to 1944 when the British finally lost patience with him over the 'Quit India' campaign. The Japanese army was at the gates of India, and Gandhi proposed that India should be left in the hands of God and the Japanese resisted by soul force. The British took a more pragmatic line. They were kept in a palace of the Aga Khan (Kasturba died here), and this is now the **Gandhi National Memorial** (9am–12.30pm and 1.30–6pm daily). If you've seen one, you've seen them all.

Pune's main claim to fame over recent years has been the **Rajneesh Ashram**. What you make of Rajneesh is up to you. Like Spike Milligan, another distinguished ex-resident of Poona, he had a highly developed sense of humour. Much of the obloquy heaped on him was the fault of a lunatic fringe of his followers. One thing is for sure: if you are unhinged already you will have a lot more fun spending your money here than on psychiatrists.

The **Pataleshwar temple**, dedicated to Shiva, is another minor variation on the rock-cut theme.

The **Empress Botanical Gardens** are attractive and well kept, and the **Bund Gardens**, along the River Mala, are popular for an evening stroll.

A nice enough place, Poona does not really rate very high in tourist terms. If you want to make a stopover on the inland route between Bombay and Goa, Bijapur and Hampi are better bets.

 **Excursions** The Western Ghats offer some good **trekking**, much of it around the lakes which provide Bombay's water and Shivaji's old forts. **Mahabaleswar**, 120km/75 miles from Pune, is a popular hill resort (1370m) noted for its huge rainfall during the monsoon.

Information. Tourist counter in station (useless, and surly with it). Guided tours from station, very rushed.

Arrival and departure
Airport. On route from Bombay VT (3hrs) to Madras (21¼hrs), Hyderabad (12¼hrs), and Goa (19½hrs). Buses and taxis from Bombay.

Accommodation
National Hotel, opposite station, has convenience if nothing else in its favour. Other similar places in this area.

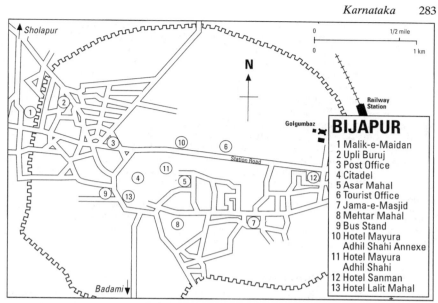

BIJAPUR

1 Malik-e-Maidan
2 Upli Buruj
3 Post Office
4 Citadel
5 Asar Mahal
6 Tourist Office
7 Jama-e-Masjid
8 Mehtar Mahal
9 Bus Stand
10 Hotel Mayura
   Adhil Shahi Annexe
11 Hotel Mayura
   Adhil Shahi
12 Hotel Sanman
13 Hotel Lalit Mahal

Eating and drinking

Neelam, near station. Mod/Exp. Indian. Good non-veg food. Many cheaper eating places nearby.

KARNATAKA

Karnataka consists mainly of the old dominions of the Maharaja of Mysore. Like Maharashtra much of the hinterland is still thickly forested and produces quality hardwood such as sandal and teak, and eucalyptus. The state produces 85% of India's raw silk, and near the new capital of Bangalore are the Kolar gold mines. Bangalore itself is an important industrial centre.

BIJAPUR

Bijapur is one of the unsung glories of India. From 1490 to 1686 it was the capital of the Adil Shahi kingdom, which superseded Vijayanagar (Hampi) as the dominant local power, and stretched to Goa in the west and as far as Thanjavur in the south. The outer walls of this great city were once 48km/30 miles in circumference; today the fort, itself 9km around, accommodates a sleepy country town. A profusion of imposing buildings stands as a reminder of a great past.

A colossal dome

Near the railway station is the **Gol Gumbaz*****, the colossal tomb of Muhammed Adil Shah (1626–1656). This is by far the largest masonry-domed building in the world though the dome itself, at 37.5m diameter, is slightly smaller than St Peter's in Rome. The tomb is 60m/196ft square outside and 41m/135ft inside. The dome is 3m thick at its base, rather less on top, and its highest point 55m above the floor. The huge weight of the dome, which would otherwise tend to push the walls outwards, is counteracted by the mass of the pendentives (the masonry in the corners of the chamber that reduces its size to that of the dome).

Under the centre of the dome is the grave of Muhammed; to the east are his youngest wife and grandson, to the west his eldest wife and favourite mistress, a Hindu dancing girl. From inside the tomb winding steps in the thickness of the walls lead up to the roof and the seven-storeyed corner towers. From the terrace around the dome outside you can see all the other monuments of Bijapur, and also the remains of the walls which enclosed the tomb's gardens. The whispering gallery (whispering? in India?) below the dome is wide enough to race karts round, and you can spend a happy few minutes clicking your fingers and listening to the ten-fold echo. The tomb opens at 6am, and you need to be here very soon after to enjoy it in peace.

The gatehouse, which constituted a music gallery, now houses a **museum**. One real oddity is a diagram of the human body made up of the words Allah and Mohammed and showing the significance of different parts according to Sufi philosophy. Miniatures include a Picasso-ish one of a Muslim saint.

More tombs and monuments

Right on the other side of town, outside the Mecca Gate and city walls is the **Ibrahim Rauza*****, the tomb of Ibrahim Adil Shah II (1580–1626). This is quite a contrast, being delicate and very ornate. On the outside can be seen remains of the painting which once covered the whole tomb. This is mostly in geometrical patterns but above one of the entrances are cypress trees and a tree of life. The carved inscriptions are marvellous. Inside, the ceiling appears to be vaulted and, when you think of the weight of the dome on top, makes you aware of the special quality of the lime mortar. Stone fillets have been used to beef up the inner colonnade. The **mosque** has a fine facade of incised plaster, and above are the intricate chajja brackets which are such a feature of Bijapur architecture. Note also the short lengths of chain with a medallion on the end cut from a single piece of stone. The mosque is now just whitewashed inside and also littered with bat droppings. Above the three steps of the mimbar are traces of painting.

Near the city gate is the **Burj-i-Sherza** (Lion Bastion), and on top of this is the **Malik-e-Maidan**** (Lord of the Battlefield), a huge 55-tonne cannon. Even to non-enthusiasts of military artefacts this is a work of art. Cast in Ahmadnagar in 1549 of bronze, the Arabic inscriptions on the exterior are as good as new, and the muzzle symbolises a Muslim lion swallowing a Hindu elephant. The cannon was brought here as spoils of war, and a later inscription tells how it was in turn captured by Aurangzeb. Visible from here is the **Upari Burj**, an oval bastion with external staircase and more guns on top. These are longer-range weapons of lesser calibre and much greater length. This tower provides the best view of the city. Below is the coppersmiths' quarter, which accounts for all the hammering.

The citadel

In the centre of the town is the unfinished **Tomb of Ali Adil Shah II**** or Bara Kaman, uncannily like the ruins of a gothic abbey. The **Gagan Mahal**** must have been one of the grandest audience halls in India. It is in a sorry state now; the roof has gone and no trace remains of the gilded decoration. Behind the facade can be seen the arches which linked it to the rest of the building. Also visible are the first floor rooms.

Monuments great...

The **Asar Mahal** was a hall of justice. Floral paintings in two of the upper rooms give an idea of how the palaces were decorated. Apparently there were also naughty scenes, but these have disappeared without trace. Outside the north gate are the original teak pillars and the rest of the woodwork which supported the canopy, obviously finer than the present crude arrangement. Two hairs of the Prophet used to be kept here, and apparently on the strength of this the place is considered too holy for women to be admitted.

The **Jama Masjid****, built in 1565, is less ornate than many Bijapur buildings, and no less impressive for that. The chajja of the main prayer hall is supported by Hindu brackets, and appears to have run right round the two wings also. The intricate mihrab is a later addition, as is the chunam floor divided up into 2250 prayer spaces. This floor is the work of Aurangzeb after he captured the place in 1686, and he also added the two unusual wings on either side of the north entrance. One of these still has a domed cupola, and the other obviously had one, perhaps to act as a minaret.

...and small

On a smaller scale the **Jal Mandir**, **Malika-Jahan Begum's mosque**, and the **Mehtar Mahal** are little gems. The major buildings used to be illuminated on Friday and Sunday nights (6.30–8.30pm). They may do it again, worth checking.

Looking at the many mosques and tombs of Bijapur which now are simply whitewashed it is important to remember that they were once brilliantly painted, especially the interiors. It is ironical that the only monument in which this decoration has survived is a church! **All Saints Church****, behind the Gagan Mahal, started life as a Muslim tomb and was converted in the last century. Usually kept locked, it is well worth finding someone to let you in to see the marvellous interior.

Bijapur is one of those very rare places where every monument is worth seeing; hiring a bike is easily the best way to get around. The atmosphere is quiet and friendly, and it is easy to spend several days very happily in Bijapur.

Practical Information *i*

Tourist Office at Hotel Mayura Adil Shahi. The little book by H Padmaraj, available here, is very helpful.

Arrival and departure. It is easy to visit Bijapur on the way from Bombay to Goa: train to Solapur from Bombay (9½hrs), Pune (5hrs), or Hyderabad (6hrs), change for Bijapur (3hrs) but check connections at Solapur. From Vasco da Gama (Goa) change at Hubli, but it is probably easier and faster to catch a bus from Panjim to Hubli and then the train.

Accommodation (STD Code 08352)

Hotel Mayura Adil Shahi Annexe, Station Road. Tel 20943. SWB Rs120 DWB Rs135. Rest. Not as good as its older partner below.

Hotel Mayura Adil Shahi (formerly Tourist Home), Station Road. Tel 20943. SWB Rs94 (around £1.90/$3.15) DWB Rs135. Rest. Bar. Built around courtyard where you can eat. Clean and comfortable.

Hotel Sanman, Station Road. Tel 21866. SWB/DWB Rs85. Rest (veg). Bar. Very neat and clean.

Lalita Mahal, near bus-stand. Tel 20761. SR Rs35 SWB Rs50 DR Rs50 DWB Rs60. Basic and rather noisy.

Eating and drinking

Naaz and *Preetam* (near Hotel Mayura). Cheap/Mod; both are good.

BADAMI

Badami has a complicated history even by the standards of this war-torn area. The Chalukya kings first built it as their capital in AD550, it was taken and destroyed in 640 by a Pallava, and became a capital again in 753, this time of the Rashtrakutas. Various other Hindu dynasties followed, then the Muslims, and finally the Marathas who lost it to the British in 1818. Badami is now just a large village in a beautiful setting dominated by two hills. The good news is that many monuments of different periods survive, the best known being four **cave temples****.

Cave temple 1 is dedicated to Shiva and has images of many other deities. In the centre of the ceiling of the porch a coiled cobra shades Shiva.

Cave temple 2 is dedicated to Vishnu, and in the porch are images of the Varaha (left) and Parasurama (right) avatars. On the ceilings of the porch are a circle of fish and swastikas. Above cave 2 is a small natural cave holy to Buddhists; the JL initials here are nothing to do with the author!

We reckon that **cave temple 3**, which dates from AD578, is among the most beautiful and best preserved in India. The quality of the statuary is remarkable; note Vishnu sitting on the coiled cobra and its seven hoods shading him from the sun. Facing that is the Narasimha man-lion avatar. Some of the bracket figures appear to be early representations of mithuna, nothing very explicit though they certainly exhibit togetherness. Elsewhere you can see the remains of interior painting. In this cave you are very aware of the benevolent aspect of Vishnu, and this makes a sharp contrast with the Shiva images in Elephanta.

Cave temple 4 is Jain, and there are two reliefs of Mahavira flanked by the 24 tirthankas. As is common there is also Hindu iconography. The inside of the front lip is shaped like the dripstones at Hampi; presumably they intended to shape the outside also.

Between caves 2 and 3 a precipitous flight of narrow steps leads up to the **south fort**.

Below cave 1 is a fine little tomb in Bijapur style. The porch for some reason is a later addition, having quite different style brackets under the eaves. The small openings are a dovecote, pigeons are often encouraged in Muslim buildings.

It seems incredible as you look at the murky green algae-laden water of the tank that any fish could live in it, yet fishermen catch catfish and something perch-like. Moving around the tank from the cave temples involves a bit of a scramble. The first of two **cave shrines** is of no interest, it may in fact have been a hermitage rather than a temple. The second, more readily accessible, is a Jain shrine. Mind your head! Under a rock a little further on is a structural shrine with a reclining figure of Hanuman.

The most interesting piece in the **museum** (10am–5pm, closed Friday) is of Lajjagauri, an image with a lotus flower instead of a head. This represents a childless woman who is ashamed to show her face, and is worshipped by women who hope to have a child.

The path up to the **north fort** is through a succession of deep clefts in the rock which closes in almost like the approach to Petra. On top are various bastions, a ruined temple, and three beehive-like structures having steps on the outside. We don't know what they are and nor does the man who runs the museum.

Arrival and departure. Train or bus from Bijapur (3½hrs) or Hospet (3½hrs, for Hampi). Station is 5km from town, a full tonga should cost around Rs15; if they won't play just walk out to the main road and catch a bus. Buses to Aihole and Pattadakal.

Accommodation

Hotel Mukambika, opposite bus-stand. Tel 3267. SWB Rs60 (£1.20/$2) DWB Rs110. Very good value.

Hotel Mayura Chalukya (Tel 3246), formerly Karnataka Tourism's Tourist Bungalow, is acceptable and little more expensive than Mukambika.

Eating and drinking

Hotel Kanchan. Ind non-veg. Cheap/Mod. Open air. Good food, watch out for the monkeys.

Hotel Sanman is said to be good, but we were driven out by loud music.

Aihole

Aihole was the capital of the Chalukya kings between the fourth and seventh centuries AD before they moved to Badami. Many old temples stand around the village. The Ladkhan temple (named after not a Hindu god but the Muslim squatter who took it over) is seen as a prototype for later buildings. While these temples do display the early stages of the development of Hindu architecture their appeal is limited; Aihole's real attractions are its peace and the opportunity to see something of rural life.

Information. Descriptive booklet from the museum.

Arrival and departure. Bus from Badami (2hrs) and Pattadakal (½hr).

Accommodation. *Tourist Rest House*. Tel Amingad 641. Not expensive.

Pattadakal

This is another place, like Aihole, to see Chalukyan temples in both northern and southern (Dravidian) styles. Most are in a single group near the village. A little further away the large northern-style Papnath temple, dating from around AD800, is similar to the Kailasha temple at Ellora, and is adorned with scenes from the Ramayana. Some of these temples are of impressive size, but the detailing is pretty crude.

Arrival and departure. On bus route from Badami (1½hrs) to Aihole (½hr).

Accommodation. None.

HAMPI

Hampi is the name used by travellers for the once magnificent city of Vijayanagar, part of which is now occupied by the village of Hampi. Vijayanagar is set in a stark landscape of rocky outcrops. In the 1960s and 1970s the calm atmosphere and beauty attracted long-term visitors, and Hampi vied with Manali and Goa as a hippy resort. A few hardy souls linger on.

When the Hoysala kingdom based on Halebid and Belur collapsed under Muslim onslaught in 1326 another branch of the family established itself here. Over a period of 200 years they built Vijayanagar, one of the richest and largest cities in the Deccan. Eventually, in 1565, the forces of Bijapur and Golkonda (Hyderabad) combined and, after the battle of Talikota, sacked the place. Despite their stated objective of leaving not one stone upon another there are many haunting reminders of Hampi's past glories.

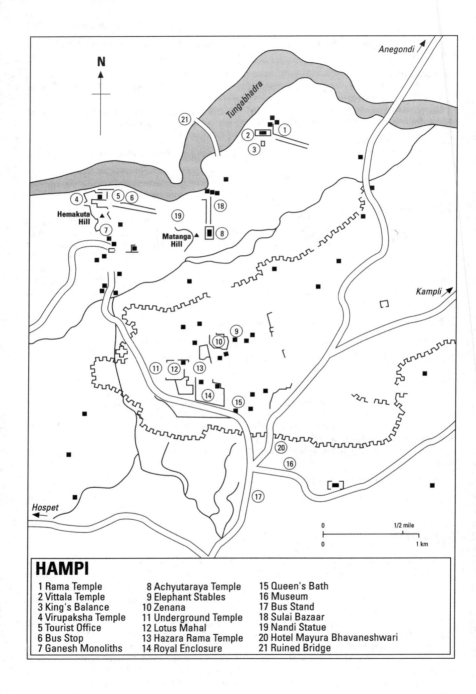

HAMPI

1 Rama Temple
2 Vittala Temple
3 King's Balance
4 Virupaksha Temple
5 Tourist Office
6 Bus Stop
7 Ganesh Monoliths

8 Achyutaraya Temple
9 Elephant Stables
10 Zenana
11 Underground Temple
12 Lotus Mahal
13 Hazara Rama Temple
14 Royal Enclosure

15 Queen's Bath
16 Museum
17 Bus Stand
18 Sulai Bazaar
19 Nandi Statue
20 Hotel Mayura Bhavaneshwari
21 Ruined Bridge

One of the most notable features in the layout of Vijayanagar is the wide bazaar in front of each major temple to provide space for the car festival when the gods were taken out in procession. The main bazaar, now occupied by the village of Hampi, fronts the **Virupaksha Temple***, still a popular place of pilgrimage. An ugly shed houses the temple cars. At the far end of this bazaar is a monolithic **statue of Nandi***. Note how some of the huge boulders here and elsewhere have lines of holes, like perforations, where masons had prepared to split off slabs. The style of building, using colossal pieces of stone, matches the rugged surroundings. Backtrack slightly and take the path signposted to the Vitthala Temple. This leads you alongside the Tungabhadra River and through a natural rock arch to the **Kodanda Rama Temple°**. Following the river bank you pass the stone piers of the **old bridge***.

The **Vitthala Temple*** is the crowning glory of the Vijayanagar style. Its strength and purposefulness symbolise a vigorous nation at the height of its powers. The great sculpted pillars which support it have subsidiary columns which give a musical note when struck. Massive slabs of stone, two of which remain, formed the roof. The superstructure of this temple, like that of most buildings in Vijayanagar, was of brick and stucco, and this has eroded badly compared with the granite lower courses. The **Kalyana Mandapa**, close to the main temple, was the marriage hall of the temple images. Note the frieze of ducks around the dripstone eaves. Traces of interior painting remain; all these buildings were once completely painted, the main structure in white and all the statuary in bright colours. The most important shrines were covered from top to bottom in gilded copper plates. You can get an idea of the effect from the modern temples on the road from Hospet to Hampi. This may seem garish, but the medieval cathedrals of Europe were painted in much the same way. The most unusual feature of this temple is the superb stone car in front of it. The wheels of this used to turn but, as pilgrims believed that they gained merit by doing so, the axles have become worn and the wheels are now cemented in place.

Passing the **King's Balance***, where the king was weighed against jewels and precious metals, head for Sulai Bazaar, at the end of which is **Achutya Raya Temple**. This is notable only for the procession of elephants around the base of the cloister. Take the small gate behind the sanctum and follow the path past a brightly coloured shrine and along the irrigation channel until you reach the steps up the **holy hill*** of Matanga-Parvatam. The temple on top is dedicated to Vishnu in his Parasurama (Rama with sword) avatar, but the real reason for braving the precarious steps is the stunning view. The horizon is a craggy lunar landscape, yet fields of sugar cane ruffled by a light breeze look like a surrounding lake.

From the foot of the hill head south crossing three water channels, and enter the citadel area of the city. The zenana enclosure contains the **Lotus Mahal**** and a couple of watchtowers. Outside are the **Elephant Stables***, more probably a rest house or, like the so-called elephant stables in Fatehpur Sikri, quarters for zenana servants. Note the fit of the stones in the zenana walls: as in other places around the world this was achieved by bevelling the mating surfaces and filling the angle with rubble, not quite as clever as it appears.

The **Temple of Hazara Rama**** (Temple of One Thousand Ramas) was the king's personal place of worship. The country around Vijayanagar has long been associated with places mentioned in the Ramayana, and friezes depict the events of this epic. In the adjacent **Royal Enclosure*** are the various palace buildings, but these suffered worst in the sack. The throne platform, water system, and new excavations are worth a quick look. Note the stone gates lying by the road outside the throne platform.

The **museum**** in Kamalpur village is good, and its centrepiece is a huge relief model of Vijayanagar. It takes nearly an hour to walk back from here to Hampi bazaar along the road. Don't miss the **Underground Temple***; it was built like this so that the lingam should always be surrounded by cooling water. This also supports quite a few fish and at least one freshwater crab of a good size. A little further on is a huge **natural arch***.

Information. Tourist office in Hospet at Taluka (District) Offices. The museum sells an excellent handbook (Rs4), and Malligi Tourist Home has *Hampi Ruins* by Longhurst (Rs30). Near the end of Hampi bazaar is a display of photographs taken in 1856 and contemporary shots of the same views. These are also available in book form (Rs125).

Arrival and departure. The bus service from Hospet to Hampi (30mins) is pretty dreadful and worse coming back in the evening. In theory buses leave from platform 10, but unless you watch out on the other side of the building you have little chance of a seat. The position is even worse at weekends. The less frequent buses to Kamalpur can be better. Hampi buses call at Kamalpur on the way back to Hospet.

A motorised cycle rickshaw costs about Rs50 each way and is preferable to a scooter rickshaw or taxi (Rs100) as you can look around. The alternative is to hire a bike in Hospet. The ride is fairly level and, after you turn off the main road at a sign advertising the KSTDC restaurant, quiet and pleasant.

Accommodation (STD Code 0839)
Hotel Mayura Bhavaneshvari, Kamalpur village. Tel 5374. Rest. New KSTDC place, reasonable and recommended.
Inspection Bungalow, Kamalpur village. DWB Rs40. Converted from an old temple. Lovely place to stay, but only two rooms so don't hold your breath. Reserve at Public Works Department office in Hospet.
In Hampi village *Rahul Guest House* and *Shanti Guest House* (Tel 51368) are adequate. Ask at chai shops about the cheaper and very basic *rooms* available in the village.

Eating and drinking
Mayura Lotus Mahal, near Hazara Rama Temple. Usually only a thali. Beer and soft drinks.
Om Shankar, by river near Rama Temple. Last hippy hang-out in Hampi. 'Special menu' offers tortoise and crab.
Several cheap vegetarian restaurants in Hampi bazaar.

HOSPET

Hospet is the railway terminus and a useful base for exploring Hampi (Vijayanagar).

Information. Guided tours of Vijayanagar can be booked through Malligi Tourist Home.

Arrival and departure. Direct train to Hospet from Vasco da Gama (13hrs), Margao (12hrs), Bijapur (7½hrs), Badami (3½hrs); also through coaches from Bangalore and Madras. The station is well away from the hotels; take a cycle rickshaw (Rs10).
Buses do the same routes as the trains, but tend to be uncomfortable and little faster. From Halebid, Belur, and Hassan you have to change in Shimoga.

Accommodation (STD Code 08394)
Malligi Tourist Home, Jambuntha Road. Tel 58101. SR Rs65 (£1.30/$2.15) DWB Rs100–175 DWB A/C Rs250/300. Rest (veg, good). Bar. Friendly people, clean rooms, good place to stay. Also the only place we have ever seen a double mosquito net; how civilised.
Hotel Vishwa, Station Road (opposite bus-stand). Tel 57171. SWB Rs60 DWB Rs100. Rest (veg, good). Good clean hotel.
Lokare Lodge, Station Road. Tel 8147. SR Rs30–40 SWB Rs50 DWB Rs70–85. If all else fails.

Eating and drinking

Eagle Garden, opposite Malligi. Ind. Cheap/Mod. Bar. Huge menu, food nothing special, and so dim you can't see it anyway. But there's beer.

BELGAUM

Aranyaka Adventures, BC 71/3 Elphinstone Road, Camp, Belgaum run adventure wildlife safaris in this area, no reports yet.

GOA TO MYSORE

The coast from Goa down to Kochi is very attractive, but holds little of interest for the traveller; better to head inland.

Jog Falls

The highest waterfalls in India make a good place to break the journey between Goa and Hassan or Mysore. The River Sharavathi falls 250m (820ft) into a wooded gorge. The river divides into four separate falls: Raja (formerly known as the Horseshoe), Roarer, Rocket, and Rani (formerly La Dame Blanche). The Raja is largest and drops sheer into the chasm, the others producing more delicate sprays and patterns of water.

The falls are truly spectacular soon after the monsoon (and pretty well invisible during it), but the hydro-electric schemes greatly reduce flow at other times. They are, nevertheless, well worth seeing. Several points above give a good view, and it is possible to walk down to the bottom of the falls, though proper shoes must be worn, and the rocks are slippery. The wet areas are notorious for leeches; watch out for them and do not brush against the undergrowth. Rainbows play and birds, which nest in the rock faces, flit through the spray. The pool at the foot of the falls is 40m/132ft deep and popular with local fishermen.

An Olympic swimming pool makes a hot weather visit pleasant.

Information. Tourist office adjacent to Woodlands Hotel. Possibility of visits to dams, power houses, etc.

Arrival and departure. Bus from Karwar (6½hrs); heading south to Mangalore from Jog check the bus passes through Honavar and change there. For Mysore, bus to Sagar (1hr) and change there.

Train to Talgappa from Bangalore (11½hrs), also first-class through coach from Mysore (18¾hrs) and Hassan (14hrs), second-class passengers have to change trains. Bus from outside Talgappa Post Office, 500m from station, to falls (1hr).

Accommodation

Woodlands Hotel, adjacent to bus stop. Tel Kargal 22. Rest. Bar. Various low to moderately priced rooms. Rooms OK, but dreary restaurant and limited menu.

Several *cheap hotels* and *official rest houses* nearby, of which the *Public Works Department Bungalow* has the best view, but it is often full. There is also a *Youth Hostel*, though this is intended mainly for groups.

Hassan

In a conveniently small area between Goa and Mysore one can see two of the finest Hindu temples and the most unusual Jain place of pilgrimage anywhere in India. Hassan is a useful base for visiting the temples at Belur and Halebid.

Information. Tourist office in Vartha Bhavan, BM Road.

Arrival and departure. On Talgappa (for Jog Falls) (14hrs) to Mysore railway line. The new railway line from Mangalore is said to be pretty spectacular. The station is 2km from the town centre. Buses to Mangalore, Mysore, Sravana Belgola and Bangalore.

Accommodation. Try *Sathyaprakash Lodgings* or *Vaishnavi Lodging*, both cheap and near bus-stand. Hotel *Ambli Palika* (Tel 08172 66307) on Racecourse Road is more upmarket (Rs150–250).

Halebid

Founded around AD1000, Halebid was the centre of the Hoysala kingdom until the capital was moved to Belur perhaps a hundred years later. Its name (*hale*, old, plus *bidu*, capital) tells the story.

The **Hoysaleswara Temple***** is arguably the finest in all India. The most distinctive features of the Hoysala style are the star-shaped ground plan, lack of a tall spire, and superb sculpture. Dedicated to Shiva it has two shrines (the other for Parvati, Shiva's wife) each with a large Nandi. The friezes which cover the whole exterior are rather battered but were obviously even finer than those at Belur.

The Kedareswara Temple and some Jain temples 1km further on are very fine, but you will do better spending your time at the Hoysaleswara.

Arrival and departure. Bus from Belur (1½hrs). The Hoysaleswara Temple is 400m from the bus stop.

Accommodation. *Tourist Cottage*, opposite temple. Tel 08177 3224.

Belur

Belur is notable for the **Chenna Kesava Temple**** which is a contemporary (AD1133) of the great European cathedrals of Lincoln and Chartres. While not built on so massive a scale the artistry and workmanship lose nothing by comparison, and the state of preservation is remarkable. The carving was done by the same man as the Hoysaleswara in Halebid. The images in this and the Kappe Chenniga Raya temple in the same compound are among the very best in India. All the Hoysala temples were damaged in Muslim invasions between 1310 and 1326. Despite its poor condition the gopuram is a later addition.

Arrival and departure. Bus from Hassan (express ¾hr), also direct service to Sravana Belgola.

Accommodation. *Hotel Mayur Velapuri*. Tel 08177 2209. Rest. Bar. Another good Karnataka Tourism place. Also several basic lodges.

Sravana Belgola

Sravana Belgola is the religious centre of the Digambara (naked) sect of Jains and the major Jain place of pilgrimage in southern India. It derives its sanctity from a sage who was a pupil of one of Mahavira's disciples. He founded a hermitage here and was joined by Ashoka's grandfather, the former emperor Chandragupta, who abdicated the throne to follow his guru. The village surrounds a large tank, the name Sravana Belgola meaning 'white lake', and is dominated by two hills. The buildings around the lake were built by the kings of Mysore in the 17th and 18th centuries.

The higher hill, Indragiri, is crowned by a 17m-high **monolithic statue***** of Gomateswara (or Bahubali), a Jain saint. Freestanding, unlike those at Gwalior, it is dated precisely to AD985. This serene nude sculpture is the most beautiful piece of work, even though the lower legs are oddly out of proportion to the rest. Ant hills, a favoured lair of cobras, stand on either side and suggest that Jainism may have succeeded a snake worship cult, common enough in this part of the world. The statue's perfect condition is partly due to the tradition of anointing it with milk, honey, and ghee every 14 years or so; this is a great ceremony due next in 2005. Several other temples stand on the hill.

The other hill, Chandragiri, is less of a climb. On top are **temples*** in Dravidian style, like southern Hindu ones, and stone light towers. Back in the town is a math or monastery where the guru lives; the walls are decorated with murals showing Jain holy men and kings. Like so many other places Sravana Belgola is not as quiet as it was, but is still worth a lot more time than conducted tours allow.

Information. Tourist office at foot of hill. Because you have to climb the hill barefoot always try to visit Sravana Belgola early in the day.

Arrival and departure. Bus from Hassan (2hrs) or Mysore (3hrs).

Accommodation
   Hotel Raghu, near steps to hill. Tel 08176 7238. Rest.
   SP Jain Guest House. SWB/DWB Rs80.
   Vidyananda Nilaya. DWB Rs25.

Eating and drinking
   Hotel Mahaveer. Cheap. Jain veg.
   Bus-stand café. Cheap. Vegetarian.

GOA TO MANGALORE AND MYSORE

The coastal route, whether by bus or train, is the quicker but less interesting way of getting from Goa to Kerala or Mysore.

Karwar

A staging point on the way south from Goa, with good beaches and picturesque women. The new bridge has shifted the chaos from the ferry landings to the bus-stand, and the peace and quiet elsewhere is unlikely to survive the Indian Navy's plans for a new base here.

Arrival and departure. Buses to Panjim (4½hrs), Margao (3½hrs), Mangalore (8hrs), Jog Falls (6½hrs).

Accommodation. Several *hotels* and an *Inspection Bungalow* (probably best bet).

Mangalore

Mangalore is little more than a convenient place to stay overnight between Goa and Kochi. Once the Konkan railway connects it to Goa it will lose even this distinction.

Mangalore is an important port, and most of the roofing tiles, so common all along this coast, are made in this area and then transported by sea.

Arrival and departure. Bus to Karwar (8hrs) or straight through to Margao or Panjim. Train to Ernakulam (Kochi) (10½hrs). The new line to Hassan, laid through very difficult country, will appeal to rail buffs.

Accommodation
   Panchami Hotel, directly opposite bus-stand. Tel 411 986. SWB Rs80 (around £1.60/$2.65) DWB Rs120 plus 5% tax. Rest (veg). Clean and comfortable.
   More hotels near the station and also railway *Retiring Rooms*.

Eating and drinking
Mama Mia Bar and Restaurant, about 1km from bus-stand. Mod. Good non-veg food, eat inside or out. Charming place.

Kodagu

Kodagu, as the district of Coorg is now called, is regarded as the most beautiful part of Karnataka. For a small and peaceful area it has produced a quite disproportionate number of generals and field marshals for the Indian Army. The main town is Madikeri (Mercara), on the main road from Mangalore to Mysore, and this is the best base for exploring. A useful source of information is Dervla Murphy's book *On a Shoestring to Coorg*.

MYSORE

Mysore is one of the most pleasant cities in India having clean broad streets, many parks, and a peaceful air. Restored to their throne in 1799 the Wadiyar family later developed the most advanced of all the princely states. Mysore is a typical undertaking of theirs; good in both form and function. The maharajas seem to have run things more like a business than a feudal state. This worked to their own benefit, as evidenced by the splendid palaces, and to that of their subjects who enjoyed excellent schools and hospitals. For many years after Independence the then maharaja continued as the democratic leader of the enlarged state of Karnataka.

The town centre

The **Maharaja's Palace***** was built around the turn of the century in Indo-Saracenic style with some distinctly Hoysala touches. The central octagonal **marriage hall** has a glass roof with likenesses of peacocks. The paintings of state occasions (not murals, they are on canvas) all around the ground floor walls were done by a local artist as recently as 1945. The **durbar hall** on the first floor has paintings from Hindu mythology and elaborately decorated ceilings. One side of this hall is open, looking out over the durbar ground like a very luxurious grandstand. A third hall is the **cabinet room**, in effect a hall of private audience. Note the inner row of cast metal pillars imported from Britain. Stained Belgian glass adorns the skylights, some mixed up with that from the marriage hall, and etched glass from the same source is in the windows. The magnificent throne of Mysore is placed in the cabinet hall at the time of Dussehra. We really think that this is our favourite palace anywhere, not only imposing but jolly as well.

The **Maharaja's Domestic Museum**** is open from 10am–6pm and costs an extra Rs2, well worth it to see the living quarters after the state apartments. You are free to take pictures of the outside of the palace from the grounds, but it seems you cannot get permission to take a camera in. The palace is illuminated on Sunday evenings.

The **Sri Chamarajendra Art Gallery***** in the Jagan Mohan Palace has one of the best two or three collections in India, including many modern Indian works. There is a collection of period furniture on the ground floor, and the top floor is the Rang Mahal (Painted Palace) with splendid murals, now used to display musical instruments.

The centre of Mysore is probably the most pleasant city in India to wander around, especially in the early evening; don't miss the **Devaraja Market**.

The **Rail Museum** (open 8am–1pm and 2–6pm, entry 50np plus Rs5 for a still camera) displays locomotives dating back to 1899, the Maharaja's palatial coaches

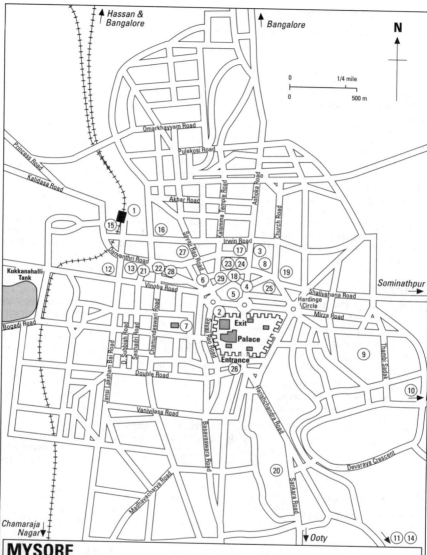

MYSORE

1 Railway Station
2 City Bus Stand
3 Post Office
4 Clock Tower Square
5 New Statue Square
6 Devaraja Market
7 Jaganmohan Palace
8 Central Bus Stand
9 Zoo
10 Lalitha Mahal Palace
11 Rajendra Vilas Imperial

12 Hotel Metropole
13 Indian Airlines
14 Chamundeswari Temple
15 Railway Museum
16 Tourist Office
17 State Bank of Mysore
18 Gandhi Square
19 Wesley Cathedral
20 Old Temples
21 Mayura Hoysala Hotel and
   Mayura Yathrinivas Hotel

22 New Gayathri Bhavan Hotel
   and Ashok Hotel
23 Hotel Dasaprakash and Akshaya
   Vegetarian Restaurant
24 Hotel Durbar
25 Ritz Hotel
26 Gun House Restaurant
27 Punjabi Restaurant
28 Kwality Restaurant
29 Shilpashri Restaurant

and ephemera. An unusual exhibit is an Austin pick-up truck converted to run on rails.

A hilltop pilgrimage

Dominating Mysore is **Chamundi Hill***** and its Chamundi, or Kali Temple. The infirm and aged can catch a bus; the rest of us will take the pilgrims' route up the thousand steps to the top. Follow the road from the main entrance of the palace behind the Gunhouse Restaurant and keep straight on. Where the main road bears right just before a group of old temples, keep straight on again. At a small café bear left past a pink-domed temple. Continue through the municipal rubbish tip, past the dhobi ghats and a pinjrapol to the steps. Two-thirds of the way up (the steps are numbered so you can check on your progress) is a huge statue of Nandi. As Kali is a form of Shiva, this is the traditional, though distant, adjunct to the temple. The temple itself (closed noon–5pm) is dwarfed by its gopuram. Non-Hindu visitors are welcome; if necessary avoid the long queue by buying a priority ticket for Rs10. A temple car is in a shed to one side of the temple, and there is a museum if you can be bothered to take your shoes off yet again. The bazaar here is unpleasantly noisy; retreat to the superb Rajendra Vilas Hotel for tea and biscuits (Rs20) or a cold beer for the same price. Chamundi Hill is more for the views than the temple.

Excursions

The **Brindaban Gardens** at Krishnarajasagar Dam (20km from the city) give you an idea how the Mughal gardens must have been in their heyday — all the fountains work and they are illuminated every evening.

Although **Somnathpur Temple** (35km from the city) is the most complete of the Hoysala temples, it somehow lacks the impact of those at Halebid and Belur. Its more convenient location, however, is useful if you have no time to see the others.

Festivals. The most important festival of the year in Mysore is Dussehra in September or October. This involves a great parade, and is worth planning your itinerary around, but book a hotel early.

Shopping. Mysore excels as a handicrafts centre. The traditional products are silk and anything that can be made from sandalwood, from soap and joss sticks to superb carvings and furniture. Other materials used to great effect are teak, rosewood and ivory; be aware of customs regulations in your own country before buying the latter.

| **Practical Information** | Tourist office near railway station. Guided tours (Rs85) include Krishnarajasagar Dam, Srirangapatna and Somnathpur Temple, but are hopelessly rushed. |

Arrival and departure. The airport was at one time served by Vayudoot, but no flights at present. Nearest working airport is Bangalore. Indian Airlines office at Hotel Mayura Hoysala.

Frequent trains from Bangalore (3¼hrs) — much preferable to the buses — and Hassan (3½hrs).

From the central bus-stand there are several services each day to Mangalore, Ootacamund (5hrs), Sravana Belgola (3hrs), and Ernakulam, one to Panjim (overnight).

Accommodation (STD Code 0821)

Rajendra Vilas Palace, Chamundi Hill. Former summer palace of the maharajas with oriental furnishings. Marvellous view directly down on to the race course. Some rooms in this fascinating place were very reasonably priced, worth checking if they still are after refurbishment.

Hotel Mayura Hoysala, Jhansi Lakshmi Bai Road. Tel 25349. SWB Rs150 DWB Rs225. Rest. Bar. Attractive old building.

Durbar Hotel, Gandhi Square. Tel 20029. SR Rs60 (£1.20/$2) DR Rs80 DWB Rs150. Rest (roof garden). Bar. Probably the best budget hotel.

New Gayatri Bhavan, Dhanvantri Road. Tel 21224. Prices similar to Durbar. Rest. Upstairs rooms preferable. Can be noisy.

Other similarly priced hotels around Gandhi Square and along Dhanvantri Road. We have heard good reports of *Hotel Dasaprakash* and *Hotel Ritz*, both in the DWB Rs150–200 range.

Eating and drinking

Hotel Metropole, Jhansi Lakshmi Bai Road. Exp (Rs150–200 per head; £3–4/$5–6.65). Ind/Cont. Bar. Excellent, well presented food and first-class service.

Gun House Restaurant and Bar, opposite entrance to palace. Mod/Exp. Ind/Chi/Cont. Bar. Very civilised, live music in the evening. Perfect place for a beer and lunch after climbing Chamundi Hill. Another of the maharaja's enterprises, and again pleasant and well managed.

Kwality, Dhanvantri Road. Tel 21464. Mod/Exp. N Ind/Chi. Bar. Excellent.

Shilpastri, opposite Durbar Hotel. Cheap/Mod. Bar. Popular roof-top eatery.

Punjabi, Dhanvantri Road. Cheap/Mod. Punjabi food, fruit juices, etc. An old travellers' favourite, but food very poor on the author's last visit.

The former maharaja's palace, the *Lalitha Mahal*, is now the top hotel and reportedly does a good buffet. Check the price before going — as in other places, prices are rising fast.

Excursions Srirangapatna

Seringapatam, as the British called it, has a long history as a religious centre, and was the early capital of the Hindu rulers of Mysore. Their throne was usurped in 1761 by one of their generals, the Muslim Haidar Ali (died 1782). He and his son Tippu Sultan carved out a substantial empire and, taking advantage of its island location, based a strong **fort** on Srirangapatna. They also, oddly enough, enhanced the local temples rather than destroying them. Until the final capture of the fort in 1799, they caused the British more trouble than all the other princes put together.

The ramparts of Srirangapatna are mostly intact, and one can see the breach made by the British, the spot near the Water Gate where Tippu Sultan died, and two large temples. The most unusual viewpoint is the ship's crows' nest on a watchtower, but everything is very spread out and of limited interest.

Outside the fort is the attractive **Daria Daulat**** (Tippu's summer palace, open 9am–5pm; entry 50np, free Friday). Murals done for Tippu by a local artist depict his forces (with many French in blue jackets) defeating the British redcoats at Pollilore in 1780. There is a good collection of prints and a model of the fortress of Srirangapatna, much easier to comprehend like this than on the ground.

In the Lalbagh the **tomb of Tippu Sultan and Haidar Ali**** (open 8am–6.30pm) is something of a throwback architecturally, resembling the Bijapur style of a couple of hundred years earlier. The most notable features are the superb polished stone arcade and the lacquered tiger-stripe (Tippu's motif) interior. The third stone inside is of Haidar Ali's wife (Tippu's mother). The stones, now concealed under coloured cloths, are supposed to be beautifully inlaid. Best visited early or late in the day, especially at 5pm when prayers are sung in the tomb, and the light is best, too. Like the Summer

Palace, the tomb is surrounded by quiet, well kept gardens, in this case with many interesting monuments.

Arrival and departure. Frequent buses from Mysore. Tongas available for local transport, but it is much better to hire a bike just down from the bus-stand. One of the entrances to the fort is nearby. For the Summer Palace head uphill (towards Mysore) and turn left where signed Gumbaz and Sangana. For the tombs turn left out of the Summer Palace and fork right after 200m, following the sign Gumbaz. Srirangapatna is included in the Mysore conducted tour.

Accommodation. *Hotel Mayura River View*, 3km from bus-stand. Tel 08227 52144. Rest. Bar. Quiet and well located by the River Cauvery. Several lodges near the bus-stand.

MYSORE TO KERALA

The main road south from Mysore runs through jungly country heading for the Nilgiri Hills and Ootacamund. The Nilgiris are the second highest in southern India. The main peak is Doda Betta (2636m/8647ft), and the hills are famous for their tea gardens. Two major wildlife reserves, Bandipur and Mudumalai, lie between Mysore and Ootacamund. Mudumalai and Ootacamund are actually in Tamil Nadu, but since most people visit them between Mysore and Kerala it is convenient to describe them here.

Bandipur National Park

Bandipur combines with the contiguous Mudumalai and Wynaad (Kerala) to form a reserve of almost 3000 sq km. Bandipur is one of the Project Tiger reserves, but your chances of seeing one are zero. In fact, since the only access to the park is a one-hour ride in a noisy bus, you are unlikely to see anything much at all. Entry to the park is Rs150, and this includes the bus tour.

Information. Forest Department, Aranya Bhavan, 18th Cross, Malleswaram, Bangalore (Tel 334 1993) or Project Tiger Office, Ashokpuram, Mysore (Tel 529 901).

Arrival and departure. The Reception Centre is on the main road from Mysore (3hrs) to Ooty (2hrs); there is a regular bus service.

Accommodation. The only low-cost accommodation is the Forest Department's bungalows, and these must be booked in advance at the offices listed above.

Mudumalai Wildlife Sanctuary

Mudumalai is notable for being the major home of wild elephants in India. The dense jungle also houses a variety of deer, bison, and a few tigers and panthers.

Theppakadu, where the Reception Centre is situated, is the main centre. Tours into the park by truck (inexpensive) or elephant run from here, and there is also a camp for working elephants. A distasteful circus act, called the Elephant Puja, takes place each evening — save your Rs20.

Heavy rain can close the park during the October to December monsoon period, and it may be closed because of fire risk in the dry season (February and March). Both Bandipur and Mudumalai should be avoided at weekends.

Information. The Wildlife Warden has an office (Tel 4098) on Coonoor Road in Ooty; book accommodation and elephant rides here to avoid taking pot luck at the sanctuary.

Arrival and departure. Theppakadu, about 10km from the Bandipur Reception

Centre, is served by regular buses on the main road between Mysore (3hrs) and Ooty (2hrs). Bus and jeep services to Masinagudi. The minibus service from Ooty to Masinagudi takes only an hour and follows a wild hilly road.

Accommodation. Inexpensive dormitory and lodge accommodation at Theppakadu, best booked in advance in Ooty. Cheap and basic accommodation is also available in Masinagudi. Private resorts exist, but tend to be expensive and far from public transport.

Ootacamund

The 'queen of hill stations', or 'Snooty Ooty' to generations of English, is not what it was. The Nilgiri Hills (*nila*, blue, plus *giri*, hills) around are still beautiful and the climate is as refreshing as ever, but the queen has middle-age spread and has become far too noisy for comfort. The **Botanical Gardens** are outstanding and the Madras Turf Club organises **races** during the season (mid-April to mid-June), but prices are highest at this time, especially for rickshaws and taxis.

Outdoor pursuits include **fishing** (carp in the lake and trout in the streams), **golf** and **walking**; details from the tourist office. Ooty is at an altitude of 2286m/7498ft, and despite being so close to the equator temperatures drop nearly to zero at night in winter.

Ooty's claim to a place in history is guaranteed, oddly enough, by snooker. The game was developed by bored British officers including Neville Chamberlain, later the British Prime Minister, in the Club in the closing years of the 19th century.

The name has recently been Indianised to Udhagamandalam, and this is how it appears in railway timetables. It will be at least 50 years before anyone other than civil servants and the most ardent nationalists call it anything but Ooty.

Information. Tourist office on Commercial Road, near Charing Cross, is little help.

Arrival and departure. Buses from Mysore (5hrs), Bangalore (9hrs) and Coimbatore (3hrs). The mountain railway from Mettupalaiyam to Ooty (4½hrs) uses Swiss-built steam locomotives, part of the route being rack and pinion. This railway is, quite frankly, the only reason for visiting Ooty. From Mettupalaiyam direct trains run to Madras (10½hrs) and Kochi (6½hrs), otherwise change at Coimbatore.

Accommodation

Hotel Tamil Nadu, Charing Cross Road. Tel 44010. DWB Rs250 (Rs400 in season).

YWCA (2km from station). Tel 42218. DWB Rs100–200 (more in season) Dorm Rs25. Rest. A little inconvenient, but quiet, and it has a lounge with log fire. You may be caught for full-board in season.

Youth Hostel, Charing Cross. Tel 43665. Dorm Rs25 (Rs45 in season). Also some rooms.

Plenty of lodges of variable quality (mostly bad) near the station and bus-stand.

BANGALORE

Twenty years ago Bangalore was still spoken of with awe. It was by any standards a model city. It enjoyed one of the most equable climates in India, and it was clean, green and quiet.

Now, however, it is one of the fastest-growing cities in Asia, its population pushing five million. Bangalore (the name means boiled beans) is India's high-tech capital and is seeing huge inward investment from multinationals as well as top local corporations. This expansion has caused the surrounding forests, which largely accounted for the pleasant climate, to be progressively cut down. The huge population increase means that the city is as crowded and noisy as anywhere else in

India. The people are still lively and friendly, but as a city it has very little to offer the traveller.

Sights are limited to **Cubbon Park** (which holds the **Government Museum**) and the **Lalbagh Botanical Gardens**.

Bangalore's one great merit is that it is, as it always has been, socially advanced. You stand a good chance of meeting liberated young Indians in its pubs and discos, and many travellers would feel that this sort of encounter makes a visit worthwhile. Start hunting in the Church Street area.

Information. Karnataka Tourism counters at airport and railway station. Its head office is at Mitra Towers, Queens Circle, and the Government of India Tourist Office at 48 Church Street; both are miles from the station. Karnataka Tourism runs city and excursion tours.

Arrival and departure. Airport, 13km from city centre. A major hub airport for Indian Airlines and most of the independents. Indian Airlines office on Kempegowda Road (Tel 221 1914). Others are Damania (Tel 558 8736), East-West (Tel 558 8282), Jet (Tel 558 8354), ModiLuft (Tel 558 2202) and Sahara (Tel 558 6976). City buses to and from airport.

Long-distance and city bus-stands are both opposite the station.

Accommodation. Travellers have suggested *Berry's Hotel* on Church Street and *Rice Bowl Restaurant*, the latter run by the Dalai Lama's sister.

Excursions

Around Bangalore

Nandi Hills, 1500m above sea level, is a resort centred on Nandidrug, a fort built by Tippu Sultan, and believed by him to be impregnable. Despite sheer drops of 300m, British forces disabused him of this notion in 1791. Bus from Bangalore; less convenient but perhaps more fun is the narrow-gauge railway line from Yelahanka Junction (15km from the centre of Bangalore) to Nandi (1½hrs), 4km from the foot of the hill. This line goes on to Kolar Gold Fields, the deepest gold mine in the world. In theory you can arrange to visit this, but 'security' considerations will almost certainly prevent foreigners from doing so.

GOA

Ten years ago only the dedicated traveller knew Goa, its wonderful beaches, good food, cheap beer and relaxed attitude towards the simple pleasures of life. Now it is firmly established as a package tourist's destination. No matter, if you know where to go it is still one of the best places to take time out from the rigours of travelling in India.

History

The Portuguese presence in India dates from 1498 when Vasco da Gama landed at Calicut, and subsequently a trading post was set up in Kochi. Difficult relations with the Zamorin of Calicut, the local ruler, caused them to look north to Goa, then part of the kingdom of Bijapur. Goa was already a substantial port for pilgrims on the way to Mecca, and for the import of horses from Arabia. After one false start Afonso de Albuquerque took Goa in 1510, and later governors greatly extended the territory. Initially development centred on what has become known as Old Goa, some distance up the Mandovi River. This site proved very unhealthy, and a terrible outbreak of plague in 1738 prompted a gradual move to Panjim.

Goa was the capital of Portugal's eastern empire and the seat of the viceroy, but Portuguese maritime power was in eclipse by the middle of the 17th century, and Goa became something of a backwater. Despite the British withdrawal from India in 1947 (and the French leaving Pondicherry and their smaller settlements in 1954), Portugal dragged its heels over negotiations with the Indian goverment, which eventually launched an invasion in 1961. What little resistance there was came mostly from former harijans in the Portuguese army who reckoned they were better off the way they were. It was, incidentally, this invasion and the failure to avoid war with China shortly afterwards that largely lost India its once influential place in world politics. Goa, Daman and Diu constituted a Union Territory ruled mainly from Delhi until 1987, when Goa became a self-governing state of the Union of India.

Contrary to first impressions, perhaps, Christians account for only about a third of the population of Goa, the rest being Hindus and a small Muslim minority. The Inquisition did little for religious harmony, but by 1835 the Portuguese had suppressed not only that but all the religious orders as well. The tolerance that ensued is seen at its best in the shared enjoyment of the many religious festivals. These often have a very Latin flavour with bands, processions and firecrackers. The biggest takes place in the three days before Lent when the streets of Panjim and Margao are taken over for the pageants and dancing of Carnival. Christmas is celebrated in similar fashion, and there are feasts for saints' days throughout the year. The great Hindu festivals such as Holi and Diwali are equally popular.

Eating and drinking

Food and drink in Goa are in a class of their own. Obviously, fish and shellfish dominate menus and can be very good indeed. The days of lobster (actually crayfish) for Rs3 are long gone, but prawns, king fish and sunfish are all cheap and tasty. Many people abjure pork after appreciating the vital part the pigs play in keeping Goa clean and sanitary. Vindaloos (hot and sour curries quite unlike the dish of that name in your local tandoori restaurant) come from Goa, and there are several other specialities. Our first encounter with Goa sausage was not a success — we likened it to curried gristle stuffed into a heavy-duty condom. Happily we have had some very good *chorizos* since then. If you are staying any time at all, try to find a place where you can cook for yourself. The restaurants are good, but you should be able to make more of the superb ingredients than they do, and at less cost.

Beer is readily available and the cheapest in India. The local firewater is distilled from either cashew juice or coconut sap, and called feni. It is a popular misconception that cashew feni is made from the nuts. It isn't; each nut grows on the outside of a fruit like a small pimento. The juice is pressed from these (you can buy it in season) and then fermented to make urrack (again sold in this form in season). It is this that is distilled to produce feni. Wines can be quite good. Adega de Velha is a white demi-sec that is palatable if served cold enough, and there is now a proper brut methode champenoise called San Beneditto (Rs110; around £2.20/$3.65). You can even get port of a sort, and now sherry!

Behaviour

Goa still has its reputation as one of the original hippy havens, and great fun it was, too; lying around getting stoned, a free and easy approach to sex, and all that. The trouble was that the locals weren't half as amused as the hippies. So came the backlash. Nudity is now totally unacceptable, and toplessness tolerated only well away from the more public beaches.

Fancy a smoke? Wait till you get home. There were very good reasons for a crackdown on drugs, but the Goa police have got out of hand. As usual only minor offenders get picked up, and the totally innocent have had drugs planted on them. This was bad enough when a couple of hundred rupees would solve the problem.

Lately there have been instances of police bullying victims into handing over *all* their money. Anjuna and Vagator are the favourite targets — be careful and keep your eyes and ears open.

PANJIM

Officially now Panaji, though only Maharashtrians call it that, Panjim is the capital of Goa and makes no secret of its Portuguese ancestry. Near the steamer wharf is the **Secretariat**, built on the site of a palace of Adil Shah of Bijapur and used as a residence by the Portuguese viceroy. On a little green nearby is a strange **statue of the Abbé Faria**, a churchman who practised therapeutic hypnotism and inspired a character in *The Count of Monte Christo*.

Overlooking much of Panjim is the **Cathedral of the Immaculate Conception** approached by zig-zag staircases. The elegant villas of the former rulers are on the hill behind, but Panjim is not really a place for sightseeing. Panjim is for relaxing in little bars, enjoying good food and just watching the world go by.

Under Portuguese rule houses had to be colour-washed (white was reserved for churches) after each monsoon. This legacy continued for many years, but now Panjim seems to be going downhill. The holes in the pavements, the noise, the piles of rubbish and the smell of urine all too common elsewhere have reached here.

Festivals. As mentioned in the background section festivals have a unique flavour in Goa. Check at the tourist office what will be going on during your stay. There are many Christain festivals, the most important being the Feast of St Francis Xavier in Old Goa. Liberation Day is 19 December; there is a military parade in Panjim and a flypast of aircraft (which include Bears) from the Naval Air Station at Dabolim.

Information. Goa Tourism at bus-stand and in Rua Afonso de Albuquerque, which is the street parallel to the one along the ferry wharf; head office at Tourist Home over the bridge on way to bus-stand. Useful map available. Various conducted tours and river trips. Government of India Tourist Office opposite cathedral. *Goa* by JM Richards (Vikas Publishing) is excellent.

Arrival and departure. Airport at Dabolim, 29km from Panjim. Indian Airlines flights from Delhi, Bombay, Bangalore, Kochi and Trivandrum. The new independent airlines all serve Goa. Indian Airlines office (Tel 224 067) in Bandodkar Marg, Panjim and at airport (Tel 222 788). Indian Airlines bus from Dabolim to Panjim. Heading for Margao, and arriving on the first flight from Bombay, get through baggage reclaim as fast as possible and see if the 'paper taxi' is still running. This is actually a minibus that takes the Bombay papers to Margao and also carries a few passengers.

Train from Bombay (24hrs) with a change at Miraj, or from Bangalore (20hrs). Services have been disrupted by conversion to broad gauge. The time from Bombay will be more than halved when the Konkan Railway starts passenger traffic. Coming from Hospet (for Hampi) or Bijapur it is easier and faster to catch a bus from Hubli than to change trains there and again in Londa, moreover the bus takes you straight to Panjim whereas the train terminates in Vasco da Gama.

Try to take a morning train when leaving so as to see the spectacular countryside on the climb to Castle Rock, especially Dudhsagar Waterfall. For some strange reason no fruit is sold on the stations on this line, so buy before leaving.

Buses from Bombay (17hrs), Mangalore (12hrs), Jog Falls (change at Karwar) and other places. Panjim bus-stand is 1km from centre.

The most pleasant way to Goa used to be the ferry from Bombay. This has at last been replaced by a high-speed catamaran, which does the run in seven hours and costs $35. Damania Airline offices make reservations; in Panjim at Liv-In Apartments, Bernard Guedes Road (Tel 220 192). Trading dhows ply this coast, and it is not impossible to hitch a ride (men only) from Bombay or Mangalore, depending on season.

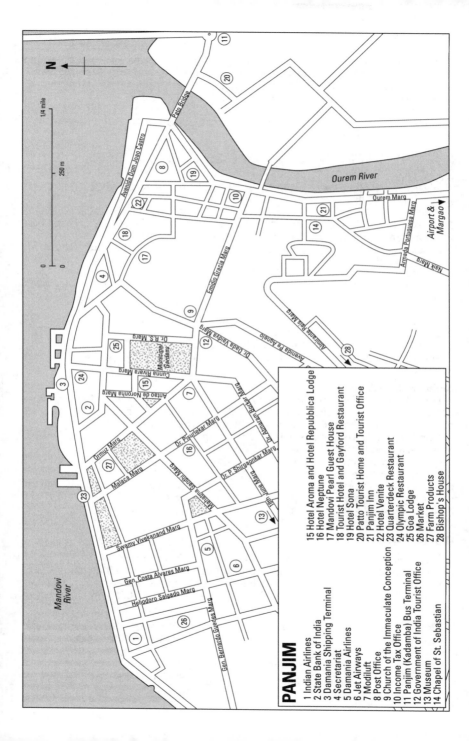

PANJIM

1 Indian Airlines
2 State Bank of India
3 Damania Shipping Terminal
4 Secretariat
5 Damania Airlines
6 Jet Airways
7 Modiluft
8 Post Office
9 Church of the Immaculate Conception
10 Income Tax Office
11 Panjim (Kadamba) Bus Terminal
12 Government of India Tourist Office
13 Museum
14 Chapel of St. Sebastian
15 Hotel Aroma and Hotel Repubblica Lodge
16 Hotel Neptune
17 Mandovi Pearl Guest House
18 Tourist Hotel and Gayford Restaurant
19 Hotel Sona
20 Patto Tourist Home and Tourist Office
21 Panjim Inn
22 Hotel Venite
23 Quarterdeck Restaurant
24 Olympic Restaurant
25 Goa Lodge
26 Market
27 Farm Products
28 Bishop's House

Getting around. It is easy to hire a motorbike or scooter in Goa, prices from around Rs150 (£3/$5) per day, less by the week. Insist on a written authority from the owner for you to use it and evidence of proper valid insurance. Do not pay any large amount of money in advance, it is not unknown for the bike (and the man who hired it to you) to disappear after a day or two. Helmets are not compulsory, but only idiots ride without them. Be warned that Goa police regard Westerners on motorcycles as a useful source of extra income.

Accommodation

Panaji Inn, Fontainhas. Tel 226 523. DWB Rs400. Rest. Bar. Comfortable rooms in old building.

Aroma Hotel, Municipal Garden Square. Tel 228 308. DR Rs250 SWB Rs350 DWB Rs475. Rest (good).

Tourist Hostel, opposite steamer wharf. Tel 227 103. SWB/DWB Rs250 (£5/$8.35) DWB A/C Rs270. Rest (location better than food these days). Bar. Probably still best value in Panjim, though our last room was shared with thousands of cockroaches.

Hotel Repubblica Lodge, opposite Secretariat. Tel 224 630. Being renovated, probably SWB Rs175 DWB Rs225. Good view from the balcony, which you'll recognise if you've seen 'The Sea Wolves'.

Hotel Neptune, Malaca Road. Tel 47727. SWB/DWB Rs180 SWB/DWB A/C Rs290. Rest. Bar.

Goa Lodge, opposite High Court. SR Rs70 DR Rs145.

Mandovi Pearl Guest House, behind Tourist Hostel. Tel 223 928. DR Rs180 3R Rs200 Dorm Rs55.

Everest, 31 January Road. SR Rs75 DR Rs110 DWB Rs1450 Dorm Rs40.

Many other small lodges in the back streets, mostly grubby and expensive for what they are.

Eating and drinking

Hotel Venite, 31 January Road, behind GPO. Tel 225 537. Goan. Mod/Exp. Bar. Closed Sunday. An airy first-floor restaurant, which offers Goan dishes seldom seen on the menu elsewhere. Friendly atmosphere and excellent value for money.

Olympic, opposite steamer wharf. Goan. Cheap. Bar. Good atmosphere and music. Mostly sea food.

Quarter Deck, river front. Goan. Cheap. Bar. Excellent location, right on river.

If you have been in India long enough to miss cheese, charcuterie and similar goodies, take heart — you can find them in Panjim. On the north side of the square to the west of the municipal Square is the *Farm Products Shop*. They sell things you thought you would never find in India.

DONA PAULA

A small resort has grown up here on the cape that divides the Zuari and Mandovi rivers. Except at weekends it is a quiet place with tourist accommodation interspersed with fishermen's houses. There are extensive views, up the Zuari river, across the estuary to Marmugao, and out to sea. Passing dhows contrast with the iron ore barges loading the bulk carriers offshore.

Arrival and departure. 6km from Panjim. Taxi, rickshaw or bus, the latter run through town centre from bus-stand. Launch service every two hours to Marmugao for Vasco da Gama.

Accommodation

Dona Paula Beach Resort, 7km from Panjim. Tel 47955. In the Rs450 (£9/$15) and over bracket, but well worth it. Rest (good). Bar. Looks across estuary to Vasco da Gama.

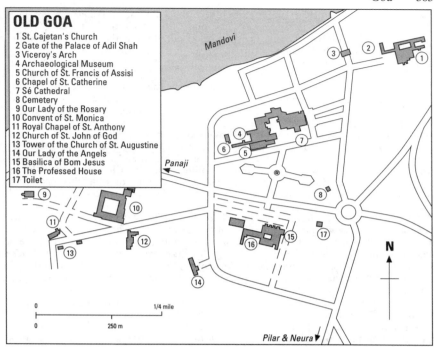

OLD GOA

1 St. Cajetan's Church
2 Gate of the Palace of Adil Shah
3 Viceroy's Arch
4 Archaeological Museum
5 Church of St. Francis of Assisi
6 Chapel of St. Catherine
7 Sé Cathedral
8 Cemetery
9 Our Lady of the Rosary
10 Convent of St. Monica
11 Royal Chapel of St. Anthony
12 Church of St. John of God
13 Tower of the Church of St. Augustine
14 Our Lady of the Angels
15 Basilica of Bom Jesus
16 The Professed House
17 Toilet

Youth Hostel, Miramar Beach. Dorm Rs25. Super location. Five minutes out of town by Dona Paula bus.

OLD GOA

Old Goa*** was the capital of Portugal's eastern empire. The main period of construction (16th and 17th centuries) bridged the transformation from renaissance to baroque architecture and this, coupled with the distance from Europe, accounts for the incredible mixture of styles in each building. Again, because building was supervised by the Jesuits, it is not a purely Portuguese style — there is much Italian influence. Despite this the artisans who did the work were locals and this is very obvious in the art; representations of the Holy Family have a very Indian look, and the best paintings are the traditional floral designs in the Church of St Francis of Assisi.

Although much of the population had already drifted away, Old Goa lingered on as a religious centre. The death knell came in 1834 when the anticlerical Portuguese government suppressed the religious orders. Most of the buildings in Old Goa were constructed of the red laterite you can see still being used. This is easily eroded by wind and rain, and neglect of the plaster coating leads to rapid decay. For this reason the few surviving churches of Old Goa are scant evidence of its former glory.

Traditionally one arrived in Old Goa by boat. Let's pretend we've done the same, so head for the river. The **Viceroy's Arch**, holding a statue of Vasco da Gama, was the formal entry to Goa for high-ranking officials. As you walk up the lane from here try to imagine that you are entering a city of 250,000 people which, in its day, compared with Rome. On all sides were grand buildings full of the riches of the Orient.

The **Church of St Cajetan**, the Italian baroque style of which is quite different from the others, is the last (1656) major church built in Old Goa. Modelled loosely on St Peter's in Rome this is, in some ways, the place's finest church. The main altar is dedicated to Our Lady of Divine Providence, as initially was the church as a whole. Both this and the pulpit are finely carved. Some of the paintings are on cloth as well as the wood panels more common in Goa. The gruesome lectern and altar in the middle of the floor are of course recent additions — vandalism of the first order in a wonderful building like this. The monastery beside the church is now a theological college. The Hindu style **arch** near this is all that remains of a palace of Adil Shah of Bijapur. Used as a residence by the Portuguese governors until 1695, it was demolished in 1820.

Over the road (climb the wall) is **Sé Cathedral** (more properly the Cathedral of St Catherine), the exterior of which is vaguely Tuscan. A tower matching the remaining one fell down in 1776. Reckoned to be the largest church in Asia, construction took from 1562 to 1619. The ceiling is barrel-vaulted, and the Chapel of the Blessed Sacrament, halfway down the left side aisle, gives an idea of what the rest of the cathedral must have looked like before the decoration was covered with whitewash.

Adjoining Sé is the **Church of St Francis of Assisi**. The main part dates from 1661, but the main door and porch belong to an earlier building. This church has the best interior in Old Goa, noted for its murals. Its associated convent, built on the site of a mosque and the largest in Goa, now houses the **museum**. Portraits of the Portuguese governors and viceroys hang here. Nearby is the **Chapel of St Catherine**, a reconstruction of the first Christian place of worship in Goa, and which marks the centre of the battle of 1510.

Most sacred of the churches is the **Basilica of Bom (Infant) Jesus**, because it shelters the ornate tomb of St Francis Xavier. Over the main altar is a statue of Ignatius Loyola, the founder of the Jesuits, and above that the Holy Trinity. The main interest in Bom Jesus, however, is in the tomb and preserved body of St Francis Xavier. The **art gallery** in the Professed House has some extraordinary paintings, an amalgam of Dali and Bosch. A niche gives a view down on to the top of the tomb of St Francis.

To the west of Bom Jesus is the Monte Santo or Holy Hill, once thick with ecclesiastical buildings. The **Convent of St Monica** (rebuilt in 1636 after a fire) was the first convent in the East, and is the only one in Old Goa still used as such. There are reported to be good murals and floral decoration inside. Walk under the three huge flying buttresses of the convent and you reach the **Church of the Rosary**. On one of the round towers buttressing the entrance porch is a little plaque inscribed: 'Deste alto assistiu Afonso de Albuquerque em 25-XI-1510 a reconquista de Goa', which translates as: 'From this spot Afonso de Albuquerque watched the recapture of Goa on 25 November 1510'. Well worth the short walk up here for the view and glimpses of Old Goa.

The ruined tower belongs to the huge **Church of St Augustine**. The monastery to which the church belonged was demolished in 1846, and most of the church collapsed in the 1930s. The tower was one of a pair, and the largest bell, second only to that in Sé Cathedral, is now in the Cathedral of the Immaculate Conception in Panjim. Recent excavation of perhaps 4m depth of rubble from the nave has uncovered beautiful Portuguese tiling, though whether there will be any left by the time you get here is another matter — the vandals are at work already.

The main churches of Old Goa have been designated a World Heritage Site. The exteriors have been repainted, this time in the correct white and, as usual, as much paint has found its way onto the floor as the walls.

Festivals. Feast of St Francis Xavier at Bom Jesus on 3 December, and a large religious procession on the fifth Monday in Lent.

Information. The Archaeological Survey of India booklet (Rs3.25) is a model of its kind and will help you really to appreciate Old Goa. *Goa* by JM Richards (Vikas Publishing) is helpful.

Arrival and departure. On bus route from Panjim to Ponda and Margao. Ask in Panjim about boats; there is no regular service at present, but the barges sometimes give lifts from the old steamer jetty. The guided tour gives you time for only Sé and Bom Jesus.

Eating and drinking. Only drinks and very basic food are available in Old Goa.

Further Afield

HEADING NORTH

Built only in 1970 the bridge over the Mandovi collapsed in 1986, killing several people. A span of its replacement fell down during reconstruction in 1990. They eventually got it fixed, and built another alongside for good measure.

Eating and drinking

O Coqueiro, Alto Porvorim (on main road from Panjim to Mapusa). Tel 7271. Mod/ Exp. Bar. *The* place to eat Goan food. Marvellous atmosphere. You must talk to the owner, Gines Viegas, a fascinating man.

Mapuca

Mapuca is the market town for northern Goa, and a visit here on Friday, when the bazaar is in full swing, is a must. You can buy anthing from dried tiddlers to a cow.

Arrival and departure. Bus from Panjim or Calangute/Baga.

Northern beaches

Even if Goa had nothing else to offer, people would still come for the beaches, mile upon mile of silver sand fringed by palm trees. Despite Goa's new popularity you can still find a place almost to yourself, just a few fishermen and the occasional sun-worshipper.

Aguada to Baga

Aguada Fort is now a five-star resort that monopolises the beach there. The author has never met anyone who has been to **Candolim**, and so to **Calangute**. Sorry chaps, you're too late. Ten years ago you could smoke three chillums before breakfast, tear all your clothes off, run screaming into the sea and nobody would bat an eyelid. Eric of Slough cruised the beaches selling his infamous hash cake and God was in his hippy heaven. Well, it's very different now, and it's hard to imagine any Western traveller wanting to stay here. The only attraction is the Book Exchange at the junction of the Baga and Calangute Beach roads, which has a huge stock — many of the thick novel variety, but lots of good stuff, too.

Arrival and departure. Bus or share taxi from Panjim.

Accommodation

The obvious place to stay is Goa Tourism's *Tourist Hostel*, though the food was very poor when last sampled. Nearby, right on the beach, the *Souza Lobo Restaurant* (good) has rooms offering minimal privacy. As elsewhere the really cheap accommodation consists of rooms in private houses. Ask around, some are in quiet locations.

Baga is still quiet and pleasant, though it is only a matter of time before the tide of concrete from Calangute engulfs it. The stream at the end of Baga Beach has the one bridge in India we would put money on not falling down; they must have had some spare shuttering for a huge box girder. A 9kg/20lb Malabar 'salmon' has been taken in this stream on a hand line.

Accommodation (STD Code 0832)

Baia do Sol. Tel 275 207. SWB/DWB Rs700. Rest (good). Bar. Delightful, spoil yourself.

Cavala. Tel 276 090. SWB/DWB Rs600. Rest. Bar. Another winner, excellent value for money, and a good restaurant too.

Hotel Riverside. Tel 276 062. SWB/DWB Rs400 (Rs300 Oct/Nov). Rest. Bar. Nice rooms, offensive music from restaurant.

Villa Fatima Beach Resort. Tel 276 059. SWB/DWB Rs150. Rest. Bar. Kitchen for guests to do their own cooking.

Jack Bar and Restaurant. DWB Rs210 Cottage Rs450 (£9/$15). Rest. Bar. Good family place run by brothers Jack and Frank. Best value in this price bracket, and may just make the best banana lassi in India.

Jack's, contact Joe Fernandes at Marvel Boutique. DR Rs130. A house over the river. About the cheapest in Baga, but the bath is a bucket from the well. Peaceful though.

Anjuna, Vagator and Chapora

Walking round the headland brings you to **Anjuna**, beloved of freaks and where you can hire windsurfers. Anjuna has long been famous for its **Flea Market** (Wednesday) and **full moon parties**; both have been in trouble with the church authorities and the police. The market is not what it used to be, with 90% of the stuff the tourist tat the wretched hawkers try to sell along the beaches. The package tourists seem to think this is the real hippy scene, so someone's happy. There is little sign at present of a resurgence of the hippy-craftsmen of old. Blatant drug-dealing will probably cause the parties to be banned again before long.

Accommodation

One or two *lodges* now in Anjuna village near the top end of the beach. *Hotel Diamond International* is inland from the end of the road at Vagator beach. Ask at restaurants about accommodation, but do not expect to find a place immediately at busy times.

Vagator. Overlooked by Chapora Fort, Vagator is even quieter than Anjuna. It is also one of the most beautiful and unspoiled parts of Goa. The walls of the fort are mostly intact, but there is absolutely nothing of interest inside, and the only point in coming up here is the view.

Accommodation (STD Code 0832)

Vagator Beach Resort. Tel 273 277. From around DWB Rs750. Rest. Bar. Attractive place with separate units scattered under the palm trees.

Eating and drinking

Mahalaxmi, right on beach. Will help you find accommodation locally; around Rs100 for a double room or a house in village for Rs800–2000 (£16–40/$26–66) per month. Ask for Ganesh.

Chapora. This tiny village is a pleasant place to stay, but Chapora Beach, along the estuary on the north side of the fort, is muddy and rocky. You have to walk round the headland to Vagator.

Accommodation

Sher Tor Villa, Chapora village. SR Rs50 DR Rs75. Traditional Goan house.

Dabholkar Tourist Houses, near boatyards. Also rooms to let.

Eating and drinking
   River Deck, Chapora village. Goan. Cheap. Very pleasant.

Arambol and Terekhol

Arambol is the quietest of the beaches regularly used by travellers. The village is picturesquely set among palm trees, and a small cluster of beach shacks caters for most needs. Around the headland is another small beach and a freshwater pool. A short walk from the village gains you the peace and isolation that used to be the hallmark of all Goa's beaches. A lot of day trippers invade Arambol village at weekends (especially January to March), but do not move far along the beach.

Arrival and departure. Buses from Betim (ferry from Panjim) to Calangute, Baga and Mapusa. Buses from Mapusa to Anjuna, Chapora and Arambol (direct or via Siolim ferry). Sometimes a weekend boat service from Baga to Arambol.

Accommodation. *Rooms* in picturesque village houses cost around Rs40 double, or Rs50 with a fan. There are a few *cottages* on the bluffs around the headland, but these are mostly let long-term.

Eating and drinking.
   Lakes Paradise Bar and Restaurant, on headland. Cheap. Goan, fish or prawn curry, etc.
   There is a small cluster of shack *restaurants* at the northern end of the beach.

Terekhol. The fort at Terekhol marks the limit of Goa's coast to the north, and is ideal for an 'away from it all' rest. The fort, now converted to a rest house, encloses a small church and has good views over land and sea.

Arrival and departure. Bus from Mapusa to Siolim, ferry to Chopdem, bus to Querim, ferry, then a walk of about 1.5km. Worth it!

Accommodation
   Hotel Terekhol Fort Heritage. Tel Panjim 220 705. DWB from Rs700 (£14/$23.35). Rest. Bar. Fort originally built by Marathas in superb isolated position. Was a fantastic bargain when run by Goa Tourism, but dubious value now, despite its super location.

VASCO DA GAMA

Vasco is now an industrial centre. For the traveller it is no more than the rail terminus for Panjim.

Information. Tourist office at Tourist Hostel.

Arrival and departure. Bus (allow 2hrs if catching a train) or taxi from Panjim. Launch from Dona Paula to Marmugao every two hours, then bus or very occasional train the short distance to Vasco da Gama.
   Trains to Bombay (24hrs) and Bangalore (20½hrs). Check under relevant sections for other destinations. For reservations try first at the Out Agency at Panjim bus-stand; Margao also has quotas.

Accommodation
   Tourist Hotel, outside station. Tel 0334 513 119. SWB Rs130 DWB Rs150.

HEADING SOUTH

The main road south from Panjim to Margao crosses the Zuari River by a bridge that took so long to build that it made the *Guinness Book of Records*. Not that you will get much time to look at it; since the Mandovi bridge fell down everyone has driven flat out over this one just in case!

The alternative route passes through Old Goa and then turns south to Ponda. In the early days of their rule the Portuguese demolished many temples. Thus those to be seen today are well inland and often tucked away in beautiful wooded country. Several are close to this road, the most notable being the **Sri Manguesh Temple****. Much of the interest here lies in the influence of the Portuguese baroque churches, which is immediately evident in the deepmal (light tower) and the exterior of the temple itself. The interior is an extraordinary mixture — romanesque columns and arches, a ceiling like that of a Portuguese house, the chandeliers of a mosque, and a purely Hindu silver-clad shrine. The tower beside the tank looks more Chinese than anything else. A big festival takes place at the end of April.

The **Shri Mahalsa** and **Shri Shantadurga Temples** are equally attractive. On the main road just outside Ponda is the **Safa Masjid**, one of very few old mosques to have survived in Goa, of minimal interest despite recent restoration.

Margao

Margao is the main town of southern Goa. Of no particular interest, it is nevertheless a pleasant town and makes a useful base for exploring both the southern beaches and hinterland. The indoor market, near the railway station, is the best in Goa. Margao's big event of the year is Carnival (last weekend before Lent). This is a big celebration with a religious procession on Sunday, and street dancing and a folk dance competition on following days.

Information. Tourist office in Tourist Hostel.

Arrival and departure. Direct bus from Panjim, also the route via Ponda, which may involve a change of bus there.

Accommodation. As in Panjim, accommodation in the town tends to be expensive and not very good. These are the best.

Hotel Metropole. Tel 223 552. SWB Rs225 DWB Rs295. Rest. Bar. Roof garden.

Goa Woodlands Hotel, opposite old bus-stand. Tel 221 121. DWB Rs150/180 (£3–3.60/$5–8) DWB A/C Rs400. Rest. Bar. Very good indeed, which means you have little chance of getting in without a booking.

Tourist Hostel. Tel 221 966. SWB Rs130 DWB Rs150–250. Rest. Bar.

Hotel Greenview, near railway station. Tel 220 151. SWB Rs80 DWB Rs100. Rest (veg). Far better than other places at this price in the same area.

Eating and drinking

Longuinhos. Goan/Cont. Cheap/Mod. Authentic Lusso-Indian charm. Bar, wine by the glass and cocktails. Continental atmosphere with good food and service. A civilised place for a meal, or just to meet friends for a drink and a snack. One of the most enjoyable restaurants in all India. And real bread rolls!

We have heard that there is a superb Chinese restaurant near the north-eastern corner of the Municipal Square. Ask at the tourist office.

Just to the west of the town bus-stand is a *Farm Shop* like the one in Panjim.

Southern beaches

These are generally much quieter than those north of Panjim. South of Vasco da Gama is an unbroken 25km of beach. The best-known section, Colva Beach, is right in the centre.

Colva. Colva village is now quite built up, and getting more so. It is not yet as crowded as one might expect, the problem is that a high percentage of the people here are precisely the type of package tourist you came to India to avoid. The author can't imagine any self-respecting traveller wanting to spend all their time in Goa at Colva, but it is at least a convenient place to travel along the beach from. Still pleasant in the evenings when day-trippers have gone, you need to walk a good kilometre to get some peace on the beach, from both vendors and voyeurs.

Accommodation

Longuinhos Beach Resort. Tel 222 918. DWB A/C Rs700. Rest. Bar. As good as the restaurant in Margao, which is high praise.

Skylark Cottages. Tel 223 669. SWB/DWB Rs225 Suite A/C Rs450. Rest. Bar. Good value. Quiet location backing onto paddy fields.

Tourist Cottages. Tel 222 287. SWB/DWB Rs250 Dorm Rs45. Rest. Bar. Plain but comfortable and very clean rooms with balconies looking towards the sea. Hot water. Special rooms (Rs250) have TV. Well kept and excellent value.

Sukhsagar Beach Resort. Tel 220 224. SWB/DWB Rs250 SWB/DWB A/C Rs390. Rest. Bar. Hard to find behind Jymi's Cottages and Silver Sands. Quiet, clean and comfortable.

Lucky Star. DWB Rs160. Rest. Bar. Clean but not cheap. Serious fly problem and smell of fish.

Jymi's Cottages. SWB/DWB Rs145 (£2.90/$4.80). Good. Mosquito nets.

Tourist Nest. Tel 223 944. SR/DR Rs80 SWB/DWB Rs125. Rest (Goan/French). Bar. Basic but clean in new block. One very special room at regular price in old house. Use of traditional Goan family sitting room.

It is still possible to find a *double room* in the village for Rs60, but don't expect much in the way of amenities.

Eating and drinking

Peacock (Mar e Sol). Goan/North Indian. Mod/Exp. Good food inside or out.

Lactancia Bar and Restaurant seems the same as ever. It preserves its rustic charm amongst the new developments, if only by the cats, dogs, chickens and piglets scratching around under the tables.

Vincy's. Rebuilt and ruined, totally devoid of character.

We are unimpressed by the beach restaurants.

North of Colva

First stop north of Colva is **Betalbatim**, often visited by Colva buses. Betalbatim now boasts a couple of beach shacks, one of which has a tame eagle (it's really a kite) that arrived with a broken wing and has settled down quite happily. Very limited accommodation nearby, ask at the shacks.

You will probably prefer to avoid **Majorda** and its resort hotel, but a little north is **Cansaulim** on the Margao-Vasco railway and bus routes and the nearby **Velsao Beach**. Velsao is certainly quiet, just one beach shack, but overlooked by a chemical works. What genius sites these places? In the village by the Church of San Tomé is a covered cemetery; these are quite common in Goa. Velsao is the last point where the beach is accessible as the road to Vasco swings inland.

Just north of the village past a small Hindu temple on the left a tarred road branches right and leads to the hilltop **Remedios Church**. You need to be feeling very energetic to walk or cycle up here, but the panoramic views, especially to the south and at sunset, justify the effort. The feast of the Three Kings is celebrated here on 6 January, and in spring you will see cashew fruit and nuts growing by the road.

South of Colva

Going south from Colva, **Benaulim** has now acquired a number of beach shacks, and many more places to stay a little inland. This has not spoiled the place, and you still have miles of beach to yourself.

Accommodation

L'Amour Beach Resort. Tel 223 270. DWB Rs250–400. Also cottages. Rest (good but slow). Bar. The first beach hotel in Benaulim and still the best located. Basic but clean and friendly.

O Palmar Cottages. Tel 223 278. DWB Rs195. Similar to L'Amour.

Green Garden Tourist Cottage. SR/DR Rs65. Very basic (shower and toilet outside) but clean and quiet.

Caravan Tourist Home, opposite Bank of Baroda. Tel 225 679. SR/DR Rs85 (£1.70/$2.85). Same standard as Green Garden.

Rosario's Inn, Vass Vaddo. DWB Rs95. Breakfast and dinner on request.

Brito's, Maria Hall, has good accommodation.

Eating and drinking

Johncy's, on beach. Goan. Cheap/Mod. Bar. Very good food, reasonably priced. Every week or so they do an excellent eat-all-you-can buffet for Rs40. Spoiled, like other places on the beach, by crass music played too loud.

Cacy-Rose, Maria Hall. Cheap/Mod. Goan. Bar. Family establishment offering good food in a quiet setting. Recommended.

Pedro's Bar. Goan. Cheap/Mod. Pleasant but, like L'Amour, has not really come to terms with having competition.

Varka, which has a very fine church, is a very quiet place to stay, and south of the Ramada Beach Resort a black-top road leads from the beach to Luis Bar (cold drinks, beer, simple food — ten-minute walk from beach) and on to **Carmona**. Varka and Carmona villages are a long way from the beach; a bike would be essential if staying there. The bus terminates at **Cavelossim**, which has an attractive church unspoiled by corrugated iron porches.

The promontory at the southernmost end of Colva Beach is now occupied by several large tourist resort and time-share developments. The kindest thing that one can say is that they are invisible from Mabor Beach and, because most visitors rarely leave the poolside, they have little impact from our point of view. In fact Carmona, Cavelossim and Mabor beaches are best reached by cycling down the beach. You may find accommodation with a family in these places but there is precious little else in the way of facilities.

Cabo da Rama

Exploring south of the Sal River involves either getting a fisherman to take you across the estuary or following the road via Margao and Cuncolim. This road passes through **Assolna**, where an unusual edifice with statues of Christ and the four apostles looks more like a war memorial than a religious monument. A covered cemetery is opposite. The road continues to the fishing village of **Bapsoro**. Just over the new bridge (it replaces a canoe ferry that was quite exciting with a bicycle) from Bapsoro to Betul is the McCla Bar and Restaurant. The track to the right leads to the wharf where manganese ore barges were loaded; the old conveyor is still there. A small fort overlooks the estuary, which is now a busy fishing port. Mint grows wild here, useful for cooking or mint tea.

Follow the road uphill from McCla Bar and take the first right over towards the two heaps of manganese ore, pass to the right of them and be prepared for a **breathtaking view** of the whole length of Colva Beach as far as Vasco da Gama. A little further towards the open sea is a small cross on the headland, from where paths lead down to the rocks. Despite the lack of real cliffs the scenery is rugged and beautiful, a change from endless beaches. Botanists and ornithologists will find plenty of interest here. A pair or two of white-bellied sea eagles patrol, occasionally swooping down to pick up a sea snake from the water. A wall is being built across this promontory for some reason; let's hope it will not impair access to this wonderful viewpoint.

Cabo da Rama Fort is quite a long haul from here via Cananguinim. All that is left of the fort is the perimeter wall, a small chapel and a few iron cannons. Amazing views, but whether you feel that they justify the effort is another matter. The author once did it on a push-bike — he must have been mad! Parts of the way are through attractive forest, but most is open, shadeless country.

Arrival and departure. Buses from Margao to Colva, Bapsoro, Betul and Cananguinim, probably also to Cabo da Rama as the road is being made up. Share-taxis (Rs3) to Colva from same place as buses. A rickshaw from the town centre to Colva costs Rs20, a taxi Rs40.

Right down south, almost on the border with Karnataka, is **Palonen**, reached by bus to Chauri (Canacona).

INLAND

Goa has no fewer than three **nature reserves**, and there is accommodation in two of them, Bondla and Molen. At **Sanguelim** there are Buddhist caves near a Portuguese fort and a waterfall. The Portuguese built many forts in Goa; one of the most accessible is **Reis Magos** over the river from Panjim.

Mention **trekking** in India and everyone thinks of the Himalayas. Yet the Western Ghats go well over 1000m and offer wild jungle terrain. You could even walk down from Pune or Mahabaleswar. More information from Captain Rebello at the Captain of Ports Office, Panjim. A festival takes place at **Sirigao** (April–May) of the Dhond tribes, whose mixture of animism and Hinduism includes firewalking.

Accommodation. Goa Tourism has accommodation at *Mayem Lake Resort* and *Molem Tourist Resort* (near a wildlife sanctuary) up in the Ghats, and cottages at the *Bondla Forest Sanctuary*, not expensive.

HEADING SOUTH FROM GOA

You have two options: straight down the coast to Mangalore and on to Kochi (see page 314), or the inland route via the Jog Falls to Mysore (see page 294).

KERALA

Unless snowy mountains are your thing you will probably find Kerala the most beautiful of the Indian states. The generous rainfall makes it brilliantly green, and its fertile farmlands support a population density of around 750/sq km, matched only by Bengal. Deserted golden beaches run all along the coast, and half the palm trees in the world must grow here. Edward Lear, a man rarely lost for a word, called it the 'coconuttery'. Not all are coconut palms, though; you will soon learn to distinguish coconut palms from the many banana trees. The palmyra grows a black fruit with a gelatinous centre, definitely an acquired taste.

The coastal strip is fairly flat, but inland the Cardamom Hills rise to over 2500m. As well as the spice for which the hills are named most of India's coffee and pepper is grown here. The coffee is good as long as you can get it strong enough, and has a distinctive caramelly flavour.

One of the fascinations of Kerala is the variety of religious communities and the accord in which they co-exist. There are many Muslims (Calicut was the centre of a Muslim state) and of course Hindus. The Malabar coast is easily accessible and, with the approval of the rulers of Kochi, many foreign ideas flourished. One of the two Jewish sects, the Black, claims to date its presence in Mattancheri to 587BC. They share a quarter and synagogue with the White Jews who arrived much later. Sadly the

Jewish population is now small and ageing, many of the young people and families having left for Israel.

Christianity was supposedly brought to Kochi by Thomas the Apostle (Doubting Thomas) in around AD50. This foundation is still represented by the Maronite Syrian Christians, their priests easily recognisable in traditional orthodox garb. The only serious persecution these three groups have ever faced resulted from the Portuguese setting up the Inquisition in Goa in 1560. The Dutch take-over a hundred years later restored peace and tolerance — and introduced yet another form of Christianity.

Kerala has for long had the highest literacy rate in India, and following a recent campaign they claim 100%. The state government reckons that this effort cost a mere Rs20 per head. It also runs the most effective health service in India. Put these two factors together with the Keralans' social awareness and you have zero population growth. Despite a declining growth rate this is still a long way off anywhere else in India. Keralans (like other southerners) tend to be looked down upon by northern Indians, not least because of their darker skins. They are, however, noted for their industriousness, and the hospital service in the rest of India would collapse without Keralan nurses, who are mostly Christian. Muslim girls often lack the education to do the job, and taboos concerning the sick deter Hindus. Kerala is not the most exciting state in India in terms of tourist attractions, but the self-confidence and communicativeness of the people easily make up for that.

KOCHI

Cochin, as it used to be called, is an important deep-water port for the south of India, and has been a major trading centre for over 2000 years. The name Kochi covers Ernakulam on the mainland, Fort Cochin and Mattancheri on the peninsula south of the harbour entrance, and Willingdon Island in the centre of the lagoon. The latter was created with material dredged from the channel and is now the main docks area.

Ernakulam

There is little of interest in Ernakulam, but it is a prosperous place, mainly because of the large number of Keralans who work in the Persian Gulf. The shops along MG Road are as good as any in India. Ernakulam is one of the points where the backwater system meets the roads. The canal bridge on Shanmugham Road overlooks a lively scene of goods being transferred from boats to lorries and vice versa.

While in Ernakulam you must take the opportunity of seeing a **Kathakali***** performance. This combination of mime and dance, the spectacular costumes and intricate make-up make Kathakali one of the world's outstanding performing arts. Two main centres, See India Foundation on Kalathi Parambil Lane and Cochin Cultural Centre on Durbar Hall Road, give performances every evening. Both give an explanation of the hundreds of movements and gestures. Arrive early to see the make-up process, which can take two hours. Art Kerala on Chittoor Road also does other Keralan dances. Full details from tourist offices.

Old Cochin

The peninsula of Mattancheri is the oldest part of Cochin; traders have come from all over the Old World and often settled here.

Many **Chinese fishing nets** are fixed in the harbour entrance (cut 1932), the men who work these having probably the finest physiques you will see in India. The **Church of St Francis*** was the first in the East to be built by Europeans, the Portuguese in 1510, though the present building dates from around 1560. The Dutch made it a Reformed Church when they siezed Cochin in 1661, and it became Anglican

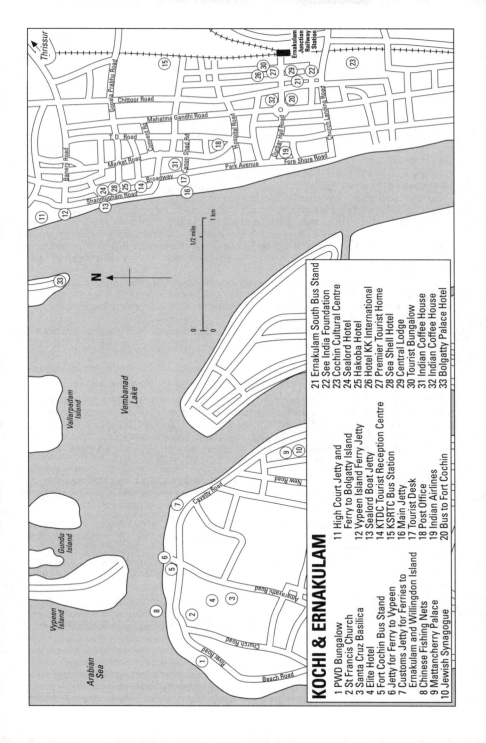

KOCHI & ERNAKULAM

1 PWD Bungalow
2 St Francis Church
3 Santa Cruz Basilica
4 Elite Hotel
5 Fort Cochin Bus Stand
6 Jetty for Ferry to Vypeen
7 Customs Jetty for Ferries to
  Ernakulam and Willingdon Island
8 Chinese Fishing Nets
9 Mattancherry Palace
10 Jewish Synagogue
11 High Court Jetty and
   Ferry to Bolgatty Island
12 Vypeen Island Ferry Jetty
13 Sealord Boat Jetty
14 KTDC Tourist Reception Centre
15 KSRTC Bus Station
16 Main Jetty
17 Tourist Desk
18 Post Office
19 Indian Airlines
20 Bus to Fort Cochin
21 Ernakulam South Bus Stand
22 See India Foundation
23 Cochin Cultural Centre
24 Sealord Hotel
25 Hakoba Hotel
26 Hotel KK International
27 Premier Tourist Home
28 Sea Shell Hotel
29 Central Lodge
30 Tourist Bungalow
31 Indian Coffee House
32 Indian Coffee House
33 Bolgatty Palace Hotel

with the arrival of the British. Vasco da Gama was buried here in 1524 before his remains were taken to Lisbon; a war memorial stands outside, and Portuguese and Dutch tablets are inside. This is one of very few places where you can see old-fashioned man-pulled punkahs in working order. Some of the houses with lovely gardens could have come straight from the stockbroker belt in Surrey, England, and, with a game of cricket on the nearby greensward, it needs only a pub to compare with an English village (there is a bar close by).

Students of artillery may be interested in the old **coastal defence batteries** on the seaward side. The area is occupied by a naval gunnery school and inaccessible, but visible from the beach. **Santa Cruz Cathedral** is effectively a late-19th century building, the Portuguese original having been destroyed by the British when they took over Cochin in 1795.

Further south in Mattancheri is the Jewish quarter and the **synagogue***, a delightful airy building that epitomises all that a place of worship should be. The floor is of 18th century blue and white Chinese tiles (no shoes allowed; closed on Saturdays). The antique and curio shops near the synagogue provide pleasant browsing. An excellent account of the Jewish communities in Cochin and elsewhere in India appears in *The Thirteenth Gate* by Tudor Parfitt (Weidenfeld and Nicholson).

In the same area is the so-called **Dutch Palace****, actually built by the Portuguese in 1515 to placate the Raja after some slight, and later restored by the Dutch. There are very fine wood carvings and also very beautiful murals depicting the Hindu epics, including some naughty ones.

Kerala processes a huge amount of coir, the rough stuff from coconuts. A cooperative on Gundu Island produces doormats, sisal for charpoys, and clouds of dust. The boat tour visits here.

Willingdon Island is visited only for the Tourist Office and the adjacent Malabar Hotel and swimming pool.

Information. Government of India Tourist Office (one of the best) on Willingdon Island; you want the ferry from the main jetty to Embarkation Jetty, take the southern ferry and you will have a long, hot walk. Tourist Reception Centre on Shanmughan Road is the place to find out about accommodation in the Bolgatty Palace and book the **harbour tour** (excellent value), which picks up nearby. Government of Kerala Tourist Information Centre in Park Avenue.

Local transport. Ferries run from the main jetty in Ernakulam to Customs Jetty on Fort Cochin and Mattancherry. Most details are posted in English, and staff are very helpful.

Arrival and departure. Airport on Willindon Island (5km from centre). Flights from Bombay, Delhi, Goa, Madras, Bangalore and Trivandrum. Indian Airlines, Durbar Hall Road, Ernakulam (Tel 370 242).

Trains to Ernakulam from Bombay (35hrs), Madras (14hrs), Mangalore (10hrs direct, 12hrs with a change at Shoranur), Ootacamund (12hrs, change at Mettupaliyam), and Trivandrum (4hrs). The station you want is Ernakulam Junction; Ernakulam Town is out of the way, and Kochi Harbour Terminal is on Willingdon Island.

Bus services to just about everywhere including Madurai. The bus-stand is 1km from Ernakulam Junction station.

Accommodation (STD Code 0484)
Near Ernakulam Junction station:
Hotel KK International, opposite station. Tel 366 010. SWB Rs110 (£2.20/$3.65) DWB Rs165 SWB A/C Rs175 DWB A/C Rs250. Rest Ind/Chi/Cont. Clean and comfortable. Superb value and the higher the room, the fewer the mosquitoes.

Tourist Bungalow, close to KK. Tel 352 412. SWB Rs55 DWB Rs95 DWB A/C Rs165. Rest. Bar. Not an official tourist bungalow, but good.

Plenty of other accommodation; *Premier Tourist Home* and *Central Lodge* are cheaper, and cheap restaurants just outside the station. This area is also a short walk from the bus-stand.

On harbour front:

Sealord Hotel, Shanmugham Road. Tel 352 682. SWB Rs350 DWB Rs450 SWB A/C Rs500 DWB A/C Rs700. Rest (two, including a roof-top Chinese). Bar. Overlooks harbour. You'd pay twice as much for this quality in the north of India.

Bolgatty Palace. Tel 355 003. SWB Rs300 DWB Rs400 SWB A/C Rs600 DWB A/C Rs700. Rest. Bar. Golf course. An old Dutch building, later the British residency, on an island in the harbour. Check at the Kerala tourist office about ferries. A bit inconvenient but well worth it for the peace and quiet.

Hotel Hakoba, Shanmugham Road. Tel 353 933. SWB Rs65 DWB Rs110 SWB A/C Rs170 DWB A/C Rs195. Rest (good). Bar.

Sea Shell, Shanmugham Road. Tel 353 807. SWB Rs55 DWB Rs85. Rest. Bar. Overlooks harbour, or did before the unbelievably ugly shopping centre was built.

In Fort Cochin:

Public Works Department Bungalow is in a super location looking out over ocean, and the *Elite* (not far away) gets good reports.

Eating and drinking

Near Ernakulam Junction station:

Alina, Shahziha Hotel, in station road. Ind/Chi. Mod. Not bad.

THE KERALA BACKWATERS

No visit to Kerala is complete without taking a boat trip through the maze of rivers, canals and lagoons between Kochi and Quilon (new name Kollam). These waterways are the sole route for commerce and passenger traffic in this soggy area. They are mostly shallow enough for the traditional hump-backed boats to be punted along, though you will see an occasional one with a big, tatty sail. Habitation is mainly along the banks and the scenery and rural sights between Kottayam and Alleppey (new name Alappuzha) can be idyllic, especially in the late afternoon and twilight.

The boat service from **Ernakulam to Kottayam** runs only at night.

The trip from **Kottayam to Alleppey** (2½hrs) is not, frankly, a patch on that between Alleppey and Quilon. The first hour is through man-made canals and has its attractions, mainly in the back-door view it gives of riverside life. After that it degenerates into broad and rather uninteresting lagoons. Better, though, than not seeing the backwaters at all.

At times the boat ploughs through a dense mat of water hyacinth, introduced to India by a misguided Englishman who thought it would brighten up his garden pond. Spread by becoming attached to the legs of water birds it has taken a liking to the tropics. At least the herons benefit from it as it helps them to fish in deeper waters. Pied and blue kingfishers abound, their favourite perches being the prosaic power lines overhead. On either side of the canal is the brilliant green of young paddy, and everywhere are coconut palms and bright flowers. Flocks of ducks abound; why is it never on the menu?

A further service runs from **Alleppey to Quilon** (8hrs, barring breakdowns). This is very beautiful, but the hard seats and vibration can be too much of a good thing. Take food and drink if you do this trip. The alternative, if you are really short of time, is to do the first two hours from **Quilon to Alamkadavu,** a bus from there takes you back to Quilon.

Kochi, Kottayam and Alleppey are the main venues for the famous **snake boat races**. These are between long narrow boats each with up to a hundred men paddling, and competition is intense. The snag is that all the events take place in August/

September, which is not a time when many Westerners would choose to be in the area.

Arrival and departure. Bus from Ernakulam to Kottayam (2hrs) and you have only a short rickshaw ride (Rs10) to the jetty. The train is slower and the station a long way from the jetty. Kill time in Kottayam, if necessary, by sampling the banana fritters in the coffee house by the jetty.

Bus from Ernakulam to Alleppey (1½hrs), and then the boat to Kottayam. From Kottayam there is a bus to Periyar, a lovely drive (4½hrs), and trains to Trivandrum (3½hrs).

Train from Quilon to Trivandrum (1½hrs) or Ernakulam (3¾hrs).

Accommodation
Alleppey (STD Code 0477)
Kuttanad Tourist Home (between jetty and bus-stand). Tel 61354. SWB Rs50 DWB Rs80 SWB A/C Rs150 DWB A/C Rs175. New and spotless.

St George's Lodgings, CCNB Road (1km from jetty). Tel 61620. SR Rs36 (72p/$1.20) DR Rs52 SWB Rs50 DWB Rs88 plus 7½%. Rest. Clean and entirely adequate, despite low prices.

Quilon (STD Code 0474)
Hotel Sudarsan, Hospital Road. Tel 75322. SWB Rs130 DWB Rs160 SWB A/C Rs250 DWB A/C Rs300. Rest (separate veg and non-veg, both very good). Bar A/C. A short walk from boat jetty, this is a luxury hotel at budget prices.

Inconveniently located out of town, but apparently attractive, is the *Tourist Bungalow*.

Eating and drinking. Try the *Indian Coffee House* and *Komala Hotel* in Alleppey.

THIRUVANANTHAPURAM

Most people race through Trivandrum, as it used to be called, on their way from the Backwaters to Kovalam. The fearfully noisy and dusty walk between the station and the bus-stand seems to justify this. This is, however, an interesting city, and it has one of the best art galleries in India. The name, incidentally, derived from Thiru-ananta-puram, means 'Abode of the Sacred Serpent'.

Trivandrum was the capital of the state of Travancore before the formation of Kerala and has some fine public buildings, notably the Secretariat. Finest of all is the **Napier Museum***** (8am–6pm, closed Monday and Wednesday morning), a truly delightful building. Mainly Keralan in style, many foreign influences can be seen at work. The stone pillars are purely Hindu, and other features are strongly reminiscent of the pagoda architecture of Himachal Pradesh and Nepal. Elsewhere can be seen links to the architecture of south-east Asia. The interior is an absolute joy — high ceilings, pastel colours and diffused light, the perfect palace for a tropical climate. The joke is that it was designed in 1872 by an Englishman, RF Chisholm! The museum has some very fine ivory carvings, and a section on Buddhist sculpture allows you to compare the Graeco-Roman art of Gandhara with that of Travancore and Burma.

The museum is surrounded by gardens with many fine trees. A short distance away is the **Sri Chitra Art Gallery***** (10am–5pm, closed Monday and Wednesday morning). The first three rooms are devoted to Indian artists of the late 19th and early 20th centuries. Here one sees the tremendous promise for an indigenous style of modern Indian painting, a promise that has not been fulfilled. Two rooms are devoted to works by Nicholas and Svetoslav Roerich (see Naggar). The rooms are scattered, and you have to be careful not to miss any. The furthest gallery is devoted to oil paintings, mainly by the two Varmas. Some of the portraiture is excellent, especially the English colonel who, beneath the gruff exterior, was clearly the life and soul of the party. The rest, unfortunately, display how Indian artists have rarely come to

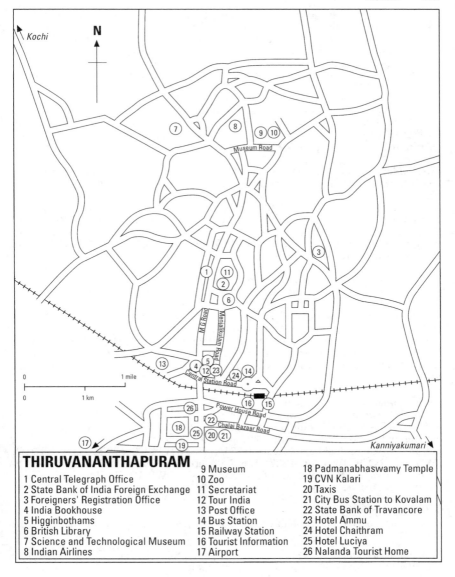

THIRUVANANTHAPURAM

1 Central Telegraph Office	9 Museum	18 Padmanabhaswamy Temple
2 State Bank of India Foreign Exchange	10 Zoo	19 CVN Kalari
3 Foreigners' Registration Office	11 Secretariat	20 Taxis
4 India Bookhouse	12 Tour India	21 City Bus Station to Kovalam
5 Higginbothams	13 Post Office	22 State Bank of Travancore
6 British Library	14 Bus Station	23 Hotel Ammu
7 Science and Technological Museum	15 Railway Station	24 Hotel Chaithram
8 Indian Airlines	16 Tourist Information	25 Hotel Luciya
	17 Airport	26 Nalanda Tourist Home

terms with this medium. Upstairs are copies of cave, temple and palace murals, useful given the poor condition and inaccessibility of most of the originals.

The **Science and Technology Museum** is also reported to be good.

Tour India (see below) lay on a **Backwater trip** in traditional boats followed by a walk back (two hours overall) with a full briefing on local flora and fauna, village life and coir production. The price includes green coconuts, the milk of which is said to be as good as a saline glucose solution. Just the thing in this climate.

At **Veli Tourist Village** (9km from town centre) you can go off and explore a backwater on your own. A rowing boat for four people costs Rs20 per hour, a kayak Rs10, water scooters Rs50/150 for 15 minutes (but a staff member will go with you), and a windsurfer Rs20 per hour. This backwater is separated from the sea by a raised beach where you are quite likely to see fishermen hauling in their nets. Birdlife is abundant on the lagoon, mostly cormorants and egrets, and also gulls trying to catch the litle fish skittering out of your way. The Youth Hostel here has dorm beds for Rs20.

Kerala has its own martial art, **kalari-payattu****, which arguably spawned karate and all the others. No visit to Trivandrum is complete without a visit to CVN Kalari in West Fort to see an early morning training session and a weapons display. More info from Tour India (see below).

Information. Kerala Tourist Development Corporation at Tourist Reception Centre near Central Bus Station. Government of Kerala information counters at railway station, Central Bus Station, Park View (near museum) and airport. Government of India counter at airport. Despite (or perhaps because of) all these places most people find a warmer welcome at Tour India, a couple of hundred metres up MG Road from the railway bridge. We rarely plug individual companies; this plug is an acknowledgement of the enthusiasm and helpfulness of Babu Verghese and his staff. They really know what they are talking about.

Arrival and departure. Airport 9km from town centre. Indian Airlines office (Tel 436 870) at Mascot Junction near museum. Bus service from office, apparently rather erratic. Flights to Colombo and Maldives as well as internal.

Rail from Kanniyakumari (2½hrs), Quilon (1½hrs) and Ernakulam (4hrs). See under Ernakulam for more distant destinations.

Two bus-stands, Central (opposite railway station) for long-distance buses and City for local services and Kovalam. From Central Bus Station to Quilon, Kottayam, Kochi (Ernakulam) and Kanniyakumari. Full details on getting to Kovalam in that section.

Accommodation (STD Code 0471)

Hotel Chaithram, Station Road. Tel 330 977. SWB Rs250 DWB Rs350 SWB A/C Rs550 DWB A/C Rs750, plus 10% tax and 10% SC. Rest (2). Bar (perhaps). A real bargain, only a government body could price it this cheap.

Hotel Ammu, Manjalikulam Road. Tel 331 937. SWB Rs100 (£2/$3.35) DWB Rs125 SWB A/C Rs250 DWB A/C Rs275 plus 7.5% tax. Rest.

Omkar Lodge, MG Road. Tel 78503. SWB Rs75 DWB Rs120. Rest (veg). Clean but front rooms are noisy.

Nalanda Tourist Home, MG Road. Tel 71864. SWB Rs55 DWB Rs80. Very similar to Omkar.

More inexpensive, and probably quieter, hotels past Hotel Ammu in Manjalikulam Road.

Eating and drinking

Omkar, MG Road. Ind veg. Cheap. Good thalis.

Chicken Corner, MG Road. Ind (non-veg). Cheap/Mod.

KOVALAM

Kovalam ranks second only to Goa among India's beach resorts. There is a lot less of it, of course, though many find the small bays between rocky headlands and the sharply rising ground behind more interesting than Goa's mainly flat straight beaches.

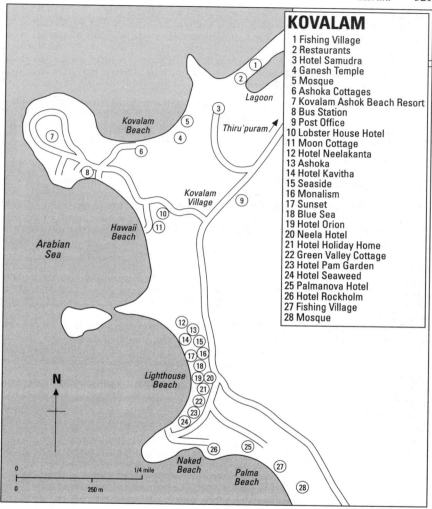

KOVALAM

1 Fishing Village
2 Restaurants
3 Hotel Samudra
4 Ganesh Temple
5 Mosque
6 Ashoka Cottages
7 Kovalam Ashok Beach Resort
8 Bus Station
9 Post Office
10 Lobster House Hotel
11 Moon Cottage
12 Hotel Neelakanta
13 Ashoka
14 Hotel Kavitha
15 Seaside
16 Monalism
17 Sunset
18 Blue Sea
19 Hotel Orion
20 Neela Hotel
21 Hotel Holiday Home
22 Green Valley Cottage
23 Hotel Pam Garden
24 Hotel Seaweed
25 Palmanova Hotel
26 Hotel Rockholm
27 Fishing Village
28 Mosque

Starting from the east, **Palma Beach** is probably quietest, except at weekends when kids play football there. Next door is what the locals, for reasons lost in the mists of time, call **Naked Beach**.

Lighthouse Beach is Kovalam's main drag, an unbroken chain of cafés and restaurants along the fringe of the beach. Sounds awful, actually rather fun, and you can always walk round the corner to **Hawaii Beach**, which is much quieter.

Kovalam Beach itself, partly reserved for the Ashok Beach Resort, is across the headland. Pleasant enough, the snag is that tour buses come down here, and especially at weekends it can be crowded and boring. Ashok Beach Resort rent out a sailing dinghy at Rs250 for two hours, also windsurfers, and water skiing costs Rs400 per hour.

Past the Hotel Samudra is a fishing village and quiet beach. Three kinds of boat are used by the fishermen, the simplest being the true catamaran. The word catamaran derives from the Tamil *kattu*, to bind, and *maram*, tree; and in their simplest form the boats are just that, logs lashed together. Be careful about trips on the lagoon with fishermen; it is said that the price goes up when it's time to return! Be careful about swimming, too; the beaches look gentle, but the currents are treacherous. Check with the lifeguards on Lighthouse Beach.

Arrival and departure. Bus from City bus-stand in Trivandrum. Share-taxis from just outside bus-stand. Arriving in Kovalam get off the bus at the Lobster House Hotel rather than at the end of the road, then you have only a short walk downhill to the beach. Direct buses from Kovalam to Ernakulam and Kanniyakumari.

Accommodation (STD Code 0471)

Hotel Rockholm, Lighthouse Road. Tel 480 306. SWB Rs750 DWB Rs800. Rest. Very attractive place, most rooms have balconies and overlook the sea.

Hotel Samudra. Tel 480 089. SWB Rs500/750 DWB Rs720/960 DWB A/C Rs1700, plus 10% SC plus tax. Rest. Bar. Quietly located right on the beach past Ashok Beach Resort.

Lobster House Hotel. SWB/DWB Rs350 (£7/$11.65). Rest. Spotless, away from the beach and secure.

Moon Cottage, on beach path from Lobster House. SR/DR Rs125/150. Rest. Bar. Good food and atmosphere.

Cheaper hotels are mostly behind the restaurants on Lighthouse Beach. A major factor in your choice should be security, a lot of thieving goes on in Kovalam. Try to avoid ground-floor rooms and keep everything of value well away from the windows.

Prices in Kovalam have rocketed with the arrival of package tourists. You should get a hefty discount outside the peak December and January season.

For any hotel other than Samudra or Kovalam Ashok get off the bus at the Lobster House Hotel and take the path down; this is much quicker than walking from the bus-stand at the end of the road.

Near Kovalam is *Surya Samudra*. This small resort is being built by a German professor who teaches at Madras University. He buys old Keralan houses, reassembles them in a great location overlooking the sea, and installs modern bathrooms. Peaceful, with good food, and highly recommended. Around Rs2000 daily for two; full details from Tour India in Trivandrum.

Eating and drinking. Just take your pick from the places lining Lighthouse Beach; the *Sunshine* is a favourite of the author, with good seafood, music and company.

PERIYAR WILDLIFE SANCTUARY

Periyar, equidistant from Kottayam and Madurai, is a convenient way to short-circuit the southernmost part of India. The sanctuary is centred on Periyar Lake, and is home to elephants, gaur (the Indian bison), wild boar, and a few tigers. The game, sometimes whole families of wild elephants snorkelling through the water, can be observed from motorboats.

The lake is artificial, designed to generate power for Kerala and irrigate a dry tract of Tamil Nadu. It is not, however, an open expanse of water, being fragmented into many creeks and surrounded by jungly hills. Kerala Tourism run four or five **boat trips** (first 7am, last 4pm), and the Forest Service two (first trip 7am, last 3.30pm). The latter tend to be more crowded but cheaper (Rs6). Early booking of the KTDC boats at Aranya Nivas (see 'Accommodation') is essential, especially for the last trip of the day (the best); if you are early enough, you can book a whole boat for as little as Rs300 (£6/$10). When the lake level is very low there is a long hot walk to water deep enough to load the boats; this at least gives you an opportunity to see the shoals of giant tadpoles in the shallow pools beside the path.

Forest treks (sound more like rambles really) start at 8.30am from the Information Centre (report at 8.15am), last three hours, and cost Rs20. You can also do longer treks with private guides.

Elephant rides, Rs30 (60p/$1) for up to four people, start at 10am. These are more for the ride than in any serious hope of seeing game. Book at Information Centre.

Spending several days here — and away from the herd it is a much nicer place to relax than the hill stations like Ooty and Kodaikanal — consider the Forest Rest Houses. They are located on remote parts of the lake, and all have watchtowers attached. The cost is only Rs50 per person per night, plus boat transport at Rs45. Advance booking can be made through the Information Centre. Over-exploitation has reduced the chances of seeing much game on the regular boat trips, so this is definitely the best bet.

Information. The Forest Information Office, by the landing stage in front of Aranya Nivas, has some useful displays, but is less helpful than it used to be. Book here for their two boats, treks and elephant rides. Although referred to by visitors as Periyar, the area around the landing stage is in fact Thekkady.

Arrival and departure. The first half of the hour-long walk from Kumily to Thekkady (there are also regular buses) is rather shadeless, and you will also be annoyed by vehicle horns. One or two little cafés provide cold drinks. After that paths through the forest parallel the road at a distance of 50–100m, and this is preferable to walking along the road. You can see a wide variey of birds, butterflies and insects, and probably monkeys of one kind or another.

Accommodation (STD Code 04869)

Lake Palace. Tel 22023. SWB Rs1450 (full-board) DWB Rs2900 (full-board). Rest. Bar. On the lake itself and accessible only by boat. Sounds very expensive, but you don't get many opportunities to stay in a maharaja's hunting lodge, or to experience total peace and quiet in India.

Aranya Nivas. Tel 22023. SWB Rs895 DWB Rs995 SWB A/C Rs1075 DWB A/C Rs1995 (includes breakfast) plus 10% SC and 15% tax. Rest (Ind/Chi/Cont; four-course lunch or dinner Rs200 or buffet Rs150, possible to spend less). Bar (beer Rs35/40). Comfortable, well kept, old-fashioned place.

Periyar House. Tel 22026. SR Rs75 DR Rs75 SWB Rs135 DWB Rs350 plus 10% SC and 10% tax. Rest (veg/non-veg). Bar (beer Rs25/30). Cool, clean rooms with hot water; check that yours is not near the dormitories used by coach parties. Nice gardens. Excellent if you can get in, which is unlikely without booking.

Reservations for all three of the above places in Thekkady can be made at the Tourist Reception Centres in Trivandrum and Kochi.

Huts and watchtowers Rs50 per person plus Rs45 for boat. Advance booking usually essential at Forest Information Centre, Thekkady.

KUMILY

Kumily is a straggling one-street town on the border of Tamil Nadu and Kerala. Kumily and Periyar are in the Cardamom Hills, and many spice merchants deal in this and other spices.

Information. See under Periyar.

Arrival and departure. Bus from Kochi via Kottayam (6½hrs, but an hour less going down), Kottayam (4½hrs), Madurai (4hrs), Kodaikanal (5hrs). Note that from Kochi or Trivandrum you can catch a bus to Alleppey and then the boat to Kottayam. Buses for Periyar from Madurai and Kodaikanal mostly terminate at the border in Kumily, and it is best for late arrivals to find accommodation there rather than risk the limited number of rooms at Thekkady being full. Buses from Kerala will usually drop you at Periyar House, Aranya Nivas or in Kumily, as will the express from Madurai, which goes on to Kochi. The drive from Kottayam is much more attractive than that from Madurai, best views from right of bus going up.

Accommodation (STD Code 04869)

Lake Queen Tourist Home. Tel 22086. SWB Rs50 DWB Rs100. Rest (Ind/Chi/Cont). Good basic place.

Muckumkal Tourist Home. Tel 22070. SWB Rs55 (£1.10/$1.85) DWB Rs110 DWB A/C Rs360. Rest (good). Bar. Hot water in rooms.

Mini Lodge. SR Rs45 DWB Rs90. Rooms small but clean.

Rani Lodge. SWB Rs60 DWB Rs95.

Eating and drinking

Hotel Paris. Good. Ideal for breakfast. Same man owns *Paris Restaurant* (veg only).

All these places are in the main street. Rani and Mini lodges are well set back, so may be less noisy. Several more places in the first 100m of the Thekkady road, branch left at end of main street. *Hotel Ambadi* (Tel 22192), about 500m further on, is moderately priced (around Rs250 double), and should be quieter than anywhere in town, worth a look.

OFF THE BEATEN TRACK IN KERALA

Iddukki, where there is a large dam and lake surrounded by forest, has been a popular away-from-it-all retreat for years. Now, by all accounts, you are constantly hassled to buy drugs. Try instead **Kattapani**, which is between Kumily and Idduki, surrounded by tea and coffee plantations and very peaceful (try the Tourist Home).

The **Padmanabhapuram Palace** (9am–5pm, closed Monday) between Trivandrum and Kanniyakumari is probably worth a visit. The **Hill Palace Museum** at Tripunithura (9am–5pm, closed Monday), 13km from Ernakulam, is interesting and will be more so when they display the Travancore crown jewels. The nearby **Chhottanikara temple** is not worth the visit, whatever you may hear about people knocking nails into trees with their heads and the like.

There are beautiful beaches all along the coast and many little ports including **Mahé**, which was formerly a French colony. Traditional dhows are built in **Beypore**, but Tim Severin (*The Sindbad Voyage*) makes it sound even more horrible than Veraval.

South-Eastern India

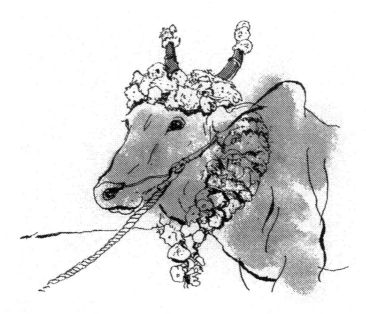

Ceremonial Bull, Madurai

Tamil Nadu — Andhra Pradesh — Orissa

The languages of the two southern states belong to the Dravidian group; Tamil (more a culture than just a language) is spoken in Tamil Nadu, and Telugu in Andhra Pradesh, though Urdu is common in Hyderabad and other Muslim centres. Oriya, the language of Orissa, has an Indo-Aryan base incorporating earlier elements and some Assamese influence.

Handicrafts. Most of this area produces ivory and sandalwood carvings, silks and leatherwork. Hyderabad is famous for its pearls and carpets, and bidri ware (iron with a gold or silver inlay) is still produced. Shell and palm products are common along the coast.

Climate. Tamil Nadu experiences the north-east monsoon from October to December, and temperature and humidity are high all year round, often going above 40°C in May and June. The hills can be surprisingly cold in winter. Hyderabad is as hot but less humid in summer, and a lot cooler (22°C) in winter.

The best time to visit Orissa is from November to March, when the average temperature is around 17°C. The temperature and humidity increase thereafter, until the monsoon arrives in June.

SOUTH-EASTERN INDIA

MAHARASHTRA

ORISSA

MADHYA PRADESH

Bhubaneswar
Khurda
Berhampur   Puri
Chilka Lake

Aurangabad

Palampet
Warangal

Bombay
Secunderabad
Hyderabad
Waltair

Wadi

Vijayawada

Goa
Guntakal

ANDHRA PRADESH

Bay of Bengal

Chittoor

Bangalore   Kanchipuram   Madras
Hosur   Chigleput   Cholamandal
                          Mahabalipuram

Hogenakal   Villupuram
Mudumalai   Yercaud   Pondicherry
Ootacamund Salem   Chidambaram
            Erode   TAMIL
Coimbatore   NADU
        Tiruchirapalli   Tranquebar
        Thanjavur   Nagappattinam
        Dingidul
Kodaikanal Madurai   *Pt. Calimere*

Coromandel Coast

N

Rameswaram

Courtallam

Tirunelveli
Thir'puram   Tiruchendur   Sri Lanka
        Kanniyakumari

| 0 | | 100 miles |
| 0 | | 200 km |

TAMIL NADU

After a while one gets used to the contrasting scenery across India, but **Tamil Nadu** probably offers more variety than any other single state. Its coastal plain, much wider than that on the west coast, is tropical with dense growth and long sandy beaches. Not too far away, though, are the hills to provide relief from the heat and humidity. These hills are varied and beautiful, with many rivers and waterfalls, and settlements of primitive tribal people.

The Tamils are more cohesive than the members of any other state and deeply conscious of their cultural heritage. There were riots a few years ago when they suspected that northern politicians were trying to foist Hindi on them. Here you will be most conscious of Dravidian influence: the ebullient temple architecture is purely Indian. Muslim invaders did little more than nibble at the edge of Tamil Nadu.

For some reason, Nadu is usually pronounced 'Nahd', without the terminal 'u'.

KANNIYAKUMARI

Cape Comorin, now titled Kanniyakumari, is the Land's End of India. The waters of the Indian Ocean, the Bay of Bengal and the Arabian Sea meet here, and this has long made it an important place of pilgrimage. Its calm inspired men like Mahatma Gandhi and Swami Vivekananda, and there are memorials to both.

The main objective for the pilgrims, however, is the **Temple of Devi Kanya** (the Virgin Goddess), one of the incarnations of Shiva's wife Parvati. Non-Hindus may enter as long they wear a dhoti (loincloth) and go bare-chested. The multi-coloured sand on the beach nearby represents the coloured rice thrown, like confetti, at the goddess's unconsummated wedding. The beaches here are not safe for bathing. A small bathing ghat at the southernmost tip of land is; most people will prefer to go the short distance to Vattakottai (see below).

The **Gandhi Mandapam*** is the memorial built over the place where a portion of his ashes rested before committal to the sea. The weird lines belie the intended harmony of its ecumenical design. A hole in the roof allows the sun to shine on the memorial stone on 2 October, Gandhi's birthday. Gandhi shared his birthday, incidentally, with Marshals Hindenburg and Foch, Groucho Marx (undoubtedly more to his taste) and, oddly enough, Lal Bahadur Shastri, India's second prime minister.

Swami Vivekananda achieved a brief fame towards the end of the last century by preaching a universal gospel. An adulatory biography by Romain-Rolland is available. Whatever you make of this the **Vivekananda Rock Memorial**** is altogether grander than Gandhi's. Completed in 1970, it is built of red and black granite on the islet where he meditated and achieved enlightenment, and incorporates architectural themes from all over India. A frequent ferry service (7–11am and 2–5pm, fare Rs3 plus Rs5 entry fee) takes you there. The footprints of the goddess can be seen, and there is a panoramic view of the town from the candy-striped temple to the towering spire of the Catholic church. Photography is banned on the island.

Visit **St Mary's Church*** (Catholic) and walk back along the shore through the fishing village, smelly but friendly. True catamarans (see Kovalam) are made here. A good view of this area, and the hills behind, can be had from the ferry jetty. The best view of all is from the **Lighthouse*** (open 3–5pm, fee Re1), again no photography. You can reflect, as you look south, that there is no land between you and the Antarctic.

The **Circular Fort*** at Vattakottai, 6km away, is hardly circular. Basically square in plan it has pointed bastions at three corners and a large semi-circular battery jutting right out into the sea at the fourth. The arms and RV monogram over the gate signify Ravi Varma, Maharaja of Travancore in the 18th century. Like the larger Udayagiri Fort this was built for him by de Lannoy, a Dutch general in his service. Construction is of large blocks of granite tightly fitted together with no external mortar. The merlons, in contrast, are rendered brick. Surrounded by sand and palm trees this is a proper romantic fort. The attractive beach has the same multi-coloured sand as Kanniyakumari and looks safe for bathing. A taxi costs Rs25–30 (50–60p/85 cents–

$1), best to get together a party and share. It is also possible to bus to Vattakottai village, though the walk from there is definitely a country kilometre.

The real novelty of Kanniyakumari is that you can watch the sun rise from one ocean and set in another. Full-moon time provides a simultaneous sunset and moonrise. This can be watched from the shore; the best viewpoint is the roof of the Tri-Sea Lodge.

Not so many years ago Kanniyakumari was a quiet reflective place where one could happily spend several days. Few people will find it like that now. One can hardly begrudge the Indians wanting to travel in their own country, but why does that have to mean spoliation? Crowds, noise, cheap and nasty trinket stalls; you might as well go to Southend on a bank holiday. Consider how much time you have, and remember you can go from Kottayam to Madurai via Periyar.

Information. Government of Tamil Nadu Tourist Office near Gandhi Mandapam.

Arrival and departure. By train from Trivandrum (2¼hrs). The once weekly Him-Sagar Express runs direct from Kanniyakumari to Jammu via Ernakulam, Madras, and Delhi; at 3730km/2331 miles and just over 3½days this is the longest ride on Indian Railways.

Bus from Trivandrum (2½hrs), Kovalam (3hrs), Ernakulam, and Madurai (6hrs). The bus claiming to go to Rameswaram in 7½hrs takes at least 2hrs longer. It is, moreover, a bumpy, boring and miserable ride. Seats on some buses bookable. The railway station and 'New Modern' bus-stand are probably the best of their kind in India.

Accommodation

Hotel Tamil Nadu. Tel 71257. DWB Rs250 plus 15% tax. Rest. Bar. Hot water. All rooms in the new block face the sea, but rooms in the original building have more character.

Kerala House. Tel 71229. Slightly lower prices than Hotel Tamil Nadu. Rest (basic). Older building, fine view over the sea.

Kaveri Lodge. DWB Rs125 (£2.50/$4.15). Hidden away behind Tri-Sea Lodge and Narmadha Hotel.

Youth Hostel, near Hotel Tamil Nadu. Dorm Rs25.

Slightly cheaper hotels in the bazaar area, but very noisy. Also *Retiring Rooms* at both station and bus-stand.

Eating and drinking

Chicken Corner. Cheap. Non-veg.

Hotel Keerthi, opposite police station. Basic, but recognisable food.

TIRUCHENDUR

A large and attractive temple right on the seashore is dedicated to Subramanian (a common name in Tamil Nadu, usually abbreviated to Subu). Subramanian is the southern equivalent of Kartikkeya or Skanda, the elder son of Shiva and Parvati and the god of war; his legends and characteristics appear to have overlaid those of an older Tamil god Murugan. Six important temples, including this one, are dedicated to Murugan, who seems to have been a pretty lively character, his worship being of a bacchanalian and orgiastic nature.

Arrival and departure. Bus (78km/49 miles) from Kanniyakumari, bus or train to Tirunelveli to travel on to Madurai.

Accommodation. *Hotel Tamil Nadu* or cheap pilgrim accommodation near temple.

RAMESWARAM

Rameswaram claims, like several other towns, to be the second holiest place of Hinduism, in this case because Rama himself built the **Ramanathaswami Temple** in favour of Shiva. The main feature is the corridors, two of them 200m long and lined with hundreds of pillars. Very impressive, the catch is that this is all you are allowed to see. Not worth the effort of getting there.

Few travellers ever went to Rameswaram except to catch the ferry to Sri Lanka. Now there seems no point at all.

Information. Tourist office on railway station.

Arrival and departure. Train from Madras (18hrs) or Madurai (5¼hrs). The road link to Rameswaram is finally complete (six years late), so buses now run straight through. Check the section on Kanniyakumari.

Accommodation

Hotel Tamil Nadu (Tourist Bungalow). Tel 21277. DWB Rs125/150 DWB A/C Rs275 Dorm Rs25. Rest. Bar.

Youth Hostel, adjoining above. Dorm Rs20.

MADURAI

Madurai is a bustling town with a friendly atmosphere, an absolute must when you are in the south of India. The main attraction for travellers, as for countless pilgrims, is the great Meenakshi Temple.

History

Madurai is a very old town; legend says that it was founded by Pandaia, a daughter of Hercules, and subsequently ruled by women. It is known for certain that a Pandaya king sent an ambassador to Rome around 20BC and that there was trade with the Roman empire. The Cholas ran it for a time, but the Pandayas were soon back. Their heyday ran from the ninth century AD up to 1310, and they actually spread their influence as far as Sri Lanka, sacking Anuradhapura in 1001. Marco Polo reckoned it the finest kingdom in the world but in 1310, shortly after his visit, it was conquered by a general of the Muslim Sultan of Delhi. He took a colossal amount of booty back to Delhi but, as was often the way, the man he left in charge set up his own state in Madurai. This was conquered by the kings of Vijayanagar (Hampi). When Vijayanagar broke up after the battle of Talikota in 1565 a branch of the royal family, the Nayaks, established themselves here. Madurai again became the main centre of Tamil learning.

As an aside, a clever Jesuit, Robert de Nobili, settled in Madurai in 1606. He had some success in converting brahmins by accepting their views on caste and certain other rituals.

Temple of the Fish-Eyed Goddess

The **Temple of Meenakshi***** was the centre of the old town, and the main streets were arranged concentrically around it. The four Veli Streets mark the line of the old city walls, demolished around 1840 when the East India Company developed the town. The temple compound is well over 200m square and has a tall gopuram in each wall. More of these tapering towers are inside the walls, some poking out through the extensive flat roofs. All are covered in sculpted figures, a thousand or more on the larger ones.

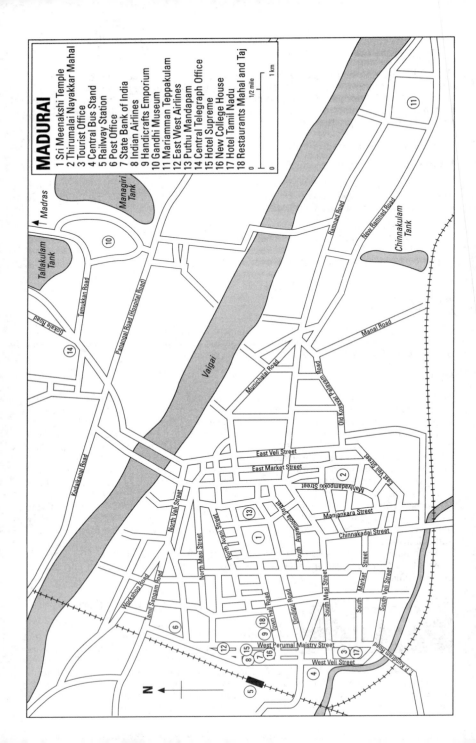

MADURAI

1 Sri Meenakshi Temple
2 Thirumalai Nayakkar Mahal
3 Tourist Office
4 Central Bus Stand
5 Railway Station
6 Post Office
7 State Bank of India
8 Indian Airlines
9 Handicrafts Emporium
10 Gandhi Museum
11 Mariamman Teppakulam
12 East West Airlines
13 Puthu Mandapam
14 Central Telegraph Office
15 Hotel Supreme
16 New College House
17 Hotel Tamil Nadu
18 Restaurants Mahal and Taj

0 — 1 km
0 — 1/2 mile

Madras

Managiri Tank
Tallakulam Tank
Chinnakulam Tank

Vaigai

Tamukkan Road
Gokhale Road
Kodaikanal Road
Panangal Road (Hospital Road)
Ramad Road
New Ramad Road
Manal Road
Munchalai Road
Old Natarajan Road
Workshop Road
Tamil Sangam Road

East Veli Street
East Market Street
Manjyadampokku Street
Manjankara Street
Chinnakadai Street
East Veli Street

North Veli Street
North Avani Street
North Masi Street
South Avani Street

West Perumal Maistry Street
West Veli Street
Dindul Road
Town Hall Road
South Masi Street
South Market Street
South Veli Street
T.P. Kumaran Road

N

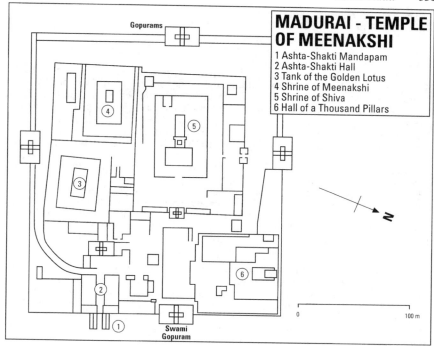

MADURAI - TEMPLE OF MEENAKSHI

1 Ashta-Shakti Mandapam
2 Ashta-Shakti Hall
3 Tank of the Golden Lotus
4 Shrine of Meenakshi
5 Shrine of Shiva
6 Hall of a Thousand Pillars

Although you can enter through any of the gopurams the most impressive way is through the **Ashta-Shakti Mandapam** on the east side. Inside is the hall of the eight (ashta) goddesses (shaktis) with fine sculpture and paintings. This is now a lively bazaar. Statues of Ganesh and his brother Subramanya (the southern version of Kartikkeya) guard the entrance to the temple itelf. Straight ahead from here is the Temple of Meenakshi. On the way is the Tank of the Golden Lotus surrounded by colonnades; the murals that adorned the walls have deteriorated badly but some of the ceiling paintings have been beautifully restored. In one corner is a cage of parakeets, the bird favoured by Meenakshi.

There are in fact two main shrines in the temple; one to Shiva adjoins Meenakshi's. Every night at 9.30pm (10pm on Friday) Shiva is taken in a musical procession to spend the night in Meenakshi's shrine. Most of the pilgrims have gone, the temple is quiet, and this is when one is most aware of its elemental power.

Just to the right of the entrance is the **Kalyana Mandapam**, normally locked, but a little bakshish will get you in. The ceiling is much more attractive than the stone slabs in the rest of the building, and there are two unusual circular paintings, presumably mandalas, on the end wall. This is the marriage hall of Meenakshi and Shiva, though it appears to be a later addition.

The **Hall of a Thousand Pillars** is actually older than the main structure of the temple, having been built in 1560. In some ways this is not as impressive as the Puthu Mandapa (see below). Most of the pillars, while all different patterns, are rather ordinary. One of the so-called musical pillars is near the entrance. The custodian will provide you with a baton, but the sounds are strictly for the tone deaf. The museum that now occupies the hall has some interesting displays; good bronzes and a lot of information on Hindu iconography. The snag is that the showcases and placards have cluttered the hall to the point where it is hard to judge its size any more.

The attitude of the temple trustees is refreshing as visitors are welcome to visit any part of the temple except the very sanctuaries. Photography is now permitted throughout the day for a R10 fee.

Across the road from the **Swami Gopuram** (in the east wall) is the **Puthu Mandapa*** (Thirumalai Choultry), built at the same time as the temple by King Tirumala Nayak (1623–1660). This was an audience chamber where the king could meet his god as the Shiva image from the temple used to spend ten days here each spring. The king and his family are represented by the group of sculptures halfway down the hall, and there is a canopied dais for the god. The outer corridors are now a bazaar (mostly of tailors), yet the sculpture here is easily a match for any in the temple. You will probably have to go to the far end to find the custodian to let you in (more bakshish). Across the road from this point is the base of the **Raya Gopuram**, never completed but intended to be the tallest in India.

It used to be possible to climb one of the gopurams for a good view of the temple and town. The gopuram is now closed after a number of suicide attempts, all of them successful. Rauf Green-Eyes, who runs a Kashmiri emporium at Thirumalai Lodge, 25 West Chitrai Street, will take you up on the roof, from where you can at least see the golden dome over the Meenakshi shrine. He will probably expect you to buy something afterwards.

Tirumalai's palace. The early 17th-century **Palace of Tirumalai Nayak****, the builder of the temple, is actually only about a quarter of the original building. Some restoration was done around 1870 by Lord Napier when he was governor of Madras, and the incongruous entrance dates from this time. More work has been done recently.

The entrance leads to a courtyard flanked by colonnades of squat, chunam-covered pillars. Directly ahead is the king's throne in a domed octagonal chamber called Swarga Vilasam (Celestial Pavilion) and forming a hall of public audience. Behind is the large, ornate hall of private audience. This, like the rest of the palace, is Hindu-Saracenic in style — and looks uncommonly like a Victorian-Gothic swimming pool.

The courtyard is the setting for a very good **sound and light show**** each evening at 6.30pm; it costs Rs2/5 and tells the story of King Tirumalai Nayak.

Festivals and bullfighting

Many **festivals** take place throughout the year, most involving colourful processions of temple elephants around the town. At other times the elephants collect alms from pilgrims in the buses parked around the temple; their trunks reach right into the buses, and they pass the money up to the mahout.

An event unique to this part of India occurs in nearby villages at the time of Pongal, a harvest festival in mid-January. This is comparable to **the running of the bulls** in Pamplona, though of course the animals come to no harm, which is more than can be said for some of the human participants! This is seen at its best in an informal setting at Kancharampettai, where the bulls are garlanded and have banknotes attached to their horns. The animals are turned loose, and the young bloods of the village try to grab the prizes. A larger and more regimented event takes place at Allanganallur the following day where the idea is to wrestle the bulls to the ground. The tourist office in Madurai arranges excursions to these events, but avoid being herded into special enclosures. About a week later the **floating festival** takes place during the evening on the **Mariammanan Teppakulam*** about 5km from the town centre. This huge tank with a colourful temple in the middle merits a visit at other times.

Madurai is an important industrial town despite its spiritual air. The air-raid sirens that wake you in the morning are summoning workers to the textile mills, not heralding the start of war.

Practical *i* **Information**	Tamil Nadu Tourism office on West Veli Street adjoining Tourist Bungalow, and at station and airport.

Arrival and departure. Airport (10km/6 miles). Indian Airlines office (Tel 26795) on West Veli Street near station.

By rail from Madras (8½hrs by the second-class only Vaigai Express, others take at least two hours longer). The Vaigai Express is alright if you have a reservation, with reasonably comfortable padded-chair cars. Rameswaram (6½hrs) and Trichy (7hrs). Trichy has a rail connection to Nagappatinam where the Penang ferry (if they ever reinstate it) calls before Madras.

Separate bus-stands on West Veli Street for local, state and private operators. Buses to Periyar, Kodaikanal, Kochi and Kanniyakumari (7hrs, faster than the train). The town bus service is excellent, ordered queues and not too crowded.

Accommodation

Hotel Tamil Nadu (formerly Tourist Bungalow), West Veli Street (near station). Tel 37470. DWB Rs170 DWB A/C Rs250 Non A/C plus 10% tax, A/C plus 15% tax Dorm Rs20. Rest (veg/non-veg). Bar.

Hotel Supreme, West Perumal Maistry Street. Tel 36331. DWB Rs235 DWB A/C Rs355. Non A/C plus 10% tax, A/C plus 15% tax. Rest (two, including roof garden, N/S Indian food). Bar. Comfortable marble-floored rooms. Excellent value and quiet.

New College House, (100m from station). Tel 24311. SWB Rs70 (£1.40/$2.35) DWB Rs138 SWB A/C Rs127 SWB A/C Rs205, all plus 10% tax. Rest (good, veg only). Huge place; it pays to pick a room away from the water pumps, etc.

There are cheaper places, the ones we have seen being pretty horrible. *Hotel Krishna* in Town Hall Road and *Radhakrishna Lodge* near the temple are worth a look.

Eating and drinking

Mahal, Town Hall Road. A/C. Ind/Chi/Cont. Mod/Exp. Good food (north Indian), nice decor, and first-class service.

Taj, Town Hall Road. A/C. North Indian. Mod. Used to be excellent, but we had two poor meals there recently. May be worth trying, and still best for real food at breakfast.

Eating out for less than Rs15–20 means vegetarian. Madurai is notable for the number and quality of its fruit juice stalls.

KODAIKANAL

At one time Kodaikanal was a quiet, inexpensive alternative to Ootacamund. Times change, and the wreckers have moved in. Trees have been felled, a tremendous amount of building is going on and prices have rocketed. Hill stations were established not just for escape from the heat, but also all the other pressures of life on the Indian plains; attract too many people, let in too many vehicles with blaring horns, and you destroy the whole point of such havens.

There is a positive side. It's cool (altitude 2133m/7000ft), and the **lake** provides boating and carp fishing. **Trout fishing** is available in nearby streams, which are stocked (day ticket Rs6, Rs10 for the week, if you can catch the man in his office). The 18-hole **golf course** costs Rs40 plus Rs25 for club hire, and Rs15 for a caddy. You buy balls from the pro for Rs10 and sell them back for Rs5! The nice clubhouse has a bar.

Coaker's Walk (see below) gives a panoramic view of the plains, and **Bryant Park**, at the eastern end of the lake, is a mass of flowers.

Kodaikanal is a good trekking base; Perumal Peak (2234m/7328ft) is an easy day's walk from Perumalmalai village (bus). The more ambitious can try the 2695m/8840ft-high Anai Mudi Peak (the highest in South India), and it should be possible to walk down to Periyar from there along the ridge.

Information. Tamil Nadu information office near the bus-stand has the bus times and that's about all. Map of sorts available. Fisheries Office just past the telephone exchange. Forest Office, just off the main road opposite the turning to Hotel Tamil Nadu, has a little information on trekking. Contact Subu at the Boat Club on the same subject. Maps (1 inch:4 miles) may or may not be available from Director of Survey and Land Records, Madras.

Arrival and departure. Bus from Madurai (4hrs) or Periyar (5hrs), also from Kodaikanal Road on Trichy–Madurai railway line and Palani (ancient hilltop temple here).

Accommodation (STD Code 04542)

Hotel Tamil Nadu, Fern Hill Road. Tel 41336. SWB/DWB Rs400 (250) Dorm Rs40 (30) plus 20% tax. Rest (Ind/Cont). Bar. Very out of the way. Comfortable (hot water) but no view. Seems typical of prices in Kodai; not long ago a room cost only Rs70. Dorm beds in *Youth Hostel*.

Yagappa Lodge, Noyce Road (near Coaker's Walk — down past Zum-Zum, which is not recommended). Tel 41235. SWB Rs100 (£2/$3.35) DWB Rs150 Dorm Rs40. Rest. Nothing special, but constant hot water.

Green Lands Youth Hostel, near Coaker's Walk. Tel 41099. DWB Rs150 (100) Dorm Rs40 (30). Rest. Nice atmosphere, splendid view, undoubtedly the best value in Kodai. They organise trekking (probably more like rambling), Rs50 per day including food.

Eating and drinking

Tibetan Brothers. Cheap/Mod. Sort of 'hippy-international' fare, and none the worse for that.

The Hilltop is not bad, in an aseptic way, and the *Boat Club* was good on a previous visit.

The season is from 1 April to 30 June, and lower out-of-season prices are given in brackets. Moves are afoot to institute a second season (and raise prices again) in September and October.

OTHER HILL STATIONS

The scenery around Hosur, on the road from Bangalore to Madras, has been compared with England, and Hogenakal has waterfalls on the River Cauvery. Better known hill resorts include Courtallam and Yercaud.

TIRUCHIRAPALLI

Trichinopoly, as it was known to the British, is usually sensibly abbreviated to 'Trichy'. The author had read enthusiastic reports about the **Rock Fort** perched 83m above the city, and liking forts went along expecting a proper one with battlements and guns; what you actually find is another load of old Hindu temples that you aren't allowed into, though at least there is a good view from the top of the hill. Certainly the town is a lot more attractive from up here than at ground level.

It is from the Rock Fort that you can best judge the scale of the colossal **Raghunathaswami Temple** at Srirangam, 3.5km away in a straight line. Set on an island in the Cauvery River, the outer walls enclose an area 750m by 870m. The

Rajagopuram gateway was stuck for centuries at the 15m mark. Construction resumed in 1980, and the 73m-high tower is now the tallest of its kind in Asia. Impressive enough, but artistically not a patch on older efforts. More of the temple interior is open to non-Hindus than used to be the case, but it's hard to work up much enthusiasm when the ground is blistering the soles of your feet.

Trichy is still in the naive stage of tourism, and you will be beset by highly optimistic beggars, children, rickshaw-walas and hoteliers.

Information. Tourist office near bus-stand, also a counter at the station open mornings and evenings.

Arrival and departure. Airport, flights to Sri Lanka as well as internal. Indian Airlines office at 4A Dindigul Road (Tel 42233).

Important rail junction; the station you want is Trichy Junction. Nagappatinam (6hrs), Madurai (3¾hrs), Madras (10hrs), Pondicherry (9¾hrs) and Rameswaram (6hrs).

Main and express bus-stands are 800m from the station, many routes including Madurai (2½hrs). A No 1 city bus from the railway station or bus-stand will take you to the Rock Fort and Srirangam.

Accommodation

Hotel Tamil Nadu, McDonald's Road. Tel 40383. SWB Rs90 DWB Rs160 SWB A/C Rs190 DWB A/C Rs290. Rest. Bar. Another unit on Racecourse Road has dorm beds at Rs40 but is rather out of the way.

Hotel Aristo, Dindigul Road, 500m from station. Tel 41818. SWB Rs65 DWB Rs90 (£1.80/$3). Rest. Bar. Nice garden.

Selvam Lodge, Junction Road, straight ahead out of station. DWB Rs70/110. Rest (see below).

Hotel Ashby (Tel 40652) on Junction Road is reasonable and sounds a little like the Fairlawn in Calcutta, and it has a bar.

Eating and drinking

Hotel Aristo, Dindigul Road. Exp. Limited choice of Western food nicely cooked and well served in the garden.

Selvam Lodge. Cheap/Mod. Ind. Several restaurants on the premises, the roof-top being most pleasant.

The station refreshment room has eggs for breakfast.

THANJAVUR

Thanjavur (Tanjore) was an important centre during the Chola era from the tenth to the 14th century, and the great **Temple of Brihadiswara**** dates from this time. The tower over the sanctuary rises to 65m and is topped with a carved block of stone reckoned to weigh 89 tonnes. The ramp along which this was inched into place was 6km long. It is usual for Shiva temples to have a statue of Nandi, the bull, facing the entrance and this one is huge. The cloisters that surround the enclosure have many, many lingams and interesting, but rather tatty murals. The temple itself is closed to non-Hindus.

The old palace buildings house a **museum and library**; the **tower** of the former gives a good view over the town. Danes will be interested in the **Schwartz Church*** nearby.

At Manora (65km) a 30m tower put up by a local raja commemorates the British victory at Waterloo. This showed remarkable prescience since, according to the tourist brochure, it was built in 1814.

Information. Tourist office just outside the railway station opposite the GPO.

Arrival and departure. On Trichy (1½hrs)–Madras (8hrs) chord line. Train (4hrs) or bus (3½hrs) from Madurai. Buses to Trichy, Pondicherry, etc.

Accommodation

Hotel Tamil Nadu (Tourist Bungalow), Gandhi Road. Tel 21421. SWB Rs125 DWB Rs150 DWB A/C Rs380. Rest. Bar. Good. Also another unit (Tel 20365) on Trichy Road.

Cheaper lodges between Hotel Tamil Nadu and the station.

THANJAVUR TO PONDICHERRY

The **Point Calimere Wildlife Sanctuary** has wide saltflats that attract many estuarine and sea birds from November to January. There is said to be a good beach, and deep-sea fishing may be possible. Access by rail to Kodikkaral or by bus. Forestry Rest House.

Tranquebar (which sounds like a brand of whisky) was a Danish colony from 1616 until 1845 when they sold it to the East India Company. The castle, the Dansborg, and several fine churches survive. This was the site of the first Protestant mission in India in 1706. Georgina Harding's *Tranquebar: A Season in South India* is fascinating. Good beach, limited accommodation. Access by bus from Thanjavur or rail.

Tamil Nadu has the highest concentration of magnificent temples in all India. Tourist officials and locals will encourage you to visit these, overlooking the fact that substantial parts of many are closed to non-Hindus. Attitudes are becoming more relaxed but, even where a priest takes you into a sanctum, you will often be made to feel unwelcome. Always ask before travelling.

Chidambaram was one of the capitals of the Chola empire (907–1310), and its temples are said to be the oldest in south India. According to legend, Vira Chola Raja (927–997) dreamt of Shiva dancing on the shore with Parvati, a dance representing the power of creation.

Accordingly the raja built a golden shrine dedicated to Shiva Nataraja (or Natesa), the Lord of the Cosmic Dance. Around this has grown the present temple in a precinct 600m by 400m with a tall gopuram in each wall. The main shrine (theoretically closed to non-Hindus, but entry is possible) has a magnificent bronze statue of Shiva Nataraja. A Thousand-Pillared Hall (there are actually 984) and other important shrines stand in the main courtyard. The temple is closed noon–4.30pm, the best time to visit being for evening puja.

Information. Tourist office (Tel 22739) at Hotel Tamil Nadu.

Arrival and departure. Train from Madras (5hrs), Madurai (8½hrs), Thanjavur (2½hrs) and Trichy (4hrs). Bus to Pondicherry (68km/43 miles).

Accommodation. *Hotel Tamil Nadu* (Tel 22323), rooms from Rs100. There are also cheaper places.

PONDICHERRY

Pondicherry and the smaller enclaves of Karaikal (also in Tamil Nadu), Yanam (Andhra Pradesh), Mahé (Kerala) and Chandernagore (upstream from Calcutta) were all that remained of French imperial aspirations in India after the wars of the 18th century. Unlike the Portuguese the French negotiated a settlement with independent India; Chandernagore became part of Bengal in 1951, and the remaining territories were handed over in 1954. The French were not the first to see the potential of Pondicherry; a Roman town unearthed at nearby Arikamedu in 1945 predated other European settlement by 1500 years.

Pondicherry is a town of some charm. It lacks the interest it might have had because the British razed the place in 1762, so nothing remains of the fortifications or early buildings. Nevertheless, its streets are clean and quiet by Indian standards, and the French connection has given it a character all of its own. The area around the Governor's Residence is just like a French provincial town, plus bougainvillea of course, and the police wear képis, though their Lee-Enfields rather spoil the effect. You could be disappointed if you expected a sort of Goa with a French flavour, a trap the author fell into on his first visit. Be fair, and see Pondicherry in its own light.

The most attractive part of the town is the **sea front****, of which you get a good view from the new pier. The best bit of beach is between the pier and the Park Guest House. Nearby is a **statue of Dupleix** who, given a little more support from Paris, might have made all India a French dominion. The **War Memorial** must have been considered very outré when first built, modernist to a fault. Around the back is a relief showing the arrival of Dupleix in Pondicherry in 1742. The **Gandhi memorial** flatters neither the town nor the man. The **museum** (10am–5pm, closed Monday) is good, having a fine display of furniture and ephemera of the colonial period.

The **Grand Bazaar**** is Pondicherry's main market. Very crowded, here are all the necessities of Indian life. At the south end colourful, cheerful fishwives sell piles of assorted prawns, rays, crab, shark and dozens of kinds of little fish, all absolutely fresh. Oh, for somewhere to cook it yourself!

The **Church of Our Lady of Immaculate Conception** is attractive enough in a Romanesque sort of way. Very plain inside, it lacks all those monuments with which the British clutter their churches, and which make them so interesting and tell so much of the colonial way of life. The **Place Jeanne d'Arc** is actually an unkempt garden, now half occupied by a tennis court. One guesses that the statue once stood elsewhere. The **Botanical Garden**, between the bus-stands and the station, is worth a look.

The Aurobindo Ashram

And so to the **Sri Aurobindo Ashram**. This is a very strange place, and some visitors pick up bad vibes. It is unpleasant to see devotees abasing themselves before the memorials of two persons who, whatever they achieved materially, were no more than minor seers. Go, observe quietly, and make up your own mind.

Pondicherry has Indianised itself in a way Goa has resisted. Many street names have been changed, statues removed, and so on.

Practical Information *i*

Tourist office on sea front near remains of old pier. Conducted tour daily.

Arrival and departure. Train from Villupuram (1hr), which is on Madras (2¼hrs)–Trichy (2¼hrs) line. There is a direct train from Madras (5hrs) but you arrive late in the evening. Bus from Madras (4hrs) and Mahabalipuram.

Accommodation (STD Code 0413)

Grand Hotel d'Europe, Rue Suffren. SWB Rs400 (full-board) DWB Rs800 (full-board) plus 10%. Rest. Bar. Reputedly offers genuine French cuisine, lunch/dinner Rs75/85. Advance reservation for both rooms and meals essential.

Park Guest House, Goubert Ave. Tel 34412. SWB Rs150 DWB Rs200. Rest. Very comfortable. Mainly for ashram visitors, so no drinking or smoking.

Shanti Guest House, Rue Suffren. Tel 26473. DR Rs60 DWB Rs125. Clean and airy.

State Tourist Home, Indira Nagar (near station). Tel 26145. SWB Rs50 (£1/$1.65) DWB Rs90 DWB A/C Rs180. Rest. Best value in town, despite location (and shocks from the shower), and consequently often full.

Bungalows, huts, and French restaurant at Serenity Beach north of Pondicherry; information from a house in Rue Dumas near the intersection with Bazaar St Laurent.

Eating and drinking
Charlies/Copa Cabana. Cheap/Mod. Ind/Chi/Cont. The Copa Cabana upstairs is nicely done in bamboo and banana palm thatch, one of few places where you can enjoy a beer with your meal, very civilised.

Spencers Fiesta Restaurant, near New Pier. Mod. Upstairs bar has a good selection of drink, including port and vermouth, and a view out to sea. The interesting menu includes fillet steak with onions, chips and all the trimmings.

Several Vietnamese restaurants, the *Blue Diamond* (Rue Dumas) not bad. The **Hotel Aristo** has a roof-top restaurant, good food (even pheasant!), but you wait for ages and cannot have a beer in the same place. Beware the grisly restaurant downstairs. The Alliance Française has a *Club Gastronomie Française* claiming to provide French cuisine. This having been a French colony there must surely be a nice little bar somewhere; let us know if you find it.

AUROVILLE

Aurobindo was a Bengali freedom fighter who sought political asylum in Pondicherry in 1910. Settling down to found his ashram he formed an alliance with a Frenchwoman, the wife of the consul in fact, who became known as The Mother. Aurobindo died in 1950, and before The Mother followed him in 1973 she conceived an international community where all should live in a spirit of light and understanding.

The Mother's brief was that 'Auroville wants to be a universal town where men and women of all countries are able to live in peace and progressive harmony above all creeds, all politics and all nationalities. The purpose of Auroville is to realise human unity'. Fine sentiments; unfortunately harmony between the Aurovilians and the Sri Aurobindo Society proved elusive. The Society sought to control Auroville, and this was resented by the people who were doing the hard work. The matter has been resolved, up to a point, by the Indian government taking control of the whole project.

Auroville is planned as a circular city, and its geographical centre is the **Matrimandir****. The upper part of this huge spherical building is occupied by a meditation chamber reached by spiral ramps. The office is manned 9am–1pm and you can get information on visiting. The inauguration of Auroville took place in the adjacent **amphitheatre** on 28 February 1968 when the city's charter and soil from 124 different countries were placed in the lotus-shaped urn.

Progress on these buildings, and the residential and industrial colonies, has been slow. The Aurovilians blame this on the obstructive behaviour of the controllers of the ashram in keeping them short of funds. An air of sensible idealism inspires Auroville, and the pioneers have good relations with the locals. This is not the case in Pondicherry where there is considerable resentment of the ashram's wealth and influence.

Information. The only source of information on Auroville in Pondicherry town is La Boutique d'Auroville on Nehru Street. The Auroville Information Centre in Bharat Niwas (1km from the Matrimandir) puts on a video show about Auroville at 2.30pm on Wednesdays. Also a shop there.

Arrival and departure. Auroville is 12km from Pondicherry, and its various elements are scattered over a large area. The conducted tour of Pondicherry calls here, or a scooter rickshaw tour of the main sites will cost Rs75–100 (£1.50–2/$2.50–3.35), but the best way is simply to hire a bike and potter around on your own.

MAHABALIPURAM

Mahabalipuram offers some remarkable temple architecture in a quiet seaside setting. This is another of those resorts like Goa, Diu, Kovalam and Puri that caters well for Western visitors, which makes it a very pleasant place to stay and relax.

In the time of the Pallava dynasty (third to ninth centuries AD) Mahabalipuram was the seaport for their capital in Kanchipuram, and the temples, dating from this period, testify to its former wealth. Like Madras there was no actual harbour, but links extended to south-east Asia and beyond the Middle East to Rome.

The ridge

West of the village is a granite ridge, and on the eastern side is a huge bas-relief, probably the largest in the world, known as **Arjuna's Penance*****. Some idea of its scale may be had from two elephants, which are each 5m long. Over 1000 finely sculpted figures are converging on the cleft in the centre of the rock, obviously to witness a great event. But what? The Mahabharata relates how Arjuna, Krishna's companion in arms, did penance to Shiva for the lives he had taken in battle. Shiva is readily identified by his matted locks, and the emaciated ascetic is said to be Arjuna.

The alternative interpretation links the same figures to the descent of the Ganges. The ascetic figure represents Bhagiratha begging Brahma to allow the Ganges, source of all goodness, to flow down to earth. The flood thus unleashed threatens to destroy mankind, but Shiva catches the water in his matted locks and controls the flow. Given that the cleft symbolises the Ganges this seems to be the more likely explanation. The sculptor had a sense of humour too; note the cat too starry-eyed to bother with the mice playing around its feet. In fact there is an awful lot of detail to enjoy here.

The **Krishna Mandapa*** to the south is a cave temple. A relief of pastoral scenes includes Krishna lifting up the mountain at Goverdhan to shelter villagers from the rain. It is best to head north from here and then work your way south down the ridge.

Several more **cave temples*** are cut into the ridge and have reliefs showing familiar scenes; refer to the section on Ellora for details. The large balanced rock is known as **Krishna's Butterball**.

The **Rayala Gopuram**, over Arjuna's Penance, never got above the base level. It was perhaps a victim of the same event that left so many other monuments unfinished. The **New Lighthouse** is open in the afternoon, a good view but photography is prohibited. Its predecessor, known as the Old Lighthouse, was in fact a temple.

The five rathas

Descending the path at the southern end of the ridge you come to a group of **five rathas****. A ratha is the car or wagon on which deities are taken in procession; these are, in effect, scale models of Dravidian temple styles carved out of solid lumps of rock. The popular names of the rathas derive from the five Pandava brothers, the epic heroes of the Mahabharata. The Ratha of Draupadi (wife of the brothers) is more likely to have been dedicated to Durga as suggested by the lion outside and the figure inside cutting off his hair as an offering. The adjacent Ratha of Arjuna resembles the Kailasha Temple at Ellora with which it is contemporary. This is dedicated to Indra,

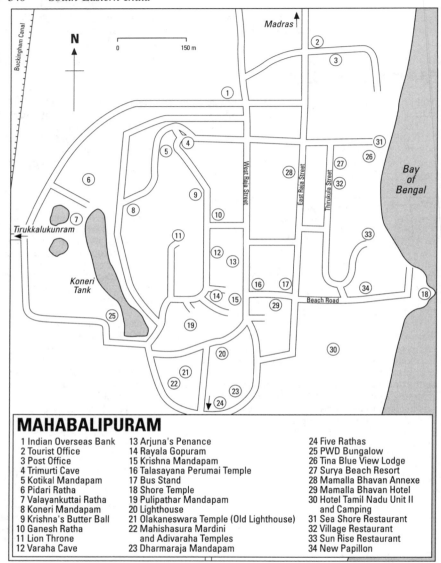

MAHABALIPURAM

1 Indian Overseas Bank
2 Tourist Office
3 Post Office
4 Trimurti Cave
5 Kotikal Mandapam
6 Pidari Ratha
7 Valayankuttai Ratha
8 Koneri Mandapam
9 Krishna's Butter Ball
10 Ganesh Ratha
11 Lion Throne
12 Varaha Cave

13 Arjuna's Penance
14 Rayala Gopuram
15 Krishna Mandapam
16 Talasayana Perumai Temple
17 Bus Stand
18 Shore Temple
19 Pulipathar Mandapam
20 Lighthouse
21 Olakaneswara Temple (Old Lighthouse)
22 Mahishasura Mardini
   and Adivaraha Temples
23 Dharmaraja Mandapam

24 Five Rathas
25 PWD Bungalow
26 Tina Blue View Lodge
27 Surya Beach Resort
28 Mamalla Bhavan Annexe
29 Mamalla Bhavan Hotel
30 Hotel Tamil Nadu Unit II
   and Camping
31 Sea Shore Restaurant
32 Village Restaurant
33 Sun Rise Restaurant
34 New Papillon

and his elephant stands nearby. The Bhima Ratha is an unfinished two-storey edifice perhaps inspired by the wooden huts of the Toda tribes in the Nilgiri Hills. The Yudhistra Ratha (usually known as the Dharmaraja after the Pandava's father) is the largest and dedicated to Shiva in one of his leonine Pallava forms as Narasimhavarman. Finally comes the Sahadeva Nakula Ratha, named after the last two brothers, which resembles a Buddhist chaitya or chapel.

The shore temples

Mamallapuram, the earlier form of the name, means seven temples. This referred to a group of seven temples and enclosures built on the beach. These **shore temples**** represented the first attempt by the Pallavas at structural stonework. Before this their temporal buildings were presumably made of timber and brick, none having survived, and the temples as in so many other places in India were cut from solid rock.

The early Pallava kings were Buddhists and later Jains. By the time of the dynasty's golden age (AD 650–750) worship of Shiva held sway. The many bulls in the courtyard indicate that this is a Shiva temple, yet behind the main shrine is another dedicated to Jalasayana, Vishnu in his form of 'sleeper on the waves', a fair description of the temple. The lingam in the other shrine again shows allegiance to Shiva. The carvings on the temples have been badly eroded by salt and sand, but somehow it doesn't matter. This is a romantic place and especially so at sunrise.

It was previously believed that the works at Mahabalipuram were commissioned by a number of different Pallava kings in the period AD600–728 (and in the order described above). Recently discovered inscriptions now confirm that all were the work of Narasimhavarman II (otherwise Rajasimhan) (AD700–728), clear evidence of the wealth and power of his kingdom.

Other interests

The **beach** south of the shore temple is pleasant; be prepared to walk some way to avoid the day trippers. Swimming can be dangerous, the beach shelves steeply and currents are strong.

A **sculpture school** has been founded in recent years to keep the old arts alive, and the chinking sounds from this and other artisans can be heard in much of Mahabalipuram. There are said to be some good **yoga** teachers in the village and nearby.

| **Practical Information** *i* | Tourist office on main street. TN Tourism produces a good, if fancily worded, booklet on the monuments. |

Arrival and departure. 60km from Madras. Included in the temple tour from Madras, but you can easily get there by bus (19A or 68 from High Court). Also buses to Thirukkalikundram and Kanchipuram.

Accommodation (STD Code 04113)

Silver Sands Beach Resort (2km from bus-stand). Tel 2228 or Madras 477 444. SWB Rs200 DWB Rs300. Rest. Bar. Large beach resort with many facilities including beach barbecue. Prices are for the *Budget Tourist Complex*; there are also much more expensive rooms. Highly recommended.

Surya Beach Resort. Tel 2292 SWB Rs125 DWB Rs200 Cottages Rs350–550 plus 15% tax. Rest. Camping. Quiet location beside a small lake.

Mamalla Bhavan Annexe, East Raja Street. Tel 2260. SWB/DWB Rs150 (£3/$5) plus 10% tax SWB/DWB A/C Rs250 plus 15% tax and 10% SC. Rest (veg, tandoori as well as thalis).

Tina Blue View. Tel 2319. SWB Rs60 DWB Rs100. Rest. Bar. Mosquito nets. Garden adjoining beach. Own buffalo for milk. Quiet, airy roof terrace.

Mamalla Bhavan, in square by bus-stand. Tel 2250. SWB/DWB Rs45. Rest. Much better than anything else at the same price, but early morning noise from the temple.

The *Public Works Department Rest House*, on the other side of the ridge from town, is isolated and quiet. A TN Tourism *Youth Hostel* (Rs20) is off the shore road. Various other lodges, mostly disgusting. Very, very basic rooms available in village near Five Rathas, about Rs250 per week.

Eating and drinking

Rose Garden. Cheap/Mod. Very good seafood, including crayfish.

Sunrise, behind Rose Garden, and very similar.

Tina Blue View. Mod. Ind/Chi/Cont. Located upstairs, good view and cool.

Mamalla Bhavan. Cheap. South Indian. Different thalis in back room. Good.

Barbecue at Silver Sands on Sunday.

Crocodile Bank. This crocodile farm was set up to provide stocks of the once numerous crocodiles for wildlife reserves. Funny how such cute hatchlings can grow up to be so ugly and dangerous. The farm is located 14km north of Mahabalipuram on the Madras road, and any bus will drop you there. It's also possible to cycle.

Tiger Cave, on the way to Crocodile Bank, is described as a cave temple. It has a shrine to Durga, but is of minimal interest. **Thirukkalikundram** (*thiru*, sacred, plus *kaliku*, eagles, plus *kundram*, hill) is a small village dominated by its temple atop a 160m hill. The priests here feed a pair of kites reputed to fly down from Varanasi and return each day. This is a round trip of 3000km/1875 miles as the crow flies. The spectacle takes place any time between 11am and 2pm and easily justifies the sweaty slog up the hill. The hilltop also gives an aerial view of a large temple at its base, may be worth a look.

Take a bus from Mahabalipuram or Chingleput on Madras–Trichy railway line. Perhaps a direct bus from Kanchipuram, otherwise change in Chingleput. Quite possible by cycle (a level 14km/9 miles) from Mahabalipuram. The temple tour from Madras calls here, usually too late to see the kites.

KANCHIPURAM

Kanchipuram, Conjeeveram to the British, is the only one of India's seven holy cities in the south. It is also the only one where Shiva and Vishnu are equally revered. Its prosperity first as capital of the Pallava kingdom and later as a trading centre enabled the construction of many remarkable temples.

History

It is said that Buddha visited Kanchipuram and built temples there. No traces remain, but there is no doubt that the town was established as a place of learning and a local centre well before the Christian era. Its golden age came under the Pallava kings from AD600 onwards. The Pallavas were in constant conflict with the Chalukyas based on Badami, but expanded their kingdom well beyond Madras in the north and to Tiruchirapalli and Thanjavur in the south.

The Pallavas were overthrown early in the tenth century by the Cholas who expanded Hindu influence to south-east Asia and Indonesia. They in turn were conquered by the Pandyas of Madurai. Eventually Kanchipuram became part of the Vijayanagar empire and, when that fell, came under the control of the Muslim Nawab of Arcot. Despite all these changes Tamil Nadu remained a prosperous place and building continued. Even the Muslims ruled with a lighter hand than in the north.

In the 18th century this part of Tamil Nadu became a battleground for the French and the British, each making up for their own small numbers by backing rival factions of the Muslim ruling hierarchy. In 1751 Clive captured Kanchipuram from a French and Muslim force holding the great temple. Kanchipuram settled down under British rule as a wealthy religious and silk-producing town.

The temple town

The **Kailasanatha Temple** is notable for being a purely Dravidian design dating from the Pallava era (early eighth century), though the front is a Chola addition. It is dedicated to Shiva as Lord of Mount Kailash. The temple was once brightly painted; slight remains of this can be seen in the shrines round the courtyard.

The basis of the **Ekambareshwara Temple** is Pallava with Chola additions. The 57m-high gopuram and outer wall date from the Vijayanagar period (16th century). There are two theories about the attribution of this temple. The name can refer to Shiva as the Naked Lord, in other words as leader of the ascetics. Alternatively it could be a corruption of Lord of the Mango Tree. There is a mango tree supposedly several thousand years old in one of the courtyards, but whether the name was made to fit this or the other way round is a matter for conjecture. This is about as far as you can go, but the gopuram provides a view of the rest. The Thousand-Pillar Hall actually has only 540. The tower of the mandapa, over 60m high, was built by a Vijayanagar king in 1509. The temple was used as a fortress in the Anglo-French Carnatic War, which did it no good at all.

The **Kamakshiamman Temple** was built by the Cholas in the 14th century. It is dedicated to Parvati (Shiva's wife) in her Shakti form. Shakti can be crudely translated as sexual energy, which makes it very popular with newly-weds.

The **Vaikuntaperumal Temple** is one of the oldest, having been built by King Nandivarman around AD735. Dedicated to Vishnu it has the alternative name of Venkatanatha, the Lord of the Hills. The relief around the shrine depicts the war between the Pallavas and the Chalukyas.

The **Varadarajaperumal Temple** is huge. Varadaraja means Lord of the World and applies to Vishnu. Swami is sometimes added to the name; this is Vishnu again as a guru or teacher. The mandapa is known as the Marriage Hall, but this was for a marriage of the gods, not humans. The 96 pillars are carved with avatars of Vishnu in Vijayanagar style. Note also the European soldier, perhaps a Portuguese as they aided Vijayanagar against the Muslims.

Festivals

As in other holy towns there are frequent festivals, and it is a good idea to check whether any major ones will take place during your visit. The Kamakshiamman Temple has a very lively car festival in February–March and lesser festivities every week, well worth planning for.

Holy Kanchipuram may be, but it is a noisy, dusty place where one gets little respite from beggars and hustlers.

Arrival and departure. Bus services from Madras and from Chingleput on Madras–Trichy railway line. Also a branch line from Chingleput, probably much slower than the bus. Included in the temple tour from Madras.

Accommodation

Hotel Tamil Nadu, Kamatchi Amman Sannathi Street (near station). Tel 22552. SWB/DWB Rs150 (£3/$5) SWB/DWB A/C Rs300. Rest.

There are also less expensive hotels near the bus-stand.

MADRAS

Madras is a strange place. No-one ever enthuses about it, but it is pleasant enough and most people find themselves staying longer than they had planned. Madras was the first major settlement of the East India Company, and a fort and factory were built in 1644. This later grew into the present Fort St George and became the centre of the struggle for supremacy in India between the English and the French.

Fort St George

The entry to **Fort St George***** is through the Sea Gate, once right on the beach. Before the harbour was built, ships had to unload both passengers and goods into small boats that brought them through the dangerous surf onto this beach. The collection of captured cannons in front of the museum is worth a look, some with Arabic and Chinese inscriptions. Another has the C7 monogram of Christian VII showing it to have come from Tranquebar, which the British purchased from the Danes in 1845. The grey building behind the flagstaff housed the council chamber and secretariat, and still fulfills its original function as the state assembly of Tamil Nadu meets here.

The best thing in the **museum** (9am–5pm, closed Friday) is a model of the fort in its definitive form during the first half of the 19th century. Fort St George was essentially a landward defence; the walls you see as you enter were only a battery covering the shore. Land reclamation for the new harbour has left this high and dry, and modern encroachments make it hard to see the elaborate western defences. Prints engraved by the Daniells, English artists who travelled in India around the turn of the 19th century, show how monuments in Madurai and elsewhere looked at that time. The portrait gallery on the first floor was an exchange for the merchants of the East India Company.

The interior of the fort is marred by modern administrative buildings, but you will easily find the **Church of St Mary**, the oldest (1680) Anglican church in India. Robert Clive was married here, it is linked with Elihu Yale who founded the university, and the many memorials make fascinating reading. **Clive Corner** preserves ephemera associated with the empire builder, ask at the ASI office behind the church.

The fort withstood a French siege in 1759, something its smaller predecessor had failed to do in 1746. Eventually it was superseded by the Napier Battery to the south; this was demolished a few years ago. A matching battery stood in the south of the city. These fortifications were necessary; quite apart from all the trouble with the French, not to mention Hyder Ali and Tippu Sultan, Madras was bombarded in both World Wars. In 1914 the German cruiser *Emden* made one of her startling appearances, and in the Second World War Japanese aircraft dropped bombs. The museum has mementoes of both occasions.

Around town

North of the fort is the **High Court** in Indo-Saracenic style. The lighthouse in one of the towers is officially closed to the public, but a little bakshish might gain you an unparalleled view of the city. The old city of Georgetown (impolitely known as Black Town until 1905) lies north of the fort and is quite cosmopolitan; there is even an Armenian quarter and church. The **Moore Market** was fascinating, and should by now have been repaired after fire damage.

The spire visible from Egmore Station belongs to the **Church of St Andrew***, otherwise known as the Scots Kirk. This most attractive church is built on a circular plan.

The **Museum** is one of the three national museums of India. What you make of this

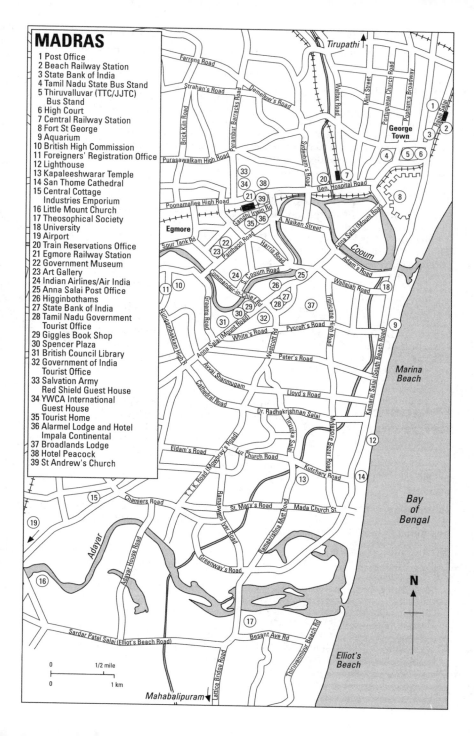

MADRAS

1 Post Office
2 Beach Railway Station
3 State Bank of India
4 Tamil Nadu State Bus Stand
5 Thiruvalluvar (TTC/JJTC)
   Bus Stand
6 High Court
7 Central Railway Station
8 Fort St George
9 Aquarium
10 British High Commission
11 Foreigners' Registration Office
12 Lighthouse
13 Kapaleeshwarar Temple
14 San Thome Cathedral
15 Central Cottage
   Industries Emporium
16 Little Mount Church
17 Theosophical Society
18 University
19 Airport
20 Train Reservations Office
21 Egmore Railway Station
22 Government Museum
23 Art Gallery
24 Indian Airlines/Air India
25 Anna Salai Post Office
26 Higginbothams
27 State Bank of India
28 Tamil Nadu Government
   Tourist Office
29 Giggles Book Shop
30 Spencer Plaza
31 British Council Library
32 Government of India
   Tourist Office
33 Salvation Army
   Red Shield Guest House
34 YWCA International
   Guest House
35 Tourist Home
36 Alarmel Lodge and Hotel
   Impala Continental
37 Broadlands Lodge
38 Hotel Peacock
39 St Andrew's Church

place is up to you, and will probably depend on how many Indian museums you have seen already. The exhibits are tremendously varied and mostly inadequately captioned, though at least we learn that boomerangs are not unique to Australia. Easily the best part is the large collection of bronze statuary, many of the same quality as the famed Shiva Nataraj (the Cosmic Dancer) of Chidambaram. Outside are the spoils of war from British expeditions to China and also Manila in 1762 (nothing about that in our school history books).

The adjoining **Art Gallery** is of interest only for the Mughal and Rajput miniatures, though there is hardly any information about them. The gallery, as a whole, is not a patch on those in Trivandrum and Mysore. This and the museum are really more notable for their fine buildings than the contents.

The beach and British worthies

Two main roads lead south from the old part of Madras. Mount Road originated as the link between Fort St George and **St Thomas' Mount** where, tradition has it, Thomas the Apostle was martyred. The Marina follows the line of the beach to **San Thomé Cathedral**, where Thomas is supposedly buried. Sharks discourage sea bathing, but a swimming pool and aquarium are along here. The new lighthouse (open 2–4pm every day and also 10am–noon on Sunday) is near the cathedral.

Madras is the only Indian city not to have removed its British statues, and these symbols of the Raj stand alongside heroes of the fight for independence. Queen Victoria sits imperiously outside the University, Edward VII looks out from a beautiful little garden over Mount Road, and George V presides over the War Memorial. By far the grandest statue, however, is of the obscure Sir Thomas Munro, Governor of Madras in the early 19th century. So why have the statues remained in Madras? A local explained to the author: 'We have put up statues of our own heroes, and these English people are as much a part of our history as they are of yours. Why should they not stay?'

Practical Information *i*

Culture. Madras is a major cultural centre. Visiting in winter you will have a chance to see the various forms of Indian **dance and drama**, and perhaps to hear classical **Carnatic music**. Performances are not a daily occurrence, the tourist office will provide details. The main Carnatic music and dance festival takes place in the first two weeks of January. The Theosophical Society is based here, and there are many **yoga ashrams**.

Information. Government of India Tourist Office on Mount Road, the main shopping street. Conducted tours of city and day tours of southern temples. Street map (with bus routes) available from booksellers.

Arrival and departure. Airport, 16km from centre, international as well as local flights. Trains and a bus service both from Egmore, the latter calling at the Indian Airlines office, 19 Marshalls Road (Tel 825 1677).

By train from Kochi (12hrs), Madurai (11½hrs) but check under Madurai, Pondicherry (4½hrs), Hyderabad (16hrs), Calcutta (27¼hrs by Coromandel Express, 32½hrs or more for others), Bombay (24hrs), Delhi (34hrs), and Goa (28½hrs, change in Bangalore). There are two terminal stations, Egmore (metre gauge for the south) and Central (broad gauge for most other destinations); a few trains also depart from Madras Beach. Tourist quota reservations for all destinations at Central.

Express and local bus-stands are separate but both close to High Court. The local bus service is good.

Accommodation

Hotel Impala, opposite Egmore station. Tel 825 0484. SWB Rs145 (£2.90/$4.80) DWB Rs207/270 DWB A/C Rs330 including taxes. Rest (veg, room service).

Hotel Peacock, Poonamalee High Road. Tel 39081. SWB Rs125 DWB Rs175 SWB A/C Rs175/225 DWB A/C Rs235/300. Rest. Bar.

Tourist Home, opposite Egmore station. Tel 825 0079. SWB Rs15 DWB Rs235 plus 15%.

Alarmel Lodge, opposite Egmore station. Tel 825 1248. SR Rs55 DR Rs80.

Broadlands Lodge, Near Star Cinema, Triplicane. Tel 845 573. SR Rs90 DR Rs149 SWB Rs100 DWB Rs190 Penthouse Rs225 (super). Also dorm beds on the roof. Another of those famous old 'overland' places everyone passes through. On mature reflection, we would say that this is the main attraction of Madras.

YWCA, Poonamalee High Road. Tel 532 4234. SWB Rs300 DWB Rs350 (including breakfast). Rest. Parking. Camping. Well located and quiet.

The YMCA is at 74 Ritherdon Road (over tracks from Egmore). The Salvation Army's *Red Shield Hostel* (Tel 532 1821) is also on Ritherdon Road, Dorm Rs25 and some rooms. Tamil Nadu Tourism's *Youth Hostel* (Rs40) is on EVR Road near Central Station. The *YHA* is miles away in Adyar, very inconvenient. We looked at several places in Georgetown, the old part of the city, but would not recommend any; however the *Malaysia Lodge* still has a following.

Eating and drinking

Delhi (Coronation) Durbar, corner of Mount Road and Wallaja Road. Mod. Ind/Chi/Cont. Roof garden. Some of the best Indian food to be found at these prices; tell them to go easy on the chillis.

Thousands of vegetarian thali restaurants all over the city. Many other restaurants around Egmore and along Mount Road. There are restaurants here run by Chinese, but they're not a patch on those in Bombay and Calcutta. For the rest it's thalis, thalis, thalis. If you can find a recognisable breakfast near Broadlands, let the author know.

ANDHRA PRADESH

The parts of Andhra Pradesh you are most likely to visit were part of the great Muslim state of Hyderabad, but that was land-locked while Andhra has a coastline of nearly 1000km. In 1947 the Nizam (hereditary ruler of Hyderabad) was unwilling to join India and be submerged in a Hindu majority. He vacillated between opting for Pakistan or independence, but the following year his state was invaded and incorporated in India anyway.

HYDERABAD

Hyderabad, now the capital of Andhra Pradesh and for long India's fifth city (now overtaken by Bangalore), was formerly the capital of the Muslim state of Hyderabad. The city was founded in 1589 as a successor to Golconda, the site of which had proved very unhealthy. Captured by Aurangzeb at the second attempt in 1687, its real prominence began in 1724 when the Mughal viceroy declared his independence of Delhi. Hyderabad was the second largest of the princely states (after Kashmir), and its ruler, the Nizam, was traditionally the richest man in the world.

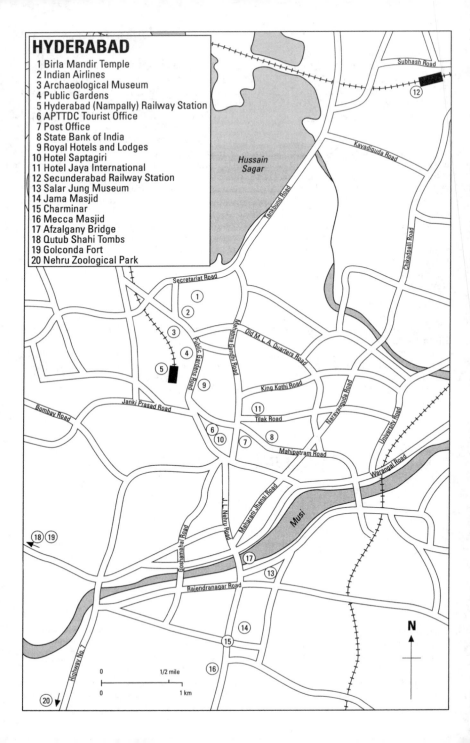

HYDERABAD

1 Birla Mandir Temple
2 Indian Airlines
3 Archaeological Museum
4 Public Gardens
5 Hyderabad (Nampally) Railway Station
6 APTTDC Tourist Office
7 Post Office
8 State Bank of India
9 Royal Hotels and Lodges
10 Hotel Saptagiri
11 Hotel Jaya International
12 Secunderabad Railway Station
13 Salar Jung Museum
14 Jama Masjid
15 Charminar
16 Mecca Masjid
17 Afzalgany Bridge
18 Qutub Shahi Tombs
19 Golconda Fort
20 Nehru Zoological Park

Subhash Road

Kavadiguda Road

Hussain
Sagar

Tankbund Road

Chikadpalli Road

Secretariat Road

Old M. L. A. Quarters Road

Mahatma Gandhi Road

Public Gardens Road

King Kothi Road

Narayanguda Road

University Road

Janki Prasad Road

Bombay Road

Tilak Road

Mahipatram Road

Warangal Road

J. L. Nehru Road

Maharani Jhansi Road

Goshamahal Road

Musi

Rajendranagar Road

Highway No. 7

N

0   1/2 mile

0   1 km

The old city

The walled city of Hyderabad was laid out south of the River Musi. The best entry is Afzalganj bridge, which leads onto one of the two straight roads that quarter the old city. At the inter-section of these roads is the elegant **Charminar*****, a building that symbolises Hyderabad (and lends its name to a popular brand of cigarette). The 'four minarets' (56m high) of the name stand at the corners of the 30m-square arch. You used to be able to climb one of these to visit the mosque at second-floor level and get a good view over the city, though there is some doubt about access at present. The Charminar was built in 1591 by Muhammad Quli Qutb in thanksgiving for the end of a terrible outbreak of plague. Electricity supply permitting, it is lit up early every evening.

The nearby **Mecca Masjid**** may just be the most attractive large mosque in India, despite the unsightly bird screens. The arched facade and four minarets are dated 1614, and the gateway was added by Aurangzeb in 1692. The name supposedly derives from the incorporation of a brick brought from Mecca. Note the use of huge slabs of stone in the facade. A long pavilion in the courtyard covers the simple tombs of the Nizams.

The **Jama Masjid**, which elsewhere would be the main mosque of the city, is down a narrow lane on the other side of the Charminar. You should walk back through the **bazaars**** between here and Afzal Ganj bridge — they are very colourful with Hyderabad's traditional products of textiles, bidriware (hammering coloured wire into engraved iron or steel objects) and jewellery. As well as trade in the diamonds and gems mined locally Hyderabad has long been an entrepot for pearl trading, and you will see pearls being graded, drilled and made up into strings.

The hereditary prime ministers of Hyderabad were great collectors and patrons of the arts. Their collection, mainly the work of Salar Jung III who died in 1949, is in the **Salar Jung Museum***** (open 10am–5pm, closed Friday) near Afzalganj Bridge. This is absolutely outstanding, so allow plenty of time. The collection is in an ugly new building next to the old palace.

The new town and around

The **Public Gardens** near Nampally station are pretty, and the police pipe band plays every Sunday evening; very British, but they include two thotas, a keyless twin-reed instrument similar to a medieval European instrument called a bombard. The **Archaeological Museum** (10.30am–5pm, closed Friday) is in the park. A little north of the gardens on a hilltop is a white marble temple endowed by the Birlas, one of India's leading families of industrialists. These Birla temples are always very beautiful, and the benefactors see to it that people of all castes and religions are welcome.

Several spectacular palaces around the city are closed to the public, not least because of a long-running vendetta against the Nizam's descendants by the tax authorities, who accuse them of concealing untold riches the state would like to expropriate.

The **Nehru Zoological Park** (closed Monday) is probably the best in India, and a sure way of seeing Asian lions. Best visited early in the morning before the animals' siesta.

Secunderabad

Hyderabad is in effect a twin city. The second element, Secunderabad, originated as an island of British territory. It remains the main rail terminus for Hyderabad, and the best jewellery shops are in the Pot Bazaar, near the station. The name is a variant of Sikander or Alexander.

What the newspapers call communal unrest can make it difficult to visit Hyderabad. It might be remarked here that large parts of Indian newspapers and radio and television news are in code. Communal unrest is a euphemism most commonly indicating that Hindus are killing Muslims or vice versa, less often that caste Hindus are having a go at untouchables (scheduled castes) or that Shia and Sunni Muslims have fallen out. In the first case the trouble is rarely spontaneous, especially in a place like Hyderabad where the former princely rulers (in this case Muslim) took care to maintain religious harmony.

Practical Information

Tourist office on railway station. Guided tours are available; those by private operators can be very disorganised and those of the tourist board too rushed.

Local transport. Good bus service with destinations shown in English. For Golconda (11km from Hyderabad centre) take 119 or 142 from Nampally or 80 from Afzal Ganj. Bus-stand in front of Secunderabad station for buses (No 80) to Hyderabad. A bicycle might be fun for the ride out to Golconda, but would be anything but in the crazy town traffic.

Arrival and departure. Airport (8km). Indian Airlines on Secretariat Road in Saifabad (Tel 236 902), 2km from Nampally.

The broad gauge station in Hyderabad is Nampally, but many trains terminate in Secunderabad 6km away (check carefully when leaving); frequent bus service between the two. Trains to Bombay (15¼hrs), Bangalore (16½hrs) for Mysore, Madras (15hrs), Kochi (28¾hrs) and Delhi (26½hrs). Metre gauge from Secunderabad to Aurangabad (12¼hrs), but a broad gauge line is under construction, also Ajmer (37hrs) and Jaipur (40¾hrs). Beware of the Fast Passenger between Ajmer and Hyderabad, which is scheduled for 52hrs and probably takes even longer.

Accommodation
Hotel Jaya International, near Abids Circle, 1km from the station. Tel 232 929. SWB R150 DWB Rs200 SWB A/C Rs300 DWB A/C Rs400. Rest (good).

Saptagiri Hotel, off Station Road, 750m from station. Tel 503 601. SWB Rs120 DWB Rs 175 DWB A/C Rs295. Best value around.

Cheap places such as *Royal Lodge*, *Royal Hotel* and *Hotel Imperial* directly opposite Hyderabad (Nampally) railway station. All are in the order of SWB Rs85 (£1.70/$2.80) DWB Rs150 (£3/$5). None has much more than convenience to recommend it. The *Retiring Rooms* at Secunderabad station are acceptable, and ideal for an early train.

Eating and drinking
Café Simla, Nampally (near station). Cheap/Mod. Try khunbani-ka-meetha, apricot purée with a sort of custard.

Excursions

Golconda

Before the rule of the Nizams the capital of this area was at Golconda, which was the base of the Qutb Shahi kings. The city was founded in 1565 after the battle of Talikota, which marked the final defeat of Vijayanagar. Aurangzeb captured the fort when he took Hyderabad in 1687, and imprisoned the last king in Daulatabad.

The outer wall of **Golconda Fort***** is about 8km around, and has nine gates and no fewer than 87 towers and bastions, a few still having old cannons on top. The extension on the north-east was added in 1724 when the Nizam declared his independence. The inner fort, the Bala Hisar, towers 100m above the plain. Most of the buildings inside the citadel are in a ruinous state, and the most interesting feature is the way even a quiet sound will carry from the main gate to the very summit. The palace at the top has a throne on the roof from which the ruler could survey his domain. Ruined maybe, but a fascinating place.

The first time the author visited Golconda, slogging up the steps to the citadel, he was mystified by bugles blaring, cheering and the rattle of musketry. Could this be the reenactment of some long-forgotten battle? The making of a Bollywood epic, perhaps? Or was he in a time warp? Excited, he rather tentatively stuck his head over battlements and saw — nothing. Yet the sound effects continued. The following day he read that the army football cup final had been played in the camp below, which presumably accounted for the cheering. The rest was down to normal cantonment activity and an over-fertile imagination.

Like Hyderabad in later years Golconda was a famous diamond-cutting and marketing centre, and the huge Koh-i-Noor diamond (found in the Warangal area in 1623) took a circuitous route from here to England's Crown Jewels.

A little to the north of the fort (walkable) are the **tombs**** of six of the seven Qutb Shahi kings. The exception is Abul Hasan Tana Shah, the last of the line, who ended his days in Daulatabad. The most poignant is that of Sultan Quli Qutb Shah, founder of the dynasty, who was murdered by his son at the age of 90. The tombs are well preserved (like most of the historic buildings in Hyderabad) and worth seeing. The clearest view of the fort is from here.

Information. A useful little booklet and plan is available.

Arrival and departure. See under Hyderabad.

ORISSA

Orissa is included here because it is visited mainly on the way from Madras to Calcutta. Culturally and historically it belongs to northern India rather than the south. There seems to be little more to say about it except that, with 45 per cent of its area covered with forest or jungle, it probably has more trees than people. In the inland areas many of those people are tribals who still maintain in varying degrees their original way of life. A permit is required to visit tribal areas, and a car and interpreter would be essential. Read *A Goddess in the Stones* by Norman Lewis for a fascinating account of the way of life.

PURI

Puri is one of the most important pilgrimage towns in India. The pilgrims' destination is the **Jagannatha Temple**, which may be highly impressive but is closed to non-Hindus. The tower of the library opposite provides a view, though this strikes us as being pointless. How can you appreciate a place of worship without experiencing the atmosphere?

Every year the three grotesque images from the temple are taken in processsion to their summer home. The massive carriage for Jagannatha has 16 wheels over 2m in diameter and is dragged down the broad main street by thousands of men. The carriages of Jagannatha's brother and sister are smaller. The old story of devotees throwing themselves to their deaths under the wheels is apparently much exaggerated, but the word juggernaut has still made its mark in English. At this time there are huge crowds, no accommodation, a serious health risk and difficulties over photography. At other times a colourful bazaar occupies the main street, and small replicas of the images can be bought.

Exploring

A small travellers' colony has grown up to the east of town near the fishing village, and this makes a good place to break the journey to Calcutta (or recover afterwards). The restaurants serve good inexpensive seafood, and parts of the **beach** are OK for sunbathing, though the water is heavily polluted. For clean water and peace you need to walk quite some distance past the fishing village (heading away from Puri). The beach is very exposed, and the currents can be dangerous. The so-called lifeguards are doddering old men who probably couldn't save themselves from the surf. Puri is worth a day or two, but not really any longer.

Handicrafts. The local people do some nice work with palm and shells, and at **Pipli**, on the way to Bhubaneswar, are many shops selling pretty, brightly coloured wall hangings.

Practical Information *i*

Tourist offices in Station Road and in the station itself. Orissa Tourism runs a tour of Konarak, Dhauli, Bhubaneswar and Udayagiri Hill. This is contracted out to a private operator who uses video coaches. If you specify 'non-video' you get seats in the cab, which is cramped, hot and noisy. This tour also wastes a lot of time at a zoo. Similar strictures apply to the tour of Chilka Lake.

Arrival and departure. Direct train from Calcutta (11hrs) and Delhi (37hrs), the latter passing through Lucknow (28½hrs), Varanasi (23½hrs) and Gaya (19½hrs). Coming from Madras it is possible to change trains at Khurda Road, but a bus from Bhubaneswar will be faster.

Accommodation (STD Code 06752)

South-Eastern Railway Hotel, Chakratirtha Road. Tel 22063. SWB Rs335 DWB Rs475 (£9.50/$15.80; includes breakfast). Rest (good, lunch or dinner Rs90 for non-residents, cheaper for children and Rs25 for the dog). Bar (beer Rs40 inside or on the terrace). Splendid establishment, well maintained, where the efficient bearers still wear the uniform of the Bengal and Nagpur Railway.

Hotel Holiday Resort, Chakratirtha Road. Tel 22440. DWB Rs450 Cottage D Rs650. Rest (Mod/Exp, good). Bar. Coffee shop. Modern quality hotel with good gardens and friendly staff.

Hotel Z, Chakratirtha Road. Tel 22554. SR Rs75 DR Rs150 DWB Rs250 Dorm Rs40. Rest. Attractive old house with clean bright rooms.

Sea and Sand Guest House, off Chakratirtha Road. DR Rs80 DWB Rs100. Friendly.

Travellers Inn, near Hotel Z. Tel 23592. SR Rs40 DR Rs75 SWB Rs60 DWB Rs95. Basic.

Beware of *Sri Balajee Lodge*, where the man pays commission to rickshaw-wallahs and makes a rotten din at 5.30 in the morning. Many other hotels, including the good *Panthanivas Tourist Bungalow*, but geared mainly to pilgrims and Indian holiday-makers. Our selection is intended for relaxation.

Eating and drinking

Xanadu, Chakratirtha Road. Ind/Cont. Cheap/Mod. Excellent fish, prawns and pancakes.

Many others on this road, including *Mickey Mouse*!

Excursions

Konarak

The **Sun Temple***** was one of the largest in all India. In a high-walled enclosure the temple consists of three main elements: a separate dancing hall (the Nritya Mandapa), the porch (Jagamohan), and the shrine with the spire (Deul) over it. These last two elements take the form of a huge carriage (like that of Jagannatha), having 24 wheels and being covered with sculpture, much of it erotic. While the stone of which the temple is mainly built has eroded badly, the architraves of the Jagamohan entrances and some of the statues are of harder, greenish chlorite, which gives a better idea of the original workmanship. Construction began perhaps as early as the ninth century AD, and it is uncertain whether the spire was ever completed; if so it would have been at least 70m high — more than half as high again as the Jagamohan.

The temple was for centuries a landmark for sailors who called it the Black Pagoda, in contrast to the White Pagoda of Jagannatha in Puri. The use of wrought iron beams in the roof of the Jagamohan gave rise to a legend of the temple luring ships on to the shore.

Information. ASI booklet from local vendors, check the price before buying.

Arrival and departure. Bus from Puri (1hr), also jeeps and tempos, or Bhubaneswar (1½hrs).

Accommodation. *Tourist Bungalow* near temple and several lodges.

Bhubaneswar

The new capital of Orissa (Cuttack preceded it) has many temples in the distinctive Orissan style. The largest and most impressive, the **Lingaraj**, is closed to non-Hindus. Nearby, surrounded by mango trees, is Siddharanya (the grove of perfect beings), which contains a number of temples. The smallest, the **Mukteswara***, is also the best. It has some superb sculpture outside, and is most unusual among these Orissan temples for its ornate interior. This is just by the road to Puri.

Udayagiri (Sunrise Hill, 10km out of town) has a large number of caves, one carved as a tiger's head with the entrance through the mouth. This is badly eroded, and if you have already seen larger and better preserved cave temples elsewhere there is little point in coming here. Nearby is **Khandagiri** with more of the same and a Jain temple on top.

Dhauli (8km from Bhubaneswar on the Puri road) has an Ashokan rock edict and, on the strength of this, a Japanese peace stupa. This looks like the set for a sci-fi film, not at all as attractive as the one at Rajgir.

Information. Government of India Tourist Office and Orissa Tourism both near Tourist Bungalow. Orissa Tourism also at station and airport. The ASI publishes guide books to both Bhubaneswar and Udayagiri/Khandagiri.

Arrival and departure. Airport. On Madras (19hrs)–Calcutta (6hrs) main line, branch line to Puri (3hrs, faster by bus).

Chilka Lake

Chilka Lake is an important wetland that attracts flocks of wild fowl in December and January. The lake, scarcely separated from the sea, covers around 1000 sq km.

Accommodation. Orissa Tourism has *Tourist Bungalows* at both Barkul and Rambha. Check carefully that boats are available for exploring the lake, because there is not much point in going otherwise.

North-Eastern India

Toy Train to Darjeeling

West Bengal — Sikkim — Assam and the Hill States

Background

This area consists of the states of Assam, Sikkim, Nagaland, Manipur, Tripura, Meghalaya, Arunachal Pradesh and Mizoram, and a small part of West Bengal. It is varied country including the paddies of the Brahmaputra valley, the tea estates of the hills, and the great mountains of Arunachal and Sikkim. Much of the land is covered by dense rain forest, and Cherrapunji, near Shillong, is reckoned to be the wettest place in the world. Over 1000cm/394 inches of rain falls in the average year, and the all-time record is 2280cm/898 inches.

Sadly most of these states are racked by severe social problems. The unaggressive nature of the local people and low population density have encouraged 'foreigners', mostly Bangladeshis and Indian Bengalis, to move in. Their rapid domination of trade and administration has led to fears of cultural disintegration and, in turn, to serious civil disorder. Strikes and violence have become all too common, and activists at one time demanded that the central government deport everyone who was not established as a resident before 1951. The Indians, like the British before them, have always been very touchy about people visiting this area. Fighting took place in Arunachal in 1962 between Indian and Chinese troops, and border security has greatly concerned India ever since.

Season. For Darjeeling March–June (spring) and September–November (autumn); for Sikkim February–May and October–December. Avoid this area during the monsoon (June–September).

The hill states are best visited during winter and spring; rains are heavy from May–September.

WEST BENGAL

When India was partitioned in 1947 the formation of East Pakistan from the predominantly Muslim province of East Bengal virtually cut off Assam and its neighbouring states from the main part of India. A narrow corridor along the foot of the mountains was left to India, and all communications that had previously run over Pakistani territory had to be rerouted through this.

NEW JALPAIGURI AND SILIGURI

New Jalpaiguri is the junction for the famous narrow gauge railway, the 'Toy Train', to Darjeeling. It and the neighbouring Siliguri are really just a long main road leading from New Jalpaiguri station. The town is hot, scruffy and very noisy, best travelled through as fast as possible.

Information. Tourist offices in New Jalpaiguri station and on main street. Permits for Sikkim obtainable at the SNT bus-stand on the main street, near the main bus-stand and Siliguri Junction station. Permits are not at present required for Darjeeling.

Arrival and departure. Nearest airport is Bagdogra (12km from Siliguri), flights to Delhi and Calcutta. Indian Airlines office (Tel 20 692) at Hotel Sinclairs on main road in Siliguri.

Broad gauge railway lines from Calcutta (11¼hrs) and Delhi (28½hrs). Trains from Calcutta depart from Howrah and Sealdah stations, check carefully. Some Delhi trains pass through Mughal Sarai (for Varanasi) and Patna. Also metre gauge trains from Lucknow and Varanasi, slow compared with broad gauge but useful if the latter are fully booked.

The Toy Train for Darjeeling is best boarded at New Jalpaiguri straight off the mainline train. If you have to stay in Siliguri (God help you) you can catch it at either Siliguri Town or Siliguri Junction stations. Second class is always very crowded between New Jalpaiguri and Siliguri, but most passengers get off before the climb starts.

Bus services (from Siliguri) to Darjeeling, Gangtok (4½hrs), Kalimpong, Kathmandu, and perhaps Patna. Share-taxis to Darjeeling from Siliguri or Bagdogra airport are not too expensive. Buses also run to Calcutta, only for when the trains are full.

Accommodation. The railway *Retiring Rooms* (DWB Rs60 Dorm Rs18) are the best bet. A new hotel has recently been built just outside the station. There are lots more in Siliguri, mostly fiendishly noisy; take a cycle rickshaw. Near the Sikkim bus-stand, and quieter than most, is *Siliguri Lodge* (not to be confused with WB Tourism's *Siliguri Tourist Lodge*), priced around DR Rs100 (£2/$3.35) and DWB Rs150.

THE TOY TRAIN

The Toy Train, which chuffs slowly up to Darjeeling, is one of India's great transport experiences. Now that the more accessible Simla mountain railway is dieselised, the Darjeeling–Himalayan Railway is probably the most exciting ride in northern India. In fact, it is probably the best reason for making this long detour from the plains.

The 82km/51 miles Darjeeling–Himalayan Railway (its official name) was built in 1879–81 on a 2ft (61cm) gauge, and has a maximum gradient of 1 in 20. It climbs from Siliguri, only 119m/390ft above sea level, to Darjeeling at 2134m/7000ft. The flat section of the line as far as Sukna used to be operated by miniature Pacific locos, and these may still be in the shed at New Jalpaiguri. Railway workshops are located at Tindharia (860m/2822ft). 10km/6.5 miles past here is Pagla Jhora (Mad Stream) marked by a huge bare scar on the hillside where underground watercourses cause frequent landslides. This is the usual reason for the lower part of the line being out of commission. The highest point on the line is at Ghoom (2258m/7407ft); an important Buddhist monastery stands near here.

The line employs both reversing stations and loops to deal with the gradients, and at times it runs down the main street of straggling mountain villages. Unlike the other three mountain railways this is a real working line, not just a tourist amenity, and it is much used by the local people. Some visitors are annoyed by the youngsters jumping on and off the train, but this really is just part of the fun — as of course is being covered in soot and deafened by the whistle.

The Darj has been at risk for a number of years because of the cost of maintaining both the track and the antiquated stock. At last its value as a tourist amenity has been recognised, and improvements in the service can be expected.

Arrival and departure. The Toy Train runs two services daily, both in the morning, up to Darjeeling. From Calcutta Sealdah the overnight 3143 Darjeeling Mail connects directly with the 9am train; the Howrah 5659 Kamrup Express may just make the 7.15am train. As at Matheran 'down trains' go up the hill and vice versa, the railway rule that down trains run away from the terminus taking precedent over logic. Scheduled time is 8½hrs up (actually often longer) and a little less on the way down.

Landslides, mainly during and just after the monsoon, often put the train out of commission; check in Calcutta whether it is running. The upper section from Kurseong to Darjeeling (30km/19 miles) can be working even when the lower section is not.

DARJEELING

Darjeeling, situated on the crest of a hill at 2134m, is one of the most enjoyable and interesting of all the hill stations, commanding spectacular views in all directions (particularly of Kanchenjunga).

Background

Darjeeling — the name means 'place of the thunderbolt' — was founded in 1816 as a rest centre away from steamy Bengal for the troops of the British East India Company. The town grew through the 19th century, but was something of an oddity among Indian hill stations in that it was never a major resort for the British upper crust. It became primarily a Nepalese town that was a convenient centre for tea planters. Later the pleasant climate attracted many schools and retired people.

The population now is a mixture of Gurkhas, Sherpas and Newars from Nepal, Bengalis, Tibetans, Butias from Tibet, Lepchas from Assam and Burma, and Dupkas from Bhutan. During the season the fashionable and wealthy come up from Calcutta, and the prices go up too. Actually there are two seasons, from April to mid-June and from mid-September to November. Durga Puja (the local form of Dussehra) occurs during the latter period and is one of the most popular festivals in this region.

Political and ecological problems

Recently the Nepalese (mainly Gurkha) presence and the mutual antipathy between them and the Communist Party of India (Marxist) government of West Bengal has caused a lot of trouble. The Gorkha National Liberation Front was founded in the early 1980s to represent the 60% of India's 1.5 million Gurkhas living around the Darjeeling and Kalimpong area. Impetus was given to their demands for self-government in 1986 when 10,000 Nepalis were evicted from Meghalaya where locals feared they were taking over. A strike called in West Bengal led to fighting between GNLF and CPI(M) factions and many deaths.

The central government then took the opportunity of embarrassing the West Bengal government with Rajiv Gandhi, then prime minister, accusing it of neglecting the area. Further violence ensued and eventually in 1988 agreement was reached on the formation of the Darjeeling Gorkha Hill Council. No sooner was this in command than it found itself paying a heavy political price to its supporters. Uncontrolled settlement is causing serious deforestation and exacerbating the already marginal water supply position.

Around town

The town is pleasant; stroll around Chaurastra and The Mall at the top of the hill, where many buildings still retain an English feel with their gardens full of dahlias, roses and hollyhocks. These contrast with the local flora, and especially the wonderful deodar trees. Near Chaurastra is **Step Aside**, the home of Bengali leader CR Das. The upper floor is preserved as a rather morbid memorial to him.

Above Chaurastra is **Observatory Hill*** with a cave temple; far below is an old gompa, **Bhutia Bustee**. It is very small, with only one monk. The guardian figures painted by the door are particularly fine. Walking north and looking down you should spot the red tin roof of the **Tibetan refugee self-help centre****, this having been established in 1959. The production of traditional handicrafts is their main occupation, and you can see the work in progress. Among other things they produce excellent carpets at slightly lower prices than in Kathmandu. There is also a chang shop and a beautiful gompa containing some superb tankas. They breed pedigree Tibetan dogs, too.

At North Point is the **Passenger Ropeway****, the first cablecar built in India. Originally 8km long it ran 1311m/4300ft down to Singla Bazaar in the Rangit Valley. At present only the upper stage operates, but this is still a spectacular ride. The cablecar runs every day except Sunday, advance booking advisable (Rs30 return; 60p/$1).

On the path from North Point up to the Himalayan Mountaineering Institute is the **Snow Leopard Breeding Centre**, your only realistic chance of seeing these elusive animals, though the author is inclined to think that not seeing them at all is better than seeing them in cages. The **Himalayan Mountaineering Institute**** has a very interesting museum (open 9am–5pm) where you can discover the history of Himalayan exploration and mountaineering, and view Sir Edmund Hillary's tin plate, Sherpa Tenzing's left glove, and a great assortment of other exhibits. Close to the main building are a hothouse for Himalayan plants and the telescope house. This houses a powerful German instrument presented by Hitler to the commander of the Nepalese army, who donated it some years ago. Above the institute is the cremation place of Sherpa Tenzing, where a museum about him is being developed. Nearby is the **zoo**; the cages are small but the animals do look healthy. A little bakshish to the keeper of the pandas might get you into the enclosure with them. The **Natural History Museum** near Chaurastra contains a lot of stuffed things.

In the lower part of town is the interesting **bazaar**, with plenty of warm clothing if you need it. **Lloyds Botanical Gardens** are below here and very pleasant. There is an excellent collection of native trees and flowers, and an orchid house.

Practical Information

Permits are no longer required for Darjeeling and Kalimpong. See under Gangtok for Sikkim permits.

Information. Tourist office at 1 Nehru Road, Chaurastra. Conducted tours available.

Arrival and departure. Airport at Bagdogra 90km away; bus or taxi direct or via Siliguri. The bus from Siliguri (4hrs) is much faster than the train and follows almost the same route. See the Practical Information section for details of the route from Kathmandu.

Accommodation (STD Code 0354)

Windamere Hotel, Observatory Hill. Tel 54041. SWB $59 (full-board) DWB $89 (full-board) Suite $98 (full-board). Rest. Bar. Drawing room. If you can afford it, this is the place to stay. *Life* magazine says this is the kind of place Americans look for in Britain, often in vain. It reminded Colette of the Bower House Inn in Eskdale, Cumbria. All the rooms have fireplaces and are beautifully decorated in old English style. Food is Western and said to be very good; lunch or dinner $9, non-residents must book in advance.

The Darjeeling Club. Tel 54348. DWB Rs700 (Rs500 off season or Rs1000 full-board). Rest (Ind/Cont). Bar. Library, billiards room, table tennis. Formerly the Tea Planters Club. Bedrooms very old-fashioned and all have wood fires. Much renovation taking place.

Hotel Bellevue, The Mall. Tel 54075. DWB Rs350 (£7/$11.65). Bar. Large, comfortable rooms and lounge. Morning hot water.

Tower View, near TV tower, Rockville. DWB Rs80. Dorm Rs30. Rest. Run by the charming Krishna who served 20 years in a British Gurkha regiment. He keeps a data book on all aspects of the area including Sikkim and trekking. Nice rooms, good views, a real pleasure to stay.

Hotel Pagoda. DR Rs80 DWB Rs150 Dorm Rs30. Bucket hot water. Clean.

Hotel Prestige. Tel 3199. DWB Rs120–150. Very clean, good value.

Hotel Everest. DWB Rs90–100. Not bad and has a good view, but is not (as it claims) a youth hostel.

Youth Hostel, Dr Zakir Husain Road. Tel 2290. Dorm Rs25 (Rs20 for YHA members). Also some double rooms. Quite a walk from town, but well worth it. Fabulous views.

Eating and drinking

Dekavas, Nehru Road. Ind/Cont. Cheap/Mod. Pizzas, noodles, and so on, all good. A friendly meeting place.

Glenary's Confectionery, Nehru Road. Very good bakers — little cakes, birthday cakes, chocolates, cheese and other goodies. Upstairs is a very English tea room. Try afternoon tea with scones and jam or a selection of dainty cakes and just imagine a *thé dansant* in the 1930s.

Keventer's Snack Bar, Nehru Road. Cheap/Mod. Cunningly replicates the decor, cuisine and service of the baser sort of transport café. Just the place for a huge greasy fry-up when you're fed up of idlis, dosas and all the rest of that vegetarian stuff.

Plenty of inexpensive Tibetan eateries. All restaurants close very early in the evening.

Excursions

You can arrange to visit a **tea estate** if you wish, but don't expect to be drinking extra-special tea in Darjeeling, it's almost all exported. Not far from Darjeeling there are several other places worth visiting. **Ghoom** is a pleasant little place with a very old and fine gompa. Just above Ghoom is Tiger Hill, a fine vantage point to see the **sunrise over Kanchenjunga**; you should get up early to see this at least once, though clouds often obscure the view. The **racecourse** at Lebong is the smallest in the world; meetings are held in spring and autumn. **Kurseong**, lower and milder than Darjeeling, is an orchid growing and breeding centre.

Kalimpong can be reached by jeep from Darjeeling bus-stand. It is much lower and quieter than Darjeeling with an interesting bazaar. There are pleasant walks around and some gompas. The road from Ghoom drops dramatically down the mountainside to cross the Teesta river.

Trekking

Trekkers have not yet over-run the mountains around Darjeeling. There are some rewarding routes and distances are not great. The mountain people are friendly, cheerful and honest. Walking to Sandakphu (3636m) takes a mere two days. Bus or taxi to Manaybhanjang, from where there is a steep 11km stage to Tonglu. Tonglu to Sandakphu is 22km, and it is possible to go a further 21km to Phalut. Return the same way or via Raman and Rimbik. Chai, basic supplies and accommodation (Youth Hostels and bungalows) are available *en route*. For detailed information go to the Youth Hostel in Darjeeling. Equipment can be hired there or at the Pineridge Hotel just off Chaurastra. The tourist office has sketch maps.

SIKKIM

Sikkim is rather different from the other states in the area, having been an independent country with its own chogyal, or king, albeit under strict British (and later Indian) supervision. By 1975, however, mass immigration, mainly from Nepal, had diluted the local Lepcha population to perhaps only 15%. Agitation for a more populist form of government in which their interests were represented turned to violence. The Indian government, always worried by the Chinese threat to its northern borders, quickly seized the excuse to intervene. Sikkim was then, by a legal device, incorporated in the Indian union, an event greeted with something less than enthusiasm by much of the population.

A word of caution is appropriate here. Sikkim is often imagined to be a remote Himalayan kingdom, and its capital Gangtok as being another romantic medieval city like Kathmandu or Leh. In fact the only part of Sikkim you can readily visit is not even Alpine, but sub-tropical; and Gangtok is a modern (though far from unfriendly) concrete jungle. Apart from several Buddhist monasteries Sikkim is short on conventional tourist sights. Its real attraction is for the botanist, naturalist and bird-watcher.

RANGPO TO GANGTOK

Given that Gangtok itself is not very interesting, and that you are so limited in where you can go in Sikkim, you may feel it is worth spending a bit of time on this short journey. The route is along two river valleys and very beautiful. The forest on the hillsides is almost untouched and full of wild orchids and colourful birds.

The border checkpoint is at Rangpo, where you cross from Bengal to Sikkim. From here to Singtam (11km/7 miles by road) the route follows the Teesta River. The old footpaths still exist along much of the way, and this should make a pleasant if rather sweaty walk. Many people fish in the river, which holds trout and mahseer as well as many other species. There appear to be good campsites and plentiful wood along the way.

The Teesta runs much clearer above Singtam, but the road to Gangtok leaves it here to follow a tributary, the Rongnye. At Saramsa (15km/9.5 miles on from Singtam and 14km/9 miles from Gangtok) is a well kept **orchid and cactus garden**. They may play loud Hindi film music only for the tour groups, but it does nothing for one's enjoyment of an otherwise beautiful place.

Alternatively, it is possible to follow the Teesta for a few kilometres above Singtam to Sirwan. From there a packhorse trail leads to Rumtek village and monastery, which is connected to Gangtok by road (bus service).

Accommodation. In Rangpo there is the *Tourist Reception Centre* and other accommodation. Various accommodation in Singtam.

GANGTOK

The capital of Sikkim, at an altitude of 1600m/5248ft, straddles a hill — indeed its name means 'flattened hill'. The park that occupies much of the ridge above the town is the centre of the International Flower Festival between March and May, a magnificent display of orchids. The southern end of the ridge is occupied by the **Royal Palace**, kept closed except for a religious festival in December. Within this is the **Tsuk-ka-lang**, the richly decorated Royal Chapel, a very holy place for local Buddhists. Like the palace this is mostly closed up except during the Sikkimese New Year celebrations in late February.

Higher up on top of the ridge is the small 200-year-old pagoda of **Enchey Gompa***. The interior paintings here are both beautiful and grotesque, disturbing in fact. No mere illustrations, they reach into the soul. They are very different from those in other Tibetan Buddhist monasteries, and apparently typical of the Nyingma tantric sect that controls this gompa. A major religious dance festival is celebrated here in December/January.

The **Research Institute of Tibetology**, founded by the last chogyal, is in effect a library that also displays a small collection of thankas and Tibetan artefacts. This is in the same category as the Oriental Library in Patna: absolutely invaluable if you are a serious scholar (and can read Tibetan), but of limited interest otherwise.

Near the institute is a huge **chorten** surrounded by prayer wheels. The associated **monastery** with its two large figures is of interest only if you will be seeing no other Tibetan Buddhist places. The author's happiest memory of this place, though, is of young (and not so young) monks playing football, red robes flying.

The **Orchid Sanctuary**, below the Research Institute, grows around 200 species (out of 600 or so found in Sikkim).

Lall Bazaar market is disappointing despite stalls selling a vegetable that looks a little like asparagus (and tastes vile) and incredibly smelly yak cheese. Shopping in Sikkim is notable only for the number of liquor shops and the great variety of liqueurs they stock.

Although concrete has completely taken over in Gangtok many of the smaller buildings in rural areas are still built with a wood frame and the spaces filled with wattle and daub, just like Tudor buildings in England.

Practical Information *i*

It is no longer necessary to apply far in advance for a Sikkim permit. To obtain a permit in Darjeeling get a form from the magistrate's office on Hill Cart Road and take it to the Foreigners' Regional Registration Office. There you receive another bit of paper with which you have to return to the magistrate's office. Easy enough but takes time. Specify the places you wish to visit. The permit is usually easily extended at the FRRO in Gangtok. Alternatively apply at Sikkim Tourism, 5/2 Russell Street, Calcutta, or at the FRRO in any large city. In theory it is possible to get the permit when you apply for your visa.

Tourist office on MG Marg, the main street.

Arrival and departure. Helicopter service from Bagdogra airport. Bus from Darjeeling (6hrs), Kalimpong (4hrs), and Siliguri (5½hrs). Share-taxis and Land Rovers also operate. Booking for the Diamond Express bus to Darjeeling is by the Hotel Hungry Jack near the private bus-stand.

Accommodation (STD Code 03592)

Hotel Mayur, Paljor Stadium Road. Tel 22825. SWB Rs200/325 DWB Rs250/400. Rest. Bar. Lovely rooms. The restaurant (Mod/Exp) is a bit like eating in the jungle, with plants everywhere.

Hotel Tibet, Paljor Stadium Road. Tel 22523. SWB Rs425/500 DWB Rs550/675. Rest (Snow Lion, see below). Bar. Comfortable rooms with good views.

Hotel Green, MG Marg. Tel 23354. DR Rs80 SWB Rs150/250 DWB Rs250/350. Rest (good). Bar. Best porridge in India.

Hotel Sher-e-Punjab, National Highway. Tel 22823. SR Rs65 DR Rs110 DWB Rs11500. Rest. Clean basic rooms.

Hotel Orchid, National Highway. Tel 23151. DR Rs100/150 DWB Rs300. Rest. Bar.

Hotel Hungry Jack, National Highway. DWB Rs125–150 (£2.50–3/$4.15–5). Rest (good). Bar.

Sinioichu Lodge, near Enchey Monastery. Tel 22074. SR Rs75 DR Rs100 SWB Rs125 DWB Rs175. Rest. Attractive place with comfortable lounge. Super views, but a long walk from town.

Out of season (roughly December to March and July and August) you can expect hefty discounts on these prices.

Eating and drinking

Snow Lion, Hotel Tibet. Ind/Tibetan. Mod/Exp. Excellent food in a room decorated with Tibetan paintings.

Blue Sheep, Tourist Office, MG Road. Ind/Chi. Mod. Good food.

Excursions

Rumtek monastery is the base in exile of the Kagyu sect of Tibetan Buddhism. The largest monastery of its kind outside Tibet, the buildings are all modern, albeit following strictly traditional lines. The prayer hall is very attractive but lacks that air of sanctity that comes from many years of worship. In a separate building is the chorten of Gyalwa Karmapa, the 16th leader of the sect, which enshrines his heart. He died in 1982, and several years later the leaders of the sect were still searching for his reincarnation to succeed him. Surrounding the chorten are statues of himself and his 15 predecessors. Rumtek is visible from Gangtok but it is a 24km/15 miles trip by road. There are several places to stay, the best looking being about 500m down the road from the monastery; below that is a botanical garden.

Pemayangtse Monastery (at 2085m/6843ft), founded in 1705 by the Nyingma sect, is the second oldest in Sikkim. **Tashiding Monastery** is a day's walk further into the wild, though whether you will be allowed to make it without a permit is another matter. Altogether more accessible is **Phodang Monastery**, 38km/24 miles north of Gangtok.

Trekking in Sikkim is limited to one route, Pemayangtse Monastery to Zematang, the return trek taking up to ten days. It is possible to do one extra stage to the Gocha La at well over 5000m/16,400ft and only 15km/9.5 miles from the peak of Kanchenjunga (8586m/28,162ft). The catch is that you can only do the trek as part of an organised escorted group. Sikkim Trekking and Travel Service in Gangtok quotes $35 per head per day (inclusive of porters, food and transport) for a group of four or more. In theory these rules are being relaxed, but nothing has happened yet, check before travelling. There is also talk of organising rafting on the Teesta River.

ASSAM AND THE HILL STATES

Until very recently it was virtually impossible to obtain a permit to travel anywhere in this region. A lessening in insurgency in some areas and an improvement in relations with China has recently led to some relaxation. This is an exciting new area to explore, more notable for its landscapes than man's impact.

Assam

At the time of Independence the whole of this area (plus Sylhet, now in Bangladesh) was Assam. Local independence movements have seen it broken up into seven states. There would probably need to be 27 to keep all the minority groups happy.

Guwahati (Gauhati), on the banks of the mighty Brahmaputra river, is the capital of Assam. A pleasant town, it boasts a number of interesting temples, one on an island in the river.

Kaziranga National Park is famous for its rhinos; there are over a thousand of them and they are readily visible. The best way of seeing them is from the back of an elephant; jeeps are also available, but frighten the game.

Manas Wildlife Sanctuary, on the border with Bhutan, is a Project Tiger reserve. The scenery is stunning, rhino and other game can be seen, and the rivers are famous for mahseer fishing.

Prices of accommodation and transport in Manas and Kaziranga are still low; full details from Assam Tourism offices.

Upper Assam, to the north-east, is the main centre of the tea industry, and also the source of much of India's coal and oil. This area is served by two railway lines, one each side of the Brahmaputra. These lines, and specifically the supplies they carried for the Chinese army, rather than a desire to conquer India, led to Japan's invasion in 1944. The southern line used to connect directly with the major port of Chittagong (now in Bangladesh), and at the far end is Ledo, the start of the Ledo Road, built to supply Chiang-Kai-Shek. Nearby, the town of Margherita is named, for some unfathomable reason, after a queen of Italy.

All of Assam can be visited without a permit.

Meghalaya

Meghalaya means the Land of the Clouds. The landscape is very like southern Scotland. The main town **Shillong** is a pleasant hill resort where the local Khasi people hold colourful folk dance festivals.

Meghalaya requires no permit.

Tripura

Tripura was the princely state of Tippera. Bengali influence was always strong here, and today Bengalis outnumber the local tribals by four or five to one. This is the flattest of the 'hill' states and, very like Bengal as a whole, not especially interesting.

Large influxes of Bengali peasants practising jhum (slash and burn) have had a disastrous effect on wildlife and the ecology as a whole. **Agartala** is the main town, and there are huge monolithic statues of Hindu deities at **Unakoti**.

No permit is needed for Tripura.

Mizoram

The Mizos were traditionally a warlike lot related to the Chins of Burma. This was a lawless area until 1925 when the British invaded, mainly to stop the Mizos raiding tea plantations. In contrast to almost everywhere else in India they then encouraged missionaries to move in. The result, after upheavals leading to statehood in 1986, is a peaceful and beautiful country with a Christian majority.

A Restricted Area Permit is required, issued usually only to groups of four. The whole state is open to permit holders. Applications to: Mizoram Bhavan, Circular Road, Chanakyapuri, New Delhi (Tel 301 5951); 24 Old Ballygunge Road, Calcutta (Tel 757 034); GS Road, Bhangagarh, Guwahati, Assam (Tel 564 626).

Manipur

Manipur was a princely state; menaced over the years by Burma, it sheltered under the wing of a British treaty from 1826. **Imphal**, the main town, is situated in a most attractive valley. As in nearby Kohima, bitter fighting took place here in 1944. The Manipuris are great sportsmen and claim that their version of polo was the origin of the modern game.

A Restricted Area Permit is required, issued usually only to groups of four. Access is limited to Imphal and its locality. Applications to Manipur Bhavan, Sardar Patel Marg, Chanakyapuri, New Delhi (Tel 301 3311); 25 Ashutosh Shastri Road, Calcutta (Tel 365 012); Rajgarh Road, Chandmari, Guwahati, Assam (Tel 540 707).

Nagaland

The Nagas, in their various tribes, are of Mongolian stock. They were notorious for their enthusiasm for head-hunting. During the Second World War this prowess was harnessed as they became highly effective guerillas and guides against the invading Japanese.

Kohima, the capital, was besieged by the Japanese in their drive on the Assam railways in 1944, and its defence by Indian and British army units is an epic to rank with Lucknow. Savage hand-to-hand fighting went on for a fortnight, the two front lines separated by the width of the District Commissioner's tennis court. For the first time the Japanese were fought to a standstill, then pushed back into Burma where they were annihilated.

Nagaland is in a highly unsettled state, and no permits are issued to foreigners (or Indians, for that matter). You are allowed to transit by rail.

At the time of the Japanese invasion the British troops received great support from the local villagers, and since the great battle of Kohima they have kept the extensive graveyards in impeccable condition and given a warm welcome to visits from British relatives organised by the British Legion.

Arunachal Pradesh

Arunachal Pradesh, the Land of the Sunrise, is the most remote part of India, bordered by Burma and Tibet. This is a land of great contrasts; **Namdhapa National Park**, the main attraction, varies in altitude from 200m to 4500m, ranging from sub-tropical to alpine ecosystems.

A Restricted Area Permit is required, issued usually only to groups of four. Access is limited, and you have the choice of spending $150 (£90) a day on a package tour or \$50 (£30) a day just to be there. Applications to Arunachal Bhavan, Kautilya Marg, Chanakyapuri, New Delhi (Tel 301 3915); Roxi Cinema Hall, Chowringhee Road, Calcutta (Tel 248 6500); Bhaskar Nagar, RG Baruah Road, Guwahati, Assam (Tel 562 859).

The troubles in Assam and the Hill States

The causes of unrest in this part of India have been outlined already, the main one being an influx of Bengali settlers. The effects have been exacerbated by a central government more concerned with politicking than good, strong government. As a result pressure groups have proliferated. These usually pass through a cycle of political agitation, armed insurrection, political success in forming a government, then almost instant corruption and unpopularity. In the meantime other groups have sprung up claiming to represent the true revolution. They fight the central government, the now respectable old guard, other tribal groups and factions, and one another. Nationalist principles quickly degenerate into the money-grubbing quest for power and the patronage that goes with it. The result, as usual, is hell for the ordinary people who just want to get on with their lives and enjoy a bit of the prosperity India is now achieving.

Part of the trouble stems from the way the British administered this area. Large parts of it were 'excluded areas' where the elected local legislature and bureaucracy had no remit. Control was entirely in the hands of the Governor and a few hand-picked administrators. Outsiders, from tourists to settlers, were rigidly excluded. The notion of the noble savage is a tantalising illusion, but many of these peoples had evolved a near idyllic way of life. The British aim was to protect them from the outside world until they were ready for it. After all, the first influences of Western civilisation, apart from missionaries, are usually venereal disease and alcoholism.

All this was swept away by Independence, and the guarantee in the constitution that an Indian was free to live where he liked in his own country.

Two books, readily found in second-hand bookshops, capture the magic of this area in the last days of the Raj: *Naga Path* by Ursula Graham Bower, and *Elephant Bill* by JH Williams. Life may have been simpler in those days, but it was a lot tougher and more dangerous as well.

BHUTAN

Bhutan, next door to Sikkim, is still nominally independent, but even the king cannot give you a visa if the Indians do not approve (they never do unless you want to spend a huge amount on a package tour).

A FEW WORDS OF HINDUSTANI

Hindustani is a mixture of Hindi and Urdu (plus a lot of English words) transliterated into roman characters. It is a kind of north Indian lingua franca which evolved during British rule and is still used by the Indian army.

The best book is *Cambridge Self Hindi Teacher* (Pankaj Publications, New Delhi). *Hindustani Without A Master* is a splendid little book. It will not, it is true, teach you to enquire after the health of your postillion, but who cares when you can order your Lascars to set the topgallants or tell a man he will be hanged tomorrow?

Because the Devanagri alphabet has ten vowels and 33 consonants transliteration is not precise, and pronunciation, which varies from place to place anyway, is tricky. Note especially the following:

a	as in 'cut'
ā	as in 'cart', never as in 'cat'
ai	as in 'said'
aī	as in 'why'
au	as in 'foul'
e	as in 'bet'
ē	as in 'bait'
i	as in 'hit'
ī	as in 'heat'
o	as in 'pole'
u	as in 'full'
ū	as in 'fool'
ṅ	as in French 'bon'
<u>th</u>	as in 'boathook', not as in 'the'

Try to stress each syllable equally and, if in doubt, use French pronunciation rather than English.

anyone here?	koī hai?
hallo, goodbye, greetings	namastē
thank you	shukriya (or thank you)
yes	hāṅ
no	nē, nahīn
OK	achchhā, tīk (hai)
where is...?	...kahān hai?
how far?	kitnī dūr?
to the left	bāyīn
to the right	dāhinī
come on, let's go, go away	chalāo
go (imperative)	jāo
hurry up (imperative)	jaldī karo
when is...?	...kab hai?
how much? how many?	kitnā?
what price?	kitnā paise?
rupees	rūpiyā

too much	zyādā, adhik
far too much	bahut zyādā
expensive	mahamgār
cheap	sastā
many, much, very	bahut
enough	bas
more	adhik
bad	kharāb
good	achchhā
better	behtar
best	behtarīn
clean	sāf
dirty	mailā
hot	garam
cold	thandā
large	barā (burrah)
small	chotā
soon	jaldī
today	āj
tomorrow, yesterday (!)	kal
bicycle	sāikil (cycle)
toilet	pakhānā (or latrine)
black	kālā
blue	nīlā
green	harā
red	lāl
white	safed
yellow	pīlā
what is your name? (pre-emptive strike!)	āp nām ki hai?
my name is...	mērā nām... hai

GLOSSARY

achar	pickle
adivasi	aboriginal, polite expression for tribal people
ahimsa	total non-violence
Ahmadiyya	Muslim sect that reveres Jesus
Akali	Orthodox Sikh sect
Allah o-Akbar	God is great (Muslim)
ālū, aloo	potato
andā	egg
apsara	heavenly nymph
Aryan	Indo-European (from Sanskrit *aryās* noble)
ashrām	spiritual learning establishment
ASI	Archaeological Survey of India
ātman	self, soul, the god within
avatar	one of nine guises in which Vishnu has come to earth
Ayurveda	traditional Indian medical system
bābū	usually clerk, rarely complimentary
bāgh	garden
bahrā/bearer	personal servant
Bakr-Id	Muslim festival of Abraham's offering of Ishmael
bakshīsh	tip, alms, bribe
bāndh	strike, labour dispute; dam
bāradarī	literally 12 doors, pavilion or summer house
baraf	ice
basti/bāstee	literally village, usually cramped buildings, slums
Bhagavad Gītā	The Song of God, Krishna's sermon laying down the basic laws of Hinduism, a late addition (first century AD) to the Mahabharata
bhajan	hymn, also prayer
bhang lassi	hashish and yoghurt drink mixture
Bharat	India
Bharata Natyam	North Indian classical dance
bhāt	rice (boiled)
bhavan	house, building, temple
bhel puri	fried snacks, 'Bombay mix'
bhindī	okra, ladies' fingers
bhojan	food
bīdī	cheap smoke
biryāni	rice dish
BJP	Bharatiya Janata Party, Hindu nationalist party
Boddhisatva	Buddhist saint
bogie	railway carriage or wagon
Bollywood	Bombay, in its role as the centre of Indian movie-making
Brahmā	the creator, senior god of the Hindu trinity
Brahman	the magic of the sacred word, the godhead from which

	all else comes
Brahmanism	belief in the above and the search for unity with Brahman, and thus freedom
Brāhmin	priest, member of the top caste
Buddha	The Enlightened One, ninth incarnation of Vishnu
Buddha Jayanti	Buddha's birthday
bund	embankment
chaī	tea
chaitya	Buddhist chapel
chajja	projecting eaves
chakra	wheel symbolising the cycle of death and rebirth
chālān	summons to court
chang	barley beer
chapāti	flat unleavened bread
chaplī/chappals	sandals
charas	cannabis resin, hashish
charpoy	string bed with wooden frame
chatti	tea shop
chāwal	rice (uncooked)
chhattri	literally umbrella, canopied memorial or cupola
Chief Minister	prime minister of a state
chillum	pipe for smoking charas
chīnī	sugar
chīnī nē	no sugar
chorten	memorial to Buddhist monk
chowkidar	caretaker
chūnām	hard white plaster
communalism	social conflict, religious or caste
Cong	Congress Party; letter in brackets indicates faction, e.g. (I) for Indira, the mainstream
CPI	Communist Party of India
crore	10 million, written as 1,00,00,000
dabba	packed lunch
dahī	curd, yoghurt
dalit	preferred term for harijan
darbar/durbar	meeting between a ruler and his subjects
dargah	tomb of a Muslim saint
darwaza	gateway
Deccān	literally South, the plateau of peninsular India
devadasi	dedication of young girls to the goddess Yellamma after which they become prostitutes; banned but rife in Karnataka and Maharashtra
Devi	generic word for goddess, used specifically refers to Durga, Kali or Parvati
dhāl	lentils
dharamsala	religious guest house
dharma	the rules that govern a caste Hindu's life
dharna	protest
dhobī	laundry
dhoti	loin cloth (North India)
dhow	arab sailing ship (generic)
Digambara	literally sky-clad, i.e. naked, the ascetic sect of Jain monks
dīvān	literally divan, the throne of a minister or the minister himself (diwan and dewan the same)